The Woodland Southeast

D1441180

The Woodland Southeast

Edited by

David G. Anderson
and
Robert C. Mainfort, Jr.

The University of Alabama Press
Tuscaloosa and London

9 8 7 6 5 4 3 2 1
09 08 07 06 05 04 03 02 01

Design by Virginia Horak

Cover painting by Martin Pate,
courtesy of the artist and the Southeast Archeological Center

∞

The paper on which this book is printed meets the minimum requirements of
American National Standard for Information Science–Permanence of Paper for
Printed Library Materials, ANSI Z39.48-1984.

Library of Congress Cataloging-in-Publication Data

The Woodland Southeast / edited by
David G. Anderson and Robert C. Mainfort, Jr.
p. cm.
Includes bibliographical references and index.
ISBN 0-8173-1137-8 (pbk. : alk. paper)
1. Indians of North America—Southern States—Antiquities.
2. Woodland culture—Southern States.
3. Southern States—Antiquities.
I. Anderson, David G., 1949– II. Mainfort, Robert C., 1948–
E99.W84 W66 2002
976'.01—dc21   2001005919

British Library Cataloguing-in-Publication Data available

For Judith,
who has done so much
for southeastern archaeology
in recent years

Contents

Figures

Tables

Preface

Planning for *The Woodland Southeast* began about a decade ago, when a number of members of the southeastern archaeological community recognized the pressing need for broad yet detailed readers on major periods of southeastern prehistory, at least prior to the Mississippian period, which had and continues to attract appreciable publication effort. This volume represents the culmination of this effort. Earlier volumes examined other periods: *The Paleoindian and Early Archaic Southeast* (Alabama 1996) and *The Archaeology of the Mid-Holocene Southeast* (Florida 1996) were produced under the leadership of Kenneth E. Sassaman. While the editors may assemble these volumes, they are truly a team effort. These volumes have happened because of the support of many colleagues, who gave of their time and effort to produce valuable overviews on their areas of expertise. We deeply appreciate their willingness to participate and are grateful for all the help along the way.

The call for papers that led to this volume went out in the early spring of 1998. Although the project was planned as a publication from the start, the initial impetus was an all-day symposium held on November 12, 1998, at the fifty-fifth annual meeting of the Southeastern Archaeological Conference in Greenville, South Carolina. Eighteen papers were presented, most of which are represented in this volume. The session was well attended, and a videotape record exists for those interested in seeing the initial versions of many of the papers. The manuscript was submitted to the press in January 2000 and, upon review and subsequent revision, was resubmitted in January 2001. Several additional papers were added by the editors and at the request of the reviewers, to provide for more even coverage of the region and of special topics.

In the preparation of this volume Judith Knight of the University of Alabama Press provided support and encouragement and, above all, patience. She has helped many southeastern archaeologists get their work published in recent years and is one of our community's biggest supporters. She and the staff of the press deserve all of our thanks. Copy editing was handled by Kathy Cummins, while several of the graphics were standardized by George Wingard of the Savannah River Archaeological Research Program (SRARP) of the South Carolina Institute of Archaeology and Anthropology. We appreciate the support of Mark Brooks and Richard Brooks, SRARP program directors. The camera-ready copy for this volume was produced by Virginia Horak of the Southeast Archeological Center (SEAC) of the National Park Service, Tallahassee, Florida, who worked wonders on the tables and figures alike. Her attention to detail has greatly improved the overall manuscript, and she has our deepest thanks. The extensive support and encouragement provided by SEAC Director John Ehrenhard are deeply appreciated and are a large part of the reason this volume exists. Likewise, the continued support and encouragement of Tom Green, the Director of the Arkansas Archeological Survey, are also important reasons this volume came about. At SEAC, graduate assistant Donna Freid helped assemble the references and, with Emily Yates, helped with the innumerable copying and assembly chores. These volumes require a lot of work to produce but, the editors and authors hope and believe, should serve as useful guides to our region's prehistory. The editors encourage our younger colleagues to consider producing similar volumes in the years to come.

Chapter 1

An Introduction to Woodland Archaeology in the Southeast

David G. Anderson and Robert C. Mainfort, Jr.

The Woodland period spans the interval between roughly 3000 and 1000 B.P. (radiocarbon years before present), or from circa 1200 B.C. to A.D. 1000 as calibrated in calendar years (Stuiver et al. 1998). The period has traditionally been subdivided into three subperiods, Early, Middle, and Late, to demarcate intervals characterized in general terms by the first widespread use of pottery across the Southeast, the rise and then decline of a vast panregional ceremonially based interaction network, and, finally, a period of political fragmentation, increasing agricultural intensification, and population growth in many areas, out of which the complex agricultural chiefdoms that characterize the ensuing Mississippian era arose. Griffin (1967:180–89) is perhaps the most classic statement describing these subperiods.

During the Woodland period, dramatic increases in sedentism, population, and organizational complexity occurred across the Southeast. At the beginning of the period, people across the region are assumed to have been living in small, more or less egalitarian groups loosely tied together by collective burial ritual that sometimes involved the construction of small mounds. By the end of the period some 2200 years later, densely packed civic-ceremonial centers ruled by hereditary elites had emerged in parts of the region, maize had become the predominant food crop for many peoples, and the region's ancient animal-focused and, no doubt, hunting-based religion and cosmology was being replaced by solar and warfare iconography more suited to societies dependent on intensive agriculture and whose elites were in increasing competition with one another. What happened during this roughly 2200-year span, how the changes we observe came about, and the archaeological record from this period that has been found in each part of the Southeast are examined in this volume.

What do we mean by the Woodland period in the Southeast? Archaeologically, sites and cultures from this era locally are recognized primarily by the presence of pottery (outside of those relatively restricted areas where the technology arose much earlier, as discussed by Sassaman [1993a, this volume]). A bewildering array of surface finish, paste, and vessel forms exists over the region (e.g., Broyles 1967 lists over 2000 types). Arguably more work over the past century has gone into untangling this variability than has been directed to any other research theme, providing information that many of the authors in this volume summarize when presenting local sequence data. Many ceramic attributes have proven to be highly sensitive chrono-logical markers and, as a result, our dating of sites and events within the Woodland period is far more precise than it is for earlier periods. Chrono-logical resolution on the order of one to a few centuries is possible in many parts of the region. Until fairly recently, in fact, much of the work with Woodland site assemblages in the region was directed to culture-historical reconstruction and sequence building, with discrete prehistoric phases, or archaeological cultures, commonly described and identified through refer-ence to specific pottery types. Ceramics, of course, are not the only tempo-rally diagnostic Woodland artifact category, just the most common. A range of square- to contracting-stem projectile points are also characteristic of the Woodland period, as are a variety of triangular projectile points. Woodland points are typically appreciably smaller than earlier Archaic forms, and over the course of the Woodland period point size decreased in many areas. A major reduction in size occurred near the end of the period, when the bow and arrow appears to have replaced the spear thrower across the region (Blitz 1988; Nassaney and Pyle 1999). The impact of the bow on local cultures is discussed by a number of the contributors to this volume.

The Woodland Concept

The recognition of the Woodland period as a major stage in the cultural development of the prehistoric peoples of the Eastern Woodlands dates to the 1930s (e.g., McKern 1939:309), although the term and concept were not formalized into the subdivisions now in use until somewhat later, in the 1940s and after (J. B. Griffin 1946, 1952a, 1967, 1986a:42, 1986b:609; Woodland Conference 1943). *Woodland* is now routinely used interchange-ably as both a period and a stage marker across most of the Southeast. Even where alternative terminology is still employed (e.g., J. A. Ford and Willey's [1941; Willey 1966] Burial Mound I and II and Temple Mound I and II periods; Willey and Phillips's [1958] Formative stage; or S. Williams's [1963; Stoltman 1978] Neo-Indian stage), most notably by some researchers work-ing in the lower Mississippi alluvial valley (e.g., Phillips 1970:5–8; S. Wil-liams and Brain 1983), these scholars routinely provide concordances, in the form of charts or text, linking the various constructs together. In this volume we use the term *Woodland* to refer to cultural developments in the Southeast between circa 3000 and 1000 B.P. (uncalibrated radiocarbon years), although trends extending both before and after this interval are also discussed. In areas where Woodland terminology is used differently (i.e., the Middle Atlantic region [see chapters by Hantman and Gold and by Herbert, this volume]), these differences are spelled out.

What happened during the Woodland period in the Southeast, and what makes it worthy of our research attention? Until quite recently, the onset of the Woodland was assumed to have been the time of the initial appearance of pottery across much of the region, the beginnings of elaborate burial mound ceremonialism, the emergence of sedentary village life with well-defined structures and settlements, and the first evidence for the intensive cultivation of crops (Griffin 1967:180). We now realize that the beginnings of these developments lie much deeper in the past, well back into the Archaic period (e.g., see the various papers in Sassaman and Anderson [eds.] 1996). We now know, for example, that mound construction activity has great antiquity in the Southeast, dating back into the Middle Archaic (e.g., Russo 1994, 1996a; J. Saunders et al. 1994, 1997); that the intensive cultivation of local food crops like chenopod, sunflower, and gourd was occurring in a number of Late Archaic societies (Gremillion 1996a, this volume; B. D. Smith 1992a, 1992b); that the first pottery predates the onset of the Woodland by as much as 1500 years on the lower south Atlantic seaboard (Sassaman 1993a, this volume); and that well-made structures marking the existence of semipermanent to permanent residential communities were present in many parts of the region by the Middle Archaic period and were likely present during the Early Archaic as well (Russo 1991, 1996b; Sassaman and Ledbetter 1996).

These advances in our understanding of the antiquity of plant domestication, sedentism, and mound ceremonialism in the Southeast perhaps should not have come as any great surprise to the professional archaeological community. Although the Southeast has a mild temperate climate, shelter is essential in the winter in several areas. Many parts of the region are rich in wild plant and animal resources, reducing the need for extensive mobility in their acquisition. The massive mound complexes of the Terminal Archaic Poverty Point culture, and the widespread mound-building behavior of subsequent Woodland peoples, are unlikely to have emerged nearly instantaneously without at least some antecedent (J. Gibson 1996a). Finally, everywhere in the world where the origins of agriculture have been explored, we have come to recognize that domestication is a long process, with initial steps occurring thousands of years before cultivated crops make major contributions to the diet (Cowan and Watson 1992; Gremillion 1996a, 1996b, this volume).

That our perspective about so many aspects of Woodland occupations in the Southeast has changed dramatically in recent years is a direct by-product of the truly massive amounts of archaeological fieldwork and reporting that have occurred in the past quarter century. Much of this is a result of federal environmental legislation, which has led to the funding of appreciable research as part of the review and compliance process, as well as a marked expansion in the number of professionals at universities and in the public and private sectors to handle cultural resources training, survey, and management responsibilities. Whereas a few decades ago the entire archaeological literature from the region could fit comfortably within a single researcher's office, today over one hundred thousand reports exist, and no person or organization has the capability of reading, or even accessing, this vast literature. The need for synthetic volumes like this one is thus pressing and will continue to grow.

In this volume, we have adopted a topical and geographic approach to synthesizing the vast literature on the Woodland period. Our goal is not to be inclusive—that is clearly impossible in today's world. But we have asked the contributors to highlight, as best they can, the major substantive literature in their area or topic, to guide readers interested in exploring further to the primary sources. Likewise, while we have aimed for as broad a geographic and topical coverage as possible, we have deliberately avoided subjects explored in far greater depth elsewhere. Thus, while the Woodland is sometimes known as the "Burial Mound" period (e.g., J. A. Ford and Willey 1941), the many syntheses encompassing Woodland mound and earthwork construction that have appeared obviated, we believe, the need for specialized treatment of this activity here (e.g., Mainfort [ed.] 1988; Mainfort and Sullivan [eds.] 1998; Mainfort and Walling [eds.] 1996; Pacheco [ed.] 1996; Sherrod and Rolingson 1987). In some cases, unfortunately, synthetic treatments are simply not available. Woodland period bioarchaeological research in the region, for example, is in urgent need of synthesis. While a number of excellent highly focused studies exist, the opportunity for broad synthetic research is wide open, particularly for studies of the magnitude of those produced by Owsley and Rose ([eds.] 1997) for the central and northern plains, and Rose ([ed.] 1999) for the south-central United States. Readers are encouraged to further explore and address any deficiencies found herein.

The Early Woodland Period

Although the Woodland period has been characterized historically by mound construction and ceremonialism, intensive cultivation of crops, and well-defined village life, at least at some times and in some areas, about the only clear distinction between the Archaic and Woodland periods that remains is the widespread adoption of pottery. That is, by shortly after 1000 B.C., and certainly by 700–500 B.C., people all across the Southeast were using pottery, where before this technology had been present in only a few areas (Sassaman 1993a, this volume). Many Early Woodland adaptations, however, appear so similar to those that came before that in many parts of the Southeast they are described as "Archaic with pottery." In the Southeast, the Early Woodland period usually is dated from about 1000 to 200 B.C. The former date approximately marks the widespread adoption of pottery, while the latter date is associated with the start of increased mound construction and participation in the Hopewellian exchange network in many areas.

The widespread appearance of pottery across the region that is a hallmark of the Early Woodland period has facilitated the recognition of large numbers of discrete archaeological cultures—many more than are known for earlier periods, when such obvious signatures are lacking. Four major ceramic traditions—presumed prehistoric culture areas or groups of similar or related societies—appear at this time, located in the Gulf Coastal Plain, the interior Midsouth, the South Appalachian area, and the middle Atlantic seaboard (Bense 1994:114–19; Caldwell 1958). The ceramic traditions in both the Midsouth and Middle Atlantic are characterized by cord or fabric impressions applied with a wrapped paddle, while in the South Appalachian and Gulf coastal areas more elaborate designs are common, applied with carved wooden paddles in the former area and characterized by dentate and rocker stamping and incising in the latter area. The actual separation between assemblages of these traditions is often more a matter of geography than discrete physical attributes, and surface treatments typically encompass appreciable variation, within and in addition to the major finish categories. The development or use of major traditions or horizon markers to organize and describe large numbers of assemblages is something rarely attempted today, as researchers increasingly focus on local variability. Ceramic stylistic and technological variation continues to be used, however, in combination with distributional and chronological evidence, to define many southeastern Woodland cultures, although the approaches to systematics used are clearly wanting in many areas (see O'Brien et al., this volume). Similarities in assemblages over vast areas, something long noted (e.g., Griffin 1967; Holmes 1903; Phillips 1970), continue to be an important way to link developments across the region. As information management procedures and site and assemblage records become more accessible, particularly online, such studies should receive increasing attention in the years to come (e.g., see papers in Anderson and Horak [eds.] 1995).

Excavated data pertaining to Early Woodland communities are sparse, and settlement models typically rely heavily on surface collections. Some Early Woodland cultures were characterized by communities that may have been occupied year-round with well-defined structures, large subterranean storage pits, and dense occupational middens, as in the Kellogg phase of northwest Georgia (Caldwell 1958:23–25; W. D. Wood and Bowen 1995). In the Central Mississippi Valley (D. Morse and P. Morse 1983), most reported sites are small, but several large sites are reported in western Tennessee (Mainfort 1994; Rolingson and Mainfort, this volume). Early Woodland Colbert settlement in the middle Tennessee River valley emphasized shell middens along the banks of the river, and rockshelters in the adjacent uplands were utilized intensively (Knight 1990a; Walthall 1980:114–15).

In the Duck River drainage, Long Branch phase occupations exhibit single or small isolated clusters of features (storage pits, shallow processing basins, earth ovens), suggesting short-term, occasional occupation (C. H. Faulkner and McCollough 1974:192; C. H. Faulkner and McCollough [eds.] 1982a:292–300). At the Aaron Shelton site (C. H. Faulkner, this volume), twelve features were disclosed, including storage pits, shallow basins, postholes, and two burials, suggesting that larger groups reoccupied the site on a frequent basis.

While it is dangerous to over generalize, many Early Woodland communities across the region are assumed to have been fairly small, on the order of a few structures and probably no more than fifty to sixty people. Early Woodland peoples in many areas appear to have been fairly mobile foraging populations, at best sedentary or settled only seasonally. Social organization appears in most areas to have been based on unranked or minimally ranked lineages and clans.

Early Woodland groups may have been more socially isolated than their Late Archaic ancestors in some areas. A decline in interaction appears to characterize the Early Woodland in the lower Southeast, for example, something likely related to the collapse of the Late Archaic exchange network centered on the Poverty Point site in the Lower Mississippi Valley, as well as the decline of the elaborate shell midden cultures of the south Atlantic coast. This is most manifest in the occurrence of materials used in everyday life. During the Late Archaic many of these artifacts were made of exotic materials that came from appreciable distances, while during the Early Woodland locally available materials tend to predominate. Interaction appears to have been primarily between immediately adjoining groups, and centered on collective burial ritual, sometimes at sites located at territorial boundaries.

This was not the case everywhere, however. Exchange clearly was not curtailed in Kentucky, where mortuary artifacts associated with Adena include a variety of copper objects, mica ornaments, galena, and beads of *Marginella,* freshwater pearls, and columella (W. Webb and Snow 1945; Clay, this volume). Steatite vessels occasionally occur with Colbert culture burials in northern Alabama (Walthall 1980:116). The Tchula period McCarty site in northeast Arkansas yielded an Alabama (?) greenstone celt, an adze of basalt from the St. Francois Mountains of Missouri, and copper beads (D. Morse 1986; D. Morse and P. Morse 1983:145–59). Nonlocal cherts, which regularly occur in Late Archaic lithic assemblages, however, are less common at Early Woodland sites in Kentucky (Railey 1996:87).

In most of the Southeast, little is actually known about Early Woodland mortuary practices. The quantity and variety of Adena burial mounds, which occur within the Southeast proper only in central and eastern Kentucky, are without parallel in other regions. First appearing around 500 B.C., Adena mounds themselves exhibit remarkable structural diversity (Clay 1998, this volume; W. Webb and Snow 1945). The Robbins Mound (W. Webb and Elliot 1942) and the Wright Mound (W. Webb 1940) were fairly large and covered a stratified sequence of mortuary processing crypts containing primary and secondary burials, while the Morgan Stone mound (W. Webb 1941a) covered the remains of only a few individuals. In the Robbins Mound skeletal sample, males and females are equally represented (Milner and Jefferies 1987). Circular and asymmetrical earthen enclosures are associated with some Adena mounds (Clay 1988a, 1988b, 1998), but comparable structures are unknown elsewhere in the Southeast.

The small conical Tchula period burial mounds in the North-Central Hills of Mississippi were completed during a single construction event. Although ceramic vessels were included in the mound fill, they were not associated with specific burials (J. L. Ford 1990). Nonlocal materials have not been reported. In northeast Arkansas, the flexed and semiflexed interments at the McCarty site were placed in oval pits (D. Morse 1986; D. Morse and P. Morse 1983:145–59). Fleshed, flexed inhumations and cremations occur within Long Branch phase habitation areas in south-central Tennessee (C. H. Faulkner and McCollough [eds.] 1982a:292–300). Colbert phase burials in northern Alabama typically were flexed and placed in pits within habitation areas; grave inclusions are rare (Walthall 1980:116).

Thus, during the Early Woodland period, discrete mortuary facilities like charnel structures and burial mounds appear in some areas. In some of these facilities, large numbers of people were placed or processed, indicating a fairly egalitarian form of social organization (although compared with regional population levels, the number of individuals interred in or processed through Early Woodland mounds may have been fairly low). In other areas, mound burial is assumed to have been reserved for smaller and smaller numbers of people over time, indicating appreciable status differentiation was occurring—that some individuals and perhaps their associated lineages were becoming more equal than others, probably because they were able to control long-distance exchange or ceremonial activity. How much status differentiation was actually occurring during the Early Woodland period, however, is unclear. Temporal relationships between Adena mounds are sufficiently ambiguous that these data cannot be used to support or reject this interpretation (Mainfort 1989), and data from contemporary sites in other parts of the region for ranking at this time level are equivocal at best. Not until Late Adena/Early Hopewell Middle Woodland times, from roughly 100 B.C. to A.D. 100, are presumed high-status individuals found buried in elaborate facilities. While leadership positions do not appear to have been inherited—the rise of ranked social classes does not occur until the very end of the Woodland period and is a particular hallmark of the ensuing Mississippian era—some individuals as well as their lineages and clans clearly controlled more wealth than others (cf. J. Brown 1981; Mainfort 1989). Burial mound construction is not ubiquitous over the region during the Early and subsequent Middle Woodland periods, however, and some investigators (i.e., Clay 1991, 1992) have suggested it occurs primarily in areas where subsistence stress was likely, where ritually maintained patterns of interaction could have helped groups buffer subsistence shortfalls, by making it easier to draw on the resources of neighboring areas.

Although cultivation of squash/gourd and a number of indigenous seed-producing plants, including goosefoot (chenopod), sumpweed, sunflower, knotweed, and maygrass, began prior to 1000 B.C. (e.g., Fritz 1997), most of these cultigens were first produced in quantity during the Early Woodland period (Gremillion 1998, this volume). Use of cultigens varied regionally. The large assemblage of native cultigens from Salts Cave, which dates to the Early Woodland period (P. Gardner 1987), includes an abundance of chenopod, but sumpweed, sunflower, and maygrass also are plentiful (Fritz 1993:39; P. Gardner 1987). It is likely that caches of these seeds were stored in the cave for later planting (Fritz 1997; Johannessen 1993a:61). Analyses of human paleofecal remains indicate that as much as two-thirds of the diet of the Early Woodland cave explorers in Kentucky came from domesticated chenopod, marshelder, and sunflower (Watson [ed.] 1969, 1974; Crothers et al., this volume). The potential crop yields of these species are as high as 1000 kilograms/hectare (B. D. Smith 1992c), comparable to that achievable from maize, which, however, was not widely or intensively cultivated until near the end of the Woodland period. Cold Oak shelter (Gremillion 1998), the Patrick site (Schroedl 1978a), and Rush (T. Rudolph 1991) also have produced native cultigens.

Agriculture was not universally adopted over the Southeast during the Woodland period. In some areas, particularly those rich in natural food resources like the Lower Mississippi Valley or southern Florida, only minimal evidence for agricultural food production has been found, and use of wild plant and animal food sources continued much as in earlier periods (see chapters by Kidder and Widmer, this volume). The extent to which indigenous agriculture was practiced even in areas where there is evidence for its occurrence and, particularly, the contribution native domesticates provided to overall diet remain unknown. In the absence of stable carbon isotope signatures like those conveniently left by maize, at present we simply do not know whether Early and Middle Woodland societies were heavily dependent upon these crops. Delimiting the role that agriculture, and specifically native domesticates, played during the Woodland period in the provisioning and organization of society is a major challenge facing the regional archaeological profession.

Given the extensive amount of archaeological research ongoing in the Southeast, and the increasing use of sophisticated field and laboratory procedures directed to the recovery and analysis of plant remains, however, the Eastern Woodlands is one of the best places on earth to explore the origins of agriculture and its impacts on human society (B. D. Smith 1989, 1992a). Among the research procedures that have become commonplace are water screening and flotation processing for the recovery of carbonized plant remains, the direct dating of individual seeds through accelerator mass spectrometry, stable carbon and nitrogen analyses of human bone to determine the relative contribution of maize and other foods to the diet, and use of scanning electron microscopy to determine morphological changes in plants and seeds resulting from domestication.

The Middle Woodland Period

During the Middle Woodland period, from roughly 200 B.C. to A.D. 400, there is evidence in the form of burial mound construction, shared artifacts, and iconography to suggest that societies across much of eastern North America, at least to some extent, interacted widely with one another, particularly in exchange and religious activity. While the Middle Woodland is, as a result, sometimes viewed as a period of panregional communality, we have come to realize that many diverse cultures were actually present, onto which a thin veneer of Hopewellian exchange, iconography, and ritual was overlain in some, but not all, parts of the Southeast (e.g., Anderson 1998; Griffin 1967, 1979; Mainfort 1996a; Seeman 1996; B. D. Smith 1986;

Steponaitis 1986). As most of the essays in this volume demonstrate, away from major centers little direct evidence exists for Hopewellian materials or interaction.

The apparent increase in mound construction during the Middle Woodland period does not seem to have been accompanied by major changes in community or settlement organization in most areas. While increasing status differentiation may have occurred in some areas during the Middle Woodland period, most peoples continued to live in small communities of well-made circular to oval structures. A tribal form of social organization, consisting of a number of interacting, more or less equal clans, or people claiming descent from common or mythic ancestors, was likely widespread (Anderson 2002; Knight 1990b). While hereditary leadership positions are not apparent, in some southeastern societies there is clear evidence that some clans or lineages were wealthier and more powerful than others, exercising considerable control over long-distance trade, public ceremony, and monumental construction (e.g., Mainfort 1988a, 1989). These leaders have been compared to Melanesian "big men," achieving their position through personal ability and the skillful manipulation of followers (e.g., B. D. Smith 1986:48); evidence for social ranking is, however, minimal in most areas. Even so, the accumulation of wealth, prestige, and control over ceremony and ritual within specific clans and lineages eventually led to social ranking and the emergence of hereditary leadership groups later in the Woodland in some areas.

While most people are assumed to have been buried in the traditional fashion, unquestionably following a variety of local practices, such as in communal charnel houses, or low mounds, or in individual or collective interments in or near dwellings, some individuals received unusual treatment. At a number of sites across the Southeast, small numbers of elaborate burials are found, sometimes in log-lined tombs under mound deposits. These individuals are usually accompanied by nonlocal grave goods like copper panpipes and earspools, prismatic blades, pieces of galena, cut copper and mica, and platform pipes—classic Hopewellian artifacts occurring within otherwise purely local Woodland assemblages. This highly atypical mortuary program associated with a few individuals has drawn appreciable research attention, coloring our perception of Middle Woodland life in many areas. Away from the major centers, in fact, Middle Woodland burial ceremonialism appears to have been relatively uncomplicated.

Although the Middle Woodland period often is characterized as a period during which there was a marked increase in burial mound construction, in fact, most parts of the Southeast have very few burial mounds relative to the numbers present in the Midwest. In south-central Tennessee (C. H. Faulkner 1988, this volume) and the Appalachian Summit of Tennessee

(J. Chapman and Keel 1979; Wetmore, this volume), both extensively studied regions, few Middle Woodland mounds are reported. By far the greatest concentration of burial mounds in the Southeast at this time occurs in the Copena mortuary complex of the middle Tennessee River valley (Beck 1995; Walthall 1973). Over fifty mounds are known from about two dozen sites. Roughly half of these sites have a single mound, but nine contain two mounds and one site has eight mounds.

In Copena, grave elaboration usually entailed the addition of nonlocal clays to the area surrounding the deceased. The complex mortuary processing programs seen in Ohio and Illinois (J. Brown 1979) are lacking, and virtually all Copena burials were fleshed, primary interments. Grave inclusions are few and are limited primarily to copper objects, galena, greenstone, and shell. There is a clear geographic division within the Copena area—the eastern and western sites differ in the specific artifacts that occur most frequently, and there is greater elaboration of burials in the western mounds. The eastern sites are thought to reflect an egalitarian social organization in which differentiation was based on age and personal achievement; the western mounds appear to represent societies with an emerging hierarchy in which a limited number of adults were able to accrue durable burial objects and to enlist assistance in constructing graves (Beck 1995).

More complex mortuary processing is indicated at several mound groups. At the Tunacunnhee site in northern Georgia, for example, interment modes included bundle, disarticulated, and cremation, as well as extended and flexed fleshed burials (Jefferies 1979). In northeastern Mississippi, Bynum Mound B was constructed over the remains of a charnel house with a sunken floor, and Bynum Mound D covered a small mortuary facility consisting of a rectangular floor with a fired circular pit near the center, surrounded by four large posts (Cotter and Corbett 1951). Several mounds at Pharr (Bohannon 1972) were constructed over low earthen platforms, some of which had burned areas and other probable processing features on their surface. The paucity of skeletal material at both Bynum and Pharr implies that final interment generally was not within a mound (Mainfort 1996a). At Helena Crossing, Arkansas, the excavated mounds were constructed over mortuary crypts similar to those seen commonly in Illinois (J. A. Ford 1963; Mainfort 1988b; Toth 1988). Both fleshed and cremation burials were found at the non-mound Yearwood site (Butler 1979). Relationships between habitation sites and burial mounds have received little attention in the interior Southeast, and this is an area where much more work is needed.

In general, the exotic materials and artifacts associated with the Hopewellian horizon in Ohio and Illinois occur sparingly throughout the Southeast (Seeman 1979a). The main influx of these characteristic materials and artifact styles probably was limited to only a few hundred years, between about 100 B.C. and A.D. 200 (C. H. Faulkner 1996; Mainfort 1996a; Walling et al. 1991). Especially distinctive are copper panpipes and bicymbal earspools, but beads, celts, and reel-shaped gorgets also occur. Although most Middle Woodland copper is of northern origin, some apparently derives from southeastern sources (Goad 1979). Mica from Appalachian sources is found at a number of sites across the Southeast (Seeman 1979a), as are bladelets of Flint Ridge, Ohio, flint (J. Chapman and Keel 1979; Mainfort 1986). Galena also is widespread, but the bulk has been found at Copena sites (Beck 1995; Walthall 1973).

Major southeastern Middle Woodland ceremonial centers, with their monumental construction and elaborate mortuary behavior, are thought in many cases to represent regional ceremonial and trading nodes in the widespread ceremonial and exchange network that likely originated within or was to some extent shaped by events in the Hopewellian heartlands of the Midwest (e.g., Anderson 1998; Brose 1979a; Brose and Greber [eds.] 1979; Mainfort 1988c, 1996a; Mainfort and Sullivan [eds.] 1998). In some cases direct contact or trading links to and from the Hopewell heartland in Ohio are indicated, most typically along apparently favored communications arteries such as the major river systems of the interior. Yet seemingly geographically isolated locales such as Pinson Mounds (Mainfort 1986, 1988a) and Ingomar (Rafferty 1990, this volume) also gave rise to some of the largest Middle Woodland sites in the Southeast. Along portions of the southern and middle Atlantic seaboard (see chapters by Herbert and by Hantman and Gold, this volume), such sites are extremely rare. How and why various societies participated (or chose not to participate) in the regional interaction networks is, in fact, a major opportunity for research.

In the Ohio River valley, the massive ceremonial mounds and geometric earthworks of the Middle Woodland Hopewellian culture appear to have evolved directly from the burial mound complexes of the Early Woodland Adena peoples (Clay 1998). Mound building for feasting and burial of the dead occurs in a number of areas during the Middle Woodland period, and some of the ceremonial complexes that were built, such as at Marksville in Louisiana and Pinson in west Tennessee, are enormous in scope, covering hundreds of acres, with mound and burial complexes rivaling any found in the Ohio River valley (Mainfort 1996a; Mainfort and Sullivan [eds.] 1998). Major and minor centers, in fact, emerged and declined across the Eastern Woodlands during the Middle Woodland period, organizational changes that appear to be tied to shifts in regional patterns of exchange, the success of individual leaders or lineages in specific areas, and the ripple effects that changes in one locality caused elsewhere (e.g., Anderson 1998:295–96; Clay

1991, 1992, 1998; Hantman and Gold, this volume). Pinson Mounds, for example, was a major center over a period of several centuries, from circa 100 B.C. to A.D. 500. Most of the large mounds and earthworks, however, were erected in the first several centuries of site use. Similar patterns appear to characterize the use of major centers of Ohio Hopewell in the Scioto and nearby river valleys, which had periods of florescence, seeming stability or stasis, and then decline (e.g., Pacheco 1996).

As during the Early Woodland, some centers are located in boundary areas, along drainage divides or along smaller tributaries, suggesting they continued to serve as locations where peoples from many different groups or those living throughout large areas came together in collective ceremony. Only in the Late Woodland and Mississippian periods, with the emergence of true civic-ceremonial centers, do the region's mound centers shift from serving many groups and dispersed populations to being the geographic as well as political centers of individual societies (Anderson 2002; Clay 1998).

Middle Woodland populations in many parts of the Southeast also built platform mounds, a form of public architecture that until about twenty-five years ago was thought restricted in time to the Mississippian period (Dickens 1975; Hally 1975; Mainfort 1996b; Mainfort [ed.] 1988). The construction and use of these mounds appears tied to mortuary ritual in some areas and to public consumption/feasting activities in other locations, while still others are surmounted by structures or large posts, suggesting ceremonial facilities or possible astronomical alignments. Just as we now know that mound building itself dates far earlier than we once thought, to the Middle Archaic period, we now know that platform mound construction in the Southeast dates well back into the Woodland period, almost a thousand years earlier than once recognized. Examples of major Woodland platform mounds in the Southeast include the 10-meter-high Ozier Mound at Pinson, which was built around 2000 years ago, and the 18-meter-high platform mound at Kolomoki in south Georgia, built circa A.D. 200–300. From the Middle Woodland to the Mississippian period, the function of these mounds changed, from being the probable arena of public competition and ceremony between unranked lineage heads, to serving as substructures for the residences and temples of powerful hereditary elites.

In contrast to later Terminal Woodland and Mississippian examples, Middle Woodland mound centers—large and small—do not appear to have supported large resident populations. The relatively large, bent-pole structures at sites like Bynum and Pinson Mounds are linked to short-term, specialized activities, not domestic habitation (B. D. Smith 1992c; Mainfort 1996a).

The importance of intensive agriculture and specifically the role maize may have played in the emergence and evolution of Middle Woodland society has been the subject of intensive debate for decades. Thanks to the attention directed to the collection and analysis of paleosubsistence remains that has occurred in recent years, we now believe that native domesticates like sunflower, chenopod, and marshelder were grown in parts of the Midwest and Midsouth during the Middle Woodland period (Fritz 1993; B. D. Smith 1992c), although, as noted previously, their actual importance in both subsistence and the organization of society remains unknown. Besides the carbonized plant remains themselves, however, there is evidence for fairly intensive cultivation in the form of evidence for land clearing, the manufacture and use of hoes, the construction and use of storage facilities, and the manufacture of specialized ceramic vessels for both the cooking and storage of these crops (Delcourt et al. 1998; Gremillion 1993a, 1998, this volume; B. D. Smith 1992c). Thanks to stable carbon isotope analyses we also now know that maize, a tropical cultigen first domesticated in Mesoamerica, did not become a major constituent of the diet in many areas until the very end of the Woodland period, after circa A.D. 900 (Lynott et al. 1986; Yarnell 1993). While a few specimens of maize have been securely dated to the Middle Woodland period, such as those from the Icehouse Bottom site in Tennessee and at the Edwin Harness site in Ohio, maize appears to have been a minor and archaeologically almost invisible crop for nearly a millennium. A tropical cultigen dependent on human beings throughout its life cycle, maize probably was not initially well suited to a temperate climate, and many centuries may have been required before strains developed that would thrive in the Eastern Woodlands and before people learned how to cultivate it successfully. Tobacco apparently entered the region about the same time as maize, however, and was apparently quickly adopted and became an important ceremonial plant, evidenced by the widespread occurrence of pipes in the archaeological record from this time onward (B. D. Smith 1992c).

Analyses of the source areas, distributions, and stylistic variability in Middle Woodland artifacts have a long history in the Eastern Woodlands and are helping resolve patterns of interaction (e.g., Goad 1979; Stoltman and Snow 1998). It is likely, for example, that some materials moved along the same trails used by Indian groups in the early historic era. New and innovative analyses have also focused on the occurrence of specific ceramic design motifs over large areas, particularly in the South Appalachian area where a local Middle Woodland culture known as Swift Creek occurred (F. Snow and Stephenson 1998; Stephenson et al., this volume; J. Williams and Elliott [eds.] 1998). Swift Creek complicated stamped pottery is characterized by elaborate and symbolically richly imbued design motifs, offering an almost unparalleled opportunity to explore exchange and interaction as well as questions of Middle Woodland world view and cosmology. By document-ing subtle flaws in the paddles used to produce this pottery, direct interac-tion over large areas and between many sites has been documented, while studies of clay sources have helped determine that actual vessels were mov-ing in some areas while in others it was the carved paddle stamp itself that moved (Snow and Stephenson 1998; Stoltman and Snow 1998).

Middle Woodland iconography has also proven a fertile if somewhat speculative area of study in recent years. Both plant and animal motifs as well as cosmological themes such as the quartering of the world, for ex-ample, are found in Swift Creek ceramic designs (F. Snow 1998), while classic Hopewellian vessels as well as southern variants like Marksville are dominated by avian images, typically raptors or ducks. Some of these motifs may have served as individual or lineage/community guardian spirits, while others were likely representations of more general forces of the cosmos such as the sky and underworld (Brose 1985; Penny 1985:184–89).

The Late Woodland Period

The Late Woodland period, from roughly A.D. 400 to 1000, has been viewed traditionally as a period of cultural decline and possibly turmoil across much of the East (e.g., Phillips 1970; S. Williams 1963). Until quite recently many researchers tended to overlook or simplify cultural developments during the Late Woodland period, preferring instead to focus on the societies that came both before and after, which, as a rule, had more impressive mound and mortuary complexes and, because of the existence of widespread prestige-goods exchange networks, had more spectacular artifact assemblages. Thus, southeastern Late Woodland societies have been variously described as "good gray cultures" (S. Williams 1963:297) or undistinguished and simplistic compared to what came before and after.

We now know this view is incorrect (e.g., Nassaney and Cobb 1991). As noted previously, the exotica and decorative motifs of the Hopewellian hori-zon occur infrequently over the Southeast, and there is little evidence for a diminution in mound building over time, at least on a regional scale. Thus, evidence of a Late Woodland "decline" is not readily apparent in the ar-chaeological record. The Late Woodland, in reality, is a time of appreciable cultural change. There is evidence for population growth across the region. In many areas, households and small communities became both numerous and widely scattered, filling the landscape. A major technological advance, the bow and arrow, appeared and spread rapidly and this, coupled with evi-dence for increasing pressure on food resources, may help to explain the dramatically increased evidence for warfare seen in some areas (Blitz 1988; Milner 1999; Nassaney and Pyle 1999).

In some portions of the Southeast, mound construction was curtailed during Late Woodland times. For example, no mounds are associated with the McKelvey (Walthall 1980:140) or Miller III (N. Jenkins 1982:111) cultures of the Midsouth. The Eastern Highland Rim of Tennessee also lacks Late Woodland mounds, but no Middle Woodland examples are reported either (C. H. Faulkner 1988). In fact, mound construction in the Southeast did not cease during the Late Woodland period, and it actually increased in some areas, such as in the central and lower Mississippi Valley, and along the Gulf Coastal Plain, in the heartlands of Coles Creek and Weeden Island cultures. Burial mounds are also abundant in the Watts Bar and Tellico reservoirs in eastern Tennessee; many probably are Late Woodland (Schroedl 1978b). In northern Alabama, several low conical mounds are attributed to the Late Woodland Flint River culture (Walthall 1980:136). At Pinson Mounds, two small mortuary mounds were built after the peak usage of the site (Mainfort 1988c).

Late Woodland groups also constructed platform mounds. At the Cold Springs site in northern Georgia (Jefferies 1994), one such earthwork had at least five construction stages. Other possible Late Woodland examples in Georgia include the Leake (W. D. Wood and Bowen 1995:25), Swift Creek (Jefferies 1994), and Anneewakee Creek (Dickens 1975; W. D. Wood and Bowen 1995:79) sites. Perhaps the most impressive evidence of Late Woodland mound construction in the region is Toltec Mounds in Arkansas, characterized by eighteen mounds surrounded by an earthen embankment and a ditch (Rolingson 1998a, this volume).

The Late Woodland was thus not a time of organizational decline or simplification throughout the region. Weeden Island culture societies along the Gulf Coast and the Coles Creek societies of the central and lower Mississippi Valley were as complex as any that came before. The Weeden Island mortuary complex has yielded artifacts as spectacular as any found in the region, particularly the painted ceramic effigy pots that are a hallmark of this culture (Milanich, this volume). The emergence of formal civic-ceremonial complexes, consisting of arrangements of residential and temple mounds around plazas, and occupied by hereditary elites, appears to occur in the Coles Creek culture, from circa A.D. 700 to 900 (Barker 1999; Kidder, this volume; Rolingson, this volume). For the first time mound complexes were occupied continuously and served as the geographic as well as religious centers of society. Mound complexes, formerly the intermittently used arenas of competition and mortuary ritual, now became the permanently occupied temples and residents of elites and their supporters. The arrangement of mounds at a number of these centers indicates they were laid out using standard measurement units, and at some of them significant astronomical events are highlighted by the arrangement of mounds and posts, such as summer and winter solstices (Sherrod and Rolingson 1987).

While a decline in the regionwide pattern of individual status rivalry may have occurred during the Late Woodland in some areas, clan- or lineage-based descent continued in others. By the end of the period there is clear evidence for the emergence of ranking or distinct hereditary status differences between lineages or clans in some areas, particularly in the central and lower Mississippi Valley. The Late Woodland period also witnesses the beginnings of a dramatic shift in agricultural practices in parts of the region, to intensive maize cultivation. The impact of maize production and consumption on the use of native cultigens remains unclear, in part because the latter apparently do not leave a readily identifiable chemical signature in human bone. In the American Bottom, for example, starchy seeds remain abundant after the abrupt adoption of maize circa A.D. 750 and throughout Mississippian times (Rindos and Johannessen 1991:42). Here, maize clearly was an addition to the diet, not a replacement for traditional foods.

In south-central Tennessee, moderate amounts of maize occur in circa A.D. 600 contexts in association with native domesticates (C. H. Faulkner 1988; Gremillion and Yarnell 1986). No evidence has been found, either through stable isotope analyses of skeletal remains or in the form of numerous carbonized plant remains, however, for the intensive cultivation and consumption of maize in the Coles Creek culture area, where such use of maize occurs much later (Fritz and Kidder 1993). The subsistence base of the complex Coles Creek societies that emerged in the Lower Mississippi Valley was thus comparable to what earlier Woodland societies had—wild plants and animals, supplemented by indigenous crops.

Why was there a lag of between six and eight centuries between the initial cultivation of maize in the Southeast during Middle Woodland times and its emergence as a major crop? As noted previously, in its initial form maize may not have been well suited to the temperate climate, or else people had not learned how to care for it effectively. More likely, in some parts of the region, particularly across the Atlantic and Gulf coastal plains, the natural occurrence of wild plant and animal food resources was so great that agriculture of any kind was unnecessary. In other areas, such as in the Midsouth and lower Midwest, the harvest yields from indigenous crops, coupled with their long tradition of use, may have been sufficient to preclude switching to the new cultigen. Maize may have also been a restricted crop, used primarily on ceremonial occasions, or it may have been initially harvested and eaten in the green state and hence been unsuited to long-term

storage (and, possibly, greater likelihood of preservation). The labor investment required to clear and cultivate fields of maize, additionally, may have
been sufficient to discourage its adoption. That maize emerged as the region's
dominant crop at the end of the Woodland is likely a result of, and no doubt
contributed to as well, the increasing population pressure and changes in
organization that were occurring at this time.

We have seen that between the Middle and the Late Woodland a shift in
the location of the primary centers of power or political dominance and
exchange occurred in the Eastern Woodlands, from the upper Midwest to
the lower Mississippi Valley and along the Gulf Coast. The Coles Creek and
Weeden Island societies of the lower Southeast appear to evolve without
interruption from preceding Middle Woodland Marksville/Troyville and
Santa Rosa–Swift Creek cultures. This seeming unabated development of
cultural complexity proceeded, furthermore, in the near complete absence
of evidence for the use of agricultural foodstuffs. Once intensive maize cultivation appeared after circa A.D. 800, power relations shifted again, this
time to the central Mississippi Valley, in the region extending from northeast Arkansas to the American Bottom. Many of the attributes that characterize the Mississippian period appeared in at least parts of the Southeast
during the Late Woodland, such as civic-ceremonial centers, the use of platform mounds as elite residences, shell-tempered pottery and wall-trench house
construction, and the intensive cultivation of maize. The period from roughly
A.D. 750 to 1000, formerly called the Late Woodland, is in fact now described as the Emergent Mississippian in some areas (J. Kelly 1980, 1987;
B. D. Smith [ed.] 1990), though this designation is appropriate only for areas for which there are extensive excavated data documenting not only the
importance of maize, but also the appearance of large, permanently occupied communities with public buildings. Use of the term is not widespread
over the Southeast, probably in part because of its teleological implications
and because Mississippian was late to appear (or never appeared) in some
areas, particularly in the eastern part of the region (Muller 1997:118).

Toward the very end of the Woodland period, dramatic shifts in iconography begin to occur that appear associated with the increasing importance
of agricultural food production, specifically maize, in everyday life. Solar
disks increasingly replace avian representations as a central icon in some
areas, something thought to reflect the gradual replacement of a highly individualistic and egalitarian, animal-centered hunting/guardian spirit–based
ceremonialism and ritual—with roots no doubt stretching deep into the Archaic—by a more collective, elite-directed communal ceremonialism centered on agricultural productivity and reinforcing the sacred and hereditary
position of the leadership. Individualistic expression appears to have begun

to be channeled from more traditional emphases on hunting to success in warfare and militarism. The iconography of the region thus mirrors the dramatic changes in status and social agendas that were occurring, from achieved prestige through the manipulation of foreign objects to the hereditary dominance of lineages and societies over other such groups. In contrast, changes in the underlying cosmology of the southeastern Indians, such as the quartering or layered nature of the world, appear to have been much less pronounced.

Conclusions

The 2200-year span of the Woodland period was one in which major changes occurred in the Southeast, particularly in burial patterns, long-distance exchange, mound ceremonialism, community organization, and political leadership. Our knowledge of the period has grown immensely in recent years, resulting in changes to many of our long-held beliefs about the importance of agriculture in general and maize in particular, the age of platform mounds and civic-ceremonial centers, and the emergence of complex society. The Southeast, we are coming to realize, is one of the best places in the world to explore important questions of cultural evolution. The potential database is enormous for the study of how people made use of the southern landscape down through the millennia. In the pages that follow, the contributors to this volume explore how this was done during the Woodland period in various parts of the region.

Chapter 2

Woodland Period Archaeology of the Central Mississippi Valley

Martha Ann Rolingson and Robert C. Mainfort, Jr.

The Central Mississippi Valley (D. Morse and P. Morse 1983) encompasses the northern portion of the lower Mississippi River alluvial valley (Figure 2.1). By the early 1900s, Holmes recognized the middle Mississippi Valley group as a geographic area with distinctive late prehistoric pottery and noted that "its greatest and most striking development centers about the contiguous portions of Arkansas, Missouri, Illinois, Kentucky, and Tennessee" (Holmes 1903:80), which closely corresponds to the present study area. Fisk (1944) described the geomorphology of the lower Mississippi alluvial valley, and his subdivisions of lowlands separated by older uplands have important implications for prehistoric occupation (Phillips et al. 1951). The subdivisions continue to figure prominently in regional studies (McNutt [ed.] 1996; Morse and Morse 1983; O'Brien and Dunnell [eds.] 1998; Phillips 1970), although Fisk's descriptions and interpretations have been modified by Saucier (1974, 1994).

The core area of the Central Mississippi Valley region is the alluvial valley proper, bounded by the loess bluffs of Kentucky, Tennessee, and Mississippi on the east and the escarpment of the Ozark Plateau on the west. It extends north to the confluence of the Ohio River, while the southern terminus is the mouth of the Arkansas River. In eastern Arkansas and southeast Missouri, Crowley's Ridge separates the Eastern and Western Lowlands. The St. Francis Basin, which extends nearly 200 miles between Cairo, Illinois, and Helena, Arkansas, comprises most of the Eastern Lowlands and is bounded by Crowley's Ridge on the west and on the east by the Mississippi River. The Western Lowlands parallel their eastern counterpart, but are characterized by sediments of glacial outwash deposited during the early Wisconsinan stage by braided streams of the ancestral Mississippi and Ohio rivers. The western extent of these Lowlands is the Ozark escarpment and Grand Prairie.

Since 1980, several critiques of the space-time units used to organize archaeological data in the study area have appeared (see O'Brien et al., this

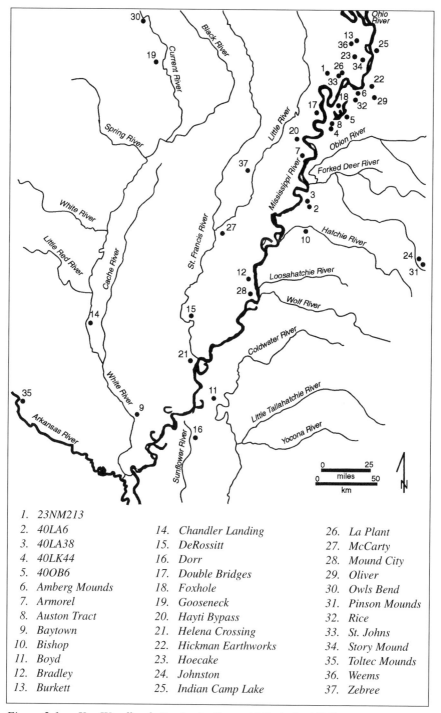

Figure 2.1 — Key Woodland sites in the Central Mississippi Valley

1. 23NM213
2. 40LA6
3. 40LA38
4. 40LK44
5. 40OB6
6. Amberg Mounds
7. Armorel
8. Auston Tract
9. Baytown
10. Bishop
11. Boyd
12. Bradley
13. Burkett
14. *Chandler Landing*
15. *DeRossitt*
16. *Dorr*
17. *Double Bridges*
18. *Foxhole*
19. *Gooseneck*
20. *Hayti Bypass*
21. *Helena Crossing*
22. *Hickman Earthworks*
23. *Hoecake*
24. *Johnston*
25. *Indian Camp Lake*
26. *La Plant*
27. *McCarty*
28. *Mound City*
29. *Oliver*
30. *Owls Bend*
31. *Pinson Mounds*
32. *Rice*
33. *St. Johns*
34. *Story Mound*
35. *Toltec Mounds*
36. *Weems*
37. *Zebree*

volume). Although not unsympathetic to many of these criticisms, we have elected to present our data along a traditional line, emphasizing the archaeological data and not forcing these data into existing culture-historical units.

Early Woodland: Tchula Period

Early Woodland is essentially synonymous with the Tchula period, which dates from about 600 B.C. to 200 B.C. (McNutt 1996a:169; D. Morse and P. Morse 1983:137, 1996:131; O'Brien and Wood 1998:174). Reported Tchula sites are rare throughout most of the study area, and few have been excavated, including McCarty in the Little River Lowland (Morse 1986), Boyd in the upper Yazoo Basin (Connaway and McGahey 1971), and Burkett (Hopgood 1969:124–33; S. Williams 1954:28–38) and Weems (J. R. Williams 1968:160–71; S. Williams 1954) in the Cairo Lowland. Few radiocarbon determinations are available and none are particularly instructive. The Burkett site has been dated to circa 100–200 B.C. (Lafferty and Price 1996:13). At the Boyd site, radiocarbon ages of 220 ± 90 B.C. and A.D. 85 ± 100 were obtained from a Tchula occupation stratum with a ceramic assemblage dominated by fabric-marked and plain surfaces (Connaway and McGahey 1971). The more recent date seems anomalous, and use of student's t-test demonstrates that the two assays probably are different (t = 2.27, p <.05). The earlier assay seems reasonable for a late Tchula occupation. The charcoal samples "were collected one small particle at a time" (Connaway and McGahey 1971:59), which may account for the range of dates obtained.

The start of the Woodland period generally is equated with the widespread appearance of pottery. While this may be valid in a general sense, pottery clearly is associated with Poverty Point contexts, including the Poverty Point site itself (in northeastern Louisiana), which dates to circa 3200 B.P. (J. Gibson 1996a). Recognition of Tchula occupations generally is based on the presence of Cormorant Cord Impressed and/or Twin Lakes Fabric Marked ceramics (Mainfort 1996b; D. Morse and P. Morse 1983:142, 144; Phillips 1970:876). Sand or grog or both often are present as paste inclusions, but it is unclear whether these represent temper in the strict sense (see Mainfort and Chapman 1994; Weaver 1963). Plain surfaces are common, while surface treatments and decoration include individual cord impressions, fabric marking, and cord marking. Some types, notably Withers Fabric Marked, occur in both Tchula and Early Marksville contexts (Phillips 1970:877; Walling et al. 1991). Less common are stamped and punctated motifs; red filming also occurs (Brookes and Taylor 1986; Morse 1986). Vessels may have tetrapodal or flat bases (Mainfort and Chapman 1994; Morse and Morse 1996), bosses below the rim (O'Brien and Wood 1998:186; Price 1986), and cord notching on rim interiors (Mainfort and Chapman 1994). Some whole vessels have triangular orifices (J. L. Ford 1990). Projectile points include expanded stemmed and corner-notched forms; medium-sized triangular Frazier points are reported at several western Tennessee sites in association with Tchula ceramics (Mainfort 1996a:14). Biconical, spherical, and perhaps some other styles of baked clay objects often are present (Morse 1986; Price 1986; see also Mainfort 1997a).

Virtually no information on Tchula period subsistence has been obtained. Floral and faunal data from the Boyd site (Connaway and McGahey 1971) are incompletely reported and not abundant. Floral remains associated with Zone 1 included acorn, black walnut, pecan, and persimmon; the scant faunal assemblage consisted almost exclusively of fish and turtle bones. Carbon isotope analysis of Tchula period human remains from the McCarty site indicates only that maize was not a subsistence staple (Morse 1986:74). Native small starchy seed crops were cultivated in the western sections of the region by roughly 1000 B.C. (Fritz 1990a, 1993), and excavations at site 23MI605 suggest that domesticated *Chenopodium* was economically important to some populations in the Central Mississippi Valley by circa 1500 B.C. (Lopinot 1999).

Most reported sites on the west side of the Mississippi River are small, but several fairly large sites (>2 hectares) are known in western Tennessee (Mainfort 1994). In Arkansas and southeast Missouri, reported Tchula period sites are located along the natural levees of rivers, as well as in swampy areas and the adjacent uplands (e.g., Price 1986).

Conical burial mounds in the North-Central Hills of Mississippi were completed during a single construction event and measure less than 3 meters high and 15 meters in diameter. Ceramic vessels were included in the mound fill, but were not associated with specific burials (J. L. Ford 1990). Mounds reported on sites in the Cairo Lowland are located on higher alluvial land surfaces. At the McCarty site, the flexed and semiflexed interments were placed in oval pits. The site yielded several artifacts fashioned from nonlocal materials: a celt of Alabama greenstone, an adze of basalt from the St. Francois Mountains of Missouri, and copper beads (perhaps from the Lake Superior region) (Morse 1986; D. Morse and P. Morse 1983:145–59).

Middle Woodland: Marksville Period

The Early Marksville period in the Lower Mississippi Valley equates with the Hopewellian horizon in the upper Midwest, which dates between approximately 200 B.C. and A.D. 300. Late Marksville (ca. A.D. 200–400) has not been documented in the Central Mississippi Valley and will not be treated; the general time period is subsumed under Late Woodland.

Many researchers, beginning with Setzler (1933a, 1933b), have characterized Marksville as culturally inferior to Hopewellian societies to the north (see Mainfort 1996a, 1997b). This position has been strongly advocated by Toth (1988:41), who states: "In short, most elements of the mortuary procedures found in various combinations in the early Marksville mounds of the Lower Valley can be traced to Hopewellian contexts in the Illinois Valley—but only in disjointed bits and pieces, not as a unified whole." This implies that Hopewellian manifestations in Illinois exhibit minimal variation (which is not the case) and the groups associated with these sites shared a universal belief system, while Marksville societies never reached such an alleged level of development. In a similar vein, Toth (1988:29) avers that the "widespread and apparently sudden presence of a number of good horizon markers" in the Lower Mississippi Valley was the result of "diffusion" and even direct contact with Hopewellian societies in Illinois.

The notion of "Marksville inferiority" is flawed on several counts. Mound construction has a far longer history in the Lower Mississippi Valley than in more northerly areas, and conical burial mounds dating to the pre-Marksville Tchula period are well documented (J. L. Ford 1990). Large Middle Woodland platform mounds are present at several sites in the Midsouth (Mainfort [ed.] 1988); none are recorded in Illinois. Enclosures, rare in Illinois (cf. Kellar 1979:106), occur at a number of sites in the Lower Mississippi Valley (Mainfort 1996a; Thunen 1988). Earthen burial platforms—not found to the north—further serve to distinguish the Middle Woodland societies of the Midsouth and Lower Mississippi Valley (Mainfort 1996a). Finally, radiocarbon evidence is equivocal on the question of cultural precedence and, if anything, supports a greater age for Marksville societies.

Within the alluvial valley proper, the best-dated site is Helena Crossing (J. A. Ford 1963), but the four dates have caused some confusion for many years, as they span the period 150 B.C. to A.D. 335, all ± 75 radiocarbon years (Crane and Griffin 1963:240–41; the standard deviations published by J. A. Ford [1963] represent a doubling of the actual figures). The two assays on Helena Crossing Mound C, Tomb D (1625 ± 75 B.P. and 1930 ± 75 B.P.) differ significantly, allowing the more recent to be rejected (Mainfort 1988b, 1996a). The remaining radiocarbon ages, especially the two earliest (150 B.C. and A.D. 20), seem compatible with the ceramic assemblage from Mound C, which exhibits several attributes characteristic of the Tchula period (i.e., tetrapodal vessels and soft, chalky ceramic pastes). At the Hayti Bypass site, charcoal from a pit containing two Marksville-related sherds and a Copena point produced an AMS date of circa A.D. 240–440 (Conner and Ray 1995:72–79).

Over forty radiocarbon determinations have been published for the Pinson Mounds site (Figure 2.2), located about 70 miles east of Memphis (Mainfort 1988a, 1988c, 1996a; Mainfort and Walling 1992). An uncalibrated assay of 205 ± 115 B.C. was obtained from a stratum under Mound 12 that contained several mortuary features and a small sample of ceramics that were primarily fabric marked. The uppermost summit of Ozier Mound (Mound 5) dates between the latter half of the first century B.C. and the first several decades A.D.; associated with this summit were mica, copper, and microblades. Four dates on tombs at the base of the northern Twin Mound, which contained several Hopewellian commodities, place construction during the first century A.D. Mound 10, a small, irregularly shaped platform mound, dates to the third century A.D.

Radiometric dates for the Bynum, Pharr, and Miller sites in northern Mississippi (Walling et al. 1991) support a time range of 200 B.C. to A.D. 200 for Early Marksville. These dates and those from Pinson Mounds show that cord marking surpassed fabric marking as the dominant ceramic surface treatment during the first century A.D. (Mainfort and Walling 1992; Walling et al. 1991); comparable data are not available for the alluvial valley proper (e.g., Morse 1988). Diagnostic Early Marksville decorative styles, such as the bird motif and crosshatched rims, both resembling Havana-Hopewell pottery, appeared by around 100 B.C. (cf. Walling et al. 1991). These decorative modes, as well as the "tubby pots" on which they consistently appear, probably were not produced after about A.D. 200 (see Toth 1988:49–50 and Fortier et al. 1989a:556–60). Ceramic pastes generally are "tempered" with particles of grog or fired clay in the alluvial valley, but in some parts of the region, including western Tennessee and western Mississippi, pastes are sandy. On the western side of the river, grog temper predominates at sites near the Mississippi River, but is replaced by sand farther to the west (e.g., Lafferty and Hess [eds.] 1996:209). The cultural significance of the technological differences is the subject of some discussion (Lafferty and Price 1996; Mainfort and Chapman 1994; Phillips et al. 1951:432). Sandy pastes also are characteristic of most of the ceramics from Pinson Mounds and presumably contemporary sites in western Tennessee (Mainfort 1986; Mainfort et al. 1997); reinforced rims ("rim folds") also are common.

Few subsistence data have been recovered. Test pits at the Indian Camp Lake site in western Kentucky produced white-tailed deer, hickory nutshell fragments, and a few seeds of American lotus and goosefoot. Hickory nuts also were associated with the probable Marksville component at site 23NM213 in southeast Missouri (R. Marshall 1965a:32). Floral and faunal

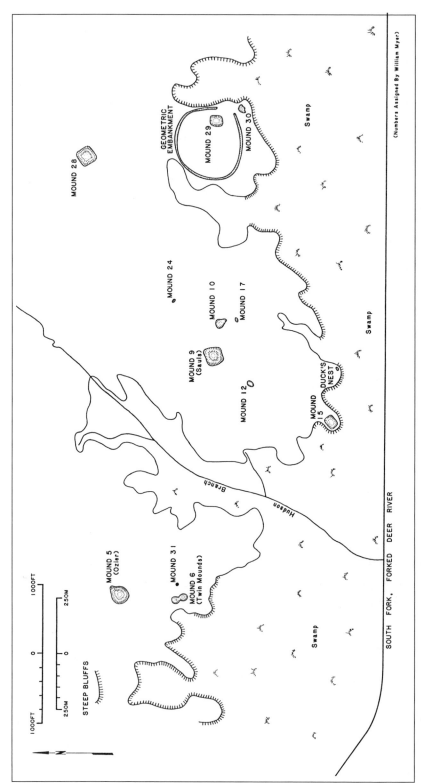

Figure 2.2 — *The Pinson Mounds site (40MD1) (Mainfort and Walling 1992:128, courtesy Midcontinental Journal of Archaeology)*

data from Zone 2 at the Boyd site (Connaway and McGahey 1971) included acorn, black walnut, pecan, hickory nuts, and persimmon. The faunal assemblage implies the importance of fish and turtles, but mammals, particularly white-tailed deer, are more prominent than in the underlying Tchula component.

Marksville habitation sites are under-reported, perhaps because of masking by later components at the same sites and the rarity of decorated ceramic types (Morse 1988), and very few have been excavated. The latter include Boyd (Connaway and McGahey 1971), La Plant, and St. Johns (R. Adams and Walker 1942:11; Toth 1988:74–81; J. R. Williams 1974:49–53); two test pits were excavated at both Indian Camp Lake (R. Lewis 1996:57; Sussenbach and Lewis 1987:93–108) and at site 23NM213 in southeast Missouri (R. Marshall 1965a:31–34). A number of sites yielding distinctive Marksville decorated types are known in northwest Mississippi (Toth 1988:89–136), and numerous sites of probable Middle Woodland age have been located in the general vicinity of Pinson Mounds (Mainfort 1986:1, 1994:15–16). Most of the latter sites are small and produce few artifacts; none have been tested. Morse and Morse (1996:126) note that in northeast Arkansas, major Marksville components are present at Armorel, Bradley, and Mound City. Available data suggest that the number of sites increased during the Middle Woodland period over that of the Early Woodland period.

Excavations at Pinson Mounds significantly changed interpretations of Middle Woodland in the Southeast (Mainfort 1996a; Mainfort [ed.] 1988). The site includes more than twelve mounds and a geometric enclosure within an area of about 160 hectares (Figure 2.2). Particularly noteworthy are the five large rectangular platform mounds, ranging in height from 2.5 to 22 meters. Primary construction and use of the site occurred between about 100 B.C. and A.D. 350 (Mainfort 1988c; Mainfort and Walling 1992). Another site with large flat-topped Middle Woodland mounds, the Johnston site, is located 4 kilometers northwest of Pinson Mounds (Kwas and Mainfort 1986).

The Helena Crossing site was a group of five conical burial mounds located on the southern end of Crowley's Ridge (J. A. Ford 1963). All of the earthworks were between 4 and 6 meters tall and approximately 30 meters in diameter. Construction of these mortuary facilities at this prominent location probably is related to territoriality (R. Chapman 1981). Very few Middle Woodland mounds are reported in the alluvial valley in Kentucky and Tennessee. The Amberg Mounds, in the northern Reelfoot Lake Basin, are a pair of conical (presumably burial) mounds of probable Middle Woodland age; each is approximately 4 meters tall and 20 meters in diameter. Six small Middle Woodland components, known only from surface collections, are reported nearby (Mainfort 1996b). A pair of mounds of equivalent size are reported at site 40LA38 in the Lauderdale County, Tennessee, bottomlands.

Two features were exposed beneath Helena Crossing Mound B. One consisted of four large logs placed on the original ground surface near the center of the mound. The second, a large submound mortuary crypt covered with four large logs, contained the remains of a young male and a mature male. Mound C was slightly larger and was structurally more complex. Four large mortuary crypts were exposed, as well as a log-covered individual tomb and a number of individuals not interred in log-covered features (J. A. Ford 1963). These facilities are very similar to presumably contemporary structures in Illinois, such as Wilson Mound 6 (Neumann and Fowler 1952). Placed with the dead were a silver-plated copper panpipe, bicymbal copper earspools, several large conch shells, a mica sheet, a copper ferrule, Wyandotte flint bladelets, and some *Marginella* beads. A number of whole and partial ceramic vessels also were recovered (most from deposits in Mound C), including tubby pots, beakers, and hemispherical bowls. Mainfort's (1988b) analysis of mortuary patterning demonstrated that Toth's (1988:40) inference that Helena Crossing represents a "stratified" society is incorrect.

Three mortuary mounds have been excavated at Pinson Mounds (Mainfort 1986, 1988a; Mainfort et al. 1985). Partial excavation of the northern Twin Mound exposed four log- and/or fabric-covered tombs at the base. All burials were primary, fleshed inhumations of adults. One tomb contained the remains of at least eight relatively young women covered by a large quantity of *Marginella* beads. Several individuals wore fiber headdresses decorated with copper ornaments, as well as freshwater pearl necklaces. At the knees of an elderly male in an adjacent tomb was a pair of engraved rattles fashioned from human parietals and decorated in the typical Hopewellian artistic style. Also found in mortuary features were a small mica mirror, a schist pendant, and a boatstone of green schist. Two smaller burial mounds date to the sixth century A.D. and are discussed later.

One of the five mounds at the Dorr site in the upper Yazoo Basin was excavated, but documentation is very limited (Peabody 1904; Toth 1988:39). There was considerable diversity in burial treatment, including eight flexed, six extended, and two bundled interments, and some isolated skulls, all interred before or during construction of the mound. Artifacts in the mound included early Marksville ceramics, a few pieces of galena, and corner-notched projectile points.

Few Middle Woodland geometric enclosures are recorded in the Midsouth (Thunen 1988, 1990), but two occur within the study area. The Hickman Earthworks complex in western Kentucky includes a rectangular enclosure paired with extended parallel embankments to form a "tuning fork"

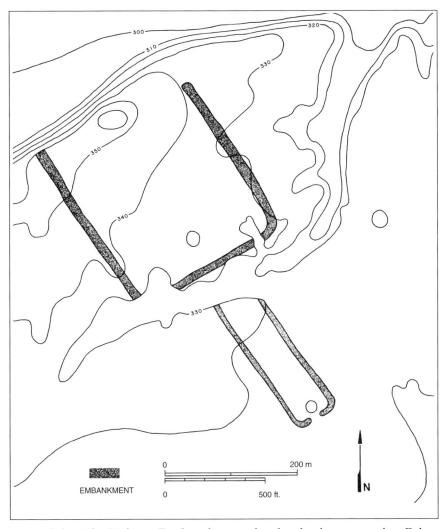

Figure 2.3 — The Hickman Earthworks mound and embankment complex, Fulton County, Kentucky (Mainfort and Carstens 1987:58, courtesy Southeastern Archaeology*)*

(Figure 2.3). This complex Middle Woodland enclosure is reminiscent of some Ohio sites. Several conical mounds are situated within the enclosure, and six more are located outside. The complex probably dates between A.D. 1 and 300 (Mainfort 1996b; Mainfort and Carstens 1987). The Pinson enclosure encompasses over 15 acres (6.7 hectares); a large, ramped flat-topped mound is located within. For over a third of its circumference, the enclosure forms a perfect circle with a diameter of about 180 meters, while the remainder is more elliptical (Thunen 1998). Although undated, the Pinson enclosure probably was constructed between about A.D. 1 and 200 (Mainfort 1988a, 1988c, 1996a).

Excavation of the uppermost summit of Pinson Mound 5 (Ozier Mound) produced a number of artifacts and nonlocal materials that suggest ritual use (Mainfort and Walling 1992). Off-mound excavations documented several possible ritual activity areas, characterized by the presence of large, ovoid, bent-pole structures and some associated mortuary features. Nonlocal materials (copper, mica, and galena, and Flint Ridge flint microblades) are associated with these localities, strengthening the case for ritual use (Mainfort 1986; Mainfort [ed.] 1980, 1996a; B. D. Smith 1992c).

Despite its large size, Pinson Mounds has produced a relatively small amount of nonlocal materials, and in general sites in the Southeast produce few of the exotic materials and artifacts associated with the Hopewellian horizon in Ohio and Illinois (Seeman 1979a). The occurrence of stylistically nonlocal ceramics at Pinson Mounds has led to the suggestion that individuals from as far away as southern Georgia and the Gulf coast participated in rituals at the site, perhaps bringing their own pottery vessels with them. Neutron activation analysis of numerous sherds seemingly contradicts this scenario (Mainfort et al. 1997), but the nonlocal origin of some vessels is supported by petrographic analysis (Stoltman and Mainfort 1999). Sites in the upper Sunflower subregion of Mississippi have produced bladelets and other artifacts of cherts from Illinois and/or Missouri, including Cobden, Burlington/Crescent Quarry, and Mill Creek, as well as novaculite (Brookes 1988). Zone 2 at the Boyd site, attributed to a Late Marksville occupation, produced bladelets, a copper fragment, mica, and a baked clay human figurine (Connaway and McGahey 1971).

Late Woodland: Baytown Period

A somewhat arbitrary date of A.D. 300–400 often is used in the study area to mark the beginning of Late Woodland, which is synonymous with the Baytown period. Baytown typically is characterized as a time of cultural "decline," referring specifically to a perceived curtailment of mortuary ceremonialism, the low frequency of decorated ceramics, and the lack of nonlocal artifacts and raw materials seen in the Marksville period (cf. Phillips 1970:901). As noted above, in the study area there are relatively few Marksville mortuary mounds, and Hopewellian decorative modes and exotica occur infrequently. Thus, such a "decline" is not readily discernible in the archaeological record. Evidence from Pinson Mounds demonstrates that mortuary mounds were constructed during Baytown times (Mainfort and Walling 1992); the lack of comparable examples elsewhere may reflect sampling error. Cultural continuity seems evident, as utilitarian ceramics and stone tools are stylistically and technologically similar to their Middle Woodland counterparts.

Nonetheless, the date of around A.D. 300 for the end of the Hopewellian horizon generally (but not specifically) is supported by data from the American Bottom (Bareis and Porter 1984; Fortier et al. 1989b; Maher 1996; Kelly, this volume), as well as the construction sequence at Pinson Mounds (Mainfort 1996a). Less well established is the end of the Baytown period, which occurred between about A.D. 700 and 900, probably at different times within the study area. Four radiometric assays (two AMS) on a Baytown component at the Hayti Bypass site place occupation between cal A.D. 400 and 600 (Conner and Ray 1995:121). These are the only secure dates on the Baytown period (as the concept is used here) within the study area.

D. Morse and P. Morse ([eds.] 1980; Morse and Morse 1983:182; see also P. Morse and D. Morse 1990:53) suggest that three dates on the Dunklin phase component at Zebree fall within the Baytown interval. There are several possible problems with their interpretation. First, two of the radiocarbon determinations (SMU-415 and 432) are virtually identical to several others associated with the subsequent Big Lake component (e.g., SMU-433, 445, and 453). Second, sand-tempered (Barnes) and shell-tempered ceramics co-occur in several dated features (e.g., Feature 238, a Big Lake pit that contained 170 Barnes, 238 Mississippi Plain, and 323 Varney Red sherds). In fact, a number of features produced large quantities of both sand-tempered and shell-tempered ceramics (Anderson 1977a:76–78, 1980:8–25). At the very least, the radiocarbon evidence suggests that the Dunklin component at Zebree postdates the Late Woodland/Baytown interval as we use the terms here. The possibility that sand-tempered and shell-tempered ceramics were partially contemporary at Zebree is worth considering, since the contemporaneity of clay-tempered and shell-tempered ceramics is fairly securely established elsewhere in the study area (e.g., Dunnell and Feathers 1991:35; Mainfort 1994, 1996b).

D. Morse and P. Morse (1990:162) cite two sixth-century radiocarbon assays from two pits at the Double Bridges site in southeast Missouri, but the dates actually have little interpretive value. The ceramics associated with one include hundreds of both clay-tempered and shell-tempered sherds, as well as baked clay objects and a sherd of Wickliffe Thick (J. R. Williams 1968:135–36). Fewer cultural materials were recovered from the other pit; clay-tempered wares predominate, with a small number of shell-tempered sherds.

Although numerous "Baytown" sites have been recorded in northeast Arkansas and southeast Missouri, the period remains very poorly documented in the Central Mississippi Valley. The only data from an unequivocal Baytown context in the study area are from the Hayti Bypass site in southeastern Missouri (Conner [ed.] 1995). In the west Tennessee interior, Late Woodland sites either are virtually absent or researchers have incorrectly attributed sites to the Middle Woodland period (Mainfort 1994) on the basis of sand-tempered/sandy-textured ceramic pastes that may continue into Late Woodland times. The Late Woodland sites in the Reelfoot Lake Basin are thought to postdate A.D. 700, as discussed later (cf. Mainfort 1994, 1996b).

Baytown assemblages are characterized primarily by clay-tempered Mulberry Creek Cord Marked ceramics and to a lesser extent, Baytown Plain (cf. D. Morse and P. Morse 1983:190). In portions of eastern Arkansas, plain surfaces are more common than cord marked. In the Little River Lowland and northern portion of the Western Lowlands, the two Middle Woodland ceramic traditions—sand-tempered and grog-tempered—continue into Baytown times (D. Morse and P. Morse 1983:182). Decoration on ceramics is very rare. Conner's (1995:122–70) detailed analysis of the ceramics from the Hayti Bypass site provides the best baseline data in the study area for the Baytown period. Jars and bowls were present in roughly equal numbers, although the total number of identifiable vessels is small. One virtually complete Mulberry Creek Cord Marked jar was recovered. The upper rim is incurved and gently everted, while the base and shoulders are rounded. Decoration was limited to lips (particularly lip punctations), and only two vessels with "rim folds" were recorded. No examples of Larto Red, Wheeler Check Stamped, or Kersey Incised were recovered, lending a measure of support to Phillips's (1970:901–2) observation that the end of the Baytown period is marked by the appearance of Wheeler Check Stamped and Baytown Plain with Coles Creek characteristics.

At the undated, but very likely Baytown age, DeRossitt site in northeastern Arkansas, a considerably different ceramic assemblage is reported. Baytown Plain outnumbers Mulberry Creek Cord Marked by a margin of roughly 2:1 (Spears 1978:153); some cord-marked rims were decorated with reed punctations. Large pans and simple bowls were the most common vessel forms. Some Evansville Punctated and Wheeler Check Stamped sherds were found in a few "more recent" pits (Spears 1978:92).

Baytown point styles include expanded base, notched, and stemmed forms (D. Morse and P. Morse 1983:188; cf. Spears 1978:146). A single Steuben Stemmed–like point was recovered from a Baytown pit at the Hayti Bypass site (J. Ray 1995:191–93). True arrow points are not present in reported Baytown components in northeast Arkansas and southeast Missouri, but Nassaney and Pyle (1999:260) argue that small, corner-notched arrow points were introduced into central Arkansas around A.D. 600.

Botanical remains from the Baytown component at the Hayti Bypass site reflect the importance of nuts, particularly hickory/pecan, acorn, and walnut. The relatively small seed assemblage includes maygrass, chenopod, and erect knotweed. A few specimens of cultivated sunflower and marshelder/ sumpweed also were recovered (Lopinot 1995:221–38). Although Morse and Morse (1983:181, 186) postulate seasonal mobility during the Baytown interval, the botanical sample from Hayti Bypass suggests year-round occupation by a society that cultivated starchy and oily seed-bearing plants and collected nuts and fruits (Lopinot et al. 1995:297). The small faunal assemblage consists of over 96 percent medium-large mammals and about 4 percent birds; notably lacking are aquatic species (Yelton 1995a). Two test pits at the Indian Camp Lake site yielded hickory and black walnut nutshell, as well as a few seeds of American lotus and goosefoot. White-tailed deer dominate the animal bone sample, but smaller mammals, fish, and reptiles also are present. Although this material has been represented as Late Woodland (e.g., R. Lewis 1996:62), the site also has Early Woodland and Mississippian components in the shallow midden, and the published data (Sussenbach and Lewis 1987:93–108) provide no basis for attributing the subsistence remains to any specific time period.

The large, multimound Hoecake site (Figure 2.4) may have begun to develop during Baytown times, although greatest use of the site occurred during the Terminal Late Woodland/Early Mississippian period (e.g., R. Lewis 1991:277–80). Another southeast Missouri site, Double Bridges, formerly included nearly two dozen mounds and may have its origin prior to A.D. 700 (J. R. Williams 1968:117–59). Located on the lower White River near the southern boundary of the study area, the large Baytown site itself includes nine mounds, but little research has been conducted there. Occupation appears to have begun during this time period and continued into the next (see Rolingson, this volume).

One of five conical mounds was excavated at the Story Mound site (not to be confused with the Story Mound at the Hoecake site) revealing one burial on the original ground surface, one burial in a shallow pit, and two pits with no burials (J. R. Williams 1968:86–99). Associated with one burial were a square of sheet copper, red ochre, and two racks of white-tailed deer antlers. The small ceramic assemblage from mound fill was primarily clay-tempered cord marked, and the mound probably dates to Baytown times.

Two burial mounds built after the inferred peak usage of Pinson Mounds date within the Baytown period. Mound 31, probably constructed during the sixth century A.D., is a low earthwork with a diameter of approximately 10

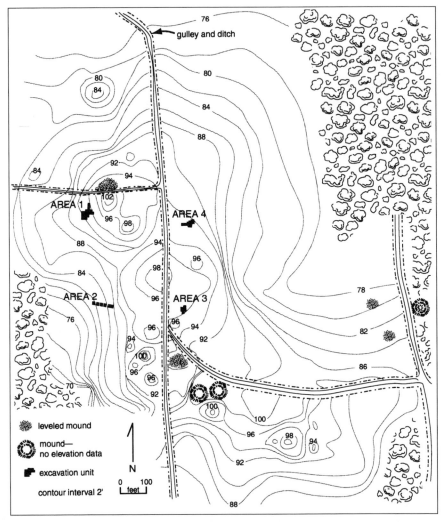

Figure 2.4 — The Hoecake site (adapted from J. R. Williams 1974:56, courtesy The Missouri Archaeologist*)*

meters. A rectangular subsoil pit near the center of the mound served as a tomb for an elderly adult male. Unidentified calcined bone, a number of ceramic sherds, and some small fragments of mica were placed around the pit periphery and covered with a U-shaped ring of subsoil. A human skull was located in a pit intrusive into the mound (Mainfort 1986, 1996a). Pinson Mound 12 was constructed on a knoll that had been utilized for mortuary purposes as early as the first or second century B.C. This small conical earthwork was constructed over a low clay platform, in the center of which was a probable crematory facility (Mainfort [ed.] 1980, 1988). Associated with this feature were the calcined remains of one or two extended individuals. Radiocarbon assays place usage during the sixth century A.D. (Mainfort 1996a).

At the Hayti Bypass site, nonlocal lithics were more numerous in Baytown contexts (12 percent) than in Mississippian (2.6 percent) and also represent a greater number of sources (J. Ray 1995:202). Although sample sizes are fairly small, these data serve notice that traditional notions of Late Woodland as a time when long-distance exchange largely ceased need to be reassessed. The copper from the Story Mound is intriguing, but the context is not securely dated. Fragments of mica and quartz crystal were associated with the small Pinson Mound 31.

Terminal Late Woodland / Early Mississippian Period

Around A.D. 700, cultures of the Baytown period began to be replaced by those of the Terminal Late Woodland/Early Mississippian period. Although the term *Coles Creek* often is used throughout the study area (Lafferty and Price 1996), such usage is inappropriate, and Coles Creek should be applied only to archaeological cultures to the south of the study area. Toltec and related sites, formerly placed within the Coles Creek construct (Phillips 1970:916–17), are now seen as representing the local indigenous Plum Bayou culture (Rolingson 1998a, this volume).

Following the Morses (D. Morse and P. Morse 1983, 1990) and researchers in the American Bottom (e.g., Bareis and Porter 1984), we view the period between about A.D. 700 and 1000 as a time during which cultural elements associated with Mississippian cultures in the study area were developed or introduced. These features include maize agriculture, relatively large towns, and shell-tempered ceramics. Of these, relatively large towns clearly developed in at least some parts of the Central Mississippi Valley prior to the use of shell-tempered ceramics (Mainfort 1994, 1996b). Although maize was grown during this period by the inhabitants of the Zebree site, its dietary importance seems minimal (Lynott et al. 1986).

The radiocarbon assays from Zebree (D. Morse and P. Morse 1980; P. Morse and D. Morse 1990) are important to dating the Terminal Late Woodland/Early Mississippian interval. At two sigma, seven of the calibrated dates that the Morses associate with the Big Lake component overlap between A.D. 900 and 1000 (excluding SMU-457 and 460), though there is considerable overlap with the Dunklin phase dates. Four dates on the Early Mississippian component at Hayti Bypass place occupation around A.D. 950–1050

(Conner and Ray 1995:72–79); both clay-tempered and shell-tempered ceramics were being produced at this time. Eleven calibrated dates from the Oliver site, in northwestern Tennessee, suggest an age of about A.D. 1000–1100 (*contra* Mainfort 1994:136). The large associated ceramic assemblage consists primarily of Mulberry Creek Cord Marked, but Varney Red, Mississippi Plain, Kimmswick Fabric Impressed, Kersey Incised, Baytown Plain, and Wickliffe Thick also are present. Toltec Mounds, a unique multimound site near Little Rock, Arkansas, is securely dated between about A.D. 700 and 1050 on the basis of fourteen radiocarbon determinations (Rolingson 1998b:24–25, this volume). Baytown Plain is by far the dominant ceramic type, followed by Larto Red; decorated types are present in very low frequency and shell-tempered wares are rare.

In the Central Mississippi Valley, the start of the Terminal Late Woodland/Early Mississippian period coincides with the appearance of Wheeler Check Stamped and Baytown Plain with Coles Creek characteristics (Phillips 1970:901–2). Despite the temporal importance ascribed to Wheeler Check Stamped (e.g., Phillips 1970), the type has rarely been found in large quantities and the distribution is discontinuous. The Foxhole site, near Reelfoot Lake, has produced a large collection of Wheeler Check Stamped (Mainfort 1996b). Two other sites in western Tennessee (40LA6 and Bishop) also have components with strong representation of check stamping. The spatial and temporal distribution of Wheeler Check Stamped in the study area is an important research topic.

There are pronounced differences in ceramics between the northern and southern portions of the study area. Particularly in the southern portion of the study area, grog-tempered Coles Creek Incised, characterized by parallel incised lines on the rims of jars and bowls, is diagnostic of Terminal Late Woodland/Coles Creek occupations. Within southeast Missouri and northeast Arkansas, the dichotomy between sand-tempered Barnes and clay-tempered Baytown ceramics continues. Shell-tempered pottery, including Varney Red and Mississippi Plain, appears by around A.D. 900. Evidence for pre–A.D. 800 Varney Red and shell-tempered ceramics in general (e.g., Lafferty and Price 1996; Lynott 1989) is fairly weak (Conner [ed.] 1995; D. Morse and P. Morse 1990; Sierzchula et al. 1994), but the issue clearly warrants further research.

Varney Red has a wide spatial distribution (see D. Morse and P. Morse 1990:154), ranging from the Ozark escarpment in southeast Missouri (Price and Price 1984) to the northern Yazoo Basin in Mississippi (R. Marshall 1987). The greatest concentration, however, appears to be in the lowlands of southeast Missouri, northeast Arkansas, and northwestern Tennessee (Mainfort 1996b). Varney Red vessel forms present at Zebree include globular jars (some of which could hold over 50 liters), salt pans, and hooded bottles. Dunnell and Feathers (1991) discuss some technological differences between sand-tempered (Barnes) and shell-tempered ceramics. Kersey Incised is a distinctive pottery type that probably is diagnostic of the latter portion of our Terminal Late Woodland/Early Mississippian construct. The type is best known from southeast Missouri (e.g., R. Marshall 1965a), but the largest collections are from northwest Tennessee (Mainfort 1994, 1996b). Kersey Incised is not reported from Zebree, and occurs only in minute amounts at most sites in the Reelfoot Lake Basin.

Artifacts from a burial mound (40OB6) on the bluffs above the Samburg site, on the east side of Reelfoot Lake, included several hooded water bottles and angular shouldered bowls resembling Lohmann and Early Stirling phase Powell Plain vessels from the American Bottom; two comparable vessels were recovered at the Hoecake site (J. R. Williams 1974:75). A red-filmed seed jar was recovered from an adjacent, non-mortuary mound (Mainfort 1996b).

Small arrow points—both triangular (Madison) as well as small notched forms (Sequoyah)—occur at sites placed within our Terminal Late Woodland/Early Mississippian construct (Lynott 1989; Mainfort 1994; D. Morse and P. Morse 1990). Side- and corner-notched dart points appear to be associated with a Varney horizon context near Reelfoot Lake, Tennessee (Mainfort 1996b). The microlithic tool industry at the Zebree site (P. Morse and D. Morse 1990:58) has not been reported at other sites within the Central Mississippi Valley. Large agricultural implements fashioned from Mill Creek chert presumably are linked to maize cultivation. At Zebree, a Mill Creek chert hoe and thirty-five polished flakes of Mill Creek chert were recovered from Big Lake phase contexts (P. Morse and D. Morse 1990:58). The Oliver site in northwestern Tennessee produced 138 polished flakes of Mill Creek chert (Mainfort 1994); the contrast with Zebree, at which investigations were far more extensive, is pronounced.

Private collections from the Foxhole site contain hundreds of bone implements, including harpoons, fishhooks, needles, awls, and punches (Mainfort 1996b). Several harpoons and other bone tools also were recovered at the Zebree site (P. Morse and D. Morse 1990). Present evidence suggests that extensive bone tool assemblages are horizon markers for the Terminal Late Woodland/Early Mississippian period, although why this would be the case is presently unfathomable.

In the Central Mississippi Valley, maize cultivation began during this time interval. Maize has been recovered from contexts at Toltec dating to around A.D. 800 (calibrated) (Rolingson 1998a; C. Smith 1996), while samples from Zebree (D. Morse and P. Morse [eds.] 1980) and the Oliver site (Mainfort

1994) date to the tenth and eleventh centuries A.D. The low frequency of reported native cultigens at Terminal Late Woodland/Early Mississippian sites in the Central Mississippi Valley relative to contemporary sites in the American Bottom is striking and should be a focus for future research. At the Oliver site, fifty-two specimens of maize were recovered from five of the forty-two features sampled. Maygrass, chenopod, and knotweed were fairly numerous, but occurred in only a few features. Virtually all of the nut remains were hickory. Of the identifiable mammalian remains, nearly two-thirds are from white-tailed deer. Especially noteworthy is the extraordinarily large number of passenger pigeon remains, which constitute almost 41 percent of the total number of specimens and represent over 100 individuals. Although historic accounts indicate that it was not uncommon for entire Native American settlements to relocate at roosts, where large numbers of pigeons were easily taken by netting or by felling trees on which thousands of birds were perched, this quantity of passenger pigeon remains is virtually unprecedented in archaeological contexts (Mainfort 1994).

Maize was recovered from one feature at Zebree that is assigned to the Dunklin phase occupation, although this is attributed to admixture from Big Lake phase deposits (D. Morse 1980:17-12). The Dunklin phase component also produced large quantities of acorn, walnuts, and hickory nutshell, with minor amounts of seeds of wild plants. Twenty-nine Big Lake phase features yielded maize. Starchy native cultigens were rare, but hickory nuts and acorns were found in large numbers. The Zebree faunal assemblage is small relative to the excavated area. Samples from the Dunklin and Big Lake components are quite similar; white-tailed deer are well represented, as are aquatic waterfowl and fish (P. Morse and D. Morse 1990).

The Early Mississippian component at Hayti Bypass yielded a small quantity of maize kernels and cobs. Native cultigens included *Chenopodium berlandieri,* little barley, maygrass, and knotweed. Hickory, pecan, and acorns dominate the charred nut assemblage (Lopinot 1995:239–52). The associated faunal assemblage is very small. Fish remains constitute over half of the assemblage, with only about one-third of the specimens being mammalian (Yelton 1995a). Test excavations at the Owls Bend site in Missouri produced remains of eleven seed taxa, primarily native cultigens (goosefoot, sunflower, little barley, sumpweed, maygrass, and gourd), but also two fragments tentatively identified as maize. Carbon isotope studies indicate that maize was not a major dietary constituent. Large amounts of hickory, acorn, and hazelnut hulls also were recovered (Lynott 1989:83–84). The roughly contemporary and nearby Gooseneck site yielded a comparable botanical assemblage, including ten specimens of maize (Lynott 1989:51–54). Neither site produced large faunal samples.

The middens on Toltec Mound D produced a large quantity of floral and faunal remains. Among charred seeds, the most abundant are an unidentified Poaceae (Type X), followed by little barley, maygrass, chenopod, and amaranth; sunflower, sumpweed, knotweed, squash, and bottle gourd also were identified. Mound D also produced numerous nutshell fragments, primarily thick-shelled hickories. White-tailed deer remains dominate the faunal assemblage, followed by squirrel, turkey, passenger pigeon, bowfin, and turtles (Rolingson 1998c:105–6). Toltec Mound S produced a small (n = 9) sample of maize from contexts dating to around A.D. 750–850 (calibrated) (Rolingson 1998b:24–25; C. Smith 1996). This is the best evidence for pre–A.D. 900 maize in the study area. The associated native grain assemblage is comparable to that from Mound D.

After circa A.D. 700, the number of reported sites in the study area increases dramatically. Some sites are quite large and include multiple mounds. The type site for the Plum Bayou culture, Toltec Mounds is the largest (40 hectares) and includes eighteen mounds surrounded by a roughly semicircular embankment and ditch (Rolingson 1998a, this volume). The largest mound stands 15 meters tall, but has not been excavated. Four low platform mounds, a large (11.5 meters) platform mound, and a burial mound have been partially excavated. Many contemporary hamlets are located in the vicinity of Toltec.

In the Reelfoot Lake Basin, the largest sites are located on the prime agricultural lands associated with relict terraces of the Mississippi River, with sizes ranging from about 2.5 to 15 hectares. Reports of artificial mounds at Rice (e.g., R. Lewis 1991, 1996) are incorrect (Mainfort 1996b). Several kilometers south of Reelfoot Lake, at least thirteen conical mounds were present at the Auston Tract and as many as fifty may have been present at site 40LK44 (Mainfort 1996b).

During the latest segment of the Terminal Late Woodland/Early Mississippian interval (Mainfort's [1996b] "Red-Filmed horizon," D. Morse and P. Morse's [1990] "Varney Horizon") in the Reelfoot Lake Basin, mounds are present at several large sites. The largest of these, Samburg, formerly had two platform mounds, one about 3 meters tall, the other about 6 meters in height, surrounded by a habitation area about 8 hectares in extent. Several apparently contemporary mound groups are located on the nearby loess bluffs overlooking the site. One blufftop mound, part of the 40OB6 group, covered the charred remains of a small structure. Eleven radiocarbon assays derived from this structure and skeletal remains from an adjacent burial mound suggest construction between about A.D. 950 and 1050. On the west side of Reelfoot Lake, the Foxhole site includes a habitation area covering at least 6 hectares, as well as a low, saddle-shaped mound (Mainfort 1996b).

The extensively excavated village at Zebree was at least partially surrounded by a ditch. The remains of nine small, rectangular wall post houses
were exposed; one structure was situated in a basin (P. Morse and D. Morse
1990). The Hoecake site in the Cairo Lowland includes at least thirty-one
mounds, ranging up to 7.5 meters in height (Figure 2.4). The mounds do not
appear to be placed with respect to an overall site plan. Fairly extensive
habitation deposits also are present. Excavated houses were all rectangular
semi-subterranean structures with walls constructed of small, individually
set poles (J. R. Williams 1974). We agree with R. Barry Lewis (1991:277)
that the primary occupation at Hoecake dates to the Terminal Late Wood-
land/Early Mississippian period. Hoecake is a very large and complex site,
and the extent of investigations by professional archaeologists is incom-
mensurate with the site's importance. The limited amount of published data
is somewhat obfuscated by attempts to define various "phases" or subphases
at the site. Over 95 percent of the excavated ceramics were obtained from
Excavation Area 1. Therefore, attempts to chronologically order the various
excavation areas (D. Morse and P. Morse 1990; J. R. Williams 1967, 1974)
are seriously compromised by overwhelming sampling problems. Unfortunately, the two published radiocarbon determinations from habitation-area
contexts at Hoecake (J. R. Williams 1974:85) are of no help in resolving
questions of site age or internal chronology.

Excavation of Story Mound 1 at the Hoecake site (not to be confused
with the Story Mound site discussed earlier) disclosed three elaborate mortuary crypts covered and lined with logs and matting (Figure 2.5) (R. Marshall
1988). No associated artifacts were found with any of the thirteen burials.
An uncorrected radiocarbon age of A.D. 640 ± 130 was obtained on a combined charcoal sample from two crypts (J. R. Williams 1974:85), which is of
little value in assessing the actual age of the mound. The purported association of some shell-tempered ceramics with mound construction is questionable (R. Lewis 1991:277–80). In the absence of associated diagnostic artifacts, we tentatively propose a Terminal Late Woodland/Early Mississippian age.

Thirty-one skeletons in twenty-one graves were excavated at the Zebree
site. All interred individuals were adults and none was accompanied by grave
goods. One grave, possibly indicative of a charnel house, contained four
males and four females, half of which were placed on deposits of mussel
shells. At Chandler Landing, a Plum Bayou culture site on the White River,
C. B. Moore (1910:340–51) excavated two accretional burial mounds that
contained a number of nonlocal artifacts and materials.

On the bluffs overlooking Reelfoot Lake, two burial mounds of the
40OB6 group have been excavated (Mainfort 1996b). One was an accretional

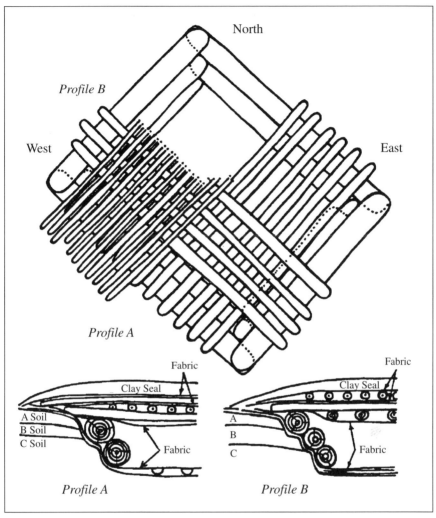

Figure 2.5 — Tomb A at the Hoecake site (courtesy Mississippi Department of Archives and History)

burial mound about 12 meters in diameter and containing the remains of over sixty individuals; most were extended, but bundle burials and cremations also were present. Among the few associated artifacts were several hooded water bottles and angular shouldered bowls, and a sandstone pipe carved in the shape of a rabbit. The second, smaller mound was located on a finger ridge to the south; unfortunately, it had been extensively vandalized and produced little useful data. Other probable burial mounds are present short distances to the north and south of 40OB6, but comparable blufftop mounds or mound groups are largely unknown to the north and south of the Reelfoot Lake Basin.

The lithic assemblage from the Samburg site includes a substantial number of white Burlington/Crescent Quarry chert flakes. This material is extremely rare at roughly contemporary sites in the Reelfoot Lake Basin. At Zebree, most of the microlithic artifacts were fashioned from Burlington/ Crescent Quarry chert (P. Morse and D. Morse 1990:58). Considerable Burlington chert debitage is present at the Hoecake site (D. Morse and P. Morse 1983:216), though it was not discussed in the excavation report (J. R. Williams 1974). Zebree also yielded a Mill Creek chert hoe and hoe flakes of Mill Creek and Dover chert. All major sites identified for this time period in the Reelfoot Lake Basin have produced specimens of Mill Creek chert, and Mill Creek hoe flakes were recovered from the Oliver site (Mainfort 1994) to the east. Quarried in southern Illinois, Mill Creek chert was used throughout a large portion of the midcontinent for agricultural implements (J. Brown et al. 1990), and it first appears in quantity in the American Bottom around A.D. 750 (J. Kelly 1990a:130). Trade in Mill Creek hoes and Burlington chert accelerated around A.D. 1000 (J. Kelly 1990a).

Copper and galena were recovered during test excavations at the Hoecake site (J. R. Williams 1974:82), but the sources of these materials have not been determined. Most burial inclusions at Chandler Landing (C. B. Moore 1910) reflect long-distance exchange; these include quartz crystals, pearl and shell beads, and copper. Conch shell, copper, and galena occur rarely at Toltec, although a variety of lithic materials (including novaculite, quartz crystals, mica, lamprophyre, and syenite) were obtained from the Ouachita Mountains (Rolingson 1998a).

Directions for Future Research

Below we present a number of research themes and topics that we consider crucial for advancing our understanding of the study area:

1. Data on the Early and Middle Woodland periods in general are lacking. Especially useful would be excavation of habitation sites, with an emphasis on recovering subsistence data.

2. The role of indigenous cultigens in Woodland subsistence within the alluvial valley is poorly documented. Botanical remains from Zebree contain minimal evidence for native domesticates or their wild relatives, but starchy annuals were of some importance at Hayti Bypass and Toltec.

3. The appearance and adoption of maize remains an important issue in the Central Mississippi Valley and elsewhere in eastern North America.

4. We agree with Lafferty and Price (1996) that radiometric dating has not always clarified the temporal sequence in the study area. Several issues are involved here. First, considerable thought must be given to context, whether in assessing existing assays or in selecting samples for dating. Second, there has been a tendency to interpret radiometric data from the Central Mississippi Valley on the basis of accepted chronologies from outside the study area; the Central Valley data should be interpreted in their own right. Possible early cultigens should be dated using AMS, not conventional dating.

5. Area researchers should discard the notion that shell temper equates solely with Mississippian and sand/grog temper equates solely with Woodland. There is ample evidence that shell and nonshell additives have considerable temporal overlap.

6. There appears to be considerable cultural diversity during the Terminal Late Woodland/Early Mississippian period, sometimes even within fairly restricted subregions such as the Reelfoot Lake Basin (Mainfort 1996b). Long-term research at the local level could unravel some of the apparent complexity.

7. Most archaeological phases within the study area were proposed on the basis of admittedly insufficient data (see Phillips 1970 *passim*). While researchers should acknowledge the historical importance of these units, attempts to align more recent data with older phases are unlikely to advance our understanding of regional prehistory.

Chapter 3

Plum Bayou Culture of the Arkansas–White River Basin

Martha Ann Rolingson

While Toltec Mounds was recognized as an important site by Cyrus Thomas (1894:243–45), investigation nevertheless languished because museum-quality artifacts were scarce (C. B. Moore 1908:557) and the landowner was protective. A brief excavation in 1966 recovered Woodland grog-tempered ceramics that were unexpectedly in association with the Mississippian characteristics of site shape, arrangement of mounds, and embankment (H. Davis 1966; Phillips 1970:916; see also Anderson 1977b). Philip Phillips surmised that "the great Toltec (Knapp) site (14-H-1) will inevitably become the type site for a phase of Coles Creek (or earlier?) date in the Lower Arkansas region" (Phillips 1970:916). The Toltec Mounds site was purchased by the state of Arkansas in 1975 and a research program and park development began in 1976 (Rolingson 1982a, 1982b). Investigations concentrated first on the site itself and on defining Plum Bayou culture (Rolingson 1982c, 1990, 1998a) and subsequently on contemporary sites in the surrounding region (Nassaney 1992a, 1994, 1996a).

Research goals and strategies were outlined in a research plan completed in 1978 (Rolingson 1982a, 1982b). At that time only three mounds were readily visible and almost nothing was known about this great site or how much of it had survived 150 years of farming. The proposed research questions included data collected by onsite fieldwork, documentary research, and offsite fieldwork. The investigations of intrasite variability and culture history were interrelated to determine the chronology of occupation and earthwork construction, extent of occupation, regional temporal relationships, internal settlement design, social context of activities, production technologies, craft specialization, mortuary practices, and evidence for sociopolitical-religious organization and distinctions expressed in these data. Research regarding the natural environment considered the natural history of the site locality, reconstruction of nineteenth-century and prehistoric environments, subsistence data, and use of local and regional resources. Investigations of associated residential communities, specialized functions of these sites, and possible hierarchical ranking of sites were outlined. Bioarchaeology, historic archaeology, the impact of historic occupation on the prehistoric data, and technical evaluations of data recovery techniques were also defined as research domains. Some of these questions have received more attention than others and while the quantity of available data has varied, all have been given some thought. An abundance of data about the Toltec site, various small sites, and Plum Bayou culture has been gathered over the years and this chapter integrates those data into a substantive overview of Plum Bayou culture and the place of the Toltec Mounds site within it.

Plum Bayou sites are distributed throughout much of the area in Arkansas drained by the Arkansas and White rivers. The majority are middens with a few features such as pits, hearths, and graves. Some sites have one to four mounds. The large overall size of the Toltec Mounds site and the number and size of mounds present establish it as an atypical site. The beginning date of occupation at Toltec is not yet known, but the earliest dates obtained so far for mound construction are in the A.D. 700s, and apparently occupation ended before A.D. 1050. The origins of both Plum Bayou culture and the Toltec Mounds site are rooted in the local Baytown culture and began sometime prior to A.D. 700.

Environment

The Toltec Mounds site is located 10 kilometers east of the Arkansas River on the bank of an ancestral channel now occupied by an underfit stream called Plum Bayou. It is on the western edge of the Mississippi Alluvial Plain physiographic region downstream from the point where the river flows out of the Arkansas River Valley region into the Arkansas Lowland subregion (Figure 3.1). This is an advantageous position within close range of diverse environments and varied resources. The Arkansas River Valley, Ouachita Mountains, and West Gulf Coastal Plain are upland regions to the west. To the east is the alluvial plain of the Arkansas and Mississippi rivers, in which the land forms are low basins created since the last glacial maximum and older, slightly elevated, land forms.

The Mississippi Alluvial Plain is composed of several lowlands divided by terraces and ridges. Ancestral river channels have meander belt ridges with higher elevations and are separated by lower floodplains or backswamps (Saucier 1994:24–29, 98–129). Basins have considerable topographic variability and even a few feet of elevation are important for the location of sites and for the composition of the bottomland hardwood forest.

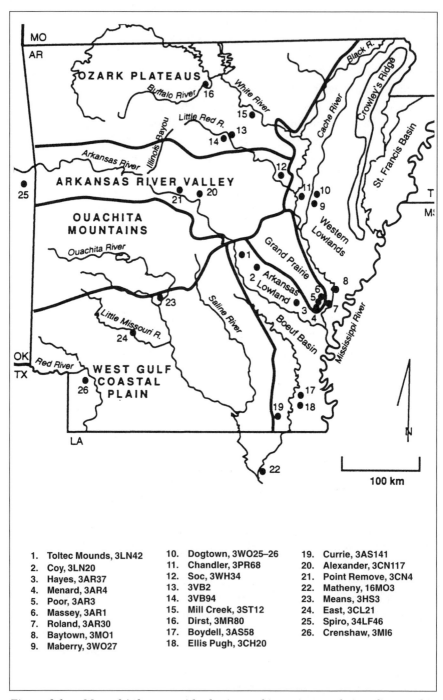

1. Toltec Mounds, 3LN42
2. Coy, 3LN20
3. Hayes, 3AR37
4. Menard, 3AR4
5. Poor, 3AR3
6. Massey, 3AR1
7. Roland, 3AR30
8. Baytown, 3MO1
9. Maberry, 3WO27

10. Dogtown, 3WO25–26
11. Chandler, 3PR68
12. Soc, 3WH34
13. 3VB2
14. 3VB94
15. Mill Creek, 3ST12
16. Dirst, 3MR80
17. Boydell, 3AS58
18. Ellis Pugh, 3CH20

19. Currie, 3AS141
20. Alexander, 3CN117
21. Point Remove, 3CN4
22. Matheny, 16MO3
23. Means, 3HS3
24. East, 3CL21
25. Spiro, 34LF46
26. Crenshaw, 3MI6

Figure 3.1 — Map of Arkansas with physiographic regions and sites discussed in the text (adapted from Rolingson 1998a:fig. 101)

The West Gulf Coastal Plain, composed of poorly consolidated sand, clay, and gravel, has a flat to rolling terrain. The Ouachita Mountains are sandstone, shale, and novaculite formations folded and faulted in northeast-to-southwest trending ridges and valleys. Lithic resources in the Ouachita Mountains were desirable and widely dispersed throughout prehistory. The Arkansas River Valley region separates the Ouachita Mountains from the Ozark Plateau, and tributaries of the river drain both of these rugged regions. The major tributaries have moderately broad floodplains where they join the Arkansas River. These uplands had a mixed hardwood and pine forest. A southern floodplain forest environment was present along the Arkansas River upstream to the Grand River in northeastern Oklahoma (J. A. Brown 1996:36).

Site Distribution

Plum Bayou sites, primarily middens, are widely distributed in the Mississippi Alluvial Plain region and lower portion of the Arkansas River Valley region, and on tributary streams in the adjacent uplands. Analysis of sites in Arkansas and adjacent states dating between A.D. 600 and 1000 (Late Woodland and Terminal Late Woodland periods) provides the data to define the extent of Plum Bayou culture within the area (Rolingson 1998d) and expand the territory suggested previously (Jeter et al. 1989:57; Nassaney 1991:206).

In the Arkansas Lowland, Plum Bayou sites are numerous, providing data on four settlement types: single household, multiple household, multiple household with single mound, and multiple mound center (Nassaney 1992a, 1996a, 1996b). In addition to Toltec, nine sites have had some excavation (Figure 3.2), including Fitzhugh (Nassaney and Hoffman 1992); Ink Bayou (D. Waddell et al. 1987); Bearskin Lake South, Clear Lake, Cross Pond, Coy (Nassaney 1996a); St. Marks Church (Guendling 1996; Nassaney 1996a), County Dairy Farm, and Quapaw Links (Guendling 1996). Some sites have Middle and Late Woodland components. Three sites within 30 kilometers of Toltec had single conical mounds (today only the one at Cross Pond survives) for which surface collections and test excavations provided data on adjacent middens. The conical mounds are undated, but probably are Woodland. The Toltec Mounds, Coy, and Hayes Mounds sites are multiple mound ceremonial centers. Toltec has eighteen mounds and is surrounded by an earthen embankment and exterior ditch. The Coy site, on Indian-Bakers Bayou 19 kilometers southeast of Toltec, has four mounds (Jeter [ed.] 1990:340; Nassaney 1996a; Palmer 1917). The Hayes Mounds site, on Bayou Meto 30 kilometers southeast of the Coy site, has four mounds.

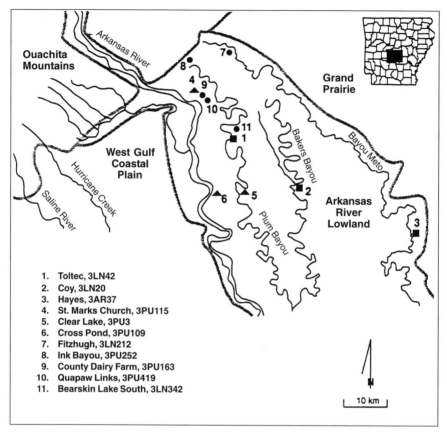

Figure 3.2 — Central Arkansas with physiographic regions and sites discussed in the text (adapted from Rolingson 1998a:fig. 97)

It has not been excavated, but materials in surface collections are typical for Plum Bayou culture (Rolingson 1998c:104).

Most of the Grand Prairie region is not well known, but sites with Plum Bayou artifacts are present (Derley 1979). Sites assigned to the Toltec phase by Phillips (1970:916–17), including Menard, Poor, and Massey, are located on the southern end of Grand Prairie near the mouth of the Arkansas River and on the lower White River. The Baytown site, on the White River, is the type site for the Late Woodland period Baytown phase and Baytown culture (Phillips 1970:903–4; Phillips et al. 1951). Recent research indicates that the occupation continued into the Terminal Late Woodland period, but so little is known about the mounds that the time of construction and full range of occupation have not been established (House 1996:143). With two large and seven low mounds, it is the largest site in the White River basin. The excavated Roland site (Scholtz 1991) on an abandoned channel of the White River, provides the largest artifact assemblage for this area.

In the Western Lowlands, a cluster of Plum Bayou sites is present at the mouth of the Little Red River and along the Cache River. Single mounds were present at each of three sites, Maberry and two Dogtown sites (House 1975:159; House and Schiffer 1975:171). The Chandler Landing site on the White River (C. B. Moore 1910:340–48; Phillips et al. 1951:444) had two burial mounds with artifacts that are similar to Plum Bayou and early Caddoan artifacts. The Soc site, on the lower Red River, is of interest because it has typical Plum Bayou ceramic types, some of which are shell tempered (Figley 1968). Sites with Plum Bayou–related materials are present on the Little Red River in the Ozarks (Baker 1974; H. Davis 1996; D. Waddell et al. 1987). The Dirst site on the Buffalo River has a Late Woodland occupation of A.D. 650–700 (Guendling et al. 1992; Sabo et al. 1990a). The Western Lowlands had a substantial Plum Bayou occupation during the Late and Terminal Late Woodland periods and rivers provided accessible corridors for communication. Archaeology along the Black River in Arkansas is less well developed, so the extent of Plum Bayou culture has not been established. Sites dating to the Terminal Late Woodland/Early Mississippian period in the St. Francis Basin are clearly different from Plum Bayou culture and Crowley's Ridge is a convenient boundary between the two regions (D. Morse and P. Morse 1990:154–62).

South of the Arkansas River, in the Boeuf Basin, the extent of Plum Bayou is not sharply defined. The Boydell site (House and Jeter 1994), with a large platform mound, has typical Plum Bayou ceramics in the early levels, but most of the platform mound was constructed in the 1200s. The non-mound Ellis Pugh and Currie sites (Rolingson 1993) have varieties of ceramics typical of Coles Creek culture farther south and occupation continued after A.D. 1050, when Plum Bayou culture had declined. The boundary between Plum Bayou and Coles Creek may have fluctuated through time in this section of the Mississippi alluvial valley (Jeter et al. 1989:161).

Plum Bayou culture extended up the Arkansas River and sites are located on the floodplain and upland tributaries (Sabo et al. 1990b:73–82). The Alexander site (Hemmings and House 1985) on Cypress Creek is multiple component, but the major occupation is Plum Bayou, contemporary with Toltec. A minor Middle Woodland period occupation (A.D. 200–500) is present, and one burial contained two cups and beads of marine whelk shell resulting from long-distance trade. The Point Remove site (H. Davis 1967), located on the floodplain, apparently once had one large and four small mounds. It is multiple component, but several sherds of Plum Bayou ceramic types were recovered from mound fill in a test excavation in the large mound. It is not clear when the mounds were constructed, as the site has a Late Mississippi period component and sites of this period are present in this segment of the valley. Upstream from Illinois Bayou, near the town of Dardanelle, the valley narrows and this may be the extent of Plum Bayou culture sites up the valley (Schambach 2001, this volume). The ceramics on Late and Terminal Late Woodland period sites on the Arkansas/Oklahoma border are different from Plum Bayou ceramics (Galm 1984:213–15; J. Rogers 1991).

South of the Arkansas River, in the Ouachita Mountains and Gulf Coastal Plain, the Fourche Maline culture was present for 1500 years. Late Fourche Maline, period 7, dates roughly A.D. 700 to 950 (Schambach 1982:138–39). Several sites (Dickinson and Lemley 1939; Schambach 1998a; Scholtz 1986; Wood and Early 1981) have low amounts of Coles Creek Incised varieties present. Mounds on these sites are Caddoan and have not been dated earlier than A.D. 1100. Farther downstream along the Ouachita River on the Gulf Coastal Plain, sites of the A.D. 800 to 1100 period are common, with occupation continuing into the Mississippi period. Middens contain varieties of Coles Creek Incised pottery that are similar to varieties present in Louisiana. This material is considered a regional variant of Coles Creek culture (Schambach [ed.] 1990:115–16).

Internal Features and Design of Sites

Non-mound sites in the alluvial floodplain are linear deposits along the higher natural levees of the oxbow lakes, while those in the uplands are generally amorphous deposits. So few midden sites have been fully excavated that there is little evidence for spatial organization of activities. At the Alexander site, a cluster of seven burials on the east edge of the site was probably a cemetery area for the Plum Bayou occupation (Hemmings and House 1985:23). The Roland site was a linear midden along the crest of a natural levee, with a mound of midden 30 meters in diameter on the highest point of the levee (Scholtz 1991:11). This midden, over a meter thick, appears to be a Terminal Late Woodland period mound with earlier Middle and Late Woodland period midden in the fill (House 1996:144).

Accurate maps of sites with two to four mounds are not available. The Coy site was excavated by Edward Palmer in 1883 (Jeter [ed.] 1990:340–41), but his notes are inadequate for locating the mounds today. His description identified four mounds: one 4 meters high and flat topped, one 3 meters high, a 2.4-meter-high burial mound, and a small, low mound. Only the largest survives, and it was tested in 1988 and 1994 (Nassaney 1996a:26–29). It has a baked clay lens 1.5 meters below the top that yielded samples used to obtain an archaeomagnetic date of A.D. 730. A posthole or pit associated with the last stage of construction above the baked clay contained charred nutshell that was radiocarbon dated to A.D. 890–1010. Although the site has an extensive midden, the deposits beneath the mound did not contain midden, indicating that at least this portion of the site had not been occupied before construction began (Nassaney 1996a:29).

Despite the prominence of the Baytown site in archaeological literature (Phillips et al. 1951), little is known about its occupations and internal chronology. It is considered to have both Baytown and Plum Bayou occupations because of the presence of Plum Bayou material culture (House 1996:143). This site has nine mounds in a rectangular plan paralleling the bank of a cutoff channel of the river with the long orientation southeast-northwest (Figure 3.3). The highest mound (6 meters) is midway along the length of the site on the edge of the bank; the second in height (3 meters) is at the southeast end of the rectangle. All other mounds are 1.5 meters or less in height. In these features the Baytown mounds are arranged similar to those at Toltec, but on a smaller scale. Stratigraphic excavations and chronometric

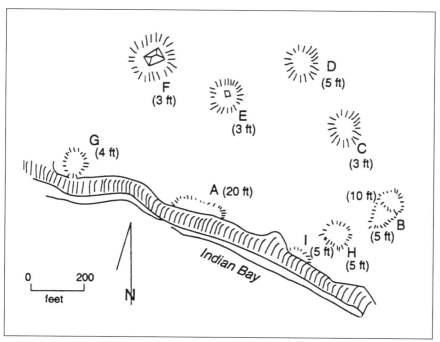

Figure 3.3 — Baytown site plan based on a 1940 map by James A. Ford, on file Arkansas Archeological Survey (adapted from Rolingson 1998a:fig. 102)

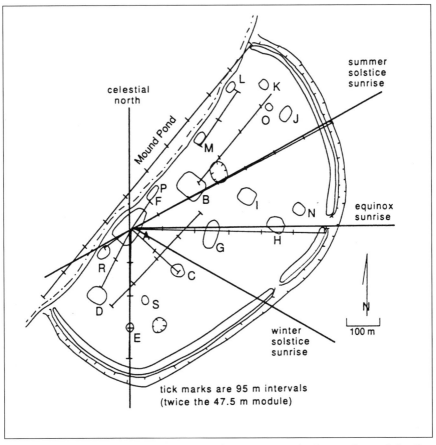

Figure 3.4 — Toltec Mounds site plan with imposition of solar angles and the distance module in relation to Mound A (adapted from Rolingson 1998a:fig. 90)

dating are needed to establish temporal relationships of mound construction and occupation. Distinguishing Plum Bayou from Baytown affiliation of sites throughout the lower White River region is, and will be, a problem until sites are excavated and chronometric dates are obtained.

The Toltec Mounds site covers 40 hectares, demarcated by the bank of an oxbow lake on one side and an earthen embankment and exterior ditch on the other sides in the form of a partial oval or C-shape (Figure 3.4). Eighteen mounds are known, ten of which border a rectangular plaza, while eight border a less well-defined plaza. The highest mound (A, 15 meters) is situated on the bank of the lake midway along the length of the rectangular plaza and the second in height (B, 11.5 meters) is at the north end. The third in height (C, 4.2 meters) is across the plaza from the highest one and the fourth in height (D, 1.5 meters) is at the south end. All other mounds were less than 1.5 meters high (Palmer 1917:423–26). The low mounds range in size from 300 square meters with a single construction stage (Mound S) to 4200 square meters resulting from multiple stages of construction (Mound G). Four of the low mounds have been partially excavated and they are earthen platforms that were extended in area when enlarged, but without much additional height. They have underlying midden; construction fill is composed of both midden and soil without artifacts collected from around the platforms. Radiocarbon dates indicate that all mounds were not in use at the same time. Mound S was used in the mid-700s, Mound E in the 800s, and Mound D was used after 900 and may have been the last to be built on the site: an archaeomagnetic date on a sub-D burned silt deposit is A.D. 830. Mounds B and G were in use throughout much of the site occupation.

Mound S had an extensive midden and animal bone deposit on the off-plaza side, covering an area larger than the small single-stage platform itself. No building was present on or beneath this platform and the midden may have resulted from community feasting activities. Mound E, built in two stages, had a concentrated midden adjacent to the platform. Mound D began as a small platform with a concentrated midden on the off-plaza side. The platform and midden were covered by a second stage of construction, doubling the mound size. This second stage had an extensive midden deposit on the off-plaza side that was then covered with a mantle of soil. Both middens contained burned clay and charcoal fragments that may have resulted from the destruction of buildings. Unfortunately, the central portion of the mound, where structural features should be present, has not been excavated. The middens could have resulted from both residential activities and feasts. A number of status-related artifacts were present in these middens. Mound G is rectangular and about 100 meters long. A test trench partially exposed a circular wall trench and pit hearth beneath it. No post molds were present in the trench, so the structure had been dismantled.

Mound C was briefly tested (Anderson 1977b; H. Davis 1966; J. E. Miller 1982:30–33) and is apparently an accretional burial mound (discussed below). An exploratory excavation in the plaza-facing corner of Mound B exposed five stages in the upper two-thirds of the mound (J. E. Miller 1982:36–41; Rolingson 1980:38). Three of the stages had middens on them and there may have been buildings on some of the stages. Both human and animal bone on the top of the mound were plowed up in the nineteenth century (Knapp 1878). Some of the soil used for fill is a clay obtained from the lake bed and a large borrow pit is adjacent to the mound. Few artifacts were present in the fill zones. The plaza appears to have been kept clean and excavation recovered remarkably few artifacts. The noteworthy feature of the plaza is a cluster of superimposed post pits and post molds 20 to 40 centimeters in diameter in the southwest portion of the plaza between Mounds A, D, and S. An earthen embankment and exterior ditch surround the site except along the lake bank. These are impressive constructions involving planning, management, and group effort. The embankment is 2.4 meters high, 18 meters wide at the base, and 1615 meters long. The northern portion was piled up on the inside of an abandoned channel forming a natural ditch; the southern portion had an excavated ditch. There are two openings in the long segment and perhaps a third on the southwest end.

The formal arrangement of the Toltec site is a result of a plan in which some mounds are aligned with positions of the sun on the horizon at the time of the summer solstice and the equinoxes (Sherrod and Rolingson 1987:26–41). The precise positions of the sun at the solstices and equinoxes are obscured by the large size of the mounds. The placement of mounds in these solar positions may have been symbolic, integrating the physical world with the cosmological world of the supernatural. Many of the mound locations are spaced on standardized distances in multiple increments of 47.5 meters measured from Mounds A and H, mounds aligned east-west. The lengths of the two plazas and the extent of the site along the lake bank are multiples of a measurement unit of 47.5 meters, while the embankment length is 34 times the distance measurement.

Subsistence

Plant and animal remains at Toltec and several small sites provide information on Plum Bayou subsistence as a mixed strategy of hunting, foraging, farming, and fishing. At Toltec, 8900 seeds from four contexts have been typed to thirty species or genera (Fritz 1988; Fritz and Powell 1998; C. Smith 1993, 1996). The native starchy seeds are primarily little barley, maygrass, chenopod, and knotweed and were cultivated, if not domesticated. The most common seeds are an as-yet unidentified grass, Poaceae Type X. Trace amounts of maize, squash, and bottle gourd are present. The maize is from deposits dating A.D. 750–800 and A.D. 950–1030. Seeds of fleshy fruits, such as persimmon, plum, and grape, are present and hickory nutshell and acorn fragments are abundant. At the Ink Bayou site, fifteen seeds include maygrass, sumpweed, chenopod, and little barley (King 1987). Maize is present in eight features, two of which are radiocarbon dated to A.D. 900–1000. At the Alexander site, twenty-seven seeds from Plum Bayou middens and features include maygrass, chenopod, sumpweed, squash, bottle gourd, knotweed, and one maize cupule (King 1985:53–57). One date on the Plum Bayou component is A.D. 750–850. Thick hickory nutshell is abundant at both Ink Bayou and Alexander.

In the Ozark Plateau region, native starchy seeds and maize were used at the Dirst site, dated to A.D. 600–800. The sample of 199 seeds includes little barley, chenopod, maygrass, amaranth, and erect knotweed (Dunavan 1992:94–95). Maize and squash were produced on a small scale. The plant remains indicate a heavy reliance on acorns, hickory nuts, and native starchy seeds (Fritz 1990b:174).

The small midden sites have more maize than does Toltec in these samples. The widespread distribution of maize indicates that it was available to everyone and that it was not a food reserved for elite members of society. It may have been consumed only in ritual contexts. Stable carbon isotope studies in the Lower Mississippi Valley show no evidence for maize consumption between A.D. 300 and A.D. 1000 (Fritz and Kidder 1993:9–11). Microwear studies of teeth indicate a reliance on starchy seeds (Burnett 1990:203–5). This pattern of plant use is present throughout the central area of eastern North America in the Late Woodland period (Johannessen 1993a).

Animal remains at Toltec and several midden sites show a heavy reliance on white-tailed deer. In addition to deer, other animals present at Toltec in large numbers are squirrel, turkey, passenger pigeon, bowfin, and aquatic turtle. Mammals, birds, fish, and turtles are all present in varying amounts, but the species reflect the availability of animals near each site. At Toltec, fifty-two species or genera of animals are identified (R. Hoffman 1998), greatly exceeding the species/genera range of smaller sites. At Ink Bayou the amount of fish is high relative to the number of birds and small mammals, and aquatic-habitat mammals, such as swamp rabbit, mink, and river otter, are present (Colburn 1987). The Fitzhugh site, located in a backswamp, is low in aquatic turtle, fish, and bird (Nassaney and Hoffman 1992). At the Alexander site, the amount of turtle is high, especially box turtle, while turkey and squirrel are the predominant bird and small mammal (Styles et al. 1985:61–63). At the Roland site, the amount of fish is high, that of birds low, and raccoon and gray squirrel are the most abundant mammals, in addition to deer (Butsch 1991). At the Dirst site, forty-five animals are identified, with white-tailed deer and elk dominant; turkey, beaver, squirrels, raccoon, and turtles are common; and fish remains are a minor part of the assemblage (Scott 1992:110–11).

Plum Bayou subsistence is characterized in the preserved remains by an apparent emphasis on deer, starchy seeds, hickory nuts, and acorns. The importance of small mammals, birds, fish, and turtles varies with local availability. This strategy is present in the central area of eastern North America (Johannessen 1993a) and is distinct from that of the Lower Mississippi Valley where densities of starchy seeds are low and maize is absent (Fritz and Kidder 1993:7–11).

Material Culture

Lithic artifacts and manufacturing waste are abundant on Plum Bayou sites in spite of the fact that stone does not occur naturally in the floodplain. Chert, sandstone, and quartzite are the most abundant materials and are available in gravel bars of the Arkansas and White rivers and their tributaries. Also present are materials from the Ouachita Mountains and Arkansas River Valley regions including novaculite, quartz crystal, quartzite, sandstone, siltstone, shale, hematite, syenite, and lamprophyre. Minor amounts of novaculite and quartz crystal are widely distributed, even at sites in the Western Lowlands where formal tools are more common than debitage (House 1975:159). When the entire Plum Bayou region is taken into consideration, the widespread distribution of materials indicates an established exchange system. The materials were readily accessible to everyone living in the western portions of the region and the Arkansas River Valley, but not to those living in the Grand Prairie, Western Lowlands, lower White River, and Boeuf Basin. Quartz crystal is noteworthy because it is present on most Late and Terminal Late Woodland sites in the Plum Bayou region; at Toltec it comprises 6 to 10 percent of the chipped lithic assemblage. It was used to make bifacially chipped arrow points and knives and the tips of crystals were used as perforators or cutting tools. The largest analyzed and quantified material culture assemblages are from the Toltec site surface collections (Anderson 1978) and Mound D excavations (T. L. Hoffman 1998). Most of the artifacts are expedient tools and flaking debris; formal tools include corner-notched and stemmed arrow points, darts, knives, bifaces, scrapers, perforators, adzes, celts, hammerstones, and pitted anvils. The bow and arrow was in use. Antler and animal bone, mostly deer and turkey, were made into flakers, awls, pins, and ulna tools (Rolingson 1998e).

The pottery is grog tempered, although crushed bone or shell is occasionally present in the paste. Shell tempering occurs in 1 percent of the plainware from the later deposits at Toltec (Rolingson 1998f:27). Ceramics at the Dirst site include shell tempering by A.D. 600–700 (Guendling et al. 1992:150). The Soc site has shell-tempered sherds with Coles Creek Incised designs (Figley 1968). A minor amount of red-filmed surface treatment is characteristic of Plum Bayou pottery, comprising as much as 11 percent in some deposits at Toltec. Vessel shapes are jars and bowls. Jars are deep subconoidal shapes, with flat bases, constricted necks, and short flaring rims.

This shape is similar to the Williams Plain jars of Fourche Maline culture (J. Brown 1996:344; Schambach 1998b:279) and is present, but not common, for Baytown Plain in the Mississippi valley (Phillips et al. 1951:78). Shapes of bowls at the Toltec site range from shallow with outsloping walls to hemispherical, apparently with rounded or slightly flattened bases (Rolingson 1998f:31–33).

Decoration of pottery is rare at all Plum Bayou sites, but the diagnostic types are Coles Creek Incised and Officer Punctated, with French Fork Incised present in trace amounts. These types make up only 4 percent of the pottery at Toltec Mound D (Rolingson 1998f:26) and they are not abundant on any site. These types can be used as temporal markers for the Terminal Late Woodland period. Plum Bayou ceramics are distinguished from those of Coles Creek culture by the smaller amounts of decorated sherds and by the absence of varieties common in the Lower Red River region in Louisiana.

Status-Related and Nonlocal Artifacts

Late and Terminal Late Woodland sites are not usually noted for the presence of nonlocal or status-related artifacts; therefore, exchange among distant groups is thought to have been minimal. Several artifacts on sites in the Arkansas River basin indicate long-distance trade during the Terminal Late Woodland period. At Toltec, two items have their sources at great distances. One is a fragment of thin copper in a midden on Mound D. The other, in the midden beneath Mound E, is a modified piece of conch shell columella with an engraved decoration reminiscent of Weeden Island and French Fork pottery designs. The copper has not been analyzed for trace elements, but it is an imported material. The columella is likely from the Gulf Coast. A copper-stained wood fragment was reported in one of the Chandler Landing mounds (C. B. Moore 1910:346).

A gastropod shell, *Leptoxis* Rafinesque, 1819 (Pleuroceridae), present in the Toltec Mound D deposits, was made into a bead. The shell probably originated in the clear streams of the Ozark Salem Plateau in southern Missouri (Rolingson 1998e:82). The source location is some distance from Toltec, but possibly within Plum Bayou territory. Biotite mica in the form of apparently unmodified pseudo-hexagonal pieces is present at Toltec. This form of mica is available locally in biotite lamprophyre outcrops and may have been collected because of the unusual appearance of the mica. Lumps of hematite and small cubes of galena probably were ground for paint. Both occur in Arkansas, but the galena may well have been imported from sources in southeastern Missouri (Walthall 1981). Modified platform pipes of red siltstone and shale, gorgets of shale, and plummets and boatstones made of a variety of raw materials including igneous stones are present in Plum Bayou sites. These artifacts may be grave goods, as at the Chandler Landing site (C. B. Moore 1910:342), but are not exclusively so, and they are present in middens at Toltec, often battered and broken. Of particular note is an owl head effigy of trachyte at Toltec. These materials are available within 40 kilometers of the Toltec site, but some of them may have their source in the more distant Magnet Cove near Hot Springs.

Animals are a source of materials for artifacts that are potentially status related. Bones of pileated and red-headed woodpeckers and barred owl are present; these birds may have been caught for their bright feathers. Small perforated disks made from deer scapula, a bead of bird bone, and hairpins of deer long bone are present at Toltec (Rolingson 1998c:108, 1998e:80–81). Some of the pottery may also be considered status related, especially unusual vessel shapes, such as beakers and square, gourd-shaped, and re-stricted-orifice bowls. The types French Fork Incised and Coles Creek Incised are rare and may have been used in special contexts; nevertheless, sherds occur in low numbers in middens throughout the Plum Bayou region.

Most of the raw materials used for both utilitarian and special artifacts are available within the Plum Bayou region or are from the Ouachita Mountains. Materials from the Ozarks are present in the Western Lowlands sites. Internal trade is evident in the fact that lithic raw materials occur throughout the region. Artifacts providing evidence for long-distance trade are rare, but the copper and conch shell indicate that some trade routes existed.

Mortuary Patterns

Plum Bayou midden sites have burials that are either extended supine or par-tially flexed and that lack grave goods, as exemplified by two burials at the Ink Bayou site (D. Waddell et al. 1987) and seven burials at the Alexander site (Hemmings and House 1985:23–24). The latter burials, in a compact cluster on the east edge of the site, had varied orientations around the compass.

At the Toltec Mounds site, remarkably few burials have been encoun-tered in ten seasons of excavation, only one of which can be assigned to the Plum Bayou occupation. This was an extended adult located near Mound C (Rolingson 1980:42). Several units on the east side of Mound C were exca-vated in 1966 (Anderson 1977b; H. Davis 1966; J. E. Miller 1982:30–33) and two burials were uncovered, an extended adult female and a partially flexed adult male with a few infant bones. The burials had been covered with soil containing midden, and the artifacts are probably accidental inclusions rather than grave goods. An unassociated Coles Creek Incised, *var. Keo* bowl was excavated near the top of the mound. In 1966, the walls of an old excavation down through the mound showed no obvious stages of construction. In 1883, Palmer (1917:424; Jeter [ed.] 1990:259–60) dug a hole 1.5 meters square and 3.3 meters deep. He abandoned the effort when he encountered wet clay, having recovered only fragments of artifacts and a Coles Creek Incised, *var. Scott* bowl. Apparently, there was little formal preparation of the graves and the mound was built up by accretion, but the excavations are hardly adequate to establish a pattern.

Palmer excavated fifty-four burials from a small mound at the Coy site. The mound was 2.4 meters high and 15 meters in diameter. The human remains were near the base on an uneven surface. He described them as "laying without any order not overlaying each other but in full length… without order as to the points of the compass…all the remains must have been covered up at the same time" (Jeter [ed.] 1990:340). Five piles of ashes were present, but the human remains had not been burned. Artifacts included a stone knife and arrow points, a modified platform pipe, a few shell-tempered sherds, and Baytown Plain and Larto Red sherds (Nassaney 1996a:26). These burials were apparently in a single layer, perhaps a group burial.

A different pattern of burial is evident in the two mounds excavated by Moore (1910:341–48) at the Chandler Landing site. Mound A was 2.3 meters high and 19.8 meters in diameter; Mound B was 1.3 meters high and 12.2 meters in diameter. Excavation was done with picks through hard clay and produced mostly decayed fragments. Human remains "were present throughout, but less frequently than would be expected in a mound of the size of the one in question…[and] a layer of bones…apparently consisting of skeletons and parts of skeletons mingled, many bones, however, being missing and others being out of place" indicated disarticulated burials (C. B. Moore 1910:342). Artifacts from the mounds were a flat-based pottery jar with notched rim; four modified platform pipes of shale; a clay elbow pipe with long stem; three polished celts; six boatstones, one of which was quartz crystal; a leaf-shaped biface 25 centimeters long; lance and arrow points; one shell and four pearl beads; and fragments of copper-stained wood. The variety and abundance of artifacts distinguishes the Chandler Landing burials from those at Coy and Toltec.

Social Context

Initial assumptions in the Toltec Mounds and Plum Bayou research were that Toltec had been occupied by a small to moderate-sized group of people and that they were an elite with higher rank than people who lived in the outlying sites. The excavations at Toltec have shown that middens are primarily associated with mounds or are thin deposits mostly concentrated around a clean plaza. Nor are middens of sufficient size to have been left by a large residential population. The Toltec site itself was occupied by a small group of people and most of the population lived in the surrounding countryside. Alternatively, the Coy site apparently has a midden with continuous distribution without a clean plaza.

The question of whether or not social inequality had developed is difficult to answer as it is a matter of complexity and scale and the criteria used in the analysis. In general, Late Woodland society in the Southeast is considered to have been egalitarian, while Mississippian society is characterized by hierarchical chiefdoms with formal inherited political offices and ascriptive social ranking (J. Scarry 1996:19). Within Mississippian society, however, there was a range of complexity and more attention has been given to ethnohistorical tribes and archaeological cultures having greater rather than less complexity. Models used in assessing ranked society are often based on southeastern tribes at the time of initial contact in the sixteenth century and on later ethnographic descriptions (Barker and Pauketat [eds.] 1992; J. Scarry [ed.] 1996; Steponaitis 1991), and these may not be applicable to the development of inequality in the Terminal Late Woodland to Mississippian transition. Plum Bayou social complexity should be considered dynamic and changing through 300 to 400 years.

Data from a 20-kilometer circle around Toltec were used by Nassaney (1992a:353–56, 1992b) to investigate the development of complexity from A.D. 1 to 1700. He used a political-economic model of social ranking in which the relative concentration of power, that is, the "ability of agents to alter, or attempt to alter, the conditions of their existence in specific social and material contexts" (Nassaney 1992a:27) is the significant dimension of variation in ranked societies. The question is how individuals exercise power to obtain and accumulate surplus and how such strategies may be resisted. Hierarchies were present in the Mississippi valley in which individuals "symbolized and enforced the separation between elite and commoners... in burial practices, residence form and location, grave goods, and status insignia" (Nassaney 1992a:31–32). Nassaney analyzed sites around Toltec for population size and density, catchment productivity, rank size and hierarchy, and earthwork construction and labor. He concluded that "clear, institutionalized relationships of social inequality had not arisen in Plum Bayou culture" (Nassaney 1992a:353, 1992b) particularly in regard to incipient elites mobilizing surplus and controlling production and exchange of either food surplus or prestige goods and in the absence of differential mortuary treatment.

There are, however, alternative models to that of a political economy controlled by elite individuals. Earle (1991) and his colleagues proposed three schemes for understanding variability in chiefdoms and distinguishing simple from complex structures. A chiefdom is defined as "a polity that organizes a regional population of thousands" (Earle 1991:1) and some degree of heritable ranking and economic stratification is associated. Simple structures are distinguished from complex structures by assessing scale of development, basis of finance, and orientation to a group or to an individual. The scale of development for a simple chiefdom is characterized by a polity in the low thousands with one level of hierarchy above the local community. A complex chiefdom has a population in the tens of thousands and at least two levels of hierarchy above the local community (Earle 1991:2–3). Plum Bayou culture has a low population density, and most people lived in small groups of households or single households without ceremonial architecture. Above the local community are several sites with one or two mounds; two small multiple mound centers (Coy and Hayes); and two large multiple mound centers (Toltec and Baytown).

The basis of finance (Earle 1991:3) distinguishes staple versus wealth finance in chiefdoms. In a simple system of staple finance, food and technological goods are mobilized and disbursed for services, and the chief provides feasts. Social position in wealth finance is defined by items of symbolic value that are obtained through long-distance trade or craft production. Plum Bayou culture has some evidence for mobilization and disbursement of food through feasts in the Toltec locality. Mound-associated midden deposits have rich and diverse animal bone (R. Hoffman 1998:92–94) in contrast to samples from small habitation sites (Rolingson 1998c:105). The association of large, diverse bone samples with elite or ritual contexts is recognized in southeastern sites (H. Jackson and Scott 1995). A regional exchange system in Plum Bayou culture is indicated by the presence of lithic resources from the Ouachita Mountains on sites in the Western Lowlands and Boeuf Basin. Novaculite, quartz crystal, syenite, and lamprophyre were dispersed throughout the Plum Bayou territory. This is not, however, a new development; Archaic and Woodland sites in eastern Arkansas generally have an abundance of novaculite, sandstone, and quartzite, and igneous rocks are common. Items of wealth and adornment at the Toltec Mounds site were made of a wide variety of materials both locally available and from neighboring regions, such as Magnet Cove and the Salem Plateau. Wealth items resulting from long-distance exchange are rare, but include copper and marine shell present at the Toltec Mounds and Chandler Landing sites.

Group structure in chiefdoms distinguishes between group-oriented cultures in which the importance of the group is defined through corporate labor constructions and planned communities, while adornment, special housing, and burials set the elite off from the non-elite in individualizing cultures (Earle 1991:3). Special burials and personal adornment, the evidence for an orientation to individuals or an elite, are not characteristic of Plum Bayou culture. Mound and earthwork construction and the formal planning of the Toltec Mounds site are evidence of an emphasis on the corporate group. The Toltec site represents a long-term investment in planning, time, and labor to produce a permanent place with conceptual or ritual identity for the corporate group. The continuity of planning may have been directed by religious specialists who lived at the center and mobilized a labor force from the region.

External Relationships

Plum Bayou culture did not exist in isolation, of course, and evidence is present for contacts in several directions. Mound construction has a long history in the Lower Mississippi Valley, and mounds are more common in Coles Creek culture than in Plum Bayou. Excavated early Coles Creek period sites contemporary with Toltec have low platform mounds, including Matheny (Kidder 1994:144), Mt. Nebo (Giardino 1984:102), Osceola (Kidder 1990), Greenhouse (Belmont 1967; J. A. Ford 1951), and Lake St. Agnes (Toth 1979a) in Louisiana, and Lake George in Mississippi (S. Williams and Brain 1983:38–56). Early stages may have burials in them; none appear to have had structures initially, although they did support structures on later stages. The organization of the site into a mound and plaza complex is characteristic of the Coles Creek period. Plum Bayou pottery decoration reflects connections with the Lower Mississippi Valley in varieties of Coles Creek Incised, French Fork Incised, and Larto Red. Several varieties are similar to varieties in the Bayland phase in the lower Yazoo (S. Williams and Brain 1983:316) now dated A.D. 700–800 by Kidder (1992a:149). The changes in decorative styles in the middle and late Coles Creek periods in the Lower Valley are not present at Toltec, where the simpler motifs continued in use. Connections extend beyond the Mississippi valley to stylistic modes common in Weeden Island culture on the Gulf Coast. The presence of marine-shell artifacts in the Arkansas River Valley is also evidence of Gulf Coast connections.

The species of cultivated native seeds and maize that have been recovered from Toltec and small Plum Bayou sites are evidence for contact with the Illinois River valley and American Bottom and distinguish Plum Bayou from Coles Creek culture, which did not rely on cultigens (Fritz and Kidder

1993:8–9). Shell-tempered pottery also reflects contacts to the northeast; the amount of shell tempering is greater in the northern Plum Bayou sites than at Toltec, and this may have been introduced from the Central Mississippi Valley. Red filming may have moved from Plum Bayou to the north end of the Western Lowlands and St. Francis Basin where it is widespread in the Varney horizon, A.D. 800 to 1000 (D. Morse and P. Morse 1990:156–59). Red filming also appeared in low frequencies in the George Reeves and Merrell phases about A.D. 900 in the American Bottom (J. Kelly et al. 1984:142, 150). Contact to the north for Plum Bayou is also indicated by the presence of copper.

Evidence for contact to the west and southwest is stronger than for other directions. The use of Ouachita Mountain lithic materials dates back centuries prior to Plum Bayou, continues through the Terminal Late Woodland, and is only reduced to near invisibility with the Mississippi period after A.D. 1000. The Ouachita Mountain lithic materials comprise less than 20 percent of the assemblage at Toltec Mound D. Most, but not all, of the raw materials could have been collected from river gravels washed out of the Ouachita Mountains. Similarities in pottery between Plum Bayou and Fourche Maline are evident in the shapes of utilitarian jars and the low incidence of decoration. Late Fourche Maline sites, such as the Means site on the Ouachita River (Schambach 1998b), have Coles Creek Incised and French Fork Incised present in low amounts. There are no known Fourche Maline mounds in the mountain and river valley regions, but there are midden sites with Caddo I period mounds built on them. In the Little Missouri River valley the multiple-mound East site was in use by A.D. 1150 to 1200 (Early [ed.] 1993:224). East Incised is one of the earliest Caddoan types in the Ouachita Basin (Early [ed.] 1993:88) and is distinctive because it is red filmed with horizontal incised lines on the rim (Suhm and Jelks 1962:41), apparently derived from a combination of Coles Creek Incised and Larto Red. The early Caddoan type Crockett Curvilinear Incised was derived from French Fork Incised (Suhm and Jelks 1962:31–33).

The Spiro and Crenshaw site occupations were in part contemporary with the late occupation at Toltec. The Spiro site is located near the juncture of the Poteau River with the Arkansas River. It has two platform, seven buried-structure, and three burial mounds. Platform mound construction began in the Harlan phase, about A.D. 1000 (J. Brown 1996:167), but the site was fully occupied during the Evans phase, A.D. 950 to 1000. Specialized structures were laid out according to important solar positions and standardized distance spacing and accretional burial mounds were begun (J. Brown 1996:167). Burials were groups of disarticulated individuals placed in layers with each layer covered with bark. Coles Creek Incised and French Fork

Incised pottery vessels, modified platform pipes, boatstones, and stone and shell beads were included as grave goods. Two burials at the base of the Craig mound had plain conch shell cups and fragments (J. Brown 1996:144). Quartz crystals and other lithic materials from the Ouachita Mountains were used. Clear connections to Toltec are present in the initial grave period, and connections to Crenshaw were important (J. Brown 1996:161).

The Crenshaw site (Schambach 1982, 1997) on the Red River was a late Fourche Maline village and ceremonial center and an early Caddoan period center with six mounds and a linear embankment. The late Fourche Maline occupation dates to about A.D. 700 to 900 (Schambach 1997:65). Some mounds are positioned according to solar alignments, but the standardized measurement was not in use (Sherrod and Rolingson 1987:63). Two mounds contain Fourche Maline burials with Coles Creek Incised and French Fork Incised vessels, arrow points, celts, bone pins, long-stemmed pipes, and shell beads. One burial had a copper ornament (W. R. Wood 1963a:8). The burials were primarily disarticulated, some of them consisting of skulls and mandibles. One mound had a mass burial of extended complete and incomplete remains in a single grave, accompanied by arrows and a few pottery vessels (Schambach 1997:62–63).

It is evident that there was contact among the three mound centers during the tenth century, which is particularly reflected in the material culture. Future research should determine whether the pottery vessels were carried from one site to another. In addition to regional exchange, highly valued materials and/or artifacts from long distances were imported to the ceremonial centers west of the Mississippi River. The Late Woodland period is often characterized as lacking in exchange of exotic goods, but the presence of copper and marine shell on the western border of the Southeast is the initial evidence for an active exchange network in the Mississippi period (J. Brown et al. 1990).

Future Directions

Research on the Toltec Mounds and other Plum Bayou sites has made a significant contribution to the archaeology of the Mississippi River valley by providing data on the region of the Arkansas and White rivers. There is no longer a gap in our knowledge between Coles Creek culture in the south and Emergent Mississippian in the north. This does not mean that all problems have been solved, and certainly new questions have been raised. Debates concerning the development of Mississippian cultures in the Mississippi valley, the transition from Woodland cultures, the development of social inequality, the significance of mound construction, and the importance of maize versus native seed crops have been going on for a long time and will continue.

Early Plum Bayou culture had relationships with the Coles Creek culture of the Lower Mississippi Valley and Gulf Coast. Late Plum Bayou was contemporary with Emergent Mississippian in the Central Mississippi Valley and there is evidence for contact between the areas. Contacts with the Fourche Maline culture to the west were sustained during the time of Plum Bayou. Plum Bayou culture is primarily Woodland in material culture, subsistence, and settlement pattern. Within Plum Bayou, two centers developed, one in the area around Toltec and one around Baytown and the Cache River area. Such places were more important than others and were maintained and used for a long period of time. The public architecture and some of the material culture are distinct from ordinary sites and the centers probably developed under the direction of leaders in simple chiefdoms. These places undoubtedly symbolized the identity of the corporate group.

The culture history of the Plum Bayou region during the 1500 years of the Woodland and Mississippi periods needs to be developed in more detail. Temporal diagnostics among ceramic and lithic artifacts are needed to refine the culture history of the region and to investigate changes in subsistence, settlement, and social inequality. The apparently abrupt termination of Plum Bayou culture needs to be explored. Plum Bayou culture and the Toltec site were in a strategic location with access to neighbors in all directions and they maintained their independence and unique cultural pattern for 400 years. Nevertheless, mound construction had ended and the population in the Arkansas Lowland appears to have declined by A.D. 1050, at a time when neighboring cultures were growing in population and developing complex societies.

Chapter 4

Woodland Period Archaeology of the Lower Mississippi Valley

Tristram R. Kidder

The Woodland is one of the best known yet paradoxically least under-stood temporal units in the Lower Mississippi Valley. Contrary to ear-lier ideas (McNutt 1996b:217; S. Williams 1963:297), the Woodland was not populated by static, "good gray" cultures, but was a time of innovation and variation. Because southeastern archaeology is often viewed through the lens of the contact era ethnohistoric record, our understanding of Wood-land behavior is conditioned by what we know of Mississippi period adapta-tion. While Mississippian peoples may have enlarged on or perfected some of the major subsistence, social, political, and economic adaptations devel-oped in the Woodland, few characteristics that define Mississippian in the Lower Mississippi Valley were truly novel.

To geologists, the Lower Mississippi Valley stretches from Cairo, Illi-nois, to the Gulf of Mexico, but my discussion is limited to the valley south of the mouth of the Arkansas River. The Mississippi River and its tributaries dominate the geography and geology of the Lower Mississippi Valley. The landforms and plant and animal communities are almost all influenced by the river or by processes affected by the river. During Woodland times the Mississippi meandered widely within its floodplain and both human and natural communities were forced to respond to this dynamic process.

Low hills and bluffs of the Upland complex mark the eastern edge of the alluvial valley. Tertiary age and older deposits form the western side of the valley. South of Natchez, Mississippi, the valley flows through coastwise deposits of the Upland, Intermediate, and Prairie complexes (Autin et al. 1991). The valley consists of the modern river, which flows within a mean-der belt of recent origin, and a complex mosaic of relict meander belts, aban-doned channels, cutoffs, and backswamps (Saucier 1974, 1994; Saucier et al. [eds.] 1996). Within the alluvial valley are landforms created before the Holocene (Autin et al. 1991; Saucier 1994), most notably Macon Ridge, which extends from southeast Arkansas to Sicily Island, Louisiana, and sepa-rates the Bartholomew-Boeuf Basin from the main portion of the valley.

The Mississippi alluvial valley has a temperate environment, with cool, wet winters and hot, humid summers. There has been little study of later Holocene climates or paleoenvironments (H. Delcourt 1976; H. Delcourt and P. Delcourt 1996), but Stahle et al. (1985) used tree ring data to document ten major droughts between A.D. 1531 and 1980. These data make it clear that the climate of the Lower Valley varied through time. Moreover, catastrophic flooding caused by changes in rainfall and moisture circulation in the eastern United States have caused significant disruption in human settlement (Kidder 1996; see also P. Brown et al. 1999; Knox 1983, 1985; Saucier 1994).

While there is some degree of microenvironmental variation within the region the plant community predominately consists of mixed hardwood forests with nut-bearing trees, notably oaks and hickories. Cypress and tupelo occur in seasonally inundated swamps, and hackberry, sweetgum, maple, and willow are found in low, poorly drained backswamp areas. Game animals are relatively abundant in the region, with deer, raccoon, opossum, squirrel, muskrat, and rabbit being the most commonly hunted species. Fish were a major food source for almost all human populations in the region. Freshwater and, near the coast, brackish-water shellfish were exploited by many groups.

The major geographic subdivisions of the Lower Mississippi Valley as defined here are the Bartholomew-Boeuf Basin of southeast Arkansas and north-central Louisiana, the Yazoo Basin of west-central Mississippi, the Tensas Basin of northeast Louisiana, the Natchez Bluffs region of southwest Mississippi, the Red River mouth region of central Louisiana, and the Mississippi River delta region of southern Louisiana (Fisk 1944; Saucier 1994) (Figure 4.1). Each region has a unique culture history. Sites discussed in the text are also shown in Figure 4.1. Although there are differences between basin-wide culture-historical sequences, archaeological data indicate a general pattern of cultural continuity since roughly 800 B.C.

The archaeological history of the region has been summarized by Neuman (1984) and D. Morse and P. Morse (1983). Jeter et al. (1989) have published the most recent extensive synthesis of the regional culture history. The culture history of the Lower Mississippi Valley is well known, but the nomenclature can be confusing. As depicted in Figure 4.2, the post-Archaic prehistory is divided into time periods that subsume numerous archaeological cultures, which, in turn, are subdivided into phases (Phillips 1970; S. Williams and Brain 1983). It is important to observe that the cultural and temporal units used here are not always concordant. Thus, for example, the Coles Creek *culture* crosses the temporal boundary of the Mississippi *period* and can be traced, as a ceramic cultural entity, up to at least circa A.D. 1200.

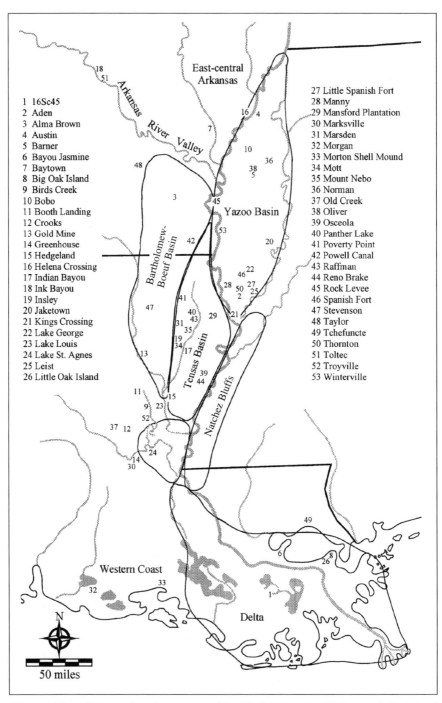

1 16Sc45
2 Aden
3 Alma Brown
4 Austin
5 Barner
6 Bayou Jasmine
7 Baytown
8 Big Oak Island
9 Birds Creek
10 Bobo
11 Booth Landing
12 Crooks
13 Gold Mine
14 Greenhouse
15 Hedgeland
16 Helena Crossing
17 Indian Bayou
18 Ink Bayou
19 Insley
20 Jaketown
21 Kings Crossing
22 Lake George
23 Lake Louis
24 Lake St. Agnes
25 Leist
26 Little Oak Island

27 Little Spanish Fort
28 Manny
29 Mansford Plantation
30 Marksville
31 Marsden
32 Morgan
33 Morton Shell Mound
34 Mott
35 Mount Nebo
36 Norman
37 Old Creek
38 Oliver
39 Osceola
40 Panther Lake
41 Poverty Point
42 Powell Canal
43 Raffman
44 Reno Brake
45 Rock Levee
46 Spanish Fort
47 Stevenson
48 Taylor
49 Tchefuncte
50 Thornton
51 Toltec
52 Troyville
53 Winterville

Figure 4.1 — Sites and major geographic subdivisions in the Lower Mississippi Valley

Date	Period	Northern LMV	Central LMV	Southern LMV
— 1600	European Contact	Various Historic Tribes	Various Historic Tribes	Various Historic Tribes
— 1400	Mississippi	Mississippian	Plaquemine	Plaquemine
— 1200 — 1000 — 800	Coles Creek	Plum Bayou / Coles Creek	Coles Creek	Coastal Coles Creek
— 600	Baytown	Baytown	Troyville	Coastal Troyville
— 400 — 200	Late Marksville	Issaquena & Plainware Phases	Issaquena & Plainware Phases	Issaquena
— 0	Early Marksville	Marksville	Marksville	Marksville
— 200 — 400 — 600 — 800	Tchula	Lake Cormorant / Tchefuncte	Tchefuncte	Tchefuncte
	Late Archaic	Poverty Point	Poverty Point	Poverty Point

Figure 4.2 — Archaeological culture history of the Lower Mississippi Valley

Tchula Period

The Tchula period is the designation for Early Woodland in the Lower Mississippi Valley (Phillips 1970). This period saw the emergence and establishment of Woodland cultural traits in the region, notably the regular use of ceramics. Tchula period sites are scattered throughout the Lower Mississippi Valley and the loess bluffs to the east. Tchula occupations appear to be relatively simple, with little evidence of social differentiation, economic specialization, or long-distance trade and exchange. The Early Woodland cultures of the Lower Mississippi Valley appear to have limited external contacts and manifest few of the seemingly more complex traits of the preceding Late Archaic.

Chronologically, Tchula is traditionally placed between 500 B.C. and A.D. 1 (S. Williams and Brain 1983), but recent dates from the Bayou Jasmine site suggest the presence of a fully developed Tchefuncte ceramic repertoire by circa 800 B.C. (Hays 1995). Tchula occupations are generally assigned to one of two archaeological cultures, distinguished by differences in ceramic decoration and style. Tchefuncte culture is found throughout the Lower Mississippi Valley, from the central Yazoo Basin south to the coast. With the exception of a notable increase in sites in the coastal region, Tchefuncte culture distribution generally mirrors that of the early Poverty Point culture settlement. The poorly known Lake Cormorant culture is located in the northern Yazoo Basin and eastward into the hills adjacent to the alluvial valley (J. L. Ford 1990; Phillips 1970; Weinstein 1995).

Tchula pottery was crude and often is classified as "temperless," but grog or sand was occasionally added (Phillips 1970:162–64; Weinstein and Rivet 1978). The ceramic fabric was usually laminated or contorted in cross section, and vessel surfaces are usually soft, implying low firing temperatures (Gertjejansen and Shenkel 1983). Bowls are the most common vessel form, followed by restricted-orifice pots or jars, and flaring-rim pots or jars. Vessels were often decorated, with incised rims and teat-leg tetrapodal and wedge-shaped supports common (J. A. Ford and Quimby 1945; Weinstein and Rivet 1978). At Tchefuncte sites on the north shore of Lake Pontchartrain, Alexander ceramics, presumably derived from the Tennessee and/or Tombigbee drainages (N. Jenkins and Krause 1986; Walthall 1980), occur (J. A. Ford and Quimby 1945). Many Tchula sites have yielded fired clay cooking balls. These objects are generally smaller than those found at Poverty Point sites and lack the typological diversity of earlier forms.

Projectile point (dart) forms do not differ greatly from those of Poverty Point times (Shenkel 1984a). Nonlocal lithics are rare, but a few Tchula sites have produced quartz crystals (Shenkel 1984a). Both flake tool and core tool reduction strategies seem to have been utilized. Ground stone tools are relatively rare and are mostly confined to utilitarian items. The Poverty Point lapidary industry was largely abandoned, and the exotic decorative items found at Poverty Point sites are absent or very rare at Tchula sites. There was a thriving Tchula bone tool industry.

Tchula subsistence remains suggest an exclusive reliance on wild plants and animals. The few botanical analyses are from sites in the coastal zone. Squash and bottle gourd were utilized at the Morton Shell Mound in coastal Louisiana (K. Byrd 1974, 1994). The squash seeds fall below the minimum size range expected for domesticated cucurbits, and the bottle gourd specimens are not considered to have been cultivated (K. Byrd 1994; Fritz and Kidder 1993). Wild seeds and fruits were also utilized at Morton Shell Mound and at the Raffman site in the Tensas Basin (Trachtenberg 1999). Neither site yielded evidence of the Native American starchy seed complex.

Faunal remains are reported from several sites along the coast, notably Morton Shell Mound (K. Byrd 1974, 1976a, 1994), and several Pontchartrain Basin sites (Shenkel 1974, 1981, 1984a). Most sites in this region consist of midden that includes large amounts of shell of the brackish water clam, *Rangia cuneata* (J. A. Ford and Quimby 1945). The dietary importance of clams is unclear. K. Byrd (1976b) notes that they would have provided a minimal amount of protein or other nutrients, but the quantity and ubiquity suggest some economic importance (Shenkel 1984b). At Morton Shell Mound, subsistence focused on deer, blue geese, box turtle, alligator, and fish. Fish were especially important at Big Oak Island and Little Oak Island, with mammals poorly represented (Shenkel 1974, 1981, 1984a; Shenkel and Gibson 1974). Shenkel (1984a:65–67) argues that Tchula period occupants in the Pontchartrain Basin were semispecialized hunter-fisher-gatherers, with food intake tailored to each site's specific habitat. The *Rangia* beds provided stable, predictable resources and became "anchors" for regional settlement.

Tchefuncte settlements are widely, but not uniformly, distributed. Most occupations are found near the coast or in the alluvial valley of the Mississippi. There are very few known Tchefuncte occupations in southeast Arkansas or the Bartholomew-Boeuf Basin of Arkansas and Louisiana, but Tchefuncte sites are well represented in the lower reaches of the Ouachita River (J. Gibson 1985a, 1985b, 1996b) and in the Felsenthal region north of the Louisiana-Arkansas border (Hemmings 1982; Weinstein and Kelley 1984). Tchefuncte sites are rare in the Natchez Bluffs east of the river. Lake Cormorant culture settlements are frequently found in small tributary stream valleys immediately east of the alluvial valley proper (J. L. Ford 1990).

Tchefuncte sites differ considerably from those associated with Poverty Point culture. Most, especially those dated relatively early, are small and structurally simple. The Tchefuncte occupation at Raffman appears to be an exception. Tchefuncte deposits are found over a roughly 500-square-meter area; a contemporary mound is located several hundred meters to the south.

Several Tchula period mounds are documented (J. Gibson 1996b; J. Gibson and Shenkel 1988). The best known Tchefuncte example is the Lafayette Mounds (J. A. Ford and Quimby 1945). Other examples have been identified in the lower Ouachita Valley at the Lake Louis and Boothe Landing sites (J. Gibson 1985a, 1996b:47–49; J. Gibson and Shenkel 1988). Burial mounds also were a part of the Lake Cormorant culture in northwest Mississippi (J. L. Ford 1990; Phillips et al. 1951:432). Most excavated Tchefuncte mounds served as mortuary facilities containing flexed or bundled burials, representing an important shift from Poverty Point mound uses (J. Gibson 1996a; J. Gibson and Shenkel 1988). Burials in Tchula mounds appear to represent communal interments, possibly drawn from dispersed communities. Tchefuncte burials also were placed in cemeteries, usually in pits excavated into midden deposits. These burials are usually flexed or interred as bundles (H. Collins 1927, 1941; J. A. Ford and Quimby 1945). Some bundle burials underwent extensive postmortem treatment, including snapping long bones while they were still green (B. A. Lewis 1991).

Early Tchula components at Jaketown and sites in the Lafayette area have yielded fiber-tempered pottery and decorated ceramics with Wheeler-like styles on local Tchefuncte pastes (J. A. Ford et al. 1955; J. A. Ford and Quimby 1945; J. Gibson 1976; Weinstein 1986, 1995). Alexander ceramics occur in the Lower Mississippi Valley, though their relationship to the emergence of Tchula ceramics or culture is unknown. Thus, it is possible to suggest that the origins of Tchula ceramics were a consequence of three trends. One was an incipient ceramic industry emerging at Poverty Point and contemporary sites. The second was the intrusion of Wheeler series ceramics or stylistic ideas from the Tennessee Valley. The last was the east-to-west movement of ideas along the Gulf. Unfortunately, if such a scenario is true, it does not explain the emergence of Tchula period cultures. It seems likely that Tchula period populations represent local populations carried over from Poverty Point times. These peoples essentially ceased to traffic in long-distance trade goods and to construct vast public works shortly after 1000 B.C. Although the transformation of Tchula from Poverty Point probably was related in some fashion to the end of the Poverty Point interaction network, the causes of such a change remain unknown.

Marksville Period

Middle Woodland in the Lower Mississippi Valley is designated the Marksville period, after the type site of the same name in Louisiana. Middle Woodland generally is subdivided into early and late periods. Early Middle Woodland societies in most of the study area are associated with the Marksville culture (Jeter and Williams 1989:127; Phillips 1970; S. Williams and Brain 1983), though in the Central Mississippi Valley (D. Morse and P. Morse 1983; Rolingson and Mainfort, this volume) the connection to Marksville culture can be questioned (cf. Jeter and Williams 1989:131–33). Marksville culture is associated with traits such as mound building, mound burial, nonlocal goods, and Hopewellian iconography. By circa A.D. 200–300, however, late Middle Woodland successors no longer participated in the mortuary, ceremonial, and exchange behaviors that define Marksville (J. Gibson 1996b). The best-known late Middle Woodland culture is Issaquena (Greengo 1964; Phillips 1970; S. Williams and Brain 1983), which was widely distributed in the southern Yazoo Basin and southward along the Mississippi River as far south as the Marksville site.

North of a poorly defined boundary from Columbia, Louisiana, to Greenwood, Mississippi, other contemporary Late Marksville period occupations are differentiated from Issaquena by ceramic assemblages with a low incidence of decorated pottery. These "plainware" groups are not recognized as an independent cultural complex, but they encompass a number of phases, such as Hegwood Bayou in the Bartholomew-Boeuf Basin (Ring 1986), Johnson in the Tensas (Phillips 1970:895), Alligator Point and Alma Brown in Arkansas (Jeter 1982; Jeter and Williams 1989; Rolingson 1993), and Porter Bayou and Paxton in the Yazoo (Phillips 1970:892, 895; S. Williams and Brain 1983:361–62).

Marksville material culture suggests an evolutionary development from Tchula. Ceramics were generally better made, with harder pastes and better surface finishes. The earliest stylistically Marksville pottery occurs on Tchefuncte-like pastes in coastal Louisiana (Shenkel 1981, 1984a, 1984b). In many instances, late Tchula wares cannot be sorted from Early Marksville ones. Although some Marksville vessels have Tchefuncte shapes and decorative characteristics (J. A. Ford and Willey 1940:65, 137–38), Marksville pottery differs stylistically from its predecessors. Distinctive decorative and iconographic styles of Early Marksville pottery include birds, curvilinear designs, stamping, and deep U-shaped incisions. These motifs, as well as specific rim modes and vessel shapes, may indicate close ties with Havana-Hopewell groups in the Illinois Valley (Toth 1979b, 1988).

Issaquena pottery is widely distributed throughout the Lower Mississippi Valley (Greengo 1964; Phillips 1970). This pottery continues many earlier themes, but lacks distinctive Marksville characteristics. The fabric is harder and better prepared, and surfaces are often smoothed or burnished. Vessel shapes are more varied, including jars, bowls, and beakers. Toward the end of the Marksville sequence, Issaquena ceramics begin to exhibit a qualitative decline in decoration. Incising and stamping are less well executed. The neat U-shaped lines of classic Marksville and Issaquena decoration change to shallow, often V-shaped incisions. Ceramic styles used for hundreds of years disappear or are liberally reinterpreted (Bitgood 1989).

Marksville lithics reflect continuity from Tchula. Contracting-stem dart points dominate the formal tool assemblage (J. A. Ford and Willey 1940:84–

105; Toth 1988). Blade tools, produced from prepared cores, occur at a few sites. Cores have not been found, suggesting that these blades were imported as finished products. A few blades were made of nonlocal chert (Toth 1988:168, 187), but most flaked lithic artifacts were made of local chert gravel. Ground stone tools are rare at Marksville sites. The most diagnostic are large, trapezoidal "greenstone" celts (Toth 1988:68, 70, plate VI), found primarily in mortuary or mound contexts. More rare are boatstones, pendants, and plummets.

Use of nonlocal artifacts and materials increases during Marksville times, though these artifacts occur in low frequency relative to Havana-Hopewell (J. Kelly, this volume). Copper earspools, marine shell beads and cups, greenstone celts, stone and pearl beads, bituminous shale and limonite pendants, cut mica, and galena have all been recovered from Marksville burial contexts (J. A. Ford and Willey 1940; Toth 1979b, 1988). The presence of these exotic artifacts is limited to the Marksville culture. Issaquena and contemporary sites produce virtually no exotic materials.

Marksville subsistence is poorly understood (Fritz and Kidder 1993). Botanical remains recently excavated at the Marksville site (McGimsey 1999) represent the only Marksville culture floral remains from the study area. Hickory (both thin- and thick-shelled) and acorn are the dominant taxa. Persimmon and palmetto seeds were recovered, along with seeds of bedstraw and wild beans. No representatives of the native starchy seed complex were found, perhaps because of sampling problems. No maize was found at Marksville (Fritz and Kidder 1993). Late Middle Woodland floral analyses are also limited. Data from Reno Brake (Fritz and Kidder 1993) and Raffman (Trachtenberg 1999) indicate that acorn was the predominant mast resource used in the alluvial bottomlands, and hickory was rare; palmetto, persimmon and other fleshy fruits (grapes and raspberries) also were important. Wild variants of some native starchy seeds were recovered from Issaquena contexts at Reno Brake (Kidder and Fritz 1993), but the quantity is very small. The presence of domesticated native crops, as well as (intrusive?) maize fragments, at Rock Levee indicates important shifts in subsistence at or around the end of Middle Woodland times (Weinstein et al. 1995).

Little can be said about Middle Woodland faunal procurement. Large and small mammals, as well as fish, are important in the assemblages from the Stevenson site in the Bartholomew-Boeuf Basin (Mariaca 1988), Mansford Plantation (K. Byrd 1979), and Rock Levee (Weinstein et al. 1995), while amphibians, reptiles, and birds occur in low frequencies. Freshwater mussels are abundant at Stevenson.

Middle Woodland settlements are widespread, but Marksville sites appear to concentrate in several areas (Toth 1988). It is unclear whether these "clusters" represent settlement preferences or modern survey practices. Non-mound Marksville occupations have been found on almost every landform in the alluvial valley of sufficient age. Settlements were located both in the alluvial areas and in upland zones adjacent to the floodplain (Toth 1988).

Issaquena sites are more common and more widespread, perhaps because of a shifting settlement pattern (S. Williams and Brain 1983:360–61). Late Middle Woodland settlements in the Yazoo Basin are clustered in the south, with distinct concentrations seemingly separated by uninhabited zones (Phillips 1970; S. Williams and Brain 1983). Late Middle Woodland "plainware" sites appear in modest quantities throughout their respective distributions (Belmont 1985).

Marksville habitation sites are small, usually no more than 1 to 2 hectares (Phillips 1970; Toth 1988), and generally consist of midden scatters with no identified site plan. Some sites, such as Norman in the Yazoo Basin, appear larger than average, but it is not known whether these represent large, contemporaneous occupations or sequential use. Based on size and lack of internal structure, most habitations could be classified as hamlets, implying small, widely dispersed population clusters. Issaquena habitation sites appear somewhat larger than Marksville ones. At Manny and Thornton, deep Issaquena deposits cover a relatively large area (Greengo 1964; Phillips 1970).

The most conspicuous elements of Early Marksville occupations are conical burial mounds. Most sites include only a single mound, but clusters of up to five earthworks have been reported. A few earthen enclosures also have been associated with Marksville (H. Jackson 1998; Mainfort 1996a; Phillips 1970; S. Williams and Brain 1983). In the southern Yazoo Basin, three or possibly four enclosures have been documented, including those at Spanish Fort, Little Spanish Fort, and Leist. These are large semicircular embankments with their ends terminating at the bank of a river. H. Jackson's (1998) work on the Little Spanish Fort embankment revealed that it was built in two episodes beginning between 150 and 100 B.C.

The largest mound site of the time is the Marksville site in Avoyelles Parish, Louisiana (see Figure 24.2). The site was enclosed by an earthwork approximately 1000 meters long and 2 meters tall (Fowke 1928; D. Jones and Kuttruff 1998). Within the enclosure are five mounds. Three are classic Middle Woodland conical structures, while two (Mounds 2 and 6) were flat-topped (Fowke 1928; Toth 1974). Early maps show a number of other earthworks adjacent to or immediately to the north of the main enclosure. Most of the excavations at Marksville were conducted prior to World War II; Toth (1974) presents a good synthesis based on the spotty documentation.

Marksville Mound 4, a large conical earthwork, was excavated extensively by Fowke and later by Setzler and Ford. The mound covered a flat-topped platform, approximately 1.5 meters tall (Toth 1974:22–28). A square pit in the center contained a "number of burials" (J. A. Ford and Willey 1940:32). The pit was covered with logs (J. A. Ford and Willey 1940:32) or, more likely, small trees or saplings (Toth 1974:figs. 10, 12–13). Upright posts supported the covering. Finally, the covered pit was sealed with seven layers of cane and clay (not cane and bark as stated by Mainfort [1996a:374]). Mainfort (1996a:374) suggests that this facility may represent a charnel house. Smaller "vaults" containing burials were placed on the surface of the primary mound. A primary mantle, containing a "few" burials, was erected over the burial platform. A second mantle covered the primary mantle and the platform (J. A. Ford and Willey 1940:32; Toth 1974:23–25). Twelve burials were recorded, as were twenty ceramic vessels, two platform pipes, fifteen projectile points, three stone knives, a quartz crystal, a copper fragment, a piece of worked shell, and a number of potsherds (J. A. Ford and Willey 1940; Fowke 1928; Toth 1974:25, table 2).

Mound 8, located to the north of the Marksville enclosure, yielded seven graves dug into the ground surface. Four ceramic vessels indicate that this mound was essentially contemporary with Mound 4. A large area on Marksville Mound 6 was excavated to roughly 0.9 meter. Even though a "habitation" level was encountered, no mound construction details were recorded, and no burials or ceramic vessels were recovered (Toth 1974:28–31). Excavations along the edges of Mound 2 provided extensive stratigraphic data, but no evidence for the function of the mound (Toth 1974; Vescelius 1957).

The second important Marksville mound site is Crooks, located 35 kilometers north of Marksville (J. A. Ford and Willey 1940). Crooks consisted of two conical mounds. Mound A had a circular base 26.2 meters across and stood 5.28 meters tall. Mound B, located to the south of Mound A, measured 17.68 meters long by 11.58 meters wide and 0.91 meters in height. Excavation of Mound A revealed "a mortuary situation unparalleled anywhere within the Hopewell world" (Mainfort 1996a:374). Within this mound were 1159 burials; thirteen interments were recovered in Mound B. The quantity of burials at Crooks suggests that this structure served a far-flung community (Mainfort 1996a).

Mound A began as a low (0.6 meter) rectangular earthen platform aligned with the cardinal directions. A single burial was found beneath the platform, and 168 interments were found within the platform itself. After the platform was built, it was evidently left open to the elements as a distinctive light zone of weathered soil developed on its surface. Pits of different sizes had been excavated into the surface of the mound and several postholes with burned edges were found. During a second episode of mortuary activity, 214 burials were placed in the center of the platform, with the mass of the burials forming a large pile (J. A. Ford and Willey 1940).

Immediately following the placement of the burials on the initial platform, it was covered with a layer of bright yellowish-brown sandy clay. Another stratum containing 270 burials was added before the initial primary mantle could weather. A stairway of logs was found on the east side of this stage of mound construction (J. A. Ford and Willey 1940:27–28). A secondary mantle, erected in two stages, formed the final dimensions of the mound. The inner stratum contained all of the 503 burials associated with this stage (J. A. Ford and Willey 1940:28–29). Most were "placed singly in small depressions," but three burials were placed in an elliptical pit that was lined with cane mats. The final stage of mound construction entailed placing backswamp clays halfway up the slope of the mound. The completed mound surface was heavily eroded, and three burials were placed in the surface of the mound after its completion.

Flexed burials were most common, followed by isolated skulls and mandibles, bundle burials, semiflexed, partially disarticulated, and, finally, extended burials. There is little patterning in the placement of burials either by type or position in the mound. More than half of the articulated burials were placed with their heads facing toward the center of the mound. Isolated skulls were common, and many skulls had been placed with or very near more complete skeletons. Some burials had been wrapped in hide or cane mat containers.

Artifacts were associated with 169 individuals, most commonly with flexed burials (J. A. Ford and Willey 1940:44–45), but only two interments had more than a single funerary artifact. Artifact frequency paralleled the number of burials in each mound stage. Thirty-six (out of 84) ceramic vessels were recovered with burials, along with thirty-eight projectile points, twenty-one ground stone items, six copper earspools, a copper bracelet, beads of copper, shell, stone, and pearl, gorgets, pendants, and six platform pipes. Red ochre and charcoal were associated with some burials.

At Big Oak Island, Shenkel (1984a, 1984b) excavated an ossuary containing at least fifty individuals, all apparently representing bundled interments. Radiocarbon dates place the mortuary activity in the first century B.C. Associated artifacts included Marksville ceramics with raptorial bird designs and classic U-shaped incising. A number of Tchefuncte ceramic types also were found in the mortuary area, and the pastes of the Marksville vessels were essentially indistinguishable from Tchefuncte Plain. Also recovered were a ceramic pipe of Tchefuncte style, three *Busycon* dippers or cups, a shell bead, a quartz bead, a rolled copper bead, a *Busycon* gouge, and a split deer-bone point.

Mound construction apparently decreased dramatically at the end of Marksville times. Issaquena mounds are not common and mound construction among contemporary "plainware" populations is poorly documented or unsubstantiated (Kidder and Ring 1986). The best evidence for Issaquena mounds comes from Thornton, where excavations revealed a possibly early Issaquena flat-topped platform with multiple construction stages (Phillips 1970:581–87). The mound was constructed over an Issaquena midden, and a midden zone on the surface of the second stage contained abundant Issaquena markers mixed with some later pottery that Phillips believed was intrusive. Excavations at the Troyville site disclosed that the substantial Issaquena deposits associated with the "Fire Level" were deposited on the surface of a low platform (W. Walker 1936:20–21), and Walker suggests that there may be at least one other Issaquena mound stage above the "Fire Level." Bitgood (1989) has demonstrated that some mound construction took place at Indian Bayou at this time. Four Alligator Bayou phase sites in southeastern Arkansas have low conical mounds, and the Alma Brown site is best known for its conical mound (Rolingson 1993).

One central question regarding Middle Woodland is the genesis of Marksville culture. Toth (1974, 1979b, 1988) and S. Williams and Brain (1983) advocate that Marksville was the outgrowth of direct contact between Tchefuncte groups and Havana-Hopewell peoples in Illinois. Others argue that Marksville was an indigenous phenomenon that developed in the Lower Mississippi Valley (J. Gibson 1996b; J. Gibson and Shenkel 1988; Shenkel 1984a) and that the Hopewellian characteristics of Marksville are adoptions of a broader pan-Southeastern set of ideas and concepts, rather than the product of direct contact. J. A. Ford and Willey (1940, 1941), however, suggested that Marksville was the stimulus for northern Hopewell.

Those advocating direct Havana-Hopewell connections point to the strong similarities between Havana and Marksville ceramics mentioned above. Additionally, some lamellar blades found at Marksville and Helena Crossing were made from northern cherts. Conical burial mounds are another possible link to societies farther north, as is the use of exotic grave furniture. Toth (1988:72) argues that "during the first century of the Christian era, and probably not much before the year A.D. 50, small groups representing the contemporaneous Bedford, Ogden, and Utica phases of the Illinois Valley penetrated down the Mississippi River in search of raw materials, to trade, to explore, or for some still unestablished reason. The movement was relatively rapid...[and] contact, of course, was with local Tchefuncte groups."

Others have noted that the nature of Hopewellian connections in the Lower Mississippi Valley was remarkably disparate (J. Gibson 1970; J. Gibson and Shenkel 1988; Mainfort 1996a) and that many traits used to argue for contact may have an indigenous background. Mound building and mound burial have deep roots in the Lower Mississippi Valley. The Marksville pattern of secondary burial below, in, or on low platforms has possible Tchefuncte antecedents at Lafayette Mounds and probably Lake Louis. The only site that reflects northern Hopewellian mortuary features is Helena Crossing (J. A. Ford 1963), and even this site poses problems for Toth's hypothesis (Mainfort 1988b, 1996a). The frequent appearance of Marksville-like designs on Tchefuncte-like pastes, as well as vessel forms (tetrapodal vessels), may suggest an indigenous basis for Marksville styles. Radiocarbon determinations suggest that Marksville cultural characteristics developed in the first century B.C., if not earlier (H. Jackson 1998; Shenkel 1984b; Walling et al. 1991).

In his overview of Middle Woodland in the Lower Mississippi Valley, Mainfort (1996a:388) rejects Toth's hypothesis. He observes that the Hopewell Intrusion model was tied to the notion that Lower Mississippi Valley cultures were inferior to those to the north and also that it imputes to northern (Havana) groups more uniformity than really exists. Data pointing to local roots for Marksville culture seem now to be relatively abundant and obvious, but it is clear the region participated in a wider Middle Woodland sphere of interaction, including direct contact between groups living in different parts of the Mississippi Valley (J. Johnson 1988; Mainfort 1988c, 1996a).

The Marksville pattern did not die out with the cessation of Hopewell-related contacts. Issaquena and the northern "plainware" phases demonstrate that the Middle Woodland was a thriving time in the Lower Mississippi Valley well after the period of Hopewellian interaction ended. These later cultures appear to be more parochial in that they were not trading so widely and their mortuary activities show less flamboyance, but they were clearly successful and well adapted to their environment.

Baytown and Coles Creek Periods

The beginning of the Late Woodland is identified by the emergence of new ceramic decorative ideas emphasizing rectilinear incising and all-over body decoration. New site types and functions, the development of increasingly more complex social institutions, and the emergence of agricultural economies around A.D. 1000 characterize the Late Woodland. Far from being a time of stasis, the Late Woodland in the Lower Mississippi Valley was a time of dynamic change and most trends that characterize Mississippi period cultures developed by the end of the Late Woodland.

Late Woodland is subdivided into two periods: Baytown and Coles Creek. During the early Late Woodland, or Baytown, period, cultures are principally differentiated by their ceramics, but they have different patterns of social and subsistence organization as well. Baytown culture occurs in the northern part of the valley, while Troyville culture developed between Vicksburg and Baton Rouge. South of Baton Rouge is the poorly defined Coastal Troyville culture (Jeter and Williams 1989:fig. 14). The succeeding Coles Creek period encompasses three cultures: Coles Creek, found throughout the interior Lower Valley; coastal Coles Creek, south of Baton Rouge; and Plum Bayou, in the Arkansas River lowlands (Rolingson, this volume).

Late Woodland pottery is technologically sophisticated; it is harder than earlier wares and vessel forms are more varied. Baytown potters used a variety of decorative techniques, including incising, stamping, punctation, cord marking, brushing, filming, and polychrome painting. Vessel types include bowls and jars, as well as effigy vessels and elaborate painted pots. Regional ceramic variation is quite marked. Baytown potters in the Yazoo Basin and in southeast Arkansas used cord marking and brushing extensively; punctation and pinching were also common. Rectilinear incising and red filming also were used extensively. Troyville potters experimented with a variety of styles, including rectilinear and curvilinear incising, punctation, stamping, and painting, and some vessels exhibit multiple techniques. Populations along the coast generally followed trends similar to those of Troyville, but painting was used far less frequently, and cord marking was not utilized.

Coles Creek pottery is well made, but stylistically less varied than Baytown ceramics. Rectilinear incising around the rim or neck of vessels is the most common decorative technique. Along the coast check stamping was common (I. Brown 1982, 1984; Neuman 1981; R. Saunders 1997). Painting and cord marking were less popular, but pinching, punctation, and rocker stamping persisted in minor amounts. Ceramic styles of the Lower Valley and the adjacent coast were shared widely along the eastern Gulf Coast (Belmont and Williams 1981; Blitz and Mann 2000:41–47; Fuller 1998; Phillips 1970). Coles Creek vessel forms include jars, bowls, and beakers (Hunter et al. 1995; A. Lee et al. 1997).

Early Baytown period sites have moderately large dart points with rounded or square bases, but around A.D. 700 arrow points, notably the Collins point and its variants, become common and seem to rapidly supplant dart points. Late Woodland stone tool technology was relatively simple and was dominated by amorphous core preparation. Nonlocal lithic materials are uncommon during the Late Woodland, as are ground stone tools.

Bone and shell tools have been recovered from Late Woodland sites, although never in large quantities. Shell hoes are associated with the Baytown occupation at Lake George (S. Williams and Brain 1983:282–84). Several shell celts or chisels made from *Busycon* were found at site 16SC45 in St. Charles Parish, Louisiana (D. D. Davis et al. 1982). A shell bead was found with a burial at Powell Canal (House 1982a), and a *Busycon* shell dipper or drinking container was recovered from a burial area at the Gold Mine site (Belmont 1980).

Exotic artifacts are rare in Late Woodland contexts. Other than the shell artifacts mentioned above, the most "exotic" artifacts recovered are polychrome painted effigy vessels (Belmont and Williams 1981; R. Jones 1979). The source of these vessels is uncertain, but based on ceramic paste characteristics they were likely locally made.

Baytown period patterns of settlement, subsistence, and social organization appear to be extremely variable. In the northern Yazoo Basin and in southeast Arkansas, Baytown sites are abundant, but mound construction was rare (House 1982b:42; McNutt 1996a:174). Some sites in the southern Yazoo Basin exhibit a circular or semicircular pattern of discrete freshwater shell middens (Phillips 1970). Sites occur across most of the region, including both in the alluvial valley and in the hills flanking the valley, and some areas were occupied for the first time (H. Collins 1932; House 1996; McNutt 1996a; Phillips 1970; Phillips et al. 1951; Weinstein et al. 1995; Weinstein and Hahn 1992; S. Williams and Brain 1983:364–66).

Powell Canal in southeast Arkansas is one of the better-known Baytown period occupations (House 1982a, 1990). Sixteen pit features and four burial pits were excavated. Fish and deer were the most important animals, as is the case at all other contemporary sites. Small mammals, turkey, turtles, and freshwater mussels also are represented. Hickory nut was the most prevalent mast species, but the nuts were not common and most were found in one feature. No domesticated cultigens were recovered.

The Rock Levee site consists of a large artifact scatter and midden along a relict channel of the Mississippi River (Weinstein et al. 1995). Major occupations date to the Late Marksville and Baytown and Coles Creek periods. A wall-trench structure foundation was identified at the southern end of the site. Most features were identified as postholes or post molds. Pits were bell-shaped, cylindrical, and basin-shaped. Most features, especially the bell-shaped pits and the wall-trench structure, probably date to the later part of the Coles Creek period (ca. A.D. 900–1000). The Baytown period occupation was seasonal and emphasized fishing during spring and summer months (Weinstein et al. 1995:303–7). Because of mixed contexts the nature of the plant food diet is uncertain. Acorn was most common in contexts assigned to late Middle Woodland and early Late Woodland periods. Hickory was also present, as were some fleshy fruits, notably persimmon. Native domesticates at Rock Levee include chenopod, sunflower, and possibly knotweed and maygrass. The seemingly early maize has not been directly dated and may be intrusive (Weinstein et al. 1995:264–85).

Native cultigens have been documented in Baytown period contexts at Toltec, Ink Bayou, and Taylor in the Arkansas River and upper Bartholomew-Boeuf Basin (M. Brown 1996; Rolingson, this volume; C. Smith 1993). Domesticated variants of these species have not been positively identified from contemporary sites south of Vicksburg (Fritz and Kidder 1993). Late Woodland sites near the mouth of the Arkansas also frequently yield specimens of an unidentified, possibly domesticated grass identified as "type-X" (M. Brown 1996:20–21; Fritz 1993; C. Scarry 1995; C. Smith 1993). Maize was cultivated in the Arkansas River valley and adjacent regions by the beginning of the Coles Creek period.

Baytown mortuary data are sparse. At Powell Canal, the four burials (containing four adults and two infants) were clustered together and share a common orientation (House 1982a:72–84); the only grave inclusion was a single shell bead. At Thornton, Phillips (1970:588–92) excavated six burials in the upper levels of a low platform mound, but the dating of these is uncertain. A single red painted ceramic vessel was found near one burial. Several burials were extended, but some consisted of a "hopeless tangle" (Phillips 1970:590) of remains, evidently caused by interments cutting into and through earlier burials.

A number of Baytown sites have mounds, but few have been adequately tested (Jeter and Williams 1989:145–46). Small conical mounds are thought to be associated with some Baytown culture sites in the northern Yazoo Basin and east-central Arkansas (McNutt 1996a:174; Phillips 1970:904, 907). Rectangular, flat-topped mounds were apparently erected at the Baytown site (House 1982b:42–44; D. Morse and P. Morse 1983; Phillips et al. 1951:table 13). Two large structures or enclosures built of single set posts were erected on the summit of the flat-topped Edwards Mound at the Oliver site (Belmont 1961:36–50; Peabody 1904; Weinstein et al. 1995:289). The largest construction was a circular enclosure or palisade measuring just over 24 meters (80 feet) in diameter. A rectangular enclosure or palisade just over 18 meters (60 feet) across was built within the circular building, but at a slightly later date. Burials placed in the surface of this construction stage were all located outside of the rectangular enclosure. Rectangular flat-topped mounds also were constructed at Manny and Thornton at this time (Phillips 1970). Baytown sites often have multiple-component occupations and surface-collected data are insufficient for pinpointing the date of mound construction.

In contrast to the northern part of the alluvial valley, groups living between Vicksburg and Baton Rouge exhibit a complex and varied pattern of social and settlement organization during the Baytown period. One of the best examples of a Baytown period mound site is Greenhouse, located near the mouth of the Red River (J. A. Ford 1951). Greenhouse had seven mounds arranged in a roughly elliptical pattern around a plaza. Although the primary construction episodes date to the Coles Creek period, the lower premound levels of the site produced many of the same "Troyville variant" ceramics noted at the Troyville site. Overlying a minor Issaquena component were Baytown period remains, represented by an oval midden ring surrounding an empty plaza. Secondary burials were evident within the midden, and clay fill episodes may have capped midden areas or were used to elevate occupation surfaces. Nine deep "bathtub-shaped fire pits" were found in the midden ridges, and burials were placed in a specific area set aside for that purpose (Belmont 1967, 1984; J. A. Ford 1951).

The Troyville mortuary program at Greenhouse included extended and semiflexed interments, possibly cremations, and dog burials—all lacking grave goods (Belmont 1967:31, 1984; J. A. Ford 1951:106–8). Long-term exposure to intense heat was evident in the bathtub-shaped pits, but as no human bone and few vessel fragments were found, they probably were not kilns or crematoria (J. A. Ford 1951:104). Ash and animal bone were found in these features, leading some to suggest that the features were used as cooking pits for communal feasting (Belmont 1980, 1984; J. A. Ford 1951:104–5).

A Baytown period mortuary area was excavated by amateurs at the Old Creek site in LaSalle Parish, Louisiana (J. Gibson 1984). No mounds or earthworks were present, but a small midden area south of the burial area may be contemporary with the cemetery. J. Gibson (1984:198) argues that this midden was the location of a charnel house or structure devoted to mortuary processing. Most interments were bundle burials, but some flexed burials were excavated, and a number of isolated crania, mandibles, and other human bone fragments were recovered. Ten of the nineteen burials contained whole or partial ceramic vessels.

Excavations at the Indian Bayou, Marsden, and Insley sites provided the stratigraphic and cultural identification of Troyville in the Tensas Basin of Louisiana. C. B. Moore (1913:41–42) described the Indian Bayou site as "a group of eight mounds… which form an irregular ellipse with two mounds facing each other and three mounds on each side." The initial occupation at Indian Bayou dates to the Issaquena phase, but most of the ceramic assemblage of Mounds C and D dates to the Baytown period (Bitgood 1989:47–48). Moore reported at least forty-two interments, but only two pots and a sandstone disk were recovered with them (Bitgood 1989:18–21; C. B. Moore 1913:42). Human and dog burials were found in Mound D.

The initial occupation at Marsden dates as early as Issaquena (Bitgood 1989:74–75). Baytown midden covered the eastern part of the site, and two bathtub-shaped fire pits were located near the edge of the site within the midden (Bitgood 1989:74). A mortuary feature contained five to nine extended individuals, one accompanied by sherds of an incised, red-filmed vessel (Bitgood 1989:69–74).

The Gold Mine site in Richland Parish, Louisiana, is one of the most intensively excavated Troyville sites (Belmont 1980, 1984; Jeter and Williams 1989:149, 151). The earliest occupation dates to Tchefuncte times, and an Issaquena midden underlies much of the site. Baytown-period occupants constructed a single low mound that included a complex stratified sequence of surfaces, occupation features (hearths, pits, and post molds), and multiple burial episodes. A row of bathtub-shaped fire pits may have been present at the southern edge of the site, but only one was excavated (Belmont 1980:7–14, 16–34, 1984:86–88). The base of this fire pit was filled with ash and "a few sherds and charred deer bones," while the upper part contained a "rich midden," evidently the result of secondary filling of the large feature depression (Belmont 1984:86). Belmont (1984:88) felt that this feature was similar to those found at Greenhouse and that they functioned as "large-scale cooking or barbeque [sic] pits." Belmont also notes that "hearths which would have sufficed for ordinary cooking abound at both Greenhouse and Gold Mine."

The Gold Mine burial program included extended, "pseudo-extended" (re-articulated skeletons), and bundle interments, plus dog burials. Skull piles, masses of long bones, and a pit with long bones deposited vertically also were found (Belmont 1980). Interments in each successive mound stratum clustered around a central hearth or hearths, and the horizontal position of the hearth changed little from level to level. Although the burial data were not fully analyzed, the skeletal inventory indicates a normal population distribution, and no age or sex class was over- or under-represented (Jerome Rose, personal communication, 1993). A conch shell cup, a red-filmed bowl, several vessel fragments, and two polychrome effigy vessels were recovered (Belmont and Williams 1981; R. Jones 1979). These do not appear to have been associated with specific individuals, but with burial concentrations instead.

At Reno Brake, four low mounds, including two burial mounds, were arranged in an oval pattern on the edge of a relict Mississippi River channel (Kidder 1990; Kidder and Fritz 1993). A ring of midden joined the mounds, but the plaza was essentially sterile. The site had multicomponent occupations, with Issaquena, Troyville, Coles Creek, and Plaquemine materials recovered from the surface. Human bone was common, and extended, flexed, bundle, and cremation burials were identified in looters' pits, erosion scars, and plowzone scatters. Ceramics exhibit considerable diversity, including polychrome pottery and red-painted duck-head effigy fragments. At least six ceramic human effigy heads were recovered, all bearing similar detail. A seventh face was modeled on the side of a small cylindrical beaker. An effigy head bearing similar facial features was recovered from Greenhouse (J. A. Ford 1951). A broken clay effigy of a human torso, painted white and wearing a red sash or belt, was also found. Exotic items include Weeden Island–like ceramics, nonlocal lithics, and a shark tooth.

One of the most enigmatic sites dating to the Baytown period is Troyville, which once consisted of nine to thirteen mounds enclosed within an embankment at the confluence of the Tensas, Little, and Ouachita rivers (W. Walker 1936). The Great Mound, estimated to have been 24.7 meters (80 feet) tall, was destroyed before archaeologists could determine the precise construction sequence, but pottery from later levels suggests Troyville affiliation (Belmont 1984; W. Walker 1936:table 1). Further work at the site yielded considerable evidence for Troyville occupation and construction, including the embankment (Cusik et al. 1994; Hunter and Baker 1979). Excavations in the Bluff Mound at Troyville, which contained twelve extended burials lacking grave goods, suggest that this was also a contemporary earthwork (W. Walker 1936).

An early Baytown period burial pit was placed in the initial platform of the Lake St. Agnes site in Avoyelles Parish, Louisiana (Toth 1979a), but Baytown mound construction is not documented south of here. Contemporary coastal sites are small and widely dispersed (K. R. Jones et al. 1994).

Troyville mortuary sites are geographically separated and probably served regional populations. Small hamlets or dwellings were widely distributed and may reflect seasonal or short-term occupations. Limited data from contemporary non-mortuary settlements suggest that populations subsisted by fishing coupled with hunting of deer, small mammals, and amphibians. Floral remains indicate a strong emphasis on nuts, notably acorn, supplemented by wild fruits, and, more rarely, starchy seeds (Kidder and Fritz 1993; Trachtenberg 1999). Squash was present, but it is not clear whether these were wild or domesticated variants. There is currently no evidence for the use of domesticated native cultigens in this region.

Toward the end of the Baytown period, regional variation appears to diminish as a new pan–Lower Valley pattern emerged. The clearest evidence for cultural change occurs at the beginning of the Coles Creek period, circa A.D. 700–800. Coles Creek is known for its distinctive pottery tradition and for the common use of flat-topped platform mounds arranged in plaza groups. The use of mounds shifted from mass mortuary functions to supporting structures for religious (?) and/or individual use. Coles Creek populations appear to increase significantly and most habitable areas of the Lower Valley were occupied (Kidder 1992a). Sites are generally larger than in earlier times. There is little evidence of long-distance trade.

Coles Creek subsistence focused on locally available wild plant and animal foods. Acorns and hickory nuts were principal dietary staples, supplemented by wild fruits, seeds, tubers, and greens. Chenopod, knotweed, and maygrass were exploited at a number of sites. In some cases these species were clearly domesticated (K. Roberts 2000), but in other instances the evidence for domestication is equivocal. Sunflower has been recovered only at the Hedgeland site (K. Roberts 2000), and tobacco was recovered at Osceola (Kidder and Fritz 1993). Maize appears for the first time during Coles Creek times, but did not become important until circa A.D. 1000 or later (Fritz and Kidder 1993; Kidder 1992b; Kidder and Fritz 1993; K. Roberts 2000). Fish and deer made up the bulk of the diet in the interior parts of the Lower Mississippi Valley (Kelley 1992; Mariaca 1988), while fish, alligator, deer, and muskrat were commonly used on the coast (R. Smith 1996). In all instances fish were among the most significant contributors to the diet.

In early Coles Creek times there was a shift in mound function. While earlier mounds were constructed to cover burials, platform mounds were constructed as the foundation for a perishable structure or structures, and burials were later deposited in them. Mortuary treatments were highly varied. For example, at Lake George, an extended prone adult male was accompanied by the bodies of thirteen infants (S. Williams and Brain 1983). At the Mount Nebo site a male was interred on his back, with an isolated human cranium on his abdomen, and deer bones were evidently buried with this individual. This grave, which also included two adult females on either side and three children, was centrally located in the mound and was the earliest burial at the site (Giardino 1984). Both the Lake George and Mount Nebo burial mounds were constructed over the remains of a large circular enclosure marked by a wall trench (Kidder 1998a; S. Williams and Brain 1983:54).

Coles Creek mortuary patterns do not reflect the inclusive character of Troyville burial sites. Bathtub-shaped pits, perhaps used for communal feasting, are absent, as are effigy vessels or figurines, and burial offerings are exceedingly rare. At Lake George a disproportionate number of interments were children. Interments of individual adults (usually males) with associated multiple individuals (often children or women) may indicate that Coles Creek society was becoming increasingly ranked (Kidder 1992a, 1998a; Kidder and Fritz 1993; Steponaitis 1986).

Large Coles Creek mound groups were built around the edges of plazas and often were enlarged both laterally and vertically in several construction phases. Open plazas apparently were an integral element of site planning. The construction of earthen platforms with structures over pre-existing mortuary facilities, as well as possible evidence of social differentiation among the burials, suggests that high-ranking individuals or lineages occupied sacred places in order to emphasize or reinforce their status. Buildings on flat-topped mound summits were not only physical symbols of elevated status, but also served to legitimize power by symbolically connecting the inhabitants with their ancestors.

Both at Mount Nebo and in Mound C at Lake George the shift in burial practices occurred at roughly A.D. 700. In the Tensas Basin, the earliest flat-topped mound groups were constructed by circa A.D. 750–800 (Wells 1998). Early mound communities commonly supported one large, flat-topped structure, with one or more smaller mounds arranged to form a rectangular or triangular plaza (S. Williams and Brain 1983). Too few of these sites have been adequately investigated to allow confident inferences about the underlying organizational processes. Not all mound communities were vacant ceremonial centers; midden deposits are frequently encountered beyond the mound flanks and often ring the mounds themselves.

It appears that the mounds and their residents were increasingly the focus of interest within the community. Mound size and complexity increases, and their function changes from encompassing public mortuary rituals to accommodating elite residents. The segregation of the whole society was not evident, however, since it appears that many people lived around the mounds, and access to the mounds and the plazas was initially relatively open. Beyond the mound communities, the bulk of the population was scattered across the landscape and continued to practice a mostly nonagricultural subsistence life-style, perhaps supplemented by horticulture.

Early Coles Creek non-mound settlements were small and widely distributed (Wells 1998). By middle to late Coles Creek times settlements generally become larger and more aggregated near the newly emerging mound centers (Wells 1997). By circa A.D. 1000–1200 there were fewer non-mound communities, but the documented examples are bigger (Brain 1978; Hally 1972; Kidder 1998a). The pattern of increasing village size and a decrease in the number of outlying communities reaches its peak at the end of Coles Creek times. Although it is tempting to attribute increasing aggregation to an increase in external threats, hostility, and perhaps warfare, there is no evidence to indicate that conflict was a major problem or significant factor in Coles Creek evolution.

The Osceola site in Tensas Parish, Louisiana, exhibits a pattern of increasing spatial exclusion and restriction of access to the interior plaza spaces over time (Kidder 1998a). Mounds A and B were built first, in the early

Coles Creek period. By the later Sundown phase, Mound C was added to form an elongated plaza. Mound F was added to the eastern edge of the mound cluster in middle Coles Creek times. Finally, Mound E was constructed just after A.D. 1000. The addition of this last mound formed a bounded plaza complemented by a low earthen midden rise identified as Mound D. The bulk of vertical accretion also was accomplished during the later Coles Creek phases, so that Mound A had at least 3 to 4 meters of construction fill added to it, and Mound E was built in a single effort.

At Lake George a similar process took place during the same interval (S. Williams and Brain 1983:332–37). Mound C, which had been the locus of earlier construction activities, was added to and expanded both vertically and horizontally. Mound construction was evidently initiated at Mound A at this time, indicating the definition of a plaza with two mounds at opposite ends of the open space. Mounds E, F, and F' were constructed or added to at this time, forming the northern boundary of a well-defined plaza. Mound B was probably built during the Coles Creek period and would have completed a virtually wholly enclosed plaza.

The Greenhouse site duplicates the pattern seen at Osceola and Lake George (Belmont 1967; J. A. Ford 1951). During the early to middle Coles Creek period two mounds were erected at opposite ends of a largely sterile plaza, bounded at its northern end by the addition of a third mound during the later Coles Creek period. Midden deposits along the southern edge of the site accumulated to form notable rises or habitation mounds that capped house floors and burial areas. Thus, the concept of a bounded plaza surrounded by mounds or other cultural features (houses, cemeteries) was in place at or prior to the beginning of the Mississippi period.

There were marked differences among and between Coles Creek populations. Mound sites were not common north of the Arkansas River, but village sites generally were larger than those farther south (Brookes 1980). Sites in the northern Yazoo Basin frequently include rectangular wall-trench structures with open corners; large, deep, bell-shaped pits; and burials distributed across the site and often associated with individual structures (Connaway 1981; Weinstein et al. 1995). Extensive surface scatters of daub are common. North of the Arkansas River, ceramics are more aligned with the Plum Bayou culture in the Arkansas Valley or with sites farther north in the Mississippi Valley (Brookes 1980; McNutt 1996b:224–25; D. Morse and P. Morse 1983:192–97; Potts and Brookes 1981).

Most sites south of the Arkansas River were small and few yielded rectangular wall-trench structures, bell-shaped pits, or burials within structures or the village remains. Daub is uncommon, suggesting that there was a shift in architectural characteristics at roughly the Arkansas River mouth. Farther south, circular structures, some with wall trenches and some with single set posts, were erected (J. A. Ford 1951; Wells 1998:103–6; Woodiel 1980) both on mound platforms and on ground surfaces (I. Brown 1985; Quimby 1951). Rectangular buildings, usually made with single posts, were built in later Coles Creek times.

Within the Coles Creek region no single community achieved preeminence within its region (Kidder 1992a, 1998a, 1998b). Mound communities clearly differ in terms of numbers of mounds and mound volume (Belmont 1985), but, at best, some communities were first among equals. For example, the Winterville site seems to be the largest community in its immediate region at this time, but it was not especially larger than nearby contemporary mound sites (Brain 1989). Similarly, Lake George was bigger, but not much bigger, than Aden, Kings Crossing, or other mound groups in the southern Yazoo Basin (Phillips 1970; S. Williams and Brain 1983). The Osceola, Raffman, and Mott sites are the largest contemporary mound communities in the Tensas Basin, but they do not dominate the physical or political landscape (Kidder 1998a). In the Mississippi River delta region data are limited, but there is no evidence that any mound group was regionally dominant (Weinstein et al. 1978; Weinstein and Kelley 1992). An exception may be the Morgan Mounds site in coastal Louisiana, which is considerably larger than any known contemporary site along the coast (I. Brown 1981; Fuller and Fuller 1987).

Coles Creek mounds have yielded few nonlocal or exotic goods, and mortuary goods are rare. In fact, the major line of evidence indicating social differentiation at this time is the mounds themselves (Kidder 1992a), although faunal evidence from Lake George and from Morgan Mounds indicates residents living on mound tops enjoyed better meat resources than other occupants of the sites (Belmont 1983; I. Brown 1984). As discussed by Rolingson (this volume), the only significant exception to these patterns is the Toltec site and the Plum Bayou culture in the Arkansas River valley.

Late Woodland peoples throughout the Lower Mississippi Valley developed sophisticated adaptations to local environments, selectively using domesticated plant foods in combination with local wild resources. The slow southward spread of native and tropical domesticated plants and the variable timing of their acceptance as an integrated element of the subsistence base suggest some dietary decisions were the result of selection from among a complicated array of economic possibilities related to the environment, demography, and social demands for surplus production. In the central and southern valley, there evidently was little immediate pressure to adopt new food sources.

During the Baytown and Troyville periods, there is little evidence of status differentiation, but differences appear with the flurry of mound building in the Coles Creek culture, though other social markers of status are not present or are difficult to detect (Wells 1998). Thus, in regard to architecture, site layout, and political organization, Coles Creek is perhaps better equated with Emergent Mississippian than with Late Woodland, as the term is traditionally understood. The absence of systematic and intensive food production south of the Arkansas River, however, distinguishes Coles Creek from Emergent Mississippian cultures elsewhere in the Southeast (B. D. Smith 1986:53–57).

Summary

Archaeological data from the Lower Mississippi Valley reveal an unbroken history of change and development dating back well before the Woodland period. The history of native societies after Late Archaic times is a story of change and continuity. These societies never abandoned their reliance on wild foods, even with the advent of maize-based economies in the eleventh and twelfth centuries. Acorn and wild fruit coupled with fish and deer provided the bulk of food resources. Other continuities include the construction of mounds. Although the function of these earthworks changed through time, their use and general plan suggest a common heritage dating back perhaps to the Middle Archaic. In contrast to surrounding regions, expressions of wealth and social status, such as those displayed in elaborate burials with grave goods, were rare; even during the Middle Woodland such expressions were distinctly different from those of their contemporaries. The Lower Mississippi Valley is clearly not one homogeneous culture area, however. Beginning at least in the early Woodland the northern, central, and southern parts of the Lower Mississippi Valley manifest adaptive behaviors that suggest the occupants have different backgrounds and emerge from different historical circumstances. In this context, it becomes obvious that differences among and between historically documented cultures in the region can be traced back into the Woodland past.

Chapter 5

Fourche Maline: A Woodland Period Culture of the Trans-Mississippi South

Frank Schambach

The Woodland period culture of the large part of the Trans-Mississippi South lying south of the Arkansas Valley in western Arkansas, eastern Oklahoma, northwest Louisiana, and northeast Texas (Figure 5.1) is called Fourche Maline culture. The most informative components of this culture are at sites in the Ouachita and Red River valleys in southwest Arkansas (Schambach 1982, 1998b; W. R. Wood 1963b; W. R. Wood and Early 1981). However, the culture also includes the Woodland period remains from the sites of the original Fourche Maline "focus" and the more recently formulated Fourche Maline "phase" (Wann, Sam, Scott, Williams, and McCutchan-McLaughlin) in the Ouachita Mountains in southeastern Oklahoma (R. Bell and Baerreis 1951; Galm 1984). In northwest Louisiana, it includes the assemblages and mounds of the Woodland period "Bellevue focus" (C. Webb 1982) and the "Coles Creek" assemblages from Late Woodland–Early Mississippi period sites such as Mounds Plantation (C. Webb and McKinney 1975). In east Texas, Fourche Maline assemblages are recognizable in the materials reported from sites as far west in the Red River valley as the Sanders site (Krieger 1946:171–99; Story 1990:302) and as far southwest as the George C. Davis site (Newell and Krieger 1949).

This populous culture (for southwest Arkansas alone we have records of about 700 sites with Fourche Maline components) materialized between 1000 and 500 B.C., lasted until around 800 A.D., then evolved into Caddo culture. Its hallmark throughout these thirteen to eighteen centuries was a robust, but mostly plain, ceramic assemblage consisting mainly of flat-bottomed, often flowerpot-shaped, jars tempered with crushed bone, grit, sand, or grog. The main types in this assemblage are Williams Plain, Cooper Boneware, and Ouachita Plain (Schambach 1998b). Other artifact types diagnostic of—but generally not limited to—Fourche Maline culture that were in vogue for significant parts of its long life are the following: Gary projectile points of several regionally and temporally significant varieties; arrow points of several types; coarsely chipped stone tools traditionally called

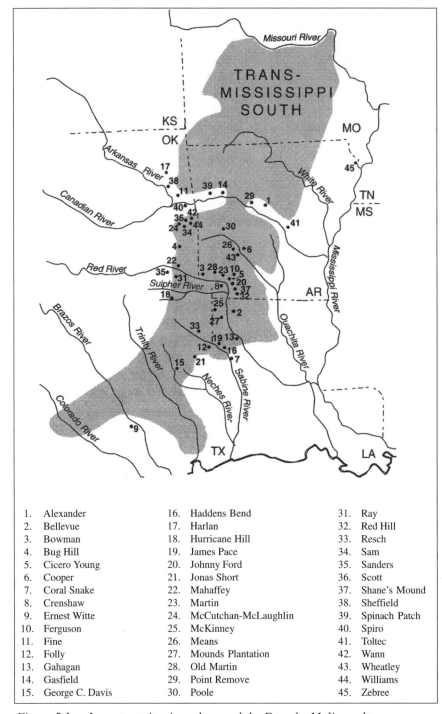

1.	Alexander	16.	Haddens Bend	31.	Ray
2.	Bellevue	17.	Harlan	32.	Red Hill
3.	Bowman	18.	Hurricane Hill	33.	Resch
4.	Bug Hill	19.	James Pace	34.	Sam
5.	Cicero Young	20.	Johnny Ford	35.	Sanders
6.	Cooper	21.	Jonas Short	36.	Scott
7.	Coral Snake	22.	Mahaffey	37.	Shane's Mound
8.	Crenshaw	23.	Martin	38.	Sheffield
9.	Ernest Witte	24.	McCutchan-McLaughlin	39.	Spinach Patch
10.	Ferguson	25.	McKinney	40.	Spiro
11.	Fine	26.	Means	41.	Toltec
12.	Folly	27.	Mounds Plantation	42.	Wann
13.	Gahagan	28.	Old Martin	43.	Wheatley
14.	Gasfield	29.	Point Remove	44.	Williams
15.	George C. Davis	30.	Poole	45.	Zebree

Figure 5.1 — Important sites in and around the Fourche Maline culture area

double-bitted "axes," but which probably were hoe-like gardening tools; boatstones; modeled-clay platform pipes; similar clay pipes called Poole pipes; and remarkably abundant stone seed grinding and nut processing equipment (Schambach 1982, 1998b).

The Fourche Maline people had a distinctive burial mound tradition (Schambach 1996a) but, unlike their Coles Creek and Plum Bayou neighbors to the east in the Lower Mississippi Valley, they had no flat-topped mound, or temple mound, tradition. They probably had a horticultural tradition based on the eastern North American starchy and oily seed complex. Their settlement pattern included small villages occupied, possibly continuously, for long periods, producing many 0.8- to 2.0-hectare sites with characteristically deep, black, middens rich in cultural debris and full of flexed or extended burials, some with modest offerings (Schambach 1982). The larger sites often yield small amounts of imported pottery of Tchefuncte, Marksville, and Coles Creek types, evidence of contact of some kind with peoples of the Lower Mississippi Valley for more than a thousand years (Schambach 1982, 1991, 1998b).

Remarkably, Fourche Maline seems to have been a culture that got by until nearly the end without stone celts, hence also without houses substantial enough to show up archaeologically (Schambach 1982:178, 185). It was a culture that did not use storage pits, which is one reason it is so difficult to obtain charcoal samples and data pertaining to diet from good contexts at Fourche Maline sites (Schambach 1982:184). On the other hand, the Fourche Maline people were probably among the first in the Southeast to adopt the bow and arrow (Nassaney and Pyle 1999:table 4), not surprising considering their location on the southwestern frontier of the Southeast. What is surprising, considering how far they were from the apparent center of the development of corn horticulture in the Southeast, the Central Mississippi Valley, is that they seem to have been among the first Southeasterners to adopt that trait (Story et al. 1990:254). Along with it they adopted, near the end of the Woodland period, a foreign mound-burial complex significantly different from their own, but similar to that expressed in Mound 72 at Cahokia (Schambach 1996a).

History of the Fourche Maline Concept

The name Fourche Maline has a long history in Oklahoma archaeology (R. Bell 1980; R. Bell and Dale 1953; Newkumet 1940; Orr 1952:242; Proctor 1957; Sharrock 1960). It comes from Fourche Maline Creek, a tributary of the Poteau River, in the Wister Valley in southeastern Oklahoma, where

WPA archaeologists applied it to a type of site that happens to be abundant along that creek—sites with deep, rich, black, apparently unstratified, Archaic, Woodland, and Mississippi period middens—rather than to an archaeologically defined culture, as we understand that term today.

When R. Bell and Baerreis (1951:19–27) described the Fourche Maline "focus" of eastern Oklahoma they included both the Archaic and the Woodland period materials found in the Wister Valley sites. Furthermore, Oklahoma archaeologists of the 1950s and early 1960s gave greater weight to the former than to the latter. For them, Fourche Maline was a fundamentally Archaic culture that took on a veneer of Woodland period traits, particularly pottery, late in its life span.

The first to identify Fourche Maline "focus" materials outside Oklahoma was W. Raymond Wood, in a report on WPA excavations at the Poole site on the upper Ouachita River in Arkansas (W. R. Wood 1963b; W. R. Wood and Early 1981). Fortunately, the Archaic period materials that are so strongly represented at the Wister Valley sites are weakly represented at the Poole site (W. R. Wood 1963b:53) where the main occupations were during the Woodland and Mississippi periods. So Wood was able to see, as I would later at other southwest Arkansas sites with similar occupation histories, a Fourche Maline assemblage practically free of the Archaic period artifacts that seemed to be part of the Fourche Maline complex in Oklahoma. His perception was sharpened by grave-lot data from two burials at Poole and two at the Wheatley site nearby on the Caddo River (W. R. Wood 1963b:figs. 8 and 23). These affirmed that the basic Fourche Maline assemblage comprised flat-bottomed, grog-tempered pots, Gary projectile points, double-bitted chipped stone "axes," modified platform pipes made of clay, and boatstones.

In 1965, picking up where Wood left off, I began working up the results of extensive WPA excavations at the Cooper and Means sites, about 35 miles down the Ouachita River from the Poole site (Schambach 1970, 1982, 1998b). On the basis of vertical and horizontal separation of components at Cooper, and on the basis of comparison of the Cooper collection with the Means collection, I isolated and identified as Fourche Maline materials similar to those from the Poole and Wheatley sites and comparable also in important respects, particularly the pottery (Schambach 1998b:83–89, table 12), to those from the Oklahoma Fourche Maline sites. On the basis of that work and comparative studies involving many other sites in southwest Arkansas, southeast Oklahoma, northeast Texas, and northwest Louisiana, I reformulated the old Oklahoma Fourche Maline focus, stripping it of its Archaic baggage and setting it forth as a "new" Woodland period culture in the Southeast, with—I anticipated—many regional and temporal phases (Figure 5.2).

	Era (Period)	*Middle Ouachita*	*Great Bend*	*Little Missouri*	*Little River*	*Ouachita Mountains*	*Low. Miss. Valley*
	LATE (7)		**Crenshaw***	Washington	**Old Martin**		Early Coles Creek
A.D.			Bowman		Old Martin		
700							
	LATE (6)	**Dutchman's Garden**		Allen's Field	Hutt	Kelly Creek	
600							Baytown
		Means		Kirkham 2			
500							
	MIDDLE (5)	Condray	Shane's Mound				Troyville
			Shane's Village				
400							
		Oak Grove	Canfield	Ferguson		Poole	
300	MIDDLE (4)						Late Marksville
		Cooper					
200							
		Ecore Fabre 1	Red Hill Mound	Kirkham 1			
100	MIDDLE (3)						Early Marksville
0							
		Ecore Fabre 2					
100							
		Lost Bayou	Cicero Young				
200	EARLY (2)	Cooper	**Field Bayou**				Tchefuncte
300							
			Johnny Ford 1				
400							
500							
600	EARLY (1)		Johnny Ford 2				
700							
800							

* *A.D. 900 ± 70; A.D. 890 ± 60*

Figure 5.2 — Fourche Maline regional and temporal phases (phases in bold, components in normal type)

Later, Altschul (1983:89, 95, table 9) obtained a series of radiocarbon dates from the Bug Hill site, in the Kiamichi River drainage of southeast Oklahoma, that confirmed that the old Fourche Maline focus was loaded with Archaic, and other, baggage. This study put the earliest Bug Hill burials at 1430 ± 110 B.C. and demonstrated that the probable span of occupation of this typical-looking "Fourche Maline–type midden mound" was 1605 ± 125 B.C. to A.D. 1500 ± 50. On the basis of radiocarbon dates on the skeletons themselves, and some contextual evidence, Altschul (1983:243) concluded that fifteen of the Bug Hill burials were probably Archaic, only five were *probably* Fourche Maline, and two were probably Early Mississippi period. Other dating projects carried out at about the same time revealed even longer spans of occupation for the Wister Valley sites (Baugh 1982; Galm 1984:table 9.3).

Chronology and Taxonomy

No valid regional phases of Fourche Maline culture have been isolated since I last summarized the information on this subject for the Fourche Maline occupation of Arkansas (Schambach 1982). Galm's (1984:fig. 9.2) Poteau Basin–based Fourche Maline phase, inappropriately named as it appeared in print two years after the publication of my (1982) definition of Fourche Maline *culture,* is a subdivision of his "Arkansas River period" and his "Southern Woodland stage." Hence, it is obviously a subperiod mistakenly called a phase, a product of "the confusion that inheres in practically all archaeological sequence formulations between culture and chronology" (Willey and Phillips 1958:28).

Some archaeologists (Perttula 1999:27; Story 1990) working in northeast Texas err in the opposite direction by assigning assemblages characterized by the long-recognized core trait complex of Fourche Maline culture to a time period while failing to acknowledge their obvious cultural affiliations. The period is Story's (1990:293) "Early Ceramic Period," described as "the span between approximately 200 B.C. and A.D. 800." Story writes, "Sites believed to date to the [Early Ceramic Period] are identified most easily by the presence of plain, usually grog-tempered sherds (type Williams Plain), double-bitted axe heads, dart points (mainly of the Gary type), and, probably late in the period, expanded stem arrow points."

Fortunately, this point of view is not unanimous among practitioners of east Texas archaeology. Bruseth (1998:51–53, fig. 3-4) understands the "Early Ceramic Period" in the conventional sense as a "period of time" and recognizes that people of the Fourche Maline culture were among the "prehistoric groups [extant in east Texas] during this time." He recognizes occupancy of the middle Red River and upper Little Red River regions in east Texas during this period by people of unnamed Fourche Maline phases and has identified "a good example of a very late Fourche Maline settlement at the Ray site… in Lamar County."

Fourche Maline and the Development of the Spiroan Tradition in the Arkansas Valley

The type sites of the old Fourche Maline focus are tantalizingly close to the "North Caddoan Area" (J. Brown 1996:36, fig. 1-7), that is, the Arkansas Valley in eastern Oklahoma and western Arkansas, and would appear to have been linked to it and the Spiro locality by the Poteau River. Nevertheless, no Fourche Maline components have been positively identified around Spiro, or elsewhere in the Arkansas Valley, and most archaeologists who know that area are of the opinion that it does not have a long history of occupation by Fourche Maline people (R. Bell 1984:221–39; J. Brown 1996:28; H. Davis et al. [eds.] 1971:7, 221–39; Galm 1984:219; Proctor 1957:90; Wyckoff 1980:519–20; Wyckoff and Brooks 1983:91). The explanation for this is Wyckoff's (1974:66) hypothesis that until around A.D. 700 (James Brown [1996:38] has upped this to A.D. 950) the "fertile bottomlands …along the Arkansas, Canadian, Illinois, and Grand Rivers" were "uninhabited." Thereafter, Fourche Maline "farmers"—not that we know the Fourche Maline people were farmers—began moving in after exhausting their own lands along Fourche Maline Creek and the Poteau River.

This hypothesized post–A.D. 950 expansion of Fourche Maline culture into the Arkansas Valley is implausible for two reasons—besides lack of evidence that it occurred. It presumes, for no stated reason, that the Arkansas Valley in eastern Oklahoma and western Arkansas was vacant prior to that time. And it presumes that the Fourche Maline immigrants developed, *de novo,* within decades of their arrival, all of the traits of the Early Mississippi period Spiroan culture of the Arkansas Valley: a charnel house–mound building complex; square, four-center-post houses with gabled roofs and extended wall-trenched doorways; *hoe* horticulture of the starchy and oily seed complex (Fritz 1989); a *shell-tempered* pottery assemblage; and the multifarious contacts with other Early Mississippi period cultures throughout the Southeast that distinguish Spiroan culture from all others of its time.

Actually, a combination of environmental and demographic factors would have kept Fourche Maline people from moving easily into the Arkansas Valley. Primary among the former would have been their centuries-old forest adaptation. The Wister Valley, where Fourche Maline Creek and all the original Fourche Maline type sites are located, lies just within the northwesternmost lobe of oak-hickory-pine forest in the Ouachitas in Oklahoma. North of that, a 60-kilometer-wide eastern lobe of the Osage Savanna environment characteristic of eastern Oklahoma (i.e., tallgrass-oak-hickory savanna) extends eastward, subsuming the territory on both sides of the Arkansas floodplain as far as the Mulberry River and the town of Ozark (Albert and Wyckoff 1984:fig. 1-1; J. Brown 1996:fig. 1.7; J. Rogers 1989:160, fig. 51; Schambach 1998a:fig. 1-1; Wyckoff 1984:fig. 1) in western Arkansas (Figure 5.1).

This environment, the same one that set limits to the westward movement of Fourche Maline culture and, later, Caddo culture, in east Texas, was evidently not one that the Fourche Maline people found congenial. For Fourche Maline hunters and gatherers, this "mosaic ... of upland dry, scrubby forests" and "tallgrass prairies" (Albert and Wyckoff 1984:24; J. Brown 1996:36; J. Rogers 1989:160; Wyckoff 1984:3) would not have been nearly as productive as the oak-hickory and oak-hickory-pine forests they inhabited throughout the Trans-Mississippi South to the south of the Arkansas Valley. To the extent that they practiced hoe or slash-and-burn horticulture, this environment would have been an even more formidable obstacle. Nothing stops people reliant on those technologies more effectively than tallgrass prairie.

Another obstacle to a Fourche Maline migration to the Arkansas Valley would have been indigenous people who *were* adapted to the Osage Savanna and the "distinctive flood plain vegetation community...along the Arkansas River...a densely vegetated area dominated by...oak-gum forest" (J. Rogers 1989:160). As Sabo and Early (1990:79) state regarding the Arkansas Valley in eastern Oklahoma, there is archaeological evidence that people were there throughout the Woodland period, but we do not know who they were "because so few well dated and/or sealed deposits have been studied, and even diagnostic artifact assemblages are difficult to identify."

Yet "a discrete Woodland period manifestation" in the Arkansas Valley (Sabo and Early 1990:76), M. Hoffman's (1977:31–41) "Gober complex," has been identified in the Ozark Reservoir area, between Van Buren and Ozark, in western Arkansas. The materialization of this taxon is guess-dated to sometime after A.D. 300 (Bond 1977:120) and it probably lasted into "the later portion of the Woodland period" (Sabo and Early 1990:77). The type components are represented at the Spinach Patch and Gasfield sites, the former on the Mulberry River, near its confluence with the Arkansas River (Bond 1977:fig. 6.1; M. Hoffman 1977:fig. 1.7), and the latter on the Arkansas about 5 miles downstream from Ozark (M. Hoffman 1977:fig. 1.5). Additional "probable" and "possible" components are recognized at eight other sites in the Ozark Reservoir area (M. Hoffman 1977:33). All of these sites are within 70 kilometers of Spiro. Like that site, they occupy an Osage Savanna floodplain environment and they are within the "North Caddoan area," as delimited by J. Brown (1996:36). Thus, the Gober complex is probably the easternmost manifestation of a much larger proto-Spiroan population that occupied the Arkansas Valley in western Arkansas and eastern Oklahoma during the Woodland period.

Fourche Maline and the Gober Complex

Despite his reservations on this matter, M. Hoffman's (1977:41) Gober complex is commonly considered Fourche Maline or Fourche Maline–related (R. Bell 1980:111–14; Galm 1984:219; Rolingson 1998d:121; Story et al. 1990:293). This is an error, although one I have helped to perpetrate (Schambach 1982:188–89). The evidence that it is—Gary projectile points and sherds of plain, flat-bottomed, clay-tempered pottery from poor contexts—is weak and ambiguous. There are, for example, plenty of both at the Alexander site, located about 150 kilometers downstream from the Ozark Reservoir, which is now considered the locus of one of the two westernmost good components of Plum Bayou culture in the Arkansas Valley (Rolingson 1998d:120–25, fig. 101), the other being at the nearby Point Remove site.

On the other hand, there is considerable evidence that the Gober complex was not Fourche Maline, nor even Fourche Maline–related (Schambach 1993a:191). The layout of the most extensively excavated of the two type sites, Spinach Patch, known through Hoffman's pioneering efforts in aerial photography in Arkansas archaeology, is like nothing in Fourche Maline culture. It appears to be the remains of a complex little village consisting of two probable mounds and a well-defined midden area surrounding a rectangular plaza. I am not alone (Sabo and Early 1990:73) in seeing similarities between it and Emergent Mississippian (J. Kelly 1990a:126) settlements such as those represented at the Zebree site (D. Morse and P. Morse 1983:228–33; P. Morse and D. Morse 1990:63) and sites farther north in the Central Mississippi Valley (J. Kelly 1990b:79). The wattle-and-daub houses postulated on the basis of daub found at the Spinach Patch and Gasfield sites (M. Hoffman 1977:35) would be, again, like nothing in Fourche Maline. Nor would the presumptive "storage-refuse pits" at Gasfield (M. Hoffman 1977:35). Nor would the Steuben projectile points (P. Morse and D. Morse 1990:54) that appear to supplement the assemblage of Gary projectile points and arrow points at Spinach Patch (see Bond 1977:fig. 6.6, *a, b, c,* and *h*).

Nor would the chipped argillite "spades," probably hoes, considered the prime diagnostic of the complex (M. Hoffman 1977:33–35).

These "spades"—fifty were found at Spinach Patch—also appear in surface collections from twenty-four of the fifty-nine sites reported for the Ozark Reservoir area. Furthermore, they appear to be characteristic of Woodland period sites in the Arkansas Valley. Specimens I consider identical have been found in remarkable quantities in Evans or Harlan phase (i.e., late Woodland and/or Early Mississippi period) contexts at Spiro (J. Brown 1996:494–95, figs. 2-86, 2-87), and hundreds more have been reported from other Arkansas Valley sites in Oklahoma (Rose et al. 1999a:26). But, remarkably, only one Ozark Reservoir site, 3FR2, produced a double-bitted chipped stone axe (M. Hoffman 1977:6, 21), and these tools have not been reported from Spiro or other Arkansas Valley sites in Oklahoma, although they are well represented at sites north of the Arkansas Valley in eastern Oklahoma (R. Bell and Dale 1953:101; Harden and Robinson 1975:111) and, of course, at countless Fourche Maline sites to the south of the Arkansas Valley in Arkansas, Oklahoma, Texas, and Louisiana as well. This split geographical distribution suggests that they were displaced as gardening tools in the Arkansas Valley by Spinach Patch–style hoes.

Considered in conjunction with the Mississippian-like features of the Spinach Patch and Gasfield sites, particularly the layout of the Spinach Patch site, this split geographical distribution further suggests that the Gober complex represents a population of Emergent Mississippian hoe-horticulturalists who were well established in the Ozark Reservoir area and the Spiro locality during the latter part of the Woodland period. These people, not the Fourche Maline immigrants postulated by Wyckoff and Brown, would have been the Woodland period progenitors of the Spiroan tradition (Phillips and Brown 1978:9–10) in the Arkansas Valley. Perhaps they were, as R. Bell (1984:239) has speculated regarding their identity, a "new group of people" who had recently "entered the region … from the east or southeast." More likely, they had been there all along. Worth considering, in either case, are the observations of Rose et al. (1998:115) that "there is dental evidence to suggest that the inhabitants of the northern Caddoan region [i.e., the Arkansas Valley in western Arkansas and eastern Oklahoma] are genetically distinct from those Caddoan groups living to the south" and that there is "not even a hint that the southern Caddo populations did not derive from the preceding Fourche Maline inhabitants." Hence the Woodland period population of this region, still unstudied bioanthropologically, probably differed from Fourche Maline and Caddo populations to the south as well.

This Woodland period, apparently proto-Spiroan, cultural manifestation in the Arkansas Valley requires a name, the better to talk about it and study it. I will call it the Mulberry River culture, in recognition of the location of the Spinach Patch site on that river. Eventually, when it is better understood, the Gober complex will comprise one or more temporal phases of this culture, as, perhaps, will the Late Woodland period Evans phase materials from Spiro.

Thus, the Woodland period cultural geography of the Arkansas Valley and the Ouachita Mountains in eastern Oklahoma and western Arkansas would have consisted of Fourche Maline people in the oak-hickory forest of the Ouachita Mountains, the northern extent of their territory in the Trans-Mississippi South; of Plum Bayou people in the Arkansas Valley at least as far west as the Point Remove site; and of Mulberry River people in the Arkansas Valley to the west of them, on either side of the Arkansas-Oklahoma state line. I envision Mulberry River culture as a Woodland period adaptation to the river bottoms of the Osage Savanna and Cherokee Prairie biotic districts of northwestern Arkansas and northeastern Oklahoma (Albert and Wyckoff 1984:fig. 1.1; J. Rogers 1989:fig. 51), with some habitation and exploitation of the river valleys of the Arkansas drainage within the Ozark Plateau. Hence, the Mulberry River people would have occupied a considerable region in the Arkansas River drainage both east and west of Spiro. If I am right in arguing that the Spiroan tradition was the ancestral Tunica tradition (Schambach 1999a), these people would have been the Woodland period builders of that tradition, just as the Fourche Maline people were the builders of the Caddo tradition.

Fourche Maline Bioanthropology

The biggest problem in the area of Fourche Maline bioanthropology is that much of our information is the result of bioanthropological work on skeletal remains that are only thought to be Fourche Maline by archaeologists with varying ideas about what Fourche Maline is and insufficient standards for the identification of particular graves as such. This is particularly true of the Oklahoma Fourche Maline sites. All that can safely be said about the human remains from these sites is that some are probably Fourche Maline. Bioanthropologists (Rose et al. 1983:241) working in the Lower Mississippi Valley and the Trans-Mississippi South noticed this years ago, cautioning that all so-called Fourche Maline skeletal collections from "such sites as Sam, Wann...McCutchan-McLaughlin...and Mahaffey...probably include individuals from the Late Archaic, Woodland, and Caddoan periods." More recently, Rose et al. (1999a:15) noted that, of all the human remains from the five "Western Ouachita Mountain Fourche Maline" sites—

Scott, Sam, Wann, McCutchan-McLaughlin, and Bug Hill—"only the Bug Hill burials have been definitely assigned to the Fourche Maline phase."

Unfortunately, these questionable Oklahoma "Fourche Maline" bio-anthropological data have been used extensively, before and since publication of these warnings, in comparisons with Mississippi period populations. This has created the probably false impression that there were abrupt and drastic changes for the worse in caries rates, infection rates, and other measures of dental and physical health and environmental stress around the time that Fourche Maline culture evolved into Caddo culture (Powell 1989:tables 6, 8–11; Rose et al. 1984:396–97, 1999b:123–25).

For example, Rose et al. (1999b:123), writing as if the problems in the Oklahoma data had never been noticed, treat the "Mahaffey skeletal series in the Red River drainage" as representative of "Woodland period subsistence" in that region, concluding: "These data are typical of a hunter/gatherer subsistence strategy: low caries rates indicating low carbohydrate consumption, low porotic hyperostosis frequency indicating adequate supply of bioavailable iron and high rates of osteoarthritis and osteophytosis indicating high biomechanical stress." But that may be because the forty-seven Mahaffey site skeletons, although "dated ... to the Woodland (Fourche Maline) period" by Perino and Bennett (1978:31), actually are mostly those of Archaic period hunter/gatherers. In fact, no one knows. Only four were accompanied by artifacts, all of which could be Archaic period as easily as Woodland. What is not in evidence at all in the graves, nor sufficiently at the site itself, is plain pottery, the *sine qua non* of Fourche Maline assemblages. Perino and Bennett (1978:73) thought that "approximately 300" of the 1502 sherds from the site were "comparable" to Williams Plain pottery, the rest being sherds of various Mississippi period types. That is not enough. The Fourche Maline assemblage from the Cooper site included 4791 sherds of Williams Plain, 1142 of Cooper Boneware, and 1097 of Ouachita Ironware, *var. De Gray* (Schambach 1998b:21–26). I would expect that much or more plain pottery of these Woodland period types from a Fourche Maline component strong enough to include forty-seven burials. And I would expect to see some in the burials, along with the other Fourche Maline diagnostics such as boatstones, double-bitted chipped stone "axes," and Poole pipes.

The problem of the validity of the so-called Fourche Maline bioanthropological data is compounded by the ambiguity over the identity of the Woodland period population of the Arkansas Valley in western Arkansas and eastern Oklahoma. There are no recorded finds of Gober complex burials. But Terminal Woodland period–Early Mississippi period Evans phase burials—which I would now call Mulberry River culture burials—were found at Spiro. As noted earlier, most archaeologists with some knowledge of this material have opined that they are not Fourche Maline; that Fourche Maline culture did not extend to the Arkansas Valley. Yet the bioanthropologists aver that "the Spiro Woodland occupation is thought [by whom, they do not say] to represent a Fourche Maline adaptation interacting with both the northern Ouachita populations and the Gober complex" (Rose et al. 1999a:20).

Last, there is the fact that Fourche Maline, as I have conceptualized it, was a *culture,* not a short-lived, monolithic "phase," as the bioanthropologists seem to perceive it. It surely had a life span of over a thousand years, ample time for the development of many temporal and regional phases, certainly more than we now realize. To the extent that the skeletal remains they consider Fourche Maline actually are Fourche Maline, they represent living populations that could have been separated in time by anywhere from a few decades to as much as eighteen centuries. This in itself would render nonsensical most current comparisons of "Fourche Maline" site populations with each other and with Archaic and Mississippi period populations.

Fourche Maline Subsistence

We know little about Fourche Maline subsistence. In fact, because of the problems with distinguishing Fourche Maline remains from those of the Woodland period occupants of the Arkansas Valley, and from those of earlier and later peoples of southeastern Oklahoma and elsewhere south of the Arkansas Valley in the Trans-Mississippi South, we know less than the literature on this subject would suggest that we do.

The most misleading information abroad at present is Fritz's (1989:85) generalization that the "Fourche Maline horticultural subsystem [was] founded on the four members of the Eastern Cultivated Starchy Seed complex probably along with gourds (both *Lagenaria* and *Cucurbita*) and the two native oily seed crops [sunflower and sumpweed]." While her study is undoubtedly accurate as far as the paleobotany goes, this statement is based on her study of the plant remains from the Early Mississippi period Copple mound at Spiro plus the *assumption* that the Woodland period ancestors of its builders were Fourche Maline people, which they almost certainly were not.

One reason for our ignorance on the subject of Fourche Maline subsistence is that so much of the Fourche Maline data is from the WPA era, when even the collection of food refuse bone did not have high priority and collection techniques were rudimentary (Schambach 1998b:79). Nor is this only a problem with WPA data. To the chagrin of those of us who thought we were doing the best that could be done in the late 1960s, after flotation processing hit the scene, collection techniques remained inadequate until the late 1980s when we learned that we should have been screening for seeds the size of poppy seeds if we really wanted to know what people of the Woodland period were eating (Fritz 1989:86–87, 1990a; Fritz and B. D. Smith 1988). So, as Fritz (1989:85) has observed, "Fourche Maline features in the Ouachitas and elsewhere might contain millions of…starchy seeds of the pre-maize Woodland period horticultural complex…just as at west-central Illinois sites of the same time periods." However, we will not know whether they do until midden samples from some securely identified Fourche Maline components, like the one represented in the deep, apparently exclusively Fourche Maline, middens at the Crenshaw site in southwest Arkansas (Schambach 1982:150–54), have been passed through flotation processing screens fine enough to catch the evidence.

In the meantime, we cannot assume that the Fourche Maline people were growers of starchy and oily seed crops. Given the ubiquity of starchy and oily seed horticulture among Woodland period cultures to the north and northeast of them (Fritz 1993:52, fig. 4-1; Johannessen 1993a:fig. 5-1; C. Scarry [ed.] 1993) it may be difficult to imagine that they might have shunned it. Yet we need look no further than their Marksville and Coles Creek neighbors to the east in the Lower Mississippi Valley to find people who did. Recent work by Fritz and Kidder (1993:2) "indicates that the Lower Mississippi Valley was not an early center of agriculture based on either tropical or temperate cultigens." Still, the Fourche Maline territory of the Ouachita Mountains and the Gulf Coastal Plain of southwest Arkansas, southeastern Oklahoma, and northeast Texas probably was not as bountiful an environment as the Lower Mississippi Valley, so the Fourche Maline people might have been more receptive to the early domesticates. And it is more likely that they would have had to have had them for their culture to have developed as it did.

There is circumstantial evidence suggesting that they did. For one thing, they had in abundance the stone pounding and grinding equipment required to process these foodstuffs (Schambach 1982:178). This equipment, consisting of bi-pitted cobblestone hammers or pestles, cobble stone manos, stone slab metates, and large, dished, and multiple-pitted stone mortars, occurs in profusion on virtually all southwest Arkansas Fourche Maline sites. In fact, it seems to be characteristic of them since it seems scarce at Archaic sites and is absent at all of the southwest Arkansas Caddo sites that we know anything about.

Second, there are the so-called "double-bitted chipped stone axes" (Schambach 1998b:fig. 61, a–d), one of the markers of the early stages of Fourche Maline culture. When I last reviewed the data on Fourche Maline culture (1982:178–79), I rejected speculation that these specimens were gardening tools, though they do not look like they would have been useful for wood cutting or woodworking. My reasoning was that, although they are ubiquitous in assemblages of the early Fourche Maline phases, they dropped out of use around the end of the Fourche Maline 4 period, about the time horticulture, by which I meant *corn* horticulture, might *possibly* have been coming in. But that was before we knew about the starchy and oily seed complex. Now, it seems possible that they were gardening tools; hoes of some sort. They are, as mentioned earlier, also abundant on sites in eastern Oklahoma north of the Arkansas Valley (R. Bell and Dale 1953:101; Harden and Robinson 1975:111), well beyond the northernmost Fourche Maline sites but within the probable geographical range of the Early and Middle Woodland starchy and oily seed horticulturalists (Fritz 1993:fig. 4-1).

The possibility that they were associated with the gardening of starchy and oily seed crops in the Fourche Maline homeland as well as the Ozarks has some interesting implications. One would be that the Fourche Maline people could not have been far behind their neighbors to the north and northeast in the Ozarks and eastern Kentucky (Fritz 1993:55) in taking up this distinctive form of horticulture. Double-bitted chipped stone axes are abundant in the earliest southwest Arkansas Fourche Maline assemblages, those at the Lost Bayou and Field Bayou phases at the Cooper and Johnny Ford sites, guess-dated to about 400 B.C. (Figure 5.2). This, in turn, could account for other aspects of their culture, such as their small-village settlement pattern. And it could account for their numbers, which *seem* to have been substantially greater than those of their Archaic period forebears.

The still-puzzling fact that these tools are missing in the latest phases of Fourche Maline culture might reflect an abandonment of some or all of the practices and tools of old-style seed-crop horticulture when corn horticulture became popular. To grow seed crops in quantity, horticulturalists must use some kind of hoe or spadelike tool to turn over the soil and make relatively large beds upon which seeds can be sown by broadcasting. Corn, on the other hand, is a hill, or row, crop that does not require large hoed, spaded, or plowed seed beds. It is easily grown using the slash-and-burn technique and digging sticks.

I think it possible that such a replacement occurred, particularly if my estimate of when double-bitted chipped stone axes went out of use happens to be a century or so too early. That, too, is possible, considering the all but complete absence of radiometric dates on Fourche Maline assemblages. Recently reported early dates on corn from early Caddo and, perhaps, late Fourche Maline, contexts at sites in northeast Texas lend credence to this scenario. According to Story (1990:254), some of the earliest corn from the Davis site, long well known for yielding large amounts of possibly early corn (V. Jones 1949), may date "back perhaps to ca. A.D. 800." This corn, collected during Story's 1968–1970 excavations, amounted to 156 cobs, over 11,000 cupules, 7 "shank" fragments, and 68 stalk fragments (R. Ford 1997:table 11).

Story's A.D. 800 estimate is bolstered by a recent report (Bruseth 1998:53) of a floated sample of "numerous corn cupules and corn cob fragments," identified by Fritz, from a feature at the Ray site in northeast Texas. The dates on this feature are cal A.D. 820/840/860 ± 90. Bruseth considers the Ray site a "good example of a very late Fourche Maline settlement." Distinguishing between a very late Fourche Maline settlement and a very early Caddo settlement would have to be arbitrary, but this would probably be, at least, a transitional component—as would an occupation dating to A.D. 800 at the Davis site.

So it looks as if late Fourche Maline/early Caddo people in east Texas had corn by around A.D. 800, during the Fourche Maline 7 period. That would not be out of bounds either temporally or geographically, considering the recently published date of A.D. 700 to 750 for securely identified early corn from a good context in Mound S at the Toltec site in central Arkansas (C. Smith 1996:69). Possibly, they were growing it in quantity, to judge from the George C. Davis site collections. On the other hand, stable carbon isotope values from Fourche Maline 7 period Crenshaw phase and Old Martin phase skeletons from the Crenshaw and Old Martin sites in southwest Arkansas indicate that those people, living *between* Toltec and east Texas, were not corn-eaters (Rose et al. 1998:117, table 6-2). However, Rose et al. add: "It should be pointed out that Fritz thinks that stable carbon isotopes cannot identify seasonal consumption of maize on the order of 10 to 15 percent of the diet." Thus we cannot necessarily rely on this technique to identify the earliest corn-eaters, assuming that the late Fourche Maline/early Caddo added corn gradually to their (still hypothetical) starchy and oily seed horticultural complex, which they almost certainly would have done.

Rose et al. (1984:396–97, 1999a:17) have suggested that caries rates in excess of two caries per person might be indicative of regular corn consumption. By that standard, the seven Fourche Maline 4 skeletons from the Ferguson site (Schambach 1972:6) are, as Rose and colleagues put it, "definitely within the maize consumption range" with a rate of 4.3 caries per person. I am as certain as one can be about such things that the Ferguson site skeletons I identified as Fourche Maline *are* all Fourche Maline, having done so on the basis of grave offerings (double-bitted chipped stone axes and boatstones with some of the skeletons), position and orientation of the skeletons, location of the graves, and condition of the bone. Hence, we can be reasonably sure that the Fourche Maline 4 period occupants of the Ferguson site really had a caries rate of 4.3 per person. That looks anomalously high because the rate for the populations from the Oklahoma sites that have long been generally accepted as Fourche Maline (i.e., Mahaffey, Sam, Wann, and McCutchan-McLaughlin) is only 0.1 to 1.6 caries per person (Rose et al. 1984). But, as noted earlier, we do not know which, if any, of the skeletons from these sites are Fourche Maline: they may be mostly Archaic period. In that case, the Ferguson site caries rate would be more representative of certain aspects of Fourche Maline diet in general during the middle Fourche Maline era than it may have seemed to be.

Still, this would not necessarily mean the middle Fourche Maline people were corn-eaters. Indeed, having searched diligently in some very rich-looking Fourche Maline middens at the Ferguson site without finding a trace of corn (Schambach 1972:6), I doubt that they were. Fritz and Kidder (1993:10) point out with respect to similarly high-looking caries rates among certain non-corn-eating and non-horticultural Coles Creek populations in the Lower Mississippi Valley that corn is only one of the starchy and sugary foods that can boost caries rates when consumed frequently. Examples they mention are acorns, persimmons, and the Woodland starchy seed complex, not that the latter seems to have boosted the caries rates of Woodland and Early Mississippi period consumers in eastern Oklahoma (Rose et al. 1999a:29). All of these are worth considering in the case of the Ferguson site skeletons.

Considering the location of the George C. Davis site on the far southwestern edge of the Southeastern Woodlands, one would be bound to wonder whether the Late Woodland–Early Mississippi period corn found there was introduced from the Southwest. However, R. Ford (1997) identifies it as primarily Eastern Complex, concluding, "It is reasonable to argue that the Eastern Complex evolved in the Middle West and was introduced to the Davis site from a northern or eastern source." How, then, did it make its way from the Late Woodland sources in the American Bottom from which, I presume, it would have come (C. Cobb and Nassaney 1995:209; Johannessen 1993a:62–63; C. Scarry 1993a:82) to the late Fourche Maline/early Caddo populations of east Texas and, presumably, those of southeast Oklahoma, southwest Arkansas, and northwest Louisiana as well?

The proximate source may have been people of the Plum Bayou culture of the Arkansas River valley in central Arkansas, with whom the Fourche Maline people were apparently in contact circa A.D. 700–900 (Rolingson 1998d:126). Corn "does not seem to have been an important part of the diet" at Toltec, or at least not the daily diet (Rolingson 1998c:106), yet that need not have precluded transmission of the corn horticulture complex to others. Certainly, the source would not have been the non-corn-eating, *non-horticultural* peoples of the Lower Mississippi Valley (Fritz and Kidder 1993:2) to the east of Fourche Maline country. Nor does it look as if it was the non-corn-eating, starchy and oily seed crop horticulturalists of the Arkansas Valley of western Arkansas and eastern Oklahoma. In neither of these areas did people have much, if anything, to do with corn until around A.D. 1200, and in the latter area corn probably was not grown until around A.D. 1400 (Fritz and Kidder 1993:11, Rose et al. 1999a:29).

Rose et al.'s (1998:118–19) conclusion that "significant maize consumption [was] absent prior to A.D. 1100 among Late Baytown and Early Mississippi period groups" of the Central Mississippi Valley in eastern Arkansas raises the possibility that corn did not reach either Toltec or Fourche Maline country via simple group-to-group, or "down the line," diffusion southwestward from the American Bottom. Considering the apparent ceremonial significance of corn at Toltec, and perhaps at the Davis site, and the tendency for it to appear earliest in ceremonial contexts elsewhere as well (C. Scarry 1993a:90), it seems that some more complex form of diffusion may have been involved. The corn horticultural complex may have traveled in conjunction with the foreign prestige goods, such as copper beads and artifacts made from whelk shells, that, as C. Cobb and Nassaney (1995:212) observe, appear in Fourche Maline contexts late in the Woodland period.

Fourche Maline Culture and Caddo Culture

My suggestion (Schambach 1998b:128), made originally in my 1970 dissertation, that Fourche Maline culture is "a plausible, early local ancestor of Caddoan culture in the Trans-Mississippi South" has been strengthened almost to the point of certainty by fieldwork and research since then (Schambach 1982, 1991, 1993a, 1993b, 1997, 1998a, 1998b). Most archaeologists interested in Caddo culture appear to share my opinion (Bruseth 1998:53; Early 1982:86, 2000:126; Jeter et al. 1989:196; Kidder 1998b; Perttula 1992:13; J. Rogers 1991:232). Furthermore, bioanthropologists who have concerned themselves with this problem (Rose 1984:252; Rose et al. 1998:114–15; Rose et al. 1999a:24–25) conclude that there is "not even a hint that the southern Caddo populations did not derive from the preceding Fourche Maline inhabitants" (Rose et al. 1998:115). Note, however, that here Rose and his colleagues specify "southern Caddo populations." In addition, they go on to say that "there is dental evidence to suggest that the inhabitants of the northern Caddoan region are genetically distinct from those Caddoan groups living to the south." I am not surprised.

The only dissenter on the role of the Fourche Maline people as the ancestral Caddo is Story (1990:323), whose view is "there was no one center or sequence of early Caddoan development, nor an antecedent 'Mother' culture. Rather there are indications of several distinct, yet related, developments that might usefully be called subtraditions." These she identifies as the Arkansas Valley subtradition, the Woodland Edge subtradition, the Red River subtradition, and the Piney Woods subtradition. The difficulty in this view (an accurate statement of the traditional model of Caddo area archaeology, by one of its major practitioners) is the assumption that these entities are in fact *subtraditions* of an entity that could be called "Caddoan" culture. I believe they represent different *traditions,* and that only one of them, the "Red River subtradition," which subsumes the sites in the territory in southwest Arkansas, southeast Oklahoma, northeast Texas, and northwest Louisiana that was occupied by the Caddo on the eve of European contact, can be called a Caddo tradition on historical and archaeological grounds. I have argued that the "Arkansas Valley subtradition" is a distinct tradition that was neither Caddo, nor Caddoan, but probably Tunican (Schambach 1993a, 1999b). I have also demonstrated that the organizing concept behind the "Woodland Edge subtradition," the old "Sanders focus" (Krieger 1946), is an incorrect construct based on the misinterpretation of the Sanders site as the type site for a Red River valley focus when it was actually an outpost of Spiroan traders from the Arkansas Valley (Schambach 1999a, 2000a, 2000b).

Story's (1990:318–19) admittedly tentative "Piney Woods subtradition" is another example of an invalid construct based on the misinterpretation of one assemblage, this one from the James Pace site in the Sabine River valley in west-central Louisiana. Finding it remarkable, for a Caddo area site, because it "produced so many LMV-like sherds," particularly sherds of diverse varieties of the type Coles Creek Incised—and *no* sherds of Caddo types (Story 1990:318–19, table 77)—Story jumps to the conclusion that it "may represent...a different culture complex and different regional sequence" within the "Caddoan" area. In fact, it is close enough to the border between the Lower Mississippi Valley and the Trans-Mississippi South, as I drew it more than thirty years ago (Schambach 1998b:fig. 4), when the Pace site had yet to be found, to suggest that it is a Coles Creek site, pure and simple, located at or near the northern limits of the territory occupied by Lower Mississippi Valley peoples in southwestern Louisiana. Coles Creek people probably occupied the Sabine Valley as far north as Toledo Bend, just as— contrary to what used to be the conventional wisdom in Caddo area archaeology—they and Lower Mississippi Valley peoples before them as far back as Poverty Point times occupied the Ouachita Valley all the way up to Camden, Arkansas (Kidder 1998b). Not surprisingly, the early Woodland period Resch site, with its excellent Tchefuncte pottery (C. Webb et al. 1969:fig. 8, *d,* and fig. 9), is located about fifteen miles farther up the Sabine in northeast Texas.

Let me emphasize, though, that Fourche Maline culture as I described it in 1982 really *was* too inclusive. Obviously, I no longer include any of the Arkansas Valley materials such as the Evans phase remains at the Spiro and Harlan sites, and the Gober complex, that I ascribed to it then (Schambach 1982:182). Nor does it include, as I suggested it might based on preliminary reports (Schambach 1982:188), any materials from the extraordinary Archaic through Woodland period cemetery at the Ernest Witte site on the lower Brazos River (G. Hall 1981; Story 1990:237–42). This site is south of the border of the Trans-Mississippi South, even as defined in 1982 (Schambach 1982:fig. 7-1), and it has not produced a Fourche Maline assemblage.

Fourche Maline Culture and the Genesis of the Early Caddo Burial Mound Tradition

The most important unsolved problem in late Fourche Maline/early Caddo archaeology is that of the origin of the extraordinary Caddo mound-burial complex of the Early Mississippi period. Whence the complex of social and religious concepts exemplified by the deep tombs of important people buried with their pottery, textiles, celts, and Osage orange bows, and with their characteristically Mississippian prestige goods of shell, copper, and other materials from throughout eastern North America, at all of the *earliest*-known Caddo ceremonial centers: Crenshaw and Bowman (Durham and Davis 1975; Schambach 1982, 1996b; W. R. Wood 1963c) in the Red River valley in Arkansas; Mounds Plantation and Gahagan (C. Webb and Dodd 1939; C. Webb and McKinney 1975) farther down the Red River in Louisiana; and George C. Davis (Story 1997, 1998) in central east Texas?

Although I was once confident that all of this could be derived from the interesting and unusual Fourche Maline mound-burial complex (Schambach 1982:182), my recent study of it leads me to conclude that it cannot (Schambach 1996a). Apart from a common core concept that mound burial was for a privileged few, rather than the masses, and a shared concept of interring artifacts of exotic materials with the dead, I find much in the way of concepts as well as artifacts that must have come from Middle Woodland through Early Mississippi period societies to the northeast of the Fourche Maline–Caddo area.

To make a long story (Schambach 1996a) short, the earliest evidences, so far, of the Fourche Maline burial mound tradition are inconspicuous, dome-shaped mounds covering the remains of crematoria, located away from habitation sites along the bluffs bordering rivers and streams. The two excavated examples, dating to around 200 B.C., are the Cicero Young mound (Schambach

1982) on a bluff overlooking the Red River valley in Arkansas and the Belle-vue mound (Fulton and Webb 1953; C. Webb 1982) overlooking Bodcaw Bayou in northwest Louisiana. These contain small quantities of cremated human remains and artifacts, also cremated, but the remains of most of the bodies and offerings disposed of in the crematoria they demarcate were apparently buried in cremation cemeteries like those at the Johnny Ford site in the Red River valley in southwest Arkansas (Schambach 1982:145–46) and the Hurricane Hill site on the upper Sulphur River in northeast Texas (Perttula [ed.] 1999:387).

Shane's mound (Schambach 1982:149), located a mile from the Cicero Young mound, and the Jonas Short mound (McClurkan et al. 1980) in the Angelina River valley in east Texas, represent a second stage in the evolution of this tradition. Despite the distance between them, they were very similar. Both were valley, rather than bluff-edge, mounds. Like Cicero Young and Bellevue, both covered central pits containing cremated human bone. But in these mounds the pits also contained Hopewell-looking Early to Middle Woodland period prestige goods, including two copper bracelets (Jonas Short) and (from Shane's mound) an owl effigy "boatstone" carved from bone (probably human) and a disc-shaped pendant, 10.8 centimeters in diameter, cut from a human skull. Significantly, both mounds also contained small additional deposits of prestige goods that had been laid on intermediate surfaces, probably along with fragmentary human remains, and covered with soil as the mounds were built.

The custom of building mounds over crematoria seems to have gone out of style around A.D. 100, judging from evidence from the Red Hill mound (Schambach 1982:147), about five miles down the bluff line from the Cicero Young mound; from the McKinney mound (C. Webb 1982:262–63) in northwest Louisiana; and from the Coral Snake mound (Story 1990:283) on the Sabine River in west-central Louisiana. However, the interring of small deposits of artifacts (including exotic pottery and copper ornaments), cremated human remains, and *parts* of uncremated bodies on intermediate mound surfaces continued and intensified. Thus, by around A.D. 300, Fourche Maline mounds seem to have become primarily repositories for human remains and offerings interred in that way rather than primarily coverings for crematoria. We have no data from excavated mounds dating to the interval between A.D. 300 and A.D. 600–700, the probable date of the earliest Fourche Maline mound at Crenshaw, Mound D. Yet there, and in the first two construction stages of Mound C, best known for the deep, intrusive, early Caddo tombs it contained (Durham and Davis 1975), we find the same mound-surface deposits of human remains (although now almost invariably skulls, mandibles, and teeth) and artifacts.

This old and characteristically Fourche Maline mode of interring skulls, mandibles, teeth, and offerings in mounds is totally unlike the classic early Caddo tombs. I see no evidence and no possibility that the one evolved into the other. Rather it seems that the Fourche Maline practice was simply terminated somewhere between A.D. 800 and A.D. 900 when the earliest-known tomb of the early Caddo pattern was emplaced in Mound C at Crenshaw. This tomb, W. R. Wood's (1963a, 1963c) Burial 42, consisted of the skeletons of eight people lying extended and supine in a *burial pit* at least 55 centimeters deep that originated from some higher surface within the mound. Apparently contemporaneous with this were three extraordinary burials that were, unfortunately, excavated and only poorly recorded by the looters who had preceded Wood at Mound C (Durham and Davis 1975:12, 33–36, 75–78, figs. 4, 17, 22). These consisted of large numbers of skeletons representing full-fleshed corpses that had been placed side by side in long rows, either on a mound surface or in grave pits.

As far as I know, there is only one other place in the Southeast where similarly laid-out group burials were being placed in mounds at roughly the same time as these: Mound 72 at Cahokia (Fowler 1991, 1997:fig.6.33; Fowler et al. 1999). These graves also contain what I consider the earliest essentially Mississippian trade goods (copper artifacts, polished petaloid celts of igneous rock, and Copena bifaces) yet recovered in the Caddo area. Hence they appear to be an epiphenomenon of the earliest participation of the late Fourche Maline/early Caddo people in the developing Mississippian interaction sphere. The basis for this participation—the main reason for the interest of the Early Mississippians in the Fourche Maline people of the Red River valley—was, I hypothesize, powerful, flat-shooting bows of Osage orange, or bois d'arc, a resource unique to a small area in the Red River valley in northeast Texas that the Fourche Maline people had probably begun to exploit hundreds of years earlier (Schambach 1995, 2000a, 2000b).

Thus, we come full circle. The old idea that the development of Mississippian culture in the American Bottom was the result of a "blending of local and Caddoan influences" has been replaced by the realization that there is no longer "any need to perceive…[it as]…having been introduced from somewhere else" (J. Kelly 1990a:142–43). And in the Caddo area, the reverse has happened. What remains unchanged is the near certainty that there was consequential interaction of some kind between these areas toward the end of the Woodland period.

Chapter 6

The Woodland Period in the Northern Ozarks of Missouri

Paul P. Kreisa, Richard Edging, and Steven R. Ahler

An understanding of the Woodland period in the northern Ozarks is as dependent upon past archaeological models as on current archaeological data. The lack of well-documented chronological markers, whether projectile points or pottery, has resulted in an interpretation of the Woodland period that stresses an ebb and flow of population into what has been characterized as a marginal environment. For the past ten years, large-scale surveys, supplemented by test and large-area excavations at numerous sites, have been conducted at Fort Leonard Wood, located in the central portion of the northern Ozarks. These projects have resulted in a large database for all of prehistory and history, including the Woodland period (Figure 6.1). This increase in data has led us to interpret the Woodland period in this region as, in contrast to earlier models, exhibiting continuity of population and a logical adaptation to the northern Ozarks environment.

Our focus, then, is on data from three counties, Pulaski, Phelps, and Maries, in the north-central Ozarks. This three-county study area is part of the Salem Plateau (eastern) portion of the northern Ozark Highland and, in that physiographic region, the eastern portion of the Osage-Gasconade Hills (M. Rafferty 1980). The dissected landscape of this region is characterized by a rolling topography of upland interfluvial plateaus that are separated by deeply entrenched stream valleys. Fort Leonard Wood occupies part of the dissected uplands between the Big Piney River and Roubidoux Creek (Figure 6.2). Both streams flow northward and are tributaries of the Gasconade River, which is part of the Missouri River drainage. Caves, rockshelters, solution cavities, and sinkholes are plentiful along both major and minor stream valleys and were significant factors in prehistoric settlement (Atwood 1940).

At present, many of the upland ridges are covered by oak-hickory forest and scattered junipers, while the floodplains are covered by dense deciduous forests. While this region often has been described as a socially and physically marginal environment, this characterization probably is based

Years B.P.	Period	Subperiod	Horizon – Phase
Present	Historic		
500	Mississippian		Late Maramec Spring Phase
1000		Late	Early Maramec Spring Phase
1600	Woodland	Middle	Spring Creek Complex
2500		Early	
3000	Archaic	Late	Sedalia Phase or James River Complex

Figure 6.1 — Northern Ozarks Woodland period chronology

more on the rugged topography and difficult travel conditions presented to historic settlers than on scarcity of food resources (see for instance Sauer 1920). Prior to historic settlement and land clearing, the uplands were covered primarily in oak barrens, with scattered openings of prairie and oak savannas and occasional stands of pine. Steeper hillslopes and floodplains supported mesic oak-hickory forests or mixed bottomland communities (Nelson 1987; Schoolcraft 1853; Steyermark 1963). Environmental conditions described in early historic accounts (e.g., Schoolcraft 1853) are assumed to have prevailed during the Woodland period, with very little change caused by long-term climatic fluctuations or human activities.

Previous Archaeological Research

Previous archaeological research in the northern Ozarks can be characterized as geographically extensive, but with excavations focusing on a few large or rich sites (e.g., Fowke 1922; Geier 1975; R. Marshall 1963, 1965b; McGrath 1977; McMillan 1963, 1965; Reeder 1982, 1988). Complementing this historical trajectory is the Fort Leonard Wood program. It has, based on its cultural resource management objective, provided intensive data gath-

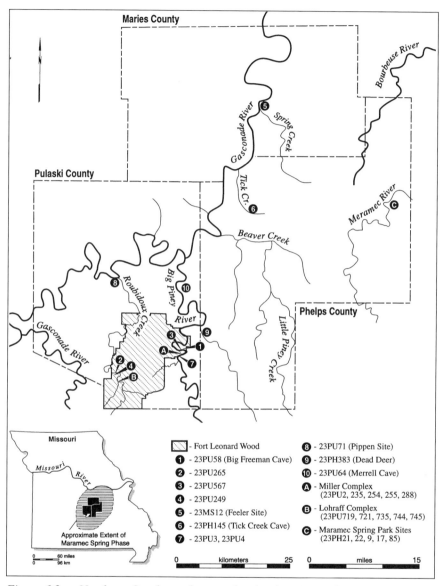

Figure 6.2 — Northern Ozarks study area showing locations of sites mentioned in the text

ering in one restricted portion of the northern Ozarks. As of 1999, 52,000 acres have been surveyed and over 300 prehistoric sites located; Phase II testing has been conducted at forty-five sites and expanded excavations conducted at an additional five sites. The scale of this work makes the Fort Leonard Wood database the most detailed in the study area. Data from projects outside of Fort Leonard Wood provide additional information on site types not present or yet to be investigated. The combination of information from Fort Leonard Wood and its surrounding area provides a relatively robust database with which to evaluate prior interpretations of the northern Ozarks Woodland period, as well as to attempt explanations of the patterns of human behavior observed in the archaeological record.

Much of the tone and orientation of discussion concerning the prehistory of the northern Ozarks, including that of the Woodland period, was set by Carl Chapman in the late 1940s. Chapman (1948a, 1948b) defined two themes regarding the prehistoric occupation of the northern Ozarks: cultural conservatism or the continuation of earlier patterns after the disappearance of these lifeways in other regions, and low or no population during particular time periods. The theme of a low population entailed a proposed use of the area by hunting groups, or its maintenance as an uninhabited buffer zone between cultural groups (C. Chapman 1980:69). Willey and Phillips (1958) accepted much of this interpretation in their classic *Method and Theory in American Archaeology*. Populations characterized as the Ozark Bluff Dweller culture were thought to have remained at an Archaic stage of development into the Woodland period. In Willey and Phillips's view, the Ozarks were impervious to cultural influences from centers of development, such as those in the Mississippi River valley. James Brown (1984) was later to successfully counter this argument for the southern Ozarks region, but to date this view continues to be accepted by most researchers for the northern Ozarks region.

Early Woodland

Though Early Woodland expressions are well defined in much of the Southeast (e.g., east Tennessee, northern Alabama, Atlantic coast regions), Early Woodland manifestations are difficult to identify in the Midwest (see Farnsworth and Emerson [eds.] 1986). Well-defined Early Woodland expressions generally are limited to portions of the Illinois and Mississippi river valleys where distinctive ceramic and projectile point styles have been identified in dated and stratified contexts. The northern Ozarks region lacks a well-defined local Early Woodland expression. Chapman (1980) and others working in the region expressed the opinion that the northern Ozarks may have been essentially devoid of human occupation during the Early Woodland. Even the most recent synthesis of Missouri prehistory (O'Brien and Wood 1998) includes only passing mention of possible Early Woodland manifestations in the northern Ozarks, and a recent paper synthesizing the

Maramec Spring phase (Reeder 1999) asserts that there was no existing population with Woodland adaptive strategies present in the region prior to the
Late Woodland period.

Excavations at several stratified cave and rockshelter sites in the region
(Verkamp Shelter [R. Marshall 1965b]; Tick Creek Cave [R. Roberts 1965];
Miller Cave [Fowke 1922; Markman 1993]) produced ample evidence of
Late Archaic and Late Woodland habitation but lacked any evidence of early
pottery that could be temporally, stylistically, or technologically linked with
established Early Woodland ceramic types such as Alexander, Crab Orchard,
Marion Thick, or Black Sand. Projectile point types characteristic of the
Terminal Archaic or Early Woodland periods in the Illinois and Mississippi
river valleys (Terminal Archaic Barbed Cluster or Kramer points [Justice
1987]) were also absent. Recent inspection of over 1200 Missouri site file
records for the three-county study area divulged only nine sites with identified Early Woodland components. For four of these, age assignment was
based on unillustrated points or contracting-stem points that may not represent Early Woodland period occupation. Thus it is not surprising that an
Early Woodland manifestation for the northern Ozarks had not been defined.

Only recently have excavations provided direct evidence of projectile
points associated with the Early Woodland time period. Three sites at Fort
Leonard Wood have yielded radiocarbon dates in the Early Woodland time
range (Table 6.1). One site (23PU606) consisted of a surface hearth exposed
in an eroding bankline about 2.6 meters below ground surface (Ahler and
Albertson 1996:84–88). Charcoal, ash, flakes, and fire-cracked rock were
associated, but no projectile points were recovered. This feature yielded
AMS radiocarbon assay results of cal 960 ± 50 B.C. (USGS-CAMS 626) and
cal 1080 ± 50 B.C. (USGS-CAMS 627). Recent excavations on the talus
slope of a small rockshelter (23PU719) provided a sample of bone, lithics,
ceramics, and mussel shell from a stratified Woodland sequence in bluff-
base colluvial deposits (Ahler et al. 1999). One level produced charcoal
dated to cal 900 ± 70 B.C. (ISGS-4085), but no ceramics or projectile points
were associated with this stratum.

The best information about possible Early Woodland artifact assemblages
was derived from excavations conducted at 23PU58, Big Freeman Cave
(Ahler et al. 1997; see Figure 6.2). Test units placed at the dripline and
within the front chamber documented intact strata radiocarbon dated to cal
830 ± 80 B.C. (ISGS-3543) and cal 770 ± 70 B.C. (ISGS-3540), respectively.
The sample from the cave interior was obtained from contexts about 20
centimeters below ceramic-bearing deposits, and the dripline sample was
also from aceramic deposits. These dated Early Woodland strata contained

Table 6.1 — Woodland Period Radiocarbon Dates from Fort Leonard Wood Sites

Site	Sample Number	Calibrated Date	Citation
23PU606	USGS-CAMS-627	1255 (1126) 1012 B.C.	Ahler and Albertson 1996
23PU606	USGS-CAMS-626	1000 (964) 843 B.C.	Ahler and Albertson 1996
23PU719	ISGS-4085	990 (910) 830 B.C.	Ahler et al. 1999
23PU58	ISGS-3543	820 (780) 410 B.C.	Ahler et al. 1997
23PU58	ISGS-3540	800 (780) 540 B.C.	Ahler et al. 1997
23PU249	BETA-78611	350 (185) 100 B.C.	Ahler et al. 1995a
23PU264	BETA-101932	330 (180) 100 B.C.	Childress and Weaver 1998
23PU249	BETA-78613	370 (100) B.C. A.D. 75	Ahler et al. 1995a
23PU209	ISGS-3888	95 (21) B.C. A.D. 63	Ahler et al. 1998
23PU265	BETA-78616	A.D. 135 (235) 320	Ahler et al. 1995a
23PU265	BETA-78614	A.D. 120 (250) 415	Ahler et al. 1995a
23PU567	ISGS-3366	A.D. 240 (340) 420	Ahler et al. 1997
23PU235	BETA-78609	A.D. 260 (410) 440	Ahler et al. 1995a
23PU211	ISGS-3818	A.D. 396 (430) 540	Ahler et al. 1998
23PU492	BETA-81619	A.D. 428 (541) 603	Kreisa (ed.) 1995
23PU58	BETA-88676	A.D. 440 (575) 640	Kreisa et al. 1996
23PU719	ISGS-4086	A.D. 540 (600) 650	Ahler et al. 1999
23PU567	ISGS-3363	A.D. 550 (620) 660	Ahler et al. 1997
23PU235	BETA-79715	A.D. 575 (620) 650	Ahler et al. 1995b
23PU235	BETA-79719	A.D. 605 (640) 660	Ahler et al. 1995b
23PU264	BETA-101931	A.D. 620 (660) 695	Childress and Weaver 1998
23PU58	BETA-88675	A.D. 660 (690) 860	Kreisa et al. 1996
23PU313	GX10411G	A.D. 660 (790) 1000	Niquette 1984
23PU210	ISGS-3815	A.D. 673 (740) 878	Ahler et al. 1998
23PU249	BETA-78612	A.D. 690 (785) 885	Ahler et al. 1995a
23PU172	BETA-78608	A.D. 890 (980) 1020	Ahler et al. 1995a
23PU565	ISGS-3364	A.D. 890 (980) 1020	Ahler et al. 1997
23PU235	BETA-79714	A.D. 1020 (1040) 1175	Ahler et al. 1995b
23PU235	BETA-79721	A.D. 1015 (1040) 1180	Ahler et al. 1995b
23PU492	BETA-81618	A.D. 1003 (1144) 1155	Kreisa (ed.) 1995
23PU421	BETA-86171	A.D. 1300 (1340) 1410	Kreisa et al. 1996
23PU719	ISGS-4083	A.D. 1300 (1365) 1420	Ahler et al. 1999
23PU249	BETA-78610	A.D. 1310 (1420) 1455	Ahler et al. 1995a
23PU614	ISGS-A-0017	A.D. 1320 (1410) 1430	Ahler et al. 1999

Note: Calibrated date includes a one-sigma date range and a date mean in parentheses. In cases of multiple intercepts of the mean, an average of the intercepts is presented. Date calibrations were generated using Stuiver and Reimer (1993).

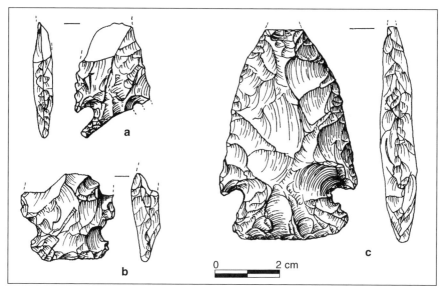

Figure 6.3 — Early Woodland projectile points: a, McMillan category CB2; b, untyped convex-base side-notched; c, Reeder category ES2

associated bone, mussel shell, and lithic artifacts, including a few projectile points. One point (Figure 6.3, *a*) has a concave base and may represent a variant of McMillan (1965) category CB2. Other diagnostic artifacts recovered from Early Woodland strata in the main chamber include a convex-base side-notched specimen (Figure 6.3, *b*) with the haft element noticeably narrower than the blade, and a Reeder (1988) category ES2 point (Figure 6.3, *c*) with a broad haft element.

Several of these point types have been recovered from other aceramic contexts assigned to Late Archaic through Middle Woodland periods, but the excavations at Big Freeman Cave provide one of the few examples of radiocarbon-dated contexts for these point styles. Of most importance is the possible documentation of a distinctive side-notched point type (Figure 6.3, *b*) that has not been found in other contexts and that may be truly diagnostic of Early Woodland occupations in the region.

These findings indicate that an Early Woodland manifestation is present in the northern Ozarks, but it is apparently distinct from contemporary assemblages in neighboring regions. Northern Ozarks Early Woodland is apparently an aceramic expression, and some of the associated projectile point forms may have been made during the Late Archaic and Middle Woodland periods as well, making Early Woodland difficult to identify as a separate manifestation. A narrow-hafted side-notched point form, however, may be diagnostic exclusively for the Early Woodland period. Recent examination of drawings and photographs of points in the Missouri site files identified two additional sites containing this point form. This suggests that a regional Early Woodland population was maintained in the northern Ozarks and that the archaeological signature of this population has not been adequately defined in contrast to earlier and later aceramic cultural expressions.

Middle Woodland

Until recently, archaeologists also have been uncertain as to the nature of occupation of the northern Ozarks during the Middle Woodland, mostly because of the rarity of diagnostic Hopewell pottery. The few diagnostic Middle Woodland ceramics found suggested ties to the Mississippi River valley, but the low numbers suggested that the northern Ozarks was not a part of the Hopewell Interaction Sphere. Because of this, it was thought by many that the region was unoccupied or at best a hinterland. Chapman (1980) supported this interpretation on the basis of the rarity of ceramic artifacts and suggested that the region was used as a buffer for cultures to the east and west. Clearly the region was not close to Hopewellian centers such as the lower Illinois Havana-Hopewell, the central Mississippi River, the Big Bend Missouri Valley sites, or the so-called Kansas City Hopewell areas (Kay 1980; O'Brien and Wood 1998). Coupled with the virtual invisibility of archaeological data from the Early Woodland, it was easy to construct a northern Ozarks marginality paradigm for this period.

Key to any treatment of Middle Woodland is the understanding of local differences in lithics and ceramics and their association with dateable intact deposits. This often is a difficult proposition in caves and rockshelters, where the majority of these sites have witnessed vandalism and bioturbation. Fort Leonard Wood survey and testing projects have identified seventeen Middle Woodland sites, eleven of which are identified on the basis of the surface recovery of temporally diagnostic Kings Corner-Notched or Snyders projectile points (Figure 6.4, *a*). The remaining six sites contain artifacts or dated intact Middle Woodland deposits. Seven radiocarbon dates have been obtained from five of these sites, all caves or rockshelters, providing a chronometric range of 200 B.C. to A.D. 400 for Fort Leonard Wood Middle Woodland components (Table 6.1). Hopewell or Hopewell-like ceramics are all but absent at Fort Leonard Wood. There, the Hopewell-like pottery consists of one dentate stamped sherd with a row of small punctations, from 23PU265 (Figure 6.4, *b*), one dentate rocker-stamped sherd from 23PU719 (Figure 6.4, *c*), and a rimsherd with cross-hatched rim decoration, reed punctates

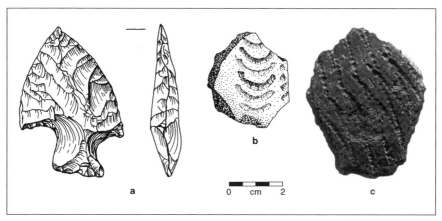

Figure 6.4 — Middle Woodland artifacts: a, Kings Corner-Notched projectile point; b, dentate stamped sherd; c, dentate rocker-stamped sherd

below the rim, and incised line decorations on the body from Miller Cave (23PU2). O'Brien and Wood (1998) identify ceramics from the nearby Tick Creek Cave in the Gasconade drainage as possible Havana types. In contrast, eastern Missouri sites such as Burkemper, Creve Coeur, La Plant, and 23MA3 produced sizable quantities of Havana pottery (O'Brien 1985; O'Brien and Wood 1998), and to the north in Callaway County, Havana-like pottery such as Neteler and Naples with stamped designs similar to those in the lower Illinois Valley has been found. Aside from Hopewellian ceramics, thin grit-tempered pottery similar to Middle Woodland utilitarian wares from other parts of the Midwest has been identified in low frequencies at two sites in the Fort Leonard Wood area, 23PU719 and 23PH17. Pottery from 23PU719, associated with a Middle Woodland radiocarbon date, has affinities with the Baytown Plain–Mulberry Creek Cord Marked complex of the lower Mississippi River valley (Ahler et al. 1998).

While earlier researchers (e.g., C. Chapman 1980; J. B. Griffin 1958; Kay 1980) proposed that the distribution of Havana styles was a result of migration lured by bison, others suggested the distribution was simply the spread of styles following various drainages from the western Illinois core area around A.D. 100. However appealing the scenario that Havana pottery styles diffused westward, most pottery dating to the Middle Woodland period in Missouri is undecorated. The near absence of stamped or incised pottery has encouraged some to assume that large regions of the state had been abandoned or were used ephemerally during the period.

If Middle Woodland pottery, albeit non-Hopewellian, is present to a limited extent in the northern Ozarks, a firmer basis for recognizing this period is a suite of projectile points and radiocarbon assays (Ahler et al. 1995a, 1995b, 1997, 1998; Kreisa et al. 1996; Reeder 1988). Reeder (1988:196) has stressed that although a Middle Woodland ceramic expression is elusive, lithic artifacts are abundant. Point types such as Snyders, Steuben, Manker, Ansell, and Kings Corner-Notched are well represented in the Gasconade drainage. Additionally, although such situations are mainly reported from caves and rockshelters, a few open sites such as Feeler have aceramic components between Late Archaic and Late Woodland strata. Similar components identified at Tick Creek Cave and Williams Shelter have supported this characterization of northern Ozarks Middle Woodland occupations. These and other sites led Reeder (1988) to propose a Middle Woodland Spring Creek complex. It is likely that the Spring Creek complex extended across much of the Gasconade drainage during the initial four centuries A.D. Although rare, Middle Woodland ceramics clearly are associated with this complex.

Another key area of investigation is northern Ozarks Middle Woodland plant use. In the central Mississippi and lower Illinois river valleys the subsistence base grew from an existing group that included chenopod, sunflower, marshelder, and cucurbits. Maygrass, knotweed, and little barley became increasingly abundant throughout the Middle Woodland period (Asch and Asch 1978, 1985a; Watson 1985). In eastern Missouri, botanical evidence from the Burkemper site (O'Brien 1996) is comparable to the ubiquity of starchy seeds in Middle Woodland features from the lower Illinois and central Mississippi River valleys. In contrast, analysis of numerous flotation samples obtained from Middle Woodland components at Fort Leonard Wood has yielded no data indicative of increased cultigen utilization. Specific starchy seeds like goosefoot and maygrass are present, but in very low numbers.

The recovery of diagnostic projectile points, stratigraphic positioning, and a suite of radiocarbon dates have clearly shown that a Middle Woodland presence exists within some areas of the Gasconade drainage, but as with the Early Woodland period, defining a local Middle Woodland phase continues to be difficult (Ahler et al. 1998). Although some evidence of distinctive ceramic styles is present, evidence of exchange networks, mound building, and the intensive use of cultigens is absent. Thin grit-tempered pottery similar to Middle Woodland utilitarian wares from other parts of the Midwest has been identified in low frequencies in this area. Other artifacts traditionally used as markers of the Middle Woodland such as Snyders or Kings Corner-Notched points are present in dated contexts at sites 23PU235, 23PU249, 23PU265, and 23PU567 (Figure 6.2). All of these sites contain strata that date between about 1600 and 2100 years ago, and all of these strata have produced aceramic assemblages (Ahler et al. 1998).

While certain Middle Woodland ceramics and projectile points occur, it is doubtful that other cultural patterns common in the midcontinent such as intensive use of native cultigens, complex settlement hierarchy, social differentiation in mortuary practices, and participation in panregional exchange are expressed in any northern Ozarks Middle Woodland manifestation.

Late Woodland

Over the past 50 years, four individuals—Carl Chapman, Richard Marshall, R. Bruce McMillan, and Robert Reeder—have largely been responsible for the definition of Late Woodland in the northern Ozarks. Initially, Chapman (1948b) defined the Highland aspect of the Woodland tradition based on Fowke (1922) and Fenenga (1938), as well as his own research, and identified grit-tempered pottery as characteristic. A decade later R. Marshall (1963, 1965b, 1966) revised the Highland aspect on the basis of excavations at a number of sites along the Bourbeuse and Meramec rivers. Excavations at rockshelters, mounds, and open-air "refuse areas" were used to define the Maramec Spring phase. Maramec Cord Marked and Plain ceramics characterized this phase, although small amounts of ceramics tempered with quartzite, chert, sand, and fired clay were present. Associated projectile points included Scallorn, Crisp Ovate, Rice Side-Notched, and Kings Corner-Notched. McMillan (1963:115–19) expanded the phase geographically into the Gasconade River drainage and elaborated on the traits of associated material culture.

Reeder (1988:204) later reviewed and redefined the Maramec Spring phase. He characterized this construct as distinctive and readily recognized as a result of the relatively widespread presence of pottery, but at the same time as ambiguous because of the problem of mixture of deposits at investigated sites. From a review of excavations, Reeder (1988:206, 208) identified an early Maramec Spring phase associated with only Late Woodland material culture and a late Maramec Spring phase associated with low frequencies of Mississippian material culture. The introduction of Mississippian material culture appeared to occur sometime during the tenth century A.D., although only six Late Woodland radiocarbon dates from four sites in the northern Ozarks were available to Reeder during his study. More recently, Reeder (1999) has provided a detailed discussion of the history, geographical extent, components, material culture, and chronology of this phase, although he no longer divides it into early and late subphases.

Late Woodland components, easily recognized by cord-marked or plain limestone/dolomite-tempered ceramics, frequently are encountered during site excavations at Fort Leonard Wood. Of forty-two sites tested, twenty-six have Late Woodland components (Ahler et al. 1995a, 1995b, 1996, 1997, 1998, 1999; Childress and Weaver 1998; Kreisa [ed.] 1995; Kreisa et al. 1996). These include caves and rockshelters, plus ridge crest and terrace open-air sites. Securely dated contexts, though, are mainly from caves and rockshelters. While it is not unusual to find Late Woodland projectile points at open-air sites, corresponding intact deposits are rare. Only one open-air site, 23PU614, has yielded ceramics associated with a feature and radiocarbon date (Ahler et al. 1999). In addition, previous investigations have shown that the numerous cairns (Niquette 1984) and three petroglyph sites (Ahler et al. 1999) in the area date to the Late Woodland period. While a great number of Late Woodland sites have been identified, the data here discussed are from eighteen components at fourteen sites having securely dated contexts, as well as from other nearby Late Woodland sites (see Figure 6.2).

Early Maramec Spring Subphase (A.D. 400–900)
Early Maramec Spring components originally were defined as having only Late Woodland material culture (Reeder 1988:208). While recent investigations have found this artifact pattern to be substantially true, a few instances of chronologically early components with minimal Mississippian traits have been found. The date of A.D. 400 for the beginning of the Maramec Spring phase is based on the co-occurrence of Maramec ceramics with Kings Corner-Notched and Rice Side-Notched projectile points as identified in an Archaeological Survey of Missouri site file review recently conducted by one of the authors. Earlier Middle Woodland components in the area appear to be associated with Snyders and Kings Corner-Notched points and with few or no ceramics. The continued use of Kings Corner-Notched points between the Middle Woodland and Late Woodland periods may indicate population continuity between the two periods, although Reeder (1999) has recently suggested an absence of Woodland populations in the area prior to the Maramec Spring phase. Ten securely dated early Late Woodland components have been excavated at Fort Leonard Wood, nine at enclosed sites and one from a cairn. Twelve radiocarbon dates from these ten sites document a continuity of occupation throughout the early subphase (Table 6.1).

Projectile points from the early Maramec Spring components include Kings Corner-Notched, Rice Side-Notched, Gary Contracting Stemmed, Langtry, triangular, Scallorn, Klunk Side-Notched, Koster Side-Notched, Lowe Flared Base, Cupp, and untyped flake points (Figure 6.5, *a–g*). Of the eighty total projectile points from the early Maramec Spring assemblages, exactly one-half are small arrow points and one-half are larger side-notched, corner-notched, or stemmed forms. Most numerous, both in terms of num-

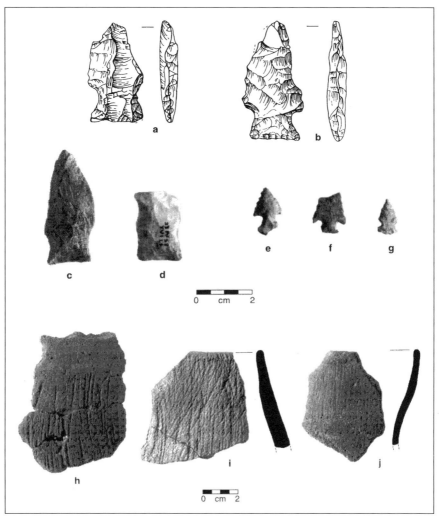

Figure 6.5 — Late Woodland artifacts: a–b, Kings Corner-Notched projectile points; c–d, Rice Side-Notched projectile points; e–g, Scallorn projectile points; h–j, Maramec Cord Marked ceramics

ber of sites (4) and total number (30), are Rice Side-Notched points. Smaller arrow points consisting of Scallorn (3 sites, 23 points), untyped flake (3 sites, 5 points), and triangular (2 sites, 8 points) are next most common. As common as the latter two point types is Kings Corner-Notched, five of which were found at two sites. Aside from Langtry, which was found at two sites, all other point types associated with the early subphase consist of one to two examples from a single site.

The ceramic assemblage is numerically dominated by Maramec Plain and Cord Marked, although a few non-dolomite–tempered ceramics are present (Figure 6.5, *h–j*). The Maramec series ceramics are either plain or cord-marked jars; only single examples of incised and knot-fabric (net?) impressed Maramec sherds have been found. Other temper types identified include grog, grit, sand, and shell. The former three tempers are minor components of assemblages, having been found at a single site each. Shell tempering, a hallmark of the Mississippian time period and culture in the Mississippi River valley to the east, has been found at three early Maramec Spring sites at Fort Leonard Wood, although only five shell-tempered sherds, including one from a bowl, have been found. Shell-tempered pottery was also recovered at Merrell Cave (23PH64), where a date of A.D. 723 would suggest an association with this early subphase. The ceramics and radiocarbon date, however, are not directly associated (Yelton 1995b). The cultural origin of shell-tempered sherds in the northern Ozarks is presently unknown. The presence of a shell-tempered bowl, highly unusual for the Maramec series, might suggest their importation into the northern Ozarks. In contrast, ceramics with mixed shell and dolomite temper at 23PU235 suggest local manufacture (Ahler et al. 1995b).

The presence and degree of preservation of subsistence-related data, both botanical and faunal, vary widely among sites (Kreisa et al. 1996). Most ubiquitous within botanical assemblages are nuts, including walnut, hickory, and acorn. Starchy seeds, such as chenopod, amaranth, and knotweed, are present, but in small numbers. So-called tropical cultigens, maize and cucurbits, are also present in small amounts. Maize is present in three of nine assemblages, while cucurbits are present in only one of nine assemblages. Among the three assemblages with maize, only one to three kernel fragments have been recovered in each. Faunal assemblages, when of a large size, exhibit a great diversity of species. Mammal remains tend to dominate, although large and diverse fish and bird assemblages are present at some sites. Not surprisingly, white-tailed deer appear to have provided a substantial portion of the meat used by the region's inhabitants.

Late Maramec Spring Subphase
Reeder (1988:208) defined the late subphase as an essentially Late Woodland manifestation with additional Mississippian traits, with the division between the two subphases occurring after A.D. 910 (Reeder 1988:208). We have taken the beginning of this subphase to be A.D. 900, with the viewpoint that the initial 100 years may possibly represent an admixture of early and late subphase attributes. Nine radiocarbon assays from eight different sites date the late subphase in the Fort Leonard Wood area (Table 6.1). Six assays

date to the initial three centuries (A.D. 900–1200) while three date rather late, from the fourteenth through mid-fifteenth centuries (A.D. 1300–1450). Dates attributed to the thirteenth century are lacking, but this probably represents a matter of sampling rather than a lack of occupation. This suite of radiocarbon dates suggests a continuous and late occupation of the northern Ozarks.

Projectile point forms after A.D. 900 consist of arrow points such as Scallorn, Reed Side-Notched, triangular, and untyped flake points (Figure 6.5, *e–g*), although a few Rice Side-Notched and Kings Side-Notched points are present. In three assemblages dating to the initial century of the late subphase, Rice Side-Notched and Kings Corner-Notched forms comprise 75 percent of the projectile points found. After approximately A.D. 1000, 86 percent of the projectile points found are small arrow forms, such as Scallorn and untyped flake points. The data also indicate an apparent decrease in the variety of point types between the early and late subphases.

Shell-tempered sherds are present at six of ten late components, although Maramec series sherds continue to dominate all assemblages. Shell-tempered sherds are present on the surface and in disturbed contexts at one of the other four sites, while the final three have small (fewer than 50 sherds) assemblages. This suggests that shell-tempered sherds are ubiquitous in large late subphase assemblages. Similar to the earlier portion of the Maramec Spring subphase, most vessels, whether Maramec series or shell tempered, are plain or cord-marked jars. Other forms identified include a shell-tempered bowl and a possible pan or plate fragment (Ahler et al. 1998). Surfaces are predominantly plain or cord-marked, although occasional knot- or fabric-impressed, incised, and red-slipped sherds are present. Punctated sherds have also been found in disturbed contexts.

Subsistence remains associated with the late subphase components are remarkably similar to those discussed above for the early subphase components, perhaps because of the similarity of preservational and site-use constraints. Nuts are the most prevalent botanical subsistence item, while seeds, maize, and cucurbits are present but uncommon. Maize was found in three of ten assemblages while cucurbits were found in two of ten components. No more than four maize fragments have been found in the dated late components at any single site. Interestingly, no beans, common in some late prehistoric cultures (Rossen and Edging 1987), have been found at late subphase sites. Also similar to the early subphase, larger faunal assemblages exhibit a diversity of species with mammals dominant.

Late Woodland Settlement Patterns
Coincident with the increase, visibility, and identifiability of Late Wood-

land sites in the northern Ozarks is what appears to be a substantial reorganization of settlement, with at least two major changes from earlier patterns of Woodland settlement in the area. First, large village sites with numerous pit features are present during the Late Woodland period. Cairns, petroglyphs, caves and rockshelters, and smaller open-air sites also occur. The large, multiseason village is perhaps the archaeologically most impressive, but poorly understood, site type at Fort Leonard Wood. Four such villages, Feeler (Reeder 1982, 1988, 1999), Dead Deer (Reeder 1999), Kimberlin (Geier 1975), and Pippen (McMillan 1965), have been excavated in close proximity to the installation (Figure 6.2). Radiocarbon dates from two of these sites place the Late Woodland occupation between roughly A.D. 875 and 1100. These village sites evidence a number of similarities: all are large (over 2 hectares), contain midden or numerous features, and have yielded large artifact samples. Excavations at Feeler and Dead Deer revealed numerous storage/refuse pits, hearths, postmolds, and midden areas, and botanical remains including nuts, seeds, and maize (Reeder 1982, 1988, 1999).

Second, large-scale surveys conducted at Fort Leonard Wood indicate that some of the Late Woodland site types appear to have been organized into spatially coherent site complexes. A site complex has been defined as a set of spatially clustered sites that are temporally and functionally related and may consist of cave, rockshelter, cairn, rock art, and blufftop and alluvial base camps and extractive sites. Two of the more intensively investigated site complexes, Miller Cave and Lohraff, share many structural similarities. Both are organized around large upland peninsulas adjacent to major streams, the Big Piney River and Roubidoux Creek (Figure 6.2). Both include cairn, petroglyph, cave and rockshelter, and smaller open-air specialized function encampments. Large village sites also may be associated with such complexes, but this has yet to be documented.

The Miller Cave complex is located along the Big Piney River (Figure 6.2). Investigations at two cave/rockshelter sites, an open-air site, cairns, and a petroglyph complex suggest the presence of a wide range of site functions (Ahler et al. 1995a, 1995b). The two closed sites are Miller and Sadie's Cave. Miller Cave has been greatly impacted by looting, but investigations in the 1920s and 1990s provided evidence of site use as a mortuary and ritual location based on the presence of a number of human and two dog burials. Supporting this interpretation is a complex of three rock cairns (23PU254) located along the bluff crest above Miller Cave. In contrast, excavations at nearby Sadie's Cave recovered a generalized faunal and floral assemblage and a specialized tool assemblage. Lithic reduction focused on biface production, while tools centered on cutting and hide working. This site is interpreted as a short-term specialized field camp. Between Miller

Cave and Sadie's Cave is the Miller Petroglyphs site. This site, now heavily damaged, consisted of a number of zoomorphs and bisected ovals (Ahler et al. 1995b). Above the two closed sites is 23PU288, an open-air bluff-crest site. Excavations indicate that a highest density of material is near the bluff crest above the two cave sites that represents discrete, short-term, relatively intense occupational episodes (Ahler et al. 1995b). The lithic assemblage suggests a focus on biface production and maintenance.

Researchers have suggested that populations occupying the Miller Cave complex resided at two sites located to the south on floodplain terraces of the Big Piney River (Ahler et al. 1995b). Investigations of these sites, 23PU3 and 23PU4, are restricted to descriptions made in the 1920s (Fowke 1922). Site 23PU3 is described as a village with house mounds. Mortars and pottery, as well as stone tools, were found at this site. The other, 23PU4, is described as once having a ditched embankment that enclosed house mounds. Pottery, stone tools, and animal bone were also abundant.

The second example of a site complex is the newly discovered grouping of Late Woodland sites known as the Lohraff complex (Ahler et al. 1999; Kreisa and Adams 1999). The complex is located on and around the Lohraff Peninsula, which is created by Roubidoux Creek and its floodplain (Figure 6.2). This complex includes a cairn, a petroglyph site, a large open-air habitation site on the bluff crest, a cave and two rockshelters at various elevations along the bluff slope, and a small open-air habitation site at the base of the bluff on a floodplain terrace. A number of other sites without diagnostic Late Woodland artifacts are present in the immediate vicinity of these sites. These floodplain terrace sites can be characterized as generally small, with low densities and diversities of artifacts suggestive of relatively short-term camps (Kreisa and Adams 1999). As of 2000, test excavations have been conducted only at two of the rockshelters and two open-air sites, while nonintrusive data collection has been conducted at the petroglyph site (Ahler et al. 1999; Kreisa 2000).

Juxtaposed between cairn, blufftop, cave, and creek are the Lohraff Petroglyphs. While some of the motifs at this site are common in Missouri, some are unique and highly suggestive of dichotomous earth and sky aspects of Native American cosmology (Figure 6.6). The earth motifs can be separated into two groups: vulvar motifs and an anthropomorphic shaman motif. Vulvar motifs, consisting of partially bisected circle/oval elements, are also found at the Miller Cave and Ramsey Cave complexes and at other sites in southeastern and eastern Missouri. The vulvar motif represents female or fertility motifs similar to those that other researchers have called the Earth Mother or Mother Corn, a female deity known to most Eastern Woodland and Plains tribes (Diaz-Granados 1999; R. Hall 1997; Prentice 1986).

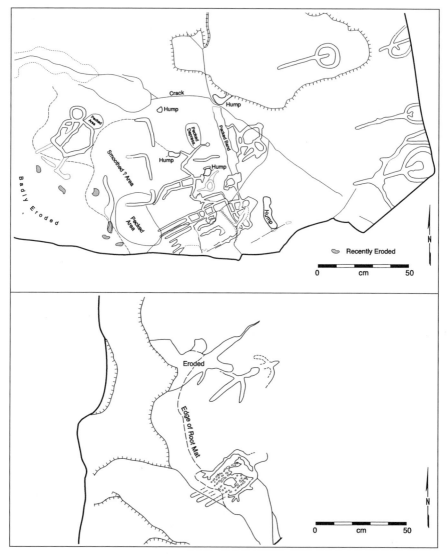

Figure 6.6 — The Lohraff Petroglyphs

R. Hall (1997:56) suggests that the bisected oval may represent a mortar and pestle, or Ho´-e-ga, the Osage ritual name for earth. Located on the same rock but clearly separated from the vulvar motifs is a shaman or priest figure (Figure 6.6). The Lohraff shaman figure seems to be stylistically unique to Fort Leonard Wood, but conceptually very similar to those seen in the Plains region (Ambrose 1998:65; Diaz-Granados 1999:216; Edging 2000; O'Neill 1981).

Just north of the shaman but on a separate rock are motifs that further support the concept of an earth/sky dichotomy (Figure 6.6). One is a spotted bird that could represent an eagle, hawk, or owl, discernible by its claws hanging down at its sides like hands, clearly defined shoulders, three tail feathers, and a pecked breast (Diaz-Granados 1999:217; Edging 2000). The Osage are reported to consider the spotted hawk or eagle their most important creature. Many North American oral traditions contain twin sons of the Earth Mother called the "thunderers," one civilized and the other wild. In several of these widespread oral traditions, the wild boy is symbolically killed and then resurrected as a spotted hawk or eagle. The presence of this motif could symbolize a vision quest in which a person seeks a guiding spirit that is then carved on a boulder (Diaz-Granados 1999:217). The motif could also be a territorial marker for a sky clan group to honor the spotted eagle or hawk. The other motifs located on this rock are bird forms that may also represent symbols of sky. The Miller Petroglyphs reportedly contained a winged zoomorph image, which Mark Wagner et al. (1999) interpret as representing a stylized Mississippian-era falcon warrior associated with the Southeastern Ceremonial Complex and which is clearly a sky motif. It is clear that both the Miller and Lohraff petroglyph sites at Fort Leonard Wood were chosen with regard to visual and physical relationships, but it is not clear whether the locations were sacred or whether the sacredness was the result of events that took place at the location. This may be a moot point, in that, as Diaz-Granados (1993:96) suggests, petroglyphs combine the power of place and the power of imagery, juxtaposing the natural and cultural worlds.

The association of rock art with habitation, processing, and ritual sites such as cairns within Late Woodland site complexes documented at Fort Leonard Wood has contextual implications for the interpretation of late prehistoric settlement systems. Rock art as a medium for the transmission of knowledge related to social events (such as death or burial) or to ideology and cosmology and the close proximity of rock art to habitation and processing sites in these site complexes suggest the extent to which the sacred and secular were interconnected. Ongoing archaeological research centering on these site complexes provides a unique opportunity to investigate this interconnection of the sacred and secular in the Late Woodland period, our last archaeological link to the Historic-era tribes in the northern Ozarks.

Conclusions

The recent increase in archaeological fieldwork in the northern Ozarks, with the Fort Leonard Wood archaeological program a key component, has greatly increased our understanding of the Woodland period in this region. This fieldwork has led us to interpret the archaeological record as evidencing cultural and population continuity rather than periodic abandonment, based on an increased ability to identify Early and Middle Woodland sites. The growing body of evidence appears to support a continuation of resident populations at least from the Late Archaic through the Late Woodland period. But for this same time span, there is little evidence for change in resource base or climatic factors. Changes in social conditions are a different, and perhaps more elusive, matter.

Our interpretation of population continuity is based on the radiocarbon dates and associated assemblages discussed above. Clearly, populations were present in the study area throughout the Woodland period. One problem in recognizing them has been the paucity of ceramics associated with the Early Woodland and Middle Woodland periods. The general lack of ceramics has lessened archaeologists' ability to identify components, leading some to deny their existence in the study area and others to question the nature of resident populations. While the increased number of Early Woodland and Middle Woodland radiocarbon dates should show that the former position lacks validity, arguments concerning the latter position are more in the realm of chronological systematics. We view the Early Woodland and Middle Woodland as essentially temporal constructs *sensu* Stoltman (1978), and hence Woodland period populations are present in the northern Ozarks. The cultural affinity and adaptive strategies and lifeways of those populations are separate questions that remain open to discussion. This problem appears, in part, to be related to the degree of interaction between northern Ozarks Woodland period populations and cultures in adjacent regions that fit current archaeological understanding of Early Woodland and Middle Woodland cultures.

The degree of interaction between northern Ozarks populations and Middle Woodland Hopewell and later Mississippian centers remains uncertain, but appears to have been minimal. The resident population was almost certainly aware of these cultural manifestations, but may have intentionally chosen to limit social, political, and economic interactions. The relative geographic isolation of the northern Ozarks provides an excellent opportunity to reexamine and formally test ideas of cultural conservatism and marginality. The present data suggest that while there was limited interregional contact between the inhabitants of the northern Ozarks and those in surrounding areas, the northern Ozarks was by no means completely isolated. Limited contact and interaction with surrounding groups, adherence to a well-established hunting/gathering subsistence pattern, and possible long-term population stability are factors that suggest local Early and Middle Woodland populations may be identified by a unique material culture that is distinct from that of better-documented contemporary groups inhabiting the Missouri and Mississippi river valleys. Even the substantial reorganization of settlement, subsistence, and material culture evident at the beginning of the Late Woodland period is apparently dissimilar to trends in settlement and social reorganization documented in other regions in the Midsouth and Midwest (D. Braun 1977; J. Brown 1984; Tainter 1977). The northern Ozarks again appears to have retained its own unique cultural expressions in spite of massive changes in technology, settlement, subsistence, ideology, and social organization that are well documented for surrounding regions during the Woodland period.

Chapter 7

Woodland Period Archaeology in the American Bottom

John E. Kelly

B etween 600 B.C. and A.D. 1000 much of the eastern United States was a dynamic cultural landscape involving the interaction of human populations of varying sizes and levels of intensity. Evidence for this interaction is expressed archaeologically in stylistic affinities and the actual presence of artifactual materials. This presentation focuses on the context of the 1600 years of Woodland interaction between those populations in the Southeast and those of the lower Midwest, especially the area of the American Bottom.

As noted by James B. Griffin (1986a:42):

> The term Woodland for archaeological cultures was adapted from the ethnographic culture area divided into northeast and southeast regions. Woodland archaeological complexes were soon divided into Early, Middle, and Late by stratigraphy and superposition recognized in Illinois in the early 1930s and then carried to the New York area and the Southeast with the relief labor excavations, providing supportive data by stratigraphy and comparative studies in the mid-to-late 1930s.

Griffin was also a participant in the 1941 Woodland Conference, which produced the classic trait list from this gathering of soon-to-be-famous archaeologists (Woodland Conference 1943). More detail on regional Woodland cultures appeared in Griffin's edited tribute to Fay-Cooper Cole (Griffin [ed.] 1952), which is an important point of departure for any discussion of the Woodland tradition. Although we have come considerably further in our attempts to understand the dynamics of those early ceramic-producing societies and their histories, we have a long way to go.

There is no doubt that Griffin had the best grasp of the overall culture-historical framework in which we continue to work. His trips to see collections and excavations were undoubtedly the source of this intuitive inspiration, by which he understood and communicated the way in which archaeo-

logical materials were distributed in time and space. He knew the direction-
ality of change particularly as it regarded ceramics. It is in this spirit that I
will attempt to convey the nature of the Woodland tradition in the American
Bottom and its relationship to coeval complexes in the Midwest and Southeast. I will focus especially on the continuity of occupation within the American Bottom. One implicit, if not explicit, tendency we have is to assume that
the occupation of a region was relatively continuous in time and space. Of
course we know that this was probably not the case and that the degree of
continuity is perhaps not as great as is generally suspected. In part this can
be attributed to the relatively low density of population until the end of the
Woodland tradition when the density began to increase (J. Kelly 1992).

The term *American Bottom* originally was employed in the late eigh-
teenth century to delineate the eastern Mississippi floodplain between Alton,
Illinois, and the mouth of the Kaskaskia River at Chester, Illinois (Figure
7.1). Archaeologically, most employ the term to embrace a larger area that
incorporates the adjacent uplands (e.g., Bareis and Porter 1984; J. Kelly
1990a). To understand the changes within the American Bottom it is critical
to look beyond the bluff crests bordering the Mississippi Valley. Even given
some low population densities, the interaction of the various groups across
the landscape of the midcontinent was quite dynamic.

My perspective is presented from atop Monks Mound, located at the
northern part of the American Bottom. I will draw on the recent and not-so-
recent works of researchers not only in the American Bottom, but also in the
adjoining regions of western and southern Illinois and eastern Missouri.
Within the past two decades, many individuals have been involved in the
study of the various episodes of the Woodland tradition.

The American Bottom Database

Most researchers look to the more recent investigative results as the basis
for securing some sense of the Woodland tradition in the American Bottom.
Certainly the FAI-270 work (Bareis and Porter 1984) of the late 1970s and
1980s was critical in the establishment of the overall superstructure. Studies
of the Woodland tradition, however, extend back to the beginning of the
century with the survey and testing efforts of Warren King Moorehead in
the 1920s at a number of sites outside of the large Mississippian center of
Cahokia (J. Kelly 1999). Sites such as the Wood River Mounds (a.k.a. Grassy
Lake site) (J. Kelly 2000; Moorehead 1929:62–64), Sullivan's Mound (a.k.a.
Clark's Mound) (Moorehead 1929:56–57), and the Aluminum Ore Mound
(a.k.a. the Lohmann site) (J. Kelly 1999) produced a scattering of Woodland

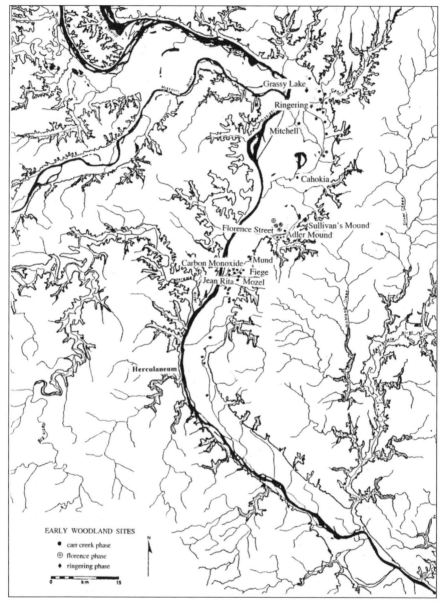

Figure 7.1 — Distribution of Early Woodland sites in the American Bottom

materials covering the entire sequence. While Moorehead recognized some of the cultural differences, a viable contextual framework did not emerge until the next decade with the development of the Midwestern taxonomic system.

Systematic survey and excavation in the region really began with the WPA work across the river in Jefferson County, Missouri, with the combined efforts of the young professional Robert McCormack Adams and the enthusiastic amateur Frank Magre (R. Adams and Magre 1939). J. B. Griffin (1941) had an important hand in sorting out some of the differences in the ceramic assemblages for this portion of the region. In 1949, Griffin and Spaulding (1952) established the Central Mississippi Valley Survey and began a systematic examination of amateur collections. During the 1940s and 1950s amateur work in the region was at its peak, filling an important void, given the lack of any in-place professionals. Preston Holder was, for a brief period in the 1950s, the first professional at a local institution (Washington University) to conduct work in the region (Pauketat 1993), mostly at Cahokia and other nearby Mississippian sites. Fowler (1959) conducted excavations farther south in the region at Modoc Rock Shelter, a predominately Archaic location, although the upper deposits contained evidence of Woodland through Mississippian activity.

The first systematic surveys that resulted in an analysis and discussion of the culture-historical sequence in the American Bottom were the surveys conducted by Munson (1971) and Harn (1971). These surveys came about as a result of the multi-institutional highway salvage work conducted at the Mississippian mound centers of Cahokia and Mitchell in the early 1960s. In addition to survey work, excavations were conducted by Porter (1963) at sites with Woodland occupations, including Grassy Lake and Indian Creek. Nearly a decade after Munson's and Harn's surveys, Keith Brandt of the University of Wisconsin-Milwaukee conducted follow-up surveys on some of the same sites. In the late 1960s and early 1970s, a statewide initiative, put in motion as a result of the 1966 Historic Preservation Act, resulted in the survey of numerous regions within the state of Illinois (see M. K. Brown [ed.] 1981). For the American Bottom, surveys were implemented across the entire region from the mouth of the Kaskaskia (Fortier 1981; Porter 1972) to the uplands east of the American Bottom (Denny and Anderson 1972, 1974). Except for Schroeder's (1997) dissertation research in the southern two-thirds of the American Bottom region, much of this earlier work remains unreported. Schroeder's work was an integral part of Milner's (1998) reexamination of the collections in the southern part of the region.

With the implementation of cultural resource management laws in the 1960s and 1970s, the amount of survey work increased, especially with regard to proposed highway projects. Certainly the most publicized has been the FAI-270 project, which was initiated with an extensive survey corridor. The project received national recognition for the mitigation efforts on over twenty sites that covered most of the cultural continuum in the region and resulted in the clear formulation of the Woodland sequence in the American Bottom. Since the early 1990s, with new legislation in Illinois, other development projects have been included in the process and have added much new data to our understanding of the Woodland occupations. It simply is not possible to tabulate all of the work that has occurred. Given the forces of development that are randomly and rapidly erasing the local archaeological record, such work is increasingly important.

The Early Woodland

The Woodland period traditionally has been parsed into tripartite divisions or periods. The dates for the beginnings and ends of these periods vary from one region to the next. The onset of the Woodland tradition in the Midwest can be equated almost solely with the introduction of ceramics (Farnsworth and Emerson [eds.] 1986). Along the coast and portions of the interior Southeast, ceramics had already been produced for over 1000 years (Sassaman 1993a, this volume). The thick-walled, flat-bottomed pots of the greater Midwest comprise a northern ceramic tradition that appears earlier in the northeast, with the Vinette I series, and over several centuries spread farther west, where similar vessels have been designated Fayette Thick in northern Kentucky and other parts of the middle Ohio River drainage (Farnsworth and Emerson [eds.] 1986). Similar ceramics known as Swannanoa extend down the west flank of the Appalachians into east Tennessee (Keel 1976). In the northern and western parts of the Midwest along the upper Mississippi River, by 600 B.C., Marion Thick pottery and Kramer points comprise a complex known as Marion culture (Munson 1966). A number of phases have been assigned to this complex for each of the subregions in which it occurs. In certain respects the distribution is discontinuous.

Three Early Woodland phases have been identified in the American Bottom: Carr Creek, Florence, and Ringering (Figures 7.1 and 7.2). A fourth construct, the Columbia complex, is included as a late element in the broader Florence culture (Emerson and Fortier 1986). Until recently the scattered Black Sand materials recovered were left without any other designation. The latest excavations at the Ringering site (B. Evans et al. 1997) resulted in the recovery of Black Sand materials from feature contexts, and Evans (1994, 1995) has proposed that these materials warrant the creation of a new phase for Black Sand materials in the American Bottom known as Ringering.

Marion Culture: Carr Creek Phase
In general, Marion Thick vessels are undecorated, thick-walled cauldrons

Dates A.D./B.C. (calibrated)	Cultural Periods	Cultures	American Bottom Phases (north)	(south)
1000 ·	Emergent Mississippian			
900 ·				
800 ·	Late Woodland		Sponemann	
700 ·			Patrick	Patrick
600 ·				
500 ·			Mund	Mund
400 ·			Rosewood	Rosewood
300 ·	Middle Woodland	Pike-Baehr	Hill Lake	Hill Lake
200 ·				
100 ·		Havana-Hopewell	Holding II	Holding II
0 ·			Holding I	Holding I
100 ·		Early Havana	Cement Hollow	Cement Hollow
200 ·	Early Woodland	Black Sand	Ringering	
300 ·				
400 ·			Florence	
500 ·				
600 ·		Marion	Carr Creek	Carr Creek
700 ·				
800 ·	Late Archaic			

Figure 7.2 — American Bottom Woodland chronology (adapted from Bareis and Porter 1984; Fortier et al. 1989b; Kelly 1990a; McElrath and Fortier 2000)

with exterior and interior textured surfaces. Some vessels exhibit thinner walls. Most vessels are coarsely tempered with grit, although Porter (1974) has also demonstrated the use of grog. The only possible decoration might be the individual cord impressions on some Marion Thick sherds (D. Morgan 1992:135), but no decorative pattern is yet evident. Griffin (1952b:98, 100) noted a sherd with a Black Sand Incised decoration on the exterior and a Marion Thick style of horizontal cord marking on the interior, thus suggesting the possible continuity of Marion into Black Sand.

In addition to the ubiquitous diagnostics of Marion Thick and Kramer points, Red Ochre cache blades from mortuary contexts are considered an integral part of Marion culture (Esarey 1986). As attested to by the Carr Creek phase in the American Bottom, there is a discontinuity between Marion culture and the terminal Late Archaic Prairie Lake phase. Significant differences extend beyond the mere presence or introduction of ceramics. Most notable are the stylistic breaks in the projectile point forms and broad changes in settlement systems, from the larger sedentary communities of the Late Archaic Prairie Lake phase to the smaller seasonal encampments of the Early Woodland Carr Creek phase. Examination of Prairie Lake phase sites excavated to date (Fortier et al. 1998) suggests that the large Missouri-Pacific site is an exception, although several large Prairie Lake sites are evident along the Wood River Terrace in the northern American Bottom (B. Evans 1995; Linder et al. 1978). Another consideration in the interpretation of a large site such as Missouri-Pacific is that the Prairie Lake phase lasts several centuries, from circa 1100 to 600 B.C. uncalibrated (Fortier et al. 1998). Thus the occupation, or occupations, at Missouri-Pacific probably represent multiple reuses of an optimally located site. Nonetheless it appears that large base camps may be the exception in the settlement pattern and that the smaller sites are more apt to represent the norm and thus be more in line, at least in size, with the subsequent Early Woodland occupations.

Carr Creek phase sites in the American Bottom are concentrated in at least three areas (Figure 7.1). The heaviest concentration occurs in the area between Prairie Lake and Long Slash Creek. A second area is in the northern portion of the American Bottom along the Wood River Terrace, and a third, smaller cluster occurs near the junction of Prairie du Pont Creek and Goose Lake. A recent survey of the alluvial fan near the bluffs has added evidence for the concentration of Carr Creek phase activity in this area (Booth and Koldehoff 1999). The nearby Adler mound (J. A. Williams and Lacampagne 1982) may be part of this complex, if not of the following Florence phase. Scattered evidence of Marion culture occurs in intervening areas such as the uplands, where a Marion culture site was excavated, and on the floodplain near Cahokia Mounds, where a small cluster of shallow pits was excavated

(Witty 1993). Beneath Sullivan's Mound on the bluffs southeast of Cahokia, Moorehead (1929) excavated features containing Marion Thick sherds (Kelly 1999). Other excavations include recent work at the Ringering site (B. Evans 1995) and the recovery of Marion Thick from a feature at the Mitchell site (Porter 1974).

Most excavations, however, have been centered around the sites in the Carr Creek locale, including work at the Jean Rita (Linder 1974), Carbon Monoxide (Fortier 1985a), Fiege (Fortier 1985b), and Mund (Fortier 1983) sites. More recently, I have uncovered similar small activity loci at the Mozel site near Columbia, Illinois (Kelly 2001). With the possible exception of Jean Rita, which was only tested, these excavations revealed small concentrations of lithic and ceramic debris with few, if any, associated pit features. Most Carr Creek phase sites are located on low-lying, yet better-drained soils, which contrasts with the Prairie Lake phase sites that are preferentially located on poorly drained clayey soils. Paleoenvironmental evidence suggests changes in local hydrology (B. Evans 1995). In fact, the break between the Late Archaic and Early Woodland coincides with the Scandic climatic episode (Wendland and Bryson 1974).

In the uplands to the east and west of the Mississippi River trench, only a few Marion culture sites have been recorded. In a literature search to the west, Harl (1995) noted only one site with Early Woodland ceramics; otherwise any occupation is restricted to diagnostic lithics such as the Kramer points. Except for some possible Red Ochre cache blades near Herculeanum (R. Adams and Magre 1939), Griffin also noted the paucity of Early Woodland activity in the Jefferson County area. To the east, scattered Early Woodland activity has been recorded. A survey of a portion of Richland Creek, the first major drainage system east of the American Bottom, disclosed another cluster of Marion culture occupations (Denny 1976), but to date none have been investigated in detail.

A concentration of Marion culture sites also occurs in the lower Illinois River valley (Farnsworth and Asch 1986). In the Sny Bottom locale of the Mississippi Valley to the west, excavations revealed a well-documented continuous sequence from the Marion culture into the early Middle Woodland. Perhaps the largest or most intensively occupied site to be excavated was Ambrose Flick (Stafford [ed.] 1992), where a Black Sand occupation (Kinderhook phase) is located stratigraphically above two components of the local variant of Marion culture. Radiocarbon dates are consistent with the stratigraphy. Excavations revealed a variety of Marion culture features, including hearths, pits, and refuse areas, and Red Ochre cache blades were recovered from a non-mortuary context. A Red Ochre cache blade base was recovered from the Mozel site in the American Bottom. Ambrose Flick yielded a large quantity of little barley, as well as traces of chenopodium and maygrass, which along with squash were cultivated by the Marion culture inhabitants (Asch and Sidell 1992).

The American Bottom represents the southern distribution of Marion Thick and hence Marion culture. To the south of the Kaskaskia River, the general consensus is that the Crab Orchard tradition, with its distinctive fabric-impressed urns, has its beginnings in the Early Woodland (Butler and Jefferies 1986; Maxwell 1951; Muller 1986). Although introduced in the Early Woodland, Crab Orchard fabric-impressed ceramics are a part of a strong tradition that persists into the Middle Woodland period of southern Illinois as far north as the southern part of the American Bottom. Griffin (1952b:98) noted the co-occurrence of Crab Orchard fabric-impressed sherds with Marion Thick sherds in the uplands to the east of the American Bottom.

Florence Culture: Florence Phase

As with the preceding Late Archaic/Early Woodland transition, a discontinuous shift also occurs within the Early Woodland between the Carr Creek and subsequent Florence phases, although production of Kramer points continued, as did the use of some flat-bottomed jars. On the basis of an overlap of radiocarbon assays, Emerson and Fortier (1986) suggest that the Florence phase represents an intrusion into the region and is in part contemporary with the Carr Creek phase. Even if the Florence phase is an influx of new peoples, they probably did not travel far. More significant is the possible short-lived nature not only of the Florence Street site occupation (Emerson 1983), but also of the overall complex, given its restricted occurrence around Goose Lake (Figure 7.1).

Excavations at the Florence Street site uncovered a unique buried Early Woodland occupation consisting of a circular structure with associated features (Emerson 1983). The lithic and ceramic assemblage at Florence is similar to that obtained from the Peisker site in the lower Illinois River valley. Farnsworth and Asch (1986) argue, however, that Florence series pottery co-occurs with the Black Sand ceramics as part of the Cypress phase Black Sand occupation in the lower Illinois River valley and that Florence ceramics are imports into that area. If the Florence phase was relatively short-lived, the American Bottom Florence populations ultimately may have moved north into the lower Illinois River valley. While continued use of Kramer points indicates continuity with Marion culture, new point forms include contracting stem types of the Belknap cluster: Bradshaw stemmed and a distinctive knife form known as the Goose Lake knife or Peisker Diamonds. Also introduced at this time were humpbacked scrapers, which persist well into Middle Woodland.

Except for the fabric-impressed ceramics, little direct evidence exists for the interaction between the Southeast and Midwest during this time interval. The Florence phase exhibits influence from the Lower Mississippi Valley in the form of decorative ceramic elements, as first noted by Perino (1966) based on his excavations at the Peisker site, and possibly grog tempering. The decorative elements include fingernail pinching and incisions that are similar to the arced stamping evident to the south. While exhibiting similar methods of decorative technique and motif, American Bottom populations do not appear to reflect demographic movements, but instead widely shared modes of decoration.

Black Sand Culture: Ringering Phase

During the subsequent Black Sand culture of western Illinois, which at present is primarily an aggregate of sites in the northern American Bottom along the Wood River Terrace (B. Evans 1994, 1995) (Figure 7.1), there is an elaboration of ceramic decoration. As originally conceived, Black Sand culture was characterized by Liverpool Cord Marked and its decorative equivalent Black Sand Incised ceramics (J. B. Griffin 1952b). Incising is used to create rectilinear motifs in bands around the vessel orifice—a technique that can be readily linked to Alexander Incised and other roughly coeval types from the Midsouth (J. B. Griffin 1986a, 1986b). One of the basic research problems with Black Sand culture is its source. Munson (1986) argues that the complex is intrusive in the Illinois Valley, presumably from the west and northwest by non-ceramic proto–Black Sand populations, and that the later Middle Woodland Havana tradition of the central Illinois River valley is a descendant of Marion culture. Others, such as Griffin (1986b), are extremely skeptical of such propositions and maintain that Havana ceramics can be derived from Morton Incised and Fettie Incised, which in turn are derivatives of Black Sand. Nonetheless the decorative techniques are a product of the interaction occurring between the Illinois country and the upper part of the Lower Mississippi Valley and the adjacent upland Midsouth to the east (Farnsworth 1986).

If we are to comprehend interaction during the period from 400 to 100 B.C., the early Crab Orchard culture of southern Illinois must be better understood. One possible variant of the early Crab Orchard tradition is Baumer, a term introduced by Willis (1941) based on excavations near the Kincaid site. Baumer is similar to the grit-tempered ceramics of the Crab Orchard tradition, but is limestone tempered. Strong affinities with Crab Orchard were noted by Maxwell (1951) and have been reiterated by more recent authors (Butler and Jefferies 1986; Muller 1986). Perhaps the most intriguing aspect of Baumer ceramics is the decorative modes, which include cord

impressions, incisions, punctation, and collared sherds that seem to have
ties with Tchula period materials in southeast Missouri (Price 1986) and
northeast Arkansas (D. Morse and P. Morse 1983). The cord-impressed sherds
are reminiscent of the type Cormorant Cord Impressed defined for materials
in northwest Mississippi (Phillips 1970; Phillips et al. 1951). Resolving the
spatial distribution of these materials is an important first step toward understanding interaction between societies throughout the Midsouth and Lower
Mississippi Valley north into Illinois.

The Middle Woodland

The Middle Woodland period represents the first major cultural climax in
the Midwest. Attempts to characterize Middle Woodland societies as
chiefdoms cultivating maize have been laid to rest (D. Braun 1977), but
elaborate ritual and burial ceremonialism were widespread, transcending
the various regional sequences, in what has been called the Hopewell Interaction Sphere (Caldwell 1964). While occasional traces of maize are present
(Riley et al. 1994), it was a minor crop overshadowed by the numerous
native cultigens that had emerged and taken root in the broad-spectrum subsistence cycle (B. D. Smith 1992c).

The northern two-thirds of Illinois are encompassed within the Havana
tradition, which extends into northern Indiana, southern Wisconsin, and eastern Missouri and Iowa. As discussed earlier, the enduring Crab Orchard
tradition of southern Illinois's Shawnee Hills has roots extending back into
the Early Woodland and that are in turn linked with the fabric-impressed
wares of the Tennessee drainage to the south. Griffin (1952c) argued that the
direct descendant of Black Sand was the Morton complex consisting of
Morton Incised, Sister Creeks Punctated, and Neteler Stamped, *var. Crescent.* The decorative techniques of these ceramics were applied to the surfaces of the Middle Woodland utilitarian wares Havana Cord Marked and
Havana Plain. Although Griffin initially characterized them as Early Woodland wares, these types mark the appearance of Middle Woodland in western Illinois.

The onset of the Middle Woodland was not abrupt. Continuity is evident in the incised chevrons of Black Sand, Morton Incised, and Fettie Incised. In fact, Griffin (1952b) considered the latter two types as Early Woodland wares, while others such as Cantwell (1980) included them in early
Havana. To Cantwell (1980) the onset of the Havana ceramic tradition begins with the appearance of Havana Cord Marked and Plain vessels. Her
analysis of excavated materials from Dickson Camp resulted in the formula-

tion of the Caldwell phase, which preceded the Fulton phase defined at the nearby Pond site in the central Illinois River valley (J. B. Griffin et al. 1970).

Maher (1996) synthesized data from twenty-three Middle Woodland sites across the American Bottom region. Most sites are clustered in the northern corner of the American Bottom (Figure 7.3), but several other locales are represented, including the area west of the Mississippi River in the lower portion of the Missouri River drainage; a cluster in the central portion of the American Bottom floodplain; and another group farther south in the lower Kaskaskia drainage. The inclusion of sites from the latter locale with American Bottom assemblages may need to be rethought and a separate sequence formulated for that region, given the higher frequency of Crab Orchard fabric-impressed ceramics that occurs.

The American Bottom Middle Woodland sequence essentially mirrors the sequence to the north in the Illinois River valley, although there are differences. The four phases currently defined for the American Bottom consist of an early Havana, Cement Hollow phase; two Havana-Hopewell phases, Holding I and Holding II; and a Pike-Baehr, Hill Lake phase (Figure 7.2). Four possible settlement types have been proposed for the American Bottom region, with different settlement patterns for each phase (Fortier et al. 1989a:567; see also Maher 1996).

Holding is the largest and most intensely occupied site excavated in the region and provided the first clearly Hopewell-related materials in the immediate area (Fortier et al. 1989b). With the Holding and Dash Reeves sites being possible exceptions to the norm, the other excavated Middle Woodland sites in the region are much smaller and are generally restricted to single settlements of limited duration. Smaller sites, like the earlier Florence Street site, are important because they provide evidence of short-lived occupations of human activity.

Early Havana Culture: Cement Hollow Phase and Before
As with the Late Archaic to Early Woodland transition, there is little evidence for continuity from the Early Woodland into the Middle Woodland. While there is Black Sand occupation in the area to the north of Cahokia, the evidence for some type of "Initial Havana" comparable to the Caldwell and Fulton phases (Cantwell 1980) of the central Illinois River is relatively sparse. A single Morton Incised rim was recovered from the Range site (J. Kelly et al. 1987), and a possible Morton Incised sherd was collected from the surface of the Nochta site (Linder et al. 1978). The other Early/Middle Woodland transitional types—Sister Creeks Punctated and Neteler Stamped—are also relatively rare. To the north in the lower Illinois River valley, there is a similar lack of early Havana, although Griffin et al. (1970:8) proposed a

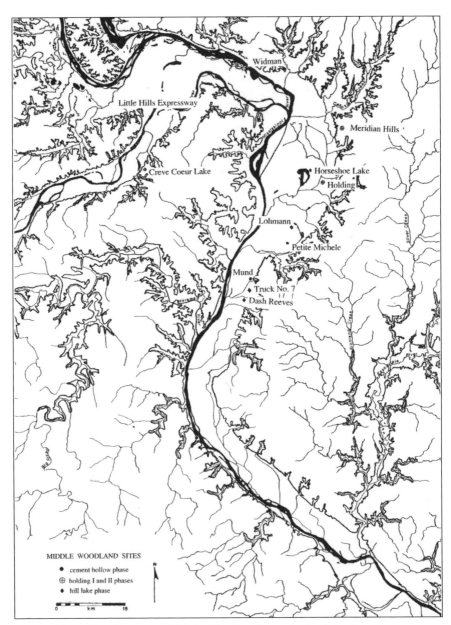

Figure 7.3 — Distribution of Middle Woodland sites in the American Bottom

Calhoun phase for the pre-Hopewell materials from the Snyders site, located in the uplands to the west of the valley. Farnsworth and Asch (1986) have noted a lack of continuity from Black Sand to the Havana-Hopewell Mound House phase in the lower Illinois River valley.

The Cement Hollow phase is characterized by Havana Plain and Cord Marked ceramics and the decorated Havana types, which involve a variety of techniques such as "zoning, punctating, chevron stamping, ovoid stamping, linear stamping, oval impressing, and dentate stamping" (Fortier et al. 1984:83). Few if any Hopewell ceramics have been identified. Diagnostic lithics consist of Manker points and disk scrapers and a substantial quantity of Cobden/Dongola chert from southern Illinois sources. Cement Hollow phase occupations have been identified from excavations at three single-component sites: Mund (Finney 1983), Petite Michele (Fortier 1998; Maher 1996), and Widman (Wolforth et al. 1990). A fourth excavated site in the uplands to the southeast remains to be fully reported (Brad Koldehoff, personal communication, 1993) and was not included in Maher's analysis. Maher did include nine additional sites considered to have a Cement Hollow phase component on the basis of ceramics. Except for the extensive occupation at Petite Michele, the remaining sites are small, limited-term occupations. A settlement model for the Cement Hollow phase includes two settlement types: residential camps such as Indian Creek and Petite Michele and extractive loci such as Mund (Fortier et al. 1989a).

For the American Bottom, one major unresolved question is whether there is continuity from the Black Sand Ringering phase into the early Havana Cement Hollow phase, or whether the lack of these materials reflects another hiatus. Based on site distribution, with Black Sand components clustered in the north and the later Cement Hollow assemblages dispersed in a number of different areas, it appears that any occupation is also even more limited. Fortier (1998:355) has noted that "in terms of subsistence, settlement patterning, and technology, early Middle Woodland Cement Hollow phase occupations differ imperceptibly from previous Early Woodland settlements in this area." While there is no question that small occupations of limited duration occur throughout the Early Woodland and early Middle Woodland, the differences in settlement patterns are dramatic, with a clear concentration of Carr Creek, Florence, and Ringering phase sites in separate areas of the American Bottom. In contrast, in the distribution of surface materials indicative of the early Havana sites, the pattern is less concentrated and more dispersed. Unlike Fortier et al. (1989b), B. D. Smith (1992c) notes that these early sites were composed of one or two households in close proximity to aquatic resources on the floodplain or near the point where upland valley streams open onto the Mississippi floodplain.

One frequent problem regarding the identification of Middle Woodland sites is the lack of diagnostic artifacts in surface collections (Wolforth et al. 1990). For example, the Widman site produced no Middle Woodland artifacts during three separate pedestrian surveys.

Evidence for interaction with groups outside the region consists of the early Hopewell vessels from Widman and Cobden/Dongola chert bifaces and debitage, derived from quarries in southern Illinois, which were present at all excavated sites. Other isolated exotic items include a copper celt with an infant burial at Petite Michele and mica recovered from flotation samples at this site (Maher 1996). Nonlocal materials include galena and hematite, which could have been derived from sources both within and just west of the American Bottom.

The American Bottom represents the southernmost extension of the Havana ceramic tradition, with occasional occurrences of fabric-impressed Crab Orchard wares (Finney 1983). Ovoid dentate stamping occurs widely at this time, although Havana Plain and Cord Marked vessels with exterior cord-wrapped stick impressions on the lip are most common locally.

In contrast to Early Woodland, there is greater emphasis on the use of starchy seeds (K. Parker 1989). Cultigens such as squash, however, have yet to be identified, although they do appear appreciably earlier at Late Archaic (Fortier et al. 1998) and Early Woodland (Johannessen 1984) sites in the region. Seeds and fruits also were collected and are part of this broad-spectrum subsistence strategy. Nuts, especially hickory, are ubiquitous and hazelnut and black walnut are also present. Faunal remains are rare, reflecting problems of preservation.

Havana-Hopewell Cultural Climax: The Holding I and II Phases

The Cement Hollow phase is followed by an early Holding I phase, which marks the beginning of the Hopewellian infusion throughout the Midwest and Southeast; the peak of Hopewellian activity coincides with the Holding I phase (Fortier 1998; Maher 1996). The Holding I phase is characterized by Havana Cord Marked and Havana Plain, with the lack of any early Havana ceramic types, and the appearance of Hopewell Zone Incised and Hopewell Zone Stamped (Maher 1996). Use of Havana ceramics continued during the Holding II phase, but Pike Rocker Stamped appears in frequency equal to or greater than that of the Havana utility wares. Also appearing are traces of Pike Brushed, limestone tempering, bowls, and channeled rims. Cross-hatching of the upper rim is more prevalent than the lip notching. Although Hopewellian artifacts and raw materials are present during the Holding I and II phases, they are not common (Maher 1996) and with few excavated mortuary sites, little else can be said.

A concentration of sites northeast of Cahokia includes larger communities such as Holding on the floodplain and Meridian Hills in the uplands (J. A. Williams 1993) and smaller extractive sites in both settings. Large mounds such as Sugar Loaf and Fox Hill are located on the bluff crest and may be contemporaneous, although their cultural affiliation is unresolved. Most of the documented Middle Woodland activity occurs in the Madison County area of the northern American Bottom, with a second area of activity to the south in the Goose Lake to Hill Lake segments of the Bottom.

A number of Middle Woodland sites have been investigated in the uplands bordering the lower Missouri Valley to the west. The Little Hills Expressway (Lopinot 1990) and Creve Coeur Lake (Blake 1942) sites have been assigned to the Holding I phase (Maher 1996); both sites also have earlier Cement Hollow and later Hill Lake components. In addition to native seed cultigens, maize was identified at the Holding site from the Holding I phase context (Riley et al. 1994).

Pike-Baehr Post–Havana-Hopewell Cultural Climax: The Hill Lake Phase

The terminal part of the Middle Woodland period in the American Bottom is represented by the Hill Lake phase, a complex equivalent to the Pike-Baehr of the Illinois River valley to the north. Pike Brushed ceramics are abundant, while Havana pottery is very rare. Grog and limestone are generally the predominate ceramic tempers. Many of the Hopewellian ceramic decorative elements such as zone incising and stamping disappear, as do Hopewellian raw materials. Bladelet production continues, however, at sites such as Dash Reeves. The Hill Lake phase was defined on the basis of Fortier's (1985c) excavations at the Truck No. 7 site, which is one of the most important Middle Woodland investigations to date because of the limited duration of the late Middle Woodland household. Fortier posited a fall/winter occupation, although there is nothing to preclude year-round occupation. A large, 10-meter diameter structure was uncovered, with associated facilities both inside and outside. One kilometer to the south, a more extensive occupation was found at the Dash Reeves site (Maher 1996). Other excavated late Middle Woodland sites in the Cahokia area include a mortuary area near the Mississippian mound at the Horseshoe Lake site (Wiant and Harn 1994).

Some degree of occupational continuity is evident throughout the Middle Woodland, although the occupations appear dispersed, with some areas nearly devoid of occupation. For example, extensive areal surveys in various parts of the American Bottom, such as the area around Horseshoe Lake (Lopinot et al. 1998; Pauketat et al. 1998), have produced little evidence of Middle Woodland activity. Ultimately it may be possible to delineate Middle Woodland territories in the American Bottom and track the spatial movement of the different occupations through time.

The American Bottom is on the southern fringe of the Havana tradition and, while participating in the Hopewell Interaction Sphere, did not exhibit the elaborate burial ceremonialism and the intensity of occupation seen to the north. The only excavated mortuary site is the Solto site in St. Charles County, Missouri, although Maher (1996) tested several mounds that could be assigned to the Middle Woodland based on diagnostic materials in the fill. There has been some suggestion that the American Bottom was virtually depopulated at the end of the Middle Woodland (McElrath and Fortier 2000). The subsequent early Late Woodland Rosewood phase exhibits some stylistic vestiges of Middle Woodland, but the differences are more pronounced than the similarities. Of course much of what we perceive is a product of our excavated sample.

While the Midwest had already established its own unique identity during the Middle Woodland, the earlier influences from the south during the Early Woodland appear to have been reversed. Toth (1988) suggests that much of Lower Mississippi Valley Marksville culture can be attributed to interaction with Havana-Hopewell societies to the north in Illinois, citing as evidence ceramic motifs, blade technology, and the mortuary program. While connections may have been quite strong up and down the valley, when we turn to the uplands of the Midsouth, as documented by work at the Pinson Mounds complex (Mainfort 1988c, 1996a), affinities are more evident to the east and south, with few if any connections to the north except perhaps through Ohio Hopewell. J. Brown (1979) has discussed the possible diffusion of the Illinois mortuary program of log tombs into the south, but Brose (1988) and others have noted such tombs are spatially widespread.

It is not clear whether Crab Orchard societies were an impediment to the interaction that undoubtedly was occurring elsewhere, but a portion of the Crab Orchard area contained the gray cherts sought by Middle Woodland populations to the north. Hofman (1980) has discussed the possible linkages with the Southeast, noting the ceramics and lithics present at the large Crab Orchard Twenhafel site on the Mississippi floodplain west of the Shawnee Hills. There are also connections to the Middle Woodland complexes to the north in the form of Havana ceramics and Burlington chert blades. In many respects there is a research lacuna between the St. Louis area and southeast Missouri.

The Late Woodland

Late Woodland has been described as the product of "good gray" cultures (S. Williams 1963:297). Although sandwiched between the more elaborate Hopewell and Mississippian, Late Woodland is an important stage in the evolution of eastern Woodland societies, and the shift from Middle Woodland to Late Woodland has been the subject of much discussion. At the fore-front of this dialogue was Griffin's (1960) article on climatic change, which was invoked as a source of this transformation. An underlying assumption was the importance of maize cultivation and the effects of changing climate on agriculture. The realization beginning in the 1970s of the important role native cultigens played in the subsistence regimes of Middle and Late Woodland societies has altered many of the earlier models (D. Braun 1977). Other scenarios, such as Hall's (1980) "Schmoo effect," have provided alternative perspectives.

In the late 1970s and early 1980s, D. Braun (1977, 1983, 1985a) vigorously and systematically tackled the complex problem regarding the shift from Middle Woodland to Late Woodland, invoking a multivariate approach. Essentially, he characterized the changes as linked to subsistence shifts, specifically to an intense focus on the cultivation of a variety of starchy seed plants and other cultigens. The small dispersed communities of the area were linked through alliances such as marriages, feasts, and other events that bring people together. Braun's model is applicable over a very large area.

In the American Bottom, the FAI-270 investigations helped refine the Late Woodland chronology initially established by Munson (1971) and Harn (1971). The present American Bottom sequence (Figure 7.2) is the result of multi-institutional investigative efforts in the Bottom, with occasional forays into the uplands. One major modification to the terminal part of the Late Woodland in the Cahokia area is the Emergent Mississippian, discussed at length elsewhere (J. Kelly 1990a, 1990b). Three Late Woodland phases, Rosewood, Mund, and Patrick, are defined throughout the American Bottom, with a fourth, the Sponemann phase, found only in the area to the north of Cahokia (Figure 7.4). Revised regional chronology (Fortier and Jackson 2000; McElrath and Fortier 2000) indicates a period from A.D. 400 to 900.

Initial Late Woodland: Rosewood and Mund Phases
The earliest phase, Rosewood (A.D. 400–500), is the local equivalent of the Weaver and White Hall complexes to the north. While we have often assumed that Rosewood was directly derived from the Hill Lake phase, McElrath and Fortier (2000) have rightly pointed out that there is little evidence for stylistic and concomitant demographic continuity in the greater American Bottom. Stylistic connections are evident, however, in the noding and exterior cord-wrapped stick impressions on much thinner walled subconoidal jars. Such ceramic decorative elements decrease significantly by the Mund phase (A.D. 500–650), although excavations at the Cunningham site in the northern American Bottom have defined a ceramic assemblage

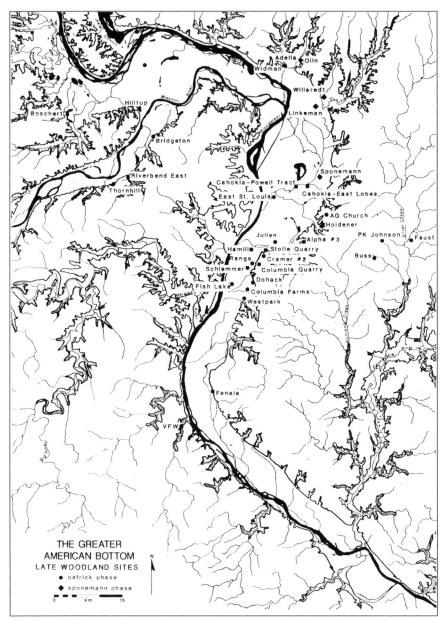

Figure 7.4 — Distribution of Late Woodland sites in the American Bottom

intermediate between the two phases (McElrath and Fortier 2000). The lithic assemblage is characterized by expanding stemmed dart points derived from Middle Woodland antecedents such as Steuben Expanding Stemmed.

It appears that the area may have been briefly abandoned at the end of the Middle Woodland before populations began to be reestablished from the north, east, and south. A greater degree of uninterrupted occupation exists farther to the north in the Illinois River valley, between Peoria and Kampsville. Presumably the same uninterrupted occupation is evident in the area of the Crab Orchard tradition of southern Illinois with the emergence of Raymond, although the eventual demise of fabric-impressing as a surface treatment in favor of cord marking has not been fully studied. D. Braun (1985b) has emphasized the decrease in vessel wall thickness from Middle Woodland into the early episodes of the Late Woodland throughout much of the Midwest.

A distinct contrast is apparent between Middle Woodland and the subsequent early Late Woodland Rosewood phase settlement distributions. In the latter, there is a clear dispersal into the upland interior, with most settlements indicative of small, dispersed homesteads and hamlets. Floodplain settlements are restricted to the alluvial fans and Pleistocene terrace remnants (Figure 7.4). The lack of occupation on the floodplain proper may reflect hydrologic conditions in which occupation of any duration on the Mississippi bottoms was subject to flooding.

As during the Middle Woodland, subsistence was broad based. Wild plants and animals employed in the diet reflect selected species from a variety of niches in proximity to each site. At the core of the subsistence regime were the various native cultigens, especially the starchy seed suite (Simon 2000). An occasional maize fragment is present, but this tropical domesticate is not a significant part of the plant assemblage. As noted by D. Braun and others, changes in ceramic technology such as thinner vessel walls reflect changes in methods of food preparation and the importance of starchy seeds in the diet.

Terminal Late Woodland: Patrick and Sponemann Phases

The subsequent Patrick phase on one hand represents the climax of Late Woodland societies in the American Bottom and on the other the foundation for the development and diversification of Emergent Mississippian societies. In fact, Fortier (1991) characterized the Patrick phase and its descendant hybrid Sponemann phase as "Formative Emergent Mississippian." There was a modest change in settlement distribution and community plans sometime after approximately A.D. 650 with the onset of the Patrick phase. An increased frequency in sites and increased ubiquity of settlements occur throughout the region, both on the floodplain and in the adjacent uplands (Figure 7.4). Larger village sites are distributed primarily in the bottoms, but also occur in some areas of the uplands to the east and west. Again, it must be emphasized that the distribution was discontinuous, with a greater variety of environmental niches being occupied.

The Patrick phase ceramic assemblage is characterized by an increase in decorative elements, especially interior lip impressions and occasional zoomorphic lip lugs. Jars continue to be the primary vessel form, but bowls reappear. Other aspects of the cultural inventory are more elaborate, with small clay and stone stemmed pipes and discoidals, ceramic disks, and occasional limestone hoes. Small, stemmed arrow points are evident by the Patrick phase, marking the introduction of the bow and arrow. Some recent discussions (e.g., Shott 1993) have focused on the introduction of this new weaponry prior to A.D. 650. Although changes in material cultural are noticeable, subsistence activities continue to reflect a pattern that extends back into the Middle Woodland.

A range of Patrick phase settlement types has been identified (Bareis and Porter 1984; J. Kelly 1990b). These include isolated homesteads, hamlets, and small villages with populations under one hundred. Also present are small sites of limited duration. Smaller settlements, such as the Little Hills Expressway site (Lopinot 1990) in the uplands to the west in Missouri, appear to be the most common form. Larger communities were located on the floodplain and along the bluff crest, although I have identified a portion of a possible village at the Dugan site in the interior uplands to the southeast.

Small rectilinear and keyhole-shaped domiciles are clustered throughout each village. The most complete pattern at the Range site (Figure 7.5) in the American Bottom has provided important insights into the organization of Late Woodland society (J. Kelly 1990a, 1990b; J. Kelly et al. 1984, 1987). Individual house clusters are interpreted as separate household groups of varying size distributed around a central community square. The northeast-southwest division within the community is unique in a number of ways. First, the largest structures in the two largest clusters oppose each other. The northeast household node is contiguous with a unique quadrilateral pattern of four limestone-floored pits on the edge of the square. A large pit adjacent to this cluster contained a dog with puppies in the birth canal. Along the northwest margins of this group of four pits is an isolated house. This complex has ritual implications that are associated with the northeast segment of the village. Second, this half of the community has the lowest frequency of keyhole houses, while the opposing side has the highest frequency.

The keyhole house form, with its distinctive appendage, has been examined primarily from a functional perspective (Fortier et al. 1984; J. Kelly et al. 1987). While the position of the ramps facing away from the prevailing winds suggests entries, it is possible the keyhole is imbued with a certain

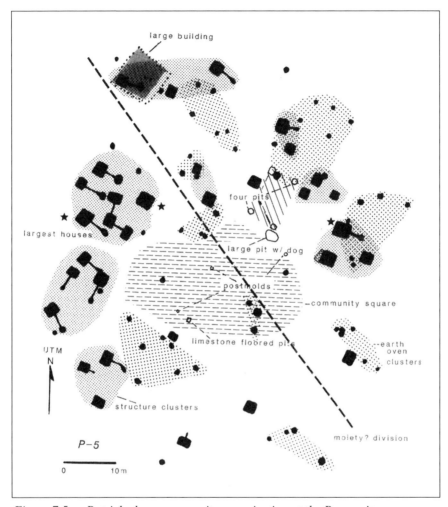

Figure 7.5 — Patrick phase community organization at the Range site

level of overt male symbolism. It is also possible to see the ramps as an entry into the mother's womb, so that there could be a possible female aspect to their interpretation. Regardless of such symbolic speculations, the keyhole houses are found primarily on the southwest side of the village.

The opposition of clusters and differing house forms is indicative of a dual community social division or moiety organization. Ethnographically, the division of Native American societies into moieties is widespread, and in some Midwestern societies like the Winnebago (Radin 1923) and Osage (Bailey 1995), social organization is portrayed in the community plans. The moieties and their associated clans were exogamous, and there were roles for each segment that served to complement each other and thus bind the community together as a whole. Another aspect of this duality was the symbolism and cosmology associated with each segment. Much like the difference between male and female, moieties, while in clear opposition, represented the biological and symbolic wedding of individuals from these different segments. This, as well as other events, served to link them and thus give them community cohesion.

A large structure on the northwest edge of the Range village may have functioned as a place in which some form of integration through a non-kin group such as a sodality could be maintained. It is important to emphasize the peripheral nature of these features that later functioned during early Emergent Mississippian as centrally located corporate buildings (J. Kelly 1990b). What was lacking within these communities, we suspect, was any clear mechanism for continuity of leadership positions. As in earlier decades these positions probably continued to be fluid and not ascribed. These were the proverbial "big-men." Certainly these individuals were not on the same level as those individuals interred with their sumptuary displays in the earlier Middle Woodland tombs.

We know that women occupied chiefly positions within southeastern chiefdoms, and there is nothing to preclude comparable roles within the Late Woodland. I suspect, however, at this time males may have dominated these fleeting positions as village heads. Prezzano (1997) has pointed out in the case of the matrilineal Iroquois that while women did not occupy chiefly positions, they did control who became chief and who was removed. During Emergent Mississippian, when matriarchal lines may have emerged, women may have had a very substantial stake and role in determining who was in power. The fluid nature of political offices and the competition for them, especially with the emergence of larger settlements, provides a basis for inferring the extremely fragile nature of community stability. The sequence of settlements at Range and their sedentary yet impermanent nature reinforces the fusion and fission of these villages over a number of decades within this nearly two-century period. At one time Patrick phase society was thought to be organized along the lines of segmentary lineages (J. Kelly 1990a, 1990b). While this is still a possibility, I am now less convinced.

The widespread distribution of similar ceramic styles for the Patrick phase suggests that the residence pattern was one of patrilocality. It is important to remember attempts to infer such residence patterns archaeologically have been severely critiqued. Allen and Richardson (1971) initially noted the difficulties of using kinship reconstruction within the context of cultural anthropology, but a brief discussion of their article by P. Watson (1977:385–86) offers some possible remedies.

Braun and Plog (1982) criticized kinship reconstruction by archaeologists and instead focused on the context of style and the use of Wobst's (1977) theory of information exchange as a mechanism for understanding ceramic similarities. Some earlier studies assumed that the transmission of ceramic production and style concepts was from mother to daughter; more recent studies emphasize the dispensing of stylistic information within a broader social arena. It is interesting to note that one argument examines generational transmission (i.e., diachronic), while the other is synchronic in its perspective. Both approaches need to be considered. The widespread similarity of styles across a large area of Illinois would seem to argue for potters, probably women, marrying and residing outside their group. Thus males would have remained resident in the area of birth. It would have been within this context that young males would have learned hunting techniques. In the uplands, males presumably would have assumed responsibility for hunting areas. Control of hunting territories may have been a potential source of conflict. Whether we can correctly infer a general pattern of patrilocality is worth considering.

No Patrick phase cemeteries have been excavated in the American Bottom, but in the lower Illinois River valley immediately to the north, some human remains exhibit evidence of traumatic death caused by the new weapon of choice, the bow and arrow. This may reflect conflict over male hunting territories. In many respects this reinforces the segmentary nature of Late Woodland society. The question is, how were subsequent societies able to extricate themselves from this cycle of violence?

The Sponemann phase is a short-lived Late Woodland manifestation identified in the northern American Bottom floodplain (Fortier and Jackson 2000) and the Scott AFB locale of Silver Creek (Holley 2000). There are two aspects of the Sponemann site that stand out. One is the sudden appearance of maize in 30 percent of the features; the other is the co-occurrence of two separate ceramic traditions within a single archaeological complex. One complex is a typical Patrick phase assemblage of grog-tempered cord-marked pottery with S-twisted cords and often decorated with interior cord-wrapped stick impressions. The other assemblage, dominated by chert and other rock tempering (Canteen Cord Marked) and textured with Z-twist cordage, is characterized by castellated or peaked jar rims with exterior lip impressions. This latter form conforms in many respects to the Ralls/Yokem phase assemblages that extend northward up the Mississippi Valley toward Hannibal, Missouri. Essentially what we have is the amalgamation yet segregation of two Late Woodland societies, with the Ralls/Yokem manifestation extending southward into the northern part of the American Bottom. The extensive excavations at the Sponemann site provided little information about the organization of the village(s); resolution of this problem may extend outside of the area examined.

A number of other sites have been identified that could be assigned to the Sponemann phase. These include some of the mounds at the Grassy Lake site, where a peaked-rim vessel and copper were found interred with an individual (J. Kelly 2000). Another is the nearby Vaughn Branch site assigned to the Patrick phase by D. Jackson (1996), although the high frequency of decorated rims with both interior and exterior lip impressions and the suggestion of a peaked-rim vessel would suggest otherwise. It differs from Sponemann, however, in that, among the identifiable cord-twists, no Z-twisted cords were present.

Another interesting assemblage was found at the McAdams phase O'Donnell site in the uplands overlooking the Illinois-Mississippi confluence to the north of the American Bottom (Goatley et al. 1996). The thirteen vessels recovered exhibit a high frequency of interior rim impressions with peaked rims and exterior punctations. The McAdams phase differs from the Sponemann phase in having a higher frequency of cord-wrapped stick impressions and a lack of exterior lip notching. In many respects this rather unique occupation is similar to that indicated in the Boschert site assemblage (Geller and Crampton 1987), located 30 kilometers to the west in Missouri. There may be merit in the proposed McAdams phase, although a much more comprehensive study needs to be completed of the surrounding area in order to understand the local context of these materials. Regarding the late radiocarbon assays (A.D. 1000), I would urge that suites of dates be run on short-lived materials such as nutshell or seeds.

These data suggest the northern end of the study area was a dynamic social landscape, particularly across the prairie peninsula to the north. This dynamism may be linked to a matrilocal resident pattern, in which ceramic diversity is a result of ceramic production by women potters. Up the lower Illinois Valley to the north and into the northeastern Ozarks and the Meramec Valley to the west, other changes were occurring that ultimately led toward the emergence of the large Early Mississippian center of Cahokia.

The above pattern in the American Bottom of dispersal into the uplands and subsequent population increases also has been observed by Green (1993) in west-central Illinois and by Hargrave et al. (1991) in southern Illinois. These demographic shifts were, in part, a complex interplay of population increases and societal change (Buikstra et al. 1986). In essence, starchy seeds provided the basis for a gruel that could be readily fed to infants allowing for a decrease in time between births and an increase in the number of births. This would have resulted in additional family members who could be involved in the intense suite of activities associated with the cultivation, harvesting, and processing of starchy seeds. At the heart of these changes were women (Watson and Kennedy 1991). Not only was their biological role an integral element, but equally important were the social changes vis-à-vis the innovations in ceramic technology, as they related to food production and preparation, that accompanied some major subsistence changes. The role of women in the cultivation of the gardens, the harvesting of the fruits of their labor, and the preparation of foods must have had a tremendous impact on the development of Emergent Mississippian societies. I believe that during the Emergent Mississippian, women continued to be important in all roles of society, as they held the key to fertility at all levels—biologically, agriculturally, socially, and ritually.

Another technological addition was the bow and arrow, which may appear prior to A.D. 650 and which originated outside the Midwest. This hunting technology undoubtedly spread rapidly over the region, and while its efficiency in hunting has been questioned (Shott 1993), it was undoubtedly useful in individual hunting of deer as opposed to communal hunts. Certainly this new weaponry was also useful in societal conflicts.

Continuity between the Late Woodland and Emergent Mississippian is assumed, with at least two ceramic traditions at the onset of the Emergent Mississippian within the region. One, Pulcher, is centered on the manufacture of vessels with limestone tempering and the other, Late Bluff, on the continued use of grog and grit temper in the northern third of the region. As noted earlier, investigations at a number of sites in the area, however, have revealed the presence of another complex, Sponemann, that precedes the latter Late Bluff tradition. What is unique is the co-occurrence of two separate Late Woodland ceramic complexes at a number sites that date to the ninth century, along with a significant increase in the ubiquity of maize. One of the ceramic assemblages is indigenous and has its antecedents in the Patrick phase. The other includes the peaked or castellated vessels with exterior notching and chert tempering and is related to similar complexes to the north along the Mississippi River. This suggests that segments of those populations expanding into the region coexisted with Patrick phase populations within the same communities. What is important is the short-lived nature of the Sponemann phase, and I have suggested little continuity exists between Sponemann and the subsequent Late Bluff complexes (J. Kelly 1990a, 1990b). The region may have been largely abandoned for several decades, with the early Late Bluff populations being derived from the Jersey Bluff populations to the north. Farther south, the Pulcher tradition can be derived from the Maramec Spring complexes of the northern Ozarks (J. Kelly 1990a, 1990b), but the dynamics are considerably different from those to the north. It is important to emphasize that such cultural dynamics are not endemic only to the American Bottom, but are widespread during the latter part of the Late Woodland in the Midwest.

Summary

Looking back at the 1500 years that comprise the Woodland complexes in the American Bottom, a number of items stand out. At the scale of the American Bottom, the distribution of Early and Middle Woodland sites is characterized by patterns of geographic and temporal discontinuity. Nonetheless, this sparsely populated region had clear linkages to other societies in adjacent regions. In turn we can see some of the connections with populations farther south along the Mississippi Valley and into the upland Midsouth. While not overly strong, they do exist and certainly warrant more extensive examination.

These demographic fluctuations can be traced back into the Archaic. A noticeable gap in cultural continuity exists between the end of the Late Archaic and the onset of Early Woodland. This boundary may coincide with the intensification of plant cultivation in the midcontinent (B. D. Smith 1993; Watson and Kennedy 1991). The extent to which the American Bottom was abandoned at the end of the Archaic period is presently unclear.

The earliest Woodland ceramics are derived from technologies introduced from the northeast. Within a few centuries additional changes are evident, with the advent of decorative methods and elements whose sources are present in the earlier assemblages of the Lower Mississippi Valley. Again, there is presently no evidence of continuity between the end of the Early Woodland and the onset of Middle Woodland. Shifts in the American Bottom Middle Woodland cultural assemblages parallel the changes occurring in the Havana complexes immediately to the north. The southern margins of the Havana tradition extend southward into the American Bottom. Influences extending up from the south are restricted to the fine cherts and fabric-impressed Crab Orchard ceramics of southern Illinois. The lithic raw materials from the Ozarks, along the southwestern margins of the American Bottom, make their way south into the Lower Mississippi Valley.

There is also no evidence of continuity between the Middle Woodland and the subsequent Late Woodland. It is during the Late Woodland period that there are significant population increases and the establishment of larger multihousehold communities. Intensification of crop production along with modifications in ceramic technology for cooking purposes highlight the importance of females in these transformations. By the end of the Late Woodland, maize begins to take on increased economic importance as an addition to the suite of native starchy seeds. Finally, adoption of the bow and arrow represents a technological item that accentuates male individuality. While Late Woodland ceramics are somewhat unattractive, they provide important insights into the strong similarities present over a broad geographic area of the Midwest and even farther south along the Mississippi Valley and the upland Midsouth. Of particular importance is the manner in which the Late Woodland complexes of the American Bottom represent the cultural roots from which Cahokia Mississippian society emerged.

Chapter 8

Deconstructing the Woodland Sequence from the Heartland: A Review of Recent Research Directions in the Upper Ohio Valley

R. Berle Clay

In this chapter I review the Woodland period culture sequence (ca. 1000 B.C.–A.D. 1000) for the middle Ohio River valley with two goals. These are, first, to provide a new and informative approach to a well-known topic and, second, reference the significant, growing body of literature that I feel is shaping our interpretation of the topic today. As defined here, the upper Ohio Valley includes the main stem of the Ohio and its northern and southern tributaries between the Great Miami and Kanawha rivers (Figure 8.1).

I have chosen to highlight three aspects of the region's culture history. They are not the only aspects that might be mentioned, rather three that seem to tie into some current questions involved in regional interpretation. The first of these I call simply "cultural pluralism." The second I refer to as "event centered" archaeological sites. The final aspect might be called "the question of domestic sites."

My rationale for using this approach, in contrast to a more traditional culture-historical one, stems from the following. First, an excellent culture-historical interpretation has already been published (Seeman 1992a) and I cannot improve on it. Second, however, I deal with the archaeological history of a region that I call the Woodland "Heartland" because it first gave the American public a feel for its prehistoric past through the writings of Atwater (1820), Squier and Davis (1848), Whittlesey (1850), Rafinesque (1824), and others. The three chosen aspects deal with important questions concerning that archaeological perception.

Because of its history, the Heartland has had much to live down. For example, non–Native American mound builders were an early interpretation of the builders of the mounds and earthworks. This prompted the Smithsonian mound survey (C. Thomas 1894) as a corrective, one that only partly moved public opinion away from the exotic explanation to a more believable one. But while public understanding was modified by the

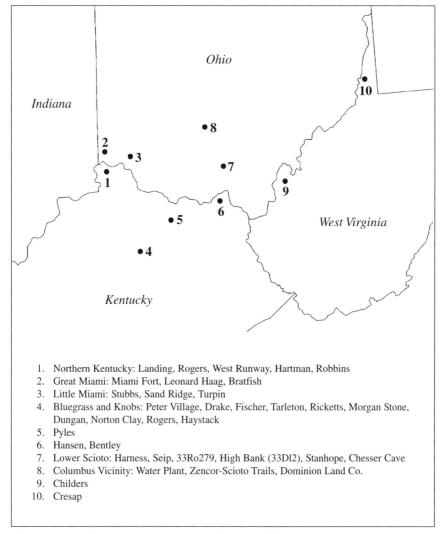

Figure 8.1 — General location of sites discussed in the text

Smithsonian Institution's efforts, earlier interpretations live on today in fringe literature.

Fifty years later it was the Heartland that gave North American archaeology the Burial Mound One and Burial Mound Two stages (J. A. Ford and Willey 1941). I believe such developmental generalizations were counterproductive even when proposed, but they proved extremely popular as Eastern United States archaeology professionalized. By the late 1950s, for example, Adena was being interpreted as "perhaps the earliest Formative culture in Eastern North America" (Willey and Phillips 1958:157), and its accomplishments equated with those of the formative cultures of the Valley of Mexico, including agriculture and monumental public works. Some (W. Webb and Snow 1945:328–29; Spaulding 1952) saw it as a direct migration from Mesoamerica. These writings, latter-day burial mound "stage" thinking, indicate a widely held belief that Heartland mounds and earthworks were the products of a maize-based agricultural society now debunked by almost two generations of ethnobotanical research (Wymer 1992, 1997), although some (Prufer 1997) remain unconvinced. Yet I find that this interpretation is still taught in regional universities, if not actually in a form still involving corn agriculture, at least in one implying its sociopolitical complexity.

The Heartland has produce a notable lineage of local archaeologists: Moorehead (1892, 1909), Mills (1902, 1917), Shetrone (1920, 1930), Fowke (1902), Greenman (1932), and Webb (W. Webb and Snow 1945; W. Webb and Baby 1957) before World War II, and at a later date R. Morgan (1952), James B. Griffin (1943a, 1945a, 1946, 1952c, 1958, 1979, 1997), Dragoo (1963, 1964, 1976), and Prufer (1964, 1968, 1997; Prufer and McKenzie 1965). These have forged our working understanding of its Woodland sequence in spite of the heavy developmental implications assumed by those generally working outside the region. But we are only just moving away from their view of the region dominated by a sequence of regionwide cultural periods.

This reappraisal started about 1970 with a review of Adena (Swartz [ed.] 1971) and gained momentum with the publication of a seminal Hopewell survey in 1979 (Brose and Greber [eds.] 1979). In the past two decades the process of reanalysis and reformulation has accelerated (Dancey and Pacheco [eds.] 1997; Mainfort and Sullivan [eds.] 1998; Pacheco [ed.] 1996; Pollack et al. [eds.] 1985), stimulated by the expansion of data collecting with public archaeology.

The Heartland sequence circa 1970 was dominated by hallowed culture-historical constructs, such as Early Woodland Adena, Middle Woodland Hopewell, and Late Woodland Newtown. Through the years these were integrated in time and space with concepts like the Scioto tradition (Prufer and McKenzie 1965; Shane 1971), the Hopewell Interaction Sphere (Caldwell 1964; Streuver 1964), the southeastern and Hopewell ceramic series (Prufer 1968), and the intrusive mound horizon (R. Morgan 1952:93; Seeman 1992b).

With new data and somewhat different questions in mind, these concepts have become less and less necessary; in some cases increasingly restrictive. I have chosen to concentrate on the three aspects of Heartland Woodland cultures noted above, not to ignore the accomplishments of earlier researchers couched in their own terms, but to try to avoid the heavy connotations that their culture-historical discourse tends to evoke. Others (Seeman 1996:305), using somewhat different terms, have announced a similar intent in their own writing on the Heartland.

Cultural Pluralism in the Heartland

Heartland Woodland societies tend to fragment under scrutiny. I mean by this that they tend to dissolve into fluid groups of people, seemingly on the move. Therefore, at practically any point in the sequence we now have to deal with culture diversity in small and great ways. This reality makes past large-scale culture-historical formulations (i.e., Adena) less defensible as the terms with which to address the whole period. Unfortunately, this cultural diversity also has a "fractal" quality to it. Depending upon the level of analysis, it would appear that basic patterns repeat themselves throughout the Heartland.

For example, I see fragmentation reflected in ceramics. Yet Heartland ceramic variation has all too often been downplayed, passed off as irrelevant free variation (e.g., the concept of Woodland Ware [Haag 1942a]), or at an opposite extreme endowed with highly specific meanings (e.g., the southeastern and Hopewell series [Prufer 1968:10–13]). This is possible because of the seeming monotony of much of the Heartland ceramics that, along with much cord-marked pottery of the Eastern United States, has prompted one writer to call them "good gray cultures" (S. Williams 1963:297).

Again, diversity often is masked by the penchant that the region's inhabitants had for trading specific artifacts over wide areas, seen in its most attenuated form in the Hopewell Interaction Sphere (Caldwell 1964; Seeman 1979a). This behavior, which had its roots in the earlier Archaic period, has at times tended to give the region a deceptive sense of cultural uniformity. But on closer analysis it is being demonstrated (Ruhl and Seeman 1998) that at least some of these very same "traded" artifacts can be reinterpreted as local approximations to regionwide patterns, perhaps "fractal" expressions.

Pluralism is not a novel analytical starting point. For example, in 1971 Shane (1971:142) wrote, "[Y]ou really cannot deal with cultures in the sense of an Adena culture....What you have to look at are local sequences that have developed in ecologically meaningful areas, and the development of local cultures." Others, like Brose (1979a) and Greber (1994) in speaking of Hopewell and Adena, have expressed similar thoughts. Finally, for all who will listen, J. Brown (1992:81) has recently and forcefully stated that the continued use of Adena and Hopewell employs "rubrics trapped in the perspectives of the pre–World War II period in which they were conceived."

Yet archaeologists have resisted attempts to embrace Heartland pluralism at least by redefining culture history in cultural phases of reasonable
time/space dimensions. For example, with the exception of one writer who
has boldly proposed a Twin Mounds phase to characterize Hopewell in the
Great Miami Valley (Hawkins 1996), Hopewell remains a taxonomic sacred
cow. Even when new culture-historical constructs are proposed, like
Newtown, a relative latecomer in the 1950s (J. B. Griffin 1952c), they tend
to expand rapidly in time and space.

Probably because of their histories, culture-historical units in the Heartland continue to take the form of regional stages. For example, as recently
as 1998, a dissertation persists in juxtaposing Middle Woodland Scioto tradition Hopewellian Subphases 1 and 2 of the Late Developmental subperiod
with Late Woodland Newtown Subphases 1 through 3 of the Intermediate
period (R. Riggs 1998). All these units, so it would appear, are meant to
apply to the Heartland as a whole.

Pluralism implies phrasing culture dynamics in the social interaction of
variable groups. In this process, archaeologists must be very careful in their
choice of descriptive terms. For example, J. Brown (1992:81–82) has ad-
vised caution in the use of the term *village*. For him an Illinois model of
settlement development driven by the ultimate emergence of Mississippian
farming society cannot be exported directly to the Heartland as a heuristic
device. Settlement remained scattered and seemingly isolated throughout
the Heartland Woodland. All too often the evidence has been misinterpreted
to suggest that nucleation occurred, driven by fuzziness in the term *nucleation* or preconceptions about social evolution (cf. Converse 1993; J. B.
Griffin 1997).

It has taken some time for this aspect of pluralism to sink in and only
recently (Dancey 1991, 1992, 1996; Dancey and Pacheco 1997; Pacheco
1996, 1997) have there been notable attempts to search for a more adequate
explanation for shifting settlement size. To analytically embrace the chronic
fragmentation of Heartland social groups is to deny the time-honored formulation that the complexity of its mounds and earthworks requires complex social organization.

Only after A.D. 900 did corn agriculture become important. Even then,
nucleated settlement is difficult to identify. The slow adaptation to corn agriculture in the region may best be viewed as the relatively independent
adoption of new cropping practices by small groups (Shott and Jefferies
1992:56). This indicates just how far Heartland social evolution was removed from evolution in the dynamic American Bottom of Illinois. It never
produced a settlement system even remotely similar in complexity to an
"Emergent Mississippian" cultural level.

For an illustration of the implications of pluralism, consider the first *major* ceramic-producing Woodland cultures of the Heartland characterized by thick, grit-tempered ceramics that are felt to have blanketed this portion of the Midwest by 600 B.C., if not earlier (Dragoo 1976:16). James B. Griffin (1943a, 1945a) first defined these ceramics when he named Fayette Thick with central Kentucky materials. Fayette Thick *became* Heartland Early Woodland following its identification at the Cresap mound in West Virginia (Dragoo 1963:127) where, it was suggested, it "is known from many Adena mounds" as reported by William S. Webb. Fayette Thick became *the* ceramic hallmark of an elusive early Adena, despite the contemporary comment (McMichael 1971:95) that it might best be relegated to a pre-Adena Early Woodland.

In 1983, I recovered the ceramics from a portion of the Peter earthwork (W. Webb 1943a), Griffin's type site (Clay 1985, 1988a, 1988b). I compared them with a collection of thick pottery from the Dominion Land Co. site at Columbus, Ohio, which had also been called Fayette Thick (W. Webb and Baby 1957:20) and concluded that these were not the same type. Cramer (1989) subsequently redefined the Ohio sherds as "Dominion Thick." This is not simply a use of new type names to correct earlier oversimplification, but the recognition of basic stylistic variability in thick pottery. Consider the context of these sherds, their typological differences, and new distribution data from northern Kentucky and the mouth of the Great Miami, and the landscape in which these early ceramics were being used becomes considerably more sharply focused—and culturally pluralistic—than it had been for Dragoo.

Thick, early pottery occurs in tight association, not as mound fill inclusions, in only a few early mounds (Clay 1980) and Cresap may not be one of them. One example of tight association is the Hartman mound near Cincinnati (W. Webb 1943b) with a calibrated date of 407 B.C. (2400 ± 150, 450 B.C. [M-2241]), an early burial mound quite unlike later structures identified with the late Adena Robbins complex (Dragoo 1963:207–8). At the same time there are mounds that by mortuary ritual appear to be only slightly later in time, but lack any pottery at all—sites in Kentucky like Ricketts (Funkhouser and Webb 1935; W. Webb and Funkhouser 1940), Drake (W. Webb 1941b), Fischer (W. Webb and Haag 1947), and Tarleton. If thick pottery was used in grave-side ritual as I have suggested for Adena Plain (Clay 1984), then it was rarely used in early burial mounds and only in certain parts of the Heartland.

At Peter, Kentucky, Fayette Thick occurs consistently with pinched surface decoration on up to 16 percent of the sherds and this association distinguishes it from other sites with thick pottery. James B. Griffin (1943a, 1945a) recognized that this decoration has "southern" analogies in the Alexander pottery of the middle Tennessee Valley. To these may be added pinched pottery from the Falls of the Ohio in Kentucky called Zorn Punctate (Mocas 1988), poorly known western Kentucky analogues in pottery in the Green River valley (L. Hanson 1960), Alexander Pinched itself on the lower Tennessee in Kentucky (Rolingson and Schwartz 1966:43–45) and in the Black Bottom of Illinois (F. Cole et al. 1951:200), and, dramatically, the Florence Street phase ceramics from the American Bottom (Emerson et al. [eds.] 1983).

Fayette Thick has a limited distribution in central Kentucky, occurring at only three excavated sites (W. Webb 1940, 1943a) and rarely in surface collections. I have interpreted the Peter earthwork as a meeting place for dispersed site users (Clay 1988a). The ceramic variability suggests that it may have attracted individuals from a wide area who made large pots at the site, reflecting several ceramic templates. These were used during activities that may have involved the excavation of ores and manufacture of barite/galena artifacts such as atlatl weights and white pigment cones. New evidence is also suggesting that the pottery may be associated with Boyle chert sources along the southern margins of the Bluegrass (Rick Matchet, personal communication, 2000).

The Ohio context of Dominion Plain is only suggestive (Cramer 1989). It is associated with a "ceremonial circle" type earthwork that should date after 100 B.C. (Clay 1987), but a series of radiocarbon dates suggests that it could occur several centuries earlier (C. Carr and Haas 1996:45, table 4). Further, the pottery occurs in the fill of a mound within the circle containing a Hopewellian bladelet and covering a post circle that could be Hopewell. Putting all this together, Dominion Thick may occur with an earthwork, later in form than the Peter enclosure. It is probably not associated with the later burial mound additions inside. Moreover, the ceramic type would seem to be a local product in the upper Scioto drainage. Peter and Dominion Land Co. appear to be isolated occurrences of sites having thick pottery with an enclosure, although the enclosures are of different form and significance (Clay 1987). In both, the site form and the associated ceramic would appear to indicate outposts of ceramic variability in a non-ceramic-using area.

A similar situation may also occur in the central Scioto Valley. An intensive survey of the Chillicothe floodplain vicinity (Prufer 1967a) did not reveal a distribution of sites with thick pottery, although it may occur in upland rockshelters (Mark Seeman, personal communication, 1999). Yet at least one earthwork in the valley—33Ro279 near Mound City with features similar to those of Peter Village (an interior bank and an external ditch according to Squier and Davis [Seeman 1981a])—may indicate a site context similar in shape to the Peter enclosure.

A more coherent distribution of sites with thick pottery, suggesting resident potters, is beginning to emerge at the mouth of the Little Miami River
and the Hartman mound is part of this distribution. But it is stretching typology to call the thick pottery from this subarea Fayette Thick, nor is it Dominion Thick, and I now refer to it as "Hartman Plain." Six other finds have
considerably broadened our understanding of this distribution and its absolute dating. At the West Runway site in upland Boone County, Kentucky, 3D
Environmental excavated a site with thirty-eight Hartman Plain sherds
(Bergman et al. 1998; Duerksen et al. 1995). Parts of West Runway may
date as early as 600 B.C. In addition, Cultural Resource Analysts has recovered the same pottery from sites on the floodplain at the mouth of the Great
Miami in southeast Indiana that may date in part somewhat earlier than West
Runway. Finally, Indiana State excavated a deeply buried context with
Hartman Plain somewhat downstream at the Bratfish site (Anslinger
1993:62). Reconsideration of existing collections also suggests that the type
was recovered from the base of the stratified Haag (Reidhead and Limp
1974) and Turpin (R. Riggs 1986) sites on the Great and Little Miami rivers,
and possibly from Miami Fort at the mouth of the Miami River.

These sites place the pottery in a variety of contexts including mounds,
earthworks, and hunting and gathering camps perhaps focused on the floodplains of the Ohio and its tributaries combined with less intensive (i.e., West
Runway) use of the adjoining uplands (Bergman et al. 1998). With the
Hartman burial mound included, the pottery makes a nice linkage between
domestic sites and detached cemeteries. Hartman would seem to be an early
example of a distinctive ritual pattern emphasizing the grave-side feasting
(Clay 1998:16–17) that continued through circa A.D. 400 in the Heartland
(but see Abrams 1992a for a somewhat different interpretation of the relationship between the domestic and mortuary side of "Adena," possibly suggesting regional variation). Finally, the possible occurrence at Miami Fort
puts the type in a large enclosure at some early point in its long period of
use, a context perhaps analogous to the Peter or Dominion Land Co. enclosures.

The West Runway excavators have emphasized the similarities between
Hartman Plain and Marion Thick (Bergman et al. 1998; Duerksen et al.
1995:82) from the Carr Creek phase of the American Bottom. The pottery
may be more closely related, however, to the contemporaneous thick, plain-
surfaced pottery, earlier than Zorn Punctate, at the Falls of the Ohio downriver.
In fact, its occurrence in the Heartland can be viewed as the upriver extension of a distinctive ceramic-using culture that can be identified between
circa 600 B.C. and 400 B.C. or later at the Falls (Stephen T. Mocas, personal
communication, 1998).

The variability and uneven distribution of thick pottery in the Heartland indicate one of two scenarios or perhaps a combination of the two. The first is that the general dispersion of social groups in the region included both ceramic and aceramic groups. A second possibility is that population was concentrated in the Ohio Valley below the Scioto and scattered, or nonexistent, elsewhere. In this view main stem inhabitants, and perhaps those from other regions as well, sporadically (perhaps systematically) used the "hinterlands" through special-use sites like Dominion Land Co., Peter, and perhaps 33Ro279, while conducting similar activities at Miami Fort in the area of actual site occupancy.

I expect that a true explanation involves elements of both viewpoints. Thus, at this time (to ca. 350 B.C.) population may have been generally low level *and* concentrated in the Ohio Valley *and* there may have been ceramic and aceramic groups existing side by side.

The similarity with the distribution of Marion sites in the Mississippi and Illinois valleys is striking. As reconstructed (Emerson 1986:625–29), Marion phases were not uniformly distributed. While the Carr Creek phase occurs in the American Bottom, there is no corresponding phase on the lower Illinois where Marion ceramics are virtually absent. Yet in the central Illinois Valley they become important in the Marion phase. Just this sort of on again/off again distribution of thick ceramics is possibly present in the Heartland.

For the American Bottom, archaeologists have stressed what they see as a dramatic shift in population distribution between the Terminal Archaic and the subsequent Carr Creek phase. The transition witnessed the end of the use of concentrated floodplain base camps, replaced by a generalization of floodplain and upland land use in small Woodland hunting and gathering sites. A similar and contemporaneous shift in settlement may also have taken place in the Heartland. Cultural pluralism—reflecting increasing cultural "distance" between individual groups—may have gone along with this shift if it had not already been a less-than-obvious feature of Late Archaic life. I, for one, see the burial mounds that characterize Heartland after about 400 B.C. as communal responses by scattered groups to the centripetal forces working against Woodland settlement aggregation (Clay 1998:16–17). I feel that mortuary ceremonies may reflect the working out of rights and obligations *between* dispersed affiliated groups on the death of specific affines. Others would tie the mound cemeteries more tightly to specific social groups as corporate monuments to group territoriality (McConaughty 1990).

Whatever the explanation, the beginnings of local earthwork and burial mound construction lay in this pluralistic, thinly populated landscape and their appearance, communal or corporate, may be a product of settlement dispersal. The Hartman mound is a local example. Away from the river, for example, at the Ricketts mound in central Kentucky, burial mounds also were built (or shortly would be built), but with no evidence that ceramics were used in grave-side rituals. Leaving aside ceramics, this suggests that there was cultural variability among mound builders. Treating all these sites *simply* as Adena may be counterproductive.

Event-Centered Archaeological Sites

To turn to my second aspect—event-centered archaeological sites—a significant characteristic of the corporate/ceremonial archaeological sites of the Heartland Middle Woodland called Adena and Hopewell is that they are accretional: they reflect activities occurring over time (Clay 1986). This is not simply a case of stratigraphic interpretation (that is, A is earlier than B); it is much more complex. When you parse the burial mounds or earthworks into their temporal parts they seem to reflect series of activities. I have always been impressed by the potential behavioral variability that could follow sequentially in the formation of a single mound, ostensibly only a mortuary site (Clay 1986, 1998). Others also have documented this variation with detailed analyses (Abrams 1992b).

The Landing mound (Figure 8.2) in Kentucky, probably dating around A.D. 100 and generally called "Adena," is a good example of the phenomenon (W. Webb 1943c). Below the mound there was a sequence of three pre-mound structures. The order of construction is not clear but the three were built and used sequentially: they were never in use at the same time. One was a spiral fence of posts. A second was a circle of loosely paired posts and a third was a rectangular enclosure with straight walls of paired posts on three sides open on the fourth. These constructions were followed by burials. Ultimately a burial mound covered the burials and all traces of the structures and made it impossible to use the site for other than additional burial episodes.

It is difficult to interpret how these constructions were used and I think it is doubtful that any represented roofed interior spaces. This question aside, all could have been, in Riordan's (1998:73) terms, "passive controlling enclosures" demarcating ritually important spaces. Like other structures below mounds, they lack features that might suggest they were used for domestic activities. But they certainly controlled visual, and to a certain extent physical, access to a delimited area. At some point burials were made on the ground surface and later the burial mound was built over them. This action transformed them from activity contexts to cemeteries. In a simplistic but

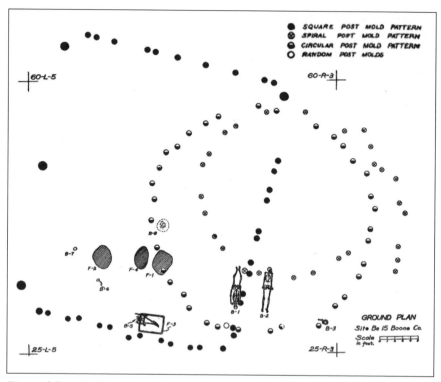

Figure 8.2 — Webb's plan of features below the Landing mound in northern Kentucky (Webb 1943b:fig. 2)

profound sense, once the mound was started no more structures could be built.

Because they differed in shape the structures probably formatted somewhat different activities or were built by work groups with different ideas of how the same activities should be staged. In addition, there is no evidence that any individual structure was repaired or rebuilt and all three were demolished after use. I submit that the three are related to different "event episodes." Perhaps they were successive acts in an unfolding drama, although the linking script is not clear and may be more complex than Seeman's (1986) suggestion that such sites were "mortuary camps." This is what I mean by "event-centered" archaeological sites.

The "great house" below the Edwin Harness mound in Ohio dating around A.D. 300 (Greber 1983) represents another level of complexity. Although a complex building with conjoined rooms and internal segmentation, there is a suggestion that it was built on an area of the Harness site that lacked previous structures. It was burned or possibly dismantled after a period of use and was not replaced. A mound then ended any use of the mound area for activities that followed it. Although the events shaped by the great house were considerably more complex than those in evidence prior to the Landing mound, in all cases buildings were constructed to begin an event and destroyed to terminate it. When the archaeologist is attuned to the potential for behavioral variability in site formation, the reconstruction of Hopewellian corporate ceremonial centers can become quite complex. In her masterful parsing of the development of the complex Seip enclosure through time, Greber (1997:214–16) reconstructs an event sequence fitting right in with the much simpler example from the Landing mound.

Elsewhere, below Adena mounds and in the vicinity of Hopewellian earthworks like the Stubbs enclosure (Frank Cowan, personal communication, 1998), multiple structures succeed one another with no real "pattern." It is as if actors came together to construct contexts for their actions, then demolished them and moved on to new events. There is a "moveable feast" character to corporate/ceremonial life in the Heartland Woodland, which may have centered on feasting (Clay 1984), especially in its "Middle Woodland" excrescencies, which is highly characteristic. This is not apparent if you treat earthwork sites simply as the sum of their parts. For far too long and for obvious reasons, because the earthworks are spectacular, we have viewed the Middle Woodland landscape of, say, the Scioto Valley as if it were a Squier and Davis (1848:map II) map of multiple earthworks and mounds. The predictable result has been a richly subdivided and structured cultural landscape that some have been content to analyze at that level (cf. Lepper 1996; J. Marshall 1996; Romain 1996). In reality in both space and time it may have been far more "discontinuous."

One thread of *continuity* is becoming apparent. Beginning as early as 400 B.C. in sites called Adena, but increasingly in somewhat later sites called Hopewell, earthworks were built to contain human behavior. Where the large earthworks have been examined, at least some of them (e.g., Riordan 1995, 1996, 1998) would seem to provide continuity over time to the structures within them. Where archaeologists have been able to get away from a fascination with the total pattern of earthworks and concentrate on their sequential development and modifications, surprising results become apparent.

At Peter, around 350 B.C., there was an early example of enclosure evolution, from stockade to ditch and bank (Clay 1985, 1987). At the Pollack works in Ohio dating from about A.D. 1 to A.D. 200, Riordan (1995, 1998) has sketched out spectacular changes in the nature of a hilltop enclosure through time that may be related to the evolution of events inside. Finally, at High Bank, Greber (personal communication, 1998) is in the process of demonstrating evolution in the nature of this significant enclosure through time, an analytical direction she has followed so well in her treatment of Seip (Greber 1997). I am sure her excavations will produce a dynamic history for this complex site such that it will no longer be viewed simply as the impressive conjoined circle and octagon mapped by Squier and Davis (1848:map XVI). But in the cases of Peter and Pollack, at least, there is the possibility that the enclosures alternatively "defended" the interior and "demarcated" ceremonial precincts without the defensive overtones.

Inside these enclosures, just as below the individual mounds, there may have been discontinuity in human activities. In fact, with the exception of the Peter earthwork, which is relatively simple and early, the later earthworks of the Heartland, like Pollack, Fort Ancient (Connolly 1997:258–69), and Seip (Greber 1997) would seem to have served as "macro" formats for complex activities. While the earthworks articulated activities in what Prufer (1964) recognized as vacant ceremonial centers and may have increased in importance over time because of this, by their evolving characters they suggest shifts in those activities as well.

Understanding why this was so is a complex problem. Undoubtedly they reflect importantly on the *nature,* not simply the *level,* of Heartland social complexity. Despite past reconstructions (Willey and Phillips 1958) that interpreted Adena and Hopewell as "Formative stage" cultures, social complexity may have been at a relatively low level. Prufer's (1964, 1997) derivative suggestion of Hopewellian ceremonial sites as vacant centers—a concept that is seeing a partial renaissance (Dancey and Pacheco 1997:8–10; Pacheco 1996, 1997)—was misleading to the extent that it posited an elite *Hopewell* population supported by a non-elite *indigenous* population. In addition, indiscriminate use of other ethnographic analogies has been more counterproductive than not (Clay 1992). Nevertheless, it must be recognized that mechanisms existed for dispersed and culturally pluralistic social groups to mesh together as the occasion demanded to build complex structures. In addition, they could maintain and develop large enclosed spaces like earthworks over a period of time and, within them, exchange a wide array of specialized artifacts in the context of elaborate and protracted funeral rites.

The Question of Domestic Structures

The final aspect of the Heartland is what I have called "the question of domestic structures." Here I wish to highlight the trajectory of architectural development in the Heartland, distinctive in that it apparently is not like the progressions that were being followed contemporaneously in other areas.

Structures, in the form of possible houses, become archaeologically visible in the Heartland for the first time about 150 B.C. in examples preserved below burial mounds like Morgan Stone (W. Webb 1941a) or Robbins (W. Webb and Elliot 1942) in Kentucky. Fieldwork in and near some corporate/ceremonial sites in the Heartland has demonstrated the presence of substantial structures (Clay 1998; Frank Cowan, personal communication concerning the Stubbs earthwork vicinity, 1998). They also occurred set apart from mounds and earthworks in seeming isolation (Clay and Niquette 1989, 1992).

There is nothing "indefinite" about these buildings although there is some question whether all were roofed. While the major paired post circles associated with burial mounds may, in some cases, have been much too large to cover (Clay 1998; W. Webb and Snow 1945), the rectangular and compound structures associated with both mounds and earthworks (Baby and Langlois 1979:figs. 4-3, 4-4; J. Brown 1979:figs. 27-1, 27-2; Greber 1979, 1983:fig. 2-4) probably were covered.

Data from some Hopewellian enclosures suggest that some of these structures may have been residential (Connolly 1997:269). Others, probably the majority, were more tightly tied to specific events associated with the earthwork (Baby and Langlois 1979:18; Greber 1997:214–15). Domestic or otherwise, their existence may have been predicated on those events and they seem to have been built for events or processes, both mortuary and nonmortuary, and then abandoned.

By and large the contemporary *domestic structures* are nowhere as elaborate and they have been very difficult to identify (Bush 1975; Carskadden and Gregg 1974; Dancey 1991; Kozarek 1987, 1997; Lepper and Yerkes 1997; Prufer and McKenzie 1965). A possible exception is the structure defined at the Twin Mounds site in Ohio (Hawkins 1996), interpreted as domestic in use even though it is located in the vicinity of a major earthwork.

The general lack of domestic facilities has contributed to the low visibility of domestic sites, perplexing to those who feel that mound and earthwork construction called for a large supporting population. If so, where was it housed? The recognition of the problem and its correction through the recognition of the significance of minor surface sites have made the presence of Middle Woodland settlement far more visible (Dancey and Pacheco 1997:table 1.1).

After circa A.D. 400, settlement pattern followed an unpredictable course generalized in two "stages," the "early" Late Woodland, to about A.D. 700, and "late" Late Woodland until A.D. 1000. The sequence is unpredictable because the Heartland did not develop toward increasing complexity resulting in agricultural Fort Ancient communities circa A.D. 1100. These stages may be an over-generalization, for there may be considerable regional variation and the culprit has been a tendency to view much of the Late Woodland as "Newtown" (J. B. Griffin 1952c). This is a culture-historical term that, as others have indicated (Ahler 1988:118–21; R. Riggs 1986:3), seems to have gotten out of hand in terms of space, time, and typology.

In the early Late Woodland the corporate/ceremonial structures of an earlier time disappeared altogether. This is an architectural revolution that has contributed to the interpretation of "Hopewellian" as one half of a dual regional tradition (Prufer 1964; Prufer and McKenzie 1965). In this view, the corporate/ceremonial buildings of the previous 300 to 500 years are ascribed to a Hopewellian elite that was specifically not the local "Scioto tradition."

In their places, for a time and in certain areas, were some of the larger and apparently most concentrated Late Woodland sites in the Heartland. In fact, these are sites that have at times been confused as the domestic villages actually associated with the mounds and earthworks (Dancey and Pacheco 1997:17). We now have considerable excavated data on these sites, but their interpretation is ambiguous.

The major excavated Late Woodland sites of the early Late Woodland are Rogers (Kreinbrink 1992a, 1992b), Hansen (Ahler 1988), Pyles (Railey [ed.] 1984), and Bentley (Henderson and Pollack 1985) in Kentucky; Leonard Haag in Indiana (Reidhead 1981; Reidhead and Limp 1974); Turpin and Sand Ridge (R. Riggs 1986, 1998), Water Plant (Dancey 1988; Dancey et al. 1987), Lichliter (Allman 1957), and Zencor-Scioto Trails in Ohio; and Childers (Shott 1990; Shott and Jefferies 1992) in West Virginia. The data vary in quality and, between incomplete data and reporting and ambiguous dating, these sites are a shaky house of cards upon which to build settlement models (Dancey 1992:26). Nevertheless, in comparison with those of earlier periods, the data are considerable. Furthermore, they do not present a consistent picture of human settlement, for pluralism was just as true of the Late Woodland as it was of the Early Woodland.

An important group of sites (Water Plant and Zencor-Scioto Trails) is concentrated in south-central Ohio. To these may be added the unexcavated examples of High Bank (33DL2), Swinehart Village (33FA7), and Ety (33FR47) (Dancey et al. 1987:73) and the excavated Childers site (Shott 1990) on the Ohio near Gallipolis. All are enclosed on one side by a ditch and embankment while the other side is defined by a river bank. Yet within the enclosed area of these sites, *as we know them at present,* one looks in vain for *substantial* domestic facilities. This is not to say they do not exist, but to argue that the identified single post oval enclosures reflect short-term and repetitive use in contrast to long-term habitation.

In discussing Water Plant, the excavators (Dancey 1988; Dancey et al. 1987) identify eleven feature clusters that they interpret as households. Because they are discrete (i.e., can be distinguished one from another with the discontinuous distribution of tool types), they suggest that there were multiple, contemporaneous households and that the whole site may have been occupied for a relatively brief period of time. Yet the excavators were unable to distinguish any structures associated with them and one must assume that built shelter was minimal. There is a possibility that evidence for structures was removed by site stripping (William S. Dancey, personal communication, 1998), but the case of Water Plant is repeated elsewhere.

At nearby Zencor-Scioto Trails, excavated over two periods but never completely published, possibly two oval structures were identified (notes of the Ohio Historical Society). Because the dates appear to be somewhat later than Water Plant, it has been suggested that the sites may have been occupied in sequence (Dancey et al. 1987:73).

The only other excavated example is Childers, where total site stripping revealed 193 features in a ditched enclosure (Shott and Jefferies 1992:54, fig. 8-1). The structural evidence is reduced to one area (Shott 1990:269) in which linking of scattered post molds suggests an oval building that was possibly rebuilt (Figure 8.3). The hypothetical linking of postholes into circular structures is unconvincing (Shott 1990:fig. 7.26), although it is possible that one or more curved screens are involved. Especially troublesome is Feature 175 inside, which consumes the bulk of its "floor space" (Shott 1990:fig. 9-10). This feature was "the deepest and largest-volume features [*sic*] discovered during UKPCRA investigations at Childers" (Shott 1990:231), probably over 2 meters deep and 2 meters wide. Short on artifact content, the feature filled through a number of episodes with "perishable household debris" (Shott 1990:231). I view the posthole alignments near this mother of all garbage pits as associated with the pit and not the area's contemporaneous or subsequent use as a house.

While the excavators cite ethnographic evidence for the association of oval structures with semisedentary groups with limited agriculture (the case at Childers), they gloss over the real inadequacies of this example as an oval structure. They reconstruct the population of the site at about 100 (Shott and Jefferies 1992:53), but no other evidence of shelter was revealed (although an unknown portion of it had been destroyed by riverbank cutting).

Perhaps the ditch and embankment give these sites a distinctive character and has most affected their interpretation as domestic aggregate sites, if not actually "nucleated" settlements. The Water Plant ditch (Dancey et al. 1987:fig. 31) was 1.6 meters deep and about 4.25 meters wide (Dancey et al. 1987:26). An associated embankment is assumed, but could not be demonstrated and there was no palisade associated with the feature. A ditch clearly is indicated on air photographs of Zencor-Scioto Trails (William S. Dancey,

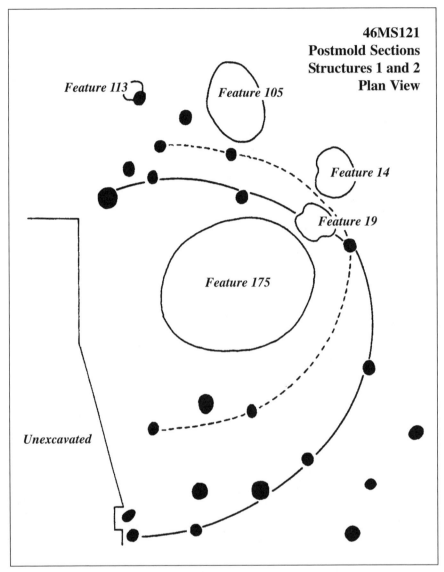

Figure 8.3 — Houses (?) at the Childers site

personal communication, 1998) and combinations of ditch/embankment are still preserved at unexcavated examples. The Childers ditch (Shott 1990:fig. 7.28) was similar in dimensions to the Water Plant example yet neither embankment nor palisade could be identified.

The interpretation of these is critical. They have been glossed as defensive features in discussions of Heartland village origins (Dancey 1992:27), perhaps responses to "predation by neighboring Hopewellians experiencing population growth at a time of climatic stress on food resources" after A.D. 400. In this view both household aggregation, and the defending ditch, represent defensive responses.

Others question this interpretation in the absence of palisades. Thus, in discussing the roughly contemporaneous Greenwood Village in northeast Ohio, Belovich (1998:178) suggests that the ditches at that site "clearly did not function as fortifications" in contrast to their function at Late Prehistoric Whittlesey sites that had both ditches and palisades. I suggest that increasingly they will be seen as nondefensive, space-marking features. Interestingly, they may look "backward" in conceptualization to the type of enclosures associated with Hopewell.

Other examples of structures in non-ditched sites dating to this early Late Woodland stage suffer from a "connect the dots at all costs" weakness in definition, or worse. Two adjacent sites, Hansen (Ahler 1988) and Bentley (Henderson and Pollack 1985), are cited as examples of "substantial" Late Woodland settlements (Railey 1996:115). They occur near a major Hopewellian earthwork in Kentucky: Bentley is literally adjacent to its walls while Hansen is somewhat over 1 kilometer away. Both sites are clearly multicomponent.

At least two circular structures seem to be proposed for Bentley (Henderson and Pollack 1985:155, fig. 7.6). The site includes Middle Woodland (Hopewellian), Late Woodland, Late Prehistoric, and Historic components, however, and neither circular structures, nor circular *Woodland* structures, would appear to be adequately demonstrated in the available documentation (Henderson and Pollack 1985). Disconcertingly, features at one point assigned to a Late Woodland Newtown component (Henderson and Pollack 1985:fig. 6) are elsewhere assigned to the Historic component (Pollack and Henderson 1984:fig. 8), and the Historic component is, rather, a Historic component confounded with a Late Prehistoric Fort Ancient occupation. Despite the laudable attempt, Bentley illustrates the real difficulty in subdividing multicomponent sites into their respective temporal/cultural parts.

Hansen is also multicomponent with Middle Woodland and Late Woodland occupations. Three possible oval posthole patterns have been proposed, with rebuilding stages (Ahler 1988:127–38). These are resolved into a temporal sequence suggesting structural change through time. Ahler (1988:138) ventures the opinion that "the Hansen site structures provide the best architectural data available for the Newtown phase." The structure plans, however, are unimpressive, suggesting a lack of substantial domestic structures.

Other Newtown components lack even ambiguous structural detail. Although a fair amount of the Rogers site in northern Kentucky was excavated

(Kreinbrink 1992a, 1992b), no house patterns have been identified at either of the discrete midden areas. It has been fancifully suggested that these middens reflect the existence of "some form of social dualism (perhaps a moiety division) within the village society" (Railey 1991:66), all without any convincing evidence. More believably, it is suggested (Kreinbrink 1992b:100) that the middens are different in age, as indicated by several lines of artifact analysis including the ceramics. In fact, with temporally distinct occupations, Rogers reinforces Dancey's observations from Water Plant that occupations in this early Late Woodland time may have been relatively short term. At Rogers settlement shifted laterally, perhaps relatively rapidly.

Finally, two sites that have been involved in the formulation of Newtown for some time—Sand Ridge and Leonard Haag—lack any evidence for structures at all. A third, Turpin, which is perhaps the archetypical Newtown site (J. B. Griffin 1952c; Oehler 1973), does have a reported rectangular structure (Oehler 1973:photo 6, p. 6), but given the shape of this feature I am inclined to associate the building with the major Late Prehistoric Fort Ancient component. Perhaps the most substantial domestic structures that are felt to be associated with the early Late Woodland in the Heartland are the three examples from the Lichliter site near Dayton (Allman 1957). As best as they can be reconstructed, these are of quite a different order from the examples noted from Zencor-Scioto Trails, Childers, and Hansen. They are circular, possibly completely or partially "double walled," with two lines of postholes. In his discussion of the Hansen site, Ahler (1988:137) points out that these structures are "reminiscent of large Middle Woodland structures which are usually found in association with Adena or Hopewell mortuary sites. ... These structures are not comparable to those from Hansen, and may represent a Middle Woodland component at Lichliter." The implication of this comment is that the Lichliter site must be multicomponent, but the pottery Allman (1957:68) illustrates would seem to be Late Woodland.

Additional confusion about the nature of early Late Woodland settlement has been created by the claim that substantial, structured, oval, nucleated settlements are associated with "Newtown" in northern and eastern Kentucky (Railey 1991:66–69, 1996:115–17) beginning as early as A.D. 300. This claim stems from the publication of the Pyles site in northern Kentucky by the William S. Webb Archaeological Society, interpreted as a circular, doughnut-shaped midden reflecting a circular settlement around an open "center" (Railey [ed.] 1984:fig. 5-1, p. 29). "As many as six stone mounds" (Railey [ed.] 1984:30) are interpreted as part of the site, although the two remaining ones (Railey [ed.] 1984:fig. 5-1) would seem, lacking any excavation information from them, to be simply rock piles beside a typical central Kentucky drywall rock fence that bisects the site. At least two other very similar sites, Gillespie and Mays Lick, are said to exist nearby.

One radiocarbon assay of A.D. 360 ± 120 (1590 ± 120 B.P.) has been obtained from Pyles along with two thermoluminescence (TL) dates on burned chert flakes of A.D. 1000 and later. On the strength of these, Pyles is considered to date from roughly A.D. 300 to 500. In fact, there is little firm idea where the site dates and the artifacts suggest that it is multicomponent. Various chert artifacts point to Archaic and Late Prehistoric components. Because Ohio Flint Ridge chert is significantly associated with the northern "portion" of the village, and Newman cherts with the southern half, one archaeologist has suggested that "village symmetry at Pyles may have been predicated on internal divisions within the village society" (reported in Railey 1991:66) and the possibility that the distribution reflects time is not considered. The ceramic collection, given the frequency of certain attributes like distinctive "shoulders," more likely dates circa A.D. 600.

A controlled surface collection and limited excavation at the site revealed various pit features, but no structures and no palisade or other feature defining the edge of the circular midden. Real questions are raised regarding the cleared center of the doughnut that was free of cultural midden constituents. Because of a high concentration of "occluded phosphates," it was interpreted, among other things, as the area where the inhabitants of the site prepared vegetative materials and habitually defecated (Railey [ed.] 1984:91). Furthermore, in this center the women and children gathered while "warriors engaged intruders around the periphery, discharging weapons from behind houses" (Railey [ed.] 1984:120). In summary, few published interpretations of Pyles seem to be solidly supported by any data, yet it is considered a significant demonstration of settlement construction for the Late Woodland.

To the examples of Water Plant, Childers, Hansen, Rogers, and other sites must be added an increasing use of rockshelter sites in the Heartland Late Woodland through time, represented by sites like Rogers (Cowan 1975), Haystack (Cowan 1979), Stanhope (Seeman and Prufer 1988), Chesser Cave (Prufer 1967b), and many others. All suggest that Heartland cultures staunchly resisted "village" life until they adopted corn agriculture after A.D. 900. Finally, this is certainly echoed in the dispersed nature of Late Woodland burial. The many stone burial mounds or cairns, like Hawkins Ridge (unpublished notes, Cincinnati Museum of Natural History), Sparks, Chilton (Funkhouser and Webb 1937), Dungan, and Norton Clay (Clay 1984), and the practice of burying in earlier burial mounds (sometimes called "intrusive mound culture"), look backwards in time to Middle Woodland practices with considerable simplification and not forward to the Late Prehistoric. Yet despite this, in a group of sites dating around A.D. 500–600, larger sites were built and used on an intermittent basis.

While it is clear that Woodland cultures of the Heartland did not lack open-air domestic shelter, it is obvious that it was minimal and ephemeral in contrast to the demonstrably domestic, substantial structures of the Late Prehistoric. Furthermore, in contrast with surrounding regions, domestic architecture does not seem to have been used to differentiate space within the settlement in a meaningful way beyond the suggestion that some sites, like Pyles, were arranged in a circle. For example, the contrast between summer and winter structures and possibly individual and corporate structures found in Owl Hollow phase sites of central Tennessee and somewhat foreshadowed by clustered single post structures in the McFarland phase (Kline et al. 1982:69–71; C. H. Faulkner, this volume) remains resolutely lacking. In speaking of the McFarland phase, although he could just as well be describing the Heartland, Seeman (1992a:14) notes, following Dean Snow (1980:71), that the lack of "overlapping postmold patterns, structural repair, superimposed features, dump areas, or a concern with reusing storage pits for refuse … suggest *sedentism* but not *permanence*" (emphasis in the original). Here, then, is perhaps the critical lesson of the "question of domestic structures" today.

As a final irony, settlement became even simpler through time in the Heartland after A.D. 700. Commenting on the settlement pattern of the late Late Woodland Parkline phase on the lower Kanawha, Niquette and Kerr (1993:53) note that "the data suggests that small, highly-mobile groups lived primarily on the banks of medium to large rivers. Winter occupations probably occurred in rockshelters. The only site type recognized in the region is the small camp."

I assume—with no particular enthusiasm for the explanation because the linkage is complex and controversial—that the particular character of Heartland habitation was closely related to Woodland economics. This involved a continuing emphasis on hunting and gathering, registered in an increasingly efficient hunting kit (Seeman 1992b), coupled with a commitment to the cultivation of a suite of local plants. As Wymer (1987:211–13) points out, the distinctive agricultural mix was probably a constant through much of the Woodland period. As such, the factor of agriculture per se probably cannot be used to explain the dramatic development or decline of the corporate/ceremonial centers of the Heartland. It probably *does* explain in part the continuing, perhaps universal, relevance of the "question of domestic structures," as I have touched on it above. Yet this mixed economic strategy never even remotely began the process of reformatting use of the Heartland in a way that was so dramatically true of the Mississippi Valley. Changes came with the Late Prehistoric, corn-using Fort Ancient culture. But even after A.D. 1000, older patterns of dispersed settlement are perhaps still apparent in the tendency of Fort Ancient groups to cyclically reoccupy village locations, rather than use them intensively over long periods of times like their downriver Mississippian neighbors.

Summing Up

While I have used Early Woodland ceramic materials to discuss cultural pluralism, Middle Woodland corporate/ceremonial structures to present "event-centered" archaeology, and Late Woodland settlement plans as an entrée to dispersed residence, it should be clear that all three apply to all three subperiods of the Heartland Woodland. In fashioning interpretations of Heartland cultural development all should be integrated into the explanation.

To state it more explicitly, throughout the Woodland we are dealing with cultural pluralism at a number of levels. For example, in the Early Woodland it may be expressed in differential adoption and use of ceramics. In the Middle Woodland it may be reflected in differences in the localized production of "Interaction Sphere" materials to a regional pattern, in regional expressions of Adena/Hopewell "ceremonialism," and in the disconnected nature of event-centered corporate/ceremonial sites. In the Late Woodland perhaps it is expressed in ceramic differences, for example, shifts in cordage twist (Maslowski 1984), in differing patterns for the exploitation of regional chert resources, and in the individualism and dispersal of mortuary sites. In any case, pluralism as an analytical starting point would seem to be called for although it may be typologically difficult to operationalize.

This pluralism perhaps in part explains what I have termed "event-centered" archaeology, or the seeming tendency of Heartland archaeological sites to reflect discontinuous and shifting local activities. However complex, the earthwork/mound complexes of Hopewell grew out of series of event-like "happenings." I visualize these, as I have sketched them elsewhere for Adena alone (Clay 1998), as products of somewhat fluid ceremonial groups that came together for a variety of activities including, importantly, mortuary ritual. If we were able to parse the large and complex sites into sequential activities—an archaeological research direction that has become increasingly important in the Heartland—I am sure this would become apparent. Confounding earlier interpretations of Hopewell, complexity in the *social structure* of Heartland social groups should perhaps be replaced by complexity in the *social relations* between relatively simply structured social groups.

Finally, the domestic arrangements notable in Heartland Late Woodland are no more baffling than the domestic arrangements of the earlier Middle Woodland. The Heartland is marked by an ambiguity of settlement, despite the complexity of its corporate/ceremonial sites. Despite Middle Woodland corporate/ceremonial sites, despite large Late Woodland domestic sites defined in part by ditches and banks, and despite a certain type of agriculture, the attractions of hunting, gathering, and foraging seem to have tugged the Heartland Native Americans toward a resolutely dispersed and dispersing way of life. This surely must be taken into account in any attempts to understand life-styles in the region.

Acknowledgments

I would like to thank William S. Dancey and Mark Seeman, in particular, for reprints, miscellaneous archaeological facts about a subject they know so well, and critical comments. They can hardly be held to account if I have not heeded their wisdom or criticisms. N'omi Greber, Frank Cowan, and Rick Matchet have all helpfully provided me with insights on their continuing work. Any comments I make on this work should be held accountable to their ultimate interpretations. Finally I would also like to thank Steve Creasman and Charles Niquette for critical comments and input.

Chapter 9

Woodland Cultures of the Elk and Duck River Valleys, Tennessee: Continuity and Change

Charles H. Faulkner

Tennessee sits astride an environmental Mason-Dixon line between the Deep South Coastal Plain in west Tennessee and the oak-hickory woodlands in east Tennessee stretching east and north into the Ohio Valley and beyond. This has been a problem for Tennessee archaeologists as they wrestled with the term *Woodland,* since its relationship to crushed-rock-tempered, textured-surface pottery (see, for example, Sears 1948) seems to be more at home in the prehistoric culture history of the Midwest and Northeast than the Southeast. Nevertheless, the term was embraced by T. M. N. Lewis and Madeline Kneberg (1946:4), who called Woodland a "pattern." Later Kneberg (1952) wrote about Tennessee Woodland "people" who were divided into early, middle, and late groups, following the lead of James B. Griffin (1952a), who popularized the term as a period designator.

When archaeological mitigation began in the Normandy Reservoir in the upper Duck River valley of Tennessee in 1972, the project archaeologists debated how to use this term of culture-historical integration that was still current in Tennessee prehistory. Since no culture-historical scheme had been established for this virtually unstudied region of the Eastern Highland Rim, and a workable and familiar organizational/descriptive tool was needed for space-time synthesis, the units of period, tradition, phase, and component were selected. Woodland was designated a period and divided into Early, Middle, and Late time segments. Within periods, phases were defined by traditions, using the definition of Willey and Phillips (1958:37) of "a temporal continuity represented by persistent configurations in single technologies or other systems of related forms." In this scheme, cultures (i.e., phases) are largely defined by patterned and interrelated traditions. Woodland cultural traditions best demonstrating increment and change in Normandy archaeological assemblages include projectile points, pottery, burials, subsistence, housing, and community patterning. This chapter will focus on Woodland population dynamics in the southern portion of the Eastern Highland Rim of Tennessee, especially as reflected in community patterning.

Field Methodology

The Normandy Archaeological Project was conducted in the upper Duck River valley to collect archaeological data from sites threatened by construction of the Tennessee Valley Authority Normandy Reservoir (Figure 9.1). A survey of the 72 miles of shoreline began in 1972, followed by Phase II testing and Phase III mitigation, which ended in 1976 when the Normandy Dam was completed and the 3200-acre reservoir lake was filled. A total of 170 prehistoric sites was located in the floodplain, older alluvial terraces, valley slopes and bluffs, and uplands. Two hundred and forty-seven prehistoric components were identified by period on these sites. Woodland components included seven Early Woodland; forty Middle Woodland; sixteen Late Woodland; and eleven unidentifiable Woodland (C. H. Faulkner and McCollough 1973).

After completion of the survey, sites were selected for Phase II testing on the basis of two major research goals: to establish a cultural history of the upper Duck River valley, particularly for the past 4000 years, and to determine how these prehistoric people adapted to the unique environment of the Eastern Highland Rim. The sites selected were characterized by midden deposits containing well-preserved faunal and floral remains, deeply buried strata, well-represented components of several major time periods, and well-preserved sub-plowzone features, especially structural remains.

Testing consisted of the excavation of 5-by-5-foot (1.5-by-1.5-meter) units placed within a permanent grid using either a random or intuitive sampling scheme, or both schemes, depending on site size, surface conditions, and surface concentrations of identified component material. Twenty-one sites were tested (C. H. Faulkner and McCollough 1974; Keel 1978; McCollough and Faulkner [eds.] 1976). Twenty-two Woodland components were identified, primarily from sub-plowzone features. These included three Early Woodland, twelve Middle Woodland, and seven Late Woodland components. The previously suggested rarity of Early Woodland components and an intensity of Middle Woodland occupation in the upper Duck Valley was verified in the testing phase.

Fourteen tested sites were selected for intensive Phase III mitigation on the basis of presence of subsistence data, preserved middens, and well-defined features. If midden deposits were revealed below the plowzone, additional hand-excavated multiple-unit blocks were opened in these areas (R.

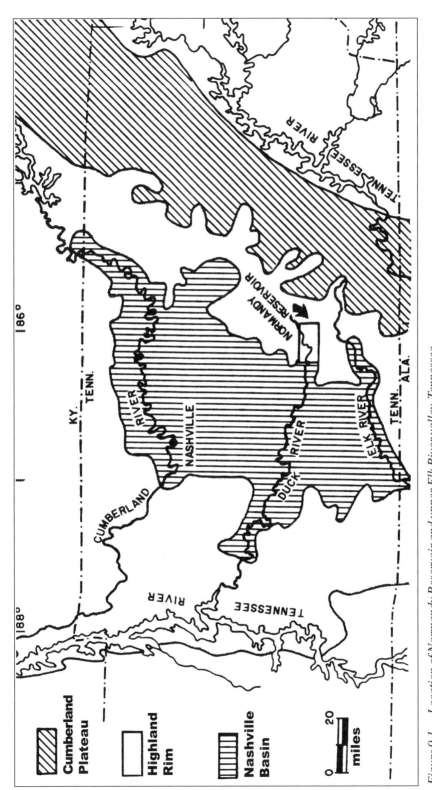

Figure 9.1 — Location of Normandy Reservoir and upper Elk River valley, Tennessee

Davis 1978; C. H. Faulkner 1977a, 1977b; C. H. Faulkner and McCollough 1974:176–257). When subsoil was encountered directly below the plowzone, which often was the case on the intensively cultivated and deflated Normandy Reservoir sites, the plowzone was removed with a pan scraper. This enabled us to gather extensive data on domestic patterns, the scope of which was unprecedented for the Woodland period in the southeastern United States. Identified Woodland components included six Early Woodland, fourteen Middle Woodland, and seven Late Woodland (C. H. Faulkner and McCollough [eds.] 1978, 1982a, 1982b; McCollough and Faulkner [eds.] 1978). Testing hypotheses about Middle Woodland settlement, community, and subsistence patterns in the Eastern Highland Rim continued after the Normandy Reservoir Project from 1976 to 1982 with National Science Foundation grants (J. Cobb 1985; J. Cobb and Faulkner 1978; C. H. Faulkner 1988; Kline et al. 1982). Additional sites were excavated outside the reservoir zone in the upland areas bordering the Duck River valley and adjacent upper Elk River valley where an intensive Middle Woodland occupation had been previously identified in the Tims Ford Reservoir (Faulkner [ed.] 1968). This three-decade systematic study of Woodland cultures occupying the upper Duck and Elk river valleys has provided a detailed regional framework for this period in the Eastern Highland Rim of Tennessee.

Watts Bar Phase

The earliest Woodland culture in the upper Duck River valley was first identified by a tradition of quartz-tempered, fabric-marked pottery. This pottery is almost identical to Watts Bar Fabric Marked in the eastern Tennessee Valley where it is profuse on large, intensively occupied Early Woodland sites (Lafferty 1981; T. Lewis and Kneberg 1957). Only two sites in the Normandy Reservoir, Nowlin II and Banks III, produced Watts Bar features; deep conical or deep circular storage pits and shallow circular basins, similar to circular storage pits and basins found on earlier Late Archaic sites in the same area (C. H. Faulkner and McCollough 1982). These features contained Watts Bar Fabric Marked pottery, Adena-like stemmed and Wade corner-notched points, the latter indicating the continuity of a stemmed/notched point tradition from the Late Archaic period. Two features on the Nowlin II site produced radiocarbon dates[1] of 2625 ± 140 B.P. (750 B.C.) and 2350 ±

---

[1] *All radiocarbon dates in this chapter have been calibrated using OxCal (Bronk Ramsey 1994, 1995), giving dates representing the median of a 95 percent confidence interval for the calibrated determinations.*

125 B.P. (475 B.C.) (Keel 1978:163). Except for two storage pits on the Nowlin II site, Watts Bar features were singular occurrences and ranged from 12 to 18 meters apart. This indicates a very small population of nuclear families occupying these sites for a single season, with many years elapsing before they returned to the same site. The Watts Bar phase has not been identified in the upper Elk Valley, suggesting the upper Duck Valley may be on the western boundary of this phase in the Tennessee Valley.

Long Branch Phase

This phase appears in the Eastern Highland Rim after 400 B.C. Significant changes in the artifact inventory include the replacement of quartz tempering with limestone tempering in the fabric-marked ceramic tradition and the appearance of a new tradition of stemless triangular points. Four sites (Banks I, 40CF34; Banks V, 40CF111; Jernigan II, 40CF37; and Aaron Shelton, 40CF69) provided information on community patterning with storage pits and shallow food-processing basins continuing to dominate the pattern and earth ovens making an appearance on these sites.

Two of these sites, Banks I and Banks V, continued the pattern seen in the preceding Watts Bar phase: single or small isolated clusters of features suggesting short-term, occasional occupation. On the former site, a large basin-shaped earth oven found in block excavations gave a radiocarbon date of 2156 ± 80 B.P. (215 B.C.), the earliest date for a Woodland earth oven in the reservoir (C. H. Faulkner and McCollough 1974:192). At Banks V, a single trash-filled storage pit produced a radiocarbon date of 2341 ± 90 B.P. (500 B.C.) (J. Cobb 1978:198, 314–15). No other Woodland features were found in the vicinity in this area of the site.

More frequent reoccupation of the same site is seen at the Jernigan II and Aaron Shelton sites. At the former site there were three clusters of features about 18 to 24 meters apart. These clusters contained varying combinations of storage pits, shallow processing basins, and earth ovens, and all clusters had associated burials, one group containing four burial pits. The flesh burials were flexed in shallow oval graves. One burial was radiocarbon dated at 2106 ± 555 B.P. (200 B.C.) (C. H. Faulkner and McCollough [eds.] 1982a:292–300).

Unlike at the Jernigan II site, the twelve Long Branch features at the Aaron Shelton site were generally concentrated in a single 18 by 18–meter area. These features included storage pits, shallow basins, at least two postholes, and two burials, one a flexed flesh inhumation in a shallow oval basin and another a redeposited cremation in a small pit. Charcoal from a shallow basin gave a radiocarbon date of 2166 ± 110 B.P. (200 B.C.) (M. Wagner 1980:182–97).

The larger clusters of features at the Jernigan and Aaron Shelton sites suggest a changing community pattern of larger groups reoccupying the same site on a more frequent basis, foreshadowing the more permanent occupation of sites seen in the succeeding Neel and McFarland phases. In fact, Mark Wagner (1980) places the Woodland component at Aaron Shelton in the early McFarland phase, an indication of the marked continuity between the Long Branch and McFarland phases. The closest relationship of the Long Branch phase in the upper Duck Valley appears to be with the Colbert culture of northern Alabama (Walthall 1980).

Neel Phase

Community size and configuration in the upper Duck and Elk river valleys changed dramatically between approximately 200 B.C. and A.D. 200. These domestic discontinuities mark the appearance of the Neel phase, which, based on radiocarbon dates, overlapped both the Long Branch and McFarland phases. Because the former appears to be ancestral to the latter, it has been suggested that Neel phase sites were simply cultural variants in the late Long Branch–early McFarland settlement system, functioning as special mortuary camps (C. H. Faulkner 1988:81).

Two Neel phase sites, Yearwood (40LN16) in the upper Elk Valley and Parks (40CF5) in the upper Duck Valley, could represent such mortuary sites. At Yearwood, eleven square, circular, and open-sided structures were found in three clusters dated with five radiocarbon determinations ranging from 1980 ± 60 B.P. (15 B.C.) to 1800 ± 75 B.P. (A.D. 235). Cremation burials and the presence of exotic materials such as copper, mica, galena, Flint Ridge chert, quartz crystals, and rocker-stamped ceramics indicate Yearwood was a gathering point for the redistribution of exotic goods within what has been called the Hopewell Interaction Sphere, as well as a place to ritually dispose of the dead (Butler 1979).

At the Parks site, seven square to rectangular structures ranging from 161 square meters to 264 square meters were grouped on the northwest edge of this large multicomponent site. Hearths were the most common interior installations, followed by earth ovens and cache storage pits; most of these features occurred in the corners or along the wall line. An earth oven carbon 14 dated at 2170 ± 185 B.P. (300 B.C.) contained numerous artifacts including a rectangular siltstone pipe, an antler atlatl handle, and sherds from a limestone-tempered red-filmed vessel (Bacon 1982). A cremation in a cluster near these structures was radiocarbon dated at 2205 ± 125 B.P. (350 B.C.) (T. Brown 1982a:450).

Small domestic sites are also present in the Neel settlement system in the upper Duck River valley. An intensively rebuilt round pole dwelling with a central hearth dated 2065 ± 60 B.P. (80 B.C.) was found at the Eoff I site (40CF32A) (Figure 9.2), suggesting repeated occupation of the same locality by the Neel people, possibly on an annual basis (C. H. Faulkner 1977a).

What appears to be a Neel phase habitation site has also been excavated on Aenon Creek in the middle Duck River valley. Storage facilities, an earth oven, and a redeposited cremation produced radiocarbon dates of 2400 ± 70 B.P. (580 B.C.), 2220 ± 60 B.P. (280 B.C.), and 1880 ± 70 B.P. (A.D. 105) (Bentz [ed.] 1995).

Companion domestic sites to Neel phase mortuary sites are also found in the upper Elk Valley. The Brickyard site (40FR13) had a small Neel component consisting of a cluster of at least three features and postholes, one of them a large fire pit radiocarbon dated at 2285 ± 110 B.P. (450 B.C.). Predominant ceramics are limestone-tempered cord-marked and plain with a minor occurrence of rocker-stamped pottery (Butler 1968).

The Hyatt site (40GL45) is a larger Neel phase site on upper Richland Creek, a tributary of the Elk River. Features consisted of fifty-six pit features including a hearth, storage facilities, earth ovens, and numerous scattered postholes. The earliest Woodland date from these features is 1900 ± 80 B.P. (A.D. 80); the latest 1640 ± 90 B.P. (A.D. 405). Plain and cord-marked vessels with podal supports appear to dominate the ceramic assemblage with a minority of dentate rocker-stamped vessels. Trade material includes quartz crystal and mica (McIlvenna 1994).

The radiocarbon dates at the Hyatt site support a temporal overlapping of the Neel and McFarland phases, but with the former appearing earlier and centered in the Elk River drainage. The temporal precedence of the Neel phase has also been suggested by Futato (1982), who sees a close relationship to the Lick Creek phase in the Bear Creek watershed of northwestern Alabama. The Neel phase also appears to be related to the Middle Woodland component at the Walling site in the Wheeler Basin of northern Alabama (Walthall 1973:391–422) and the Hopewell assemblage at the Tunacunnhee site in northwest Georgia (Jefferies 1976, 1979).

McFarland Phase

The Neel domestic traditions of triangular and expanded stemmed projectile points and limestone-tempered pottery are also found in the McFarland

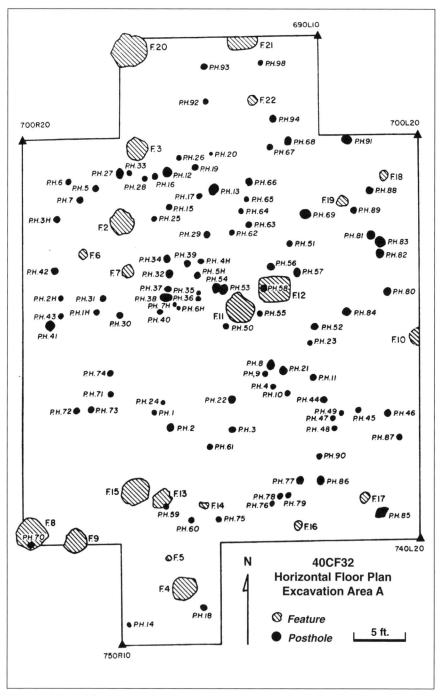

Figure 9.2 — Plan view of Neel phase structure area, Eoff I site (from Faulkner 1977a)

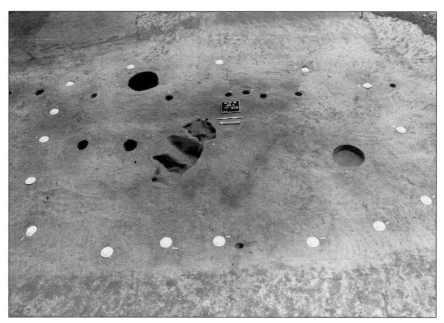

Figure 9.3 — McFarland phase Structure II, Eoff I site. Storage pit appears at upper left; shallow basin at lower right. Feature in center is partially excavated tree fall (from Faulkner and McCollough [eds.] 1982b).

phase. Unlike the Neel phase, cord marking is a minor surface treatment with fabric-marked vessels being common in early McFarland and check-stamped vessels predominating on later McFarland sites. Significant changes continue to occur in demography, community patterning, trade, and ceremonial activity. The early McFarland community plan is found at site 40FR47 in the upper Elk River valley and the Eoff I and Ewell III sites in the upper Duck Valley. Tims Ford Reservoir construction in 1970 exposed a series of discrete outdoor activity areas adjacent to an oval structure on site 40FR47 dated at 1895 ± 95 B.P. (A.D. 115) (Bacon 1975; Bacon and Merryman 1973). Pan stripping of the Eoff I site revealed three single dwellings with oval to round tensioned pole wall-roof frameworks from 6.4 to 8.2 meters in diameter and spaced from 73 to 128 meters apart along the first terrace with an open food preparation and storage zone located at some distance from the dwellings. One of these structures dated to 1855 ± 145 B.P. (A.D. 175) (C. H. Faulkner 1982) (Figure 9.3). At the Ewell III site, nine clusters of McFarland pits and an earth oven were found in an area 15 to 46 meters from two structural areas: one of semicircular or cabana structures in the central portion of the terrace and the other an oval enclosed pole structure at the west end with a cemetery between the windbreaks and oval structure. Four radio-carbon assays from features at Ewell III have a mean date of A.D. 125 (DuVall 1977, 1982).

The above McFarland structures and accompanying features mark a distinctive community pattern that characterizes this phase for the next 200 years. These small villages were highly structured into discrete dwelling and food-processing zones. Houses consistently contain from one to three cylindrical storage pits along one wall and a shallow basin near the opposite wall. Most food preparation and additional storage took place in an intensively utilized zone some distance from the dwellings. Both open shelters and fully enclosed structures occur, sometimes in different areas of the site. The enclosed houses seem to have been infrequently repaired or rebuilt, indicating an intensive but short-term occupation.

Late McFarland villages were larger, with the McFarland site proper (40CF48) having at least three contemporary pole houses with contiguous walls (Figure 9.4). These structures and two others excavated on the site were substantially built round to slightly oval pole dwellings rather uniform in size, averaging 6.6 by 6.5 meters. Five carbon 14 dates from the McFarland site have a weighted average of A.D. 200 (Kline et al. 1982:68). The substantial architecture and clustered houses at McFarland suggest a more permanent occupation, probably because of an increasing reliance on cultivated weedy annuals such as goosefoot and maygrass, domesticated sunflower, sumpweed, squash, and maize (Crites 1978a, 1978b, 1985; Kline et al. 1982).

During the McFarland phase the burial mode shifted from flesh inhumations and cremations interspersed throughout the domestic area to predominantly cremation cemeteries. It is also possible that mortuary camps like Parks continued to be utilized, but few exotic goods are found on McFarland sites and it appears that these people were not active participants in the Hopewell Interaction Sphere.

The most dramatic change in the spiritual realm was the construction of the Old Stone Fort, a stone and earth-walled ceremonial enclosure at the confluence of the Big and Little Duck rivers (C. H. Faulkner 1996). Initial construction at the Old Stone Fort began about 1920 ± 85 B.P. (A.D. 70). While the function of this site is still a subject of speculation, cremated human bone was reportedly found in the walls in 1928 (Cox 1929), and this enclosure has been recently identified as a possible solar observatory (Pearsall and Malone 1991).

The similarity of the McFarland phase to surrounding archaeological complexes appears to be more widespread than such similarities in either the preceding Neel or the succeeding Owl Hollow phase. It had ties to the Copena complex or culture to the south (Futato 1982:109–10; Walthall

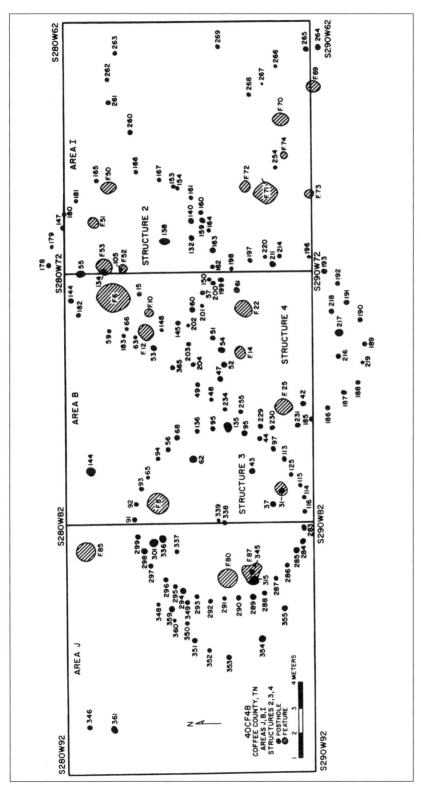

Figure 9.4 — Plan view of McFarland phase houses on McFarland site (from Kline et al. 1982)

1980:116–31), to a McFarland-like component at the Duncan Tract site (40TR27) on the Cumberland River to the north (McNutt and Weaver 1983:289–90), and to the Candy Creek–Connestee components in the eastern Tennessee Valley (J. Chapman and Keel 1979).

Owl Hollow Phase

By A.D. 300, new traditions had emerged in the Eastern Highland Rim in the Owl Hollow phase, named after the large and intensively occupied type site in the upper Elk Valley. Owl Hollow villages appear even more highly organized than the preceding McFarland villages, and unlike the preceding McFarland phase settlement pattern, villages in the upper Duck Valley are only located in the broader river valley of the lower Normandy Reservoir zone. Another difference is that the only known Owl Hollow sites were intensively occupied, creating dense middens; small camps with a few scattered features do not seem to occur in this phase.

The most striking characteristic of the Owl Hollow phase is the dual structure pattern of large oval double earth-oven winter houses and companion warm-season oval or square pole houses (C. H. Faulkner 1977b). These structures were sometimes arranged on a circular midden ring around a debris-free open area or "plaza," the midden being largely formed from burned limestone and ash from the large interior heating and cooking ovens in the winter houses. Occasional maize in the food-processing pits and large storage features around both warm- and cold-season structures indicates a growing dependency on gardening in the wider floodplains of the upper Duck Valley (Crites 1978b). Burial patterns are not clearly defined although two cremation clusters and four flesh burials have been attributed to this phase at the Banks III site (T. Brown 1982b:138–39). Continuity with the preceding McFarland phase in the sacred sphere is also indicated by the latest construction date of A.D. 505 for the Old Stone Fort.

Early Owl Hollow villages are characterized by two different community patterns. One is a large village represented by the type site in the upper Elk Valley. The Owl Hollow village was concentrically structured, with earth-oven winter lodges situated around the periphery of the midden ring and the lightly framed summer houses forming an interior circle of buildings around an open plaza area. One of the winter lodges was at least 10 to 12 meters in diameter and the interior earth ovens produced carbon 14 dates of 1675 ± 60 B.P. (A.D. 385) and 1855 ± 95 B.P. (A.D. 170) (J. Cobb and Faulkner 1978).

The early Owl Hollow community pattern is different in the upper Duck Valley, where large circular middens are absent, the dwellings do not exhibit extensive rebuilding, and storage pits are infrequent around houses. Single paired winter-summer houses appear to be typical, the best example being Structures I and II at the Banks III site (Figure 9.5). Artifact content from earth ovens and postholes indicates an early occupation, but radiocarbon dates from these features have such a large standard deviation that their reliability is dubious (C. H. Faulkner and McCollough 1974:272–80).

Late Owl Hollow sites show an increase in the size of the winter lodge and a spread of sites from the main river alluvial floodplain into the upland tributaries (C. H. Faulkner 1988:92–95). Typical large earth-oven houses include Structure III at the Banks III site, measuring 12.1 by 10.4 meters with a mean radiocarbon date from three assays of circa A.D. 591 (C. H. Faulkner and McCollough 1974:283–88); a double-oven house on the Eoff I site, measuring 13.7 by 11.3 meters with a radiocarbon date of 1485 ± 60 B.P. (A.D. 545) and an archaeomagnetic date of A.D. 300 for an interior oven (J. Cobb 1982:159–65); and the large (13.7 by 10.6 meters) Structure I on the Banks V site (Figure 9.6), with a mean radiocarbon date of A.D. 515 from two interior ovens (J. Cobb 1978:105–70).

The Owl Hollow phase may have existed in the upper Elk and Duck River valleys until the ninth century A.D. Unfortunately, little is known about post–A.D. 600 community patterns since only two Owl Hollow sites have

Figure 9.5 — Owl Hollow phase Structure II, Banks III site (from Faulkner and McCollough 1974)

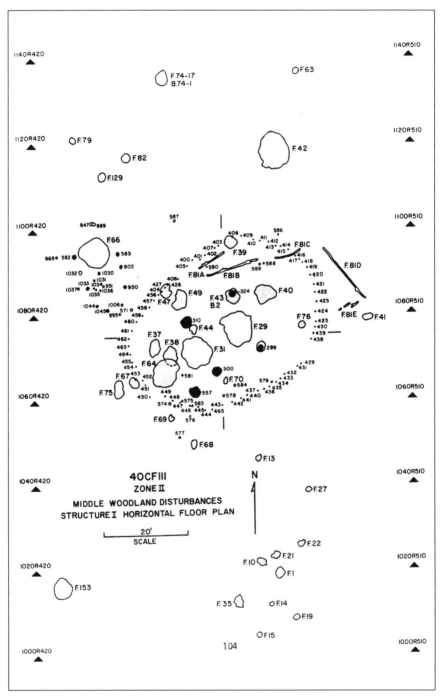

Figure 9.6 — Plan view of Owl Hollow phase Structure I, Banks V site (from Cobb 1978)

been tested from this time period and no complete structural remains have been found.

The deep, rich midden at the Raus site (40BD46) on Thompson Creek, a tributary of the Duck River, was trenched and a radiocarbon date of 1335 ± 60 B.P. (A.D. 725) was obtained from the base of the midden. An alignment of seven postholes, two redeposited cremations, and a possible crematory basin were excavated (J. Cobb and Faulkner 1978:38–39). The Hamby site (40CF214) on Betsy Willis Creek about 2 kilometers north of the Elk River was tested with eighteen widely spaced 2 by 2-meter units. Nine subsurface features were found, the most significant being two large storage pits, one producing radiocarbon dates of 1045 ± 110 B.P. (A.D. 975) and 1140 ± 55 B.P. (A.D. 890) (J. Cobb and Faulkner 1978:116–21).

The discontinuities between the McFarland and Owl Hollow phases are also seen in their respective technologies. Pottery is still largely limestone tempered, but the surface treatment on Owl Hollow vessels is simple stamped on early sites and largely plain surfaced in later components. Projectile points are shallow side-notched or lanceolate "spike" forms. Another distinctive Owl Hollow lithic artifact is the chert microtool (J. Cobb and Faulkner 1978).

While simple-stamped pottery and side-notched/spike projectile points are found in several late Middle Woodland contexts in the Midsouth, the distinctive double-oven winter houses seem to be particularly characteristic for the Eastern Highland Rim of Tennessee. The only other published description of a double-oven house is from the Tombigbee drainage: a Late Miller II structure measuring 11.0 by 8.8 meters with large interior support posts flanking two earth ovens (N. Jenkins and Ensor 1981). In the middle Duck River valley of Tennessee, the late Middle Woodland component at the Edmondson Bridge site produced Owl Hollow–like projectile points and ceramics that were associated with three large oval-rectanguloid structures (Bentz 1986). Interestingly, the closest relationship of the Owl Hollow phase may be to the La Motte culture in the lower Wabash Valley where the community pattern is characterized by circular middens around a debris-free plaza and intensively rebuilt round and rectangular houses (Pace 1973; Winters 1963).

Mason Phase

The Mason phase, appearing in the upper Duck and Elk river valleys circa A.D. 800, represents a major break in the technological and social traditions that had existed in this area for centuries. Ceramics are now tempered with crushed chert and have textured surfaces of cord marking and net impressing. The small triangular projectile point makes its appearance at this time (Duggan 1982; C. H. Faulkner 1968).

Besides these marked discontinuities in technology, a major change also occurs in community patterning. The highly organized villages of the preceding McFarland and Owl Hollow phases are now replaced by smaller dispersed habitation sites with variably placed and configured features. At the Mason type site on the Elk River, the village has a distinctive central area dominated by a cemetery (C. H. Faulkner 1968:fig. 3). Two large bell-shaped storage pits filled with refuse were radiocarbon dated at 1180 ± 85 B.P. (A.D. 835) and 1060 ± 90 B.P. (A.D. 970). Mason sites in the upper Duck drainage appear to be less intensively occupied. The Mason occupation at the Parks site had a structure adjacent to a cluster of refuse-filled storage pits, some containing flesh burials (T. Brown 1982a:531–36). However, large food-processing and storage facilities are rare on other Mason sites in the Normandy Reservoir. At the Jernigan II site, the Mason phase is represented by a dwelling and two flesh burials (C. H. Faulkner and McCollough [eds.] 1982a:303–5). Features around a Mason structure at the Ewell III site include four earth ovens and a small storage pit. One of the earth ovens was radiocarbon dated at 980 ± 75 B.P. (A.D. 1055) (DuVall 1977:89–90, 1982:58–59).

Unlike the dwellings on McFarland and Owl Hollow sites, Mason houses tend to be ill-defined with erratically placed wall posts spaced from 1 to 3 meters apart. None was rebuilt. Enclosed oval pole structures were found at the Jernigan II and Parks sites. The former measures 6 by 9 meters with a central basin hearth and large support post (C. H. Faulkner and McCollough [eds.] 1982a:204–7) (Figure 9.7). The Parks site structure was constructed of flexible poles with a diameter of about 7 meters. It was intruded by the storage pit/inhumation cluster; one of these pits was radiocarbon dated to 875 ± 50 B.P. (A.D. 1140) (T. Brown 1982a:439). The dwelling at the Ewell III site was a roughly square (7 by 7 meter) shed or cabana-like structure with one open end. A central interior earth oven was radiocarbon dated at 965 ± 70 B.P. (A.D. 1090) (DuVall 1982:72–79).

The sacred sphere of inhabitants of Mason phase sites also differs from that of their predecessors. The Old Stone Fort ceremonial enclosure was abandoned by this time. Burials were now exclusively flesh inhumations, and there was great variation in the interment mode. Three types of cemeteries occurred. At the type site a flexed adult was placed in a shallow oval grave beneath a large rock-filled pit on which an intense fire burned. Oval graves of a flexed child and an adult were located on opposite sides of the rock pit (C. H. Faulkner 1968:35–39). At the Parks site, flexed bodies had been placed in a cluster of refuse-filled storage pits (T. Brown 1982a:401–45). The two Mason burials at the Jernigan II site were flexed in shaft and

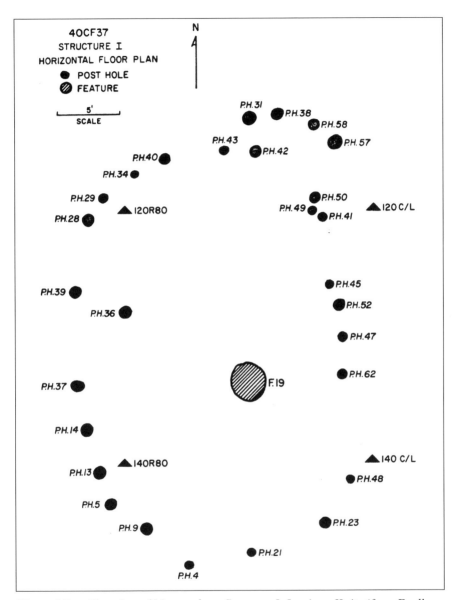

Figure 9.7 — Plan view of Mason phase Structure I, Jernigan II site (from Faulkner and McCollough 1982)

chamber graves (McCollough and DuVall 1976:43–52; McCollough et al. 1979).

Despite the general similarity of the Mason artifact assemblage to the Hamilton "focus" of the eastern Tennessee Valley (T. Lewis and Kneberg

1946) and the McKelvey culture of northern Alabama (Walthall 1980:137–41), there do not appear to be any close cultural analogs to the Mason phase outside of the upper Elk and Duck river valleys of middle Tennessee. Evidence of contact with early Mississippian culture is found at the type site and at Mason phase sites in the Normandy Reservoir. The above carbon 14 dates support the overlapping of these cultures in time. Interestingly, some of the most similar Late Woodland culture traits such as net-impressed ceramics and shaft and chamber graves are shared with Late Woodland groups in the North Carolina Piedmont (McCollough et al. 1979:185–86).

Conclusions

During the approximately 2000 years of Woodland occupation of the Eastern Highland Rim, cultural traditions waxed and waned as cultural phases appeared, flourished, and eventually disappeared from the archaeological record. Demographic fluctuations and cultural influences entering the Eastern Highland Rim from surrounding regions of the Eastern Woodlands were probably major factors in explaining these cultural dynamics. Demographic fluctuation in this and other areas of North America during the prehistoric period is probably one of the most interesting, yet understudied aspects of lifeways during this time.

In the upper Duck River valley, there was a marked change in community patterns and an obvious decrease in population during the Early Woodland period. This phenomenon of depopulation has also been noted in the lower Illinois River valley where there were dramatic shifts in settlement patterns and widespread dispersal of the population over the landscape (Emerson 1986:629). Conversely, other regions of the Midsouth witnessed a marked population increase after 1000 B.C. in the Watts Bar and Long Branch cultures of the eastern Tennessee Valley, represented by numerous large sites with deep, rich middens (Lafferty 1981; McCollough and Faulkner 1973; Schroedl 1978a). These regional population differences have not been studied in depth in the Midsouth.

While there appears to be a population decline in the Early Woodland period, the sixfold increase in number of sites during the Middle Woodland period indicates a significant population increase in the upper Duck Valley during this time. Multiple causal factors have been proposed, including interaction throughout a similar environment of the southern outliers of the Prairie Peninsula (C. H. Faulkner 1988), horticultural intensification of herbaceous annuals and the appearance of maize in the diet (Crites 1978a, 1985), and the establishment of a regional ceremonial center at the Old Stone Fort

(C. H. Faulkner 1996). On the basis of the number and size of sites, population may have again declined during the Late Woodland period. Gardening with maize as a constituent continued during this time (McMahan 1983), but major differences in the technological inventory and community patterns suggest a discontinuity after a long period of relative cultural stasis.

Evidence of contact with surrounding regions is found in prehistoric cultures of the upper Duck and Elk river valleys throughout the Woodland period. Intensity and direction of contact, however, shift through time. In the Early Woodland, cultural traditions in these valleys resembled those in the middle Tennessee Valley of northern Alabama and the upper reaches of this river system in east Tennessee. Contacts to the north are evident during the Neel phase when trade is established with the Hopewell cultures of Illinois and Ohio, although the roots of this phase appear to be to the south. During the succeeding McFarland phase, participation in the Hopewell Interaction Sphere seems to decline and there is a strong relationship to the Copena culture of the middle Tennessee Valley despite the fact that the latter manifestation maintained a relationship to Ohio Hopewell (Walthall 1979). Relationships are again oriented to the north in the Owl Hollow phase, which has affinities to the La Motte culture of the lower Wabash Valley. This focus to the north is abruptly broken by the Mason phase, which seems regionally restricted and surprisingly shows some affinities to Late Woodland cultures on the Carolina Piedmont.

Are these similarities between regions the result of stimulus diffusion, occasional contact (trade), or migration of entire ethnic groups? These culture-historical questions have fallen out of favor in American archaeology in recent years, but in reality are at the heart of understanding the temporal and social relationships between the numerous Woodland cultures that existed for 2000 years in southeastern prehistory. However, the ability to answer such questions is not provided by the data presently at hand, and answers are beyond the scope of this chapter. Nevertheless, it is important for southeastern archaeologists to answer them at a future date. To do so we need innovative research designs to address such questions about Woodland cultural dynamics on a regional scale, followed by intensive survey, predictive testing, and careful excavation of an adequate sample of Woodland communities. Numerous chronometric dates are essential. These dates should then be subjected to quantitative treatments to determine what overlapping and non-overlapping of phases should look like in radiocarbon terms. When these final questions are answered, we will be able, we hope, to say who these people really were, and terms like *Woodland* will be obsolete.

Chapter 10

Woodland Period Settlement Patterning in the Northern Gulf Coastal Plain of Alabama, Mississippi, and Tennessee

Janet Rafferty

The portion of the Midsouth considered in this chapter is the area west and south of the highland rim in western Tennessee, plus north-central Mississippi and west-central Alabama. It includes the central part of the Tennessee River valley, the Tombigbee, Black Warrior, and lower Alabama River valleys, and the upland coastal plain adjacent to these valleys (Figure 10.1). The Mississippi River valley proper is excluded from consideration, although the upland areas east of the river that drain into it are included. The study area was occupied in prehistoric times by people who made pottery diagnostic of the Gulf Formational and Middle and Late Woodland cultural periods, including the Wheeler, Alexander, Tchula, Copena, Miller, Marksville, West Jefferson, and Baytown phases and pottery types (N. Jenkins and Krause 1986; N. Jenkins et al. 1986; Jennings 1941; Mainfort and Chapman 1994; Phillips 1970; Walthall 1980; Walthall and Jenkins 1976). The time span considered is from circa 800 B.C. to A.D. 1050 (Figure 10.2). This includes the time from the beginning of fiber- and sand-tempered pottery making in the Tennessee and Tombigbee basins at circa 800 B.C. (Walthall 1980:87) and of grog-tempered pottery in the eastern uplands of the central Mississippi Valley at circa 300–400 B.C. (Peacock 1996a) to the beginning of mussel shell as an important pottery temper at circa A.D. 1000–1050 (Welch 1990) in the former area and circa A.D. 700–800 (D. Morse and P. Morse 1983:201, 1990:156) in the latter area.

The focus of the current chapter on settlement patterns precludes detailed consideration of other topics of importance to Woodland period regional archaeology, although a short overview of ceramic and lithic modes and regional chronology is given. Other topics, such as subsistence data and information on warfare, are reviewed briefly.

~

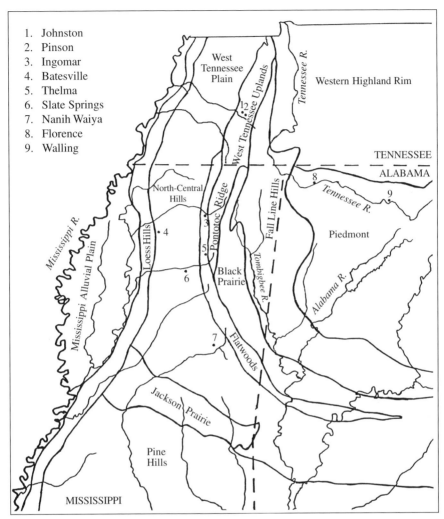

1. Johnston
2. Pinson
3. Ingomar
4. Batesville
5. Thelma
6. Slate Springs
7. Nanih Waiya
8. Florence
9. Walling

Figure 10.1 — Physiographic provinces and locations of flat-topped Woodland mounds

Chronology: Ceramic and Lithic Styles

The Gulf Formational cultural period, which represents the earliest pottery in the Tennessee and Tombigbee River valleys, is defined by fiber-tempered plain, punctate, and dentate stamped Wheeler and sand-tempered punctate, pinched, and incised Alexander styles (N. Jenkins et al. 1986; Walthall and Jenkins 1976). In the western part of the study area, it is coincident with Tchefuncte pottery and followed by Tchula styles (N. Jenkins et al. 1986),

Date	Northwest Mississippi (1)	West Tennessee (2)	Northeast Mississippi (3)	Northwest Alabama Bear Creek (4)	Northwest Alabama Pickwick to West Wheeler Basin (5)	North-Central Alabama (6)
1100					West Jefferson	
1000						
900						
800			Miller III	Miller III	McKelvey	
700		Late Woodland/ Baytown		Lost Creek		Flint River
600						
500	Baytown					
400			Miller II	Copena		Bell Hill
300					Copena	
200	Marksville	Middle Woodland		Lick Creek		Walling
100			Miller I			
0						Green Mountain
100	Tchula			Colbert	Colbert	
200						Colbert II
300		Early Woodland				
400						Colbert I
500			Broken Pumpkin Creek			
600		Gulf Formational		Bluff Creek	Bluff Creek	
700						Gulf Formational
800						

(1) Peacock 1996b, Phillips 1970; (2) Smith 1996; (3) Jenkins 1982; (4) Futato 1989, Walthall 1980; (5) Walthall 1980; (6) Knight 1990a

Figure 10.2 — Cultural periods in the lower Midsouth

the former characterized by untempered and poorly wedged plainwares (Phillips 1970:162–64) and the latter by cord-impressed, red-slipped, and fabric-marked grog-tempered pottery (Mainfort and Chapman 1994; Phillips 1970:878–80). While usually classified as Woodland, Tchula pottery from northwest Mississippi and west Tennessee has similarities in temper to Tchefuncte pottery of the Mississippi River delta and Gulf Coast (N. Jenkins et al. 1986:551; Mainfort 1994); on the other hand, wares classified by decoration as Tchula in southeast Missouri are more similar to Alexander pottery in that they are sand-tempered (Price 1986). Tchula seems to be the earliest pottery-making tradition over much of west Tennessee and northwest Mississippi, especially in upland areas where neither Tchefuncte nor Wheeler nor Alexander pottery is present (J. L. Ford 1989; Peacock 1996a, 1997a).

Woodland pottery is recognized by the common use of fabric-marked and cord-marked surface treatments (Jennings 1941:196–99), although check stamping also is important in the eastern part of the study area (P. Jackson 1996:13; Walthall 1980). Tempering agents used in the region during Early and Middle Woodland times largely seem to have followed environmental zones until, in the Late Woodland, grog tempering replaced other modes everywhere. Thus, both grog and sand temper were in use in the central Mississippi Valley, depending on whether braided-stream deposits were present on the surface to serve as a source of sand or whether the available clay was from backswamps, in which case it was tempered with grog (D. Morse and P. Morse 1983:138–39). At first, grog tempering also predominated in the uplands to the east of the main river valley, including the upper reaches of Mississippi River tributaries such as the Forked Deer, Obion, and Tallahatchie rivers, but it was replaced by sand temper (Mainfort 1994; Peacock 1997a) as people took advantage of locally abundant sand deposits or of sandy clays. Farther to the east, in the Tombigbee Valley and surrounding uplands, sand temper was commonly used from the Gulf Formational through Middle Woodland periods, a span of 1000 to 1400 years (N. Jenkins and Krause 1986; Mainfort 1986:35; G. Smith 1979:47). This area has abundant sandy clay and sand for pottery making. In the middle Tennessee River valley, pottery was tempered with crushed limestone for 1000 years, in Colbert and Copena times (Walthall 1980:112). As a result of differences in surface geology, predominant temper modes have chronological meaning within each of these areas, but are not useful in integrating across areas.

In analyzing Woodland pottery from the region, controversies occasionally have arisen over whether it is important or possible to distinguish grog-tempered pottery with sandy paste from that with non-sandy paste (J. L. Ford 1989; Mainfort 1994; Mainfort and Chapman 1994; Peacock 1997a;

G. Smith 1979:76–77) and whether to use the size or amount of grog or sand particles as a distinguishing feature (Connaway 1980; Mainfort 1994). Such disputes can be resolved best by using less ambiguous temper categories, so that pottery can be classified consistently (cf. Mainfort 1994; Mainfort and Chapman 1994; Peacock 1997a); materials analysis also may be helpful in some cases (cf. Metcalf 1992). If the goal is purely descriptive (i.e., there is no attempt to infer chronological or functional information using these classes), it is not advisable to spend time in such sorting, however distinct and well-defined the categories.

The most extensive discussion of Woodland stone tool styles for the region is in the Gainesville Lake project lithics volume (Ensor 1981). This includes sections on projectile point typology and chronology that extensively update and supplement Woodland type descriptions in the Alabama projectile point guide (Cambron and Hulse 1975) and the Normandy Reservoir reports in Tennessee (C. H. Faulkner and McCollough 1973). Another major compilation is the Mississippi point type guide (McGahey 2000). Projectile point–based seriations of collections from northeast Mississippi are presented in J. Rafferty (1994); for Gulf Formational through Middle Woodland points, the modes that were found to be most useful for devising chronologically sensitive types were unmodified stem bases, in which the stem base displays either a striking platform or cortex, and small to medium point size. Illustrations in the Mississippi point type guide (McGahey 2000) show that many Gulf Formational through Middle Woodland projectile point types display these features.

Stemmed projectile point styles were replaced in Late Woodland times by small triangular, ovate, and side-notched forms usually identified as arrow points (Blitz 1988; McGahey 2000), although the ovate ones probably also served as knives (Peacock 1986). McGahey (1999:3–4) discusses a peak in the use of Kosciusko quartzite, which outcrops in a north-south band through the center of Mississippi, to make Collins and Madison points during Late Woodland times. Extensive settlement in the north-central hills of Mississippi during the Late Woodland period, as discussed below, may partly explain the great increase in use of this raw material then.

Land Use and Settlement Patterns: Analytic Dimensions

In examining Woodland or any other settlement patterns, most data will come from archaeological survey rather than from excavation, since survey provides the large number of assemblages required to study artifact and site distributions. Whether based on survey or excavation data, a number of dimensions can be used to analyze settlement pattern change. These dimensions mostly provide devices to examine spatial aggregates of artifacts (site-based assemblages), rather than individual objects (G. Jones and Beck 1992:168–72). The dimension most commonly applied to the Woodland period is site function, referring to how a place was used. Although assemblages are sometimes recognized as palimpsests of many kinds of uses, this is usually either ignored or held to not disrupt in a major way the archaeologist's ability to investigate site functions (e.g., Blakeman 1975a, 1976; J. Johnson 1988; J. Rafferty 1980, 1996). Function is inferred from site setting and feature and artifact function, so that a variety of burial sites (earthen and stone mounds, burial caves, cemetery areas), geometric earthworks, habitation sites (base camps, temporary camps, hamlets, villages), and special-purpose sites (ceremonial encampments, extractive camps, hunting camps) have been assigned to the Woodland cultural period or to Woodland phases in the region (Brooms 1980; Futato 1988; N. Jenkins 1982; Mainfort 1986, 1988a, 1996a; Mainfort and Walling 1992; J. Rafferty 1990, 1996; Thunen 1998; Walthall 1973, 1980; Walthall and DeJarnette 1974).

Annual residential mobility forms a second dimension used in settlement pattern studies (J. Kelly 1992; J. Rafferty 1985); nucleation (or aggregation) forms a third (Dancey 1991, 1996; Pacheco 1996). Archaeologists have termed a particular site a base camp or a village, a temporary camp or a hamlet, on the basis of differing mobility models, with differences in nucleation also recognized by these terms. Sedentary settlements are those occupied year-round for at least one year (J. Rafferty 1985), with varying kinds of residential mobility recognized below that threshold and various kinds of short- and long-term sedentary settlement recognized above it. Nucleation and dispersion are two ends of a dimension referring to occupation size and, ultimately, related to the number of people who lived at the place during any one occupation. Usually, degree of nucleation is assessed using information on the size of artifact scatters or non-overlapping feature clusters assignable to a particular component at a site (e.g., N. Jenkins 1974; Jeter 1977).

In the lower Midsouth, small concentrations of Woodland artifacts, especially if distributed in a variety of environmental settings, usually are attributed to seasonally mobile populations and treated as transitory or extractive camps (Futato 1987:128, 227; N. Jenkins 1982:52, 63, 72, 94, 110; Jeter 1977:130; Mistovich 1988). Larger sites with higher artifact density, usually with midden development, have been classified either as base camps (N. Jenkins 1982:54, 63, 72, 94, 110; Mistovich 1988; Welch 1990) or as sedentary settlements-cum-villages (Jeter 1977; J. Rafferty and Starr 1986). Size thus has been used to indicate aggregation, mobility, and site function, with these being confounded—although site size may be an indicator of all three dimensions, additional measures must be used to differentiate mobility states, site function, and nucleation.

Two other settlement pattern dimensions are duration, also often called permanence, and continuity of settlement patterning. Both of these depend on use of dating methods to measure the time over which artifacts accumulated or the contemporaneity of site occupation (G. Jones and Beck 1992). Duration is taken to mean the length of site use resulting in deposition of a continuous record of chronologically sensitive artifact styles (Dunnell 1970), however those are defined; duration is measured from beginning to end of such spans (J. Rafferty 1994). A site may not have been occupied either continuously or "permanently" under this definition. In fact, it is arguable whether any occupation can be held to be permanent, in the sense of having been unchanging or at a place that was never abandoned (Cameron 1993:3).

Major continuities and discontinuities in distribution of occupations also deserve attention as part of understanding settlement pattern change (Dewar 1991; Dewar and McBride 1992; J. Rafferty 1996), particularly as they relate to environmental constraints, resource availability, and cultural stability and evolution. The extent to which temporally discrete occupations were congruent at a particular place (cf. Binford 1980; Dewar and McBride 1992) is a formation process problem. The necessity to use spatial association to date and interpret nondiagnostic artifacts (G. Jones and Beck 1992) has been a strength and a difficulty with both site and siteless approaches to recording surface artifact locations (Dunnell 1992; Dunnell and Dancey 1983).

Characterizations of other aspects of settlement pattern change—evolution of hierarchical organization, demographic change, and range constriction—depend on controlling the above dimensions to make higher-level inferences. As noted for Woodland as well as other periods (Nassaney and Cobb 1991:295–96), population growth or decline cannot be assessed unless one controls first for duration of site use, degree of nucleation, and mobility patterns; it is unlikely that site area or number of sites ever is related in a simple way to number of people, although this simple equation often is made. Similarly, site hierarchies cannot be identified until contemporaneity, presence of sedentary settlement, and parameters of site function have been determined, since sites in a hierarchy must serve different centralized, and sometimes competitive, functions in a contemporary settlement system (Hodder and Orton 1976:55–69).

There is no necessary correspondence among these settlement pattern dimensions and so usually no reason a priori to believe they bear invariant relationships to one another. Nonetheless, they often are conflated. For example, sedentary settlements, which minimally represent year-round occupation for one year, are sometimes said to be permanent (Futato 1987:227).

Similarly, the term *village* has been used to refer to a place inhabited year-round (i.e., a sedentary settlement), to a nucleated camp or nucleated sedentary settlement, or to a long-duration and continuously occupied nucleated sedentary settlement. The prevalent confusion is well illustrated by an example: "The density of artifact types normally found in base camp context is indicative of a sedentary lifeway at a more or less permanent village site" (Jolly 1971:32). A recent non-Woodland example shows that such confusion continues to be common: "One implication of such tool forms [expedient and heavy tools] is that the Early Archaic people of Florida were more sedentary, that is that they lived at least part of the year in permanent villages" (J. J. Miller 1998:61). While separate terms are not necessarily needed for each of these and other uses, it is nonetheless important to differentiate conceptually among them.

These settlement pattern dimensions have not been applied consistently in intensive analyses of Woodland data from the region. Whether changes in mobility, nucleation, duration, and continuity occurred and whether they were gradual or abrupt are empirical questions; so also is the question of whether site use and settlement patterning fluctuated between extreme states along these dimensions or maintained a steady trajectory of change or did some of both. Extensive archaeological survey work done in the lower Midsouth in the past ten to fifteen years has begun to make studies of such issues possible. This is especially the case for the Woodland period, since occupations dating from 1000 B.C. to A.D. 1000 are numerous.

Survey Data from Northeast Mississippi: A Case Study

Extensive archaeological survey in the Tombigbee River valley began in conjunction with planning for the Natchez Trace Parkway, stretching from Nashville to Natchez and located largely in upland parts of the river drainage. One result of early work along the Parkway was the basic Miller chronological sequence, devised by Jennings (1941). The next major advance in knowledge came with work on the Tennessee-Tombigbee Waterway, from the early 1970s through the mid-1980s. Open-field survey predominated, and hundreds of sites were recorded along the route of the waterway (Atkinson and Elliott 1978; Blakeman 1975a, 1976; N. Jenkins et al. 1975; Rucker 1974; Thorne 1976). Analysis of these data (Blakeman 1975a, 1976; J. Rafferty 1980) revealed that proportionately more sites with Archaic components were located in the northern section and more sites with Mississippian components were located in the central portion of the river valley. Woodland sites were found throughout, but with larger Late Woodland occupations tending to be more common in the Black Belt or Black Prairie portion (Futato 1987:227; N. Jenkins 1982).

To show the potential of survey data to address settlement pattern continuity and change, a database has been compiled that includes information on the large number of sites recorded in the uplands of northeast Mississippi over the past twenty-five years. It includes 855 assemblages with Gulf Formational and/or Woodland components, defined by the presence in surface or shovel test collections of fiber-, grog-, or sand-tempered pottery, the latter counted only in the absence of shell-tempered sherds or if cord-marked or fabric-marked sherds were present. Sand-tempered pottery has been shown to be associated consistently with both live shell- and fossil shell-tempered wares (J. Rafferty 1995a, 1998), so its mere presence in a collection is no longer adequate to identify a Woodland component.

Though several dozen of the sites in this compilation have been subjected to some excavation, excavation data were excluded from the initial analysis on grounds of non-comparability. The area studied is the western part of the upper central Tombigbee drainage and the far eastern reaches of the Mississippi River drainage in northeast Mississippi. It has been shown in the course of seriations done of survey collections that this entire area is within the sphere of the Miller tradition (Peacock 1997a; J. Rafferty 1994).

Five site distributions were generated, one for each of the cultural periods from Gulf Formational through Late Woodland, using UTM coordinates. The maps in Figures 10.3 through 10.6 include 472 of the 855 sites, since not all assemblages had the precise diagnostics required. The same sites are marked repeatedly if they produced diagnostic pottery modes from more than one period. The first two distributions are of sites that had fiber-tempered pottery or produced sand-tempered pinched and punctate sherds, diagnostic respectively of the middle and late Gulf Formational periods, 800 to 300 B.C. The third displays the distribution of sand-tempered fabric-marked sherds, indicative of Miller I components (300 B.C.–A.D. 150) and the fourth the distribution of sand-tempered cord-marked pottery, most closely associated with Miller II occupations and dating from circa A.D. 150 to 600. Finally, the distribution of grog-tempered cord-marked pottery is displayed. It is diagnostic of Miller III, from circa A.D. 600 to 1050. In using these styles as diagnostics, it is recognized that their temporal ranges overlap; they serve as a device to examine settlement pattern change on a gross temporal scale, not as markers for phases regarded as internally homogeneous.

While not representing complete coverage, these data show that survey has been extensive and intensive enough to begin to suggest patterns of change through both space and time. The assemblages with fiber-tempered pottery are widely distributed (Figure 10.3), but show a tendency for the

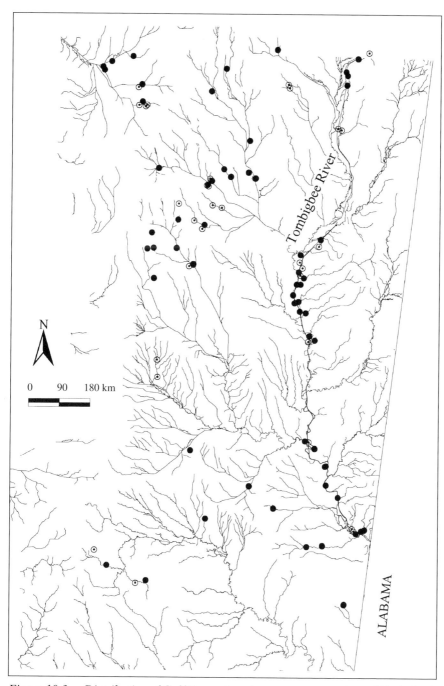

Figure 10.3 — Distribution of Gulf Formational components, northeast Mississippi: assemblages with fiber-tempered (solid circle) and/or sand-tempered pinched or punctate pottery (dotted circle)

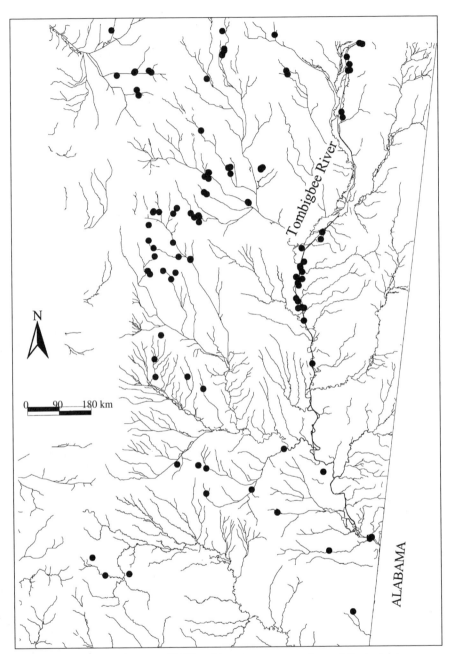

Figure 10.4 — Distribution of Miller I components, northeast Mississippi: assemblages with sand-tempered fabric-marked pottery

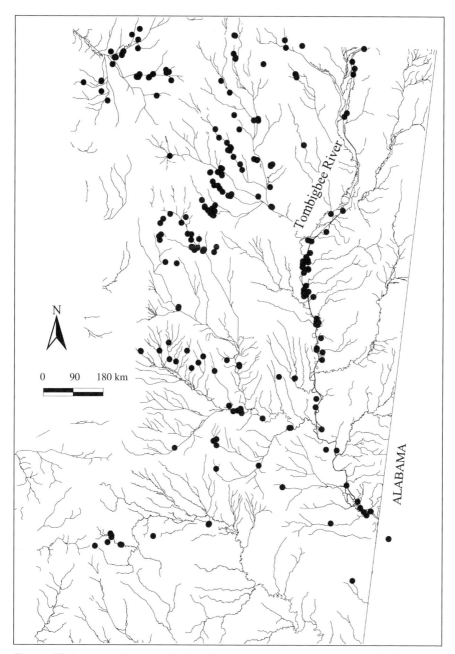

Figure 10.5 — Distribution of Miller II components, northeast Mississippi: assemblages with sand-tempered cord-marked pottery

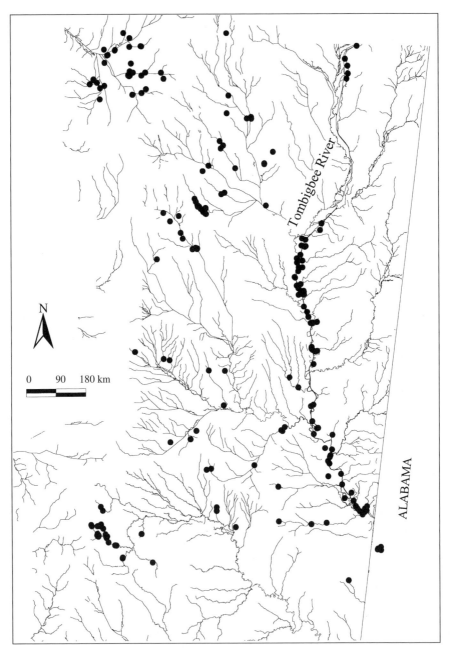

Figure 10.6 — Distribution of Miller III components, northeast Mississippi: assemblages with grog-tempered cord-marked pottery

highest site density to be along the Tombigbee River and the lowest to be in the southwest portion of the region. The distribution of sites with sand-tempered pinched and punctate sherds is similar; these pottery types probably were largely contemporary with fiber-tempered wares. There are relatively few locations shown, most likely as a result of sampling error, as many of the assemblages are small, and the requirement that certain decorative styles be present further reduced their number.

Sand-tempered fabric-marked pottery is distributed in much the same areas, but with more assemblages represented (Figure 10.4). Assemblages containing this type are found as commonly in the west-central area (Lee and Chickasaw counties) as along the river. This holds true for the sand-tempered cord-marked sherd distribution also (Figure 10.5), with a third fairly dense concentration in the northwesternmost region. Finally, during the Late Woodland period, as represented by grog-tempered cord-marked pottery, another dense concentration is evident in the southwestern area (Figure 10.6).

The most striking aspect of these data is the evidence they give of continuity in settlement patterns, at least with reference to habitation activities, over this large area (15,000 square kilometers) and through nearly 2000 years. One main change evident at this macro-scale is in-filling, in which already-settled areas came to contain more sites through time. No major settlement pattern shifts are evident, although there are areas in which few sites were used in the earlier periods but high site density pertained later. This contrasts with other areas where settlement remains at low density throughout. Long-term Woodland settlement continuity has been noted previously for smaller areas within the region (J. Rafferty 1996).

There are a number of possible explanations for these patterns of continuity. One is population growth, with existing sites continuing to be used while new ones came into use. This might occur by populations budding off from established settlements to form new ones (Dancey and Pacheco 1997:9). Another possibility is that settlements changed from more nucleated to more dispersed, so that a greater number of smaller sites were occupied with no population increase. A third scenario would involve a change in duration of site use, so that more sites were in use because each one was used for less time. These ideas all work under the assumption that the entire sequence of settlement represented was sedentary (J. Rafferty 1994) and that most of the sites visible to this method were used for habitation. This assumption cannot be critically examined at this time, although more data from small occupations will provide the basis for doing so in the future.

If one subarea is examined, changes through time can be seen in more detail. It appears from the distribution of components in Figure 10.7, representing the southeasternmost segment of the larger map, that new sites were

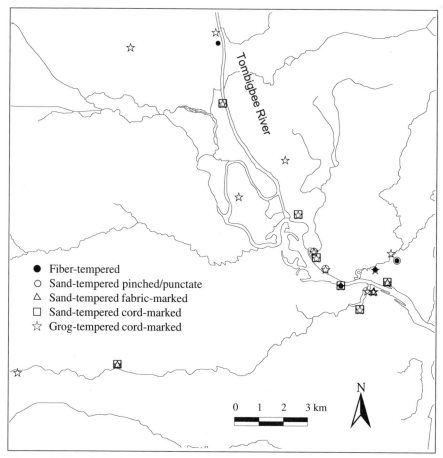

Figure 10.7 — Distribution of Gulf Formational through Miller III components, southeast subarea

being occupied mostly along the river. In Late Woodland times, a number of sites came into use that had no earlier Woodland or Gulf Formational occupation. This map also displays the biased picture caused by lack of extensive survey away from the Tombigbee River in this area, so that a fair representation of changes in the interior and along the lower Noxubee River is not given.

The patterns of assemblage duration derived from survey data are shown in Figure 10.8. For purposes of comparison, the durations are shown as lasting for the entire length of each cultural period for which diagnostics are present in the assemblages. Thirty-nine assemblages that showed discontinuities in occupation are not included; they are almost equally distributed over all possibilities (i.e., there are nine assemblages showing Gulf

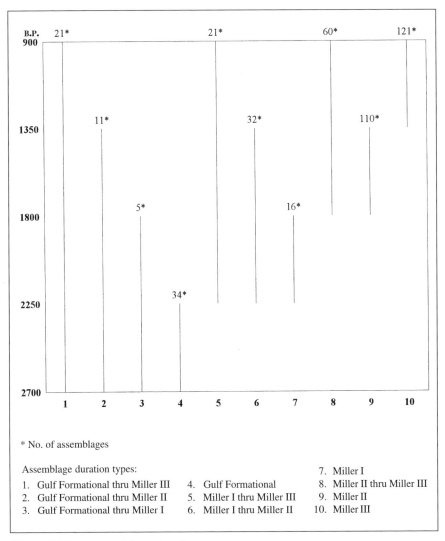

Figure 10.8 — Assemblage durations

Formational and Miller II sherds, with no Miller I; six showing Miller I and Miller III modes with no Miller II, etc.). Similar diagrams, in hypothetical form, have been displayed by others (Dancey and Pacheco 1997:22; Dewar and McBride 1992:235), but enough data have been controlled in this case to allow examination of actual patterns of change (cf. Dewar 1991). These data confirm that some (about 5 percent) of the assemblages represent long-duration habitation through all four cultural periods and that the number of moderate-duration assemblages—those indicating occupation over two to three periods—increases through time. The number of places occupied in only one period also increases through time, with the number of such sites increasing by 350 percent from Miller I to Miller II times (Figure 10.8). This kind of analysis is a beginning, but much more work on mobility, site function, nucleation, contemporaneity, and how mound building correlated with habitation density and dispersion is needed to obtain fuller understanding of the evolutionary changes that occurred in this part of the region.

These data provide a glimpse of the mass of Woodland settlement pattern information available from archaeological surveys. Information gained from excavations carried out in the area, which mostly have focused on sites in the main Tombigbee River valley, confirms the presence of numerous long-duration Woodland sites used for sedentary habitation. Examples of sites occupied from Gulf Formational through Miller III times, and in the Mississippian period as well, are Kellogg village (Atkinson et al. 1980), Shell Bluff (Futato 1987), and Tibbee Creek (O'Hear et al. 1981). Other sites, such as the Sanders site (O'Hear 1990), the Mingo site (Jolly 1971), the Self and Okashua sites (Wynn and Atkinson 1976), L. A. Strickland (O'Hear and Conn 1978), Cofferdam (Blakeman et al. 1976), River Cut (J. Rafferty and Starr 1986), and 1Pi61 (N. Jenkins and Ensor 1981), arguably were used for sedentary habitation purposes, but for a shorter duration, the first two producing Gulf Formational assemblages, the second three Miller I or II assemblages, and the latter three being primarily occupied during Miller III times. The larger picture derived from regional survey data should allow better use to be made of excavated assemblages in understanding site function and settlement pattern change. Approaching such data via concepts that can be used to focus on both continuity and change should be a fruitful avenue to understanding the evolution of Woodland settlement patterns.

Woodland Settlement Pattern Archaeology: A Regional Perspective

As demonstrated above, an indispensable source of information for understanding settlement patterns is archaeological survey. Survey efforts, long focused on the main river valleys, have turned increasingly to the upland and interior areas of the Black Prairie/Black Belt, Pontotoc Ridge, Flatwoods, North-Central Hills, and Fall Line Hills physiographic provinces (Figure 10.1). This change is due partly to a planned effort to learn more about the archaeology of these areas, as state agency archaeologists (Brookes and Connaway 1977; Broster and Schneider 1977; Mainfort 1994; P. Patterson 1990; Sparks 1987; Stubbs 1983) and university crews (Blakeman 1975b; J. Johnson et al. 1991; J. Rafferty 1994, 1996; G. Smith 1979) worked in many of the counties in northeast Mississippi, west Tennessee, and northwest Alabama. It also has been due partly to good luck, as the Mississippi and Tennessee Departments of Transportation (Gray 1993; C. Jenkins et al. 1997; Weaver et al. 1996), Soil Conservation Service (J. Johnson et al. 1984; Mistovich 1987; Peterson 1979a, 1979b), U.S. Army Corps of Engineers (J. Johnson and Thorne 1987), and U.S. Forest Service (Blitz 1984; Peacock 1996a, 1996b, 1997a) began to fund compliance-driven survey in the tributary valleys and national forests of the interior.

An important finding has been that some of these areas contain a tremendous number of relatively short-duration Woodland habitation sites. In the Holly Springs National Forest of Mississippi, an archaeologically unknown area has been filled in, largely by recording, as of 1998, 183 small Tchula period sites located on narrow dissected ridges well removed from major river valleys (Peacock 1996a, 1997a). Two newly found or confirmed conical mounds also have been recorded in the region, both apparently affiliated with the Tchula period (David Fant, personal communication, 1998; Peacock 1996a). These add to earlier work by J. L. Ford (1990) on similar mounds. Thus a cultural period the components of which had been believed until recently to be confined largely to the Mississippi River valley was found to have left numerous short-duration habitation sites, as well as mounds, in the uplands.

Excavation at one small Tchula habitation site, the Fulmer site in southwest Tennessee, produced an assemblage containing large quantities of pottery, with nearly 13,000 sherds and sherdlets recovered from the 277-square-meter excavated area (more than 60 percent of the main site area) (Weaver et al. 1996). Partially reconstructable Tchula vessels were common, with a minimum vessel count of seventy-nine. Only a few features (two small pits and a hearth) were found. Testing of several similar sites in Mississippi has confirmed that the deposits generally are shallow, although artifacts can be translocated to considerable depths in sandy soils (Peacock and Fant 1998). No features other than pottery concentrations have been found at these sites but, as at Fulmer, artifact distributions and pottery cross-mends indicate that integrity is high (Peacock 1996a). Not all the sites were occupied contemporaneously, although all fall within the span of a few hundred years, from perhaps 250 B.C. to A.D. 300 (Peacock 1996a:18, 1997a).

It seems fair to characterize the bulk of Tchula settlements in this area as dispersed, with short-duration occupations predominating. The Fulmer site excavators interpreted it as representing a short-term sedentary occupation, on the basis of the number and variety of pottery vessels in the assemblage, internal site organization, artifact diversity, distance to water, and ceramic to lithic ratio (Weaver et al. 1996:172–73). A somewhat similar pattern may be present farther north in Tennessee, as small Tchula sites are common in the Obion and Forked Deer valleys but with a few larger sites, two or more hectares in size, also known (Mainfort 1994:63–66, 73–95). In the region, Woodland settlement pattern continuity is low over the longer term, as most uplands apparently were not occupied before Tchula and were abandoned at the end of the period, possibly in favor of nucleated settlements associated with mounds (Peacock 1996a; Weaver et al. 1996:167–71). Upland areas were not to be reoccupied until historic times.

Another result of concentrating work in the interior regions has been the identification of several flat-topped ramped mounds as being of Woodland rather than Mississippian construction. Investigation along these lines began with Woodland dates and pottery from Pinson Mounds in Tennessee (Mainfort 1986, 1988a, 1996a), continued with work at Ingomar Mounds in northeast Mississippi that confirmed their Middle Woodland affiliation (J. Rafferty 1987, 1990), and has since resulted in identification of several flat-topped mounds at other sites as being of Woodland construction (Figure 10.1). For Tchula, the most prominent example is the Batesville Mounds group in north-west Mississippi (M. Holland-Lilly 1996; J. Johnson 1996; J. Johnson et al. 2001). Besides Pinson, where work continues to record newly identified mounds (Norton 1997), and Ingomar, other flat-topped mounds that are likely affiliated with the Middle Woodland Miller I and II phases include the Johnston (Kwas and Mainfort 1986) and Savannah mounds in Tennessee (Welch 1998) and the Slate Springs mound in north-central Mississippi (Baca 1993). Copena or likely Copena-affiliated flat-topped mounds include the Walling truncated mound in north-central Alabama (Knight 1990a) and the Florence mound in Florence, Alabama (H. Johnson and Boudreaux 1998). The Nanih Waiya mound in central Mississippi also may be of Early or Middle Woodland age, on the basis of analysis of ceramics from the surrounding fields and the confirmation that a geometric earthwork is present (Carleton 1999). Finally, the Thelma mound group in northeast Mississippi has produced one Late Woodland radiocarbon date (J. Johnson and Atkinson 1987).

Many of these Woodland flat-topped mounds, including Pinson (Mainfort 1986:9), Ingomar (McGahey 1971:10), Walling (Walthall 1980:240), and Florence (Walthall 1980:234) had been recorded or discussed in earlier literature under the assumption that they were constructed during Mississippian times. It is still possible that the Thelma mounds were of Mississippian construction (J. Rafferty 1995b), but most of the others have been assigned decisively to the Middle Woodland, on the basis of artifacts and absolute dates.

The functions of Middle Woodland flat-topped mounds within sites and in the larger settlement pattern remain problematic. They tend to share some traits, including ramps and orientation to the cardinal directions through the

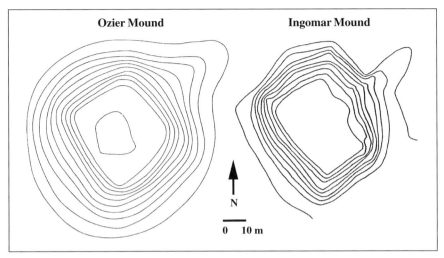

Figure 10.9 — Plan maps, Ozier Mound (based on photogrammetry) at Pinson Mounds, Tennessee, and Ingomar Mound 14, Mississippi (courtesy Midcontinental Journal of Archaeology *and* Mississippi Archaeology)

corners (Figure 10.9). Knight (1990a:158–64) holds that the Walling truncated mound was used for communal feasting, on the basis of a predominance of meat-bearing deer bones on a midden-rich surface in the mound, which also contained an unusual diversity of plant remains. Evidence of manufacture of artifacts from copper and chert obtained from exotic source areas also was present at Walling. Features included surface hearths, small pits, and three holes for 1-meter-diameter posts, as well as many smaller postholes (Knight 1990a:160–61). This and Ozier Mound (Figure 10.9) at the Pinson Mounds site in Tennessee are the two most extensively excavated of such mounds. At Ozier, there was no evidence of a midden deposit on the topmost buried surface, nor were large or small postholes found; some small burned surfaces were uncovered (Mainfort and Walling 1992). Overall the flat-topped Walling and Ozier mounds are not very similar in feature or artifact content; feasting does not seem to have been an important activity carried out at the latter mound. It is inadvisable to equate formal and functional similarity in understanding these mounds.

A number of assemblages from other early work at Woodland multimound sites in the Tennessee and Tombigbee valleys have been reanalyzed recently. These include the Brogan mound and village (Baca and Peacock 1996), as well as the Bynum, Pharr, and Miller sites in northeast Mississippi (Walling et al. 1991), where earlier work was done, respectively, by Cotter and Corbett (1951), Bohannon (1972), and Jennings (1941). The recent work provided a suite of new radiocarbon dates (Walling et al. 1991:61) confirming the temporal sequence of mound construction and pottery styles for the Middle Woodland Miller I and II phases in the Tombigbee Valley (Figure 10.2).

Habitation evidence is either unknown or seems to be relatively light at most of the large Middle Woodland mound sites in the north-south strip from Tennessee to Mississippi; in contrast, village-size areas of habitation debris are documented in association with Batesville Mounds (M. Holland-Lilly 1996) and Walling Mound (Knight 1990a) farther to the west and east, respectively. Most Middle Woodland habitation sites in the central region are hamlet-sized (J. Rafferty 1994, 1996), so thinking about the relationship between mounds and habitation sites would be fruitfully focused on the evolution of dispersed sedentary settlement patterns, with an apt comparison being Ohio Hopewell (Dancey 1991, 1996; Pacheco 1996).

That this part of the Midsouth, a relatively narrow north-south band of land in the interior, was a focus of Middle Woodland mound building, including a number of truncated mounds, is a revelation that should cause rethinking of Woodland, and possibly of Mississippian, settlement patterns. In particular, it challenges us to reexamine ideas about hierarchical political organization, which often is attributed on the basis of site hierarchies, in which sites within a sedentary settlement pattern differ in size and number of public structures (Hodder and Orton 1976; Nassaney and Cobb 1991). Are these Middle Woodland mound sites properly thought of as indications of hierarchical political organization? Goad (1979) argues that Copena sites represent such a hierarchy, but Knight (1990a:162) believes that mound construction occurred in short spurts, so that a fixed site hierarchy was not typical of the Copena phase. Pluckhahn (1996:208), following Knight (1990a) and Mainfort (1988a), argues that Woodland platform mound sites were not chiefly centers because they were not population or administrative centers. The implication is that an apparent site hierarchy (characterized by the coexistence of places containing many mounds, several mounds, and single mounds) can exist without indicating hierarchical political organization. Crucial to understanding the relationships among these mounds and to Woodland habitation sites is information about occupation duration, continuity of mound building, kinds of features and artifacts found in mounds, and contemporaneity. The question of Middle and Late Woodland flat-topped mounds in the Southeast is discussed for broader geographic areas by Jefferies (1994), Knight (1990a), and Pluckhahn (1996).

Settlement pattern variables must be compared with changes in diet, population structure, evidence of warfare, and many other factors before explanation can be claimed. Brief discussion of the current state of knowledge with reference to these topics is all that is possible here.

Subsistence Data

The settlement pattern changes identified above, including increasing numbers of sites over time, in-filling, and the beginning and end of construction of conical and flat-topped mounds, do not appear to be explained in any simple way by subsistence changes. Analysis of charred floral remains from Gulf Formational and Woodland sites in the Tombigbee River valley has shown little evidence for agricultural subsistence or even the regular presence of either native or tropical cultigens, at least until Late Woodland times. Two sunflower seeds were recovered from the Sanders site in Clay County, Mississippi, a Gulf Formational midden; no other cultigens were identified in the 10,000 floral specimens examined (C. Scarry 1990:92–96).

Caddell (1982) discusses the data gathered from major excavations along the middle Tombigbee River in the 1970s, particularly from 107 features (mostly of Miller II and Miller III date) from five sites in the Gainesville Lake area in Alabama. In two instances, concentrations of goosefoot (*Chenopodium* sp.) and maygrass (*Phalaris caroliniana*) seeds were recovered; the goosefoot seed sizes are within the range of modern wild seeds (Caddell 1982:34). Caddell's work was done prior to that of B. D. Smith (1985a, 1985b) and Fritz (Fritz and B. D. Smith 1988), which differentiated eastern North American wild and cultivated *Chenopodium* using testa thickness and seed shape. Thus, it is unknown whether the seeds analyzed by Caddell might be identified as domesticates on the basis of such traits. Maygrass is regarded as a cultivar based on its association with other native domesticates rather than on morphological grounds (Gremillion 1993a:152). Johannessen (1993a:63–66) assesses as negligible the evidence from the Tombigbee and Black Warrior valleys for Late Woodland agriculture based on native cultigens.

Maize was present in a number of Miller III contexts in the central Tombigbee Valley. These include assemblages from four sites in the Gainesville Lake area (Caddell 1982), with corn in 23 percent of the forty-seven Miller III features and structures analyzed. Other Miller III contexts with maize include two features from the Cofferdam site in Lowndes County, Mississippi (Blakeman et al. 1976), and several features from the Lubbub Creek site in Alabama, including two smudge pits filled with charred corn (Caddell 1983:201–3). Although the chronological assignments of some of these features are in doubt (J. Rafferty and Starr 1986:135), there is enough evidence to indicate that maize was grown in Late Woodland times in the central Tombigbee Valley. However, it is unlikely to have formed a major part of the diet. Analysis of wear patterns and caries rates on human teeth from burials at three sites that respectively displayed Middle Archaic, Late

Woodland, and Mississippian components (Hogue and Erwin 1993) showed that the Late Woodland Miller III patterns were pre-agricultural in character.

In northern Alabama, there are data indicating that native cultigens, including sunflower, chenopod, and others, were in use by Middle Woodland Copena times; maize also was present in small amounts (C. Scarry 1990). This is interpreted as evidence of horticulture, with consumption occurring in ritual contexts (C. Scarry 1986, 1993b). How important such cultigens were in the diet is unknown. By the Late Woodland period, corn had become more important: maize was found to be ubiquitous in West Jefferson sites in the Black Warrior Valley, being present in more than 90 percent of features (C. Scarry 1993b:165), with a considerable increase noted in its use between early and late West Jefferson times (C. Scarry 1993b:166–67). This evidence for differences in timing of the evolution of maize dependence among the Tombigbee, Tennessee, and Black Warrior valleys might be expected, given the variable pace likely to characterize the coevolutionary relationships that existed between human beings and their cultivars (Hart 1999).

Faunal remains provide evidence that diet breadth increased during Woodland times in the Tombigbee Valley. Deer greatly predominated in the Gulf Formational Sanders site assemblage, although twenty-one small mammals, turkey, reptiles, and fish were present in the sample (Scott 1990), as were shellfish. Analysis of nearly 50,000 pieces of bone from Gainesville Lake area sites, most from late Miller II to late Miller III features, showed that deer made up decreasing proportions of the diet, while small mammals, turtles, fish, turkey, and shellfish became more important (Woodrick 1981:138). Formal niche width calculations were done to compare Miller III and Mississippian faunal assemblages from the Tibbee Creek site; they showed that the Mississippian component displayed even greater diet breadth than the Miller III component (C. Jenkins 1993). The patterns shown in regional Woodland faunal materials are well summarized by Jackson and Scott (this volume). In summary, the available data on subsistence show increased diet breadth, with significant contributions made by maize only at the end of the Late Woodland period and no evidence for high use levels of native cultigens.

Warfare

The existence of intergroup conflict during Woodland times in the region has been noted primarily during analysis of human skeletal remains. Evidence is most clearly present in Late Woodland times, when the skeletal population available for study is large. No systematic analysis of extant Miller

III burials has been done to search for evidence of trauma, but projectile points and projectile wounds have been noted on one skeleton from the River Cut site in Mississippi (K. Turner 1986:132) and on several from 1Pi61 in Alabama (M. C. Hill 1981:238–39), the former victim being a male and the latter group composed of three adult females, one subadult male, and three adult males. That seven of eighty-six skeletons from 1Pi61, most assigned Miller III dates, had projectile points in their bodies indicates a fairly high degree of conflict in the central Tombigbee Valley. No fortified Woodland sites have been identified, so conflict might have taken the form of raiding or small-scale attacks.

Conclusions

One challenge is to apply settlement pattern concepts consistently to a large body of systematically recovered data, as opposed to focusing, as archaeologists so often have, on analyses of individual Woodland assemblages from sites chosen for excavation in a scattershot manner. Regional knowledge of artifact distributions must begin to provide the main context for understanding settlement patterns and how they changed during the Woodland period.

Chapter 11

Woodland Cultural and Chronological Trends on the Southern Gulf Coastal Plain: Recent Research in the Pine Hills of Southeastern Mississippi

H. Edwin Jackson, Melissa L. Higgins, and Robert E. Reams

Historically, archaeological research in Mississippi has been concentrated along the Mississippi River alluvial valley and in northeastern Mississippi in the Tombigbee drainage (J. Rafferty, this volume). Southern Mississippi, particularly the southern Longleaf Pine Hills region (Figure 11.1), has received considerably less attention from archaeologists. Consequently, regional syntheses of southeastern prehistory such as those by B. D. Smith (1986) and Bense (1994) have avoided including this area in broad cultural or interactive patterns or have assumed relationships with better known regions without empirical basis. The few attempts to place the Woodland stage prehistory of southeastern Mississippi in culture-historical context have relied almost exclusively on one or another framework developed elsewhere, most often the Lower Mississippi Valley sequence (e.g., C. Brown et al. 1996; R. Rogers 1988; Tesar 1974). A growing corpus of data suggests considerable variation through time in the sources, intensity, and character of prehistoric cultural influences that affected local traditions and adaptations.

The historical lack of attention to the southern Pine Hills has promoted the misconception that the area is impoverished archaeologically, which often exerts itself in the context of cultural resource management. The assumption that the region has little to offer archaeologically becomes a self-fulfilling prophecy, since it affects decisions about survey coverage and whether sites have potential to produce significant information. The misconception is furthered by the concentration of CRM activities in areas (primarily uplands) most likely to produce small artifact scatters that have been presumed to represent procurement activities or ephemeral occupations. In fact, the recent excavations at one "small lithic scatter," 22JO699 (see Figure 11.1 for general locations of sites discussed in the text), demonstrated a much more extensive archaeological record than was anticipated (H. Jack-

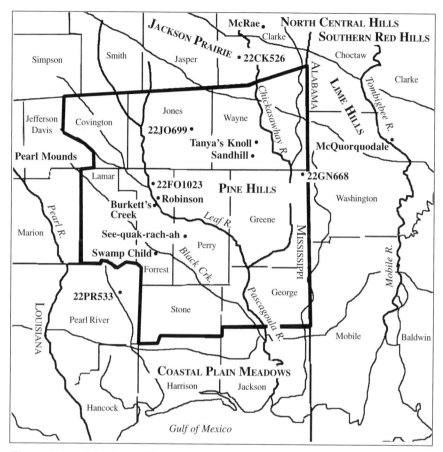

Figure 11.1 — Physiographic regions and major sites in southern Mississippi

son et al. 1995). This work suggests that insufficient attention has been paid to adequate sampling and recovery, as well as to possible chronological differences and intersite variability. This likely has masked important variation in settlement and land use trends over time. Adequate interpretation of small upland sites may require different methods of inquiry from those applied to regions with more substantial archaeological sites. While local occupations are clearly of a different sort than the dramatic expressions in the major river valleys of the Midsouth, there exists a substantial and important archaeological record of the past human adaptations to this physiographic region.

There is also a conceptual basis for the tendency to write off the southern Pine Hills archaeological record. Using historical documents and ecological studies, Lewis Larson's (1980:38–47) landmark study of Mississippian cultural ecology argued that the region, "the Pine Barrens" in his terminology, was too impoverished in terms both of wild faunal and floral resources and of soil fertility to support Mississippian populations. Consequently, Larson (1980:221) argued that the Pine Hills were largely unoccupied during late prehistoric times. Although Larson was concerned specifically with the nature of Mississippian period land and resource use (and his study was focused on the Georgia area), his conclusions have been used by some to argue that the southern longleaf pine forest was only a sporadically used hinterland during earlier prehistoric periods as well. For instance, Keller (1982), working in the longleaf pine forests of central Louisiana, noted that the majority of sites in that area were small lithic scatters. These he interpreted to represent single episodes of game butchering, reflecting a resource-specific exploitation of the Pine Hills by peoples who inhabited other physiographic or environmental zones.

This chapter represents an attempt to articulate the Pine Hills archaeological record of the Gulf Formational and Woodland stages of prehistory (ca. 1200 B.C.–A.D. 1100; Figure 11.2) with the broader patterns of the Midsouth. We begin the discussion with the Gulf Formational stage, which in the Southeast is marked by the invention of pottery containers (N. Jenkins and Krause 1986; Sassaman, this volume; Walthall and Jenkins 1976). The construct incorporates what had been included previously as the latter half of the Late Archaic and the Early Woodland periods (Walthall and Jenkins 1976:43).

We focus on that portion of the Pine Hills and adjacent physiographic regions bordered by the Pearl River in Mississippi and Tombigbee-Mobile rivers in Alabama.

Physiographic Setting

The Pine Hills physiographic region is an extensive belt running from southern Virginia to eastern Texas. In Mississippi, the area is characterized by rolling topography, with hilltop to streambed elevation differences of as much as 30 meters because of stream dissection. Linear narrow to broad, relatively flat ridges are divided by often steep V-shaped ravines. The floodplains of several major drainages, including the Pearl, Leaf, Chickasawhay, and Pascagoula rivers in Mississippi and the Escatawpa and Tombigbee rivers in Alabama, subdivide the uplands.

Surficial geology consists of Tertiary marine deposits and Quaternary alluvium on which generally acidic clayey to sandy soils have formed. Some near-surface strata, such as the Citronelle formation, contain considerable deposits of gravels that were used as lithic raw material. Other formations

Years	Stage	Period	Culture/Tradition		
1700	Protohistoric		*Miss. Valley/ Miss. Gulf Coast*	*NE Miss./West Central Ala.*	*Southwest Alabama*
1500			Natchezan	Choctaw	Bear Point Phase
	Mississippian		Mississippian/ Plaquemine	Moundville/ Summerville	Pensacola Phase
1200	Woodland	Late	Coles Creek	Miller III	Weeden Island
			Baytown		
		Middle	Issaquena	Miller II	Porter/Santa Rosa
			Marksville	Miller I	
A.D./B.C.	Gulf Formational	Late	Tchefuncte	Alexander	Bayou La Batre
200		Middle	Poverty Point	Wheeler	Unnamed Fiber Tempered
800		Early			
1400					
2000	Archaic	Late			
5000		Middle			
		Early			
8000	Paleoindian	Late			
		Middle			
		Early			
11,500					

Figure 11.2 — Chronological framework for the southeast Mississippi Pine Hills

provide sandstone, some of which is sufficiently silicified to be suitable for chipped stone tools. The Pine Hills region is bordered on the north by the Jackson Prairie or Lime Hills and on the south by the Coastal Plain mead-ows. The Lime Hills and adjoining Buhrstone Cuesta of the southern Red Hills were important source areas for Tallahatta quartzite, used extensively in the region during the Archaic and locally throughout the Woodland stage (e.g., Campbell et al. 1988).

Upland forests are dominated by southern yellow pines (longleaf being the dominant species historically), while streams support a mixed pine and hardwood vegetation cover. Interspersed in the upland pine forests are variably sized patches of sub-xeric vegetation concentrated on deep, coarse, sandy soils. These "islands" contain a significantly different plant community and range in size from as small as 1 to as large as 100 hectares. On these patches, pines are replaced by scrub oaks (bluejack, blackjack) associated with a unique vegetative assemblage that includes prickly pear cactus and a lichen ground cover. Gopher tortoises prefer these xeric patches, and deer are drawn to them in the fall by oak masts. Overall they appear to represent important resource patches for prehistoric foragers. Until recently, little attention has been paid locally to these distinctive ecosystems by biologists or archaeologists, but recent research indicates that they had a significant role in determining prehistoric settlement location (S. Keith 1998; M. Reams 1996).

Previous Research

Little professional attention was paid to the Pine Hills prior to 1970. C. B. Moore (1901a, 1905a) explored the Tombigbee River in Alabama, restricting his investigations to sites located along the river. In the 1920s, Henry Collins conducted the first professional excavations in southeastern Mississippi at the McRae mound and three other small mound groups at the headwaters of the Chickasawhay River north of the Pine Hills in Clarke, Lauderdale, and Wayne counties (Blitz 1986). During the 1930s, WPA and other federally funded archaeology was carried out in many parts of the Southeast, but the Pine Hills was largely ignored. In Alabama, WPA archaeologists excavated a number of sites in Clarke County, in the Pine Hills, but east of the Tombigbee (Futato 1989:351), including the McQuorquodale mound (Wimberly and Tourtelot 1941). Wimberly (1960) used these sites in Clarke County and others in Mobile County to construct the first local ceramic typology.

Activity before 1970 remained intermittent in Alabama, focusing mainly on the Mobile River delta and Mobile Bay area (e.g., Trickey 1958), and was nonexistent in southeastern Mississippi. Between 1970 and 1980 several small surveys were conducted in southeastern Mississippi in the Tallahala (Atkinson and Elliott 1979; Tesar 1974) and Tallahoma (Penman 1980) drainages, all north of the Pine Hills.

The first systematic archaeological investigation in the Pine Hills section of southeastern Mississippi was a transect survey to collect data with which to construct a predictive model of settlement location (Padgett and Heisler 1979). The survey included seven randomly drawn transects, 0.4 kilometer (1/4 mile) wide and 6.7 kilometers (4 miles) long in north Forrest, Jones, and Covington counties. A total of fifty-one sites were identified, but since the primary objective of the study was to examine the relationship between site location and a series of environmental variables, site testing was minimal and artifact samples were small.

Systematic survey at least in the National Forests of Mississippi began in the 1980s. DeLeon (1981) used land management–based reconnaissance data from the DeSoto National Forest to identify the physiographic variables most likely to have played a role in settlement locations in the Black Creek Basin south of the Leaf River. There were very few excavations in the 1980s. Jerome Voss conducted several small-scale testing projects as part of the University of Southern Mississippi's field school program. Voss focused on the habitation of low terraces adjacent to the Leaf River floodplain near Hattiesburg. McMakin (1995, 1996) used lithic data from the Gulf Formational Robinson site to demonstrate a post-Archaic reduction in residential mobility.

R. Marshall (1982a) surveyed portions of Archusa Creek, north of the Pine Hills in Clarke County. The survey identified thirty sites, four with Middle Gulf Formational components, eighteen with Late Gulf Formational components, and twelve with Woodland period materials. Excavation at 22CK526 revealed an extensive occupation. Machine excavation of an area approximately 65 by 36 meters uncovered forty features, most of which were small pits, 30 to 45 centimeters in diameter. These contained fired clay, sandstone, cultural material, and, in one case, burned acorn (R. Marshall 1982a:45). Alexander types dominate the collection, including Alexander Pinched, Alexander Incised, and Smithsonia Zoned Incised. Tchefuncte and Bayou La Batre types were also collected (R. Marshall 1982a).

By the late 1980s archaeological survey in the Pine Hills increased. In Alabama, among the largest scale survey and testing programs was conducted by New World Research along a corridor for a proposed pipeline just east of the state line (Campbell et al. 1988; P. Thomas and Campbell 1987). The surveyed right-of-way crossed five physiographic zones, the Coastal Plain meadows, the Pine Hills, the Lime Hills, the Buhrstone Hills, and the southern Red Hills through Mobile, Washington, and Choctaw counties, which permitted an evaluation of variation in the prehistoric use of the zones over time. The survey recorded 216 sites, of which sixty-six with Gulf Formational or Woodland components were selected for Phase II testing

(Campbell et al. 1988). The data provided important new information on culture-historical issues, on differences in lithic material use, and also on changes in how the uplands were used over time. Importantly, it began to link the area with the better known sequence of the Tombigbee watershed, and the resulting information is useful for examining links between southeastern Mississippi and southwestern and west-central Alabama.

Recent Research

CRM activity has increased in Mississippi since the late 1980s. Improved methods and more exhaustive survey coverage in the DeSoto National Forest have increased site numbers dramatically. In addition, numerous small projects (e.g., H. Jackson et al. 1995; R. Reams 1995) and several corridor surveys in the southern (Athens et al. 1993) and eastern (C. Brown et al. 1996) sections of the study area have added to the growing database.

With two exceptions, excavation in the Pine Hills has been limited to site testing, although the number of sites examined has risen dramatically. National Forest sites examined include Swamp Child in southern Forrest County (Dunn 1999), See-quak-rach-ah in Perry County (H. Jackson et al. 1995), 22JO699 in Jones County (H. Jackson et al. 1999), Tanya's Knoll in Wayne County (M. Reams 1996), and Sandhill in Wayne County (S. Keith 1998). Excavations by Robert Reams at Swamp Child, located on a terrace in a sub-xeric area overlooking Black Creek, demonstrated the influences that the southern end of the study area received from the coastal region. Ten 1 by 1-meter and seven 2 by 2-meter units were excavated, with cultural deposits as deep as 70 centimeters. Several clusters of fire-hardened clay were noted, but no evidence for structures or storage facilities. The multicomponent site has Late Gulf Formational, Middle Woodland, and Late Woodland occupations. Plainwares include Tchefuncte, Baldwin, and Baytown Plain. Decorated ceramic types include Marksville Incised, Mulberry Creek Cord Marked, and Weeden Island Incised.

Robert Reams's (H. Jackson et al. 1995) excavation at See-quak-rach-ah, a multicomponent site south of the Leaf River, revealed an apparent storage pit, as well as a cache of tested cobbles. Melissa Reams (1996) tested Tanya's Knoll, a small 2-acre site on a sub-xeric stream terrace knoll. Cultural deposits reached 60 centimeters deep, representing two to three prehistoric components. The latest Late Woodland component is represented by Mulberry Creek Cord Marked, *var. Tallahala,* pottery in association with Collins stemmed arrow points. Deeper deposits represent possibly Late Paleoindian or more likely Early to Middle Archaic occupations, characterized by a preponderance of nonlocal lithic materials including Tallahatta quartzite, an unnamed silicified sandstone, Kosciusko quartzite, and Coastal Plain agate. In contrast, Woodland lithics are restricted mainly to local gravel cherts, suggesting a shift in site function or reduction in territory size.

In 1996, the University of Southern Mississippi summer archaeological field school excavated at Sandhill, a 5-hectare site located in an extensive 95-hectare sub-xeric setting. Excavation was limited to twelve 1 by 1-meter units. The site contained intact stratified deposits up to 150 centimeters deep, spanning the Late Paleoindian through Late Woodland periods (S. Keith 1998:3). Material from the site has been the subject of two master's theses, one by Scot Keith (1998) on the changing lithic organization through time and a second by Grace Keith (1997), which used the ceramics from the site as part of a technological study of the region's ceramic tradition. The latter study identified Wheeler Plain, Alexander Pinched, and Bayou La Batre Plain, as well as Tchefuncte Plain, representing Middle and Late Gulf Formational occupations. Marksville Incised, a rare example of Santa Rosa Stamped, Furr's Cord Marked, and Mulberry Creek Cord Marked represent Middle and Late Woodland components (G. Keith 1997:88–90). The diversity of ceramics peaks during the Middle Woodland and decreases during the Late Woodland, despite a larger sample associated with the latter (G. Keith 1997:154). In addition to ceramics, excavation produced a number of concentrations of baked clay (with little inclusion of sand or grit) associated with the Woodland components. These appear to be the byproducts of ceramic production and/or daub; in either case they are thought to be indicative of a residential site function (G. Keith 1997:157). Other classes of features were not identified, although the coarse sandy matrix of the soil does not lend itself to preservation of features.

Other, mainly CRM-initiated, excavations in the Pine Hills provide additional new comparative data. Several sites with Woodland or Gulf Formational components have been excavated near Hattiesburg. Burkett's Creek is located on the edge of the first terrace above the Leaf River floodplain, along the bank of a small tributary (H. Jackson 1995). Excavation there was limited to the part of the site to be impacted by construction of a wastewater treatment facility and included a 2-percent stratified random sample of the southwest half (1700 square meters) of the site comprised of 1 by 1-meter units and four blocks of contiguous excavation units. In all, 85 square meters were excavated. Diagnostic artifacts collected during the investigation indicate a long occupational history, with components dating from the Middle and Late Archaic, Gulf Formational, Middle and Late Woodland, and Mississippian. At the locus of the 1994 excavations, the Middle Woodland occupation appears to be the most extensive. The excavation provided a basis for defining several new varieties of Late Gulf Formational ceramics and a new Middle Woodland projectile point type. Two varieties of Tchefuncte Plain were defined: a soft-paste, often clay-tempered ware, *var. Burkett;* and a sandy-paste, clay-tempered ware, *var. Goode Lake* (H. Jackson 1995). Both have widespread distributions both north and south of the present study area (H. Jackson 1995; R. Marshall 1982a, 1982b). Two varieties of Baldwin Plain, *vars. James Street* and *Durbin,* are tentatively suggested to differentiate Late Gulf Formational from Middle Woodland sand-tempered plainwares. Burkett's Creek points, particularly narrow, contracting-stem points similar to some varieties of Gary points, are locally associated with Middle Woodland material. Decorated ceramics include Basin Bayou Incised, Furr's Cord Marked, and Mulberry Creek Cord Marked. Associated lithic debris suggests the site served as a residential camp situated to take advantage of a nearby cobble chert source as well as floodplain resources. Despite considerable excavation, no evidence for structures or storage or processing facilities was encountered.

22FO1023 is an upland site located not far from the edge of the Leaf River floodplain where testing (a 1 percent sample, 27 1 by 1-meter units) revealed a Late Woodland component represented by a small number of grog-tempered plain sherds (Baytown Plain), two Collins points, and two fragments of what could be triangular points (H. Jackson and McLaurin-Wright 2000). The paucity of ceramics and diagnostic stone tools, the absence of features, and an emphasis on core reduction apparently to produce tools transported off the site all point to a special-purpose use of the location, probably as a hunting stand.

22PR533 is situated on a terrace of a tributary of the Wolf River in Pearl River County (C. Brown et al. 1996). Excavations there, the most extensive in the area to date, exposed 140 square meters in three blocks that documented an extensive Middle Woodland component. The occupation is interpreted as a seasonal residential camp. Features include a possible daub concentration, several fired clay and sandstone concentrations, one with a date of A.D. 340, a pit hearth with a date of A.D. 110, and a concentration of ceramics dated A.D. 514 (all dates calibrated intercepts) (C. Brown et al. 1996). The latter date is from a single vessel of bone-tempered Turkey Paw Cord Marked. Turkey Paw Plain, Turkey Paw Fabric Impressed, Marksville Incised, Churupa Punctated, and Baytown Plain were also identified. Turkey Paw ceramics, heretofore associated with the Miller II period in the Tombigbee watershed, dominate the Middle Woodland assemblage and distinguish 22PR533 from nearby coastal Middle Woodland components (C. Brown et al. 1996). Turkey Paw Cord Marked was also found recently at 22JO699 (H. Jackson et al. 1999), suggesting a much broader distribution than previously realized and that the type may have gone unidentified in other collections from the area. Small utilized flakes appear to be associated with stone features, and together these are interpreted to represent plant processing.

Near the Mississippi-Alabama border, testing at 22GN668 identified several post-Archaic components (H. Jackson and Fields 2000). They include a small Middle Gulf Formational occupation represented by two fiber-tempered Wheeler Plain sherds and a significant Middle Woodland component represented by Mabin Stamped, Marksville Incised, and Baldwin Plain ceramics and Tombigbee stemmed and Washington side-notched points. One or more Late Woodland components are represented by Mulberry Creek Cord Marked, Evansville Punctated, and fragments of several arrow points. Several features appear to be associated with Woodland use of the site, including sandstone concentrations interpreted to represent hearths and a pit feature that produced a date of cal A.D. 770–790. Differences in lithic raw material use are interpreted to reflect changes over time and suggest a reduction in territory size from the Archaic to Woodland.

In an attempt to bring together the data accumulating from survey-level investigations of the study area, H. Edwin Jackson et al. (1995) reexamined approximately 600 Gulf Formational and Woodland survey collections curated by the University of Southern Mississippi or by the U.S. Forest Service through 1995. These represent an eight-county area straddling the Leaf River in southeastern Mississippi (see Figure 11.1). Because of the intensive survey coverage in the DeSoto National Forest, the majority of sites are recorded in the counties in which it is located, especially Perry County, which contains a third of the sites examined. Forrest, Jones, and Wayne counties also contribute large numbers of sites to the study. Of the 600 ceramic-producing sites, 436 included decorated or otherwise diagnostic sherds that could be assigned to one of seven chronological periods spanning the Middle Gulf Formational through Mississippian. Ceramics were classified according to best fit with Lower Mississippi Valley, coastal Mississippi-Alabama, and Miller types, relying on the standard definitions developed in those archaeological areas (N. Jenkins 1981; Phillips 1970; Wimberly 1960), as well as definitions for local types (e.g., Atkinson and Elliott 1979; H. Jackson 1995). The recently discovered presence of Turkey Paw ceramics notwithstanding, the results of more recent investigations tend to bear out patterns discerned by this distributional study. The data from this study are incorporated into the following discussion to bolster the information gained by the investigations described above.

~

Woodland Cultures in the Southern Pine Hills

In the remainder of this chapter we summarize some of the apparent trends
in cultural affiliations during the Woodland stage. Basic distributions of
chronologically and culturally diagnostic types are used to plot the changes
in cultural influences over time.

Demographic Trends

Figure 11.3 plots the numbers of components assigned to each of seven chronological periods from Middle Gulf Formational through the Protohistoric,
based on the presence of diagnostic ceramics. At present, the data suggest
that occupations characterized by fiber-tempered ceramics are infrequent in
the area. However, if Bayou La Batre wares were contemporaneous with
Wheeler ceramics as is believed by some (Campbell et al. 1988), this would
increase the Middle Gulf Formational component count somewhat. Moreover, it is not unreasonable to expect that some (uncounted) Middle Gulf
Formational components simply lack ceramics. Regardless, site numbers

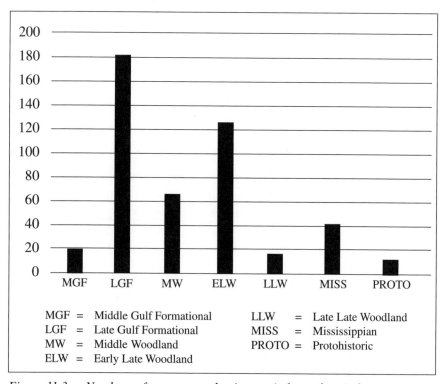

Figure 11.3 — Numbers of components by time period or subperiod

and presumably population appear to increase in the Late Gulf Formational through early Late Woodland, or about 500 B.C. to about 800 A.D. Middle and early Late Woodland site counts are depressed because neither Baytown Plain nor Baldwin Plain can be confidently sorted chronologically, therefore, sites with only these plain ceramics were omitted from consideration. The possible misidentification of Turkey Paw Plain and Cord Marked as Baytown Plain and Mulberry Creek Cord Marked would overestimate early Late Woodland components at the expense of (late) Middle Woodland ones. One clear pattern is the decrease in population after the early Late Woodland. Although the pattern may be exaggerated by having excluded sites represented only by Baytown Plain, late varieties of this type can be distinguished from earlier ones, and the former are found on significantly fewer sites. Low regional population levels persist through the Mississippian period, components of which are easily recognized. Even fewer Protohistoric components have been identified, despite or perhaps because of the large number of known historic Choctaw sites just to the north in Jasper and Clarke counties.

Gulf Formational Stage (Terminal Archaic, Early Woodland)
In Mississippi and Alabama, fiber-tempered Wheeler series pottery is the earliest pottery now recognized. It made its appearance between 1500 and 1100 B.C., coinciding with the beginning of the Middle Gulf Formational (N. Jenkins and Krause 1986; D. Morgan 1992). Bayou La Batre ceramics may have been introduced in the Mobile Bay area during this interval, where they persisted into the Late Gulf Formational (Campbell et al. 1988).

Wheeler Plain is found mainly in the eastern part of the study area (Figure 11.4), suggesting influence from the Tombigbee drainage rather than from the coastal or Lower Mississippi Valley Poverty Point cultural variants. No decorated fiber-tempered pottery has been found. In contrast, a variety of decorated Wheeler types are reported in Washington County, Alabama, just north of the Pine Hills (Campbell et al. 1988). Sites in southeast Mississippi producing Wheeler ceramics include Sandhill, nearby 22WA678 (S. Keith 1998), and 22GN668 (H. Jackson and Fields 2000). Wheeler ceramics are also recorded for sites south of the Leaf River in the Black Creek District of the DeSoto National Forest (H. Jackson et al. 1995). Sand-tempered ceramics classified as Bayou La Batre are patchily distributed in low numbers. These may represent either Middle or Late Gulf Formational components. We somewhat arbitrarily include them in the discussion here as representing part of the introduction of ceramic technology into the Pine Hills. Some early dates in the Mobile Bay area (Trickey and Holmes 1971) and the possible association of Poverty Point diagnostics and Bayou La Batre

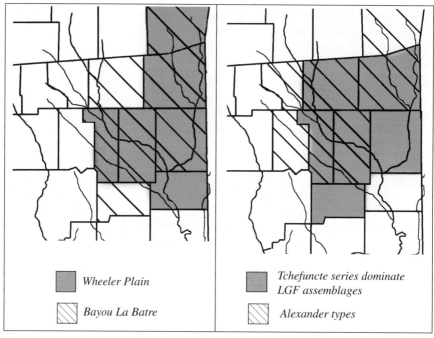

Figure 11.4 — Middle (left) and Late (right) Gulf Formational ceramic distributions

ceramics at Applestreet on the Mississippi Gulf coast (Blitz and Mann 2000) lend weak support to this suggestion. The manufacture of Bayou La Batre wares clearly persists into the Late Gulf Formational (Blitz and Mann 2000; Campbell et al. 1988). In the study area, the type is identified mainly on the basis of vessel supports and coarse sand paste. Sherds with crushed stone or grit inclusions, a common feature of Bayou La Batre ceramics in coastal Alabama, are rare, as are decorated Bayou La Batre types. Campbell et al. (1988) found no Bayou La Batre ceramics in their investigations in southwestern Alabama and suggest that at least by Late Gulf Formational times, this complex was limited in distribution to the Mobile Bay area and western Mississippi Gulf coast.

The Middle Gulf Formational period coincides temporally with the florescence of the Poverty Point culture in the Lower Mississippi Valley and along the Gulf coast. There are several large Poverty Point components on the Mississippi coast including Claiborne on the Pearl River and Applestreet in Jackson County (Blitz and Mann 2000; D. Morgan 1992). No Poverty Point sites have been recorded in the Pine Hills region, although at least four sites have produced sherds from steatite vessels, a diagnostic trade item of the Poverty Point interaction sphere.

The Mobile Bay pipeline site testing in southwestern Alabama documented nine Middle Gulf Formational components, all but one located north of the Pine Hills (Campbell et al. 1988). Like the preceding Late Archaic components, these seem to be situated to take advantage of the Tallahatta quartzite outcrops. Sites that do seem to be residential are situated near (now) intermittent streams, suggesting wet season (late fall-winter) use of the uplands. In contrast to most other periods, the Middle Gulf Formational shows a significant minority of Fort Payne and Camden cherts from northern Alabama. Campbell et al. (1988) suggest the possibility of seasonal excursions by northern or river valley populations into the southern Red Hills to exploit Tallahatta quartzite. Richard Marshall's (1982a) Archusa Creek survey, also north of the Pine Hills, produced examples of Wheeler ceramics from four sites, again pointing to a denser occupation to the north.

The Late Gulf Formational evidence from the study area (Figure 11.4) indicates interaction primarily with the Tombigbee drainage and the Lower Mississippi Valley/western Gulf coast. These areas are represented by Alexander, Tchefuncte, and, if persisting into this interval locally, Bayou La Batre types. Tchefuncte types more often occur south and west of the Leaf River, while Alexander types were identified primarily in collections north of the river. Numerically, Tchefuncte wares dominate Late Gulf Formational assemblages, in large part because Tchefuncte Plain can be identified readily. However, among decorated types, Alexander types with incised, pinched, punctated and stamped designs far outnumber examples of Tchefuncte decorated types. Alexander decorations occur on local sand-tempered pottery and also on what appear to be imported wares. Unfortunately, Late Gulf Formational sand-tempered plainware cannot be distinguished from later Baldwin Plain, a problem also noted by Ned Jenkins (1981) in west-central Alabama and by Jay Johnson (1988) in the North-Central Hills region of Mississippi. In the absence of decorated sherds, therefore, Alexander components are likely to be under-represented in the analysis. The other contemporaneous sand-tempered type, Bayou La Batre Plain, found mainly in the Mobile Bay area, was identified in the eastern two-thirds of the study area, though as noted above could represent earlier components. Sherds identified as Bayou La Batre grade into the sandy-paste Tchefuncte Plain, *var. Goode Lake,* and Baldwin Plain depending on density and size of sand inclusions.

There are few excavations of sites with Late Gulf Formational components in and near the Pine Hills of Mississippi. At the Sandhill site, Alexander Pinched and Bayou La Batre Plain were identified, but not Tchefuncte series types (S. Keith 1998:154). Excavation at Burkett's Creek (H. Jackson 1995:65–66) produced a small number of Tchefuncte Plain sherds. Sand-tempered plain sherds were also recovered that could date as early as the

Late Gulf Formational. South of the project area, Richard Marshall (1982b) excavated several sites with Tchefuncte components on Goode Lake.

The Mobile Bay pipeline corridor investigations in southwestern Alabama revealed fourteen Late Gulf Formational components, two of which were located in the Pine Hills. Alexander types dominate assemblages and no Tchefuncte types were identified (Campbell et al. 1988). The more northerly sites display a slightly different and broader distribution than occurred in the preceding Middle Gulf Formational, with southernmost sites associated with the Escatawpa River drainage. Testing data demonstrate a clear Alexander affiliation, rather than Bayou La Batre or Tchefuncte. Overall the settlement data suggest a more generalized use of southwestern Alabama, rather than the narrow Tallahatta quartzite exploitation focus of the preceding Middle Gulf Formational.

In sum, by Late Gulf Formational times, the local ceramic tradition of the northern Pine Hills appears to be more similar to that found to the north and east, characterized by Alexander ceramics. In the southern Pine Hills, south of the Leaf River, Tchefuncte wares typify the local ceramic assemblage. Population size appears to have increased and residential sites appear to be more common.

Woodland Stage

As noted in the previous section, the insertion of the Gulf Formational stage between the Archaic and Woodland stages forces the Woodland discussion to begin with what traditionally has been referred to as the Middle Woodland period (200 B.C.–500 A.D.). In general, the period is marked by renewed intersocietal trade of exotic items, particularly in the early half of the period (e.g., Toth 1988). These items, including galena, copper artifacts, mica cutouts, and nonlocal lithic materials, were intended for or at least often ended up as burial inclusions. A broad similarity in ceramic decorative motifs further suggests broad interaction (e.g., Toth 1988), though the decorative techniques and artistic roots can be found in the preceding time period (Shenkel 1984b). In addition, burial mound construction intensifies.

Southeastern Mississippi is on the margins of three distinctive Middle Woodland culture areas (Figure 11.5). To the west in the Lower Mississippi Valley and south along the Gulf coast is the Marksville culture (Blitz and Mann 2000). To the southeast in the Mobile Bay area is what is called Porter Middle Woodland culture or the Porter phase of the Santa Rosa culture of the eastern Gulf coastal region (e.g., Walthall 1980). North, along the Tombigbee River in west-central Alabama and northeastern Mississippi, is the Miller culture (N. Jenkins and Krause 1986). Miller II corresponds to the Middle Woodland time interval. All shared mound use in burial ceremo-

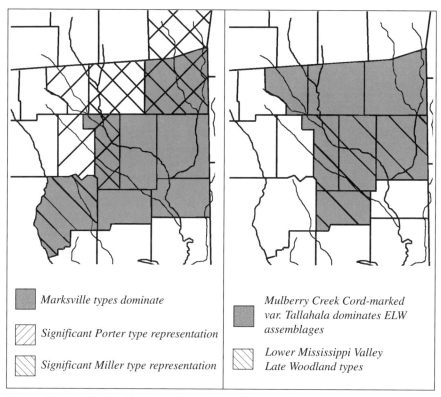

Figure 11.5 — Middle (left) and Late (right) Woodland ceramic distributions

nialism and evidence of links to the broader exchange system, at least in the early half of the period. Specific burial programs, material culture traits, and presumably also local adaptations differed in these three cultures. By late Middle Woodland times, interaction beyond the local level decreased significantly.

Nearby excavated examples of Middle Woodland mounds include the McRae mound in Clarke County (Blitz 1986) and the McQuorquodale mound near Mobile (Wimberly and Tourtelot 1941). The McRae mound, estimated to have been one and a half meters high and 14 meters in diameter, produced a copper and silver panpipe and several blade-like flakes of nonlocal material (Blitz 1986). The ceramics assemblage is particularly interesting in its variability. Early Middle Woodland Miller I ceramics include Furr's Cord Marked (the single most abundant decorated type) and Saltillo Fabric Impressed. Types typically found in the Pine Hills pointing to Porter and/or Marksville Middle Woodland connections include Alligator Bayou Stamped, Santa Rosa Stamped, Marksville Incised, and Marksville Stamped. Swift

Creek Complicated Stamped, Keith Incised, and Santa Rosa Stamped suggest interaction with Santa Rosa–Swift Creek populations farther east (Blitz 1986). The McQuorquodale mound in Clarke County is associated with the Porter Middle Woodland of the Mobile Bay region. It is a low mound approximately 1 meter high and 20 meters in diameter. WPA excavation of the mound revealed two building stages. Six burials were laid on the surface of the first construction stage and four additional burials were added to the upper stage (Wimberly and Tourtelot 1941). Hopewellian artifacts collected include a copper bead and earspool, galena, mica, greenstone celts, and a stone cone-shaped cup. In contrast to these examples, no burial mounds or Hopewellian items are currently known in the Pine Hills, at least in southeast Mississippi.

As in the preceding period, ceramics in southeast Mississippi suggest influences from the Lower Mississippi Valley, Mobile Bay area, and west-central Alabama–northeast Mississippi (Figure 11.5). Both grog-tempered and sand-tempered ceramics are present in Middle Woodland site collections. The most common decorated types are those with wide-lined curvilinear designs, which are classified as Marksville Incised when grog tempered and Basin Bayou Incised when sand tempered. Grog-tempered Marksville decorated types found in the area include Mabin Stamped, Marksville Stamped, and Churupa Punctated. Other Porter sand-tempered decorated types include Alligator Bayou Stamped and Santa Rosa Punctated (Wimberly 1960). Marksville types commonly occur in Porter assemblages (Campbell et al. 1988; Wimberly 1960) and would seem to represent a continuum of east-west interaction in the Pine Hills and along the Gulf coast. However, Porter types coincide closely with the distribution of Miller ceramic types. The pattern suggests that the sherds classified as Porter-related may actually be the result of applying Marksville designs to the local sand-tempered ware, the latter mainly being a function of Miller influences from the north. This would help to explain why those types with grog-tempered Marksville counterparts have been identified.

Sand-tempered Baldwin Plain, Saltillo Fabric Impressed, and Furr's Cord Marked are considered to be Miller II Middle Woodland types. Nearly all have been found in southeastern Mississippi (G. Keith 1997; S. Keith 1998:153; H. Jackson et al. 1995). Recently, bone-tempered Turkey Paw Plain and Turkey Paw Cord Marked sherds were identified at 22PR533 in Pearl River County (C. Brown et al. 1996) and at 22JO699 in Jones County (H. Jackson et al. 1999), as well as on sites tested along the Mobile Bay pipeline corridor (Campbell et al. 1988). Bone-tempered types occur as a minor part of Middle Woodland assemblages in north Mississippi (N. Jenkins and Krause 1986:66; also Atkinson et al. 1980:127–29; J. Rafferty 1986a:47).

Along the Mobile Bay pipeline corridor, Miller II sites are mainly north of the Pine Hills and appear to represent temporary occupations in the vicinity of Tallahatta quartzite quarries (Campbell et al. 1988). However, they do extend southward into the Pine Hills, where ferruginous sandstone acquisition appears to have been the objective (Campbell et al. 1988:10–53). In contrast, the Pine Hills region west of the state line is well populated during the Middle Woodland interval, and local populations may have peaked during this period (H. Jackson et al. 1999). To date, investigated Middle Woodland sites appear to represent seasonal residential camps (C. Brown et al. 1996; H. Jackson et al. 1999).

The Late Woodland period encompasses the time span from roughly A.D. 500 to 1200. During the early part of the period, southeastern Mississippi is generally considered to be an extension of the Baytown culture, a broadly distributed cultural complex defined in the Lower Mississippi Valley and stretching eastward into west-central and northwestern Alabama (N. Jenkins 1981:25; N. Jenkins and Krause 1986). In coastal counties and sometimes farther north, Weeden Island ceramics are sometimes included in Late Woodland assemblages, suggesting contacts with populations to the east. In the Tombigbee Valley, the Late Woodland Miller III period is considered to begin when grog use as temper exceeds the use of sand (N. Jenkins and Krause 1986:73). In southeast Mississippi, grog-tempered plain and cordmarked wares are typical for the first half of the Late Woodland period, though use of sand-tempered wares may persist (H. Jackson et al. 1999). Late Woodland grog-tempered ceramic wares are technically differentiated from those of the Middle Woodland, although many sites have both Middle and Late Woodland components, suggesting the same continuum of occupation found east of the state line. Among the most common local ceramic varieties is Mulberry Creek Cord Marked, *var. Tallahala* (Atkinson and Blakeman 1975; Atkinson and Elliott 1979), which serves as a marker for early Late Woodland (Figure 11.5). In southeastern Mississippi, it is often associated with the Collins point, which appears to be the earliest true arrow point in the area and is taken by some archaeologists to indicate the local introduction of the bow (Blitz 1988; McGahey 1999). Other types considered to represent early Late Woodland components are Alligator Incised, apparently late varieties of Churupa Punctated, and rare examples of Wakulla Check Stamped. For the most part, Mulberry Creek Cord Marked defines the early Late Woodland, as it does to the north and northwest of the study area. A clear Miller association is evident, particularly with the area just to the north of the Pine Hills (Atkinson and Elliott 1979). The Lower Mississippi Valley types Churupa and Alligator Incised are found in each county represented by more than six early Late Woodland sites, with somewhat greater representation in the southern part of the study area, indicating possible coastal or western ties. A single site in Perry County, the Beaumont Gravel Pit, produced an example of sand-tempered Wakulla Checked Stamped. Scot Keith (1998) has suggested that the middle Late Woodland components at the Sandhill site reflect decreased mobility and a shift to greater reliance on logistically organized procurement. In this interpretation, the Sandhill site represents a residential base camp. Dunn (1999) has proposed a similar interpretation of the Woodland settlement system that included the Swamp Child site.

By the latter half of the Late Woodland period, some parts of the Southeast, notably the Lower Mississippi Valley, see the appearance of large ceremonial centers, marked by truncated pyramidal mounds organized around central plazas. Late Woodland mounds were constructed at several sites on the Pearl River to the west, but none have been identified in the Pascagoula River basin. On the Pearl River, the Pearl Mounds in Lawrence County comprise the largest recorded Late Woodland mound site, covering more than 13 hectares and once including as many as fifteen mounds. Analysis of ceramics by Mann (1988) indicates a Coles Creek through Mississippian occupation with clear affinities with the Natchez Bluffs region. Other smaller Woodland mounds are recorded along the lower portion of the Pearl River (Mississippi Department of Archives and History site files) as well as along the Mississippi coast (Blitz and Mann 2000).

For southeast Mississippi, the latter half of the Late Woodland period is presently somewhat enigmatic. Wares and decorated types thought to represent this period are equivalent to Coles Creek varieties found in the Pearl River valley (Mann 1988) and Lower Mississippi Valley (e.g., Phillips 1970). Types identified include Coles Creek Incised, Mazique Incised, Evansville Punctated, and L'eau Noire Incised (H. Jackson et al. 1995). Triangular arrow points occur east of the state line (Campbell et al. 1988) and the Bayougoula point type may be introduced in southeast Mississippi during this interval as well. The number of sites producing these materials is drastically lower than the number of early Late Woodland sites. One possible explanation is that cord marking persisted longer in the area than to the west (D. Morgan 1992:262). Alternatively, there may have been a shift in population to larger river valleys.

Our ceramic distribution study identified late Late Woodland components at only ten sites in Perry County and four sites in Forrest County, all associated with either the Leaf River or Black Creek. In Greene County a minor late Late Woodland occupation is indicated by grog- and shell-tempered Evansville Punctated and possible triangular arrow-point fragments (H. Jackson and Fields 2000). Coastal connections during this subperiod, at least in the southern portion of the Pine Hills, are indicated at Swamp Child on Black Creek, which produced a Weeden Island Incised sherd. Another Weeden Island–like vessel fragment from Stone County to the south is from apparently local grog-tempered ware. The remainder of sites in both counties produced Mississippi Valley diagnostics. In the southern part of the study area, a number of shell-tempered cord-marked sherds have also been recovered, which may fall into this late Late Woodland time bracket. Farther east, at 22GN668, several grog- and shell-tempered sherds of Evansville Punctated provide evidence of a late Late Woodland component there. In sum, a clear westward shift in cultural affiliation seems apparent in the area.

In contrast, in southwestern Alabama, Miller III site distributions along the Mobile Bay pipeline continue the pattern set during Miller II (Campbell et al. 1988), with concentration in physiographic zones north of the Pine Hills. Miller III sites are distinguished on the basis of Mulberry Creek Cord Marked, Withers Fabric Marked, and the presence of small triangular points. Later Miller III components have higher percentages of grog-tempered ceramics (Campbell et al. 1988; N. Jenkins and Krause 1986). In the Pine Hills, Porter types are thought to persist and later Woodland sites, categorized as a "Porter continuum," were identified on the basis of Mulberry Creek Cord Marked and the presence of small triangular points. Evaluation of whether the "continuum" reflects a persistence of Porter types into the Late Woodland or, more likely, the repeated use of site locations creating mixed assemblages requires further investigation.

Conclusions

This study is intended to lay a groundwork for examining a series of cultural and ecological issues related to prehistoric occupation of the southern pine forest. To simply dismiss this part of the South as unimportant in prehistory can no longer suffice. It has a plentiful archaeological record, though as we have noted, population reaches its peak prior to the end of the Late Woodland. Multiple cultural influences, the mechanisms of which are not presently clear, affected the local ceramic inventory. These influences certainly varied during the Gulf Formational and Woodland eras, but the preliminary results of this study suggest that local populations remained articulated with the regions that surrounded them, through exchange, perhaps marriage, and other social processes. Over time the influences from northeastern Mississippi, which are quite pronounced during the Late Gulf Formational through early Late Woodland, diminish, so that by the late Late Woodland we see a strong alignment with the western Lower Mississippi Valley cultures, along with some coastal influence. The strong early northern connections fill a distributional void between the Alexander-producing cultures of northeastern Mississippi and the Tchefuncte cultures of coastal Louisiana. A broad sand-tempered horizon is suggested, which may require either an expansion of the Alexander concept or formulation of a broader category that encompasses a large part of the Midsouth.

Although we had expected clinal distributions that might point to variable connections that might differentiate local populations, in fact the region appears relatively homogeneous until late prehistoric times. Some distinctions between north and south are apparent during the Late Gulf Formational–Middle Woodland interval, but these diminish by the early Late Woodland. By the latter half of the Late Woodland, certain parts of the study area appear to have been abandoned or at least much differently used.

Presumably the apparent population decrease after the early Late Woodland can be related to environmental factors tied to intensification of agricultural production or else the impact of population consolidation under the control of emerging chiefdoms. The particular combination of factors that affected southeastern Mississippi should be illuminated by archaeological work along the major drainages, including the Chickasawhay and Leaf, and, more important, the Pascagoula, which they form. Two possibilities warrant examination by future research. The first is that the region was abandoned as a locus of settlement and was thereafter used primarily seasonally by segments of larger populations. Knight's (1984) interpretation of the Mobile Bay late prehistoric sequence implies seasonal dispersal into the interior. An alternative interpretation is the persistence of scattered and shifting farmsteads occupied by a much-reduced local population. Such a pattern is documented historically for the Choctaw and represented by historic aboriginal sites just to the north of the area considered here.

Chapter 12

The Woodland Period in the Appalachian Summit of Western North Carolina and the Ridge and Valley Province of Eastern Tennessee

Ruth Y. Wetmore

This regional perspective of the Woodland period examines two physiographic provinces: the Appalachian Summit and the Ridge and Valley province. Emphasis is on fieldwork results and published cultural syntheses of these two areas. The study areas are briefly defined, followed by references to previous work and a summary of the current understanding of—or differences in the understanding of—each region's cultural-temporal phases.

The Study Area

The Appalachian Summit

Kroeber (1939:95) originally used the term *Appalachian Summit* to describe a cultural and natural area comprising the highest portion of the Appalachian Mountains chain. The Appalachian Summit area is contained within Fenneman's (1938) Southern Blue Ridge province, bordered on the east by the Piedmont Plateau province and on the west by the Ridge and Valley and Interior Plateau provinces (Figure 12.1).

The 6,000-square-mile portion of the Appalachian Summit in North Carolina contains the highest peaks in the Appalachian Mountains system, with forty peaks over 6000 feet in elevation (Stuckey 1965:19–20). Drainage systems have cut the original landform into a series of deep, steep-sided valleys separated by narrow ridges, and most of the region's streams follow the Hiwassee, French Broad, or Little Tennessee River westward to the Tennessee River (Purrington 1983:89). The state line between Tennessee and North Carolina follows the ridgeline of the Appalachian chain. The Tennessee portion of the Appalachian Summit is an approximately 25-mile-wide strip adjoining North Carolina, including the Unaka and Smoky mountains (Aswell and Bunce 1939:7).

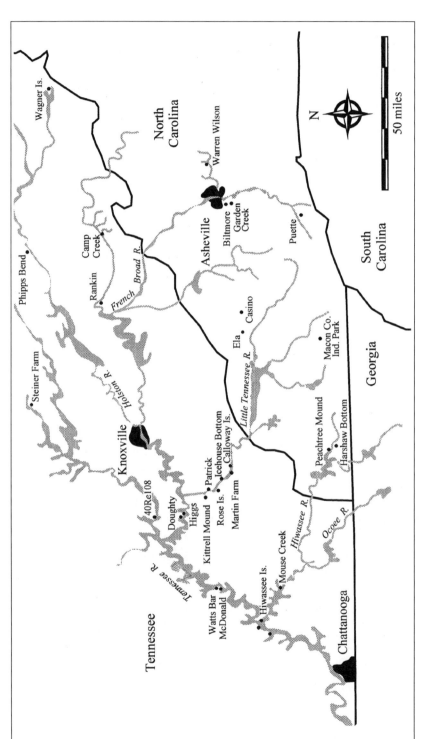

Figure 12.1 — Archaeological sites in western North Carolina and eastern Tennessee

Rainfall and temperatures vary widely, as a result of differences in to-pography, altitude, wind direction, and thermal belts (Barry 1992; Dunbar 1966). Prevailing winds from the southwest carry moisture from the Gulf and Atlantic coasts, and lower elevations farther from the escarpment re-ceive less precipitation. Mean annual rainfall in western North Carolina ranges from over 80 to 37 inches (Kitchline 1941:1044). Despite local tem-perature differences, the frost-free season is about 150 to 180 days (W. Lee 1955:9). The western slope of the Blue Ridge in Tennessee has an average annual rainfall of 44 inches, with precipitation on the eastern mountain slope between 48 and 60 inches. This area averages 190 frost-free days per year, with temperatures approximately three degrees centigrade cooler than in the Ridge and Valley province to the west (Williamson 1941:1127–28).

Temperate deciduous forests predominate in the Appalachian Summit, although the introduction of pines and the chestnut blight of the 1920s have altered the aboriginal landscape. The Woodland plant resources of the Ap-palachian Summit probably supported larger animal and human populations than would have been possible in a more homogeneous environment (Purrington 1983:93). Numerous berry, plant, and root varieties provided food and medicine in addition to acorn and nut resources (E. Braun 1950:173–213). Deer, black bear, opossum, raccoon, beaver, turkey, ducks, geese, and fish were major sources of food and clothing (Bass 1977:10–11; Goodwin 1977; Keel 1976:9–10).

Because a small portion of Tennessee lies in the Appalachian Summit, most archaeological data come from North Carolina. Significant exceptions are studies by Bass (1977) in the Great Smoky Mountains and Clifford Boyd (1986) in the Watauga Reservoir.

The Ridge and Valley Province

The Ridge and Valley region is bounded on the east by the Appalachian Summit and on the west by the Cumberland Plateau and extends northeast-southwest from the Virginia line to northern Georgia and Alabama. The el-evation, number of ridges, and degree of relief between ridges and valleys decline from northeast to southwest (Fenneman 1938). The area averages 190 frost-free days per year (Williamson 1941:1125–26) with a mean an-nual rainfall of 46 to 54 inches. As it is lower than the Cumberland Plateau and Blue Ridge areas, this province averages three degrees Centigrade warmer than regions to the east and west (Schroedl et al. 1990:178).

Modern climate and forest conditions in east Tennessee were established by 4000 years ago (H. Delcourt and P. Delcourt 1985), with oak-chestnut forests covering much of the area during Woodland times (E. Braun 1950). Floral and faunal resources are similar to, but not as diverse as, those of the

Appalachian Summit because of fewer microenvironments and more homogeneous terrain. Multidisciplinary research has compiled a 10,000-year record of human impacts on the region's ecosystem (J. Chapman et al. 1982). Changes in forest composition indicate that aboriginal land clearing had a significant effect on the region's environment by 1050 B.P. (Cridlebaugh 1984).

Much of the archaeological work in the southeastern Ridge and Valley province has been conducted in the Chickamauga (T. Lewis and Kneberg 1941, 1946), lower Little Tennessee (R. Davis 1990), and Tellico River basins (Kimball [ed.] 1985) to mitigate areas now covered by Tennessee Valley Authority dams. Northeastern Tennessee has provided information from the Watauga Reservoir (C. Boyd 1986), Norris Basin (W. Webb 1938), and Phipps Bend (Lafferty 1981).

The Woodland Sequences

The broad temporal divisions of Archaic, Woodland, and Mississippian periods were established during the early twentieth century, on the basis of stratigraphy, artifact types, and subsistence or settlement patterns (T. Lewis and Kneberg 1941, 1946; Setzler and Jennings 1941). The Woodland period is distinguished from the preceding Archaic period by the appearance of pottery, the cultivation of domesticated plants, increased sedentism, and indications of greater social complexity (Fagan 1991). Each period is further divided into culture-historical phases or complexes (Figure 12.2). In both provinces, Woodland cultural phases are defined by the occurrence of specific ceramic types—and in the Ridge and Valley province, by the comparative frequencies of specific ceramic types—in stratigraphic deposits or features having cultural integrity (Schroedl et al. 1990:179).

The earliest systematic archaeology in the Appalachian Summit was at the Peachtree mound, where Setzler and Jennings (1941) identified Woodland, Mississippian, and Cherokee occupations. Woodland period subdivisions and phases were defined during the Cherokee Archaeological Project, investigations conducted by the University of North Carolina–Chapel Hill Research Laboratories of Archaeology: Early Woodland, Swannanoa; early Middle Woodland, Pigeon; and late Middle Woodland, Connestee (Keel 1976:219–31). No Late Woodland phase was identified (Keel 1976:239).

In the Ridge and Valley province, Thomas Lewis and Madeline Kneberg (1941, 1946) established the first chronology based on work in the Chickamauga Basin and Hiwassee Island. Subsequent researchers produced new terms and definitions for phases and ceramic types in this and other

Dates AD /BC	Cultural Periods	E. Tennessee Phase (* Ceramics)	W. North Carolina Phase (* Ceramics)
2000 —	Historic	Overhill Cherokee	Cherokee *Qualla
1500 —	Mississippian	Dallas and Mouse Creek Hiwassee Island Martin Farm	Mississippian *Pisgah
1000 —	Late Woodland	Woodland IV (A.D. 600–900)	
500 —	Middle Woodland	Woodland III Icehouse Bottom *Connestee *Candy Creek (A.D. 350–600)	*Connestee (A.D. 200–900)
0 —		Woodland II Patrick II and I *Candy Creek *Long Branch (200 B.C. – A.D. 350)	*Pigeon (200 B.C. – A.D. 200)
500 —	Early Woodland	Woodland I *Phipps *Long Branch *Watts Bar *Swannanoa (900–350 B.C.)	*Swannanoa (700–200 B.C.)
1000 —	Late Archaic		

Figure 12.2 — Woodland chronology for western North Carolina and eastern Tennessee (after Keel 1976; Kimball 1985; Wetmore, Robinson, and Moore 1996)

areas. These changes are summarized below, to help correlate terminology in reports spanning half a century.

Lewis and Kneberg divided the Early Woodland period (2850–1750 B.P.) into two phases, Watts Bar and Long Branch. The Middle Woodland period (1750–1350 B.P.) had one phase, Candy Creek. The Late Woodland period (1350–1050 B.P.) contained the Hamilton phase, to which a Roane-Rhea phase was later added. Larson (1959) proposed a Middle Woodland Greeneville complex (later deleted) during which both quartz-tempered Watts Bar and limestone-tempered Long Branch ceramics were used. McCollough and Faulkner (1973) identified a locally made Swannanoa ceramic type distinct from the Watts Bar and the Appalachian Summit Swannanoa types. They also proposed dividing the Middle Woodland Long Branch phase into Phipps and Long Branch phases.

R. P. Stephen Davis (1990:56) based his chronology on statistical analyses of ceramic assemblages in the lower Little Tennessee River valley. The Woodland I, Bacon Bend ceramic cluster replaced the earlier Watts Bar designation. Woodland II, Patrick I and II ceramic clusters replaced the former Long Branch and Greeneville units (Kimball [ed.] 1985:126). Woodland III, Icehouse Bottom and Westmoreland-Barber ceramic assemblages replaced the previous Candy Creek and Connestee phases. The Hamilton focus or phase is now recognized as a burial mound complex including both Late Woodland and Mississippian periods rather than the final Woodland phase (Schroedl et al. 1985:8). More recently, a Woodland IV period was proposed (Schroedl and Boyd 1991).

Figure 12.2 outlines the current regional chronology, and representative radiocarbon dates are listed in Table 12.1. As the rate and type of cultural change vary by practice, area, and descriptive organizational framework, dates and phase names in the text will not always agree with those in Table 12.1 and Figure 12.2.

The Early Woodland Period

Appalachian Summit, Swannanoa Phase (600–200 b.c.)
The model for Early Woodland settlement and subsistence assumes small, relatively mobile groups moving frequently to utilize seasonal and environmentally variable resources available within their territory. This model is based on site location data from the Smoky Mountains (Bass 1977) and Watauga River valley (Purrington 1976:133–35). The presence of Swannanoa sites in all microenvironments is believed to indicate a broad adaptation to local resources (Purrington 1983:132). Purrington interpreted the negligible increase in Swannanoa floodplain sites in the Watauga Valley as a sign of little reliance on horticulture, although Keel (1976:24-27) found buried Swannanoa components at Tuckaseegee and Garden Creek (Ward and Davis 1999:145). Continuity of settlement patterns from the Late Archaic to the Early Woodland is suggested by the general similarity of landform use (Bass 1977:77; Purrington 1976:116; Wetmore 1993:144).

Table 12.1 — Selected Woodland Appalachian Summit and Ridge and Valley Radiocarbon Dates (from Stuiver et al. 1998, Calib 4.3 Program)

Site	Context	Period (Phase)	Conventional Radiocarbon (B.P.)	Calibrated Age (1-Sigma) max cal ages (cal ages) min cal ages	Lab No.	Reference
Casino	Feat. 2	MW Pigeon	1740 ± 70	A.D. 235 (260, 281, 291, 297, 322) 399	B-98153	Riggs et al. 1997
Ela	Feat. 41	MW Connestee	1580 ± 60	A.D. 416 (437, 454, 457, 522, 527) 556	B-69802	Wetmore 1990
Biltmore I	Sq. 4, Lev. 3	MW Connestee	1520 ± 60	A.D. 435 (542) 618	B-69804	Moore 1984
Harshaw	Feat. CB1	MW Connestee	1490 ± 70	A.D. 475 (598) 643	B-69798	Robinson 1989
Harshaw	F-10B, Lev. A	MW Connestee	1460 ± 90	A.D. 536 (605, 610, 616) 660	B-69797	Robinson 1989
Puette	Feat. 1	MW Connestee	1460 ± 60	A.D. 542 (605, 610, 616) 653	B-66768	Wetmore et al. 1996
Ela	Feat. 102	MW Connestee	1420 ± 60	A.D. 600 (643) 662	B-69803	Wetmore 1990
Biltmore II	Feat. 1	MW Connestee	1380 ± 70	A.D. 622 (658) 685	B-?????	Hall and Baker 1993
MCIP	FS240, Unit 1	MW Connestee	1370 ± 70	A.D. 622 (660) 689	Uga-2174	Collins 1977
Cane Creek	Feat. 1	LW Connestee	1340 ± 90	A.D. 640 (666) 775	B-98035	Wetmore et al. 1996
Cullowhee	Feat. 18	LW Connestee	1260 ± 80	A.D. 665 (723, 740, 771) 886	B-69964	Moore 1984
Garden Creek	Mound No. 2	LW Connestee	1145 ± 85	A.D. 778 (893) 992	GX-0593	Keel 1976
Phipps Bend	Feat. 44, Zone B	Woodland I Swannanoa	2940 ± 105	B.C. 1368 (1205, 1205, 1188, 1181, 1149, 1144, 1129) 998	UGa-2095	Lafferty 1981
Phipps Bend	Feat. 56	Woodland I Swannanoa	2690 ± 200	B.C. 1047 (828) 552	GX-2487	Lafferty 1981

Table 12.1 (cont.) — Selected Woodland Appalachian Summit and Ridge and Valley Radiocarbon Dates (from Stuiver et al. 1998, Calib 4.3 Program)

Site	Context	Period (Phase)	Conventional Radiocarbon (B.P.)	Calibrated Age (1-Sigma) max cal ages (cal ages) min cal ages	Lab No.	Reference
Bacon Bend	T-6	Woodland I	2430 ± 180	B.C. 799 (498, 493, 483, 465, 449, 441, 426, 424, 413) 262	GX-1570	Salo 1969; Lafferty 1981; Schroedl 1978b
Camp Creek	Level C	Woodland I Swannanoa	2050 ± 250	B.C. 390 (46) cal A.D. 238	M-516	Lewis and Kneberg 1957
Patrick	Feat. 101	Woodland I Swannanoa	1810 ± 165	A.D. 27 (236) 415	GX-5245	Schroedl 1978b
Patrick	Feat. 86	Woodland III	1365 ± 145	A.D. 544 (661) 779	GX-5243	Schroedl 1978b
Icehouse Bottom	Feat. 607	Woodland II	1680 ± 80	A.D. 256 (388) 431	UGa-1882	Chapman and Keel 1979
Icehouse Bottom	Feat. 598	Woodland III	1480 ± 135	A.D. 426 (600) 665	GX-5046	Chapman and Keel 1979
Icehouse Bottom	Feat. 35	Woodland III	1365 ± 90	A.D. 616 (661) 766	GX-2154	Gleeson (ed.) 1970; Chapman and Keel 1979
Phipps Bend	Feat. 8	Woodland III	1370 ± 65	A.D. 624 (660) 688	DIC-982	Lafferty 1981
Westmoreland-Barber	Feat. 37	Woodland III	1325 ± 105	A.D. 640 (679) 779	GX-0573	Faulkner and Graham 1966
Icehouse Bottom	Feat. 87	Woodland III	1345 ± 90	A.D. 624 (664) 773	GX-2487	Chapman 1973
Wagner Island I	Feat. 1	Woodland III	1320 ± 150	A.D. 602 (683) 888	GX-10246	Riggs 1985
Wagner Island II	Feat. 2	Woodland III	1290 ± 155	A.D. 621 (691, 703, 708, 753, 758) 939	GX-10245	Riggs 1985
Kittrell Mound	tomb	Woodland III	1465 ± 175	A.D. 417 (603) 758	GX-11436	Chapman 1987
Kittrell Mound	mound	Woodland III	1295 ± 90	A.D. 657 (690, 755, 755) 849	GX-11436	Chapman 1987

Keel (1976:230–31) attributed Swannanoa ceramics to resident Archaic populations, while Holden (1966:61) noted the similarity of this thick, grit-tempered, cord- or fabric-impressed pottery to North Carolina Piedmont Badin ceramics (Coe 1964). At present, no Swannanoa radiocarbon dates have been reported from the Appalachian Summit (Eastman 1994a). Swannanoa stemmed and Plott short-stemmed projectile points are associated with this phase, as are bar gorgets, net weights, ocher, and the continued use of steatite vessels (Keel 1976:230). Post molds at the Warren Wilson site indicate fairly permanent housing, although no structure outlines were defined (Ward and Davis 1999:143). Subsistence information is limited. A Swannanoa context nutshell sample from Warren Wilson contained 46.6 percent acorn, 29.8 percent hickory, and 23.6 percent walnut (Yarnell and Black 1985:100).

Ridge and Valley, Woodland I, Bacon Bend Phase (900–600 B.C.)

Quartz-tempered Watts Bar (T. Lewis and Kneberg 1957:7) and Swannanoa (Lafferty 1981:498) ceramics are diagnostic of the Woodland I, Bacon Bend phase in the Ridge and Valley area. More recently, limestone-tempered Long Branch fabric-impressed sherds also have been considered an Early Woodland type, while cord-marked Long Branch sherds are associated with Woodland II or III periods (Schroedl 1978a:226). Large triangular and stemmed projectile points appear on sites of this period (T. Lewis and Kneberg 1957:48).

The appearance of fairly large village sites, often with deep middens, is interpreted as the result of seasonal, semipermanent, or year-round occupation. At Watts Bar, a well-defined Woodland I living floor had six shallow, fired-clay surface hearths ranging in diameter from 0.55 meter to 1.1 meters and containing fire-cracked rock (Calabrese 1976:18–23). Some sites show evidence of continued domestication of plant species and increased burial ceremonialism (J. Chapman 1985a:59).

Analysis of aboriginal settlement patterns in the lower Little Tennessee River valley showed that forty-nine of the fifty-four sites with Woodland I components were located on first and second river terraces, a stronger riverine focus than during the preceding Late Archaic Iddins phase (R. Davis 1990:226–27). Using site categories based on Binford's (1980) model for collector settlement systems, Davis (1990) classified these sites into three categories on the basis of sherd counts and the presence or absence of features and/or midden accumulations, identifying twenty-two large base camps or residential sites, five small base camps, twenty-five logistical or temporary field camps, and two indeterminate sites.

The 6-acre Camp Creek site was interpreted as a semipermanent village with a fairly large settled population. An uncorrected radiocarbon age of

2050 ± 250 B.P. was obtained from the lower part of the midden (T. Lewis and Kneberg 1957:48) (Table 12.1). Typical Woodland I artifacts included large triangular projectile points/knives, biconical pipes, birdstones, gorgets, and red ocher in burials. Although it was reportedly a single-component Woodland I occupation, Watts Bar sherds comprised only 34 percent of the Camp Creek ceramics (T. Lewis and Kneberg 1957:7), while two-thirds of the ceramics and 64 percent of the projectile points/knives were Woodland II types, indicating a significant later component.

The remains of deer, elk, bear, wild turkey, woodchuck, small rodents, turtles, and mussels were found in Camp Creek midden deposits (T. Lewis and Kneberg 1957:5). Woodland I faunal remains from Patrick, Calloway, and Rose Island revealed a dietary emphasis on white-tailed deer, supplemented by turkey, bear, raccoon, turtles, and fish (Bogan 1982:41). Freshwater mussels are uncommon in Woodland I and II archaeological assemblages along the Little Tennessee River. At the Patrick site, fewer than a dozen mussels and gastropods were found in Early Woodland contexts, although fifteen edible plant species were represented (Schroedl 1978a:193, 223–24).

Phipps Bend sites exhibited good bone preservation despite small samples. Remains of white-tailed deer, raccoon, fish, turtles, freshwater mussels, and gastropods were recovered from 40HW44. The same fauna were present at 40HW45, together with elk, beaver, squirrel, dog or wolf, turkey, and loon, but no turtle or fish remains were identified (Lafferty 1981). At 40HW44, charred nutshell in Feature 44 was 20.4 percent acorn, 8.7 percent hickory, and 2.4 percent walnut; the rest of the sample (68.5 percent) was wood charcoal and unidentified material. Contemporary features at 40HW45 contained chenopods, pigweed, pokeweed, bean, grape, and grass seeds (Lafferty 1981:401–3).

At the Higgs site, shellfish use appeared to decrease from Late Archaic to Woodland I times. The Woodland I features associated with Structure II contained 39 percent of the bivalves and 9 percent of the gastropods recovered at the site (McCollough and Faulkner 1973:148–53). Domesticated sunflower seeds were present in Archaic contexts at Higgs, but were absent from Woodland I contexts there. Hickory nut and walnut shell were recorded, and chenopods were present in one Woodland I feature (Brewer 1973:142–44).

Nearly all the mammal bone identified from Stratum 1-6 at 40RE108 on the Clinch River was from deer, with beaver, squirrel, rabbit, mouse, and mole represented by single bones. Turkey, box turtle, and three species of fish were present in this stratum, as were the remains of twenty mussel and seven gastropod species (Schroedl 1990:75–77). Even though freshwater mussels are low in nutritional value compared with other animal food sources, their year-round availability provided a useful supplement to the diet (Parmalee and Klippel 1974). Because mussel species occupy different habitats, it was determined that Woodland I people at 40RE108 collected shellfish primarily from standing water close to shore (Parmalee and Bogan 1986:36). The three major nut species found here in Woodland I contexts were hickory (81.6 percent), walnut (12.7 percent), and acorn (5.7 percent) (Schroedl 1990:70).

Few of the fifty-eight burials recorded during excavation at Camp Creek were described in the report. Multiple burials were present, but most graves contained single, flexed individuals in well-defined pits. Grave goods were present in about one-third of the burials, while a few contained copper or marine-shell trade items (T. Lewis and Kneberg 1957:32–37). Triangular projectile points lodged in bones or located within body cavities indicated that some met violent deaths (T. Lewis and Kneberg 1957:44).

At the Rankin site, 164 human burials were excavated, but characteristics were only summarized in the report (D. Smith and Hodges 1968:39–44). Most graves contained tightly flexed individuals interred in separate circular, flat-bottomed pits; several bodies were missing heads or limbs. Seven cremations were identified, some of them later Mississippian burials. Fewer than half of the Rankin site burials contained grave goods. These were generally associated with adult males or children and included projectile points, tools, shell beads, pendants, and gorgets. Some items were deliberately broken. Red ocher was present in 55 percent of the burials and graphite appeared less frequently. The use of red ochre in burials is associated with the practice of shamanism and in eastern North America has been identified archaeologically in Late Archaic contexts (J. Brown 1997:473).

At Phipps Bend, fourteen burials similar to those described above were excavated from 40HW44 and 40HW45. Bodies were tightly or partly flexed, and most individuals were accompanied by grave goods. One older male was buried with forty-four bear teeth—presumably sewn to his clothing—and items suggesting tool making and hunting activities. Four individuals (29 percent) apparently died violently, on the basis of disarticulated or missing bones (Lafferty 1981:152–57).

Several Woodland I sites contained dog burials. At Camp Creek, three small dogs were buried in separate graves, while a fourth was placed below the body of an adult male (T. Lewis and Kneberg 1957:40). An unspecified number of dog burials were excavated at the Rankin site, many of them apparently from refuse pits (D. Smith and Hodges 1968). Two separate burials at 40HW45 contained medium-sized dogs; their articulation and lack of cut marks on the bones suggested intentional burial (Lafferty 1981:20).

The Middle Woodland Period

Appalachian Summit, Pigeon Phase (200 B.C.–A.D. 200)
Minor shifts from upland to valley locations between the Swannanoa and Pigeon phases are documented in the Smoky Mountains (Bass 1977), upper Watauga Valley (Purrington 1983), and Little Tennessee, Pigeon, and French Broad river valleys (Keel 1976). Pigeon ceramics are characterized by crushed-quartz temper and check-stamped, simple-stamped, or plain surface finishes (Keel 1976). Pigeon side-notched, Garden Creek triangular, and Copena triangular projectile points are typical of this phase. A few limestone-tempered Candy Creek sherds are found on Pigeon sites (Keel 1976:229; Purrington 1983:135).

Excavations at the Casino site were too limited to reveal the extent of the Pigeon occupation there, but Feature 2 provided an uncorrected radiocarbon date of 1740 ± 70 B.P. (B. Riggs et al. 1997:99) (Table 12.1) and botanical information. Nut species present, in decreasing order of weight, were acorn, hazelnut, hickory, walnut, and American chestnut. Sumpweed, honey locust, and domesticated *Chenopodium* also were identified (Crites 1997:93–95). The only other reported Pigeon phase botanical sample for this region is from Warren Wilson, where one stratum of Feature 141 contained chenopod, knotweed, sedge, and nut fragments in an undisturbed Pigeon-Connestee context (Yarnell 1976:219). The presence of pit facilities containing cultivated and wild plants at the Casino site suggests that it functioned as more than a temporary camp. Nonlocal lithic raw materials and Wright Check Stamped ceramics additionally indicate early interactions with Ridge and Valley province populations (B. Riggs et al. 1997:99).

Ridge and Valley, Woodland II, Patrick Phases (200 B.C.–A.D. 350)
Largely on the basis of work at Martin Farm, the former Middle Woodland Long Branch phase was redefined as the Woodland II period, with either one Patrick phase (R. Davis 1990:230) or two (Schroedl et al. 1985:8). At the Patrick site (Schroedl (1978a) two separate Patrick occupations were identified by pottery type frequencies. The earlier Greeneville unit included both quartz-tempered Watts Bar and limestone-tempered Long Branch ceramics. A feature or unit was defined as a Patrick I phase if the earlier quartz-tempered sherds constituted more than half the ceramic sample; the designation was Patrick II when limestone-tempered sherds predominated (McCollough and Faulkner 1973:93). Greeneville, Camp Creek, and Nolichucky projectile points are diagnostic of the Woodland II period (Kimball [ed.] 1985:277).

In the Little Tennessee River valley, 62 (7 percent) of the 894 identified cultural components were assigned to the Patrick phase. Seventeen sites

identified as large base camps were interpreted as semipermanent sites occupied by large groups for extended periods of time, rather than as permanent settlements. The remainder consisted of eight small base camps, twenty-
six logistical camps/residences, and eleven limited-activity hunting camps
(R. Davis 1990:231, 233). Excavations at the Patrick site revealed heavy
midden accumulation and a variety of Patrick phase features, including charcoal concentrations, hearths, ovens, and rock pavements. Postholes were
present, but did not form patterns complete enough to define structures. Similar features were documented in the sub-plowzone midden at Rose Island
and Calloway Island (J. Chapman 1975, 1979). At the Patrick site, thirteen
burials appeared to be single primary inhumations, eleven of them articulated. Other burial types included one multiple and two single secondary
inhumations, two probable bundle reburials, and one cremation. Only four
burials—one of which was Mississippian—contained grave goods (Schroedl
1978a:45–46).

The Woodland II phase level at the Patrick site contained elk, white-
tailed deer, dog, raccoon, squirrel, beaver, mountain lion, bobcat, turkey,
duck, turtle, and four fish species, but few mussels. More than 80 percent of
the nutshell was hickory. This level contained a mixture of wild and cultivated plants, including Asteraceae, *Chenopodium* sp., pigweed, sumpweed,
pokeweed, bearsfoot, purslane, sumac, maygrass, honey locust, knotweed,
persimmon, grape, several berry varieties, gourds, beans, and squash. The
sunflower seeds showed domestic characteristics, while the sumpweed appeared to be in an early stage of domestication; squash and gourd were probably established cultigens (Schroedl 1978b:228–31).

At Phipps Bend sites, hickory nutshell constituted 90.7 percent of the
nut species found in Patrick I contexts, followed by walnut (6.7 percent) and
acorn (2.6 percent). By the Woodland II phase, this shifted to 23 percent
hickory, 62.3 percent walnut, and 14.7 percent acorn (Lafferty 1981:423).
Of the nutshell recovered in the Tellico Reservoir, 83 percent was hickory,
12 percent acorn, and 5 percent walnut (Yarnell and Black 1985:100). Seeds
from Woodland I features at 40HW44 were from *Chenopodium* sp., pigweed, honey locust, pawpaw, persimmon, grape, grass, and legumes (Lafferty
1981:405). Faunal remains included deer, elk, beaver, raccoon, turkey, and
terrapin, with a great increase in freshwater mollusks (Lafferty 1981:144–
48). Similar subsistence patterns were observed at the Higgs and Doughty
sites (McCollough and Faulkner 1973).

Icehouse Bottom was a large, semipermanent residential site with at
least seven or eight living surfaces. Evidence of major habitat disturbance
and agriculture, including a small amount of maize, was identified in Woodland II components, and these levels contained 98 percent of the plant re-

mains recovered at the site. Hickory (87 percent) constituted the largest proportion of nutshell from this occupation, followed by walnut, acorn, and small traces of hazelnut (Cridlebaugh 1981:15, 174–75). Maize probably was added to a well-established group of native cultigens or domesticates such as *Chenopodium* spp., *Phalaris caroliniana,* maygrass, knotweed, sumpweed, and sunflower, and it did not become significant in the archaeological record until about 1150 to 1050 B.P. (J. Chapman and Crites 1987).

Eight radiocarbon assays were obtained from six Woodland features at Icehouse Bottom (Cridlebaugh 1981:178), but only sample Uga-1882 was within the Woodland II period with a calibrated date of A.D. 256 (388) 431 at one sigma (Eastman 1994a:59) (Table 12.1). Connestee and Candy Creek series sherds were associated in all levels of Stratum II from which the radiocarbon dates were taken (Cridlebaugh 1981:156).

The presence at Icehouse Bottom (J. Chapman 1973) of nonlocal Hopewell materials—small prismatic blades and cores of Flint Ridge, Ohio, chert, Hopewell rocker-stamped sherds, Connestee sherds, and cut mica—marks participation in the Hopewell Interaction Sphere (Caldwell 1964). No Woodland burials were found there, despite extensive excavations (Gleeson [ed.] 1970, 1971). This contrasts sharply with the numerous burials recorded from other large Middle Woodland sites such as the nearby Patrick site (Schroedl 1978a). Jefferson Chapman (1973:39) proposed that ridgeline burial mounds were used, and four mounds near Icehouse Bottom were reported by Cyrus Thomas (1894:388). The Stiner Farm stone mound group in the Norris Basin contained mica and cut bear mandibles (W. Webb 1938), suggestive of Hopewell involvement or influence (J. Chapman 1987:63).

Appalachian Summit, Connestee Phase (A.D. 200–950)
First identified as a late Middle Woodland phase with an estimated termination around 1350 B.P. (Keel 1976:221), this phase appears to have continued several centuries later. Fine sand-tempered Connestee ceramics—generally with plain, brushed, or simple-stamped surface finishes—are characteristic of this phase and show a clear developmental relationship with earlier Pigeon ceramics (Ward and Davis 1999).

The greater number and size of Connestee sites on floodplains and terraces during this phase may indicate increased sedentism (Purrington 1983:139). Upland sites continue to be present, suggesting continued and perhaps more specialized use of resources found there. The first earthen mounds in the Appalachian Summit appear during the Connestee phase, and a small earth mound with two construction stages was investigated at Garden Creek (Mound No. 2). The first stage was a yellow clay platform 0.5

meter high, which supported one or more structures. A second substructure mound was constructed later over the earlier platform (Keel 1976:220–21, 224). At the base of the mound, post molds outlined a rectangular Connestee structure (6.1 meters by 6.4 meters) with posts set in individual trenches (Figure 12.3). There was no evidence of an interior fireplace or the use of daub (Keel 1976:220). At Ela, eight circular structures between 7 and 8 meters in diameter were interpreted as Connestee phase dwellings. All but one of these lacked hearths, the exception having two hearths. Three of the smaller structures also contained storage pits (Wetmore 1996:224).

Connestee phase interaction and exchange with other nearby regions as well as with eastern Tennessee has long been recognized (Holden 1966; Keel 1976). Small numbers of Swift Creek, Napier, and Candy Creek sherds appear in Connestee contexts at a number of Appalachian Summit sites (Bass 1977; L. Hall and Baker 1993; Holden 1966; Keel 1976; D. Moore 1984; Robinson 1989; Wetmore 1990, 1993). In the Ridge and Valley province, Connestee sherds were found at the Higgs (McCollough and Faulkner 1973:87) and Patrick sites (Schroedl 1978a:97). Connestee sherds were reported from Icehouse Bottom (J. Chapman 1973:74), but subsequent analysis indicated their local manufacture (Cridlebaugh 1981:161).

Material from the pre-mound midden at Garden Creek included Flint Ridge, Ohio, flint bladelets, polyhedral cores, and trade vessels or copies of Ohio ceramics and figurines, indicative of participation in the Hopewell Interaction Sphere (J. Chapman and Keel 1979; Keel 1976). Petrographic analysis of nonlocal ceramics revealed that southeastern vessel sherds—including some from Garden Creek and Icehouse Bottom—occur on Ohio sites, although Ohio sherds rarely appear on southeastern sites. Stoltman (1998) interpreted this asymmetric distribution as the discard of southeastern utilitarian ceramics that were intended for personal use by traders, rather than being trade goods. Western North Carolina has long been suggested as the source of mica traded into Ohio, where it is documented at more than 100 Hopewell sites (Brose and Greber [eds.] 1979; Stoltman 1998). Jefferson Chapman and Keel (1979) identified trail networks linking western North Carolina with Hopewell sites.

Several models of Hopewell exchange have been proposed. Caldwell (1964:136–38) interpreted the Hopewell Interaction Sphere as relating to religious and mortuary matters, hypothesizing that regional interaction was associated with an increase in the rate of innovation. Streuver and Houart's (1972) model suggested an established network with varying levels and forms of exchange, while Goad (1979) offered an alternative model of independent, regional exchanges operating according to various cultural, geographic, or temporal frameworks. Garden Creek and Icehouse Bottom were two of

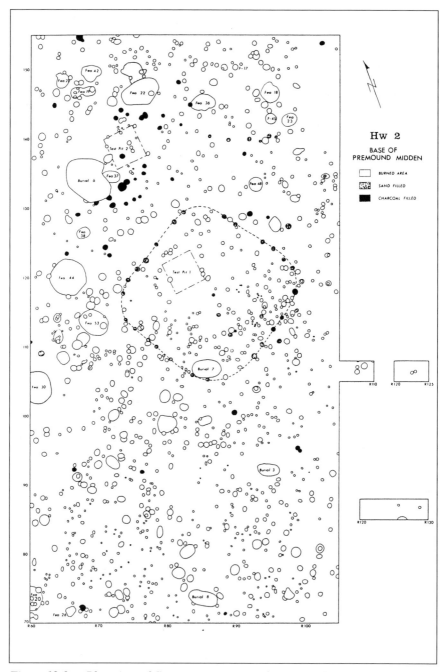

Figure 12.3 — Plan view of Connestee stratum at base of Old Village midden, Garden Creek Mound No. 2 (31Hw2) (from Keel 1976:99, courtesy University of Tennessee Press)

the six sites identified as Hopewellian ceremonial encampments in the South-east (Walthall 1985:244).

Acorn, hickory, and walnut shell have been recovered from Connestee contexts at several sites. At Harshaw Bottom, hickory constituted a majority of the nutshell from Connestee features, although the acorn:hickory ratios indicated that acorn was probably the more important food source (Gremillion 1989). Seeds identified in Connestee contexts included chenopods, sunflower, little barley, maygrass, knotweed, and cattail. Fleshy fruits were represented by grape, cherry, blueberry/huckleberry, raspberry/blackberry, and hackberry (Gremillion 1989; Holm n.d.; Oliver 1988; G. Wagner 1991; Yarnell 1976:219; Yarnell and Black 1985).

Woodland III, Icehouse Bottom Phase (A.D. 350–600)

Earlier chronologies placed the Candy Creek phase prior to the Connestee phase in the Woodland II period, but Kimball's (1985) ceramic analysis dem-onstrated the contemporaneity of these two ceramic series at Icehouse Bot-tom, which became diagnostic of the newly defined Icehouse Bottom phase. Connestee triangular and Bradley Spike projectile points are associated with this phase, which Kimball (1985:277) considered as a Middle to Late Wood-land continuum from 1600 to 1050 B.P.

In the Little Tennessee River valley, 87 of 894 identified cultural com-ponents were from this phase, and they occurred on all but one landform. Most sites (85 percent) were situated within the Little Tennessee River val-ley. On the basis of artifact classes and density, twenty-one large and seven small base camps, forty-three logistical camps, and sixteen logistical camp-sites for the procurement of specific resources were identified (R. Davis 1990:192, 235). At the Patrick site, elk, white-tailed deer, raccoon, wolf/ dog, beaver, turkey, box and soft-shelled turtle, fish, and shellfish were re-covered from the Woodland III level, which produced uncalibrated radio-carbon ages of 1430 ± 155 and 1365 ± 145 B.P. (Schroedl 1978a:193) (Table 12.1).

Although preservation of faunal remains at Icehouse Bottom was poor, deer bone was the most numerous in Woodland III contexts, with bear, turtle, freshwater drumfish, and birds also represented. The majority of plant re-mains were available in late summer and early fall, with no evidence of cultivated marshelder or sunflower (J. Chapman 1973:117, 126, 131). Fairly high percentages of bedstraw, chenopods, maygrass, and maize were recov-ered, with lesser amounts of cleavers, pokeweed, knotweed, bearsfoot, plum, and grape. Plant food remains revealed that lower terraces, bottomlands, and disturbed land accounted for 60 percent of the habitats exploited (Cridlebaugh 1984:173).

At Tunacunnhee (9DD25), which is also in the Ridge and Valley province, Hopewellian artifacts and a radiocarbon date of 1800 B.P. were obtained from four stone mounds (Jefferies 1976).

Two Woodland III radiocarbon dates were obtained from Wagner Island in the Watauga Reservoir. At 40JN89, Feature 1 was a basin-shaped pit containing limestone-tempered sherds, a Hamilton projectile point, and charred hickory nutshell, which yielded an uncorrected radiocarbon assay result of 1290 ± 155 B.P. Nearby at 40JN90, an uncalibrated radiocarbon age of 1320 ± 150 B.P. was obtained from a rock-filled hearth containing wood charcoal and sherds with limestone or mixed limestone and crushed-quartz temper. A chert Hamilton projectile point and debitage were in close proximity (B. Riggs 1985).

The Late Woodland Period

Appalachian Summit, Unnamed Phase
No Late Woodland phase has been defined explicitly for this region. When the Appalachian Summit cultural sequence was established, radiocarbon dates associated with the Mississippian period began around 950 B.P. (Keel 1976:234). With only a single Woodland date from the region, Keel (1976:239) proposed that the Connestee phase "probably lasted until about A.D. 600 [1350 B.P.], at which time it had evolved into a transition phase which would develop into the Pisgah phase." It is generally assumed that the Connestee phase continued until the appearance of Mississippian assemblages, as no changes in material culture or subsistence or settlement patterns have been identified that would indicate an intervening cultural manifestation between the Connestee and Pisgah phases. The predominance of calibrated Connestee phase radiocarbon dates more recent than 1350 B.P. appears to support this position (Wetmore et al. 2000).

At Cane Creek, Keel and Egloff (1984:14–24) named the sand-tempered ceramics for the site, describing them as "almost identical" with Connestee series vessels in paste, surface finishes, and form. Only eight sherds did not fit this classification: three Early Woodland Swannanoa sherds (Keel 1976:32), three Middle Woodland Candy Creek cord-marked sherds (T. Lewis and Kneberg 1946:101), and two Mississippian Burke Complicated Stamped sherds (Keeler 1971:34–35). Three burials were reported: one adolescent and an adult female beside an infant. A shell disk bead was associated with the woman, while a necklace of shell beads and 274 *Marginella* beads were found with the infant (Keel and Egloff 1984:44). An occupation range of 1250 to 950 B.P. was proposed for this single-occupation site, on the basis of ceramics and small triangular projectile points (Keel and Egloff 1984:44). During subsequent work at Cane Creek, a calibrated date of A.D. 640 (666) 775 (one sigma) was obtained from a rock-filled hearth containing Connestee ceramics (Wetmore et al. 2000) (Table 12.1).

Features containing Connestee ceramics at other Appalachian Summit sites have yielded calibrated age ranges from A.D. 600–660 at Ela to A.D. 778–992 at Garden Creek (Mound No. 2) (Table 12.1). Connestee simple-stamped sherds were recovered from a dated feature at the Macon County Industrial Park (S. Collins 1977), the Puette site (Wetmore 1993), and two features at Harshaw Bottom, one of which also contained Swift Creek sherds (Robinson 1989). Connestee plain sherds also were present at the sites mentioned above and at a Biltmore site (D. Moore 1984). A second Biltmore site nearby contained sherds that fell well within Keel's (1976) range of Connestee series ceramics in both form and temper, except their rectilinear complicated stamped design was suggestive of Napier ceramics. This feature produced a calibrated date of A.D. 622 (658) 685 at one sigma (L. Hall and Baker 1993).

Ridge and Valley, Woodland IV (A.D. 600–900)

The Late Woodland Hamilton phase in east Tennessee originally was defined as the final Woodland phase, characterized by limestone-tempered ceramics, small triangular Hamilton projectile points, shell middens, and burial mounds (T. Lewis and Kneberg 1941, 1946). Year-round site occupation and heavy dependence on shellfish was proposed, although no structures were identified. McCollough and Faulkner (1973) suggested an alternate model based on investigations at the Higgs and Doughty sites, two shell middens where shellfish were not the major food source. Evidence of a structure at Higgs raised the possibility of seasonal, rather than year-round, occupation (McCollough and Faulkner 1973:100).

As more radiocarbon dates were obtained, previously defined "diagnostic" characteristics were found to occur in more than one temporal period. This was particularly true of burial mound usage, which extended from Late Woodland to Historic times. Radiocarbon ages obtained from sequential construction stages of three burial mounds at the McDonald site ranged from 1275 ± 150 B.P. to 795 ± 100 B.P. (Schroedl 1973:5). Their initial construction stages were nearly contemporary, and at least two of the mounds continued to be used after 950 B.P. (Schroedl 1973). The Kittrell mound in the lower Little Tennessee River valley yielded uncalibrated radiocarbon dates of 1465 ± 175 B.P. for charcoal within the mound's fill and 1295 ± 90 B.P. for a sample from the central tomb fill (J. Chapman 1987:60) (Table 12.1). A reanalysis of early records and collections from the Mouse Creek site led

Sullivan (1989:56) to conclude that initial construction of the Hamilton phase mound there began during the Late Woodland period.

Burial mound construction and burial customs have been reported by Thomas Lewis and Kneberg (1946), Schroedl (1973, 1978b), and Jefferson Chapman (1987). Patricia Cole (1975) analyzed mortuary patterns at Late Woodland mounds statistically to infer characteristics of Late Woodland social organization. Comparisons of age, sex, and grave associations indicated egalitarian societies. Mortuary patterns at three mound groups suggested that subregional groups, perhaps lineages, constructed and maintained individual mounds or groups of mounds. The mounds may have marked territorial boundaries and strengthened group ties in addition to their mortuary function (P. Cole 1975:82).

Closing Comments

The large and comprehensive excavations and analyses conducted in the Ridge and Valley province provide a clearer picture of aboriginal life and change than currently exists for the Appalachian Summit. While Woodland settlement patterns and regional contacts are known for some areas, Appalachian Summit data on subsistence patterns, sociopolitical organization, and models of cultural dynamics remain sparse.

While looking for patterns in the archaeological record, it is useful to remember that cultural systems and their component parts do not change uniformly in either time or space. Definition of the Hamilton burial mound complex (P. Cole 1975) is a good example of bringing diverse lines of evidence together to define a problem for which contradictory explanations existed. The ranges of similarity and variation as well as the scale applied to cultural dynamics must be considered in designing a model (C. Cobb and Nassaney 1995).

Participation of these two provinces in the Hopewell Interaction Sphere is well documented at the Garden Creek and Icehouse Bottom sites; nonlocal sherds at sites in both regions attest to other, perhaps less formal, contacts between these two regions at other times during the Woodland period. Walthall's (1985) identification of Hopewellian ceremonial centers within a large and geographically diverse area might profitably be used to view Woodland interaction and cultural change on a larger regional scale. There may be more similarities between the two provinces considered here and their neighbors in other directions than between each other.

Several approaches have been employed to understand cultural dynamics and beliefs. Artifacts, ethnology, and the direct historical approach have been used to interpret Hopewell symbolism (J. Brown 1979; R. Hall 1979) and other Woodland beliefs (Brose 1985). Architecture, including that of mounds, earthworks, sweat lodges, and other ritual spaces, has been examined for insight into Woodland kinship groups (P. Cole 1975) and sacred geography (J. Rudolph 1984).

An unresolved question in both the Appalachian Summit and Ridge and Valley provinces involves the transition from Late Woodland to Mississippian culture. Three models have been proposed to describe this process in eastern Tennessee: (1) migration or ethnic replacement, (2) *in situ* cultural development, and (3) cultural diffusion, which includes elements of the first two models (Schroedl et al. 1990:189). In the Appalachian Summit, it has generally been argued that the change from Woodland to Mississippian culture was an *in situ* development and that the historic Cherokees were descendants of an indigenous prehistoric population (Coe 1961; Dickens 1976). While no separate phase has been identified between the Middle Woodland Connestee and Mississippian Pisgah phases, David Moore (1986:74–76) cautions that additional data on settlement patterns, site function, and chronology between 1350 and 950 B.P. are needed to settle this question. Moore also proposed an alternative model characterized by isolated groups and possible depopulation during this period, leading to diffusion of new ideas and the possible migration of new people into the area.

Tribal groups tend to be equated with their locations during early Historic times. Archaeological research and the analysis of sixteenth-century Spanish accounts in the Southeast document the cultural diversity of prehistoric populations in the two regions considered here, as well as the inherent instability of chiefdom societies (Anderson 1990, 1994; Coe 1961:59; Hudson 1997). Archaeologists cannot recover linguistic data, and Spanish accounts postdate by half a century the latest Woodland cultures considered here. Nevertheless, there may be parallels with earlier Woodland populations. The abundant evidence for regional contacts during the Woodland period suggests that Woodland populations may have had greater diversity than is generally assumed.

Acknowledgments

Thanks are due to Dr. Gerald F. Schroedl, whose comments on earlier drafts significantly improved this chapter, and to my husband, David, in appreciation for his support and computer expertise. Any errors or misrepresentations remain my responsibility.

Chapter 13

The Woodland in the Middle Atlantic: Ranking and Dynamic Political Stability

Jeffrey L. Hantman and Debra L. Gold

This chapter provides a perspective from just outside the typically described Southeast in the Woodland period. Almost a century ago, Holmes drew a line at about the Virginia–North Carolina border and suggested that this line divided north and south in terms of pottery—northern pottery was "rude ... simple and archaic," while southern pottery was "advanced and complex" (Holmes 1903:22, 145). Challenged by Holmes's division, we welcome the opportunity to begin as "outsiders looking in" to the Southeast and seek to place our research on the later prehistory of the Chesapeake and Middle Atlantic into a broader historical and geographic comparative framework, to ask ultimately whether a boundary does exist between the Middle Atlantic and the Southeast in the Woodland period.

Many excellent overviews of the Middle Atlantic have been written or compiled in recent years by Custer (1984, 1989, 1994, 1996) for Delaware, the Delmarva Peninsula, and eastern Pennsylvania, as well as the region at large, Dent (1995) for the Chesapeake region, Little (1995) for the Potomac drainage basin, and Stewart (1989, 1992, 1998a) on topical issues such as trade and ceramic origins and diversity throughout the region over a long time span. We draw extensively from these syntheses in our review, while adding our perspective from Virginia, the supposed southern terminus of the Middle Atlantic region. We begin with a brief overview of existing data on Woodland-era subsistence and settlement patterns. Next, we examine data relating to two key areas of change that mark the Middle Atlantic Woodland and that are also apparent in the Woodland Southeast. These are the shift from steatite bowls to ceramic containers and changes in mortuary practice.

Finally, we offer our interpretation of the appearance of ranking in the Middle Atlantic region. Overviews of the region, as well as individual site reports, often locate individual moments or places of an initial emergence of ranking or leadership to explain uneven, apparently hierarchical, distributional patterns of material culture. Interpretation is based largely on analogy with Melanesian big-man systems of competitive ranking (Sahlins 1963), an analogy that, many have argued, may be used cautiously for describing some prehistoric Amerindian political systems (Lightfoot and Feinman 1981, 1982). Sahlins (1972:208) also noted the close parallel between the Melanesian big man and the Plains Indian chief, and Hayden (1995) has described the long-acknowledged similar systems of competitive ranking among Northwest Coast Amerindian groups. B. D. Smith (1986) and many others have made a similar argument for certain times and places throughout the Eastern Woodlands.

We agree that this model holds much potential for understanding the emergence of ranking in the small-scale societies of the Middle Atlantic Woodland. In fact, what emerges at the larger regional scale of synthesis in the Middle Atlantic is an intriguing cultural pattern of cycling that situates the many individual "emergences of ranking" and their variable modes of expression into a coherent and long-term pattern of regional political stability previously undescribed for the Middle Atlantic Woodland period. This context allows, we think, for meaningful comparison with similar processes occurring elsewhere in the Southeast.

Boundaries in Time and Space

A now fairly long-standing consensus in the discipline, solidified by the creation of a separate Middle Atlantic journal and a separate Middle Atlantic conference, considers the Middle Atlantic to be that region located along the Atlantic coast from New York to Virginia, extending west to include the Coastal Plain, Piedmont, Blue Ridge, and Ridge and Valley physiographic provinces (Figure 13.1). Several major rivers define this region and the patterns of human interaction that occurred. These include the Delaware, Susquehanna, Potomac, Shenandoah, Rappahannock, and James. All of these flow east or south into the Chesapeake and Delaware bays, and each crosses several physiographic provinces. In this chapter, we focus on a slightly smaller definition of the Middle Atlantic, from southern New Jersey to Virginia.

Boundaries of the Middle Atlantic vis-à-vis the Southeast are, of course, arbitrary and subject to multiple interpretations as well as change over time. There are many different interpretations concerning the southern boundary of the Middle Atlantic (or, conversely, the northern boundary of the Southeast). Many archaeological overviews of the Southeast include the southern edge of the Middle Atlantic region defined above (e.g., Bense 1994; B. D. Smith 1986), but some do not (e.g., Steponaitis 1986). There is no correct way to proceed, of course, as such boundaries are imposed and fluctuate over time. Few would argue a boundary exists in the Paleoindian or Archaic

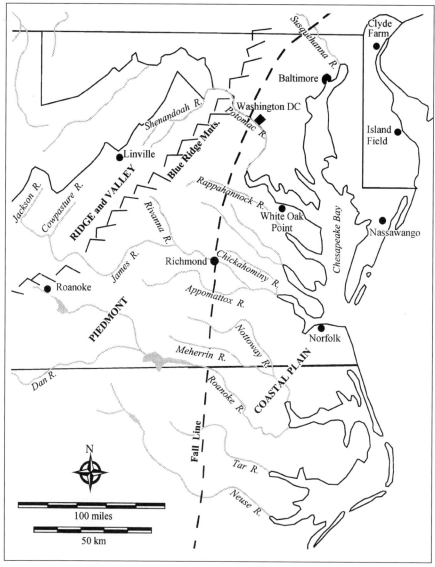

Figure 13.1 — The Middle Atlantic region, noting major river systems and prominent sites and site complexes discussed in the text

period, and the Thunderbird and Williamson sites in Virginia often are included in southeastern syntheses. On the other end of the temporal scale, Virginia's late ethnohistoric and contemporary Indian tribal histories typically are considered in overviews of the Southeast (e.g., Barker 1992; Rountree 1992), though perhaps "on the fringe" (Rountree and Turner 1994).

Beyond the well-known and well-documented Powhatan case, consideration of the linked histories of Piedmont Siouans extends unbounded from South Carolina to at least Virginia and probably north from there (Hudson 1970; Merrell 1989; Mooney 1894; Swanton 1946).

Intriguingly, it is during the Woodland and Mississippian periods that the two areas appear to be markedly differentiated and during which an archaeological boundary seems apparent. This is in part a function of the large shadow cast by the Mississippian, a phenomenon that puts the Middle Atlantic (from Virginia north) and the Southeast in noticeably different spheres of interaction. It is at least minimally accurate to say that the main icons of the Mississippian have not been noted in the Middle Atlantic, save for a few rare and isolated instances in southwest Virginia and the Potomac considered "intrusive" (Egloff and Woodward 1992:31–32). Yet, the Middle Atlantic Woodland archaeological record contains evidence for hierarchical political organization, mound building and complex mortuary ritual, and maize agriculture that is contemporary with the Mississippian farther south and west. A challenging question then emerges as to whether these are divergent or parallel, related or independent, paths to ranking and hierarchy in Eastern Woodland history. The place to start answering that question is in examining the social dynamics of the Woodland period in the Middle Atlantic territory.

A related observation concerns the *lingua franca* we use to describe archaeological stages. For reasons just reviewed, the stage termed *Woodland* in the Middle Atlantic extends from 1000 B.C. to A.D. 1600 and does not include a separate Mississippian stage (see Figure 13.2). The Late Woodland as referred to in the Middle Atlantic literature is contemporary with the Mississippian as a temporal stage elsewhere in the Southeast. To be comparable to the other chapters in the volume, we focus our discussion here primarily on the interval that Middle Atlantic archaeologists consider the Early and Middle Woodland (1000 B.C.–A.D. 1000).

Woodland Settlement and Subsistence

Traditionally, as elsewhere, the Woodland in the Middle Atlantic is said to begin circa 1000 B.C. However, a 1500- to 2000-year period immediately prior to this in the Middle Atlantic often is referred to as the Transitional period (Mouer 1991), a term first introduced by Witthoft (1953) in Pennsylvania. Following Custer (1989), many in the Middle Atlantic suggest that based strictly on patterns in the archaeological record, we should simply say that the Woodland era begins at 3000 B.C.

Approximate Dates	Chronological Period	Key Characteristics	Key Sites
3000–1000 B.C.	Transitional Period	Steatite bowl production and trade; broad-spear production; focus on riverine habitats and increased boundedness of territories; population growth; burials rare	
1000 B.C.–A.D. 200	Early Woodland	Initial ceramic production and use; continued riverine focus; decreased number of site components and diagnostic artifacts; possible clusters of residential structures (including possible pit houses) appear in archaeological record but overall pattern of mobile settlement continues; shell middens; burials rare	Clyde Farm; Delaware Park; White Oak Point
700 B.C.–A.D. 200	Early Woodland	Coiled, conoidal, cord- or net-marked ceramics common on nearly all sites; great regional variety in temper and surface treatment; "Delmarva Adena" burial sites; stone and earth burial mounds in Ridge and Valley province	Nassawango Adena; Thunderbird Ranch Mound; Alger Farm
A.D. 200–1000	Middle Woodland	Increased importance of territoriality with decrease in broad-based exchange; shell-tempered pottery (Mockley ware) throughout much of the area; restricted distribution of Abbott Zoned ceramics; slab-lined mound burials in Maryland and continued use of earth and stone burial mounds in some interior areas	Burial mounds in Great Valley of Maryland; Island Field; Linville (Bowman) Mound
A.D. 1000	Late Woodland	Maize cultivation; sedentary village occupation (seems to begin circa A.D. 1200)	

Figure 13.2 — The cultural sequence in the Middle Atlantic area

The Transitional label describes the unique site types and adaptations associated with the co-occurrence of broad-spears, the production and trade of steatite bowls, and the increased focus on riverine habitats. In the northern Middle Atlantic this is labeled the Susquehanna complex, while to the south in the region it is called the Savannah River complex (Mouer 1991:11).

Patterns in subsistence and settlement that first appear in the Middle Atlantic at this time carry on largely unchanged for the next four millennia, supporting Custer's temporal systematic. In other words, the major break in the region's culture history around the Woodland era is not the traditional Archaic-Woodland boundary at 1000 B.C., but that which took place circa 3000 B.C.

Beyond diagnostic artifacts, this transition reflects a shift from a widely ranging, foraging society to a more bounded, semisedentary and territorial society—nonagricultural, but focused on the abundant wild resources of riverine and estuarine settings. Systematic surveys in central Virginia (Hantman 1985; Hantman and Klein 1992) support this interpretation, as settlements are nonrandomly associated with riverine (good arable soil) settings in the Woodland, while previously they were more evenly distributed. Stewart (1995:185) describes this change as a shift to an emphasis on "a narrower range of more highly productive resources, [including] anadromous fish, nuts, shell fish, large mammals, [and] seed and tuber producing plants." This change may have been brought on by, or at least greatly affected by, climate change and subsequent sea level rise (Mouer 1991:3). Little change in this pattern occurs until cultigens are seen with some regularity circa A.D. 900 (e.g., Potter 1993). Gallivan (1999) convincingly argues in his study of James River settlements that there is a roughly 300-year lag between the regular use of maize and the onset of sedentary village occupation. So the Woodland, as defined in the Middle Atlantic, is a time of great stability in terms of subsistence and settlement patterns. Three areas of dynamic change, however, deserve further consideration: population growth, house construction, and territoriality.

The 3000 B.C. transition begins at a time of rather dramatic population growth. In the northern half of the Middle Atlantic, researchers describe noticeable growth of, and more intensive utilization of, individual sites, producing what typically are labeled large macro-band base camps (Custer 1989). In Virginia, Mouer (1991) also suggests there is growth in site size, in the intensity of site use, and in the total number of sites. In fact, for Mouer (1991:16–22), the Transitional is a millennium and a half of dramatic population increase as measured roughly by numbers of site components and diagnostic artifacts found in regional survey. Interestingly, the number of components and diagnostic artifacts for the traditionally defined Early Woodland shows a decline, though the riverine focus remains. Systematic surveys in the Piedmont (Hantman 1985) and E. Randolph Turner's (1976) systematic survey in the Coastal Plain produced similar results.

A point of much current interest in the region is the debated presence of residential structures at some sites in the Middle Atlantic during the Woodland. Until recently, houses were nonexistent in the archaeological record for the Woodland, despite the argument for increased intensity of site utilization. Several major exceptions to this are now in the literature and frequently cited. The best known and the seeming template for all others is the large Clyde Farm site in Delaware (Custer et al. 1987). The Clyde Farm site is located in the interior swamp zone at Churchman's Marsh, an Archaic-era freshwater swamp. A 35-square-meter area of the site revealed the presence of a household cluster, which included a variety of features including a hearth that yielded a radiocarbon date of approximately 1000 B.C.

Three kilometers upstream from the Clyde Farm site at the Delaware Park site, two semisubterranean pithouses are described dating to 1850 B.C. and 790 B.C., with associated hearths producing uncalibrated dates of 740 and 730 B.C. (dates from Custer 1989). Farther south in Virginia, McLearen (1991) suggests the presence of nine above-ground houses at an Early Woodland site in the Shenandoah Valley (44WR329), with one radiocarbon date of 908 B.C. The structures are either oval or circular in shape and range in size from 10 by 16 feet to 28 by 20 feet (within the range of what Steponaitis [1986] reports for contemporary southeastern houses). All of these "house" sites also contain pit features, activity areas, and a wide variety of artifact classes (Stewart 1995), occasionally including caches of artifacts (Custer 1989). Custer (1989) suggests that it is at these sites that one sees the initial appearance of social differentiation; that is, individuals who control and benefit from control of exchange links. At present (i.e., at the turn of the millennium), archaeologists in the region are debating the issue of whether we have routinely failed to recognize ephemeral pit structures, such as those at Clyde Farm, or whether those depressions are natural phenomena. One site in Delaware is postulated to contain perhaps as many as 700 pithouse depressions. Some geoarchaeologists are skeptical of the interpretation of these depressions as "houses," and we cannot at this time resolve this particular debate.

With or without archaeologically preserved pit structures (houses), the settlement system remains one marked by mobility throughout the Woodland, and the subsistence systems are based on exploitation of wild resources. Shell middens become common in the Coastal Plain (e.g., Potter 1993), as they do elsewhere in the Southeast (Bense 1994).

Evidence for territoriality within the larger region becomes apparent by A.D. 200 (Little 1995:157–58), based largely on the distribution of ceramic tempers and lithic exchange spheres. Stewart's (1989) detailed studies of lithic exchange spheres in the Middle Atlantic show a decline in the overall volume of trade in the Early Woodland, but not in the geographic extent of the trade. The Middle Woodland data, however, suggest a more geographically limited nature of the broad-based exchange spheres, evidence that group territories had shrunk and become more clearly defined. The Early Woodland period shows a greater quantity of nonlocal items moving through the Middle Atlantic; this pattern also falls off as the more territorially bounded social systems take shape (Stewart 1989). While territoriality increases, boundaries are permeable throughout the Woodland (Curry and Kavanagh 1991).

In the remainder of this chapter we focus on those two aspects of Middle Atlantic Woodland prehistory that are of particular relevance to our interest in regional comparison, regional boundedness, and the dynamics of sociopolitical change at the regional level. These are the transition from steatite bowls to ceramic vessels and the appearance of, and change in, mortuary ritual and mound construction.

From Steatite Bowls to Abbott Zoned: Restricted and Limited Spheres of Exchange

The traditional diagnostic of the Woodland period in the Middle Atlantic is the appearance of ceramics circa 1000 B.C. Fiber-tempered pottery has not been reported in the Middle Atlantic region, although Phelps (1983) notes its presence in North Carolina. While variability and experimentation are noted, a widespread horizon style occurs in the years of initial ceramic production with the widespread distribution, but relatively low-frequency production, of steatite-tempered ceramics.

Steatite Bowls and Steatite-Tempered Clay Bowls
Prior to ceramic production, other containers—steatite bowls—were produced throughout the Late Archaic, or from circa 3000 B.C. on (see Sassaman, this volume). Two radiocarbon assays help place the approximate beginnings of the shift to steatite-tempered ceramics in the region. The earliest dated ceramics in the Middle Atlantic area are associated with an average uncorrected radiocarbon age of 1110 ± 60 B.C. at the White Oak Point shell midden on the Potomac in Virginia (Egloff 1991; Waselkov 1982). This pottery is labeled Bushnell ware and was defined by Waselkov as being tempered with some steatite, though it is not the dominant temper. These small vessels are ovoid or rectangular with flat bases and lug handles. Marcey Creek ware, dated at the earliest to 950 ± 95 B.C. (uncalibrated) at the Monacacy site also on the Potomac (Egloff 1991), is probably contemporary and is marked by a similar shape and temper, but with a much greater percentage of steatite tempering. Other names can be added to this list (e.g., Croaker

Landing), but the common diagnostic of these earliest ceramics in the Middle Atlantic is the use of fragmentary steatite as a temper in the clay matrix.

As elsewhere in the Southeast (Sassaman 1993a), a cultural connection between the stone bowls and Marcey Creek ceramics is clear in the Middle Atlantic (see C. Hoffman 1998 for a somewhat different perspective in the Northeast). Between stone bowls and Marcey Creek, the use of steatite is a constant, albeit in different form, and the shapes of the vessels are the same and quite distinctive. Michael Klein, following Sassaman, summarizes his interpretation of their use, with which we concur:

> *The vessel form, the social import of soapstone exchange, and eth-nographic observation of the use of similar vessels for stone boil-ing and serving of meats, fishes and ritual tea indicate that these bowls are better suited for processing those items most likely con-sumed during rituals, or for serving ritual drinks or foods, than for generalized cooking. The morphological similarity and widespread exchange of soapstone vessels indicate a pan regional ritual activ-ity linked by exchange ties. (M. Klein 1997:147)*

This exchange and the ritual it is attached to extended across any perceived Southeast–Middle Atlantic border. In fact, Klein (1997:147) explicitly links the rise and fall of steatite bowl production and trade in the Middle Atlantic to the "rise and fall of complex systems of exchange in the Southeast." Ste-atite bowls found in the Southeast have been identified by neutron activa-tion analyses as deriving from Middle Atlantic sources (Allen and Pennell 1978; C. Holland et al. 1981).

Sassaman (1993a) suggests that the production and exchange of soap-stone cooking technology put constraints on the adoption of pottery and that soapstone traders perceived pottery as a threat to the perpetuation of ex-change relations and actively thwarted its spread. This hypothesis could also explain the delay in adoption of ceramics in the Middle Atlantic. Michael Klein's (1997) distributional analysis suggests a more focused image of that social dynamic in the Middle Atlantic. While steatite bowls are noted through-out the Middle Atlantic, they do not occur on all sites and access was most likely restricted to a segment of the population. Custer (1987a:100) adds that steatite bowls commonly co-occur with other nonlocal lithics. This, as well as the presence of soapstone bowls and other long-distance exchange items, suggests the presence of individuals who controlled access both to trade and to the status-bearing ritual associated with the bowls.

One must ask why the shift from steatite bowls to steatite-tempered ce-ramic bowls occurred, particularly as the introduction of Marcey Creek pottery offered no particular functional advantage (M. Klein 1997). What Marcey Creek pottery did provide was greater ease of access to the materials needed for bowl production and a reduction in labor. In the Middle Atlantic, Marcey Creek ceramics are more widely distributed than soapstone bowls (Stewart 1989:57), but they are not evenly distributed. Michael Klein (1997:149) observed that "the abundance of these ceramics thins to the north of the Potomac and the fall line of the Delaware and Susquehanna Rivers, south of the James, and west of the Blue Ridge. Thus Marcey Creek pottery production correlated far more closely with the Piedmont sources of soapstone than did soapstone bowl manufacture." We suggest that where social groups had ready access to soapstone, that is, in the Piedmont, they challenged by emulation the formerly limited nature of the stone bowl exchange sphere by producing identical vessels containing the ritually significant soapstone, even if that soapstone was only in fragmentary form. In other words, the network of those with access to soapstone or soapstone-tempered vessels was broadened, and the authority of the more limited number of individuals who had controlled soapstone bowl production and trade was challenged by Piedmont potters using local clay mixed with soapstone.

Such evening out, or opening up, of access continues through the Woodland in this same medium. Marcey Creek ceramics were produced in greater numbers than were Late Archaic–Transitional era stone bowls, but in limited number compared with later ceramic industries. Recent excavation at a stratified site in the Piedmont of the James River in Virginia shows the predominance of Marcey Creek pottery in Early Woodland levels of the site, but later ceramics were produced in far greater number and appear on far more sites (Gallivan and Hantman 1998). This seems to be a common pattern for the region.

Ceramic Production and Distribution, 700 B.C. to A.D. 900
The limited and ritually charged nature of early ceramic production gave way eventually to an increase in production of ceramic vessels and a period of relative homogeneity in access. That is, at about 700 B.C., after thousands of years of low-frequency production and limited distribution of stone bowls and then steatite-tempered bowls, containers on almost all sites become the coiled and conoidal, cord- and/or net-marked, pottery known by a multitude of names across the region (Vinette, Pope's Creek, Accokeek, Wolfe's Neck). The plethora of names reflects appreciable local regional variety in temper and surface treatment that carries on until circa A.D. 200. At that time, a new ceramic horizon occurs when shell-tempered Mockley ware unifies much of the coastal area and interior north along the Susquehanna and Delaware until circa A.D. 900. This horizon covers a vast area, though it does not in-

clude as much of the interior of Maryland and Virginia as the earlier steatite bowl and Marcey Creek patterns did. Such waxing and waning of ceramic distributions is of significance to our understanding of the formation of boundaries internal to the Middle Atlantic between coastal and interior areas. The distribution of Mockley wares supports the idea that boundaries not previously maintained begin to form at about this time (Egloff 1985; Egloff and Potter 1982). While a change is noted in this aspect of ceramic distributions, it is of equal interest that, as with their more varied predecessors, access to Mockley ceramics was unrestricted within the very large area of its production.

A significant exception to the open access and widespread distribution of the Mockley wares was the periodic occurrence of a truly distinctive ceramic type in the Middle Atlantic, Abbott Zoned decorated pottery (see Figures 13.3 and 13.4), beginning at around A.D. 200. Stewart (1998a, 1998b) has published in great detail on this phenomenon. Abbott Zoned is a distinctive decoration placed on Mockley technology and occurs at only a few places from New Jersey to the Virginia coast. Because it is even more restricted than the earlier soapstone bowl or soapstone-tempered pottery trade, Stewart, Custer, and others see Abbott Zoned as a ceramic that was used in public ceremonies and feasting. The distribution of this ceramic type may reflect the presence of a limited number of individuals who controlled access to this special-use pottery. Similarly, social ties among these "elites" were made through the marking of this distinctive decoration on the standard Mockley technology. The production and trade of Abbott Zoned extends to A.D. 950 (Stewart 1998b).

Summary of Change in Vessel Production and Distribution
To summarize the discussion of stone and ceramic vessels, we suggest the following pattern. The earliest preserved vessels were made of a raw material (steatite) that was ritually significant and moved through highly restricted exchange links. Individuals of rank appear to have controlled their production and exchange. Such control was challenged first in the Piedmont where access to clay and steatite allowed the exclusivity of the steatite bowl trade/ use to be undercut, though a long temporal lag in that process remains to be explained. The further "democratization" of vessel production and use, and the breakdown in the regional ritual associated with steatite bowls and Marcey Creek ceramics, is seen in the widespread use of clay and any locally available temper to produce vessels for more mundane practices. Later in time, however, Abbott Zoned reflects a new venue for status marking between A.D. 200 and 900, wherein ceramic decorative patterns, rather than ceramic technology, was key to such marking.

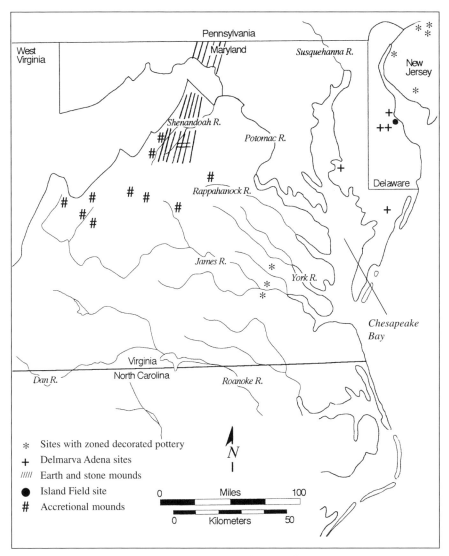

Figure 13.3 — Site and artifact distributions discussed in the text

Mortuary Ritual and Mound Construction

Burials are relatively rare in the Middle Atlantic Early Woodland, becoming more common only by the late Middle Woodland, or circa A.D. 600. Major exceptions to this include the Early Woodland phenomenon called Delmarva Adena and the stone and earth burial mounds of the Ridge and Valley province of Virginia and Maryland.

Figure 13.4 — Abbott Zoned pottery (adapted from Stewart 1998b:163; courtesy Middle Atlantic Archaeological Conference and Michael Stewart, Department of Anthropology, Temple University)

Delmarva Adena

One of the most intriguing archaeological phenomena in the prehistory of the Middle Atlantic is the presence from roughly 600 B.C. to A.D. 100 of what is called Delmarva Adena, which refers to five sites on or near the Delmarva Peninsula and two others in the Delaware Valley of New Jersey and the Susquehanna Valley in Pennsylvania (Custer 1987b; R. Thomas 1971). Dean Snow (1980) has described similar sites in New England. Delmarva Adena sites contain graves of numerous individuals, primarily multiple secondary burials and cremations, with occasional individual inhumations. Little or no evidence of domestic activity is found on these sites although caches of artifacts have been found. The link to midwestern Adena is most explicit in the distinctive trade goods that are associated with the cemeteries—the Adena bifaces, some made from Flint Ridge flint, copper from the Great Lakes, gorgets, and tubular pipes. At one cemetery, the St. Jones site, fifty burials were excavated, some associated with caches (including one with 170 bifaces, mostly of Flint Ridge flint). An area of just 8 square meters had thirty clusters of cremated bone. Red ochre covered the bifaces, copper ornaments, beads, and drilled animal teeth (Custer 1989:261).

Most of the Delmarva Adena sites were not systematically excavated, and information is drawn from nonprofessional observers and looted collections. Controlled excavation at the Nassawango Adena site disclosed seventeen subsurface pits, four of which were burial features. Artifacts associated with the burials included beads, a painted cup, and copper pendants (no flint or other Adena artifacts). Cremated and uncremated remains were together (Custer 1989).

Custer suggests that the Delmarva Adena burial sites can be broken into two groups—major mortuary-exchange centers and minor mortuary-exchange centers—on the basis of the number of Adena artifacts found in association with the burials. The major mortuary centers are not associated with habitation sites, while the minor mortuary centers are associated with micro-band base camps. Custer (1989:256–75) considers this to be evidence of ranking and the emergence of a ranked society in the Middle Atlantic. The association of individuals or small groups of individuals with long-distance, exotic trade goods is the substance of this argument. There is not a great deal of exchange, which is to say that one should not imagine a continuous flow of goods from Ohio to the Atlantic Coast; but the contact and exchange were there. There are no intervening Adena sites known in the Middle Atlantic. Adena-like artifacts are found at a few other mid-Atlantic burial sites dating to this time period as well. The Currituck site on the outer Coastal Plain contained burials with tubular pipes and gorgets, as did the nearby Riding Run site (Mouer 1991:36).

Earth and Stone Mounds

A contemporary mortuary practice of interest is seen in the numerous earth and stone mounds in the Ridge and Valley province of Virginia, Maryland, and West Virginia. These small mounds are located atop bluffs, ridges, and hills overlooking the Shenandoah River and its major tributaries. These mounds are nonaccretional, are constructed of both earth and stone, contain few burials, and usually contain grave goods including quartzite and chert projectile points, mica sheets, slate and shale gorgets, and sandstone pipes. Copper items also have been reported from a few mounds (Fowke 1894). William Gardner (1993) and colleagues have examined the mounds in the northern Shenandoah region. Ten mound sites, some containing multiple mounds, are known in this area; two have produced radiocarbon assays that range from the mid-400s B.C. to approximately A.D. 110 (W. Gardner 1986; Stewart 1981). The best known is the Thunderbird Ranch mound, part of a larger cluster of some sixteen mounds along a 1-mile stretch of the Shenandoah. The largest mound in the cluster is 24 feet in diameter and 3 feet high and capped with cobbles, which overlay four graves dug into the original ground surface. The burials were extended inhumations (W. Gardner 1993).

The vast majority of Early Woodland burials are known from earth and stone mounds. All were in very poor condition at the time of excavation (Fowke 1894; W. Gardner 1993), so there is little information on the age and sex of the individuals interred. William Gardner (1993) describes a cremation from the Lost River mound for which bioanthropological examination indicated a male, approximately 40 years of age at death. Fowke (1894:54) reports juvenile teeth from at least one mound (Alger Farm) where he notes "a pit 5 feet in diameter containing a few fragments of soft bones, among which were the teeth of a child and an adult." Both cremated and noncremated burials were interred in these mounds. Fowke (1894:54) notes "a streak of burned earth and charcoal 6 to 10 feet in breadth, apparently the remains of a fire on the surface" at the Alger Farm mound, although this does not necessarily imply that cremations occurred at the mound. Fires directly above covered burials have been noted at several mid-Atlantic sites and may date throughout the Woodland period.

Approximately 50 miles north of this group of mounds are the burial mounds of the Great Valley of Maryland, described by Fowke (1894), Schmitt (1952), and Stewart (1981). Fifteen mounds have been described, most along the Potomac River. Chronological placement is difficult as they were never systematically excavated and data are very limited. They are constructed of stone and are oval or roughly circular in shape, ranging from 12 to 20 feet in diameter and from 6 to 12 feet in height. Some graves are noted to be slab lined. These appear to be single-event burials.

Schmitt (1952) labeled these mounds part of the Mountain focus and based on the artifacts felt they were principally Middle Woodland mounds with ties to midwestern Adena and Hopewell. But the mounds are far less elaborate and contain far fewer exotic goods than most of those in the Midwest. Stewart (1995:187) observed that "the Middle Atlantic mounds are only vaguely comparable to those of Ohio Valley cultures, and the artifacts within them fail to match the range of materials, variety, or quantities seen in the Ohio Valley sites." Yet, as Stewart (1981:14) observed, "the fact that the Great Valley mounds exist in the first place, and are the final memorials of a relatively small group of individuals, forces one to assume that some form of social hierarchy existed in the area by the Early/Middle Woodland times." More recently he has noted, "We should consider the possible role of charismatic leaders in the development and maintenance of the Ridge and Valley mound building cultures and Delmarva Adena" (Stewart 1995:189).

Some areas show evidence of differentiation in mortuary treatment, as described above, but most of the region lacks comparable evidence for formal mortuary treatment in mounds. Regional variation in the structure of local social systems is evident from Early Woodland times on to an extent it had not been previously.

Middle Woodland Mortuary Patterns

Mortuary sites are poorly known for the period following the Delmarva Adena and the early earth and stone mounds. One important exception is the Island Field site in Delaware, defined by Ronald Thomas (1971, 1987) as the type site for the Webb phase/complex, dating to A.D. 600 to 900. Reexamination of the site by Custer et al. (1992) indicated an occupation span of nearly 800 years beginning around A.D. 410. The Island Field cemetery included approximately 158 individuals, almost all in single, primary interments. The majority of these (103) were associated with the Middle Woodland Webb complex. Of these 103 burials, only twenty-seven have associated grave goods in the form of caches ranging in size from fewer than five artifacts to more than twenty artifacts; the latter are quite rare. Most of the cache artifacts are utilitarian flintknapping tools (Custer et al. 1992).

Custer et al. (1992:192) point out that "most of the grave goods at the Island Field site are concentrated in only three burials which contain 406 (80%) of the 504 artifacts in grave caches. The fact that these three caches are so much larger than any of the others indicates that these individuals may have held special status positions significantly different from those of other members of the society."

The mortuary pattern changes in the later Woodland period in the Middle Atlantic, and to understand the cyclical nature of such change we must here extend our consideration to include the post–A.D. 1000 Woodland. Variation in burial practice includes individual burial pits in and around villages and group burials in ossuaries and in mounds (D. Boyd and Boyd 1992; Curry 1999). In the Piedmont and Ridge and Valley provinces of Virginia and central Pennsylvania, use of accretional burial mounds containing collective, often secondary, burials begins sometime after A.D. 900 (e.g., Clemson Island in Pennsylvania [Stewart 1990] and the Lewis Creek or Monacan mound complex in Virginia [Dunham 1994; Gold 1999; Hantman 1993; MacCord 1986]). Some of these contain hundreds of individuals, and in several of the latest mounds in Virginia that are later than A.D. 1200 more than one thousand individuals, in a single accretional mound (Dunham 1994).

These mounds, often dated to the Late Woodland (after A.D. 1000), are increasingly understood to have an earlier component pertinent to our discussion in this chapter. One of the most intriguing is the Linville (also known as Bowman) mound, located on the floodplain of Linville Creek, approximately 6 miles upstream from its confluence with the north fork of the Shenandoah River (Fowke 1894:37–44). Linville mound was excavated by Gerard Fowke in 1891 or 1892, and by that time the mound had been looted for many years. Fowke excavated the entire remaining mound, uncovering many collective secondary burial features, as well as a variety of other interment types, including single and small multiple interments (primary and secondary) and cremations. In the 1890s the mound had a basal diameter of approximately 70 feet and was approximately 3 feet high; originally it probably measured 10 to 12 feet high and was somewhat smaller in basal diameter (Dunham 1994; Fowke 1894). Artifacts found in the mound include gorgets, red ochre, shell, bone needles, stone tools of quartzite and chert, clay pipes, ceramic vessels, a panther claw, and two distinctive bone/antler combs. Fowke's narrative does not allow precise determination of the placement of these various objects, but he does indicate that many of the more elaborate grave goods were concentrated in one area. Fowke collected a small number of human bones and artifacts from Linville mound, and these were accessioned into the National Museum of Natural History. While there are no absolute dates, it has been most commonly dated to the Late Prehistoric period (A.D. 900–1600) based on similarities to other accretional burial mounds in the Lewis Creek/Monacan mound complex. Several authors, however, have suggested that at least a portion of the mound may have been used quite a bit earlier (Carpenter 1950; Stewart 1981).

Summary of Mortuary Data
While burial information is relatively scarce for the (Early and Middle) Woodland in the Middle Atlantic, this scarcity is a social phenomenon in its

own right that remains to be understood. The rarity of burial sites does establish an interesting baseline that makes the presence of some cemeteries and marked mortuary ritual behavior in the Early and Middle Woodland all the more striking. The Early Woodland (ca. 600 B.C.–A.D. 200) is marked by the distinctive Delmarva Adena pit burial type on the Coastal Plain, a burial practice clearly restricted to a few individuals. Contemporary with Delmarva Adena is the interment of individuals with grave goods, sometimes in slab-lined graves, in earth and stone mounds in the Virginia and Maryland interior. This too gives the appearance of ranking, in a burial practice restricted to certain individuals with access to nonlocal goods. The Middle Woodland (A.D. 400–1000) Island Field site and the possible early levels of the Linville mound and related sites are examples of larger cemeteries, less restricted in access, but in which certain individuals received special treatment. This pattern is replaced in the Late Woodland by tremendous variation in burial practices, including individual and multiple interments in pits within and adjacent to villages (D. Boyd and Boyd 1992) and ossuary burial in the later stages of the Late Woodland on the Coastal Plain (Curry 1999). However, a distinctive Late Woodland mode of accretional, communal, secondary burial of large numbers of individuals with few burial goods also marks the time contemporary with Mississippian (see Dunham 1994; Gold 1999; MacCord 1986). A parallel transition from Middle Woodland earth and stone burials to later earthen accretional mounds has been described in Tennessee (J. Chapman 1987)—an intriguing possible cultural tie to more southeastern regions.

Ranking, Competition, and Cyclical Patterning

We think it is clear that the local societies of the Middle Atlantic region never were isolated from neighboring regions, including the Southeast, during the Woodland period. The transition from steatite bowls to steatite-tempered bowls and the mortuary ritual patterns show connection to larger Eastern Woodland patterns. Mortuary rituals in the Adena expression on the Delmarva Peninsula and the stone cairns and mounds of the Ridge and Valley province, as well as the trade in steatite and midwestern stone, copper, and other goods moving in elite exchange spheres, link the Middle Atlantic to points west, north, and south throughout the Woodland era (see M. Klein 1997; Seeman 1981b).

The production and limited distribution of certain vessels and specialized mortuary treatment are the evidence cited in the Middle Atlantic Woodland for the emergence of ranking and elite individuals; their status positions as yet cannot be determined to be either achieved or hereditary. Yet, considered together, the appearance of such ranking shows interesting cyclical patterns, not just the emergence of an evolutionary stage, but rather evidence for the "rise and fall" of different venues of status marking. That is, rather than the single, linear, and regionwide emergence of ranked societies evolving from simple to complex, there is here a repetitive pattern of cycling in which in some limited geographically bounded systems—never the entire Middle Atlantic—a ranked individual emerged in certain places (or, perhaps more realistically, is first recognizable in the archaeological record). Individuals of temporary rank and status controlled some aspects of trade or ritual, but not all. While centuries may have passed in this way, this control was inevitably challenged by others for reasons we suspect have to do with a cultural emphasis on a community egalitarian ideology in these societies that served to check the path to greater inequality and the competition inherent in big-man systems (R. Blanton 1995:137–40; Brandewie 1991; Sahlins 1963). The evidence for this is seen in the more even distribution in each of the "status marking" items that eventually occurs. When that happens, a new marker of status emerges in other areas.

Table 13.1 summarizes the patterning in data from the Middle Atlantic for the Woodland period. This table illustrates a sequence of change in vessel production and mortuary ritual, which in both cases cycles from highly restricted, elite access, to more open, unrestricted access, then back to restricted access. The temporal offset of these patterns between vessels and mortuary practice may not be coincidental as ranked individuals or groups (lineages?) defined distinctly new avenues to control trade and mark status. A hypothetical temporal narrative posits the following sequence of competition for rank among big-man systems in the Middle Atlantic. The earliest archaeologically recognizable marker of ranking in the Middle Atlantic is the steatite bowl. The steatite bowl is, after a long span, replaced by the still somewhat restricted, but not universally accessible, steatite-tempered ceramic bowl. The status-related steatite trade links break down in the Middle Atlantic and between the Middle Atlantic and the Southeast sometime between 1000 and 700 B.C. (M. Klein 1997).

Shortly after that, and for the next eight centuries (allowing for the imprecision of chronological control in the region), marking of status shifts to mortuary ritual and control of long-distance trade, as seen in the dramatic appearance of Delmarva Adena on the Coastal Plain and earth and stone mounds in the Ridge and Valley province. Both suggest the competitive emergence of big-men with links to the Midwest (Ohio), a shift from the earlier southeastern focus. During the period of mortuary ritual as status marker, the ceramics of the Middle Atlantic show no evidence for restriction

Table 13.1 — Competitive Ranking in the Middle Atlantic Woodland: Cycles of Access and Distribution of Vessels and Mortuary Ritual

	Dates	*Distribution*	*Region*
I. Stone and Ceramic Vessels			
Steatite bowls	3000–1200 B.C.	Highly restricted	MA
Marcey Creek	1200–700 B.C.	Restricted	MA
Conoidal	700 B.C.–A.D. 200	Unrestricted	MA
Mockley wares	A.D. 200–900	Unrestricted	CP
Abbott Zoned	A.D. 200–900	Highly restricted	CP
II. Mortuary Ritual			
Delmarva Adena	600 B.C.–A.D. 200	Highly restricted	CP
Stone mounds	450 B.C.–A.D. 100	Highly restricted	RV
Island Field	A.D. 400–1000	Restricted	CP
Mounds/pit burial	A.D. 600–1000	Restricted	MA
Accretional mound	A.D. 1000–1650	Unrestricted	P, RV
Ossuaries	A.D. 1400–1650	Unrestricted	CP
Burial w/copper	A.D. 1400–1610	Highly restricted	CP

MA = distributed throughout Middle Atlantic;
CP = Coastal Plain; RV = Ridge and Valley; P = Piedmont

in access. The expected competition for rank leads to a diversity of expression and access to mortuary ritual in the period A.D. 200 to 1000. Some individuals still appear to be marked in death as persons of higher status (as at Island Field and Linville), but many have access to cemeteries who did not previously. Thus burial itself is no longer restricted to a few and is less often seen as a marker of status. At this same time, the new and very restricted mark of status is in ceramic decoration, as seen in the extremely limited but geographically dispersed distribution of Abbott Zoned. Cycling continues into the Middle Atlantic Late Woodland, where burial is open to most of the population in individual pits, multiple burial ossuaries, and accretional burial mounds. Archaeological and ethnohistoric records then suggest the access to nonlocal copper becomes the mark of status (Hantman 1990; Potter 1989).

While competition for rank apparently was defined by the ability to access nonlocal prestige goods and distinctive mortuary ritual, the territory any ranked individuals controlled was limited. At no time was the region unified under any one or more of these local ranked individuals or lineages. And, in the long term, rather than springboard any of these local big-man systems to greater or more institutionalized levels of political hierarchy, the trajectory for individual markers of high status continually appears to move in the opposite direction toward more egalitarian or even access to goods and ritual status.

There has been a tendency to say that these systems were "unstable" politically and that is why the evolution to more hierarchical systems is not commonplace in the Middle Atlantic. But while instability may have been the expected norm for local big-men, the indigenous cultural system of checks and balances on inequality was very stable over four millennia (3000 B.C.–A.D. 1000). Further, most of the Middle Atlantic Late Woodland (after A.D. 1000) does not suggest a dramatically different pattern, as it did in parts of the Southeast and Midwest.

It is not until the period immediately at or before European contact that multitiered hierarchical societies such as the Powhatan paramount chiefdom (Rountree and Turner 1998) are visible in the Middle Atlantic. The well-documented Powhatan chiefdom appears to have been quite unstable in large part because of the intense competition that Chief Powhatan suffered in the once highly contained and controlled elite copper trade (Potter 1989). As we hope this chapter makes clear, the rise and fall of a charismatic leader such as Powhatan may not have been a new-found instability, but rather a highly accelerated episode of cyclical and competitive political processes that had been part of the local cultural system since before the Woodland period began.

Finally, we began this chapter by asking whether the Middle Atlantic is part of the Southeast. As noted previously, few would posit a sharp boundary at any time prior to the Woodland period. But, as we have argued, competition in the arenas of trade and mortuary ritual—those avenues of prestige marking and exchange that link larger areas of the Americas—shifts the major connections of emergent elites in the Middle Atlantic in all directions, with particular links during the Woodland era shifting from the Southeast to the Midwest and to the north. By the Late Woodland, mortuary ritual in the southern Middle Atlantic (Virginia) shows patterns similar to those of areas of the Southeast (J. Chapman 1987), but virtually no links to the prestige exchange and mortuary ritual that marks the Mississippian. In most of the Middle Atlantic, the predominant discussion of Late Woodland linkages focuses on more northern patterns of cultural interaction and migration with Algonquian and Iroquoian groups. Thus, while the Middle Atlantic is not "outside" for most of prehistory or during the contact era, and while many of the economic and social changes of the Woodland period are common to the Southeast and Middle Atlantic, we can see how the Middle Atlantic during the Woodland is perceived archaeologically to be, and was perhaps, culturally "outside" the Southeast. It is the cycling of competitive trade and status marking with nonlocal goods and mortuary practices that, we argue, creates this pattern of change over time in macroregional patterns of interaction.

Chapter 14

A Woodland Period Prehistory of Coastal North Carolina

Joseph M. Herbert

I n eastern North Carolina, the Woodland era may be divided into Early (2200–400 B.C.), Middle (400 B.C.–A.D. 800), and Late (A.D. 800–1600) periods. This chapter focuses mainly on the three millennia comprising the first two periods. Ideally, the boundaries inscribing sociocultural periods and areas are meant to coincide with fundamental shifts in technology and major differences in social and cultural traditions. Often, though, boundaries are based on a few differences in a limited suite of material-culture traditions and are imposed more as a means of establishing chronological order and identifying spatial relationships. The development of databases necessary to formulate comprehensive and accurate models of Woodland subsistence, settlement, and social systems often lags well behind chronological and geographic studies of material culture. In many parts of eastern North Carolina, obtaining even basic subsistence data, especially for Early and Middle Woodland components, is a significant challenge. In some regions, such as the Sandhills where the preservation of organic material is very poor, subsistence models may always be inferential. Rather than deliver a malformed issue from insufficient data, this chapter attempts to fashion the preliminary framework of a cultural narrative by beginning at the beginning, documenting the evidence for material culture sequences and spatial relationships. Most often, changes in pottery styles provide the basis for developing ideas about cultural phases and boundaries in the Woodland era, and this chapter places heavy emphasis on charting regional and temporal differences in pottery-making traditions (Figures 14.1 and 14.2).

The Early Woodland period in eastern North Carolina begins about 2200 B.C. The period is distinguished from the preceding Late Archaic principally by the emergence of ceramic technology. Early Woodland pottery series such as fiber-tempered Stallings and grog-tempered Croaker Landing are what might be called cohesive traditions. Judging from the consistency of the vessel construction, the earliest pottery making seems to have been relatively well standardized. Vessels were typically thick-walled, slab-built, flat-

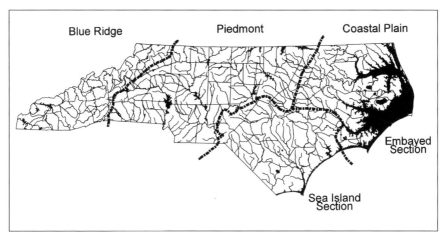

Figure 14.1 — Area map of North Carolina indicating geographic provinces

bottomed containers. In just a few centuries, however, this local regularity seems to have given way to broad-scale experimentation. On the southern and central coasts, there is slight evidence that fiber temper (Spanish moss or otherwise) continued to be added to clay, and fiber is occasionally found mixed with other tempering agents such as sand or grit. The slab-built, flat-bottomed method of construction gave way to a coil-built, paddle-and-anvil system that persisted into historic times.

The Middle Woodland period (beginning ca. 400 B.C.) is recognized primarily by a shift in ceramic technology. Middle Woodland potters raised the coil-building method to an art. The most common vessels were small, conical-based cooking pots whose walls were thinned by paddling and whose exterior surfaces were stamped with net, cordage, or fabric. By 400 B.C., ceramic vessels were an integral part of the tool kit of the working social group and were commonly transported by even the smallest parties. About this same time, stemless, triangular points (Badin and Yadkin and, possibly, Swansboro) emerge from the Late Archaic tradition of square-stemmed dart points (Savannah River and Gypsy types).

The Late Woodland period (post A.D. 800) is noted for a number of sociocultural and technological changes such as the emergence of agriculture, increased social complexity as reflected in mortuary behavior and site architecture, increased commodity exchange, and intensification of cultural regionalism. This regionalism, also expressed in pottery, is perhaps best represented by the shell-tempered pottery (White Oak and Colington series) of the central and northern coasts. The makers of Colington pottery, which is clearly bounded in geographic distribution, faithfully constructed shell-tem-

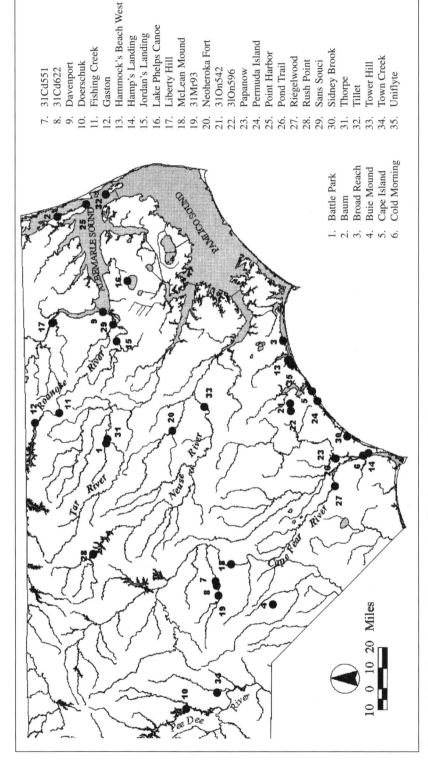

7. 31Cd551
8. 31Cd622
9. Davenport
10. Doerschuk
11. Fishing Creek
12. Gaston
13. Hammock's Beach West
14. Hamp's Landing
15. Jordan's Landing
16. Lake Phelps Canoe
17. Liberty Hill
18. McLean Mound
19. 31Mr93
20. Neoheroka Fort
21. 31On542
22. 31On596
23. Papanow
24. Permuda Island
25. Point Harbor
26. Pond Trail
27. Riegelwood
28. Rush Point
29. Sans Souci
30. Sidney Brook
31. Thorpe
32. Tillet
33. Tower Hill
34. Town Creek
35. Uniflyte

1. Battle Park
2. Baum
3. Broad Reach
4. Buie Mound
5. Cape Island
6. Cold Morning

Figure 14.2 — Locations of sites mentioned in the text and tables

pered vessels with fabric-impressed or simple-stamped surfaces, often fired in a reduced atmosphere. Their southern neighbors made very similar shell-tempered ware, with some interesting differences. White Oak does not appear to include a simple-stamped type, but does have a burnished type only rarely seen in Colington. Small triangular arrow points (Uwharrie, Clarksville, and Caraway types), marine-shell beads (primarily in burials from the latest period), and tobacco pipes are indices for these cultures.

The Early Woodland Period (2200–400 B.C.)

That portion of prehistory immediately following the development of ceramic technology generally is designated as the Early Woodland period. Studies on the lower Savannah River and Coastal Plain of South Carolina have shown that the earliest pottery made in the Atlantic coastal region (fiber-tempered Stallings) has been found in contexts dated at least as early as 2500 B.C. (Sassaman 1993a:102–10, fig. 13, appendix). As the earliest Stallings pottery is contemporary with contexts bearing Late Archaic period Savannah River phase materials, many researchers now assign the early portion of the Stallings phase to the Late Archaic period.

Regardless of cultural designations, the period from 2500 to 500 B.C. encompasses the nascence of ceramic technology along the Atlantic Coast. In the Savannah River valley, perforated soapstone disks or slabs, presumably used in basket or bladder cooking, appeared about 3000 B.C. (Sassaman 1993a:185). Soapstone-slab technology was followed by the innovation of ceramic vessel technology. Sassaman (1993a) contends that the earliest fiber-tempered vessels in the Savannah region were used as containers for boiling-stone cookery and were not placed directly on cooking fires. This may also be true of early pottery types from North Carolina, such as the Croaker Landing series (Egloff et al. 1988; Pullins et al. 1996). Early vessels along the North Carolina coast were tempered with a variety of substances including fiber (Spanish moss), soapstone, and crushed pottery. In the Sandhills types of stone such as granite, hornblende, or chlorite schist were sometimes used as tempering agents. Ingredients that reflect Piedmont sources suggest the perpetuation of the Late Archaic procurement networks by which soapstone slabs, and later vessels, along with rhyolite for projectile points and tools, were acquired (Culpepper et al. 2000; Sassaman 1993a; Waselkov 1982).

Northern Coast
Specimens of soapstone-tempered ware similar to the Early Woodland Marcey Creek series (1200–800 B.C.) of the Potomac Basin (Egloff and Pot-

ter 1982; C. Evans 1955; Manson 1948) are occasionally found in the northern part of the coast region (Phelps 1983), and rarely in the southern area (South 1960, 1976). Apparently contemporary with the Marcey Creek series is the clay- and grog-tempered Croaker Landing series (Egloff and Potter 1982; Egloff et al. 1988; C. Evans 1955; Pullins et al. 1996). Croaker Landing specimens are well represented at the Davenport site, on the Chowan River in Bertie County, and at others in the northern area of the Coastal Plain, but have not been found south of Albemarle Sound (J. Byrd 1999).

The Early Woodland coarse, sand-tempered, Deep Creek series is defined from collections north of the Neuse River (Phelps 1981, 1983). Deep Creek is comprised of cord-marked, fabric-impressed, simple-stamped, net-impressed, and plain types. Phelps (1983:31) proposed three components within the Deep Creek phase (2000–300 B.C.) characterized by trends in the popularity of various surface treatments. The earliest component is characterized by a predominance of cord marking, the middle component by a rise in the popularity of simple stamping, and the latest component by a decline in the popularity of simple stamping.

Southern and Central Coast

Examples of Stallings series ware (J. B. Griffin 1943b; Sassaman 1993a; Stoltman 1972, 1974) (2500–1100 B.C.) have been reported in collections from as far north as the Chowan Basin (Phelps 1983) and as far west as the Sandhills (Culpepper et al. 2000), though their frequency is higher in collections from the southern portion of the coast (Phelps 1983:fig. 1.4). Most of this material is plainware, having simple, smoothed exterior surfaces. There is some slight evidence for the evolution of fiber-tempering and sand-tempering traditions in the Sandhills and Sea Island section of the coast as predominantly sand-tempered specimens occasionally include fiber.

Early Woodland Thom's Creek series pottery (2000–1200 B.C.), more common on the lower Savannah River and South Carolina coast (J. B. Griffin 1945b; Phelps 1968; Sassaman 1993a; Stoltman 1974; Trinkley 1980a, 1989), is also occasionally found in collections from the southern coast of North Carolina (Phelps 1983; South 1976). In general, the Thom's Creek material that is found in assemblages from southern coastal North Carolina consists primarily of plain or reed-punctate varieties thought to be among the earliest (2000–1000 B.C.) surface-treatment types in South Carolina (Cable et al. 1998:306, fig. 113; Trinkley 1980a, 1990).

A recently identified limestone- or marl-tempered series, Hamp's Landing (Hargrove 1993; Hargrove and Eastman 1997, 1998; Herbert and Mathis 1996; Mathis 1999), has been proposed as an Early (or early Middle) Woodland type. At the type site, Hamp's Landing series pottery (Hargrove 1993) was found in an apparent stratigraphic context between and overlapping with Thom's Creek and Middle Woodland period Hanover types (Figure 14.3). Three subsequent radiocarbon dates for Hamp's Landing sherds suggest that this series is earlier than first thought. A feature containing nearly sixty-six fragments of a partially reconstructable Hamp's Landing Fabric Impressed vessel was found in a refuse-filled pit at the Cape Island site, in Onslow County, and radiocarbon dated to cal 2030 (1945) 1885 B.C. at one sigma (3610 ± 70 B.P.) (D. C. Jones et al. 1997). This was "dismissed as a spurious date" by Jones et al. (1997:38). It is, in fact, very similar to the two carbon-14 dates secured from features containing Hamp's Landing series sherds at the Riegelwood site in Columbus County (Abbott et al. 1999) and seems acceptable if Hamp's Landing is assumed to be contemporaneous

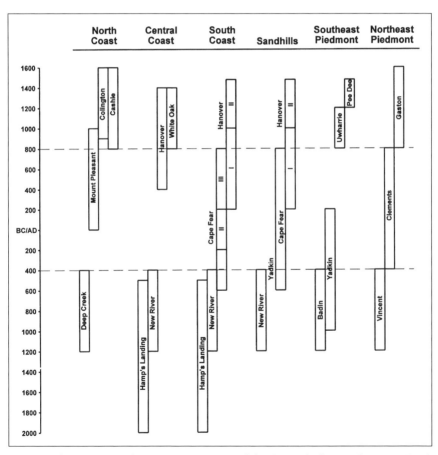

Figure 14.3 — Regional ceramic sequences of the Coastal Plain and eastern Piedmont of North Carolina

with the Thom's Creek phase (Table 14.1). Hamp's Landing series pottery
has been found in the lower Cape Fear drainage and along the coastal margin as far north as Carteret County and may be related to the limestone-
tempered Wando series (N. Adams and Trinkley 1993) found in Horry County,
South Carolina (Hargrove and Eastman 1997).

In the central coastal region, the Early Woodland sand-tempered New
River series was defined as having coarse sand in high proportions and, in
lesser amounts, granule- and pebble-sized particles (Loftfield 1976). Surface treatment types include cord marked, fabric impressed, plain, simple
stamped, and net impressed (in apparent descending order of frequency).
Two carbon-14 dates, possibly associated with New River series sherds,
were secured from the Riegelwood site (Table 14.1) (Abbott et al. 1999;
Sanborn and Abbott 1999). The earlier of the two dates is questionable, as it
predates the earliest Stallings dates by about 500 years (Herbert 1999). It is
also notable that the upper limits of the two-sigma range for this date are

Table 14.1 — Early Woodland Dates from Eastern North Carolina

Site	*Associated Pottery*	*Uncalibrated Age* B.P. [1]	*Calibrated Age* *1 Sigma* [2,] B.C.[3]
Papanow	New River Fabric Impressed	TL 2384 ± 250	684 (434) 184
Riegelwood	Hamp's Landing and New River	2470 ± 40	762 (757, 695, 541) 412
31On542	New River Smoothed	TL 2543 ± 441	987 (546) 105
Little Cedar Isle	Deep Creek	2590 ± 60	807 (796) 764
31Ht347	Yadkin I Net Impressed	TL 2962 ± 356	1319 (963) 607
Lake Phelps	Deep Creek Net Impressed	2850 ± 60	1125 (1002) 920
31Ht392	New River Net Impressed	TL 3170 ± 541	1712 (1171) 630
Papanow	New River Cord Marked	TL 3171 ± 436	1657 (1221) 785
Riegelwood	Thom's Creek Cord Marked (?)	3630 ± 70	2130 (2012, 2000, 1978) 1885
Cape Island	Hamp's Landing Fabric Impressed	3610 ± 70	2112 (1950) 1833
Riegelwood	Hamp's Landing Cord Marked	3700 ± 40	2141 (2129, 2082, 2043) 1984
Riegelwood	Hamp's Landing Simple Stamped	3700 ± 50	2193 (2129, 2082, 2043) 1982
Riegelwood	New River	4290 ± 50	2918 (2898) 2881

[1] *TL ages are calculated not on the 1950 standard, but on the assay year*
[2] *TL dates are not calibrated; the range is one standard deviation about the mean*
[3] *Maximum of cal age ranges (cal ages) minimum of cal age ranges (B.C.)*

Radiocarbon calibrations from Stuiver et al. 1998, Calib 4.3 Program

more than 1000 years earlier than the lower limits of the two-sigma range for the next earliest date possibly associated with New River series sherds. Two thermoluminescence (TL) dates for New River sherds from the Papanow site and one from site 31On542 indicate a date range for the series from about 1200 to 400 B.C. (Herbert 1997, 1999; Reid and Simpson 1996).

Most previous analyses of collections from the southern coast did not distinguish between New River and Cape Fear (e.g., South 1976; Wilde-Ramsing 1978) and, on a sherd-by-sherd basis, the distinction may be impossible. As a consequence, the frequency of the occurrence of Early Woodland coarse sand-tempered sherds in collections from the southern region is not known, but it is likely that some of the material previously identified as Middle Woodland is actually Early Woodland. Crawford's (1966) Lenoir series is also considered equivalent to the New River and Deep Creek series (Eastman et al. 1997), and Trinkley (1980b, 1990) has classified coarse, sand-tempered ware from the northern coast of South Carolina as Deep Creek.

Sandhills

The Early Woodland picture in the Sandhills is just beginning to emerge. Several TL dates recently secured from Early Woodland pottery from Fort Bragg provide the first data for understanding the regional ceramic sequence (Herbert 2000). The earliest pottery vessels in the Sandhills (1700–600 B.C.) are tempered with either sand and grit or crushed stone (mostly granitic rock) and have surfaces finished by stamping with knotted net (Table 14.1). The sand-and-grit tempered ware is classified as the New River series. The New River series is similar to or synonymous with Deep Creek II on the northern coast and contemporary with early Deptford on the South Carolina coast. The crushed-stone tempered ware is tentatively classified as Yadkin, a Middle Woodland Piedmont series tempered with a high proportion of crushed quartz and having predominantly cord-marked and fabric-impressed surfaces (Coe 1964). Current data suggest that the Piedmont Yadkin series can be expanded to include the crushed-stone tempering and net impressing of the Sandhills, on the basis of several factors. Evidence for crushed-stone tempering east of the Sandhills is very limited, and the types of rock used as temper in Sandhills wares appear to be stone types procured in the Piedmont or Blue Ridge. The few dates obtained for Yadkin series sherds are early Middle Woodland and, therefore, tentatively extending the phase to the Early Woodland seems justifiable. Evidence is too limited at this time to speculate on the nature of the relationship between the Sandhills and Piedmont Yadkin traditions, but such a relationship currently seems likely (Herbert 2000).

A cord-marked ware tempered with sand and grit, dating from about 600 to 200 B.C., is classified as Cape Fear I (Table 14.2) in northern South

Table 14.2 — Cape Fear and Associated Phases, Pottery Paste, Temper, and Surface Treatments in Northern South Carolina

Associated Phases	Estimated Age	Paste and Temper	Cord Marked	Fabric Impressed	Carved-Paddle Stamped
Cape Fear III Hanover I	A.D. 200–800	Soft to compact paste, sparse fine sand	47%	39%	14%
Cape Fear II Late Deptford Deep Creek III	200 B.C.–A.D. 200	Compact paste, moderately abundant medium sand	56%	22%	22%
Cape Fear I Early Deptford Deep Creek II	600–200 B.C.	Very hard paste, abundant medium and coarse sand	50%	23%	27%

Carolina (Cable et al. 1998). This classification expands the definition of the Cape Fear series, originally defined as a late Middle Woodland series (South 1960), to encompass these Early Woodland specimens. As such, the Cape Fear I phase coincides with early Deptford, Deep Creek II, and late New River. There appears to be some clinal variation in paste characteristics over the period such that a very hard-pasted ware with abundant medium and coarse sand shifts to a compactly pasted ware with moderately abundant medium sand (Cable et al. 1998). Although sand-and-grit tempered cord-marked sherds have been dated to the Early and Middle Woodland periods in the North Carolina Sandhills, it has not yet been established that similar trends in paste characteristics exist in the northern Sandhills specimens.

Piedmont

In the Piedmont province, the Savannah River point-type tradition appears to have evolved from a larger stemmed point to a smaller, similarly shaped version in the Terminal Late Archaic (Oliver 1985:204; South 1959:153–57; Ward 1983:70–71). The Small Savannah River Stemmed type is followed by the Gypsy Stemmed, which is somewhat smaller and made of a wider range of stone types. The Gypsy Stemmed type has been found in the earliest ceramic-bearing zones at the Doerschuk and Gaston sites along with Badin pottery and the Badin triangular points (Oliver 1985:204). In the final expression of the Savannah River–like stemmed points, the Swannanoa Stemmed types appear to follow the Gypsy Stemmed type and have been found at the Warren Wilson site in contexts with soapstone bowl fragments and triangular points (Keel 1976:196–98; Oliver 1985:207).

At the Doerschuk site on the lower Yadkin River, Coe (1952) found a rich assemblage of cultural material that he defined as the Badin focus, the first pottery-making tradition of the Early Woodland period (Coe 1952:306–7). This conclusion was reaffirmed after reanalysis of the Doerschuk site data some years later (Coe 1964:27), in which Badin series pottery was interpreted as a well-developed technology introduced to the Piedmont following a considerable period of development elsewhere. Coe (1964:27–30) refined the earlier description of the Badin series to include cord-marked, fabric-impressed, and plain types constructed of hard, compact paste with very fine river-sand temper, and he noted a similarity to the Middle Woodland Vincent series of the Roanoke River basin, in Virginia (Coe 1964:101–2; South 1959). Badin series vessel forms at the Doerschuk site were simple, straight-sided jars with conical bases, and shallow bowls with rounded bases. Neither form was commonly decorated.

No radiocarbon dates were associated with the Badin material at the Doerschuk site and this ware remains undated in North Carolina. Comparing the range of temper and surface-treatment attributes observed on Badin series sherds with those of series from adjacent areas provides some evidence for chronological placement. One hundred eight fine-sand tempered Badin series sherds with either cord-marked or fabric-impressed surfaces were also reported from the Town Creek site (Coe 1995:table 9.1). These were described as having the "look and feel" of Thom's Creek series ware (most often described as tempered with very fine sand or no temper at all). This stands in contrast to descriptions of Early Woodland pottery from the Coastal Plain such as Deep Creek and New River that is tempered with abundant coarse sand (Loftfield 1976; Phelps 1983). It is also at odds with current interpretations of the age of sand-tempered, cord-marked sherds from the adjacent Sandhills that appear to date primarily to the Middle Woodland period, about 500 B.C. to A.D. 200 (Herbert 2000). Thom's Creek series pottery is found in the southern and central Coastal Plain; however, in almost every instance it is identified by a well-smoothed exterior surface, punctate decoration, and thin-walled construction—rarely if ever is it cord-marked or fabric-impressed.

Similarities among surface treatments (cord marked, fabric and net impressed) led Ward and Davis (1999:83) to conclude that "Badin ceramics appear to be related to the Early Woodland Deep Creek wares." Net impressing is present in the Early Woodland Deep Creek and New River series, as well as in the early portion of the Middle Woodland in the Mount Pleasant and Mockley series. Net impressing does not, however, appear in the Middle Woodland Hanover or Cape Fear series, or in the Late Woodland White Oak, Colington, or Cashie series.

Middle Woodland Period (400 B.C.–A.D. 800)

Overviews typically contrast the Middle Woodland period to the antecedent Early Woodland by positing increased sedentism, a shift to more logistical collecting, intensification of horticultural activities, growing social regionalism, expansion of commodity exchange, and the emergence of social stratification. In truth, very few of these expected developments are observable in the Middle Woodland archaeological record from eastern North Carolina. Current archaeological data suggest that the Middle Woodland period in much of the Coastal Plain of North Carolina can be characterized as a time of dispersed settlement and a relatively high rate of residential mobility by groups the size of extended families using resources in very much the same manner as their Early Woodland and Archaic forebears. An increased incidence of Middle Woodland sites (as indicated by a higher frequency of Middle Woodland ceramic components) suggests little more than a population increase over the preceding Early Woodland period. Sites along the coast suggest the possibility of intensified use of marine resources, especially shellfish, but few large shell middens accreted during this time. (Potential sampling bias resulting from a sea level that may have risen as much as 2 meters over this period has not been thoroughly assessed.) Small sites, located along marsh edges in the Tidewater, upper Coastal Plain, and Sandhills, appear to be more common during this period than in the previous one (Anderson et al. 1982; Culpepper et al. 2000; T. Klein et al. 1994; Trinkley 1989). Site structure at interior marsh-edge locations suggests seasonal or short-term campsites with activities focused on bottomland resources. Trinkley (1989:78) notes "settlement fragmentation" or "splintering" beginning at the end of the Thom's Creek phase (during Deptford II) corresponding to a 2-meter rise in sea level between 1200 and 950 B.C. In contrast, on the northern coast, Phelps (1983:33) notes "a noticeable decrease in the number of small sites along the smaller tributary streams in the interior and an increase in sites along the major trunk streams and estuaries and on the coast" during the Middle Woodland Mount Pleasant phase.

An often-cited feature of the Middle Woodland period on the southern coast is the presence of a number (ca. 18) of burial mounds (Irwin et al. 1999; Keel 1970; MacCord 1966; Phelps 1983:fig. 1.4; South 1966; Wetmore 1979). Most of these were first recorded late in the nineteenth century and many have been destroyed. The McLean mound is the most intensively ex amined and records or recollections remain for at least seventeen others (Irwin et al. 1999; MacCord 1966; Phelps 1983). Culpepper et al. (2000) suggest that these mounds "seem to reflect ritualized land use and the gathering of locally dispersed, but socially allied groups for sacred activities." Mortuary behavior consisting of secondary bundle burials suggests a dispersed population transporting their dead to these ritual sites. Grave goods, including engraved stone pipes, shell gorgets, shell beads, copper, and mica, point toward interregional exchange for items possibly symbolizing personal prestige. A recent reanalysis of these mounds, particularly of materials from McLean mound, proposes that although their origins may have been in the Middle Woodland period, they also exhibit Late Woodland characteristics (Irwin et al. 1999). Two radiocarbon dates from McLean mound, cal A.D. 700 (770) 795 at one sigma (1250 ± 40 B.P.; Beta-413709) and cal A.D. 976 (1028) 1221 at one sigma (980 ± 110 B.P.), support this interpretation.

Northern Coast
The sand-and-grit tempered Middle Woodland Mount Pleasant series, found on the northern coast of North Carolina, is thought to be contemporary with the Hanover series of the south coast. (In this case, grit denotes quartzose inclusions in the granule and pebble size range, most often subrounded, but occasionally angular or subangular.) The latest Mount Pleasant date, cal A.D. 1012 (1076) 1215 at one sigma (1060 ± 80 B.P.), was derived from shell found in the midden at Rush Point. Exception is taken to the outlying date of cal A.D. 1525 (1651) 1953 at one sigma (270 ± 50 B.P.) from Feature 1 at site 31Wl170 (Hargrove 1993) until further assays demonstrate continuity in this series of dates. The relationship of the Mount Pleasant and Cape Fear series, both sand-tempered wares, is not well understood; however, Phelps (1983:35) has equated the two, suggesting they form a single series. Haag (1958) described a grit-tempered series, similar or equivalent to Mount Pleasant for the interior Coastal Plain, that may have subsumed specimens classifiable as Cape Fear. Potential differences in the paste and temper characteristics and the range of surface treatments exhibited in each series have not yet been thoroughly investigated. Mount Pleasant series sherds also resemble the Middle Woodland Vincent series (Coe 1964:101–2) of the Roanoke Rapids area of Piedmont North Carolina and Clifford Evans's (1955) Stoney Creek series from the Potomac River valley in Virginia.

Southern and Central Coast
Middle Woodland archaeological components on the southern and central coasts are identified primarily based on diagnostic ceramics. There were several changes in ceramic technology during the Middle Woodland period.

Fiber tempering is superseded by sand tempering on the South Carolina coast. Limestone tempering appears in the Hamp's Landing series on North Carolina's southern coast and in the Wando series of northern South Carolina. The size grade of sand used to temper Deep Creek series ware appears to shift from coarse to medium, and Mount Pleasant series ware exhibits an increase in the proportion of granule- and pebble-sized particles in the northern coastal region. Middle Woodland vessel shapes include larger jars with conical bases and straight walls, a transformation that emphasizes the intensified use of ceramic containers as cooking vessels. The carved-paddle stamping technique that emerged in the Refuge and Deptford phases in South Carolina and in the Hamp's Landing, Deep Creek, and New River series in North Carolina expanded to include wrapped-paddle cord marking, fabric impressing, and net impressing in the three North Carolina series. Trends in surface-treatment types during the Middle Woodland period have not been thoroughly studied, but it is significant from a typological standpoint that very few of the Middle Woodland sand-tempered specimens from the Coastal Plain have been found to exhibit simple stamping. This stands in distinct contrast to the Early Woodland Deep Creek and Hamp's Landing series. Simple stamping occurs in both the Cape Fear and Hanover series in northern South Carolina (Cable et al. 1998) and reappears in the Late Woodland Colington and Cashie series in the northern coastal region of North Carolina.

In the southern coastal area, the Middle Woodland period is dominated by two ceramic series with nearly identical arrays, but different relative frequencies of surface treatments. The Hanover series is grog tempered and the Cape Fear series is sand tempered. Loftfield's (1976) Carteret series and Crawford's (1966) Grifton series are equivalent to the Hanover series. In the original type collection from surface sites in Brunswick and New Hanover counties, about 75 percent of the Hanover series sherds are fabric impressed and 25 percent are cord marked (South 1976). The proportions are reversed for Cape Fear series sherds, with 36 percent being fabric impressed and 58 percent exhibiting cord marking. This pattern is corroborated by subsequent survey data from surface-collected assemblages from over 300 sites in New Hanover County, in which about 65 percent of the Hanover sherds are fabric impressed and 25 percent are cord marked, while 30 percent of the Cape Fear series sherds are fabric impressed and 40 percent are cord marked (Wilde-Ramsing 1978:181).

Following Coe (1952:306) and Haag (1958:108), South (1976:40) concluded that fabric impressing was an earlier technology than cord marking and surmised that the Hanover series was associated with an earlier culture phase than the Cape Fear series. In both the Deep Creek and Mount Pleasant series, however, fabric impressing is more frequent later in the series than cord marking (Phelps 1983). Based on radiocarbon dates from South and North Carolina, a conservative estimate for the temporal range of the Hanover series is 200 B.C. to A.D. 650. Although several recent dates suggest that a sand- and grog-tempered variant of the Hanover series dates well into the Late Woodland period, possibly as late as A.D. 1400 (Mathis 1999; Hargrove, personal communication, 1998), the older of the radiocarbon dates from the McLean mound, cal A.D. 700 (770) 795 at one sigma (1250 ± 40 B.P.), was an AMS assay of soot from the surface of sand/grog-tempered, fabric-impressed pottery. Some researchers subsume Hanover as a variety of the Wilmington series (Anderson et al. 1982:272; Trinkley 1990:17–18). The grog-tempered Wilmington and St. Catherines series (Caldwell 1952; DePratter 1979; Waring and Holder 1968) from the Georgia Sea Islands and south coast of South Carolina date from circa 200 B.C. to A.D. 1150 and, hence, are contemporary with part of the Hanover phase. Although these series include an array of surface treatments not seen on Hanover ceramics from North Carolina (e.g., simple stamping, check stamping, and linear check stamping), the tempering technique and geographic proximity suggest some relatedness.

The sand-tempered Deptford series (Caldwell and Waring 1939) has its origin in the Early Woodland, circa 650 B.C. (Anderson et al. 1982; Trinkley 1980b, 1990), contemporary with the later portion of the Early Woodland Deep Creek phase. Cable et al. (1998:286–97, 322–24, table 91) suggest a taxonomic sequence for the northern coast of South Carolina that merges the Deptford and Cape Fear series, recognizing three phases, each distinguished by slightly different paste characteristics and relative frequency of surface-treatment types (Table 14.2). These results suggest a trend toward softer pastes with smaller sand grains at lower proportions. Trends in surface treatment indicate a predominance of cord marking in all three phases, decreasing proportions of carved-paddle stamping (check, simple, and complicated stamped), and increasing proportions of fabric impressing at the expense of cord marking. A similar trend toward higher relative frequency of fabric impressing with a decline in simple stamping and cord marking is noted by Phelps (1983:29–32) through Deep Creek phases I–III (1000–200 B.C.) and by Herbert (2000) in the Sandhills Cape Fear series. A check-stamped, sand-tempered ware was represented in very low frequency in South's (1976) survey of Brunswick and New Hanover counties and in northern South Carolina (Cable et al. 1998), but check stamping does not appear again until about A.D. 1600 in the Piedmont as Fredricks Check Stamped (Dickens et al. 1987:189–203; Ward and Davis 1993:408).

The trends observed in paste and temper for coastal South Carolina and the North Carolina Sandhills appear to be corroborated in the central and northern coast region. Crawford's (1966) data for the middle Neuse River drainage, however, do indicate higher relative frequencies of sherds with smaller sand-grain sizes in the Tower Hill series, the later of the two sand-tempered series from that area. Possibly reversing an earlier observation of "a trend toward larger clastic temper" among Deep Creek and Mount Pleasant series assemblages (Phelps 1983:33), a fine-sand tempered ware, the Middle Town series, has recently been proposed for the Terminal Middle Woodland period in the central and northern coastal regions (David S. Phelps, personal communication, 1999). In the central outer coast region, Loftfield (1976) identified a fine-sand tempered ware as Adams Creek. Although it was initially thought to be a Late Woodland series on the basis of seriation, Loftfield (1987) later suggested it could actually be Middle Woodland and contemporaneous with either Mount Pleasant or, more likely, Cape Fear.

Sandhills
Middle Woodland sites have more archaeological visibility than Early or Late Woodland sites in the Sandhills. This pattern, also seen on the southern coast, is due in part to three factors: generally increased population size and dispersion, high residential mobility by relatively small groups, and a greater opportunity for pottery to enter into the archaeological record as a result of more routine use of ceramic cooking vessels. The Sandhills series of the Middle Woodland include grog-tempered Hanover and sand-tempered Cape Fear, both having cord-marked and fabric-impressed types. Occasionally sand-tempered, check-stamped sherds are found on southern coastal and Sandhills sites in North Carolina, and these are presumed to be related to the Deptford series. As mentioned above, check stamping also is known to occur in relatively low frequency in the Yadkin series. Cable et al. (1998) observed sand-tempered check- and simple-stamped sherds together with cord- and fabric-impressed types in Horry County, South Carolina and suggest lumping all of these types under a single Cape Fear I series. Similarly, check and simple stamping are found on grog- or clay-tempered Hanover series sherds in that region (Cable et al. 1998). Check stamping is rare among sand-tempered sherds from southern coastal North Carolina and virtually nonexistent in the Hanover and Mount Pleasant series. This suggests that the northern extent of the Middle Woodland carved-paddle stamping tradition is found in the southernmost counties of North Carolina. Considering its Deptford association, carved-paddle stamping also signals the earlier portion of the Cape Fear and Hanover series, coeval with Deptford I and II (ca. 600 B.C.–A.D. 200).

Recently there has been some progress in understanding specific variations in tempering for Middle Woodland pottery from the Sandhills through TL dating (Herbert 1999, 2000). At Fort Bragg, several net-impressed specimens tempered with crushed granitic rock have been TL dated to the Early Woodland (Table 14.3). Evidence from other sites at Fort Bragg include vessels tempered with crushed soapstone and possibly chlorite schist, exhibiting cord-marked surfaces. If, as is likely, this tradition is related to the Yadkin series, then it is reasonable to expect it to be an early variant. This conclusion derives from the fact that net impressing does not occur in the Middle Woodland Yadkin, Cape Fear, Hanover, or Mount Pleasant series, but is present in the Early Woodland Badin and Deep Creek series. There may also be some relation to the New Hope feldspar-tempered series defined for materials found in the lower Haw River valley (Claggett and Cable [eds.] 1982; McCormick 1969).

Also present in the Middle Woodland period in the Sandhills is the sand- and grit-tempered Cape Fear series (where grit denotes particle size greater than 1 millimeter), with an age range from about 400 B.C. to A.D. 400. Much like the case on the southern coast, where the series was first defined, cord marking is the predominant surface treatment found in the Sandhills Cape Fear series. Following Cable et al. (1998), the Cape Fear series is divided into three phases corresponding to variations in paste and surface-treatment characteristics (Table 14.2).

In the Sandhills, I have suggested a preliminary sequence in which the grog-tempered Hanover series comprises two temporal phases (Herbert 2000). A late Middle Woodland variety (Hanover I, A.D. 400 through 800) is characterized by pottery tempered principally with sand to which a minor amount of finely crushed grog was added. Surface treatments in this variety include cord marking, check stamping, and fabric impressing. A Late Woodland variety (Hanover II, A.D. 800 through 1500) is tempered mostly with grog with a small amount of sand included in the paste and is represented by mostly fabric-impressed sherds.

These data suggest that the Early Woodland tradition of tempering with crushed rock continued into the Middle Woodland period. Sand-and-grit tempering appears throughout the Woodland era with the addition of crushed-pottery temper beginning about A.D. 400. By Late Woodland times (post–A.D. 800), paste is tempered principally with grog with a small proportion of sand often included. Early Woodland wares are typically net impressed, Middle Woodland wares usually cord marked, and Late Woodland series most often fabric impressed. Unlike the case on the adjacent southern Coastal Plain, net impressing and check stamping seem to have persisted well into the Middle Woodland in the Sandhills.

Piedmont

In the southern Piedmont province the Middle Woodland period is distin-

Table 14.3 — Middle Woodland Dates from Eastern North Carolina

Site	*Associated Pottery*	*Uncalibrated Age* B.P. [1]	*Calibrated Age* 1 Sigma [2,3]
Tower Hill	Cashie Fabric Imp. & Plain	1230 ± 100	A.D. 673 (778) 942
Uniflyte	White Oak	1265 ± 60	A.D. 676 (721, 743, 770) 851
Thorpe	Clements Cord Marked	1265 ± 75	A.D. 665 (721, 743, 770) 878
Hammock's Beach West	Hanover Cord Marked & Fabric Imp.; White Oak	1300 ± 70	A.D. 659 (689) 778
Little Cedar Island	Mount Pleasant	1310 ± 60	A.D. 659 (687) 775
Pond Trail	Hanover Fabric Imp.	1270 ± 145	A.D. 644 (719, 746, 768) 956
Tillet	Mount Pleasant	1490 ± 85	A.D. 438 (598) 650
Hammock's Beach West	White Oak Fabric Imp.; Mockley Cord Marked & Net Imp.	1430 ± 50	A.D. 599 (640) 658
Permuda Island	White Oak Fabric Imp.	1450 ± 80	A.D. 540 (620, 634, 636) 660
31On596	Hanover Cord Marked	1329 ± 246	A.D. 439 (675) 981
Uniflyte	White Oak	1495 ± 60	A.D. 534 (564, 569, 579, 588, 597) 640
Uniflyte	White Oak	1550 ± 65	A.D. 426 (536) 600
Baum	Mount Pleasant	1590 ± 65	A.D. 409 (433) 541
Sidney Brook	Hanover Series	1560 ± 60	A.D. 425 (533) 596
31Ht344	Cape Fear II Fabric Imp.	TL 1516 ± 173	A.D. 310 (483) 656
Rush Point	Mount Pleasant	1685 ± 65	A.D. 258 (384) 426
Broad Reach	Hanover Fabric Imp.	1420 ± 90	A.D. 544 (643) 676
31Mr93	Hanover II	TL 1564 ± 314	A.D. 121 (435) 749
Point Harbor	Mount Pleasant Fabric Imp.	1670 ± 60	A.D. 261 (397) 428
31Cd622	New River Net Imp.	TL 1594 ± 272	A.D. 133 (405) 677
Liberty Hill	Mount Pleasant	1680 ± 70	A.D. 258 (388) 428
31Ht471	Cape Fear II Cord Marked	TL 2368 ± 254	623 (369) 115 B.C.
Liberty Hill	Mount Pleasant	2240 ± 60	390 (360, 273, 260) 202 B.C.
31Cd486	Cape Fear II Cord Marked	TL 2277 ± 370	648 (278 B.C.) A.D. 92
Papanow	Hanover Cord Marked	1779 ± 228	17 B.C. (A.D. 243) 536
31Ht347	Yadkin I Net Imp.	TL 1878 ± 290	169 B.C. (A.D. 121) 411
31Cd551	Cape Fear II Cord Marked	TL 1880 ± 229	110 B.C. (A.D. 119) 348
3 1Ht269	Yadkin I Net Imp.	TL 1881 ± 232	114 B.C. (A.D. 118) 350
31Ht355	Cape Fear II Cord Marked	TL 1917 ± 196	278 (82 B.C.) A.D. 114

[1] *TL ages are calculated not on the 1950 standard, but on the assay year*
[2] *TL dates are not calibrated; the range is one standard deviation about the mean*
[3] *Maximum of cal age ranges (cal ages) minimum of cal age ranges (B.C.)*

Radiocarbon calibrations from Stuiver et al. 1998, Calib 4.3 Program

guished primarily by the Yadkin ceramic series (Coe 1964:30–32). Yadkin is interpreted by Coe (1995:154) as a direct descendant of Badin reflecting a long period of gradual change. Apparent improvements in technology are evidenced by the addition of coarse, angular aggregate and surface treatments exhibiting more delicate cordage and more finely woven fabric. The shape and dimensions of Yadkin vessels are reported to be the same as those of Badin, but a major change is seen in tempering. Angular fragments of quartz (0.1–0.8 centimeter) were added to the paste in proportions commonly as high as 40 to 50 percent. About 50 percent of the Yadkin sherds from Doerschuk are fabric impressed, about 40 percent are cord marked, and 10 percent are check stamped (Dickens et al. 1987:211, table 8.22). Yadkin series sherds from Town Creek also include several surface treatment types including smoothed (or plain) (51 percent), cord marked (33 percent), simple stamped (12 percent), fabric impressed (2 percent), and check stamped (1 percent). The discovery of simple-stamped Yadkin specimens at Town Creek may be significant, since there were no simple-stamped sherds found at Doerschuk. Coe (1995:154) suggests that Yadkin at Town Creek "occurred at a late point in the ceramic continuum." He apparently came to this conclusion by noting that smoothed and cord-marked surface treatments were most common and that fabric-impressed and check-stamped types were nearly absent. Ward and Davis (1999:83), however, conclude that the presence of simple, check, and linear-check stamping "tie Yadkin phase pottery to the Early Woodland Deptford wares."

Yadkin series pottery was not dated at the Doerschuk or Town Creek sites. On the lower Haw River, a date of cal 381 (199) 67 B.C. at one sigma (2190 ± 95 B.P.) was obtained for Yadkin pottery at site 31Ch8 (Claggett and Cable [eds.] 1982:248; Eastman 1994b:6) and another date, cal 367 (193) 61 B.C. at one sigma (2170 ± 80 B.P.), was obtained at the E. Davis site (Eastman 1994b:43). In the Sandhills of South Carolina, Yadkin pottery from two features was dated at site 38Su83 (D. Blanton et al. 1986). Feature 11 was a concentration of 156 sherds from one Yadkin Fine Cord Marked vessel. Charcoal removed from the soil around the pottery dated cal 345 (165) 42 B.C. at one sigma (2130 ± 70 B.P.) (D. Blanton et al. 1986:59, table 45; Eastman 1994b:84). One of the sherds from Feature 11 was also TL dated A.D. 541–1011 (two sigma). A second feature (17), determined to be a burned tree stump, was carbon-14 dated cal 411 (393) 259 B.C. at one sigma (2330 ± 80 B.P.). Yadkin Check Stamped, Yadkin Simple Stamped, and Pee Dee Complicated Stamped sherds were recovered from the fill of Feature 17 (D. Blanton et al. 1986:61, 146–47, table 45). Dennis Blanton et al. (1986), and most subsequent reviewers (Eastman 1994a, 1994b; Ward and Davis 1999:86), have chosen to accept the carbon-14 dates as reliable Yadkin dates, ignoring contextual problems, and reject as spurious the TL date. Neverthe-less, the TL date of A.D. 776 ± 120 falls within the expected range for the Middle Woodland Yadkin phase, although the date remains a late outlier.

The archaeology of the northeastern Piedmont requires special consid-eration. The most thorough statement on the archaeology of the region con-tinues to be the results of salvage operations conducted by the Research Laboratories of Archaeology, University of North Carolina, prior to the 1955 inundation of Roanoke Rapids Lake (Coe 1964). In two months' time, sev-enty-four sites were discovered, four tested with limited excavations, and one, the Gaston site, subjected to extensive excavation. As a result of this research, three phases were delineated: Vincent, Clements, and Gaston, cor-responding to the Early, Middle, and Late Woodland periods. These three archaeological components were found, stratigraphically stacked, at both the Gaston and Thelma sites, although chronological positions were not fixed by absolute dates. The association of small, stemmed Thelma points, atlatl weights, and Vincent pottery in the lowest ceramic-bearing zone at the Thelma site suggests to Ward and Davis (1999:87–95) that the Vincent phase should be placed in the Early Woodland period. A radiocarbon date of cal A.D. 1022 (1064, 1075, 1127, 1133, 1159) 1222 at one sigma (3260 ± 90 B.P.) associ-ated with Vincent Fabric Impressed pottery and corn at site 44Fv19 (Eastman 1994b:112), however, raises questions. The possibility that Clements series pottery was mistaken for Vincent series pottery at 44Fv19 is not unlikely. Even the original analysts found it impossible at times to distinguish the two series, as the wares of both series are tempered with sand with occasional larger particles and are similarly finished by stamping with cord- or fabric-wrapped paddles (Coe 1964:101–5). Investigations at the Thorpe site yielded a date of cal A.D. 168 (774) 1278 at one sigma (2165 ± 75 B.P.) from wood charcoal found in the base of a bell-shaped pit containing Clements Cord Marked pottery (Phelps 1980).

Late Woodland Period (A.D. 800–1500)

The editors of this volume have chosen to limit the temporal extent of this volume to the Woodland era. In much of the Southeast, that means the pe-riod prior to the emergence of Mississippian culture. Archaeological mani-festations of Mississippian cultural traditions, however, are not recognized in coastal North Carolina and consequently the Late Woodland period ex-tends up to the time of European colonization. Adhering to the volume's focus, the following section presents data from only the first few centuries of the Late Woodland period, until about A.D. 1000.

During the first centuries of the Late Woodland period, economic, organizational, and ideological structures in eastern North Carolina are marked by increasing sedentism, tribalization, territoriality, and ceremonialism. The hallmark of the Mississippian economy—corn agriculture—was not well established in the Piedmont until about A.D. 1200 (Ward 1983:73). Sedentary villages, evidenced by site size, architectural styles, and storage facilities, and the remains of cultivars such as squash, beans, and corn, are particularly evident on the coast and in the Tidewater region where abundant marine resources helped to sustain village life. Current evidence suggests significant differences in residential settlement strategies in the various areas of eastern North Carolina. In the Sea Island and Sandhills sections of the Coastal Plain sites are small and broadly scattered, suggesting relatively high mobility and dispersed settlement (Culpepper et al. 2000). In the Piedmont and the Embayed section of the coast, larger village sites located along the sounds, estuaries, and major rivers and their tributaries suggest more sedentism and regionalization (Phelps 1983:39). While sites on estuaries often provide evidence for subsistence activities that focused on seasonally abundant maritime resources such as anadromous fish or shellfish, most sites seem to be located where agriculture, hunting, gathering, and fishing could all be accomplished within the same area (Phelps 1983:40). Three culture areas have been proposed for coastal North Carolina that conform to ethnohistorically recorded linguistic regions: Algonkian speakers on the northern coast and Tidewater; Iroquoian speakers on the northern interior Coastal Plain; and Siouan speakers in the Piedmont and southern Coastal Plain. Archaeologically, these culture areas are recognized by regional differences in ceramics and notable differences in burial customs and architectural forms (Loftfield 1990; Loftfield and Jones 1995).

Central and Northern Coast
The Late Woodland period in Tidewater North Carolina is considered synonymous with shell-tempered ceramics. The Colington series (Phelps 1983) is found along the coast in the northern region and the White Oak series (Loftfield 1976) in the central region. Both areas are the traditional territory of the Carolina Algonkians and are consequently related to the Rappahannock and Townsend phases in coastal Virginia and southern Maryland (Loftfield 1976; Phelps 1983). Few significant differences appear to exist between the White Oak and Colington series—both include fabric-impressed, cordmarked, and plain or smoothed types—but minor differences have been observed (Herbert and Mathis 1996; Marshall 1999). Simple stamping and incised decorations have not been confirmed in White Oak assemblages, while they are common in the Colington series. Burnishing is occasionally

seen in the White Oak series, but is not found in the Colington series. In addition, a recent study suggests a statistically significant difference among the length and frequency of paddle-edge impressions left on the interior of vessel necks (A. Marshall 1999). Future research may demonstrate additional variations, such as incising motifs, within this ceramic complex that relate to geographic region.

Phelps (1983:39) proposes that the southern extent of the Algonkian culture, and the corresponding distribution of Colington ceramics, was just south of the Neuse River (cf. Loftfield 1976). Loftfield and Jones (1995) have suggested that the distribution of Colington phase cultures during prehistoric times may have extended as far south as Onslow County. These authors cite evidence including not only shell-tempered ceramics, comparable in many respects to the Colington series, but also mortuary and architectural features; for example, ossuary burials and longhouses typical of Algonkian culture found to the north. Other interpretations suggest that the southernmost extent of the Algonkian societies was northern Pender County where some degree of interaction among Algonkian- and Iroquoian-speaking groups may have occurred (Mathis, personal communication, 2000).

The Cashie phase and pottery series were first described by Phelps (1983) and recently revised (Phelps and Heath 1998) on the basis of data recovered from the Jordan's Landing (31Br7), Neoheroka Fort (31Gr4), Sans Souci (31Br5), Thorpe (31Ns3), Battle Park (31Ns19), and Fishing Creek (31Hx61) sites. The Cashie series, dating from circa A.D. 800 to 1715, is considered contemporary with the Colington and White Oak series and, similarly, includes fabric-impressed, simple-stamped, incised, and plain types. Cashie is tempered with granule- and pebble-sized quartz particles, occasionally crushed, which often protrude simultaneously through the interior and exterior surfaces of the vessel walls. In addition, Phelps and Heath (1998) note that "perhaps as significant as any observed exterior treatment of Cashie vessels, is the dominant addition of an interior finishing treatment that is regionally unique to the series...floated and/or slipped interiors."

Cashie Simple Stamped is thought to be equivalent to Gaston Simple Stamped (Coe 1964) from the Roanoke Rapids area. In Virginia, the Branchville series (Binford 1964) in the Meherrin and Nottoway localities and the Sturgeon Head series (G. Smith 1971) are also thought to be related or equivalent. Minority surface-treatment types found in the Gaston and related series (e.g., cord marked, cob marked, and check stamped) have not been observed in the Cashie series. The earliest dates associated with Cashie pottery from the Thorpe site, a seasonally occupied site near the Tar River fall line, are cal A.D. 985 (1022) 1158 at one sigma (1000 ± 70 B.P.) and cal A.D. 1187 (1253) 1287 at one sigma (800 ± 65 B.P.). The Jordan's Landing

site, a permanently occupied, palisaded village on the Roanoke River, produced two radiocarbon dates from feature contexts, cal A.D. 1286 (1300)
1393 at one sigma (670 ± 60 B.P.) and cal A.D. 1326 (1418) 1444 at one sigma
(525 ± 70 B.P.) (J. Byrd and Heath 1997). With the additional date obtained
from the Ellis site—cal A.D. 1407 (1431) 1444 at one sigma (500 ± 50 B.P.)—
the one-sigma range for Cashie series radiocarbon dates is A.D. 985–1444.

Southern Coast

One of the most significant recent developments in understanding the Late
Woodland in the southern coastal region has been the recognition of potential for confusion regarding the distinction between shell-tempered Late
Woodland Oak Island and limestone-tempered Early Woodland Hamp's
Landing series sherds. A recent reappraisal suggested that previously analyzed "shell-tempered" assemblages from southern coastal sites may have
included a number of limestone- or marl-tempered specimens (Herbert and
Mathis 1996). A subsequent study (Mathis 1999) designed to assess this
problem by reanalyzing a portion of the collection that South (1960) used to
define the Oak Island series found that among a sample of 112 sherds (45
percent of South's original collection) none could be positively identified as
shell tempered. As researchers began to realize that much of what had been
identified as Late Woodland shell-tempered Oak Island was actually Early
Woodland Hamp's Landing series, some of the perplexity regarding surface
treatments vanished. Net-impressed, cord-marked, and simple-stamped surface treatments, problematic for a Late Woodland shell-tempered series, make
sense in an Early Woodland series. Recent studies, however, indicate a Middle
Woodland shell-tempering tradition with cord-marked and net-impressed
surface treatments present in the central coastal area (Shumate and Evans-
Shumate 2000). This series, currently unnamed but similar in many respects
to the Mockley series thought to be confined to areas north of the Albemarle,
is known only from a few sites on the central coast, and in relatively small
numbers. The ceramics may be a possible predecessor to the Colington and
White Oak series, indicating the early introduction of shell tempering into
the region (Herbert and Mathis 1996).

A second development that holds promise for the Late Woodland chronology on the southern coast pertains to filling of the gap left by the retire-
ment of the shell-tempered Oak Island series. The pottery from the McLean
and Buie mounds and the Cold Morning ossuary furnish a line of evidence
regarding Late Woodland pottery series. Seventy-five percent of the McLean
mound pottery is fabric impressed and tempered with clay, grog, or both,
and sand (Herbert 1999; Irwin et al. 1999). The presence of medium sand
along with clay or grog and the complete absence of sherds tempered exclu-

sively with clay or grog without sand distinguish these specimens as a late variety of the Hanover series. Sand-tempered, smoothed, and fabric-impressed ware is also observed in the McLean mound assemblage. Although the sand-tempered material is classifiable as Middle Woodland Cape Fear, the total absence of cord marking—the dominant surface treatment in the Cape Fear series—is notable, suggesting a late position in the Cape Fear sequence. In combination, these data suggest that both the sand-tempered and clay- or grog-tempered wares represent an early Late Woodland tradition, circa A.D. 700 to 1200. The Buie mound pottery assemblage includes mostly (79 percent) sand-tempered, burnished plainware with some (12 percent) clay- or grog-tempered sherds (Wetmore 1979:44, table 3). Fabric impressing is the minority type (about 10 percent) at the Buie mound, but is found on 86 percent of the McLean mound sherds. This suggests that the McLean mound assemblage may be somewhat earlier than that of the Buie mound (Irwin et al. 1999). Two pottery types, Cape Fear Fabric Impressed and Hamp's Landing Plain, are associated with the Cold Morning ossuary burials, dated cal A.D. 778 (984) 1163 at one sigma (1000 ± 80 B.P.) (Eastman 1994b:10; Ward and Wilson 1980). The sherds found in the Cold Morning ossuary, originally classified as Oak Island, have been reclassified as Hamp's Landing (Mathis 1999). The provenience reported for these specimens does not allow discrimination of temporal priority for one or the other series (Ward and Wilson 1980:27). Present data imply that it is more likely that the sand-tempered component in the ossuary dates to the early Late Woodland period.

Sandhills
Little is known of Late Woodland material culture and lifeways in the Sandhills. A pottery dating study from Fort Bragg provides some preliminary information about ceramic traditions (Herbert 2000). Beginning by at least A.D. 400 grog-tempered pottery appears in the region. Through the ensuing centuries grog tempering appears to displace sand-and-grit tempering. This is evident in the declining relative frequency of sand-and-grit tempered sherds and in decreasing proportions of sand included in the paste of grog-tempered vessels. By A.D. 1000, the temper is predominantly grog, with only a background (1–3 percent) of medium sand in the paste. Also during the transition from Middle to Late Woodland (A.D. 400–800) cord marking is displaced by fabric impressing. For convenience, the period from A.D. 400 to 800 may be referred to as the Hanover I phase, and the period following A.D. 800 the Hanover II phase. While Pee Dee Complicated Stamped has been found in the Sandhills, it appears to be quite rare. In the Fort Bragg reservation where over 40,000 acres have been systematically surveyed, not a single Late Woodland village site has been found. This suggests that the

poor soils and limited carrying capacity of the longleaf pine–wiregrass environment in the Sandhills proscribed sedentary life-styles based on corn agriculture.

Piedmont

In the Piedmont province, the Uwharrie phase (A.D. 1000–1200) is the earliest subdivision of the Late Woodland period. Coe (1952:307) envisioned the Uwharrie focus as the most homogeneous and widespread pottery-making culture in the central Piedmont—the cultural stock from which all later Piedmont Siouan ceramic traditions emerged and developed. Uwharrie series pottery is considered significantly different from the preceding Yadkin series in the size (larger) and quantity (higher proportion) of crushed quartz used for temper (Coe 1995:155–60). Exterior surfaces in the Uwharrie series are commonly either cord marked or net impressed and frequently scraped smooth following this application. Vessels consistently take the form of hemispherical bowls and conoidal-base jars, often having slightly restricted necks and straight, vertical rims. Uwharrie paste is tempered almost entirely with particles of crushed quartz, often so large they protrude through both sides of the vessel's walls. From his studies of the Donnaha site (31YD9) and other sites along the Great Bend area of the Yadkin Valley, Woodall (1984:76) has noted that Uwharrie ceramics exhibit "poorly mixed paste" characterized by a lamellar structure visible in cross section. Exterior surfaces bear evidence of having been shaped with paddles, often wrapped with heavy nets or cords of loosely twined strands. Jack Wilson's (1976) study of the Uwharrie ceramics from 31Ch29 indicates that about 53 percent are net impressed, 36 percent are plain, while cord-marked and fabric-impressed samples comprise 5 and 6 percent, respectively, of the sample (Dickens et al. 1987:211, table 8.22). Interior surfaces are universally scraped with a serrate-edged tool. The exterior surfaces of the vessels' necks are also sometimes scraped and crudely incised with groups of parallel lines encircling the vessels below the rims.

In the northeastern Piedmont, under what is today the Roanoke Rapids reservoir, seventy-three sites were discovered and tested by Stanley South and Lewis Binford, then (in 1955) graduate students at the University of North Carolina (Ward and Davis 1999:89). The Gaston site proved to be a large Late Woodland palisaded village site with hundreds of features including post molds delineating the palisade, house structures, fire hearths, burials (both human and canine), and garbage pits. The rich ceramic assemblage from the Gaston site indicated three major components, Vincent, Clements, and Gaston. The Late Woodland Gaston component, associated with the palisaded village occupation, was assigned a date as late as A.D. 1700 (Coe

1964:107). Coe perceived the Gaston series pottery to be "something more than a mere continuation of the Vincent-Clements tradition." Gaston ware is tempered with crushed quartz prepared in a size range from 0.5 to 5.0 millimeters resulting in a porous, granular, and rough texture. Exterior surfaces are finished primarily with simple stamping, although some cord marking, cob marking, and check stamping also occur. Vessels were usually fired in a reducing environment and interior walls were typically scraped with a serrated tool and then smoothed by hand. Rims are often folded and decorated with lip notching and neck decoration includes incising (often with a series of alternating oblique lines 4–8 centimeters long), circular punctation, or finger pinching.

Very little archaeological research has been conducted in the Roanoke Rapids region since the salvage of remains from sites flooded by the reservoir. The late Thomas Hargrove, who began his doctoral dissertation research on the region in 1997, made considerable progress reanalyzing and describing artifacts and unpublished notes from Research Laboratories of Archaeology excavations of sites in the Roanoke Rapids reservoir. Hargrove's death in 1999 marked a significant setback for archaeological research in the Roanoke River valley. With luck, another similarly gifted scholar will take up the research.

Conclusion

Ceramic chronologies are fundamental building blocks of Woodland prehistory. In most areas of eastern North Carolina, however, ceramic sequences remain only partially understood. There are many more radiocarbon dates associated with Late Woodland pottery than with pottery from earlier periods. Sandy Coastal Plain soil conditions hostile to the preservation of datable organic material, with the exception of shell middens, ensure that this will continue to be so in the foreseeable future. The application of TL dating, as exemplified in the Sandhills, appears to hold some promise. It is hoped that future studies will improve upon this framework of ceramic sequences and move beyond pottery to people the Woodland prehistory of eastern North Carolina.

Acknowledgments

This study was supported in part through a Research Fellowship from the Oak Ridge Institute for Science and Education and the United States Army Environmental Center.

Support was also provided by the Cultural Resources Management Program at Fort Bragg, and the Research Laboratories of Archaeology, University of North Carolina at Chapel Hill. Funding for the AMS date for pottery from the McLean mound was provided by a grant from Sigma Xi, the Scientific Research Society. Unpublished radiocarbon data were graciously provided by David S. Phelps. Versions of this chapter were critiqued by Mark A. Mathis and two anonymous reviewers whose comments are appreciated. David G. Anderson and Robert Mainfort, Jr., provided editorial guidance. To these individuals and institutions, I am truly grateful.

Chapter 15

Aspects of Deptford and Swift Creek of the South Atlantic and Gulf Coastal Plains

Keith Stephenson, Judith A. Bense, and Frankie Snow

The terms *Deptford* and *Swift Creek* originated as Georgia site names (Figure 15.1). Both the Deptford type site (9CH2), in the vicinity of Savannah (Caldwell 1952:315–16; Caldwell et al. n.d.; DePratter 1991:122–56; Waring and Holder 1968), and the Swift Creek type site (9BI3), near Macon (Jefferies 1994; A. Kelly 1938; A. Kelly and B. A. Smith 1975), were excavated under various relief organizations associated with the New Deal program. During this period of Depression-era archaeology, a culture-historical paradigm emphasized artifact taxonomy (Willey and Phillips 1958). Accordingly, ceramics from these sites that shared distinctive stamped surfaces were assigned the respective type site names (Caldwell and Waring 1939; Jennings and Fairbanks 1939). Also in line with the precepts of culture-historical integration, the terms *Deptford* and *Swift Creek* were extended to identify separate Woodland archaeological "cultures" located mainly in South Carolina, Georgia, and northern Florida. Chronologically, Deptford precedes Swift Creek with some temporal overlap of ceramic types, notably in southwestern Georgia (B. A. Smith 1975a, 1975b, 1977:66–67, 1979:182–83) and northwestern Florida (P. Thomas and Campbell 1985). On the Atlantic Coastal Plain, Deptford surface stamping of ceramic vessels originated between 800 and 500 B.C., and possibly as early as circa 1000 B.C. in South Carolina, and continued until at least A.D. 500 (Trinkley 1980c:9, 11, 1989, 1990). In Florida, Deptford ceramics appeared somewhat later, about 500 B.C., and persisted until A.D. 100 to 300 (Bense 1998; Milanich 1994:114; Milanich and Fairbanks 1980:66; P. Thomas and Campbell [eds.] 1993). An inventory of ninety-seven dates for Deptford contexts is presented in Table 15.1.

The early curvilinear-engraved, paddle-stamped vessels of the Swift Creek period co-occurred with Deptford pottery in the south Georgia–north Florida area at circa A.D. 100. Thereafter, Swift Creek Complicated Stamped continued until circa A.D. 600 in northeast Florida (Bense 1998) and until at least circa A.D. 800 in the interior Georgia Coastal Plain (F. Snow and

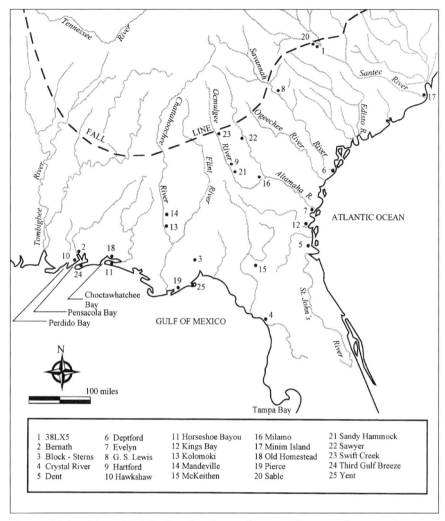

*Figure 15.1 — Major Middle Woodland period sites in the coastal zone and interior
Coastal Plain areas of northern Florida, Georgia, and South Carolina*

Stephenson 1990) as well as in portions of the Georgia Piedmont (Cable and
Raymer 1991; Cantley et al. 1997; T. Rudolph 1986, 1991; R. Webb et al.
1994; Wood et al. 1986). Swift Creek pottery is virtually nonexistent on the
South Carolina Coastal Plain (Elliott 1998:31; Sassaman et al. 1990). With
this general spatial-temporal framework, we turn to a more in-depth review
of the Deptford and Swift Creek periods emphasizing technological and socioeconomic continuities and discontinuities between the Gulf and Atlantic
regions.

Table 15.1 — Radiocarbon Dates from Deptford Period Sites

Site No.	Site Name	Radiocarbon Years B.P.	Calibrated Date (1 Sigma) * max. cal age (cal ages) min. cal ages	Lab. No.	Reference
Atlantic Coast					
38BU1214		1020 ± 70	A.D. 899 (994) 1044	Beta 40519	Trinkley 1991:91, 211
9GY-nr	South Cooper Field	1060 ± 70	A.D. 894 (991) 1025	UM 673	cited in Trinkley 1990:13, 14
38BU861	Old House Creek	1350 ± 60	A.D. 663 (691, 703, 708, 753, 758) 778	Beta 72297	Trinkley and Adams 1994:107, 108
38BU2		1265 ± 75	A.D. 652 (697) 781	UGa 6546	Espenshade et al. 1994:64
9LI26	Seaside Md. 1	1430 ± 125	A.D. 475 (640) 689	UGa 112	Caldwell 1970; cited in Milanich 1973a:55; B. A. Smith 1972:19
38BU832		1375 ± 47	A.D. 552 (625) 671	UGa 6643	Espenshade n.d.
38BU1302		1390 ± 60	A.D. 548 (618) 667	Beta 79489	Roberts and Huddleston 1998
38BU513		1410 ± 50	A.D. 541 (607) 661	UGa 6681	Roberts and Brockington 1996:76
9LI13	Wamassee B	1460 ± 90	A.D. 533 (605, 610, 616) 662	UGa 116	Caldwell 1970; cited in Milanich 1973a:55; B. A. Smith 1972:19
38BU1302		1410 ± 70	A.D. 514 (600) 661	Beta 79484	Roberts and Huddleston 1998
38BU1302		1420 ± 60	A.D. 513 (585) 649	Beta 79486	Roberts and Huddleston 1998
38BU832		1442 ± 46	A.D. 466 (556) 628	UGa 6644	Espenshade n.d.
38BU66/67	Pinkney Island	1505 ± 85	A.D. 430 (545, 560) 646	UGa 2853	Trinkley 1981:41
38BU1302		1460 ± 60	A.D. 449 (544) 612	Beta 79485	Roberts and Huddleston 1998
38CH644	Buck Hall	1499 ± 79	A.D. 380 (460) 579	UGa 6552	Poplin et al. 1993:196
38BU1302		1520 ± 60	A.D. 405 (454) 547	Beta 79490	Roberts and Huddleston 1998
38BU1302		1540 ± 50	A.D. 394 (438) 511	Beta 79487	Roberts and Huddleston 1998
38CH644	Buck Hall	1705 ± 83	A.D. 128 (243) 356	UGa 6555	Poplin et al. 1993:196
38BU861	Old House Creek	1800 ± 60	A.D. 134 (243) 339	Beta 72293	Trinkley and Adams 1994:105, 108
8DU5541	Greenfield No. 5	2190 ± 70	A.D. 80 (149) 250	Beta 131586	Kirkland and Johnson 2001:Table 53
38GE46	Minim Island	1790 ± 80	A.D. 64 (147) 260	Beta 6228	Drucker and Jackson 1984:10, 55

Table 15.1 (cont.) — Radiocarbon Dates from Deptford Period Sites

Site No.	Site Name	Radiocarbon Years B.P.	Calibrated Date (1 Sigma) * max. cal age (cal ages) min. cal ages	Lab. No.	Reference
38GE46	Minim Island	1790 ± 80	A.D. 64 (147) 260	Beta 6229	Drucker and Jackson 1984:10, 55
38BU2		1847 ± 51	A.D. 16 (79) 136	UGa nr	Espenshade et al. 1994:79
38BU927	Track	1920 ± 60	A.D. 25 (78) 131	Beta 134094	Loubser et al. 2000:158
38GE46	Minim Island	2264 ± 60	A.D. 9 (79) 140	UGa 5838	Espenshade and Brockington 1989:125, 126
38BU2		1861 ± 48	A.D. 5 (66) 125	UGa 6634	Espenshade et al. 1994:73
9CM162	Table Point	1895 ± 95	B.C. 81 (A.D. 43) 145	UGa 129	Milanich 1971a:155, 1973a:55
38GE46	Minim Island	2300 ± 49	B.C. 24 (A.D. 38) 93	UGa 5852	Espenshade and Brockington 1989:125, 126
38BU927	Track	1970 ± 120	B.C. 94 (A.D. 28, 41, 50) 133	Beta 134088	Loubser et al. 2000:158
8DU5541	Greenfield No. 5	2040 ± 40	B.C. 91 (43, 6, 4) A.D. 17	Beta 131581	Kirkland and Johnson 2001:Table 53
38BU832		1931 ± 49	B.C. 114 (30) A.D. 53	UGa 6642	Espenshade n.d.
38BU2		1946 ± 49	B.C. 106 (34) A.D. 31	UGa nr	Espenshade et al. 1994:76
38BU861	Old House Creek	2100 ± 80	B.C. 344 (146, 142, 113) 1	Beta 72295	Trinkley and Adams 1994:50, 53, 106, 108
8DU5541	Greenfield No. 5	2540 ± 60	B.C. 354 (255) 174	Beta 131583	Kirkland and Johnson 2001:Table 53
8DU5541	Greenfield No. 5	2190 ± 40	B.C. 357 (347, 321, 227, 223, 204) 175	Beta 131580	Kirkland and Johnson 2001:Table 53
8DU5541	Greenfield No. 5	2580 ± 70	B.C. 382 (342) 201	Beta 131587	Kirkland and Johnson 2001:Table 53
38BU921	Osprey Marsh	2260 ± 60	B.C. 396 (377, 266, 264) 206	Beta 74621	Gunn et al. 1995:230; Lilly and Gunn 1996:84
9LI26	Seaside Md. 1	2220 ± 100	B.C. 469 (364) 208	UGa 104	Caldwell 1970; cited in Milanich 1973a:55; B. A. Smith 1972:19
38GE46	Minim Island	2629 ± 64	B.C. 401 (369) 330	UGa 5851	Espenshade and Brockington 1989:115, 125, 126
8DU5541	Greenfield No. 5	2650 ± 60	B.C. 413 (380) 345	Beta 131588	Kirkland and Johnson 2001:Table 53
8DU5541	Greenfield No. 5	2720 ± 60	B.C. 545 (427) 383	Beta 131589	Kirkland and Johnson 2001:Table 53
8DU5541	Greenfield No. 5	2720 ± 70	B.C. 572 (427) 379	Beta 131582	Kirkland and Johnson 2001:Table 53
9CM171A	Kings Bay	2430 ± 90	B.C. 764 (498,493,483,465,449,441, 426,424,413) 397	Beta 4008	Adams (ed.) 1985:174, 358, 359
9LI26	Seaside Md. 1	2350 ± 220	B.C. 794 (506) 230	UGa SC3	Caldwell 1970; cited in Milanich 1973a:55; B. A. Smith 1972:19

Table 15.1 (cont.) — Radiocarbon Dates from Deptford Period Sites

Site No.	Site Name	Radiocarbon Years B.P.	Calibrated Date (1 Sigma) * max. cal age (cal ages) min. cal ages	Lab. No.	Reference
38BU66/67	Pinkney Island	2410 ± 80	B.C. 758 (650) 442	UGa 3513	Trinkley 1981:41
8DU68	Dent Mound	2640 ± 90	B.C. 896 (804) 779	UM 1756	Ashley 1995:26
38BU921	Osprey Marsh	2700 ± 70	B.C. 905 (830) 802	Beta 74620	Gunn et al. 1995:230; Lilly and Gunn 1996:84
South Carolina Interior Coastal Plain					
38BR170		1540 ± 40	A.D. 535 (544, 549, 558) 603	Beta 105455	Savannah Riv. Arch. Research Prog., SCIAA
38AK159		1590 ± 90	A.D. 362 (433) 598	Beta 23669	Sassaman 1989:40
38AK nr	Holley Creek	1890 ± 130	B.C. 40 (A.D. 91, 98, 126) 319	M 1373	Crane and Griffin 1966:272
38AK228 W	G.S. Lewis West	1910 ± 50	A.D. 34 (86, 102, 122) 133	Beta 157594	Savannah Riv. Arch. Research Prog., SCIAA
38AK119		1970 ± 70	B.C. 41 (A.D. 31, 38, 53) 126	Beta 118398	Savannah Riv. Arch. Research Prog., SCIAA
38AK228 W	G.S. Lewis West	2070 ± 60	B.C. 167 (50) A.D. 16	Beta 157595	Savannah Riv. Arch. Research Prog., SCIAA
38AK228 W	G.S. Lewis West	2150 ± 130	B.C. 386 (197, 190, 176) A.D. 1	Beta 23664	Savannah Riv. Arch. Research Prog., SCIAA
38AK157		2210 ± 40	B.C. 357 (347, 321, 227, 223, 204) 175	Beta 118399	Savannah Riv. Arch. Research Prog., SCIAA
38AK228 W	G.S. Lewis West	2250 ± 50	B.C. 394 (363, 269, 262) 203	Beta 23666	Savannah Riv. Arch. Research Prog., SCIAA
38SU136/137		2450 ± 60	B.C. 762 (478, 472, 411) 397	Beta 108298	Cable and Cantley 1998:248, 255, 264, Appendix H/Table H 21
38LX5		2620 ± 130	B.C. 901 (801) 544	RL 1037	Anderson 1979:Table 3
38LX5		2995 ± 110	B.C. 1405 (1258, 1233, 1218) 1020	UGa 3515	Trinkley 1980c:9,11; cited in Trinkley 1990:13
Georgia Interior Coastal Plain					
9ME60	Walker Street	2190 ± 140	B.C. 398 (347, 321, 227, 223, 204) 44	SI 264	cited in Elliott et al. 1995:119
9CY1	Mandeville	2500 ± 130	B.C. 803 (761, 680, 668, 613, 593, 569, 564) 402	M 1216	Milanich 1973a:55

Table 15.1 (cont.) — Radiocarbon Dates from Deptford Period Sites

Site No.	Site Name	Radiocarbon Years B.P.	Calibrated Date (1 Sigma) * max. cal age (cal ages) min. cal ages	Lab. No.	Reference
Gulf Coast					
8OK380		1360 ± 60	A.D. 588 (652) 690	Beta 39711	P. Thomas and Campbell [eds.] 1993:505
8OK183	Pirate's Bay	1810 ± 50	A.D. 555 (612) 657	Dicarb 2997	P. Thomas and Campbell 1985:118
8OK153		1820 ± 70	A.D. 532 (604) 663	Beta 39705	P. Thomas and Campbell [eds.] 1993:505
8OK183	Pirate's Bay	1830 ± 50	A.D. 540 (593) 644	Dicarb 2998	P. Thomas and Campbell 1985:118
8OK153		1840 ± 90	A.D. 460 (578) 662	Beta 39706	P. Thomas and Campbell [eds.] 1993:505
8OK380		1450 ± 60	A.D. 462 (560) 639	Beta 39710	P. Thomas and Campbell [eds.] 1993:505
8WL36	Horseshoe Bayou	1890 ± 70	A.D. 435 (533) 605	Beta 39723	P. Thomas and Campbell [eds.] 1993:506
8WL36	Horseshoe Bayou	1970 ± 60	A.D. 362 (429) 491	Beta 39726	P. Thomas and Campbell [eds.] 1993:546
8WL36	Horseshoe Bayou	1980 ± 70	A.D. 342 (423) 491	Beta 39725	P. Thomas and Campbell [eds.] 1993:506
8ES1287	Hawkshaw	1690 ± 60	A.D. 256 (362, 366, 383) 426	Beta 12577	Bense 1985:109
8ES1287	Hawkshaw	1700 ± 60	A.D. 224 (344, 370, 379) 423	Beta 12573	Bense 1985:109
8ES1287	Hawkshaw	1730 ± 60	A.D. 237 (261, 278, 324, 331, 335) 409	Beta 12574	Bense 1985:109
8CI1	Crystal River	1750 ± 130	A.D. 93 (258, 283, 287, 300, 320) 427	I 1367	Bullen 1966:861; Weisman 1995:39
8ES1287	Hawkshaw	1750 ± 70	A.D. 179 (258, 283, 287, 300, 320) 400	Beta 12576	Bense 1985:109
8ES1287	Hawkshaw	1770 ± 70	A.D. 132 (245, 310, 315) 383	Beta 12578	Bense 1985:109
8OK5		2115 ± 90	A.D. 136 (251) 368	nr	Mikell 1992:7; cited in P. Thomas and Campbell [eds.] 1993:546
8ES1287	Hawkshaw	1790 ± 60	A.D. 130 (240) 339	Beta 9411	Bense 1985:109
8OK183	Pirate's Bay	1830 ± 50	A.D. 127 (182, 188, 215) 243	Dicarb 2995	P. Thomas and Campbell 1985:118
8OK5		2206 ± 60	A.D. 74 (137) 228	nr	Mikell 1992:7; cited in P. Thomas and Campbell [eds.] 1993:546
8CI1	Crystal River	1870 ± 130	B.C. 17 (A.D. 129) 324	I 1366	Bullen 1966:861; Weisman 1995:39
8OK126		2270 ± 80	B.C. 13 (A.D. 79) 156	Beta 39712	P. Thomas and Campbell [eds.] 1993:505

Table 15.1 (cont.) — Radiocarbon Dates from Deptford Period Sites

Site No.	Site Name	Radiocarbon Years B.P.	Calibrated Date (1 Sigma) * max. cal age (cal ages) min. cal ages	Lab. No.	Reference
8OK126		2280 ± 80	B.C. 27 (A.D. 70) 145	Beta 39714	P. Thomas and Campbell [eds.] 1993:505
8ES1287	Hawkshaw	1950 ± 50	B.C. 36 (A.D. 34, 36, 61) 126	Beta 12575	Bense 1985:109
8ES1287	Hawkshaw	1950 ± 60	B.C. 39 (A.D. 34, 36, 61) 128	Beta 9410	Bense 1985:109
8CI1	Crystal River	1980 ± 100	B.C. 94 (A.D. 25, 43, 47) 129	I 1916	Ford 1969:29; Weisman 1995:39
8OK183	Pirate's Bay	2000 ± 55	B.C. 46 (A.D. 2, 14,16) 63	Dicarb 2996	P. Thomas and Campbell 1985:118
8WL152		2340 ± 50	B.C. 53 (A.D. 4) 60	Beta 92676	Prentice Thomas and Associates, Inc.
8WL149		2380 ± 70	B.C. 148 (43) A.D. 34	Beta 76276	Prentice Thomas and Associates, Inc.
8WL151		2520 ± 70	B.C. 345 (209) 146	Beta 92673	Prentice Thomas and Associates, Inc.
8OK126		2580 ± 70	B.C. 378 (339) 200	Beta 39713	P. Thomas and Campbell [eds.] 1993:505
8CI1	Crystal River	2300 ± 125	B.C. 503 (390) 200	I 1464	Bullen 1966:864; cited in Weisman 1995:39
8WL150		2400 ± 80	B.C. 755 (611, 600) 413	Beta 92674	Prentice Thomas and Associates, Inc.
8WL171		2840 ± 70	B.C. 760 (711) 521	Beta 92675	Prentice Thomas and Associates, Inc.
8BY9		2890 ± 70	B.C. 786 (751) 653	Beta 29512	Prentice Thomas and Associates, Inc.
8WL29	Alligator Lake	2575 ± 80	B.C. 816 (793) 544	Gx 155	Lazarus 1965b:109
8JE53	Oakland Mound	2850 ± 110	B.C. 1211 (1002) 840	No. G. 582	Morrell 1960:106

* All calibrations based on Stuiver and Reimer (1993), CALIB program (File INCAL98.14c)

nr = not reported

Deptford

There are three Deptford subregional adaptations: Atlantic, Gulf, and Coastal Plain Interior-Riverine (Figure 15.2). As Milanich (1994:113–15) points out, while the populations in the Atlantic and Gulf Deptford regions had similar subsistence economies and ceramics, the differences in developmental sequences as well as their geography make it taxonomically feasible to consider these areas separately (see Figure 15.3 for representative chronologies developed for each subregion). The Gulf subregion extends from Perdido Bay in Alabama southward to the Tampa Bay locale (Bense 1985:165; Milanich 1994:112). Representative ceramic markers include Deptford Linear Check Stamped, Deptford Bold Check Stamped, and Deptford Simple Stamped, along with several minority types (Sears 1966; Willey 1949a:353–61). The Atlantic subregion extends from central South Carolina to the mouth of the St. Johns River near Jacksonville, Florida (Milanich 1994:112). Diag-

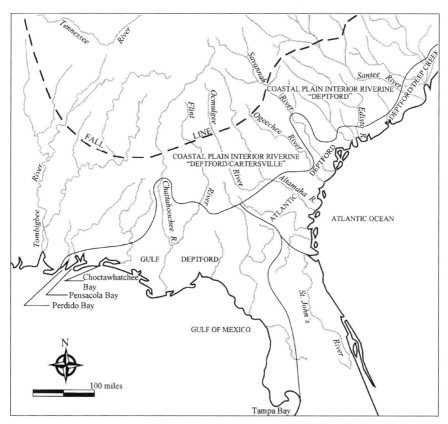

Figure 15.2 — The Deptford region (modified from Milanich 1973a:52)

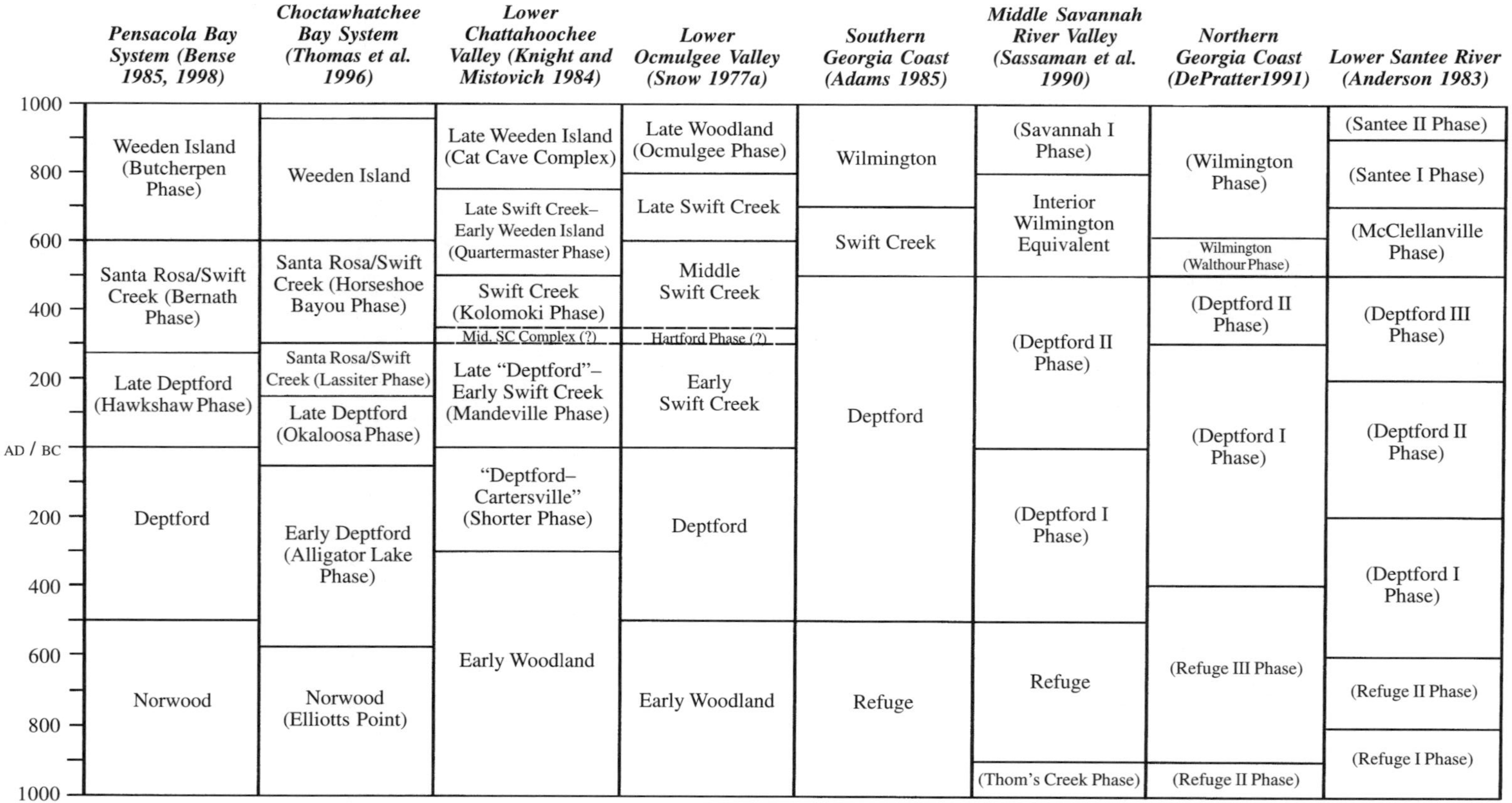

Figure 15.3 — Archaeological sequences for the coastal and interior Coastal Plain areas of northwest Florida, Georgia, and South Carolina

AD/BC	Pensacola Bay System (Bense 1985, 1998)	Choctawhatchee Bay System (Thomas et al. 1996)	Lower Chattahoochee Valley (Knight and Mistovich 1984)	Lower Ocmulgee Valley (Snow 1977a)	Southern Georgia Coast (Adams 1985)	Middle Savannah River Valley (Sassaman et al. 1990)	Northern Georgia Coast (DePratter 1991)	Lower Santee River (Anderson 1983)
AD 1000								(Santee II Phase)
AD 800	Weeden Island (Butcherpen Phase)	Weeden Island	Late Weeden Island (Cat Cave Complex)	Late Woodland (Ocmulgee Phase)	Wilmington	(Savannah I Phase)	(Wilmington Phase)	(Santee I Phase)
AD 600			Late Swift Creek–Early Weeden Island (Quartermaster Phase)	Late Swift Creek		Interior Wilmington Equivalent	Wilmington (Walthour Phase)	(McClellanville Phase)
AD 400	Santa Rosa/Swift Creek (Bernath Phase)	Santa Rosa/Swift Creek (Horseshoe Bayou Phase)	Swift Creek (Kolomoki Phase)	Middle Swift Creek	Swift Creek		(Deptford II Phase)	(Deptford III Phase)
AD 200		Santa Rosa/Swift Creek (Lassiter Phase)	Mid SC Complex (?)	Hartford Phase (?)		(Deptford II Phase)		
AD 200	Late Deptford (Hawkshaw Phase)	Late Deptford (Okaloosa Phase)	Late "Deptford"–Early Swift Creek (Mandeville Phase)	Early Swift Creek	Deptford		(Deptford I Phase)	(Deptford II Phase)
200 BC			"Deptford–Cartersville" (Shorter Phase)			(Deptford I Phase)		
200 BC	Deptford	Early Deptford (Alligator Lake Phase)		Deptford				(Deptford I Phase)
400 BC			Early Woodland					
600 BC				Early Woodland	Refuge	Refuge	(Refuge III Phase)	(Refuge II Phase)
800 BC	Norwood	Norwood (Elliotts Point)						(Refuge I Phase)
1000 BC						(Thom's Creek Phase)	(Refuge II Phase)	

nostic ceramics for this area consist of Deptford Linear Check Stamped, Deptford Check Stamped, Deptford Cord Marked, Deptford Simple Stamped, and finally Deptford Complicated Stamped, which resembles early Swift Creek and is found late in the Deptford period in minor amounts (DePratter 1991; Waring and Holder 1968). Recently, several innovative technical ceramic analyses primarily involving paste and temper characterization have been undertaken to support finer grained identification and seriation within the Deptford pottery typology (Cordell 1993; Lilly and Gunn 1996; Loubser et al. 2000). Regarding vessel form, Trinkley (1990:12–13) notes that the rounded- or flat-bottom jar with tetrapodal supports common at Gulf Deptford sites is extremely rare in the Atlantic subregion and particularly in South Carolina. Along the central South Carolina coast northward to the Cape Fear River, Deptford series ceramics occur as minority types (Trinkley 1980b, 1983:45). The interior-riverine Deptford subregion extends from the Alabama River in central Alabama, across southern Georgia, and into the western portion of the South Carolina Coastal Plain. Large Deptford settlements are located along the major river valleys with smaller sites dispersed along upland tributaries.

It has been almost three decades since Milanich (1971a, 1973a) offered the first elaborate model of Deptford settlement organization. Despite revisions, much of his scheme remains intact and it is still close to the way many archaeologists think about Deptford. He presented Deptford society primarily as coastally oriented with subsistence activities centered on hunting, gathering, and fishing circumscribed around a band level of social organization. Expanding on this model, Thomas and Larsen (1979) suggested a society of matrilineal succession on the basis of their findings at St. Catherines Island. Although Deptford burial mounds are generally unknown for the Atlantic Coast, Thomas and Larsen excavated nine presumably Deptford low, circular sand mounds containing extended and bundled burials with few and only modest grave goods. That the preponderance of identifiable interments were female led Thomas and Larsen (1979:149–50; also see Anderson 1985:48) to propose a matrilineal-based society, as was recorded for the Guale during the Historic period.

Deptford coastal sites were situated within the live oak strand that borders broad salt marshes on the offshore islands and the mainland itself. According to Milanich, camps and villages were spaced every 8 to 10 miles along the coast. At these sites, a variety of marsh animals, fish, and oysters as well as deer and turtles were used as food. Additionally, sea turtles, seals, whales, and porpoises were exploited.

Regarding settlement patterns, Milanich described Deptford groups as residing for the greatest part of the year on the coast. During certain seasons of the year, presumably the late fall and winter, whole groups, or more likely small expeditions, would migrate inland to distances of up to 40 miles along major rivers to collect ripened acorns and hickory nuts. These noncoastal, inland sites could be reached in one to three days' walking time or in a shorter time by river. With this model in mind, the following sections present a comparative review of recent developments concerning Deptford settlement and subsistence in the subregional coastal areas and the interior Coastal Plain of South Carolina and Georgia.

Atlantic Deptford

Within the past two decades, archaeological survey and excavations on the Atlantic Coastal Plain, particularly in South Carolina, have provided data that have allowed archaeologists to test this model of coastal estuary adaptation and seasonal inland migration. Researchers indeed have found numerous Deptford shell middens along the coastal estuarine areas, as Milanich predicted, but many of these shell scatters do not appear to represent the substantial camps or villages Milanich described.

The new data resulted in the recognition of great variability in Woodland shell middens (Espenshade 1993; Espenshade and Brockington 1989; Espenshade et al. 1994). Recent studies also have produced a well-developed typology based on site form and artifact content that is important for interpretations of Woodland settlement (Espenshade et al. 1994). These show that multifamily residential bases represent the largest aggregation of coastal residents at one location. These large sites are characterized by multiple or extensive shell middens where domestic and maintenance activities occurred and which may have been occupied continuously for several seasons, and possibly even year-round with periodic forays made into the interior. Thus, multifamily residential bases were strategically located so that a wide variety of food resources could be obtained from different environmental zones. Sherd density is high, along with a range of shell, bone, and sherd tools. A second site type is the single-family shell midden, which basically resembles the multifamily residential base, but is less extensive in size.

A third site type, as described by Espenshade et al. (1994), is the single-family, limited-shell site, characterized by the seasonal occupation of a small group or single family in an upland setting. Upland sites probably were established for the exploitation of deer and collection of ripened nuts during the late fall and winter. Very little shell is found at these sites, and artifact assemblage diversity is low. A final site type has been termed the oystering station. These functionally specialized sites were occupied by small work teams for short visits to gather and process primarily oysters. There is an almost total lack of vertebrate remains, as well as an absence of shell tools, bone tools, and sherd tools. These sites lack structural features and have a low frequency of pottery.

The best examples of the multifamily residential base are the sites excavated by Milanich (1971a, 1971b, 1973b), who describes coastal community patterning as comprising five to twenty structures based on counts of household refuse shell middens. Excavation revealed substantial structures with vertical wall posts anchored in shell-filled wall trenches and distributed in a linear fashion along the marsh edge. The size of these structures indicates that they probably housed nuclear families of five or six individuals. Milanich also presents evidence of a possible Deptford period ceremonial site: a dirt and shell midden ring 220 feet in diameter. Within the confines of this ring is a centrally located shell midden of unknown function. Milanich does not describe in detail what type of ceremonialism occurred, but if this large, circular feature was intentionally planned architecture, then it may have functioned much as the shell rings of the Late Archaic.

Turning next to the single-family shell midden site type, probably the best archaeological examples include Pinckney Island in Beaufort County and Minim Island in Georgetown County, South Carolina (Espenshade and Brockington 1989). The Minim Island site is an especially good example of a single-family shell midden because of its diverse artifact assemblage within a thick shell matrix. Located in the coastal estuary near the North Santee River, the Minim Island shell midden measured 40 by 13 meters. Excavations at the site consisted of a 3 by 9-meter block exposing a dense shell midden just below ground surface. Two major depositional strata were obvious in the excavation profiles. The majority of this shell deposit was a dense Deptford period oyster midden just over 1 meter thick. The Deptford deposit overlay an Early Woodland sand midden with shell. At the base of the shell deposit were numerous features. Deptford Check Stamped sherds were the most common artifact. Radiocarbon assays indicate that Deptford occupation occurred as early as 600 B.C. and lasted until 250 B.C. A later Deptford occupation that occurred from about A.D. 100 through 300 was inferred based on radiocarbon assays and the presence of Deep Creek Fabric Impressed pottery along with Deptford Check Stamped ware. Subsistence data indicate a reliance on seafood, particularly oysters and clams, while mammals seem to have been a minor food resource. According to Espenshade and Brockington (1989), there was an intensive reliance on oyster gathering in the fall, while late winter through early spring was a time of limited site use as evidenced by hardshell clam data. Thus, the Deptford remains represent a seasonally permanent encampment for a few single-family units.

Trinkley (1990) explains that most Deptford sites are not massive shell mounds, but rather thin middens formed as a series of small shell heaps that gradually accumulated into continuous masses, suggesting short periods of site use for shellfish collecting. Numerous shell middens without structural features and low artifact density have been detected in Beaufort County and are considered oystering stations (Trinkley 1991; Trinkley [ed.] 1990; Trinkley and Adams 1994).

Gulf Deptford

Milanich (1994; Milanich and Fairbanks 1980) and others have noted that, with few exceptions, Deptford sites in the Gulf region are neither deeply stratified nor found over a broad area. One explanation is that of sea-level rise and the inundation of many Deptford sites. As Milanich (1994:115) notes, archaeological evidence indicates a rise in sea level over time as confirmed through documentation of submerged Deptford sites up to half a mile from the current shoreline (Lazarus 1965a). Another factor that may account for the low number of Deptford stratified sites is that Deptford components often are located at the base of large shell middens and are exposed only through deep excavations.

Subsistence of the Gulf Deptford inhabitants was focused on fishing, gathering, and hunting in the estuaries and oak-hickory hammocks and settlement was in permanent locations along the coast. The Florida interior within 50 to 100 miles of the Gulf coast was exploited primarily to supplement coastal subsistence through hunting and collecting. The Gulf Deptford settlement pattern was one of base camps or villages surrounded by smaller satellite camps interpreted as short-term resource procurement settlements (Bense 1998; P. Thomas and Campbell [eds.] 1993).

Gulf Deptford assemblages are dominated by ceramics. For example, at the Hawkshaw site in Pensacola 15,000 sherds were recovered, but there were only eighty chipped stone, twelve bone, and twelve shell tools (Bense 1985). While the numbers are small, glimpses of technology include spears (bannerstones and chipped stone points), cordage and nets (impressions on ceramics, plummets), basketry (bone fids), fishing tools (shell and bone gigs, composite fishhooks), stone abraders and whetstones, celts, and tools for stone working (hammerstones, antler flakers, and debitage), woodworking (adzes), and leather working (awls). Personal adornment items from Hawkshaw include shell beads and bone, drilled animal teeth, and hematite cones. Deptford pottery was tempered with sand or grit, and vessels were built by the coiling and paddle-malleating method—an advance in technology over the hand-molded and fiber-tempered ware of the Late Archaic (Milanich and Fairbanks 1980:78). Vessel shapes included deep conical and globular jars, often with podal supports on the base similar to those in contemporaneous Early Woodland cultures to the west such as Bayou La Batre,

Tchefuncte, and Alexander. Early Deptford markers include Deptford Check Stamped, Linear Check Stamped, and Simple Stamped ceramics, with Deptford Cord Marked appearing late in the period. In the Pensacola Bay system, there are a minority of ceramic types in the Deptford ceramic assemblages from (or copying those of) the Lower Mississippi Valley, such as Marksville Incised. At the Hawkshaw site, Bense (1985) found that vessels decorated with these Lower Valley designs tended to be small bowls and beakers (personal eating vessels)—much different from the typical conical Deptford Check Stamped containers used for cooking.

After 100 B.C., during the late Gulf Deptford period, a new ceremonial practice appeared: burial mounds with a special sacred assemblage of materials. Sears (1962a:6–11) named this ceremonial complex Yent after the type site in eastern northwest Florida. Most Deptford Yent mounds are in eastern northwest Florida, and the best known are Crystal River, Yent, and Pierce (Brose 1979b:148; C. B. Moore 1903a; Weisman 1995). Items in Deptford mounds indicate a sacred-secular dichotomy (Milanich 1994). Imported stone, metal, and pottery items, such as plummets, copper panpipes, earspools, shell gorgets, and cups, served as prestige items for special persons. Caches of pottery included vessels made in exotic shapes such as a ram's horn or with multiple lobes and pouring spouts. Typical Deptford utilitarian types also were included. Interred human remains indicate secondary bundle burials.

The largest and most complex Gulf Deptford ceremonial center was the multiple mound Crystal River site, located in the southern portion of the culture area. This site was initially excavated by C. B. Moore (1903a, 1907, 1918) and his collection was used in Sears's (1962a) definition of the Yent complex. Bullen (1966) conducted less extensive excavations in the 1950s and 1960s. Weisman (1995) has extensively reviewed both Moore's and Bullen's data from this site. Other Gulf Deptford ceremonial locations are smaller and consist of single-mound and village sites.

Interior-Riverine Coastal Plain Deptford
Since the definitive work of Milanich (1971a, 1973a), Deptford has been considered a coastally oriented tradition. Controversy thus shadows the concept of Deptford as an adaptation to the interior Gulf and Atlantic Coastal Plains (Knight and Mistovich 1984:217–18). When considering the interior check-stamped tradition, Deptford often has been used as a generic term for the early Middle Woodland ceramic series. In particular, the check-stamped pottery of the interior Coastal Plain has been cited as more indicative of Cartersville than of Deptford (Knight and Mistovich 1984; B. A. Smith 1975a). For instance, although B. A. Smith (1975a:196) refers to the check-stamped assemblage at Mandeville as Deptford, she admits that "the check

stamped pottery from Mandeville is more similar to the north Georgia Cartersville variety than it is to the coastal Deptford variety." This indeed may hold true more for the interior Gulf Coastal Plain than for the Atlantic region.

Research over the past three decades indicates that Deptford-related ceramic types have a much broader geographical distribution than previously thought. Anderson's (1975a, 1975b) documentation of Deptford sites throughout the Coastal Plain of South Carolina suggested an adaptation to the rich resources of this interior area. Deptford ceramics reach at least as far inland as the Sable site, located in the Red Clay Hills sector, where Deptford Linear Check Stamped sherds comprise just over 70 percent of all ceramics recovered (Ryan 1972:34–42). In the neighboring county of Lexington, a Deptford site, 38LX5, was excavated in the fall line Sandhills (Anderson 1979; Trinkley 1980c).

In fact, archaeological investigations during the past decade have demonstrated that large village sites or base camps were located about 150 miles inland from the Atlantic Coast. On the interior Georgia Coastal Plain are two large sites with Deptford and Cartersville Check Stamped ceramics, Sandy Hammock along the Ocmulgee River and Sawyer on the Oconee River. A third major Deptford settlement located along the middle Savannah River in South Carolina is the Lewis West site. Archaeological investigations at the Sandy Hammock site indicate that this extensive village was probably circular in form. On the basis of check-stamped sherd distribution, the village was ring-shaped with a diameter of about 300 meters. The second large midden, recorded at the Sawyer site from density distributions of check-stamped pottery, also appears to be oval to circular in form with about the same diameter as that at the Sandy Hammock site (J. M. Williams 1996:20–21).

The best excavation data from an interior Coastal Plain site come from the Deptford base camp at Lewis West situated at the mouth of Upper Three Runs and the Savannah River (G. Hanson 1988; Sassaman et al. 1990). Located along the swamp terrace, most of the site lies beneath several feet of recent overburden from the dredging of a nearby canal. As a result, site configuration cannot be determined. Excavations at the site in 1984 and 1989 removed a 154-square-meter block through a 25-centimeter-thick midden. More than 500 cultural features were exposed including pits, postholes, and human and dog burials. Postmold patterns reveal the presence of several house structures with associated features. A number of the larger features excavated provided numerous sherds with the potential for ceramic seriation and carbonized wood material for obtaining radiocarbon dates. Over 50,000 sherds were recovered and they exhibit a broad range of decorative styles. The most numerous type present was Deptford Linear

Check Stamped (Kenion 1989). An associated minority ware was indicated by red-painted zoned sherds resembling the Deptford-related type known as Brewton Hill Zoned Punctated. A small number of Yadkin Triangular bifaces were associated with this ceramic assemblage. Also present in the midden and feature deposits was cord-marked pottery, indicative of Late Woodland occupation. Several radiocarbon assays have been obtained, confirming the presence of two distinct occupations: Deptford I/II between 300 B.C. and A.D. 100 and Savannah I from A.D. 900 to 1200.

The occurrence of numerous Deptford sites in the interior Coastal Plain up to the Fall Line some 200 miles from the coast raises questions about the primacy of the coastal adaptation among Deptford groups (Anderson 1985:44–49). Brooks and Canouts (1984) argued for year-round habitation in the lower interior Coastal Plain. In an assessment of the lower interior Coastal Plain environment, they commented that this region had abundant subsistence resources and suitable raw materials, such as stone and clay, for year-round prehistoric use. They concluded that the Milanich model of seasonal migration between the coast and interior was inappropriate for the interior lower Coastal Plain of South Carolina. Further research is needed to understand more fully the relationship of interior Deptford sites to those on the coast. The evidence of substantial Deptford base camps or villages in the upper interior Coastal Plain has resulted in a reconsideration of the long-standing model of inland migration and foraging. In line with Brooks and Canouts (1984), researchers will have to broaden their considerations of interior regional settlement patterns to include the possibility of year-round use within this region, especially in light of recent archaeological developments.

Swift Creek

The material culture of the Swift Creek period is recognized primarily by the elaborate paddle-stamped ceramics that represent the earliest complicated-stamped vessels in the eastern United States (A. Kelly 1938; McMichael 1960; Wauchope 1966; Willey 1949a; J. M. Williams and Elliott [eds.] 1998). The Swift Creek tradition has a lengthy time span, dating from about A.D. 150 in northwest Florida to around A.D. 800 in Georgia (Bense 1998; J. M. Williams and Elliott 1998). The spatial extent of Swift Creek materials is well defined, covering northwest Florida, eastern Alabama, Georgia, and the area along the lower Atlantic coast of Georgia into the upper St. Johns River area of Florida as shown in Figure 15.4 (Ashley 1992, 1995, 1998; Wauchope 1966; J. M. Williams and Elliott 1998). In Florida, Swift Creek period sites are restricted to eastern northwest Florida, or between the Aucilla

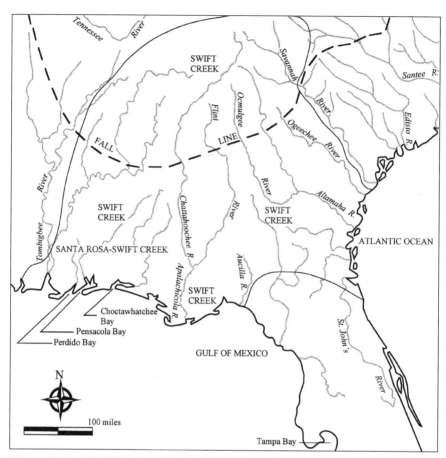

Figure 15.4 — Swift Creek region (modified from Williams and Elliott 1998:6, courtesy Frankie Snow)

River and the area just west of the Apalachicola River (Beers 1997 [also see Beers 1997 for Swift Creek botanical study]; B. C. Jones and Tesar 1996; B. C. Jones et al. 1998; Milanich 1994:121; White 1992). Ceramic variants of Marksville culture usually are found in context with Swift Creek pottery in the western Florida panhandle. These "Florida Marksville" types compose the Santa Rosa series—hence the name Santa Rosa–Swift Creek for this subregion. In northwest Florida, archaeologists have noted variation in Swift Creek and Santa Rosa–Swift Creek site structure as it relates to settlement distribution patterns. Prominent among the several site types recorded are ring-shaped middens representing circular community designs around a centralized plaza (Bense 1998; Milanich 1994:144–45; Milanich and Fairbanks 1980; P. Thomas and Campbell [eds.] 1993).

Regional Chronology

As indicated by 121 radiocarbon dates listed in Table 15.2, the Swift Creek period began at circa A.D. 150 and persisted until circa A.D. 800. A variety of ceramic attributes—including lip treatments, basal morphology, associated minor ceramic types, and variability in individual complicated stamp motifs—make Swift Creek ceramic assemblages especially well suited to fine seriation (R. Saunders 1986). Previous regional archaeological investigations have established a framework of successional phases for pottery assemblages (Figure 15.3). Arthur Kelly (1938:28), following his work at the Swift Creek type site in central Georgia, recognized three periods (early, middle, and late) in the ceramic tradition based mainly on differences in the quality of surface finish and rim treatment. Alternatively, for northwest Florida Willey (1949a:378–83, 429–35) identified only two varieties (early and late) of Swift Creek pottery, which he distinguished primarily by stratigraphic context and variation in associated ceramic types and secondarily by the corresponding stylistic traits that Kelly noted. Willey's (1949a:366, 396–97) division assigned the early variety of Swift Creek Complicated Stamped to the Santa Rosa–Swift Creek ceramic series and the late variety to the Weeden Island I pottery series.

The most detailed refinement of A. Kelly's (1938) chronology for Swift Creek was developed by Knight and Mistovich (1984:218–20) for the Chattahoochee River system of southwestern Georgia and southeastern Alabama. In this portion of the Chattahoochee River valley, early Middle Woodland sites have ceramic assemblages consisting almost entirely of the Deptford-related Cartersville Check Stamped. These sites have been assigned to the Shorter phase, which has an estimated date range of 300 B.C. to A.D. 1 (Knight and Mistovich 1984:217–18). The subsequent Mandeville phase derives from Shorter and is thought to span the A.D. 1 to 300 time interval. Excavations at sites assigned to this phase, such as the type site of Mandeville, demonstrate the development of Swift Creek Complicated Stamped from the earlier Deptford and Cartersville Checked Stamped, which occur in varying percentages in collections (Knight and Mistovich 1984:217–18). Early Swift Creek pottery is characterized by poor stamping, notched or scalloped rims, and tetrapodal supports (Caldwell 1958:39). Sites equivalent to the Mandeville phase are almost nonexistent east of the lower Chattahoochee River drainage, suggesting a continuation of the Deptford tradition in the south-central Georgia area.

Knight and Mistovich (1984:219–20) infer a developmental gap of at least 50 years for the lower Chattahoochee River valley chronology between the Mandeville and the succeeding Kolomoki phases. This interval is now filled by the transitional Swift Creek pottery assemblage recovered from the

Table 15.2 — Radiocarbon Dates from Santa Rosa–Swift Creek and Swift Creek Period Sites

Site No.	Site Name	Radiocarbon Years B.P.	Calibrated Date (1 Sigma) * max. cal age (cal ages) min. cal ages	Lab. No.	Reference
Florida Gulf Coast					
8WL176		1620 ± 70	A.D. 695 (773) 848	Beta 39719	P. Thomas and Campbell [eds.] 1993:505
8SR8	Third Gulf Breeze	1350 ± 75	A.D. 624 (663) 770	nr	Phelps 1969:18
8WL36	Horseshoe Bayou	1800 ± 60	A.D. 555 (622) 668	Beta 39722	P. Thomas and Campbell [eds.] 1993:506
8SR986	Bernath	1360 ± 60	A.D. 642 (662) 689	Beta 72072	Bense 1998:251
8WL36	Horseshoe Bayou	1750 ± 60	A.D. 611 (662) 697	Beta 39724	P. Thomas and Campbell [eds.] 1993:506
8SR986	Bernath	1460 ± 50	A.D. 544 (605, 610, 616) 647	Beta 72069	Bense 1998:251
8LI172	Otis Hare	1480 ± 70	A.D. 475 (600) 653	Beta 46703	Nancy White, pers. com. 2001
8SR8	Third Gulf Breeze	1485 ± 75	A.D. 441 (599) 653	nr	Phelps 1969:18
8LI172	Otis Hare	1530 ± 50	A.D. 431 (540) 615	Beta 46705	Nancy White, pers. com. 2001
8LI172	Otis Hare	1580 ± 80	A.D. 397 (437, 454, 457, 522, 527) 598	Beta 46706	Nancy White, pers. com. 2001
8SR986	Bernath	1590 ± 60	A.D. 411 (433) 540	Beta 72071	Bense 1998:251
8JA63		1600 ± 250	A.D. 132 (430) 664	M nr	Bullen 1958:331
8FR4	Tucker	1605 ± 325	A.D. 73 (429) 765	FSU nr	Phelps 1966:20
8SR986	Bernath	1610 ± 50	A.D. 406 (428) 534	Beta 72070	Bense 1998:251
8GU38	Overgrown Road	1650 ± 50	A.D. 343 (412) 431	Beta 25771	White 1992:24
8WL58	Old Homestead	2110 ± 70	A.D. 168 (258) 353	Beta 87796	P. Thomas et al. 1996:234
8WL58	Old Homestead	2210 ± 70	A.D. 69 (137) 236	Beta 87795	P. Thomas et al. 1996:234
8WL58	Old Homestead	2240 ± 70	A.D. 33 (108) 186	Beta 87798	P. Thomas et al. 1996:234
8WL58	Old Homestead	2270 ± 60	A.D. 12 (79) 138	Beta 87794	P. Thomas et al. 1996:234
8WL58	Old Homestead	2310 ± 60	B.C. 36 (A.D. 33) 95	Beta 87797	P. Thomas et al. 1996:234
8OK877		2340 ± 60	B.C. 73 (A.D. 4) 71	Beta 72228	Prentice Thomas and Associates, Inc.

Table 15.2 (cont.) — Radiocarbon Dates from Santa Rosa–Swift Creek and Swift Creek Period Sites

Site No.	Site Name	Radiocarbon Years B.P.	Calibrated Date (1 Sigma) * max. cal age (cal ages) min. cal ages	Lab. No.	Reference
Atlantic Coast					
9CM171A	Kings Bay	1180 ± 60	A.D. 714 (784) 873	Beta 4015	Adams (ed.) 1985:358–359
9CM171A	Kings Bay	1190 ± 60	A.D. 704 (778) 854	Beta 4012	Adams (ed.) 1985:358–359
8DU68	Dent Mound	1610 ± 70	A.D. 697 (777) 865	Beta 54645	Ashley 1995:26
9CM171A	Kings Bay	1220 ± 90	A.D. 683 (779) 957	Beta 4004	Adams (ed.) 1985:358–359
9CM171A	Kings Bay	1250 ± 60	A.D. 667 (710) 781	Beta 4429	Adams (ed.) 1985:358–359
9CM233		1300 ± 40	A.D. 680 (693, 699, 715, 749, 764) 777	Beta 157591	Dwight Kirkland, pers. com. 2001
9CM171A	Kings Bay	1320 ± 60	A.D. 665 (683) 775	Beta 3993	Adams (ed.) 1985:358–359
9CM171A	Kings Bay	1330 ± 70	A.D. 645 (674) 775	Beta 4417	Adams (ed.) 1985:358–359
9CM171A	Kings Bay	1330 ± 60	A.D. 604 (661) 698	Beta 4010	Adams (ed.) 1985:358–359
9CM171A	Kings Bay	1340 ± 80	A.D. 640 (666) 775	Beta 3988	Adams (ed.) 1985:358–359
9CM171A	Kings Bay	1360 ± 80	A.D. 619 (662) 768	Beta 3989	Adams (ed.) 1985:358–359
9CM233		1400 ± 40	A.D. 621 (652) 662	Beta 157590	Dwight Kirkland, pers. com. 2001
9MC-10-1	Sidon Plantation	1400 ± 60	A.D. 604 (652) 669	Beta 82086	Cook 1995: Appendix 4
9CM171A	Kings Bay	1410 ± 140	A.D. 584 (646) 677	Beta 3996	Adams (ed.) 1985:358–359
9CM171A	Kings Bay	1420 ± 80	A.D. 544 (643) 676	Beta 3994	Adams (ed.) 1985:358–359
9CM171A	Kings Bay	1440 ± 80	A.D. 540 (623, 628, 638) 664	Beta 4420	Adams (ed.) 1985:358–359
9MC360	Cathead Creek	1450 ± 50	A.D. 561 (620, 634, 636) 654	nr	Wayne 1987:56
9CM171A	Kings Bay	1470 ± 100	A.D. 437 (602) 661	Beta 4418	Adams (ed.) 1985:358–359
9CM171A	Kings Bay	1470 ± 80	A.D. 533 (602) 658	Beta 4005	Adams (ed.) 1985:358–359
9CM171A	Kings Bay	1410 ± 70	A.D. 493 (589) 658	Beta 4421	Adams (ed.) 1985:358–359

Table 15.2 (cont.) — Radiocarbon Dates from Santa Rosa–Swift Creek and Swift Creek Period Sites

Site No.	Site Name	Radiocarbon Years B.P.	Calibrated Date (1 Sigma) * max. cal age (cal ages) min. cal ages	Lab. No.	Reference
Georgia and Alabama Coastal Plain					
9PUv1	Hartford (village)	1070 ± 60	A.D. 785 (899, 920, 958) 992	Beta 72564	Stephenson and Snow 1994
9PUv1	Hartford (village)	1140 ± 70	A.D. 734 (885) 962	Beta 72565	Stephenson and Snow 1994
9PUv1	Hartford (village)	1200 ± 50	A.D. 779 (887) 958	Beta 72563	Stephenson and Snow 1994
1RU58	Uchee Creek Site 4	1220 ± 120	A.D. 664 (779) 978	SI nr	Chase 1978a:53
9LS23		1275 ± 60	A.D. 664 (694, 697, 717, 748, 766) 856	UGa 1706	M. T. Smith 1978
9PUo1	Hartford (mound)	1280 ± 50	A.D. 672 (693, 699, 715, 749, 764) 778	Beta 57727	F. Snow and Stephenson 1990
9PUo1	Hartford (mound)	1344 ± 74	A.D. 643 (665) 768	UGa 5986	F. Snow and Stephenson 1990
9TF37	Horse Creek	1370 ± 65	A.D. 620 (660) 756	UGa 3263	F. Snow 1992a
9PUo1	Hartford (mound)	1400 ± 50	A.D. 618 (652) 664	Beta 54001	F. Snow and Stephenson 1990
9PUv1	Hartford (village)	1410 ± 40	A.D. 617 (646) 660	Beta 145493	this chapter
9PUo1	Hartford (mound)	1510 ± 60	A.D. 441 (544, 549, 558) 636	Beta 57728	F. Snow and Stephenson 1990
9CY1	Mandeville	1420 ± 150	A.D. 439 (643) 770	M 1044	Kellar et al. 1962a:354
9PUo1	Hartford (mound)	1560 ± 40	A.D. 474 (542) 601	Beta 157592	this chapter
9ER1	Kolomoki	1545 ± 25	A.D. 432 (537) 597	I 482	Milanich et al. 1984:13
9ER1	Kolomoki	1565 ± 75	A.D. 411 (472, 478, 532) 601	I 482 c	Milanich et al. 1984:13
9PUo1	Hartford (mound)	1570 ± 50	A.D. 425 (442, 448, 468, 482, 530) 556	Beta 54000	F. Snow and Stephenson 1990
9CY1	Mandeville	1580 ± 65	A.D. 408 (437, 454, 457, 522, 527) 595	UGa 6B	B. A. Smith 1979:186–187
9CY1	Mandeville	1560 ± 70	A.D. 263 (417) 533	UGa 14B	B. A. Smith 1979:186–187
9CY1	Mandeville	1585 ± 70	A.D. 259 (403) 434	UGa 15B	B. A. Smith 1979:186–187
9PUo1	Hartford (mound)	1590 ± 40	A.D. 420 (433) 537	Beta 145494	this chapter
9PUo1	Hartford (mound)	1635 ± 78	A.D. 264 (419) 535	UGa 5837	F. Snow and Stephenson 1990
9ME21	Carmouche	1640 ± 60	A.D. 343 (417) 527	Beta 9553	Gresham et al. 1985; cited in Elliott et al. 1995:156

Table 15.2 (cont.) — Radiocarbon Dates from Santa Rosa–Swift Creek and Swift Creek Period Sites

Site No.	Site Name	Radiocarbon Years B.P.	Calibrated Date (1 Sigma) * max. cal age (cal ages) min. cal ages	Lab. No.	Reference
Georgia and Alabama Coastal Plain (cont.)					
9CY1	Mandeville	1640 ± 65	A.D. 263 (417) 533	UGa 4B	B. A. Smith 1979:186–187
9ER1	Kolomoki	1660 ± 50	A.D. 264 (407) 428	Beta 121909	Pluckhahn 2000:150
9CY1	Mandeville	1685 ± 75	A.D. 245 (384) 431	UGa 10B	B. A. Smith 1979:186–187
9CY1	Mandeville	1700 ± 65	A.D. 243 (344, 370, 379) 424	UGa 8B	B. A. Smith 1979:186–187
9CY1	Mandeville	1705 ± 70	A.D. 241 (343, 372, 377) 424	UGa 5B	B. A. Smith 1979:186–187
9ME21	Carmouche	1730 ± 60	A.D. 240 (261, 278, 324, 331, 335) 400	Beta 9555	Gresham et al. 1985; cited in Elliott et al. 1995:156
9JD8	Pike Creek	1735 ± 70	A.D. 224 (261, 279, 293, 296, 323) 411	UGa 2099	F. Snow and Trowell 1992
9ME21	Carmouche	1770 ± 140	A.D. 82 (245, 310, 315) 422	Beta 9556	Gresham et al. 1985; cited in Elliott et al. 1995:156
9CY1	Mandeville	1690 ± 85	A.D. 131 (245, 313, 315) 390	UGa 16B	B. A. Smith 1979:186–187
9CY1	Mandeville	1775 ± 120	A.D. 85 (244) 414	UGa 3B	B. A. Smith 1979:186–187
9CY1	Mandeville	1800 ± 65	A.D. 128 (238) 338	UGa 1B	B. A. Smith 1979:186–187
9CY1	Mandeville	1810 ± 70	A.D. 90 (236) 336	UGa 7B	B. A. Smith 1979:186–187
9CY1	Mandeville	1840 ± 70	A.D. 78 (134, 159, 170, 196, 209) 318	UGa 2B	B. A. Smith 1979:186–187
9WL1	Milamo	1850 ± 160	B.C. 37 (A.D. 133) 385	UGa 2992	F. Snow et al. 1992
9CY1	Mandeville	1915 ± 70	A.D. 3 (80) 213	UGa 11B	B. A. Smith 1979:186–187
9CY1	Mandeville	1860 ± 65	B.C. 36 (A.D. 69) 130	UGa 9B	B. A. Smith 1979:186–187
9ER1	Kolomoki	1920 ± 300	B.C. 355 (A.D. 78) A.D. 426	M 49	Crane 1956; cited in Sears 1992
9CY1	Mandeville	1960 ± 150	B.C. 166 (A.D. 31, 38, 53) A.D. 237	M 1042	Kellar et al. 1962a:354
9ER1	Kolomoki	2021 ± 300	B.C. 396 (38, 29, 22, 10, 1) A.D. 339	M 50	Crane 1956; cited in Sears 1992
9CE4	Halloca Creek	2020 ± 150	B.C. 202 (38, 30, 21, 11, 1) A.D. 130	M 1046	Chase 1963; cited in Elliott et al. 1995:156

Table 15.2 (cont.) — Radiocarbon Dates from Santa Rosa–Swift Creek and Swift Creek Period Sites

Site No.	Site Name	Radiocarbon Years B.P.	Calibrated Date (1 Sigma) * max. cal age (cal ages) min. cal ages	Lab. No.	Reference
Georgia and South Carolina Piedmont/Ridge and Valley					
9CO46		1010 ± 90	A.D. 904 (1020) 1157	Beta 41374	Cable and Raymer 1991:41–45, 86–90
38AN8	Simpson's Field	1020 ± 50	A.D. 980 (1018) 1146	Beta 6398	Wood et al. 1986:105
9FY106		1030 ± 60	A.D. 979 (1004, 1008, 1017) 1029	Beta 76790	Cantley et al. 1997:248
9HY39		1090 ± 70	A.D. 887 (979) 1020	Beta 68670	R. Webb et al. 1994:335
9HY39		1150 ± 90	A.D. 775 (892) 997	Beta 68673	R. Webb et al. 1994:335
9FO16	Summerour Md.	1150 ± 70	A.D. 779 (892) 982	Beta 82594	Pluckhahn 1996:198
9DO2	Aneewakee Creek	1195 ± 100	A.D. 688 (783, 789, 829, 839, 864) 980	Gx 2826	Dickens 1975
9HY39		1220 ± 50	A.D. 692 (779) 891	Beta 68674	R. Webb et al. 1994:323
9FY106		1240 ± 60	A.D. 688 (776) 886	Beta 76791	Cantley et al. 1997:246, 412
9CK130		1250 ± 75	A.D. 677 (775) 887	UGa 2393	Bowen 1982:113
38AN8	Simpson's Field	1250 ± 50	A.D. 685 (775) 882	Beta 2603	Wood et al. 1986:105
9RO53	Chase	1290 ± 60	A.D. 663 (691, 703, 708, 753, 758) 778	Beta 72137	Stanyard and Stoops 1995:198, 204
9MO487		1295 ± 111	A.D. 644 (690, 755) 886	UGa 6263	Rogers et al. 1991:54
38AN8	Simpson's Field	1340 ± 60	A.D. 644 (666) 769	Beta 7009	Wood et al. 1986:105
9DO2	Aneewakee Creek	1345 ± 85	A.D. 623 (664) 775	Gx 2825	Dickens 1975
9FY116		1350 ± 50	A.D. 651 (663) 689	Beta 76793	Cantley et al. 1997:347
9RO53	Chase	1360 ± 80	A.D. 622 (662) 764	Beta 72136	Stanyard and Stoops 1995:198, 204
9MO487		1394 ± 94	A.D. 563 (655) 757	UGa 6259	Rogers et al. 1991:54
9HY39		1400 ± 50	A.D. 603 (652) 672	Beta 68671	R. Webb et al. 1994:347
9MO487		1404 ± 90	A.D. 561 (650) 688	UGa 6260	Rogers et al. 1991:54
9GE10	Cold Springs	1410 ± 50	A.D. 604 (646) 662	Beta 145492	this chapter
9FY116		1430 ± 50	A.D. 599 (640) 658	Beta 76795	Cantley et al. 1997:341
9NE85		1500 ± 50	A.D. 444 (562, 592, 596) 639	Beta 62704	Stanyard and Stoops 1995:198, 217

Table 15.2 (cont.) — Radiocarbon Dates from Santa Rosa–Swift Creek and Swift Creek Period Sites

Site No.	Site Name	Radiocarbon Years B.P.	Calibrated Date (1 Sigma) * max. cal age (cal ages) min. cal ages	Lab. No.	Reference
Georgia and South Carolina Piedmont/Ridge and Valley (cont.)					
9MO487		1515 ± 87	A.D. 427 (543, 552, 557) 643	UGa 6262	Rogers et al. 1991:54
9GE10	Cold Springs	1505 ± 55	A.D. 439 (545, 560) 639	UGa 2364	Fish and Jefferies 1983:71
9HY39		1510 ± 50	A.D. 439 (544, 549, 558) 637	Beta 68672	R. Webb et al. 1994:358–361
9FY106		1540 ± 80	A.D. 425 (538) 617	Beta 76792	Cantley et al. 1997:250–251
9GE10	Cold Springs	1550 ± 65	A.D. 422 (536) 602	UGa 225	Caldwell 1971; cited in Fish and Jefferies 1983:71
9BR2/663	Leake	1590 ± 60	A.D. 411 (433) 540	Beta 109499	Pluckhahn 1998:125
9FY116		1590 ± 50	A.D. 416 (433) 538	Beta 76794	Cantley et al. 1997:342
9MO487		1609 ± 48	A.D. 394 (428) 537	UGa 6261	Rogers et al. 1991:54
9DA91	Miner's Creek	1620 ± 60	A.D. 387 (425) 534	Beta 41700	Chase 1991, 1998:54
9RO53	Chase	1650 ± 55	A.D. 342 (412) 432	Beta 72809	Stanyard and Stoops 1995:198, 217–220
9DA91	Miner's Creek	1720 ± 90	A.D. 235 (263, 275, 338) 422	Beta 41699	Chase 1991, 1998:54
9BR2/663	Leake	1790 ± 100	A.D. 90 (240) 383	Beta 109498	Pluckhahn 1998:127
9MG46	Little River	1840 ± 130	A.D. 27 (134, 159, 170, 196, 209) 377	Beta 13541	J. M. Williams and Shapiro 1990:146
38AN8	Simpson's Field	2030 ± 50	B.C. 109 (41, 25, 8, 3) A.D. 52	Beta 2625	Wood et al. 1986:105
9MG46	Little River	2050 ± 110	B.C. 200 (46) A.D. 72	Beta 13540	J. M. Williams and Shapiro 1990:146

* All calibrations based on Stuiver and Reimer (1993) CALIB program (File INCAL98.14c)

nr = not reported

Hartford mound site located on the middle Ocmulgee River in south-central Georgia (F. Snow and Stephenson 1998). Pottery at sites assigned to the Kolomoki phase (ca. A.D. 350–500) no longer exhibit notched or scalloped rims, but rather small folds along the vessel edge (Knight and Mistovich 1984:219–20). Additionally, vessel bases are flattened or slightly rounded without tetrapodal supports (Caldwell 1958:41). The final Swift Creek phase includes sites of the Quartermaster phase, estimated to date from circa A.D. 500 to 750 (Chase 1957, 1978b; Knight and Mistovich 1984:219–20). The pottery of this period exhibits zoned complicated-stamped designs along the waist of the vessel, wide folded rims, and both conical and flat bases (Caldwell 1958:41).

The Swift Creek tradition lasted for a period of at least 600 years, beginning about A.D. 150 and terminating around A.D. 800. In comparison with the estimated range for Ohio and Illinois Hopewell (100 B.C.–A.D. 400), it is evident that Swift Creek continued for centuries after the Hopewellian climax.

Santa Rosa–Swift Creek in Northwest Florida and Swift Creek in South Georgia

For northwest Florida, ninety-nine Santa Rosa–Swift Creek sites had been recorded in the state site files as of 1999. Much of this area has not been systematically surveyed and there are gaps in survey coverage and intensity, but several patterns or trends in the location of Santa Rosa–Swift Creek sites have been identified. The first is that there is a concentration of sites on the coastal strip; 87 percent of the sites are on or near the coast and only twelve small sites are in the interior. It thus appears that Middle Woodland populations were concentrated on the coastal strip and the interior was essentially vacant and used for special-purpose, short-term activities (Bense 1969, 1998; Milanich 1994; P. Thomas and Campbell [eds.] 1993).

A second pattern observed for Santa Rosa–Swift Creek sites is in their configuration. There are three types of midden configuration: ring middens (circular or rectangular middens and horseshoe or crescent-shaped middens), linear middens, and small midden dumps (Milanich 1994:144–45; Saunders 1998). Ring middens are large (about 100 meters in diameter), with well-formed rings, usually a meter or more high, and clean central plazas. Three Swift Creek ring middens and nine Santa Rosa–Swift Creek ring middens have been identified in northwest Florida (see Table 15.3).

In the 100 miles of coast from Panama City to Pensacola, eight site clusters have been identified (Bense 1969, 1998:260). In four of these, a ring midden is the central large settlement, and two have at least one associated burial mound. The one mound that was excavated by C. B. Moore (1902),

Table 15.3 — Selected Santa Rosa–Swift Creek and Swift Creek Village Midden Configurations in Southern Georgia and Northern Florida

Midden	Date	Mounds	Opening
Ring-Shaped Midden / Circular Midden:			
8BY74 (formerly 8BY10)	ca. A.D. 100–300	1	enclosed
8WA30	ca. A.D. 300–500	2	enclosed
8WL58 (Old Homestead)	ca. A.D. 150–450	none	enclosed
8BY26 (Baker's Landing)	ca. A.D. 150–450	none	enclosed
Rectangular Midden:			
8BY73	ca. A.D. 300–500	none	enclosed
Semicircular or Horseshoe-Shaped Midden:			
8WL36 (Horseshoe Bayou)	ca. A.D. 150–450	none	southwest
9EA1 (Kolomoki)	ca. A.D. 350–700	8	east
8SR8 (Third Gulf Breeze)	ca. A.D. 350–650	1	southeast
8SR986 (Bernath)	ca. A.D. 350–650	none	southwest
8CO17* (McKeithen)	ca. A.D. 350–475	3	northwest
9SE33 (Hare's Landing)	ca. A.D. 350–600	1	southwest (?)
9WL1 (Milamo)	ca. A.D. 400–600	2 (?)	nr
9MC360 (Cathead Creek)	ca. A.D. 400–600	none	nr
9CM171a (Kings Bay)	ca. A.D. 600	none	nr
9PU1 (Hartford)	ca. A.D. 300–600	2	southeast
nr (Torreya State Park)	ca. A.D. 750–950	none	nr
Linear or Centralized Midden:			
9SE14 (Fairchild's Landing)	ca. A.D. 350–500 and 600–900		
9CM185 (Mallard Creek)	ca. A.D. 600		

*nr = not reported; * Weeden Island period site*

Bense 1998; Bense and Watson 1977, 1979; Caldwell 1978:8, 45, fig. 7; Knight and Mistovich 1984:219–20; Milanich et al. 1984:80, 118, 198; Penton 1970; Pluckhahn 2000; R. Saunders 1986:29, 1998:162–63; Sears 1992:68–69; F. Snow and Stephenson 1990; P. Thomas and Campbell [eds.] 1993; Wayne 1987:59; Willey 1949b

Strange Bayou, contained several burials and Hopewellian prestige items. The midden rings on several of the sites have been excavated extensively, and all were composed of dense shell midden that had been formed into a well-shaped ridge. Often a few Hopewellian items are found in the refuse in the rings, such as the figurine fragments at the Third Gulf Breeze site (Phelps 1969). The plaza areas within the ring middens are well defined, and limited testing has indicated they are sterile. The ring middens were abandoned after the Santa Rosa–Swift Creek occupation, and nearby areas were occupied during the Late Swift Creek and Weeden Island periods.

Within the past two decades, investigations have been conducted at several crescent-shaped middens. At the Bernath site, the central plaza was not sterile, but contained numerous burials (Bense 1998). Seventeen burials were identified in 46 square meters, and, if these are representative, there could be 300-plus individuals buried in this plaza of 800-plus square meters. All but one of the individuals were flexed and these may represent secondary burials. The single nonflexed burial was of a particularly tall individual who was buried in the prone position facing east. No Hopewellian items were directly associated with the burials, but the interments were near the surface and had been disturbed somewhat by plowing. The midden ring is low, but well defined, and it is a black earth midden with refuse pits of shell midden (see Ruhl 2000 for botanical analyses of Bernath and related Swift Creek sites). There is no recorded burial mound near this site, but no survey has been conducted in the surrounding area to locate mounds. Like the other ring middens, Bernath was abandoned after the Santa Rosa–Swift Creek occupation and was not occupied again until the protohistoric period.

Testing at the Third Gulf Breeze site revealed that the ring midden was about a meter high and 95 meters in diameter (Doran and Piateck 1985; Willey 1949a). The plaza inside the midden arc is sterile. Interestingly, the shell midden extends outside the shell ring in the flats and is 50 to 75 centimeters thick with abundant cultural material. The midden eventually thins out between 50 and 80 meters from the ring. This midden "extension" may have served as the location of a special use or activity area. In fact, this surrounding midden contained ceramics and faunal material and it was high in phosphate content.

The Horseshoe Bayou site, on the south shore of Choctawhatchee Bay, was extensively excavated by P. Thomas and Campbell (1990, [eds.] 1993). The shell midden from the Santa Rosa–Swift Creek period was confined to the ring and a few elevated spots inside the ring, and the plaza is characterized as "swept clean." This shell midden was composed of discrete lenses of shells, with more than 330 features including trash pits, shell concentrations, hearths, and almost 200 postmolds. The overwhelming majority of the features were affiliated with the Santa Rosa–Swift Creek culture.

In contrast to the coastal adaptation of Santa Rosa–Swift Creek populations in northwest Florida are the riverine-oriented Late Swift Creek groups of interior south Georgia. A nine-year survey in the Ocmulgee Big Bend region of south Georgia revealed the near absence of sites with Early Swift Creek pottery (F. Snow 1977a:21, 1977b). This situation is attributed to the continuance of a check-stamped pottery tradition into the fourth or fifth centuries A.D. In contrast, Middle and Late Swift Creek ceramics, often along with trace amounts of Weeden Island pottery, have been located on 128 sites in the Big Bend region (F. Snow 1977a:21–22, 1977b). Although few of these sites have been tested, on the basis of surface collection density and diversity most appear as small, seasonal resource extraction sites, with several serving as central or base sites. These sites are usually located in proximity to the floodplain where a stream flows into the river, or in the floodplain on topographically high, relict sand-body landforms.

Site configuration, unfortunately, remains undefined at most of these sites; perhaps many have circular or horseshoe-shaped middens such as those described for northwest Florida. Several horseshoe-shaped middens have been described for south Georgia (see Table 15.3), such as at Kolomoki (Sears 1956a, 1992), the Kings Bay site along the Atlantic coast (R. Saunders 1986, 1998; R. Saunders et al. 1985), and the Hartford site in the Ocmulgee Big Bend region (F. Snow and Stephenson 1990). The Hartford site is a small ring midden delineated on the basis of discrete shell middens that form an arc around a central "plaza" area that opens to the southeast. Excavation has demonstrated that these shell middens were formed through refuse deposition onto the ground surface, rather than in abandoned storage pits. These midden dumps may represent the disposal activity of individual households. Given the absence of a well-formed ring midden, it appears that the site was of short duration.

Variation in site structure among Swift Creek communities indicates that material deposits often conform to a patterned configuration of horseshoe-shaped or enclosed circular middens (e.g., Milanich 1994:144; Milanich and Fairbanks 1980:118). This form of site patterning also has been recognized at Weeden Island sites such as McKeithen (Milanich et al. 1984:53–54) and Aspalaga (Milanich and Fairbanks 1980:126). These ring-shaped middens presumably reflect a similarly arranged community plan, with house structures enclosing a "plaza" or public, communal area. Within these communities, burials were placed in mounds that are often present and, when there is not a mound, within the plaza space. Most likely the villages were occupied on an annual basis by populations that dispersed periodically to special-use, resource-procurement camps, represented by smaller, ephemeral sites (e.g., Milanich 1994:145). Ring midden sites show continuity from the preceding Archaic period and possibly interior Georgia, Deptford-related check-stamped pottery traditions whose populations also inhabited circular structured villages.

Although a number of ring midden sites have been identified, little excavation has been conducted. Information obtained to date provides cursory descriptions of the elements of these constructed environments. Ring middens, whether horseshoe-shaped or an enclosed circle, often are defined by midden containing shell, either in the form of a continuous, raised midden ridge, with some ridges a meter in height, or separate, midden refuse dumps that probably represent individual structures. Ring middens most likely formed through the disposal of refuse in proximity to individual structures. Additionally, ritual cleaning of the plaza area most certainly contributed to the formation of ring middens. Excavation adjacent to and into these ring midden areas has revealed postmolds, which are often quite numerous, but no discernible architectural patterns have been noted. At both the Hartford and Kolomoki sites burned daub has been noted, suggesting that some of these structures may have been substantial (Stephenson and Snow 1993; Trowell 1998:39–40). Refuse-filled storage and cooking pits also have been noted in the middens of certain sites. The open ends of horseshoe-shaped middens do not conform to any particular pattern of orientation. Ring midden plaza areas are for the most part devoid of refuse, indicating that any communal, ritual activities occurring in this area left little debris. If debris was generated by plaza-related activities, then plaza maintenance must have followed any ritual use.

In contrast to the structured, non-mound Swift Creek ring midden sites of northwest Florida are those sites in southern and central Georgia deemed civic-ceremonial mortuary centers (*sensu* B. D. Smith 1992c:209–13). Of the nine Swift Creek ceremonial centers in Table 15.4, most are multimound complexes located in the valley basins of major waterways. All have been subjected to some degree of archaeological excavation, with intensive investigations conducted at Mandeville (Kellar et al. 1961, 1962a, 1962b), Hartford (F. Snow and Stephenson 1998), and Kolomoki (Sears 1956a, 1992;

Table 15.4 — Selected Swift Creek Civic-Ceremonial Mound Centers in Georgia

Site	*Date*	*Mounds Present*
Mandeville (9CY1)	ca. A.D. 1–250	2
Little River (9MG46)	ca. A.D. 200–400	2
Fortson Mound (9WS2)	ca. A.D. 200–400	1
Cold Springs (9GE10)	ca. A.D. 290–445	2
Hartford (9PU1)	ca. A.D. 300–450	2
Kolomoki (9EA1)	ca. A.D. 350–700	8
Milamo (9WL1)	ca. A.D. 400–600	1
Evelyn (9GN92)	ca. A.D. 400–600	4
Swift Creek (9BI3)	ca. A.D. 500–750	1

Pluckhahn 2000). Anderson (1998:279) suggests that these civic-ceremo-nial centers were strategically located along routes by which commodities, particularly marine shell, could pass from Gulf coastal extraction sites to the interior and beyond. Supporting evidence for cultural complexity and hence more elaborate trade mechanisms along the Gulf Coast as opposed to the Atlantic region is provided through comparative subsistence studies by J. Byrd (1997). Additionally, Anderson (1998) suggests that public consump-tion/feasting behavior of aggregated groups at such sites probably can be attributed to the competitive display of wealth between individuals and lin-eages of this more or less egalitarian society.

Complementing the focus on Swift Creek site types and settlement pat-terning is a research concentration on ceramic design elements and design motifs (Broyles 1968; T. Rudolph 1985, 1986, 1991; R. Saunders 1986, 1998; F. Snow 1998) in addition to studies focusing on the temporal variation of vessel rim forms (Mathews 1998; Moore 1901b; Willey 1949a) and Swift Creek Plain pottery (K. Smith 1999). Building on the pioneering effort of Broyles (1968), design analyses have focused on the reconstruction of com-plete design motifs from sherds with the ultimate objective of exploring social interaction spheres and possibly cosmology. In particular, Frankie Snow's (1975, 1977a:21–31, 1977b, 1992a, 1992b, 1994, 1998) reconstruc-tions from sherds in southern Georgia are accumulating in a database con-sisting of hundreds of different partial and complete paddle-stamped de-signs (Figure 15.5). The fact that variation exists among Swift Creek de-signs such that no two are identical becomes evident in the process of re-cording idiosyncratic "signatures" of individual designs. This results in re-covered design data that often exhibit at least one of several possible signa-ture types. Design signatures include paddle flaws such as a wood crack pattern; line anomalies caused by a paddle carver's error; design relief or topography variations due to differences in the depth to which a design was etched into the paddle; or line size sequence changes and design element attrition caused by a fragment of the wooden paddle breaking away. These incidental design attributes are not relevant to the composition of the design and would not have been replicated by an individual attempting to copy a preexisting design. Although the noted use of similar design elements re-sulted in various renditions of particular configurations, no clear examples of design copying were documented in Snow's work.

Swift Creek paddle design reconstruction studies have been employed to address questions of social interaction for both site-specific and regional perspectives. Rebecca Saunders (1986, 1998) has applied quantitative de-sign analysis at the Kings Bay site on the southern Georgia coast to explore mechanisms regarding the social organization of pottery production. Her

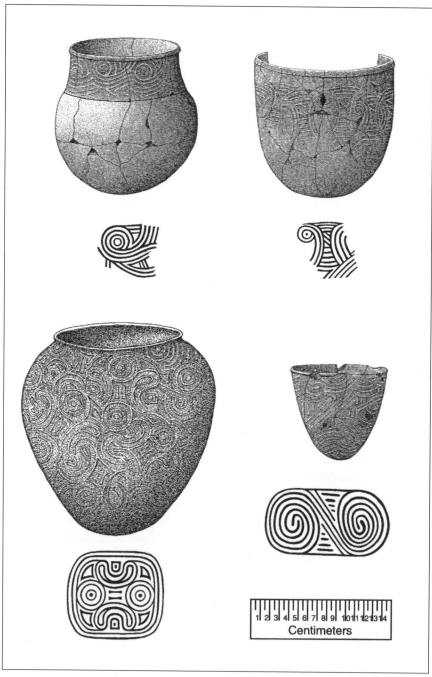

Figure 15.5 — Examples of Swift Creek vessels and reconstructed complicated stamped designs. Vessel on lower right from 9PU1; remaining vessels from 9CM233 (copyright © Frankie Snow)

analysis suggested that paddles were manufactured solely by specialists, as opposed to production at the individual household level. Implications regarding sitewide patterning in design variation revealed certain restricted distributions that might indicate lineal affiliation of clans or moieties. Intersite comparison of sherd assemblages between Kings Bay and the nearby Mallard Creek site indicates that the same population alternately occupied both locations most likely on a seasonal basis. A difference in intrasite settlement structure between the sites serves as indirect evidence for variation in site-use function (R. Saunders 1998:177).

At the regional level, analyses have revealed a wide distribution of Swift Creek pottery design contacts throughout northwestern Florida and the Georgia Coastal Plain and even into the Piedmont (Giles 2001; F. Snow 1975, 1977a:21–31, 1977b, 1992a, 1992b, 1994, 1998; F. Snow and Stephenson 1998; Trowell 1992). Moreover, Swift Creek Complicated Stamped pottery has been recovered in appreciable quantities at locations well outside its traditional area such as the Pinson Mounds site in western Tennessee (Mainfort 1986, 1988a, 1988c, 1999a), the Seip and Turner sites in Ohio (Prufer 1968:14; Rein 1974), and the Mann site in southwestern Indiana (Anderson 1998:280; Elliott 1998:26; Kellar 1979; Ruby 1997). To explore social mechanisms prompting this distribution of ceramic designs, researchers conducted compositional analyses involving sherd samples and local clay sources to determine whether this widespread distribution represents movement of the actual pottery or rather of the paddles used in creating stamped designs (Mainfort et al. 1997; B. A. Smith 1998; Stoltman and Snow 1998). The results of distributional analysis for the Georgia Coastal Plain led Stoltman and Snow (1998:153) to conclude that paddles primarily circulated among Swift Creek communities probably through social mechanisms such as marriage and residential mobility. Neutron activation analysis of Swift Creek sherds from Pinson Mounds suggests that all pottery was manufactured locally, countering previous ideas for long-distance importation of pottery from Georgia (Mainfort 1986, 1988a, 1988c), though Stoltman and Mainfort (1999a) dispute this conclusion based on petrographic analysis. Farther afield at the Mann site in Indiana, Kellar (1979) recovered complicated stamped pottery of the "Southeastern Series" from Hopewell period contexts. Ceramic studies show that the Early Swift Creek assemblage (referred to as Mann Complicated Stamped by Rein [1974]) was produced from a local, clay-tempered paste (Elliott 1998:26; Kellar 1979:103; Ruby 1997). Broyles (1968:52) noted that designs shown in photographs of pottery from the Mann site appeared identical to designs from the Early Swift Creek site at Mandeville in southwestern Georgia (B. A. Smith 1998:113). In a detailed analysis of almost 1000 sherds from the Mann site Southeastern Series assemblage, Rein (1974) found close similarities in design configurations to those of Early Swift Creek from Georgia, with at least three being identical (Ruby and Shriner 2000:6). The implications of these studies generally strengthen hypotheses for the movement of paddles, possibly as a result of trade, but more likely through the social processes promoting individual or group mobility. The sustained use of technical analyses coupled with intersite design contact studies will continue to shed light on the agencies responsible for the production and distribution of Swift Creek pottery and ultimately the spatial-temporal aspects of Swift Creek settlement systems.

Conclusions

Research on the Woodland Period Deptford and Swift Creek "cultures" in Georgia and Florida has increased in sophistication since the Depression-era recognition of these archaeological manifestations. Deptford and Swift Creek are best differentiated by their respective ceramic types. Deptford assemblages primarily include variations on check-stamped patterns as well as simple-stamped and cord-marked decorations whereas Swift Creek is recognized by elaborately applied complicated-stamped designs. The Deptford period precedes that of Swift Creek with evidence of temporal overlap in the form of ceramic co-occurrence at several sites in the lower Atlantic and Gulf Coastal Plains. Spatially, Deptford traditionally has been restricted to the coastal zones of South Carolina, Georgia, and northwest Florida with limited seasonal habitation in the lower interior river valleys. Research since the mid-1970s, however, has demonstrated that Deptford settlement is more widespread and permanent in the interior Atlantic Coastal Plain of South Carolina and Georgia. Debate surrounds the concept of Deptford occupation in the interior Georgia Coastal Plain in light of the north Georgia Cartersville Check Stamp ceramics found in appreciable numbers at sites in this area. This controversy will approach resolution not through ceramic typology semantics, but rather as archaeologists gain a better understanding of interior adaptation and settlement systems and the relationship to coastally oriented groups. Further work should incorporate settlement-specific structure and function studies.

The most promising heuristic for Swift Creek research is the coupling of technical analyses such as neutron activation and distributional studies with intersite design-contact evaluations. Swift Creek paddle-stamp design iconography has the potential to inform along multidimensional scales. Besides providing information relating to temporal and spatial concerns, design data can be employed in investigations of the social meaning of the designs used on the pottery. Thus, ceramic design analysis offers a means for reconstructing contemporaneous settlement patterns and social interaction networks over a broad area. Additionally, particular sets of designs may convey social meaning through association with particular social units such as lineages, clans, or moieties. Given that this association can be demonstrated quantitatively as well as qualitatively through technical and design analyses, the movement of information, goods, or people can be traced spatially and temporally. These and other avenues of archaeological inquiry will carry Woodland research toward a better understanding of the Deptford and Swift Creek manifestations of two millennia ago.

Acknowledgments

We thank the editors, David G. Anderson and Robert C. Mainfort, Jr., and two anonymous reviewers for their useful suggestions on earlier versions of this chapter. Additionally, we appreciate Virginia Horak's efforts in formatting the final version of the manuscript. We also express our gratitude to New South Associates, Prentice Thomas and Associates, Brockington and Associates, Southeastern Archeological Services, and TRC Garrow Associates, who generously provided reports of subject material. We especially thank Janice Campbell, Leslie Raymer, Charles Cantley, Johannes Loubser, Connie Huddleston, Chad Braley, and Dean Wood, all of whom patiently supplied specific information particularly regarding radiocarbon information.

Chapter 16

Weeden Island Cultures

Jerald T. Milanich

Weeden Island takes its name from an archaeological site on Weedon Island on the west side of Old Tampa Bay in Pinellas County, Florida, excavated by J. Walter Fewkes of the Smithsonian Institution in 1923–1924 (Fewkes 1924). Today the island, a nature preserve, retains the *Weedon* appellation, leading local residents to believe archaeologists cannot spell.

The region of the Weeden Island cultures is from Mobile Bay east to the Okefenokee Swamp, extending north into the Coastal Plain of southeast Alabama and southern Georgia. Perhaps the most famous Weeden Island site, Kolomoki, is east of the Chattahoochee River near Blakely, Georgia (see Sears 1956a). Southward, sites extend through northern Florida and down the Gulf of Mexico coast as far as Manatee and Sarasota counties just below Tampa Bay (Figure 16.1). Within that relatively large region Weeden Island cultures date within the period A.D. 200/300–1000 (for a discussion of Weeden Island chronologies see Milanich et al. 1997:10–16, 185–87).

As with other archaeological cultures in the southeastern United States, the notion of Weeden Island is closely tied to a ceramic complex first recognized in the early twentieth century (Holmes 1903:104–14, 125–28; Moore 1900, 1901b, 1902, 1903a, 1903b, 1905b, 1907, 1918) and formally defined in the 1940s (Willey 1945, 1949b; Willey and Woodbury 1942). But even from its inception archaeologists have sought to move beyond ceramic taxonomies and chronology and focus on questions of social and political structure, economic adaptations, settlement systems, and other aspects of the Weeden Island culture(s). Such studies (e.g., Brose and Percy 1974; G. Johnson 1985; G. Johnson and Kohler 1987; Kohler 1978, 1980; Milanich 1994:155–241; Milanich et al. 1997; Percy and Brose 1974; Sears 1952, 1954, 1958, 1961, 1962b, 1968; Sigler-Lavelle 1980a, 1980b; Steinen 1976, 1977, 1989, 1998; Willey 1949b:396–452, 537–49) have led to the recognition of regional Weeden Island cultures that, though apparently sharing aspects of sociopolitical structure and religion, maintained somewhat distinct environmental adaptations and exhibited other variations. Such a phenomenon is not uncommon in the Southeast where venerable taxonomies based

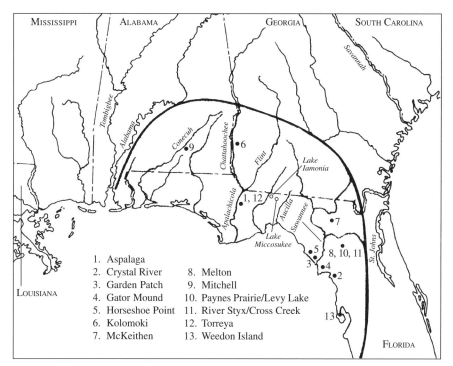

Figure 16.1 — Region of the Weeden Island cultures

on ceramic typologies are being stretched and reworked in the face of new data. A prime example of the latter, one closely tied to Weeden Island, is the Swift Creek culture (see J. M. Williams and Elliott [eds.] 1998; Stephenson et al., this volume).

The antecedents of the Weeden Island culture lie in the Swift Creek and Deptford cultures of northern Florida and southern Georgia. West and north of the Aucilla River there is considerable overlap between Swift Creek and Weeden Island settlements and ceramic inventories. East of the Aucilla River in north peninsular Florida Weeden Island is chronologically preceded by the Deptford culture. Seemingly, however, there is little overlap in Deptford and Weeden Island ceramic assemblages or site types or locations in that latter region.

Over time, descendants of the various Weeden Island cultures exhibited different evolutionary trajectories; some became Mississippian cultures, while others did not (Figure 16.2; for a short discussion of the taxonomic problems inherent in such a chart, see Milanich 1994:205–7). With its variations, Weeden Island has much to suggest to us regarding other contemporary Woodland cultures and the development of Mississippian societies.

In this chapter a short overview of the basic links between ceramics and Weeden Island chronological and cultural contexts is offered. Then several of the regional Weeden Island cultures are compared and the explanations posited by archaeologists for their similarities and differences are explored.

Pottery Types and Early Weeden Island Studies

Archaeologist Gordon R. Willey, a founding father of the Weeden Island culture (Willey 1945, 1949b; Willey and Woodbury 1942), divided its temporal range into two periods, largely on the basis of data from northwest Florida. The earlier, Weeden Island I (which I will at times refer to as the early Weeden Island period), is characterized by the presence of Swift Creek–related types of complicated-stamped pottery and Weeden Island punctated, incised, and plain ceramic types, including ornate and stylized designs and animal effigy vessels (Figures 16.3 and 16.4). The Weeden Island I period is thought to date from A.D. 200/300 to 750, though available dates suggest temporal variations in the appearance of Weeden Island ceramics across the

	NW Panhandle		North Peninsula		Peninsular Gulf Coast	
	Western	*Eastern*	*North*	*North-Central*	*Greater Tampa Bay*	*North Coast*
A.D. 1250	Pensacola	Ft. Walton				
A.D. 1000	Ft. Walton	Ft.Walton			Safety Harbor	
A.D. 750	Weeden Island II	Wakulla	Suwannee Valley		Weeden Island II variant	Weeden Island II variant
A.D. 600				Alacua		
A.D. 300	Weeden Island I	Weeden Island I				Weeden Island I
A.D. 100	Santa Rosa– Swift Creek	Swift Creek	McKeithen Weeden Island	Cades Pond		variant
500 B.C.	Deptford	Deptford	Deptford	Deptford	Manasota	Deptford

Figure 16.2 — Culture sequences in the Florida Weeden Island region, post–500 B.C.

*Figure 16.3 (right) —
Weeden Island Plain pedes-
talled effigy vessel excavated
by William H. Sears from
Mound D at the Kolomoki
site (height 34 centimeters)
(courtesy Florida Museum of
Natural History)*

*Figure 16.4 (below) —
Weeden Island Incised globular bowl with a unique wing-
nut shape and two stylized
spoonbill bird motifs from
Mound C at the McKeithen
site (mouth diameter is 13 by
15 centimeters) (courtesy
Florida Museum of Natural
History)*

region of Weeden Island cultures; for instance, compare the dates for the pre–Weeden Island Swift Creek culture in northwest Florida (Bense 1998:252–53). The Weeden Island II period assemblage (dated to A.D. 750–900/1000; the late Weeden Island period) is characterized by a decrease in popularity of complicated-stamped pottery, the presence of a new type—Wakulla Check Stamped—and a decrease in frequency of earlier Weeden Island punctated and incised types, especially elaborated designs and vessels. At Weeden Island II period sites in northern Florida and adjacent portions of Georgia and Alabama, a region referred to as the Weeden Island heartland, the most prevalent ceramics at village sites are simple bowls with check-stamped surfaces.

As archaeologists gathered new data, building on Willey's original taxonomy, it became obvious that other ceramic variations existed within the archaeological record of the Weeden Island cultures. Changes in ceramic assemblages not only occurred over time, but in space as well. For instance, Weeden Island punctated and incised ceramics typical of village sites in the heartland region in the Weeden Island I period are not found in peninsular Florida village sites. In the latter, village ceramics are almost entirely undecorated.

In the past, these regional ceramic variations have led to confusion. When Fewkes excavated the mound on Weedon Island in Old Tampa Bay, at the site that would give its name to the culture, he observed the ceramics in the mound were indeed types like those found in mounds and villages in the Weeden Island heartland region excavated earlier by Clarence B. Moore. But Fewkes also noted the ceramics in the shell midden near his mound were almost all plainware. From his report (Fewkes 1924), it is clear he was puzzled by this; nowhere does he equate the people who lived in the village and made plain pottery with the people who built the mound and were associated with Weeden Island pottery. He could not reconcile the presence of one ceramic assemblage in the mound and another in the village.

Later researchers also would be puzzled by similar intrasite ceramic variations at Weeden Island sites elsewhere in peninsular Florida, which resulted in erroneous ceramic-based cultural chronologies. For instance, in north-central Florida John Goggin placed Weeden Island–period village sites associated with plain pottery in the pre–Cades Pond period while the associated mounds with their Weeden Island vessels were assigned to the succeeding Cades Pond period (Goggin 1948:58, 1949:16, 19, 25, 35, 1950:10).

It would be William H. Sears who freed archaeologists from our constricting ceramic-based taxonomies that did not adequately take into account the ceramic-type variations within Weeden Island culture. In 1973 he published a paper on what he called the sacred-secular dichotomy. "Sacred"

vessels and artifacts found in ceremonial contexts—for example, mounds—
were not like those found in "secular" contexts—for example, villages. At
least as far as archaeologists can observe, it appears that many religious
activities took place apart from more mundane activities, those associated
with aspects of everyday life. Though archaeologists believe the human behavior reflected in Sears's model is more complex than a simple dichotomy
(Milanich et al. 1997:69, 125–26, 196), recognition of the sacred-secular phenomenon has helped clarify definition of individual Weeden Island cultures.
Still other variations within ceramic assemblages existed among Weeden
Island II cultures. Some of these are pointed out below in this chapter.

Weeden Island Cultures: Variations on a Theme

Despite the differences in Weeden Island I village ceramic assemblages, a
single, similar ceramic assemblage is found in early Weeden Island period
mounds across the entire Weeden Island region. For instance, individual
vessels from mounds at the Kolomoki site are almost indistinguishable from
vessels from mounds excavated by Clarence B. Moore in the Florida panhandle, the type site on the Florida central Gulf coast investigated by Fewkes,
the McKeithen site in north Florida, and the Crystal River site on the northern peninsular Gulf coast of Florida (also excavated by Moore). The ceremonial programs reflected in mound construction and the patterns of deposition of artifacts and human interments also share many similarities. But, as
noted above, though great similarities exist in mound-related ceramics and
activities among early Weeden Island cultures, differences among other aspects of those same cultures are apparent. Models explaining Weeden Island
cultural variations in time and space are relevant to our understanding of the
processes of evolution of pre-Columbian societies in the Southeast. Let us
now examine some of these variations, an endeavor hindered somewhat by
a lack of comparable data from all Weeden Island cultures. The available
data sets are not always comparable, with, for instance, better subsistence
information gathered in one region and better contextual information from
mounds in another region.

Early Weeden Island Cultures in
Northwest and North Peninsular Florida

Northwest Florida, the panhandle west of the Aucilla River, was the region
in which Gordon Willey first surveyed coastal Weeden Island sites in the
1940s. Along the coast of that region there is great continuity in settlement
locations between the earlier Santa Rosa–Swift Creek and Swift Creek sites

and Weeden Island I sites, though the latter are more numerous. It seems certain that these cultures practiced very similar economic adaptations, not surprisingly considering the availability of coastal resources and the desire to live in prime locations for collecting those resources.

In northwest Florida Weeden Island I coastal shell middens are found on barrier islands as well as on the adjacent mainland, usually close to freshwater sources and not far from the ecologically rich salt marsh and shallow inshore waters. As George Percy and David Brose (1974:19) have noted:

> *Although there are some exceptions, most sites do not front on open Gulf waters. Instead they tend to be concentrated on estuaries, lagoons, sounds, and small saltwater bays or coves which are relatively sheltered....[S]ites are located near a freshwater source...not more than several hundred feet from brackish or salt water, and...tidal marsh is usually near at hand.*

Such middens—dominated by combinations of oyster shells, *Rangia* clams, other shellfish, and fish bones—most likely are locations where fishing and shellfish collecting were important economic activities (Percy and Brose 1974:20).

In northwest Florida early Weeden Island sites also are found back from the coast in forested locales, but still in easy walking distance of the coast proper. These sites, most often annular middens, are thought to have been villages, and they may articulate with the special-use shelling and fishing middens nearer the coast. Like the coastal middens, many of these annular middens feature both Weeden Island I and Santa Rosa–Swift Creek or Swift Creek components (with considerable overlap).

In the interior of the eastern panhandle (east of the Apalachicola River) what are thought to be village sites first began to appear in locales well away from the coast in late Deptford and Swift Creek times, increasing in number during the Weeden Island I period. Again there is overlap between Swift Creek and early Weeden Island components in sites (Percy and Brose 1974:28). In his survey of Leon County, Florida, Louis Tesar (1980:604–6) documented clusters of Weeden Island sites around Lake Miccosukee and Lake Iamonia. I believe these site clusters, also present in the McKeithen Weeden Island and Cades Pond region, represent the continued occupation of the ecologically more productive locales by growing populations. As villages became too large to function efficiently, new villages budded off and at times older villages also were abandoned. Over time, this process resulted in clusters of villages across the landscape. It is tempting to speculate that each cluster represents an individual ethnic group whose members, though consisting of different lineages, shared an identity based in part on a common history.

Mounds, especially burial mounds, are a component of the northwest Florida early Weeden Island culture. Although village sites with a single mound are most common, several sites with multiple mounds are known. Many mounds contain both Swift Creek and Weeden Island pottery. The Swift Creek–Weeden Island I cultural continuum also is apparent at the Kolomoki site (Sears 1956a; Steinen 1998).

Immediately to the east of northwest Florida in north interior peninsular Florida (referred to here as north Florida) there does not appear to be a developmental continuum of early Weeden Island McKeithen culture out of the Swift Creek culture; there is no evidence for Swift Creek village sites east of the Aucilla River in north Florida. (There are some Swift Creek sites in extreme northeast Florida, an apparent southern extension of Georgia coastal late Swift Creek populations; see Ashley 1998.) Instead, there appears to be a relatively small Deptford occupation of the region followed by a significant early Weeden Island occupation. The latter represents either rapid population growth or the actual movement of Weeden Island peoples into what was not a heavily occupied region, or some combination of both explanations.

Named for a site in Columbia County, the McKeithen (early) Weeden Island culture villages and the associated archaeological assemblage have been well described (Milanich et al. 1997) and, as far as can be determined, are like those of the early Weeden Island period in the interior eastern panhandle. McKeithen Weeden Island sites occur in the largest numbers in the Middle Florida Hammock Belt, a higher, forested region that extends in a north-south direction through north peninsular Florida. Site types noted in field surveys include (1) villages; (2) villages with a burial mound; (3) village(s) without mounds but within 3 miles of a village with one or more mounds; (4) mound-village complexes, consisting of a village with two or more mounds; (5) isolated burial mounds (though it may be villages associated with these mounds were destroyed by modern development); and (6) special-use sites used as hunting camps, lithic quarries, or the like.

Villages were nucleated settlements, and, as in northwest Florida, village middens often are annular or horseshoe-shaped. Clusters of sites occur, also as in the panhandle, and again each probably represents a community that shared social and ceremonial ties, most likely mound building and burial activities.

Each McKeithen village is near a permanent freshwater source and all are located in mesic hammocks and within 0.5 mile of freshwater aquatic habitats, including ponds, small lakes, creeks, wet prairies or marshes, and swamps. Because this array of habitats blankets the hammock belt region of north Florida like a patchwork quilt, village locations provided residents easy access to the total range of habitat diversity.

Brenda Sigler-Lavelle (1980a, 1980b) has modeled this settlement system (and see Milanich et al. 1997:41–43, 187–89), suggesting that each village contained households that formed an interacting community bound by kinship and other social and ideological practices. As in northwest Florida, older villages budded off new villages as populations increased, resulting in clusters of villages in each of which people shared a common identity, one most likely reflected in kinship ties and social and ideological symbols and behavior.

Lineage or other kinship ties were manifested in mound burial, an explanation that holds for the northwest Florida early Weeden Island culture as well. Residents of village clusters or individual villages who shared kin ties likely were interred in that kin group's burial mound. Excavations at the McKeithen site and other sites suggest a charnel house was used to store bodies of deceased relatives before the cleaned skeletal elements were interred as bundled burials in sand mounds. At least some of the time, the charnel structure was built on a low platform mound.

At an appropriate time, the charnel house was emptied, the structure itself torn down or burned, and the human remains laid out on clean sand deposited on the same mound. Specially made ceramics used in burial (and other?) rites were also placed on the clean surface of the platform mound. Then bodies and ceramics were ritually buried under an additional sand layer. The result was a burial mound with a ceramic cache, a permanent monument, one closely tied to deceased lineage members. Sometimes this process was repeated, resulting in a burial mound with more than one layer of interments. Use of lineage charnel houses and mounds served to centralize rituals and other activities associated with burial and other ceremonies, activities presided over by religious specialists. The specialists were associated with symbols and paraphernalia, perhaps including the ceramic vessels found in mounds.

All lineages and villages were not equal in status. Within a cluster of villages, a single village or kin group might achieve higher status because of increased relative access to resources. Such an economic advantage offered that village and one or more of its kin groups an advantage in community-wide activities, such as sponsoring feasts or ceremonies, endeavors that gained higher social position. It might be that such a village was the location where burial activities occurred and a mound was erected.

Such an important village-mound complex might become a center not only for burial and communal religious activities, but also for other types of intervillage or interlineage exchange. Within that center the religious specialist(s) achieved higher social status, that of a headman or "big-man" (an anthropological term [Sahlins 1963]; at the McKeithen site at least one of the religious leaders was a woman). Such political structure might also be viewed as a "proto-chiefdom."

The importance of a Weeden Island village-mound center and its leader must have risen or fallen as economic fortunes waxed and waned. Because early Weeden Island peoples were not agriculturists, the ability of a village-mound center to maintain its competitive edge depended on its ability to successfully exploit local resources. Over time, as populations grew and locale resources were overutilized, that productive advantage declined, resulting in a loss of status and a decline in that center's importance as a focus of intervillage or interlineage exchange and communal activities. Big-man/religious leaders came and went.

In their heyday, the more important village-mound centers became elaborated symbols of wealth and status. Perhaps the best known example is the Kolomoki site with its multiple mounds, some used for burial and some perhaps platforms for structures (though as Steinen [1998] has pointed out, the McKeithen settlement pattern differs from that of the Kolomoki region where Kolomoki seems to exist in isolation without nearby, related late Swift Creek or early Weeden Island sites).

The McKeithen site with its three mounds is another example of a village-mound complex, as are the Aspalaga site in Gadsden County, Florida (Moore 1903a:481–88); Crystal River in Citrus County, Florida (Milanich 1999); and, perhaps, the Mitchell site in Covington County, Alabama (Sears n.d.). The three mounds at the McKeithen site were all excavated. One proved to be a charnel house platform mound later used as a burial mound; the second a platform mound thought to have been used for charnel activities; and the third a platform mound for the house of a religious leader/big-man, later serving as a tomb for that individual. Each of these resembles other early Weeden Island mounds at the Kolomoki site as well as mounds excavated by Moore in northwest Florida.

The same settlement-sociopolitical system modeled for the McKeithen Weeden Island region probably was present throughout the entire region of Weeden Island cultures from late Deptford times through the early Weeden Island period. It would not be surprising if it were present elsewhere in the Southeast in the Woodland period.

Late Weeden Island Cultures in Northwest and North Florida
In the eastern panhandle of Florida, including along the coast and in the interior, the late Weeden Island Wakulla culture developed after about A.D.

750 out of the Weeden Island I culture described above. Wakulla sites also are distributed in the Chattahoochee–Flint River drainage in Georgia and adjacent portions of Alabama (Dickens 1971; Jeter 1977; A. Kelly 1953; Mikell 1993; Nance 1976; Percy and Jones 1976; Sears n.d.; Steinen 1976; Walthall 1980:167–71) in the same regions where early Weeden Island sites are found. But Wakulla sites with their distinctive check-stamped village pottery are not found east of the Aucilla River in north Florida, the region of the McKeithen Weeden Island culture. The evolutionary trajectories of northwest and north Florida that differed during the period of the Swift Creek and Santa Rosa–Swift Creek cultures again diverged after A.D. 750.

The appearance of the Wakulla culture in northwest Florida is marked by changes not only in the village ceramic assemblage, but in mound ceremonialism, settlement systems, and economic emphases as well. The earliest maize kernels found thus far in Florida are from a Wakulla site just east of the Apalachicola River (Milanich 1974).

Wakulla habitation sites tend to be many more in number, but much smaller in size and less nucleated than early Weeden Island sites in the same region and some occur in localities where earlier sites are not present (Percy and Jones 1976; Tesar 1980:600–604; N. White 1981:702). George Percy and David Brose (1974:31–32) have described this pattern:

> [T]here is a very significant increase in the number of sites; also, many sites are now established in the uplands bordering the east side of the upper Apalachicola [River]. These same basic trends— new site locations and many more sites—also appear to be characteristic of scattered localities throughout the Marianna Lowlands in central Jackson County and along the lower Chattahoochee and Flint rivers in southeastern Alabama and southwestern Georgia.

Such changes are thought to correlate with "a significantly greater dependence on agriculture" by small family groups (Percy and Brose 1974:74). Slash-and-burn maize agriculture is thought to have resulted in rapid soil exhaustion, requiring shifts in settlement locales. The long-term, nucleated villages and village-mound centers of early Weeden Island times were not possible, nor were the settlement stability and interlineage and village economic cooperation represented by sites like McKeithen and Aspalaga suited to Wakulla subsistence patterns. Instead there was increased competition by smaller groups for lands for agriculture.

These same trends are reflected in the pattern of Wakulla burial mounds. Special ceramics presumably associated with interlineage and intralineage and village ceremonies no longer were made. Wakulla mounds, though most likely associated with lineage interments, do not exhibit the ceremonial and social elaboration of the earlier Weeden Island cultures. Sometimes new mounds were not even built; instead people were interred in mounds built during earlier times.

Documented Wakulla sites include special-use, short-term camps, perhaps hunting camps, and dispersed villages or hamlets characterized by discrete midden deposits, probably from individual houses. At the Torreya State Park site, thirteen such house middens representing two distinct, overlapping periods of occupation were strung out in a crescent-shaped line around the spring heads of a small creek (Percy 1971). The best estimate of households occupied at any one time is five to seven. Small burial mounds were constructed near the dispersed villages.

By A.D. 1000 or slightly before, a growing Wakulla agricultural population had spread throughout northwest Florida; new social and political phenomena were needed to help deal with a time of relative social instability (Percy and Brose 1974:32). Interaction with other southeastern peoples and the opportunity—especially in some inland locales in northwest Florida—to intensify agricultural production eventually led to the Mississippian sociopolitical, settlement, and economic systems of the Fort Walton culture (J. Scarry 1990a, 1990b). The Apalachee Indians, organized as a paramount chiefdom occupying the region between the Aucilla and Ochlockonee rivers in Florida's eastern panhandle, are early colonial period descendants of the Fort Walton peoples.

While the Weeden Island cultures immediately west of the Aucilla River were on an evolutionary trajectory toward a Mississippian way of life, those east of that river developed somewhat differently. In the early sixteenth century, the same time the Mississippian Apalachee Indians who spoke a Muskhogean language occupied the Tallahassee Red Hills region of modern Leon and Jefferson counties in Florida, interior north Florida (the McKeithen Weeden Island region) was home to a number of Timucua language–speaking chiefdoms affiliated with a non–Mississippian-derived archaeological culture. What happened? Why did north and northwest Florida evolve differently after the early Weeden Island period?

As noted above, the post–A.D. 750 Wakulla culture of northwest Florida was not present in interior north peninsular Florida. In the latter region the early Weeden Island ceramic assemblage associated with the McKeithen culture was replaced by an assemblage called Suwannee Valley (Worth 1992). Suwannee Valley ceramics, though including some check-stamped ware, are quite distinct from the Wakulla assemblage, displaying a variety of surface-roughening techniques, including cord marking, cob marking (after A.D. 1250?), punctating, and brushing. The Suwannee Valley culture and its ceramic assemblage are present in north Florida until the onset of the mission period in the late sixteenth century (K. Johnson 1991; K. Johnson and Nelson 1990).

As with the Wakulla culture, the Suwannee Valley culture is associated with sociopolitical and settlement systems unlike those of the early Weeden Island period (Milanich 1994:348–53). Initially those post–A.D. 750 systems seem to be like their counterparts in the Wakulla culture; that is, when compared to early Weeden Island McKeithen sites, Suwannee Valley village sites are not nucleated and there are many more small sites, including small dispersed villages. Extensive field surveys by Kenneth Johnson and Bruce Nelson (K. Johnson 1986, 1987; K. Johnson and Nelson 1992; K. Johnson et al. 1988) have located several hundred of these hamlet sites as well as smaller sites, probably special-use camps. Also as in the Wakulla region, many sites occur in locales little occupied in the early Weeden Island period. Although it is thought these new patterns are associated with the appearance of maize agriculture, again as in the Wakulla region, that remains to be proven.

But even if maize agriculture were present in north Florida, after A.D. 1000 the Suwannee Valley culture did not evolve into a Mississippian culture. There are no Fort Walton sites in interior north Florida. There is no Mississippian-like site hierarchy nor is there a single truncated pyramidal mound or any archaeological evidence for a class of elite individuals (Milanich 1998). The Mississippian revolution never crossed the Aucilla River into north Florida.

Even so, there is some evidence of sociopolitical changes in the Suwannee Valley region after A.D. 1000–1250 (not substantiated by radiocarbon dates), changes thought to be reflective of increasing population size and the adoption of ideas from the adjacent Fort Walton Mississippian culture. Those changes include the reappearance of nucleated villages, an increase in mound construction, and an increase in corncob-impressed pottery (signaling an increase in the importance of maize agriculture?). Clusters of Suwannee Valley village sites also appear after that time. It is likely these changes herald the formation of small agricultural chiefdoms, the archaeological equivalent of the small Timucuan chiefdoms documented for the region in the early colonial period (Milanich 1996, 1998; Worth 1998).

Why did the Suwannee Valley culture not evolve into a Mississippian cultural system? Perhaps it would have if Pánfilo de Narváez, Hernando de Soto, and the Franciscan friars had not shown up in the sixteenth and seventeenth centuries. But even so, for a half millennium the late Suwannee Valley people lived adjacent to Fort Walton peoples and borrowed little from them. I believe the answer lies in the nature of the north Florida environment, which did not offer rich soil suitable for intensive, row farming. As a consequence, maize agriculture never became as important in north Florida as in the Fort Walton region. Ethnic, linguistic, and economic differences that arose in late Weeden Island times and coalesced with the Mississippian cultural revolution persisted for hundreds of years.

Peninsular Florida Gulf Coast

Environment in large part also was responsible for the nature of Weeden Island period cultures along the peninsular Florida Gulf coast, a region where true Mississippian cultures never developed either. The sharp-eyed reader will notice that I called these coastal cultures Weeden Island *period* cultures, not simply Weeden Island cultures. In the past (Milanich 1980) I struggled with an adequate taxonomy for referring to the Gulf coast cultures and those of north-central Florida, cultures that did place Weeden Island pottery in their mounds, but whose village ceramic assemblages do not at all resemble those of the Weeden Island heartland cultures (for that matter, is the Suwannee Valley culture a Weeden Island culture?). Such thinking could lead to some wild taxonomic revisionism. For instance, is the type site on Weedon Island near St. Petersburg, Florida, from which we derive the name Weeden Island a true Weeden Island site? I concluded the best way to handle the situation was by differentiating regional Weeden Island cultures using criteria other than only ceramic typologies, recognizing that the common taxonomic bond among Weeden Island cultures was Weeden Island pottery in mounds. Such criteria include settlement patterning, economic patterns, and physiographic parameters.

Certainly it is easy to envision similarities among the early Weeden Island people of Kolomoki, Aspalaga, and McKeithen in the heartland region who made their livings by hunting, gathering, foraging, fishing, and, perhaps, gardening. Those people also made Weeden Island ceramic vessels and put them in their mounds. The Weeden Island period people of the peninsular Gulf coast did all those same things, but in ways that were qualitatively different. Theirs was a way of life centered on the resources of the coastal salt marshes and tidal streams, the shallow inshore waters of the Gulf of Mexico, and the adjacent freshwater and forested habitats. They were coastal Weeden Island people.

While the acidic soils at many inland early Weeden Island sites in the heartland region have played havoc with attempts to gather samples of plant and animal remains suitable for reconstructing dietary trends, the shell middens of coastal Weeden Island period sites offer, quite literally, food for thought. Consequently, investigations along that coast have tended to focus on midden contents and questions of environmental use rather than on larger scale surveys that might shed light on settlement changes over time, an example of our having differing data sets with which to deal.

During the Weeden Island period the Florida Gulf coast from the mouth of the Aucilla River down past Tampa Bay was not a homogeneous cultural region; differences among Weeden Island period archaeological assemblages exist, though which of those differences may be temporal and which not is not always certain. And although we might think that it is not an overly long distance from the Aucilla River to the south end of Sarasota County, Florida—an airline distance of 220 miles—the actual amount of indented shoreline is about ten times that figure. The Gulf coast of peninsular Florida offers ample geographical opportunity for archaeological variation among its Weeden Island period cultures.

The coastal region environment also offers much more than only a coastline with salt marshes and shallow Gulf waters. Those marshes are fed by numerous small and large freshwater rivers and streams (e.g., Aucilla, Suwannee, Waccasassa, Withlacoochee, Crystal, Anclote, Hillsborough, Alafia, Little Manatee, Manatee, and Myakka rivers), some of which flow out of extensive interior wetlands, such as Gulf Hammock in Levy County, Chassahowitzka Swamp in Hernando County, and the Cove of the Withlacoochee in Citrus County.

Nina Thanz Borremans (1991) has penned this cogent description of the northern portion of the coastal region, one in which water predominates:

> [T]he north peninsular Gulf coast lies within the Gulf Coastal Lowlands province....Inland from the Gulf a series of old dune lines runs parallel to the coast and interrupts the gentle westward slope....The interior coastal mainland is a patchwork of upland hammocks and ridges and lowland wetlands, including sawgrass marshes, vast cypress and hardwood swamps, and bayheads....Unlike the rest of Florida, much of the north peninsular coastline has not been ditched, diked, graded, filled or otherwise altered by modern development, giving us a glimpse of what a soggy place the Gulf coast of Florida used to be.

Before being drained, buffered with artificial islands, and stripped of its marshes, the southern portion of the coast also was "a soggy place," one that offered its Weeden Island period inhabitants a veritable larder of saltwater and freshwater fish and shellfish along with plants and animals taken from adjacent dry land locales.

The coastal Weeden Island period populations developed out of earlier coastal dwellers, including a Deptford occupation that extended south along the peninsular coast as far as Cedar Keys. There are no coastal Swift Creek sites in the region, though Swift Creek pottery appears as a minority ware at some sites in Taylor County just south of the Aucilla River.

Two geographically overlapping ceramic wares predominate in early Weeden Island period coastal middens. Pasco limestone-tempered ware tends to predominate in the northern portion of the coast, while quartz (sand)-tempered pottery is most common farther south. The exact relative percentages of wares at a single site vary greatly, though no matter what the temper, 90-plus percent of the pottery in middens is undecorated.

Shell middens—in which oyster shells most often are the predominant mollusk—line the edges of salt marshes and estuaries. Many middens are linear, several hundred yards long, while others are amorphous in shape. Rarely are any more than 5 or 6 feet high (the localities around Cedar Keys and Tampa Bay are notable exceptions). Most archaeologists assume that the larger middens, some of which probably accumulated over hundreds of years, were associated with villages.

Not all sites are on the coast. What are presumed to be special-use camps are found in the interior pine flatwoods on higher ground near water sources and wetland habitats. Some of the special-use sites contain scatters of lithics and ceramics; others are probably lithic workshops (Hemmings 1975; Padgett 1976). More intensively occupied interior villages have been found inland near extensive wetlands, such as the Cove of the Withlacoochee and the Myakka River.

Early Weeden Island burial mounds are present on the coast, though at times they are found well away from the midden/habitation areas (e.g., Gator mound in Levy County [Jones and Borremans 1991:63–64]). Moore excavated in a number of early Weeden Island burial mounds along the coast from Taylor County south to Tampa Bay, including several that, like their northern counterparts, appear to be components of village-mound centers (for summaries of Moore's mound excavations and those by other early archaeologists, see Willey 1949b:301–30). Coastal centers excavated by Moore and others include Horseshoe Point, Garden Patch, and Crystal River, the latter a major center during the time from circa A.D. 200 to 400, from just prior to the Weeden Island I period into the time when Weeden Island ceramics were used in mound ceremonies (see Milanich 1999). Although this is not quantified, it is my impression that such multiple mound centers, as well as individual burial mounds, are more densely distributed in the coastal zone than in the interior woodlands of north and northwest Florida.

Certainly the Crystal River site with its shell middens, plaza, and mounds of shell and earth (including two burial mounds, one with a surrounding platform enclosed by a circular embankment), seems to be a nucleated village-mound center like McKeithen and other northern centers. Likewise, we might expect that the many Weeden Island mounds in the coastal region are indicative of the importance of kin-based social organization.

But the morphology of the coastal zone itself may have led to some differences between coastal societies and their Weeden Island counterparts to the north. Although it was an indented shoreline with islands, coves, bays, and such rather than a single linear shore, the coastal zone with its multiple biomes was only about 10 miles wide. At any one time within that relatively narrow band, coastal populations had to vie for access to the most economically productive locales: shellfish beds, fish runs, and the like. The location of the Crystal River site in an estuary setting in one of the few places hardwood hammocks (rather than the more common pine-scrub vegetative communities) extend to the coast proper must have been one such productive place early in the first millennium A.D.

Because the distribution of resources was more circumscribed than in the interior of north and northwest Florida, coastal villages could not simply bud off new villages. As a result, the distribution (and density?) of settlements was more circumscribed and cooperation was a necessity. On the coast kinship ties and intervillage and intravillage cooperation were even more of a necessity than among interior-dwelling early Weeden Island peoples.

Does this model fit with observed archaeological patterns on the coast? I believe that it does and that it is reflected in the (as yet unquantified) greater density of burial mounds—lineage monuments—and village-mound centers in the coastal zone. Multigenerational control of specific productive locales might be reflected by the continued use of some mounds that contain multiple burial strata.

Earlier I made the point that the peninsular Gulf coast was not a homogeneous region in terms of its archaeological assemblages. Archaeologists George Luer and Marion Almy (1982) have pointed out the great archaeological continuity in the region from Tampa Bay south through Sarasota County during the time from 500 B.C. to A.D. 700, including the time in which early Weeden Island ceramics were placed in burial mounds. They have assigned the name Manasota to that archaeological culture. Thus, according to the taxonomy I have employed here, for a short time, Manasota was a Weeden Island culture. Below in this chapter in the discussion of the Cades Pond culture we shall see a similar taxonomic quirk.

Before we turn to the Cades Pond culture we should briefly consider the post–early Weeden Island period history of the coastal region. Not surprisingly in view of the relative economic conservatism of coastal cultures we see no abrupt changes after A.D. 750. Although Early Weeden Island pottery vessels no longer find their way into mounds, the people continue to occupy the same locales, often depositing their midden on top of the shell middens of the early Weeden Island period peoples. Conservatism in village ceramic types, tools, and the tried-and-true technology used to successfully live in the coastal zone makes it difficult to tell an A.D. 500 occupation from one of A.D. 1000.

But changes did take place, probably beginning in the Tampa Bay region. The shoreline of Tampa Bay, including Hillsborough and Old Tampa bays, is almost equal to the entire Gulf shoreline of the region. Its propitious waters with their fish and shellfish could support relatively large human populations, as evidenced by the extensive shell middens that once blanketed its shores. By A.D. 1000 or shortly after, larger populations and the resulting competition for the resources of Tampa Bay combined to aid in the development of the Safety Harbor culture (Mitchem 1989). Settlements became more nucleated and simple chiefdoms like those of the late Suwannee Valley culture of north Florida appeared. Small village-mound centers, many atop or beside earlier Manasota and Weeden Island period sites, were occupied around the bay shore (Luer and Almy 1981). Soon the Safety Harbor culture spread south through Sarasota County and north as far as the Withlacoochee River and Citrus County.

Like the Timucua, the colonial period Safety Harbor people around Tampa Bay were not extensive agriculturists, nor were they organized as Mississippian chiefdoms. Instead the Safety Harbor villagers continued the economic traditions that had dominated the coast for at least a millennium and a half.

Cades Pond in North-Central Florida

The Cades Pond culture occupied a portion of north-central Florida, the interior region south of the Santa Fe River and north of about Belleview; the early Cades Pond period precedes the Weeden Island I period. It is only because the later Cades Pond people put Weeden Island pottery in their mounds that we taxonomically place them under the Weeden Island rubric. As with the Weeden Island period peninsular Gulf coast cultures, 85 to 95 percent of Cades Pond village pottery is undecorated.

A great deal of Cades Pond economic and settlement data has been collected (Cumbaa 1972; Hemmings 1978; Milanich 1978; Milanich et al. 1976) and several Cades Pond mounds have been excavated (J. Bell 1883; Milanich 1994:235–41; Sears 1956b; S. Smith 1971). These sources of information have provided insights into a unique Weeden Island period cultural adaptation, one centered on the extensive freshwater wetlands present in a restricted portion of north-central Florida in eastern Alachua and western Clay and Putnam counties. Such wetlands include Paynes Prairie; Levy, Orange,

Newnans, and Lochloosa lakes; and the former extensive wetlands in the Florahome Trough, now largely drained.

As in north Florida, there is no Swift Creek occupation of north-central Florida. The evidence at hand suggests Deptford peoples (from the Gulf coast?) settled in the region, first moving into both wetland and non-wetland locales before establishing their villages almost exclusively adjacent to multiple wetlands. By circa A.D. 200, accompanied by what appears to be a rapid increase in population and a proliferation of sites, the Cades Pond culture emerged.

As with the earlier Deptford period sites, Cades Pond village sites were situated to take maximum advantage of the resources of the wetlands. Rather than locating a village on the south end of Orange Lake, for example, they instead placed their village near the north end near the freshwater wetlands of the River Styx drainage not far from Cross Creek. This strategy is true for other settlement locales as well; for example, sites are located between Paynes Prairie and Newnans Lake, between Orange Lake and Lake Lochloosa, and between Paynes Prairie and Levy Lake. From these locales the Cades Pond people had ready access to nearby hardwood oak and hickory forests. But it was the lake and marsh habitats that fueled the Cades Pond economy. Of the more than 1500 separate individuals identified in faunal collections from the Melton village site on the north side of Paynes Prairie, almost 90 percent were taken from wetlands (Cumbaa 1972).

Thus far archaeologists have identified six separate clusters of sites, each a grouping of village sites and one or more mounds. Two of the clusters—Paynes Prairie/Levy Lake and River Styx/Cross Creek—appear to be the earliest. Both contain early mounds and are adjacent to earlier Deptford sites. Perhaps populations budded off not only to colonize nearby villages, but also to move into new locales not yet inhabited. By the early Weeden Island period all six clusters were occupied.

In both of the early clusters there is at least one small burial mound surrounded by a horseshoe-shaped embankment adjacent to a village site. The embankment/mound complexes also occur in a late Deptford context in north-central Florida and resemble the complex at the Crystal River site, and all are thought to date from the first centuries A.D. Interestingly, the River Styx mound, one of the Deptford embankment/mound complexes radiocarbon dated to circa A.D. 180, contained rolled copper beads and ceramic vessels decorated with designs identical to Hopewell period village ceramics in the western Great Lakes region. The mound also contained Deptford ceramics.

The early Cades Pond period Cross Creek village-mound center features a similar earthen embankment, though one much larger than the one at

River Styx. Cross Creek's two mounds are roughly 590 feet apart with a village midden in between closer to the southernmost mound. The northerly mound, a sand burial mound, was partially enclosed by a curving trench 6 to 7 feet wide and 4 feet deep with an earthen embankment thrown up on its south (interior) side; this semicircular feature is approximately 160 feet from the mound. The southern mound, 150 by 125 feet, is a platform, perhaps a base for a structure; no burials were found in it.

Later in the Cades Pond period such embankments were no longer made. Sand burial mounds, probably used in conjunction with charnel houses, were built, though most are located some distance from villages, sometimes in close proximity to one another. As with the burial mounds from other Weeden Island cultures, these Cades Pond mounds most likely were erected as lineage burial facilities.

The Cades Pond culture was a unique adaptation to the extensive freshwater wetlands and forests of north-central Florida. The economic orientation of the Cades Pond villages certainly differed from those of the contemporary Weeden Island period populations of the Florida Gulf coast and the inland-dwelling Weeden Island people of northwest and north Florida. Even so, they no doubt shared aspects of social and political organization and the accompanying Weeden Island belief system, one closely tied to belief systems of earlier Deptford and/or Swift Creek peoples.

After circa A.D. 600 new populations moved into north-central Florida. Alachua culture people, seemingly agriculturists from south-central Georgia (Milanich 1994:333–48), began to move into the region, settling locales within the Middle Florida Hammock Belt where the best soils for agriculture were found. The archaeological assemblage and settlement systems associated with the Alachua culture are very different from those of the Cades Pond people. As the Alachua population expanded, the Cades Pond culture disappeared.

Conclusion

Weeden Island, like Swift Creek, Deptford, and certain other terms for pre-Columbian southeastern cultures, has presented researchers with taxonomic problems, problems that can be traced to reliance on ceramic types to recognize archaeological cultures. To my mind, it does not make a great deal of sense to label as Swift Creek an A.D. 100 shell midden site on the panhandle coast of Florida, an A.D. 700 site near Macon, Georgia, and a site of unknown antiquity near Brunswick, Georgia. Neither does it reveal much beyond similarities in mound ceramics to equate a Cades Pond site in the wetlands near Cross Creek, Florida, with the Kolomoki site in interior south-west Georgia.

On the other hand, if a ceramic-based taxonomy is used only to order our archaeological cultures in the grossest fashion and we then focus on other aspects of local and regional cultures—such things as settlement and subsistence systems and specific evolutionary trajectories—we can more accurately understand and model the past. This is exactly what is occurring, not only with Weeden Island and Swift Creek, but also with other southeast-ern archaeological cultures whose names have been etched in the literature for a half century or more.

The success of anthropology in explaining human behavior lies in large part in cross-cultural research. Certainly in the Southeast we continue to learn a great deal about past cultures by focusing on similarities and differ-ences among them. Does the Weeden Island model of kin-based mound build-ing, village growth and fissioning, and the waxing and waning of centers apply to other southeastern cultures? Why did the descendants of some Weeden Island cultures evolve into Mississippian cultures and others did not? These are interesting questions whose answers are now within our grasp. By focusing on locally defined cultures over time, and then comparing re-sults, we surely can learn much about the nature of Woodland period cul-tures in the Southeast.

Chapter 17

The Woodland Archaeology
of South Florida

Randolph J. Widmer

The Woodland period of south Florida shares some characteristics of other areas of the eastern United States, notably the appearance of Woodland ceramics and village life. It even participates in the Hopewell Interaction Sphere. Despite these commonalities, however, this area has radically different cultural patterns from those elsewhere in the Southeast. South Florida clearly makes the shift from Late Archaic to Woodland period coeval with this shift throughout the greater Southeast, but the adaptation that emerges is very different. Here I discuss the cultural patterns of the distinctive adaptation during the Woodland period in south Florida and explain why these divergent patterns emerged. I use the concept of the "tradition" to discuss these cultural developments persisting to the Spanish era.

Archaeological traits in south Florida during the Woodland period can readily be classified as Woodland, but the archaeology of the Woodland period of south Florida does not readily fit into the Woodland tradition. By *tradition,* I refer to a *way of life* that persisted over a relatively long period of time, not simply a series of artifact types that persisted through time (Willey and Phillips 1958). John Goggin (1949) pioneered the concept for south Florida and referred to the persistent way of life or adaptation as the Glades tradition. Goggin states:

> It is based on the exploitation of the food resources of the tropical coastal waters, with secondary dependence on game and some use of wild plant foods....The relation of the Glades Tradition to the environment is very close. All food was derived from wild products systematically gathered in their season. Seafood was perhaps the most important food source, and apparently many varieties were eaten....Other marine foods included such diverse forms as whales and echinoderms, sharks and crabs, and rays and crawfish. Even sailfish and marlin were obtained in the Gulf Stream. (Goggin 1949:28–29)

This aquatic tradition developed during the Woodland period of south Florida in response to the unique environment and the timing of its formation.

The Environment of South Florida

The environment of south Florida differs from others within the southeastern United States and is found nowhere else. More important, this environment was very different before *and* after the Woodland period because of changes around 3200 years ago and changes in the environment today in the form of draining south Florida for land reclamation, agriculture, pastures, residential developments and water for them, and the introduction of exotic flora and fauna. Prior to the Woodland period, the environment of south Florida was much drier, hence, there was less rainfall and surface water. Brackish estuaries, while present, were more limited in area and the sea level had not yet risen and stabilized near its present position. In fact, the entire coastline configuration, vegetation, and hydrology were very different from today and, more important, it was the rise in sea level that ultimately allowed the distinctive adaptation seen in south Florida during the Woodland period.

South Florida lies south of 27° latitude and is bounded by the Atlantic Ocean, the Gulf of Mexico, and the Straits of Florida (Figure 17.1). The climate is classified as Aw (tropical wet and dry) in the Köppen (1931) system with a long dry season during the winter and spring. Temperatures exceed 18° centigrade for the entire year and mean annual rainfall is greater than 1143 millimeters (44–45 inches) (T. Thomas 1974). The topography of south Florida is a flat, low peninsula some 445 kilometers wide that slopes from east to west, with the western 225 kilometers submerged to form a broad, shallow marine shelf. Prior to contemporary drainage activities, most of the exposed peninsula flooded during the wet season from June through December.

The hydric nature of south Florida is its most distinct natural feature. It includes the Kissimmee, Lake Okeechobee, Everglades (KLOE) watershed with an area of 23,400 square kilometers; the Big Cypress swamp, with an area of 6400 square kilometers; and the Peace, Myakka, and Caloosahatchee rivers (G. Parker 1984). Water enters all of these drainage systems exclusively as precipitation and flows into the coastal areas, creating brackish environments bounded on the west coast by barrier islands, and on the south and east coasts by ridges and islands formed by ancient exposed coral reefs. Off the latter, coral reefs are found near shore, with water depth dropping off precipitously to 200 meters only 10 kilometers off shore (Figure 17.2).

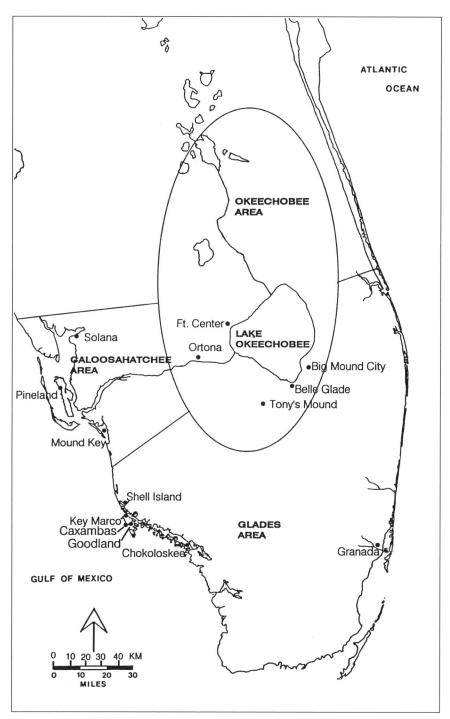

Figure 17.1 — Archaeological regions and sites in Florida

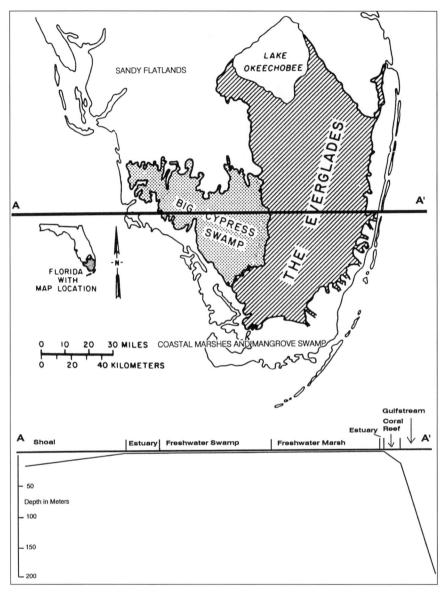

Figure 17.2 — Aquatic environments and ecosystems in south Florida

On the west coast, a series of barrier islands and mangrove keys form a vast, highly productive, bay and estuary system because most fresh water exits into the Gulf of Mexico. Figure 17.2 provides an east-west cross section of the region to illustrate how the aquatic environments are distributed in south Florida including the locations of the three major hydrological features.

Upland habitats in south Florida include vast pine sandy flatwoods in the northwest interior area and along the eastern edge of the Everglades and, more important, numerous tropical hardwood hammocks. Smaller bay islands are scattered throughout the hydric environments of south Florida. These tropical hardwood hammocks and bay islands were important locations for settlements during the Woodland period since they provided dry land for settlement.

The distinct climate, physiography, hydrology, and topography influences the type of adaptation possible in this area and also differentiates it from other Woodland period adaptations. Ironically, all of the cultural characteristics that typically define the Woodland period—settled village life, earthworks, non–fiber tempered ceramics, and agriculture—are present, but in patterns distinct from those seen elsewhere in the southeastern United States.

Chronology and Regional Variation

The Woodland period has three regional divisions: the Caloosahatchee, the Glades, and the Okeechobee, based on ceramic traditions (R. Carr and Beriault 1984; J. W. Griffin 1988). Figure 17.3 presents the basic chronological divisions for south Florida during the Woodland period in the three subregions of Florida and the ethnohistoric groups associated with these (J. W. Griffin 1988; Marquardt [ed.] 1992; W. Sears 1982; Widmer 1988).

Settlement and Community Patterns

Most Woodland period village habitation sites of the region are associated with aquatic environments. An acute problem for south Florida is the accurate dating of components at sites that make up the overall settlement pattern and, therefore, the history of this pattern through time. The reason is the persistence of undecorated ceramic bowls throughout the entire Woodland period from 1000 B.C. to A.D. 1500. In the Caloosahatchee and Okeechobee areas, most ceramics are undecorated, so periodization of sites is based primarily on ceramic cross dating or direct radiocarbon dating of deposits (Cordell 1992; W. Sears 1982; Willey 1949a). In the Glades area, however, temporally sensitive decorated wares occur, but only at around A.D. 500. The various styles of decoration have been thoroughly dated by radiocarbon assessments from stratigraphic contexts (R. Carr and Beriault 1984; J. W. Griffin 1988; Widmer 1988). Decorated ceramics are typically decorated

Dates	Archaeological Subregions and Their Historic Groups		
	Tequesta (Glades)	Calusa (Caloosahatchee)	Mayaimi (Okeechobee)
A.D. 1500–1750	Glades IIIC	Caloosahatchee V	
A.D. 1400	Glades IIIB		
A.D. 1350		Caloosahatchee IV	
A.D. 1200	Glades IIIA	Caloosahatchee III	Period IV
A.D. 1000	Glades IIC		
A.D. 900	Glades IIB		
A.D. 800		Caloosahatchee IIB	
A.D. 700	Glades IIA		Period III
A.D. 650		Caloosahatchee IIA	
A.D. 500	Glades I (Late)		
A.D. 200			Period II
500 B.C.	Glades I (Early)	Caloosahatchee I	Period I

Figure 17.3 — The Woodland chronology of south Florida

along a narrow band just below the rim and co-occur only in minor frequencies with plain bowls. Accurate dating of sites from limited surface collections is thus problematic.

Because decorated sherds necessary to date sites after A.D. 500 are extremely rare, most sites by default are assigned to the Glades I early period, that is, prior to A.D. 500. This assessment, however, is more likely a result of the small sample size than a true lack of decorated ceramics, making it difficult to assess the number of temporally distinct components or their spatial extent, without either test excavation with radiocarbon dating of the strata or full-scale excavation.

A number of large village sites in the Caloosahatchee region have been cored to determine the environment, whether the shell accumulations were cultural or natural, and the relationship of the sites to the Holocene sea level rise (Upchurch et al. 1992). Unfortunately, coring was not utilized to determine the areal growth of sites through time, and I recommend its use for such purposes. There is a desperate need for chronological assessment of sites within south Florida for a better understanding of the changes in settlement patterning through time, particularly relating to population size and density. Models of cultural development in south Florida can only be tested by adequate knowledge of the areal expansion within sites through time, to determine the history of population dynamics.

We know from existing excavation data that there are village sites over 10 hectares for all regions from the beginning of the Woodland period. Although the southwest Florida coast has two different subareas based on ceramic tradition, they are very similar in settlement patterning. In fact, settlement and community patterning has more to do with environmental setting than with ceramic tradition.

Southwest Florida Coast

In southwest Florida, habitation sites fall into three sizes: large nucleated villages over 10 hectares in area, smaller villages ranging from 3 to 4 hectares, and small sites of less than a hectare. The large village sites are located along the southwest Florida coast from Charlotte County south and are composed of huge accumulations of marine shell. They are situated directly in estuaries, often at the mouths of rivers or passes into the open Gulf of Mexico. These sites are as large as 30 hectares and often are used as modern settlements.

These sites are *not* midden, but instead are composed primarily of clean shell fill, although some areas and mounds within them may include redeposited midden. The earliest known Woodland period large village site is at Caxambas on Marco Island and dates exclusively to the early Glades I period, that is, around A.D. 300 (Cockrell 1970). The density of cultural material on these sites suggests a population density of twenty-five to fifty persons per hectare, which would yield a population of 250 to 500 for an average 10-hectare site (Widmer 1988:256). Most large coastal village sites have early Glades I components often with material dating back to 1000 B.C., but the spatial extent of these components is not understood.

The large southwest coastal village sites contain mounds and ridges composed of shell with a little quartz sand in their matrix. These mounds and ridges often are capped with a 50- to 60-centimeter mantle of dark brown/black organic loamy sand. Cultural material is more abundant in this mantle, and the dark organic content is probably the result of the decomposition of vegetation that accumulated by cultural and/or natural processes on the site surface. Ironically, these are typically midden-like in context, yet contain much less shell than the almost purely shell strata below them. These dense shell strata are very non-midden-like in terms of cultural debris. True dense organic middens are located in the valleys adjacent to the mounds, at least at the Key Marco site (John Beriault, personal communication, 1999).

Extensive excavations at two sites, Key Marco (Widmer 1996) and Shell Island, indicate that mounds served as platforms for both domestic structures and elite or temple structures. Structures have also been located on non-mound level strata at the Key Marco site, where they are interpreted as low-status residences. The structures revealed to date are quadrilateral in shape, as evidenced by linear rows of post molds. More specific information on layout of the houses is lacking because of the incredible density of post molds, even greater than is typically associated with rebuilding. These post molds extend from the dark earth mantles into the shell deposits, but also originate in the clean shell strata below the mantles.

At the Shell Island site, a complete structure on the level summit of a shell platform mound was rebuilt four times, as evidenced by four distinct superimposed strata. The level surface of the mound had an area of 30 square meters, and so by utilizing Naroll's (1962) formula of 10 square meters per person, a family size of three individuals can be determined. This would most closely correlate to a domestic structure occupied by a nuclear family.

The superimposed Shell Island structures, and the structures at Key Marco, are distinctive because they lack the typical features associated with floors at the ground surface level. No storage pits, hearths, or discrete activity areas on floors have been identified in association with the post molds in any context earlier than Glades III. These structures were probably elevated on pilings driven into these platform mounds, an idea originally proposed by Cushing (1896) at Key Marco, where he found a number of fallen pilings in the muck pond referred to as "Court of the Pile Dwellers."

At Key Marco (Widmer 1996), there is evidence of an elite structure elevated on pilings set into a shell platform mound, as well as a residential structure on a lower shell mound. At the nearby Shell Island site, another structure, roughly 30 meters square, on the summit of a shell platform mound contained four main pilings and had four construction phases. No floors were discerned on the surface of these platforms. There was actually an artifact and midden "shadow" created by the elevated floor with few artifacts found directly under the floor but many just off of the edge of the platform. Not all houses in southwest Florida need necessarily have been situated on pilings. At the Key Marco site, a number of prepared calcitic mud "floors" have been identified. These are in the upper strata of the excavation and have midden deposits adjacent to them. Some floors have post molds extending through them. Whatever their function, they remain problematic at this stage of investigation, but in the strata beneath these prepared surfaces numerous post molds are found, which seems to suggest a house elevated on piles.

One of the more startling discoveries is the existence of a *submerged* piling structure at Solana, a smaller site less than a hectare in size, in the Caloosahatchee region. Although now aerially exposed, the site originally was under water during a higher sea level stand in the past (Widmer 1986a). The submerged nature of the site was determined by the discovery of a series of doughnut-shaped rings of barnacles, mussels, and oyster that indicated sessile growth on piles. Further evidence for a submerged site is the presence of exclusively saltwater fish and mollusk remains at the site, even though the site is today located on a freshwater creek. Some marine bivalves actually were found in living position in the site sediments. This site has important implications for the settlement pattern of this area (Widmer 1986a), not only because of the potential shift in sea level and its impact on settlement pattern shifts, but more importantly because of our ability to locate sites and settlement patterns, since habitation sites may still be submerged.

I suspect that many, if not most, residential structures during the Woodland period along the southwest Florida coast actually were erected in shallow water, and that only elites, or a small fraction of the population, resided in structures on the large artificially accreted shell mounds and ridges associated with the large, conspicuous, shell-bearing sites. Cores from three large village sites in the Caloosahatchee show that all have cultural deposits that accumulated in shallow water (Upchurch et al. 1992:67), although it is not known whether these submerged deposits prograded from an aerially exposed site or were deposited initially in shallow water. In all three cases, the subsequent stratigraphic accumulations resulted in mound deposits well above the present sea level. Coring further supports my contention that sites were originally constructed on submerged sediments.

In addition to the large village sites, a number of smaller sites are composed mainly of shell and represent either small, individual-family households or fish-processing stations. Only the Solana site, composed of mostly sand with scattered shell and fishbone refuse, has been extensively excavated to determine site function (Widmer 1986a). The remains of one or perhaps two houses elevated on pilings were uncovered. The density of shell tools and ceramics is much lower here than in the large shell-bearing villages, but this may be because of the narrow span of occupation, rather than indicating any functional differences. Six radiocarbon dates from this site span the period A.D. 250 to A.D. 600.

Okeechobee Basin

In the interior region of south Florida, along the shores of Lake Okeechobee and extending up the Kissimmee drainage, are a number of extensive sites with distinctive linear mounds and circular ditches. These include Tony's Mound, Big Mound City, Ortona, Belle Glade, and the most extensively excavated site, Fort Center (Figure 17.1; Figure 17.4). Collectively referred to as "Big Circle" sites (R. Allen 1948), they are typified by semicircular narrow embankments of sand with a series of linear embankments extending from them in radial fashion. The embankments terminate in sand mounds.

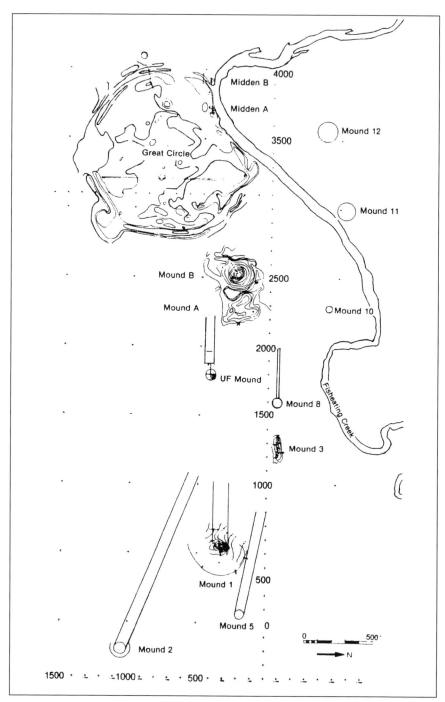

Figure 17.4 — Site plan of Fort Center (from Sears 1982:fig. 1.1, used by permission of the University Press of Florida)

Canals and circular ditches are also often associated with these sites, and large middens are sometimes found across the openings of these semicircles (Milanich 1994:283). Smaller sites with linear embankments that terminate in sand mounds, extending from smaller arc segments of circles, are also known for the area (R. Carr 1975, 1985).

Only the Belle Glade (Willey 1949a) and Fort Center (W. Sears 1982) (Figure 17.4) sites have been extensively excavated and reported. Of the fourteen numbered mounds, many of which abut linear embankments, only Mound 1 at Fort Center appears to have had a structure on its summit, as evidenced by charcoal concentrations interpreted as fireplaces and some post molds (W. Sears 1982:132), but the shape or area of this structure is not given. The structure does not appear to be prehistoric, since it has been dated to the sixteenth or seventeenth century by ceramic associations. None of the other mounds have evidence of post molds, although some have charcoal lenses on their surfaces.

Sears (1982:142–43) interprets most of these mounds, with the exception of Mounds 13, A, and B, with their linear embankments as house mounds rather than ceremonial mounds. I concur and suggest that the reason for these mounds is the high water table during the rainy season. Even during the excavation of Fort Center, many of the mounds became inundated and could not be excavated. This is important, because much of this area today has been reclaimed by drainage to produce arable land. The fact that it is still inundated by the water table suggests an even more acute problem in the past. The sand mounds provided the necessary elevation for the houses to be above this water level. The function of the linear embankments was originally probably for growing maize for ceremonial purposes and then as open activity areas after A.D. 500.

Mound 3 at Fort Center is much larger than Mounds 13, A, or B. Mound 3 is an artificially constructed mound measuring 200 by 60 meters. The mound was occupied during three periods of the site's history with gaps in this occupation. Although Sears (1982:135–36) suggests that it was a midden area, it seems more reasonable that the mound represents an elevated plaza with community-wide feasting perhaps accounting for the midden accumulation.

At the Belle Glade site, numerous post molds were reported during the excavation of a habitation mound 100 by 150 meters in extent, an area of about 2.5 hectares (6 acres). Evidently the mound is an artificial accumulation, although no specific statement to that effect is made in Willey's (1949a) report. No clear house outlines were seen, but the houses do appear to be rectangular (Willey 1949a:19). The south end of the mound had a slightly higher platform on it with a single structure on its summit.

Despite the circular earthworks, ditches, linear embankments, and mounds, none of the Lake Okeechobee Basin sites are as populous as sites in southwest Florida. The Belle Glade site with an area of 2.5 hectares would have a population of only 62 to 125, utilizing the same density calculations employed for the southwest coastal villages. Fort Center would have a population of around sixty-five, if all of the mounds were contemporaneous (which they were not) and assuming a family size of five for each of the thirteen habitation mounds (W. Sears 1982) that contained single structures.

Big Cypress and Everglades Extraction Sites

Over 350 Woodland sites have been recorded in the Big Cypress swamp (Ehrenhard and Taylor 1980; Ehrenhard et al. 1978, 1979, 1980, 1981), and just about every bay head or spot of high ground in the Everglades has a collecting station. The larger of these contain dense black earth middens with extremely dense concentrations of deer bone and human coprolites, suggesting use as temporary locations for hunting and processing deer, with the meat transferred either to permanent settlements in the Okeechobee area or to the southwest Florida coast.

Associated with these extraction sites are what I call gateway sites, located on hammocks adjacent to sloughs that run from the interior to the coast. These probably served as overnight bivouacs for making trips into the interior for hunting, fishing, and extraction of resources from the interior swamp and marsh habitat. It is not known whether they had any permanent resident population or instead were inhabited by ever-shifting hunting, collecting, and possibly trading parties making their way along these aquatic trails, as these sloughs also served as important corridors for canoe transportation and trade, linking the southern portion of the southwest Florida coast with the Okeechobee Basin area and southeast Florida.

Southeast Coastal Sites

Habitation sites on the southeastern coast of south Florida are situated on hammocks and ridges associated with rivers, bays, and inlets from the Atlantic Ocean. The largest and most important sites are at the confluence of the Miami River with Biscayne Bay with two spatially distinct sites: the Granada site on the north bank of the Miami River, and the Brickell Point site directly opposite it on the south bank. The Granada site had an area of approximately 4000 square meters and an occupation from A.D. 500 to contact. The full spatial extent of the site is unknown because it is under urban development. No post molds were reported, probably because it is almost impossible to see them in the dark black matrix, hindering our knowledge of community patterning. A 1567 account of the settlement by Lopez de Velasco (cited in Parks 1985) noted that there were twenty-eight houses surrounded by a stockade. Assuming a population of five per house, this would suggest a population of approximately 140. This seems a reasonable size for the site, with a population smaller than that of the larger sites in the Okeechobee Basin area. Floral analysis suggests that the site was not occupied year round (C. Scarry 1985), but the fauna could have supported the population year round.

A recent finding in southeast Florida is a circular pattern of postholes at Brickell Point (Robert S. Carr, personal communication, 2000), also known as the "Miami Circle" in media coverage. The "circle" consists of a number of postholes cut into the limestone bedrock. These postholes outline a structure 11.43 meters (37.5 feet) in diameter. Five calibrated radiocarbon assays have one-sigma ranges from 240 to 100 B.C., 80 B.C. to A.D. 5, A.D. 25 to 160, and A.D. 1630 to 1670 (Robert S. Carr, personal communication, 2000). Four of the five dates are early Glades I in age and would make the circle contemporary with the circular ditches at the Fort Center site, but the ditches clearly had different functions. I suggest that the "Miami Circle" functioned as a chief's house or a council house based on the following lines of reasoning.

The "Miami Circle" has an area 3.5 times larger than that of known domestic structures in southwest Florida. Utilizing Naroll's (1962) formula of 10 square meters of roofed-over area per person, the structure could have housed ten individuals, more than a typical domicile. It housed instead an important individual, such as a polygamous chief. We know from ethnohistoric sources that chiefs in south Florida had multiple wives (Hann 1991; Goggin and Sturtevant 1964; Widmer 1988). There are Spanish accounts of villagers building a chief's house on the site, and there is a specific quote by Villareal that "I teach the doctrina to the children in the house of the chief, where there are many adults present" (cited in J. W. Griffin 1985:379).

Other settlements were located in the vicinity of Miami, at Opa Locka, Golden Glades, and Surfside at Haulover Pass, which leads from Biscayne Bay into the Atlantic Ocean. These sites were investigated during the WPA era and are contemporary with the Granada and Brickell Point sites (Willey 1949a). A large settlement is also located on Matecumbe Key and may have been the location of a local chief as well.

A number of conclusions can be made about the settlement patterns in south Florida. There is definitely a gradient of settlement size and, with it, population size. Settlements along the southwest coast are much larger than those in the Okeechobee Basin, which in turn are larger than those in southeast Florida. There are also more larger settlements along the southwest

Florida coast than in the Okeechobee Basin, where they are in turn more numerous than in southeast Florida. The degree of sedentism also seems to follow this gradient, suggesting that population size and density is highest on the southwest Florida coast, followed by the Okeechobee Basin area and then southeast Florida. This gradient also applies to the degree of labor and construction efforts for mound and embankment construction and has important implications for political relationships in south Florida.

All larger habitation sites in south Florida appear to be on artificially created mounds of shell, sand, or other soil. I suspect that these served to elevate the houses from periodic inundation during the wet season. An interesting question would be whether these mounds were built in response to the A.D. 450 sea level rise (K. Walker et al. 1994a, 1994b; Widmer 1986a). At Key Marco, mounds were in place prior to the high sea stand event. There are also settlements placed directly in a shallow intertidal zone without elevated mound components. The prevalence of this site type in the settlement pattern is unknown. It is also unknown whether the larger shell-bearing habitation sites began as sites situated in the intertidal zone and then were later artificially raised by adding construction fill. In at least three examples at Shell Island and Key Marco, houses were still erected on stilts or pilings, even though they were on mounds. There is no evidence of houses erected on pilings in the Okeechobee Basin, but there is evidence for this at the Brickell Point site from my recent excavations.

Subsistence Patterns

Faunal Food Resources
Subsistence in south Florida during the Woodland period has a very distinct pattern, unlike any seen elsewhere in the Southeast. It was focused on aquatic resources, both faunal and floral. An extensive, highly specialized technology of bone, shell, and cordage was developed to specifically target the varied aquatic environments and their associated biota. The tools included gill nets of different-size mesh, with mesh sizes identical to those used today (K. Walker 1992). Cordage remains of nets were recovered from the Key Marco site (Cushing 1896; Gilliland 1975; K. Walker 1992). These nets were drift nets with floats of gourds or wooden pegs with perforated shell weights. Composite shell and bone fishhooks and gouges were utilized, as were bone spears. A number of sinkers and smaller anchors could have been used for line fishing. Tidal weirs were utilized to harvest fish. Some of these were made of shell, as in one example across Henderson Creek at Shell Island. Others undoubtedly were constructed exclusively of wood and brush

and would leave no archaeological evidence. A model of a double-hulled canoe was recovered from the Key Marco site (Cushing 1896), indicating that watercraft had the ability to exploit the shoals and deeper shelf areas of the Gulf of Mexico, a pattern verified by offshore fish remains found in the archaeological sites.

Along the southwest coast, near-shore coastal and estuarine resources—predominately fish and mollusks—account for over 90 percent of the food base in every coastal site excavated to date (K. Walker 1992; Widmer 1988). Over fifty species of fish have been reported from southwest Florida sites (K. Walker 1992:356–57). In the interior Big Cypress swamp, specialized deer hunting and processing sites are common, with dense middens consisting of coprolites and deer bone. On the southeast coast, the deep offshore waters of the Gulf Stream were exploited with long lines and even at night (Widmer 1986b), as evidenced by swordfish, mako shark, and thresher shark remains from sites in Dade County (Widmer 1986b; Willey 1949a). The near-shore reefs also were exploited, and sailfish have also been recovered in sites in Dade County. Biscayne Bay was a major whale calving area, and whaling was also practiced (Larson 1980). Sea turtles, migratory waterfowl such as ducks, geese, and loons, and wading birds, including egrets, herons, and ibis, were also exploited. Remains of monk seals, now extinct, have been recovered from a few sites in south Florida. They appear to have been an elite table fare, and their pelts elite status apparel. Freshwater fish and turtles were important in the interior sites along the Lake Okeechobee shoreline and up the Kissimmee drainage. Surprisingly, alligators, while found in archaeological sites in south Florida, are relatively uncommon. This may be because they were considered elite items, like monk seal. Throughout the Americas, caimans and alligators are thought to be powerful animal spirits that can only be associated with elites and chiefs, and so it is this elite context that probably accounts for such few remains (Furst 1968).

Floral Food Resources

In the Okeechobee Basin area, plants were also extensively utilized. Fontaneda (1944) mentions the sixteenth-century aboriginal use of three emergent aquatic root crops. The most important was probably the emergent duck potato, *Sagittaria lanciflora.* Pollen of this was found at Fort Center (E. Sears 1982:table 8.2, 126) in two of the linear earthwork mounds, 3 and 12, in samples that date from periods I, II, and III. The presence of pollen in these mound samples is important because the plants have a submerged hydric habitat. Their presence in the elevated mound context suggests the processing of the tubers took place on these mounds. Other species of *Sagittaria,* also with edible tubers, are found in the interior wetlands and marshes. Hydric plants of the lily family were also noted in the pollen samples from Fort Center, and it is likely that tubers from this family were utilized for food.

Cheno-am pollen, pigweed, and goosefoot also have been found in the Fort Center site soil samples, and these plants are often interpreted as ruderal species in south Florida (C. Scarry and Newsom 1992:394–96). At Fort Center, pollen from these plants was found in coprolites in much higher percentages than in the soil samples (E. Sears 1982:125), suggesting use as food in the Okeechobee Basin.

Numerous plants with edible fruits, reported as pollen or macrobotanical remains, have been recovered from Woodland period sites in south Florida. These include elderberry (Caprifoliaceae), prickly pear cactus (*Opuntia* sp.), cocoplum, saw palmetto, hog plum, seagrape, mastic, and cabbage palm (C. Scarry and Newsom 1992; E. Sears 1982:125). The latter six species are found in quantities suggesting intensive exploitation and greater importance in the diet, although not on the southwest coast (C. Scarry and Newsom 1992:395).

Domesticated Plants

The occurrence of maize pollen at Fort Center (E. Sears 1982:119–20), dating A.D. 1 to 500, is enigmatic, as no other maize is reported for south Florida. The exposed earthworks and drained circle at Fort Center could have been used to grow maize. Utilizing Aztec production figures—obtained from chinampa production, the highest figures for any prehispanic maize production—these ridges could apparently only have supported a population of forty individuals, a population for similar sites in the Lake Okeechobee basin suggested by Fontaneda (1944). I suggest that this maize was for ritual purposes, rather than for subsistence. Maize was made into a beer, to be used ritually to obtain an altered state of consciousness to facilitate communion with spirits. The beaker ceramic form that also appears during the Middle Woodland period in Florida is consistent with this interpretation. I suspect that early in the history of the site, the circular ditches would have been sufficient to drain the fields, but as the water table rose, raised ridges were necessary. Then with the onset of the 1.2 meter higher sea level stand at A.D. 450, maize production was no longer possible and therefore abandoned.

Remains of Cucurbita gourds (*Cucurbita pepo*) and bottle gourds (*Lagenaria siceraria*) have been found in southwest Florida at the Key Marco site (Cutler 1975; C. Scarry and Newsom 1992). These remains are of the hard-rind varieties, and while their seeds would have been edible, they appear to have been utilized primarily as net floats and never really constituted an important contribution to the diet (C. Scarry and Newsom 1992:395).

Sociopolitical Complexity and the Rise of Chiefdoms

Prehistoric aboriginal groups in south Florida developed complex political organization of the type referred to as a chiefdom. This is unusual and important because in most ethnographic cases chiefdom development is correlated with agriculture (Peebles and Kus 1977; Service 1962). An examination of sociopolitical development in south Florida, where subsistence agriculture was not utilized, can provide a better general understanding of chiefdom development by focusing on other causal variables that lead to sociopolitical complexity. Cushing (1896:413) first provided an explanation for this development, noting it was coordination of labor that required chiefs. The classic work on the sociopolitical complexity of the Calusa by Goggin and Sturtevant (1964) outlined the correlates for this complexity, linking it to the rich aquatic environment. This was followed by my model to explain how this complex adaptation developed through time (Widmer 1988).

The earliest evidence of labor coordination and perhaps sociopolitical complexity in south Florida is at Fort Center. Here circular ditches appear sometime after 500 B.C., and linear earthworks with associated mounds at their termini appear shortly after A.D. 1. I argue that the ditches originally were for drainage, but as the water table rose, it was necessary for ridged fields to be constructed for maize growing. In southeast Florida, we see the communal circular structure of the "Miami Circle" and its attendant high cost of construction as evidence of community-wide organization of labor. It is difficult to determine how labor investment relates to sociopolitical development without more supporting archaeological evidence in this case.

A low flat-topped platform mound was constructed at Fort Center, shortly after A.D. 200, with a charnel house on its summit and temporary secondary interments (W. Sears 1982:186). Adjacent to this mound was a pond with a wooden platform in its middle. A number of carved wooden animals, including otters, panthers, raptors, wolves, and birds, decorated the sides of the platform. Typical Hopewell artifacts like platform pipes, galena, and quartz crystal plummets were recovered from the mound. These carved animals probably represent totems associated with lineages. This period of ritual and probable political complexity ended at Fort Center shortly after A.D. 600. However, developments along the southwest coast were just beginning.

Temple mounds appear by A.D. 500 on the southwest Florida coast in large villages directly on the estuary fringe. By A.D. 800, temple mounds are found at all large village sites in this area. Mounds are constructed of sand and/or marine shell, with many formed from marine shell washed up after storms or hurricanes. At least two mounds from the Key Marco site span 1000 years, from A.D. 500 to A.D. 1500 (Figure 17.5). Mound C (which was

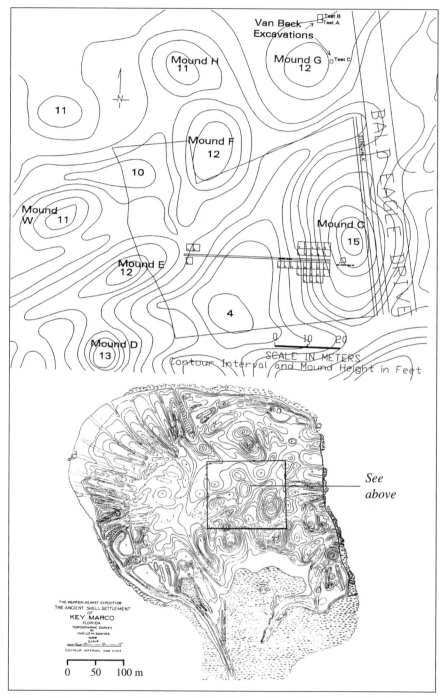

Figure 17.5 — Topographic map of Key Marco (from Cushing 1896:plate XXX)
with location of excavations in Mound C and Mound G

originally 4.6 meters in height) contained evidence for structures on its summit in the form of post molds. The slopes of this mound were covered with a veneer of nacreous pen shells that would make the mound sparkle in sunlight. The mound also contained caches of red and yellow ochre and long sections of shark as indicated by eight articulated shark vertebrae, implying that the mound served as a platform for a temple and/or chiefly residence (Widmer 1996). Excavations in Mound G showed the same time span represented in its 3 meters of stratigraphy (Van Beck and Van Beck 1965).

Large sites on the coast have impressive canal systems (Goggin and Sturtevant 1964; Luer 1989; Luer and Wheeler 1997; Wheeler 1998) with sophisticated hydrological engineering. Some actually were constructed with locks. The amount of labor to build and, more important, to maintain canals suggests a centralized form of political organization, most likely a chiefdom.

The spectacular collection of wooden artifacts excavated by Cushing from the Key Marco site, most notably the ritual artifacts, suggests the existence of chiefdoms at A.D. 500, to which many of the artifacts date (Gilliland 1975). It is likely that some of the ritual artifacts, such as masks, effigies, and stools, were actually derived from the structure on Mound C at Key Marco (Widmer 1996). In any event, these ritual artifacts are clearly derived from contexts similar to Mound C. The fact that temple mounds existed on a single location and were rebuilt over a period of 1000 years implies the existence of a unilineal principle of descent and the importance of generational depth. Both of these features correlate strongly with complex chiefdoms.

The development of a complex chiefdom in the absence of agriculture is one of the most significant problems that the archaeology of south Florida poses. In most Woodland societies, sociopolitical complexity is associated with the economic use of agriculture, but in south Florida, agriculture was never an important component of subsistence. Central to understanding the rise of sociopolitical organization in south Florida is the role of demography. There is a direct positive correlation between population size and density and sociopolitical complexity (Carneiro 1967; A. Johnson and Earle 1987), so to quantify or measure sociopolitical complexity we must have measures of population size and density. Why do we have population growth? How is population increase possible when wild food resources cannot be easily increased by cultural intervention?

The answer lies in the timing of the emergence of a rich and productive natural ecosystem. It began approximately 3200 years ago with two important events: (1) the slowing of sea level rise from a rate of 23 centimeters/100 years to 4 centimeters/100 years and (2) the rise of the sea level to a position about 1 meter below its present position (Wanless et al. 1994). By

2700 years ago, local hydrology was similar to that of today, and the physiographic characteristics of modern south Florida were fully established. This slowing of sea level rise and the raising of the water table resulted in an extremely productive aquatic environment over a much larger area than during the previous Archaic period.

Once this new environment—and its dramatically increased area of high production—was established, populations began to grow. Food gathering was facilitated by the ability to use water transportation in all areas of south Florida, whereas canoe transportation was not feasible in many areas earlier. The ability to rely almost exclusively on canoe transport dramatically increased the catchment radius from previous periods. Fishers, hunters, and foragers could go out from logistically placed villages spaced at much greater distances than if they were based on walking distance. More important, they could bring back much greater quantities of food than they could on foot. There is a forty times greater energetic advantage in using water craft over human pedestrian portage (Sanders and Santley 1985).

The ability to capture more food resulted in sedentism and an increase in population size and density. Initially the ratio of people to food was relatively low, but through time the effective carrying capacity was eventually reached. When it was, political centralization was needed to effectively resolve internal problems, notably fish redistribution. Daily fish catch is highly variable from boat to boat, due to the nature of tides, weather, and, more important, stochastic variability, more informally known to fisherfolk as "luck." These factors create a situation of continual spatial and temporal inequities in food supply, and a hereditary chiefdom hierarchy arises as a solution.

I originally modeled the increase in population size and density as a linear function, based on the limited settlement and environmental data. These data indicated little environmental change, but the history of settlement patterns was inadequate for more detailed understanding of population dynamics. This latter situation still prevails today. Sea level rise after 3200 years ago until 1932 was very slow, with a rate of only 4 centimeters/100 years, and this curve was assumed linear (Wanless 1982). There is now evidence that sea level rise during the past 3200 years was instead characterized by high-frequency oscillations, which included a high 1+ meter sea level stand at A.D. 250–500 sandwiched between two lower stands of around -0.6 meter (K. Walker et al. 1994a, 1994b; Wanless et al. 1995; Widmer 1986a).

It is necessary to reevaluate the role of an oscillating sea level curve in regard to an assumption of a linear population history. The timing of sociopolitical development also needs to be reexamined in light of a higher sea level stand between A.D. 250 and A.D. 500 (K. Walker et al. 1994a, 1994b; Widmer 1986a), since the emergence of complex chiefdoms occurs shortly after this event. I do not think that sea level change *alone* had much direct impact on population growth, and therefore sociopolitical development, because sea level rise was still very slow overall—only 4 centimeters/100 years. Since 1932, this rate of rise has increased to 38 centimeters/100 years, higher than at any time in the past 5500 years, and the effect on contemporary settlement patterns has been minimal (Wanless et al. 1994, 1995). Even recognizing the higher and lower sea level stands during the Woodland period (K. Walker et al. 1994a, 1994b), mangrove forests will simply retreat inland with increased sea stand or migrate back toward the Gulf of Mexico as sea level drops. Instead, it is the impact of hurricanes on these transgressive-regressive events that has important implications for the rise of sociopolitical complexity.

Recent before-and-after studies of the effects of hurricane Andrew and earlier hurricanes indicate that hurricanes are the most important factor reconfiguring south Florida coastlines (Tedesco et al. 1995; Wanless et al. 1994, 1995). Rising sea level acts as a charge or static buildup with little impact on coastline configuration or sedimentation. When a hurricane hits a transgressing coastline, incredible change and destruction is brought about by storm surges that range from -1 to 8+ meters in height and result in major reconfiguration of the coastline and severe impact on terrestrial and aquatic biota. All deciduous trees in hurricane Andrew's path had their leaves completely stripped (Tedesco et al. 1995).

Nine devastating hurricanes hit south Florida in the past century. There is a 1 to 7 percent probability that a category 4 or higher hurricane—one with winds in excess of 130 miles per hour—will hit the coastline of south Florida in any one year (Gentry 1984:511). The probability increases to 5 to 15 percent for lower-intensity hurricanes. Hurricanes are important factors that disrupted the cultural adaptations in south Florida, and so political systems were needed to mitigate their adverse effects. Hierarchical chiefdoms provide a mechanism for dealing with the adversity caused by hurricane disruption to existing and future food supplies, and the destruction of houses and necessary economic resources, such as nets, boats, and other fishing gear. We have ample evidence of this loss at the "Court of the Pile Dwellers" where utilitarian articles of wood were found buried in a submerged peat bog (Cushing 1896).

The hierarchical nature of a chiefdom would allow the centralized leadership to coordinate labor to rebuild after a devastating storm. At Key Marco, three rebuilding episodes of a temple mound are correlated to the aftermath of hurricanes. Massive quantities of surf clams were placed on the slopes of the mound and then covered with a veneer of pen shell. Three such episodes were recorded (Widmer 1996). These rebuilding materials became available after a storm surge had washed enormous numbers of these mollusks onto the beach. Furthermore, the previous structure on the mound summit would have been destroyed and in need of rebuilding.

Why is the complex chiefdom associated with the Calusa seen on the southwest Florida coast, but not elsewhere in Florida, despite the same potential for storm damage? The reason is that there is not a large enough population with high enough density to require the centralized organization characteristic of a chiefdom. Rebuilding and food reallocation can be accomplished within an existing simpler kin and community organization, not necessitating a more centralized political complex chiefdom.

Trade

Trade is present throughout the Woodland period in south Florida, and the nature of this trade provides an indicator of political organization and relationships within the region as well as external relationships. During the Middle Woodland period, Hopewellian artifacts like monitor pipes, probably originating from much farther north, are found at Fort Center, and olivine basalt ground stone celts from the Appalachians have been found as offerings in the postholes of the "Miami Circle." Locally, marine shell, shark teeth, and barracuda jaws were traded from the coastal regions into the interior Okeechobee sites throughout all periods of the Woodland tradition, and even into other areas of the eastern United States. Trade and interaction with political importance appears after A.D. 800. This is first indicated by the appearance of the Okeechobee area Belle Glade ceramics in southwest Florida coastal sites around A.D. 650–800. After A.D. 800, Belle Glade Plain is the predominate ceramic type in the Caloosahatchee subarea (Cordell 1992:168). By A.D. 1200, there is even greater intensity of trade and interaction with the appearance of St. Johns Check Stamped, a north Florida ceramic variety, and ceramic types such as Glades Tooled in all the subregions of south Florida. What is the reason for trading or exchanging utilitarian ceramics? I view this intraregional exchange of ceramics as a measure of the degree of social and political interaction within south Florida, specifically intermarriage. We know from historic documents (Fontaneda 1944; Hann 1991) that chiefs took wives from different villages outside their regions and the women brought with them their own local ceramics. Thus, the greater the frequency of nonlocal ceramic types in sites in south Florida, the greater the political interaction, such as alliances.

By A.D. 1300, distinctive Safety Harbor series ceramics are found in ritual contexts throughout all areas of south Florida. These ceramics are not utilitarian, but are restricted to high-status mortuary contexts (W. Sears 1973). Although originally Safety Harbor ceramics were thought to have originated from the Tampa Bay area (Willey 1949b) they now seem to be distributed from the Caloosahatchee area, and to my mind they indicate the hegemony of power focused there since no other elite ceramic complex was found throughout the region.

There is an increase in sociopolitical complexity through time in south Florida, culminating in an interregional hegemony of power over the entire region by the paramount chieftaincy that developed in the Caloosahatchee region. The inhabitants of this region later became known as the Calusa. Ethnohistoric sources clearly indicate that the paramount chief with political dominance over all south Florida was centered in the Caloosahatchee region (Fontaneda 1944; Goggin and Sturtevant 1964; Hann 1991; Widmer 1988). An intriguing question is, why would a fishing and foraging polity maintain political hegemony over an entire region? An easy answer might be to obtain elite items in trade, and indeed this did go on. Instead, I think that there is a more fundamental economic reason for this hegemony.

I suggest that the reason was the need for fishing, gathering, and hunting access in the interior areas of south Florida not originally under the control of the paramount centered on the southwest Florida coast. This is essential because carrying capacity along the southwest Florida coast can only be increased by developing more effective fishing, hunting, and gathering technology or by expanding the area from which resources can be extracted. I have suggested that ever farther forays offshore to fish are one such response to raise the effective carrying capacity (Widmer 1986b). Expansion of the terrestrial area in which fishing and foraging can be done requires political intervention. By expanding political hegemony over the entire area of south Florida, residents in southwest Florida could safely expand their catchment area, which is technically possible with canoes, into the territory of groups in other regions of south Florida.

Southwest Florida coastal groups had a larger population size and density than groups in the other areas within south Florida, and they would have had a military advantage in maintaining a dominant relationship over groups in other areas, driven by a greater need to expand food acquisition. The political hegemony the Calusa and their ancestors had over the other areas provided the means to expand food acquisition.

Conclusions

Woodland period archaeology in south Florida is a distinctive departure from that of other areas. In no other area of the Southeast does a single adaptation persist into the historic contact era. The south Florida adaptation focused on fishing, collecting, and hunting in the diverse aquatic habitats of the region. More remarkable is the observation that a complex chiefdom developed here with this natural food–based subsistence pattern. The extremely productive natural environment allowed for large population size and density along the southwestern coast of south Florida. Although maize agriculture was briefly utilized during the Hopewell era, and undoubtedly more productive maize agriculture utilized by Mississippian tradition groups to the north was known to the inhabitants of the area, it was not utilized. The reason is that the environment was not conducive to the growth of maize without modern technology, such as drainage and soil amelioration. These were beyond the capacity of the aboriginal technology of the time, although drainage and ridged fields were attempted.

This lack of subsistence agriculture is extremely important because in most areas of the world where there are high-quality aquatic environments, such as Mesoamerica, they are invariably linked with agriculture. The yields from fishing form an important protein strategy to nutritionally complement the carbohydrate-dense agricultural produce or calorie strategy (Widmer 1988). This is the ideal mix, but it is not possible in south Florida. Instead, fish met both the protein and calorie strategies. The resultant human carrying capacity will be much lower than that of the mixed strategy, which is energetically more advantageous based on the greater calories available from plants, because of their lower trophic position than fish. However, the carrying capacity will still be high enough to support a large, dense population because of extremely high primary production (Widmer 1988). This high productivity of the environment does not occur until around 2700 years ago, roughly the beginning of the Woodland period, when the sea level rises to near its present position and its rate of rise slows. This is when south Florida takes on its current configuration.

Sedentary settlement and population growth, made possible by canoe transportation and the highly productive environment, occur particularly along the southwest coast (Widmer 1988). Eventually, population grows to a point where carrying capacity is reached. It is at this point that sociopolitical complexity emerges, because any perturbation in natural environment will disrupt the balance of people and natural resources. Hurricanes, red tides, and even sudden cold fronts can disrupt the food supply. The complementary nature of the maximum availability of fish results in not enough fish at any one time (Widmer 1988) so long-term storage, as was used on the Pacific northwest coast, is not feasible. This reinforces the need for centralized political leadership for redistribution of food and labor when these catastrophes occur. This might be exacerbated by the oscillating late Holocene sea level, although the rapidity of these oscillations is poorly understood.

Nonetheless, we can characterize the entire Woodland period after A.D. 250 as being subject to the effects of both these oscillations and hurricanes. But these alone are not enough for a tributary paramount chiefdom to develop. Demographic features were also important. The southwest Florida coast has the highest population size and density, followed by the Okeechobee Basin, and then southeast Florida. Sociopolitical organization clearly follows this gradient. The dramatically larger population size and density of the southwest Florida coast results in a demographic and hence military and political dominance over the other regions.

A paramount chiefdom developed on the southwest coast to mitigate the adverse risk factors that impact the adaptive system. Population size and density was much lower in the other regions of south Florida, so there was no need nor ability to develop sociopolitical complexity comparable to that seen on the southwest Florida coast. It is both the internal and external population dynamics that result in the tributary, hegemonous political structure seen in south Florida. Ultimately, this results from a much higher carrying capacity along the southwest Florida coast, which provides the high population size and density. The higher population size and density is a greater risk in terms of disruption to resource availability, and so political centralization and redistribution of food and labor is the cultural response to this situation.

The importance of the Woodland period archaeology of south Florida is that it provides an excellent example of the dynamics of sociopolitical development and regional interaction in a situation with only natural resources. It demonstrates that sociopolitical complexity can emerge without agriculture if food sources are abundant and that this food supply is subject to the same degree of risks as, if not more than, agricultural systems.

The archaeological record, together with rich ethnohistoric resources, provides a powerful cross-cultural comparative model to utilize for other time periods and regions, not only in the Southeast, but worldwide. We are now realizing that the development of sociopolitical complexity is not a slow, lineal, continuous process, but instead may consist of a series of punctuated events with increases and decreases in sociopolitical complexity through time. This is particularly probable for adaptations that rely on natural resources, because the quality and quantity of such food resources may vary dramatically with shifts in environment. We now know that the environment was not static in the past and that cultural systems adapted to these changes. It is the demographic consequences of these changes that are important, not only within a local culture or area, but also within the region. Differences in the carrying capacities within a region affect the structure of political and social relationships within the area. The Woodland period of south Florida provides such an example.

Chapter 18

Woodland Ceramic Beginnings

Kenneth E. Sassaman

The prehistory of the southeastern United States confounds the definition of Woodland patterns set forth nearly sixty years ago by the founders of Americanist culture history (Woodland Conference 1943). Many of the defining traits of "Woodlandness" appeared some 1500 to 3000 years earlier in the preceding Archaic period. In parts of the Deep South and peninsular Florida, mound construction began nearly three millennia before Adena and Hopewell mounds were erected (Russo 1996a; J. Saunders and Allen 1994; J. Saunders et al. 1997). Relatively permanent habitation was under way in northeast Florida by 5000 B.P. (Russo 1996b). Groups in the lower Midwest and Midsouth began manipulating oily and starchy seed–bearing plants long before they became full-fledged cultigens (Gremillion 1996a). Long-distance exchange systems were operating in the lower Midwest, Midsouth, and south Atlantic area by 5500 B.P. (Jefferies 1996). And, most conspicuous, Late Archaic populations in several parts of the region made and used the continent's first pottery (Sassaman 1993a).

The recognition of precocious developments in the Archaic Southeast has caused some archaeologists to redefine the later centuries of the period as something other than Archaic. This has been especially true for the early pottery-making cultures of the Late Archaic period, which have been either promoted to the Woodland period (Trinkley 1989, 1990) or relegated to their own categories, as in the Gulf Formational (Walthall and Jenkins 1976) or Florida Transitional (Bullen 1959). Because precocious expressions of "Woodlandness" were neither panregional nor synchronous, such taxonomic innovations have had only limited utility in organizing the regional diversity of Late Archaic cultures.

Whereas the traditional taxonomic divisions between the Archaic and Woodland would seem to have outlived their usefulness, the onset of the Woodland period still holds relevance in at least one respect. Namely, by about 3000 B.P. or slightly later, ceramic vessel technology was sufficiently widespread in the greater Southeast to suggest that few, if any, populations of any consequence existed without pottery (cf. Kirchen 1997). On the surface this condition might be regarded simply as the culmination of a process of innovation diffusion that began 1500 years earlier. Instead of being the outcome of a long, continuous process, however, the widespread use of pottery after 3000 B.P. arguably resulted from the dissolution of Archaic cultural traditions that thwarted change. In other words, the widespread use of pottery had reached the revolutionary status accorded it by Bruce Smith (1986). It was revolutionary in that it coincided with, indeed was ushered in by, significant social change, and it marked a watershed in the development of cooking and storage technology that enabled more effective use of starchy and oily seeds, among other resources.

I elaborate on this argument at the close of this chapter, but my main purpose here is to provide an up-to-date summary of our knowledge about the distribution, timing, and technology of the Southeast's oldest pottery. Elsewhere I have summarized the chronology and cultural contexts of the Stallings wares of coastal South Carolina and Georgia, and the Savannah River valley, which separates these two states (Sassaman 1993a). Since issuing the results of that study, colleagues and I have continued to investigate Stallings sites in the middle Savannah River valley (Elliott et al. 1994; Ledbetter 1995; Sassaman 1993b). The radiocarbon inventory has more than doubled, and we now have many assemblages of early pottery and associated artifacts from unambiguous feature contexts. Some significant advances have likewise been made with the chronology of Florida's first pottery, the Orange series (e.g., Russo 1992; Sassaman 2001), as well as somewhat later ceramic traditions across the Southeast (e.g., Finn 1996; J. Gibson 1996a).

My presentation is divided into four sections. First I summarize the geographical distribution of early pottery traditions. This is followed by a review of the radiocarbon chronology and then a discussion of variation in vessel form and function. I conclude with a summary of the regional traditions of Early Woodland pottery (i.e., traditions dating from about 3000 to 2500 B.P.) and discuss how these deviate markedly from preceding traditions. For other treatments of early pottery in the Southeast, the reader is referred to Anderson et al. (1982), Bullen (1972), DePratter (1979), J. W. Griffin (1972), N. Jenkins et al. (1986), Stoltman (1972), and Trinkley(1980a).

Early Pottery Traditions and Their Distributions in the Southeast

Many parts of the southeastern United States hosted local pottery traditions that preceded the advent of pottery in other regions by many centuries (Figure 18.1). Within the Southeast, however, two traditions clearly had precedence over others. The Stallings series of Georgia-Carolina and the Orange

Figure 18.1 — Distributions of early pottery traditions in the southeastern United States (from Revista de Arqueología Americana, *vol. 14, 1998, used by permission)*

series of Florida have origins dating as much as 4500 radiocarbon years B.P., with Stallings having perhaps slightly greater antiquity than Orange. These traditions shared several traits, most notably fiber tempering, but they are unmistakably distinct in the application of surface decoration. Moreover, Stallings and Orange pottery do not overlap geographically in any appreciable fashion.

Stallings and Related Wares

Originally defined by James B. Griffin in 1943, Stallings is the name given to a series of types that include plain, separate punctate, linear punctate, incised, and other, minority surface treatments on fiber-tempered basins and bowls. The hallmark type for this series is a variety of linear punctate design known as "drag and jab" punctate. The namesake for the tradition, the

Stallings Island site (Claflin 1931) in the middle Savannah River, has yielded abundant drag and jab sherds, as has the Chesterfield shell ring on the south coast of South Carolina (R. Flannery 1943), from which Griffin (1943b) drew his sample for type definition. These two sites mark roughly the geographic extremes of the core area of Stallings sites along the Savannah River, an expanse of some 250 kilometers that encompasses not only much of this major river valley, but also Brier Creek and the Ogeechee River of Coastal Plain Georgia. Stallings pottery likewise occurs along the South Carolina coast to Charleston, but along most of this expanse and farther northward, the prevalent pottery is a nontempered or sand-tempered ware known as Thom's Creek (J. B. Griffin 1945b; Trinkley 1980a). In the opposite direction, along the Georgia coast, fiber-tempered pottery dominates assemblages, but here it is usually assigned to the St. Simons series (Caldwell and Waring 1939; DePratter 1979).

Like many of the early pottery traditions of the Southeast, Stallings began as an exclusively plain ware. The precedence of plain pottery was supported early on by limited, yet influential, stratigraphic excavations at the Bilbo site near the mouth of the Savannah River (Waring 1968a, 1968b). Subsequent excavations at Rabbit Mount in the middle Coastal Plain (Stoltman 1974) provided the first large assemblage of plain fiber-tempered pottery, along with radiocarbon dates suggesting origins at about 4500 B.P. Combining this evidence with other dates and stratigraphic sequences, Stoltman (1974:19) assembled the first comprehensive culture-historical sequence for Stallings manifestations in the Savannah drainage. He defined three phases of the "Stallings Culture": Stallings I, a preceramic phase; Stallings II, a ceramic phase characterized by plain fiber-tempered pottery; and Stallings III, a ceramic phase that included decorated as well as plain pottery. Although Stoltman did not provide absolute chronology for these phases, a few dates from area sites suggested that the Stallings III phase began at about 3700 radiocarbon years B.P. The current radiometric record corroborates this inference (see below).

More recently, I collected data on sherds from twenty-nine sites in the region to refine the culture-historical sequence for Stallings (Sassaman 1993a). My analysis confirmed the basics of Stoltman's model, while adding a third, late ceramic phase (ca. 3400–3000 B.P.) characterized by the resurgence of plain fiber-tempered pottery. Attention to technological, as well as stylistic traits, enabled me to demonstrate that the earliest plain pottery often was fitted with thickened or flanged lips. This proved a valuable trait for discriminating between early and late Stallings assemblages in lieu of radiometric dates or stratigraphic controls. Arguably most important in the analysis was the recognition that none of the diagnostic aspects of the

Stallings sequence was entirely synchronous or pervasive across the Savannah River region. This finding underscored the need for continued refinement of chronology and typology, as well as better theorizing about the cultural dynamics that led to such marked time-space variation.

Laying aside culture process for now, I summarize here our current understanding of the distribution of Stallings pottery within the phase designations outlined above. Plain fiber-tempered pottery with thickened or flanged lips (Stoltman's Stallings II phase) occurs in marine-shell middens of the Georgia coast and the extreme southern coast of South Carolina and at freshwater-shell middens along the Savannah River from its mouth to the lower Piedmont. The adjacent Ogeechee River of Georgia also contains freshwater-shell middens with minor traces of this early ware (Sassaman et al. 1995). Occurrences are known from a few middle Savannah sites lacking shellfish remains (e.g., Crook 1990; Ledbetter 1995), but generally the sites consist of small riverine and coastal shell middens, including the oldest known shell rings on the Georgia coast (Marrinan 1975; Waring and Larson 1968). Despite the application of different typological nomenclature for the Georgia coast, this fledgling coastal pottery cannot be discriminated from its interior, riverine counterpart on technological or stylistic grounds. What is more, there are no geographical hiatuses within its regionwide distribution to suggest the existence of distinct coastal and riverine populations.

In contrast to Stallings II, the highly decorated wares of Stoltman's Stallings III phase have much more circumscribed occurrences in the region. The hallmark linear punctate of the Stallings series is concentrated at sites in the middle Savannah River valley and on the extreme south coast of South Carolina. Dating to about 3700–3500 B.P., these sites attest to a period of cultural diversification and circumscription. Diversification is evident not so much in the stylistic expressions of pottery, but rather in the technology. If we add to the picture the various nontempered and sand-tempered wares that existed across the region, we can infer the presence of another two or three centers of settlement, notably the central Ogeechee River and the central to south coast of South Carolina. Likewise, there appears to be a separate, albeit waning, presence on the Georgia coast marked by decorative elaboration of the extant fiber-tempered tradition, which DePratter (1979) assigns to the St. Simons II phase. Areas between these cores of occupation are not devoid of Stallings pottery or its variants, but they are indeed comparatively minor occurrences. The cultural landscape during this short interval appears to have been partitioned, with large territorial buffers or abandoned land between constituent cores.

Some 200 years after stylistic elaboration and demographic clustering, Stallings groups abandoned riverine and coastal territories. In the middle

Savannah area, Stallings Island and its affiliated shell midden sites were completely abandoned by 3500 B.P. Resident populations dispersed into adjacent uplands, resuming the mobile existence of their ancestors. Pottery technology diversified to encompass a wide range of pastes and surface treatments—including a resurgence of plain wares—with no obvious geographic circumscription.

As populations of the middle Savannah area were reorganizing, many coastal sites were abandoned in apparently serial fashion from south to north. Settlement on the coast continued as new shell rings formed on the central, then north-central South Carolina coast between 3400 and 3100 B.P. Although design elements of the Stallings tradition are evident in the pottery from these late shell rings, the technology is decidedly different in both paste and vessel form. Researchers are unanimous in applying the Thom's Creek type series to these wares. Among them are varieties that are more or less restricted to the north-central coast, such as the finger-pinched variety known as Awendaw (Anderson 1975b; E. Waddell 1965). Otherwise, the Thom's Creek moniker is applied widely to any number of sand-tempered or nontempered pottery assemblages of the fourth millennium B.P. Many such assemblages come from sites across the South Carolina Coastal Plain and eastern Georgia, but not coastal Georgia. In this latter area, fiber-tempered pottery lingered on at the few, smaller coastal settlements that were occupied after 3400 B.P.

Orange

Fiber-tempered pottery appears in Florida no later than 4200 B.P., and possibly several centuries earlier. Until recently, the earliest pottery was believed to be confined to the St. Johns Basin of northeast Florida, where the Orange series of plain and incised wares was defined from collections at several freshwater-shell middens (Bullen 1955, 1972; Goggin 1952). However, fiber-tempered pottery is now known to occur across much of the state (Milanich 1994:86–104). Unfortunately, too few well-dated assemblages from outside the St. Johns area exist to infer much about the age of these extralocal occurrences.

Bullen's (1972) Orange period typology for the St. Johns area includes five subperiods. Orange 1 (4000–3650 B.P.) is characterized by the use of flat-based, rectangular containers that were tempered with fiber, had plain surfaces, thin walls, and simple rounded lips. The subsequent Orange 2 period (3650–3450 B.P.) introduced incised decorations that included concentric vertical diamonds with horizontal lines on vessels of similar form as those of the preceding period. Plain pottery persisted in abundance, and there are occasional instances of the so-called Tick Island style of incised spirals with background punctations. Orange 3 (3450–3250 B.P.) vessels include large, straight-walled and round-mouthed pots with flat bottoms and lesser numbers of shallow rectangular vessels. Decorations on Orange 3 pots include incised straight lines, some set obliquely, and a limited number of punctations or ticks. Pastes with mixtures of sand and fiber appear in Orange 4 times (3250–3000 B.P.). Coiling also appears, and decorations are limited to simple incised motifs. The final period, Orange 5 (3000–2500 B.P.), marks the replacement of fiber-tempered pottery by the chalky St. Johns wares.

The validity of Bullen's sequence for northeast Florida has not been fully tested, although in general outline it seems to have withstood what limited scrutiny it has seen (cf. Janus Research 1995). The Orange tradition does not appear to have had much of an influence in the interior Coastal Plain of Georgia, and it had only a bit of an influence on the coast of Georgia. Orange pottery has been identified at sites in the Kings Bay locality of Camden County (W. Adams [ed.] 1985) and at sites in the Okefenokee Swamp (Trowell 1979). Isolated finds of Orange-like pottery at points farther north are not unusual (e.g., Sapelo Island), although St. Simons is a more appropriate type designation for virtually all of coastal Georgia's decorated fiber-tempered ware. Thus, the St. Marys River, which today marks the boundary between northeast Florida and southeast Georgia, appears to have been a cultural boundary of sorts during the ceramic Late Archaic (Russo 1992), much as it was in later prehistoric times (Goggin 1952).

Wheeler
Fiber-tempered pottery other than the Stallings and Orange series is decidedly late in the Southeast's history of early ceramics. Most notable among the late varieties is Wheeler pottery from the Midsouth (Haag 1939a; Sears and Griffin 1950). Known primarily from sites in the middle Tennessee River area of northern Alabama, Wheeler pottery consists of wide-mouthed, flat-bottomed beakers and bowls with largely plain, but also punctate, dentate, and simple-stamped surface treatments (N. Jenkins and Krause 1986:33; N. Jenkins et al. 1986:548). Chronology for Wheeler pottery is uncertain, although it is unlikely to predate 3500 B.P. It continued well into the last half of the third millennium B.P. (N. Jenkins and Krause 1986:43), when it was accompanied by the sand-tempered Alexander series across much of Mississippi and Alabama.

Recent excavations and collections research are enhancing knowledge about the Midsouth's earliest pottery (Finn 1996; O'Hear 1996). New data on the geographical extent of fiber-tempered pottery in Alabama show a more pervasive distribution than previously seen (Finn and Goldman-Finn

1997). With the exception of the ridge-and-valley mountain range in the northeast, the entire state contains assemblages of fiber-tempered ware. Local researchers refer generally to this pottery as Wheeler (e.g., Finn and Goldman-Finn 1997; N. Jenkins et al. 1986), although O'Hear suggests that middle Tennessee River valley assemblages have properties that distinguish them from fiber-tempered assemblages elsewhere in the Midsouth. Most notably, classic Wheeler pottery from middle Tennessee River sites is thinner and more often decorated than regional counterparts (John O'Hear, personal communication, 1997).

Farther to the west are occurrences of fiber-tempered pottery in the Poverty Point area of northeast Louisiana and western Mississippi (Figure 18.1). The famous Poverty Point culture of circa 3300–3000 B.P. is not known historically as a center of early pottery production, but rather as the recipient of materials and influences from the east. Jon Gibson (1996a) has examined collections and stratigraphic data from Poverty Point to document a variety of early pottery types. In addition to fiber-tempered pottery classified as Wheeler, sherds in definite Poverty Point context include sand-tempered, clay-grit–tempered, and nontempered varieties. Although data are insufficient to establish the absolute timing of these various wares, Gibson argues convincingly that locally manufactured clay-grit–tempered and nontempered pottery predated the introduction of Wheeler pottery. This then situates Poverty Point pottery as the oldest pottery in the Lower Mississippi Valley, independent, apparently, from "external" influences. Still, the volume of early pottery sherds at Poverty Point is comparatively small, being eclipsed by the vast numbers of sherds from imported soapstone vessels. Parenthetically, the culture-historical relationship between stone vessels and early pottery is a long-standing topic of research in the Southeast, one for which I will have more to offer in later sections of this summary.

Norwood

Moving eastward once again, we find a variety of fiber-tempered wares containing varying combinations of aplastic temper. So-called "semi–fiber-tempered" pottery from sites in northwest Florida has surfaces with stick impressions and a sandy paste. Phelps (1965) introduced the Norwood type series to accommodate these wares and to distinguish them from fine-paste, incised Orange pottery. As Milanich (1994:95–97) has recently pointed out, however, not all Norwood pottery has a sandy paste, while some Orange pottery does, and designs of the Orange series occasionally appear in Norwood assemblages. The distribution, chronology, and typological validity of Norwood remain to be determined. It continues to be used as a catchall type for the semi–fiber-tempered wares of the panhandle of Florida and adjoining areas (e.g., Mikell 1997; P. Thomas and Campbell 1991) and apparently dates no earlier than 3500 B.P.

Satilla

Scores of sites in the Ocmulgee Big Bend area of south Georgia contain fiber-tempered pottery. Little of this material can be accommodated by existing typologies (e.g., Stallings, Orange, St. Simons) and hence it warrants its own typological categories. As described by Snow (1977a), Satilla wares are semi–fiber-tempered pottery with plain, simple-stamped, and check-stamped surface treatments. Sites with Satilla pottery are prevalent along the upper Satilla River, in the interriverine area between the Satilla and Ocmulgee rivers, and southwest into the Gulf-draining Alapaha River. Satilla sherds are thin, show occasional coil breaks, and have very sandy pastes. Its sandy paste and simple-stamped surfaces are consistent with the Norwood series, although Norwood does not include check-stamped surfaces.

The fiber-tempered pottery from nearby Ocmulgee River sites deviates technologically and stylistically from Satilla wares. The Ocmulgee pottery is thick and largely plain. What few decorated sherds Snow (1977a) has collected include punctated and incised varieties from sites on the Ocmulgee proper; sites with plain pottery extend into the adjoining upland tributaries. The decorated sherds include examples that fit Stallings, St. Simons, and Orange type criteria, yet they are a distinct minority. Several lines of evidence suggest that both the Satilla and Ocmulgee wares are relatively late (i.e., post–3500 B.P.; Elliott and Sassaman 1995:60–61), although absolute dates are needed to verify this supposition.

Other, Unspecified Fiber-Tempered Wares

Fiber-tempered or semi–fiber-tempered pottery can be found throughout the Georgia Coastal Plain and Fall Zone. That found in western Georgia has been identified variously as Stallings Island, Orange, or Norwood, and includes plain, incised, and punctated vessels. Some of the sherds are entirely fiber tempered, while others, presumably later in the sequence, contain fiber and grit tempering.

As noted earlier, fiber-tempered pottery is likewise widespread across much of peninsular Florida. The typological and chronological parameters of assemblages outside the St. Johns Basin remain virtually unknown, although I suspect that none of these finds will predate the oldest Orange pottery of northeast Florida. Clearly, the St. Johns sites and the nearby coastal sites of northeast Florida form a core of population and technological development that overshadows all other occurrences of early pottery in the state.

Finally, plain fiber-tempered pottery occurs at sites in the southeast Coastal Plain of North Carolina (Figure 18.1). Phelps (1983:26–28) assigns these sherds to the Stallings Plain type, despite their remoteness from the core area of Stallings pottery. Thom's Creek sherds occur with appreciable frequency in Brunswick and New Hanover counties of coastal North Carolina and have also been identified at sites in the interior Coastal Plain (Herbert 1999, this volume). Neither of these presumed extralocal expressions has been securely dated in North Carolina. Two additional pottery series of apparently local origin may date as early as the Stallings and Thom's Creek series. New River is a coarse sand-and-grit tempered ware (Loftfield 1976) with recent radiocarbon assays in excess of 4000 B.P. (Sanborn and Abbott 1999). The limestone-tempered Hamp's Landing series (Hargrove 1993) was initially defined in a stratum situated between Thom's Creek and Middle Woodland strata, although recent dates possibly push its origins into the fifth millennium B.P. (D. C. Jones et al. 1997; Sanborn and Abbott 1999). Only more dates from secure contexts will tell whether these local wares are truly coeval with, or perhaps older than, fiber-tempered wares to the south.

Radiocarbon Chronology

As shown in the foregoing section, the southeastern United States was home to a variety of early ceramic traditions. Chronologies for the oldest among them, those of the south Atlantic slope (i.e., Stallings, St. Simons, Thom's Creek, Orange), are supported by a large number of radiocarbon dates, whereas the remaining traditions are in dire need of larger samples. As more dates are obtained, we may find that south Atlantic traditions were preceded, or at least paralleled, by traditions elsewhere. For now, Stallings, St. Simons, and Orange are the oldest, followed closely by Thom's Creek.

One hundred eight radiocarbon assays are currently available for the four oldest pottery traditions. Figure 18.2 is a graphic display of the dates, subdivided by type series. Included, too, are dates for preceramic components from sites in or adjacent to locations of early pottery, as well as a series of new dates on soapstone vessels. Most of these dates have been published elsewhere (see compilations in Elliott and Sassaman 1995; Russo 1992; Sassaman 1993a, 1997; Sassaman and Anderson 1995), although many come from my largely unpublished, ongoing work in the middle Savannah River valley.

The radiocarbon record for Stallings pottery is quite robust, comprised of fifty-six assays ranging from circa 4500 to 3200 B.P. The dates are divided roughly evenly between the early Stallings phase of plain pottery and the

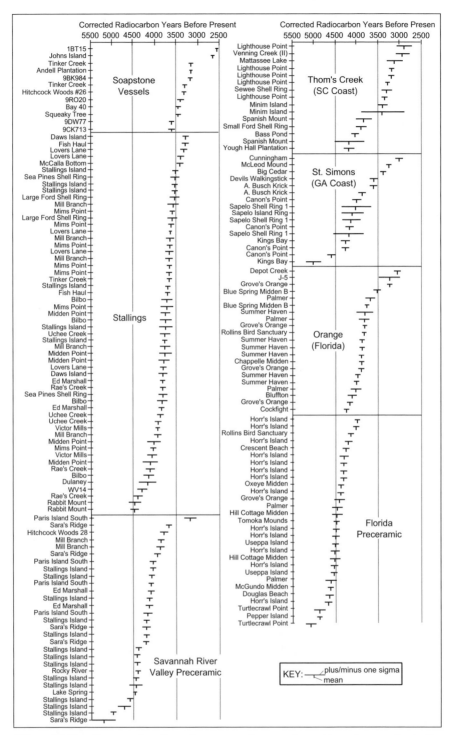

Figure 18.2 — Corrected radiocarbon assays from major early pottery series in the south Atlantic region, along with assays for select preceramic sites and soapstone vessels (from Revista de Arqueología Americana, *vol. 14, 1998, used by permission)*

"classic" Stallings era of highly decorated wares. Also occupying the eight centuries of the early Stallings phase are a series of dates designated "Savannah River Valley Preceramic." These come from habitation sites in the middle to upper Savannah River valley that not only lack pottery altogether, but also yield material assemblages quite distinct from those of their pottery-making counterparts. Before radiocarbon dating, the differences in assemblages were assumed to be temporal, as key stratified sequences suggested (e.g., Claflin 1931; C. Miller 1949). Once dates became available, particularly those from work in the Richard B. Russell Reservoir of the upper Savannah Valley (Anderson and Joseph 1988), researchers came to realize that pottery-using groups coexisted with preceramic populations for many centuries.

The radiocarbon record of early coastal pottery poses a different set of circumstances. Corrections for fractionation on marine shell have pushed back the dates for coastal pottery to at least 4500 B.P. It now seems certain that pottery in the south Atlantic region originated on the sea islands of present-day Georgia with the St. Simons series. After corrections, dates for Orange pottery from northeast Florida may be comparably old, but for now the record suggests that its local developments postdated the origins of St. Simons by a century or two. What remains so poorly documented are the centuries preceding pottery origins along most of the south Atlantic coast. Until recently, regional archaeologists assumed that preceramic occupations of the coast were either prohibited because of unstable sea levels, or, if they occurred, completely inundated and buried by rising sea levels. In the past decade, Florida archaeologists, especially Russo (1991, 1992, 1996b), have amassed evidence for preceramic coastal occupations in northeast and southwest Florida. The radiocarbon record of these occupations (Figure 18.2) suggests that they were truly preceramic; that is, they predate the appearance of Orange pottery, at least in northeast Florida. Dates postdating 4500 B.P. in Figure 18.2 are dominated by those from Horr's Island, in southwest Florida (Russo 1991). As indicated earlier, pottery in this remote location of Florida almost certainly postdates 4000 B.P. Hence, the Florida record, thus far, does not include evidence for the coexistence of pottery-using and non–pottery-using populations like those of the Savannah River valley.

Turning again northward, the inventory for Thom's Creek dates from the coast and lower Coastal Plain of South Carolina verifies that this series is generally late in the sequence of early coastal pottery (Figure 18.2). With one exception (i.e., Yough Hall) all assays predating 3500 B.P. are from sites south of Charleston. In this southern stretch of the South Carolina coast, assemblages of early pottery are mixtures of Thom's Creek and Stallings wares. The more consistently sand-tempered pottery assemblages from sites north of Charleston are younger than 3500 B.P. These occupations constitute a distinct cultural phase, one that coincides with the abandonment of many of the southerly coastal sites, as well as the freshwater-shell middens of the middle Savannah River.

Finally, I include in Figure 18.2 a series of newly acquired AMS dates on soot from sherds of soapstone vessels (Sassaman 1997). Throughout much of eastern North America, soapstone was carved into round or rectangular vessel forms, as well as a variety of other items, such as pipes and bannerstones. Archaeologists have long regarded soapstone vessels to be the technological precursor of pottery. Countering this claim, researchers working in northeast Florida and the Savannah River valley collected strati-graphic evidence to suggest just the opposite (e.g., Bullen 1972; Elliott et al. 1994). The AMS dates on vessel soot support their observations. This record shows that pottery preceded the local appearance of soapstone vessels by as much as 1000 years. None of the soapstone dates in the greater Savannah River region are older than 3500 B.P. The two slightly older ages in Figure 18.2 are from sites in the mountains of northwest Georgia, an area that did not embrace pottery until after 3500 B.P.

The relevance of this revised soapstone vessel chronology should be obvious. By repositioning the origins of soapstone vessels after the develop-ment of pottery, evolutionary or functionalist arguments based on an as-sumed stone-to-pottery sequence are rendered obsolete. How widely this revised sequence applies is not yet clear. Pottery clearly preceded stone ves-sels throughout South Carolina and Florida and most of Georgia. J. Gibson (1996a) has shown that pottery also preceded the enormous soapstone ves-sel commerce of Poverty Point exchange. I believe future research will re-verse the stone-to-pottery sequence for much of the Midsouth, and perhaps the Middle Atlantic region as well (but see Hantman and Gold, this volume).

To summarize, radiocarbon chronology for early pottery in the south Atlantic region has reached a level of detail and clarity that is unmatched in adjacent regions. Sufficient data now exist to document with considerable certainty not only the origins of pottery making in the region but also the ethnic diversity of the cultural landscape in which it emerged, as well as the technological alternatives and innovations that unfolded over the course of this early history.

Vessel Form and Function

Recent years in American archaeology have witnessed a burgeoning interest in the technofunctional aspects of prehistoric pottery (e.g., D. Braun 1983;

Hally 1986; Steponaitis 1983). Increasing attention is being diverted from the traditional pursuits of typology and culture history to inquiry centering on the actual uses of vessels and the technological decisions of potters to meet particular functional demands. With this change in emphasis has come an analytical shift from sherds to vessels. Much new information has been developed on the relationship between vessel form and vessel function, as well as the material parameters (e.g., wall thickness and temper) that affect use efficiency. More than simply information on how pots were made and used, technofunctional data reveal variation that has until now been masked by culture-historical typologies. With this newfound variation comes plenty of new opportunity to examine the cultural dynamics behind the histories of particular innovations.

Whereas the analysis of vessel form and function is becoming routine in the archaeology of late prehistoric populations, its application to early pottery lags behind. The blame for this is partly on sampling limitations. Because they involve friable, low-fired wares, early pottery assemblages generally consist of small sherds. Absent from these assemblages are the whole vessels typical of later mortuary contexts. Much to our loss, early pottery users in the Southeast did not adorn the graves of their dead with pottery. Without access to whole pots or large vessel portions, Southeastern archaeologists are seldom able to spend the many hours it takes to reassemble sherds into meaningful units. Indeed, contract archaeology, the context for most modern research, does not usually afford such expenditures.

The limited research to date on technofunctional aspects of early pottery focuses· on assemblages of Stallings and Thom's Creek pottery (Espenshade and Brockington 1989; Sassaman 1993a, 1993c; Skibo et al. 1988; Trinkley 1980a). Some useful observations have been published on the form and technology of Orange pottery (e.g., Bullen 1972; Shannon 1986), and analyses of assemblages housed at the Florida Museum of Natural History have commenced recently (Sassaman 2001). I have collected in Table 18.1 some summary data of varying quality on each of these ware groups. Stallings and St. Simons samples are combined for this purpose, as data on these wares were not separated in earlier analysis (Sassaman 1993a).

The technological history of Stallings/St. Simons pottery records the transition from indirect-heat to direct-heat cooking methods (Sassaman 1993a, 1995). Indirect-heat cooking, or "stone boiling" as it is commonly known, is a technique of moist cooking that predates the beginnings of pottery making by many millennia. Archaeological evidence for this technique is often ubiquitous. Under most circumstances, stone boiling with materials like granite, quartz, or limestone results in an abundance of cracked rock, as such materials are poor at resisting the thermal shock of rapid temperature changes. In

Table 18.1 — Technofunctional Properties of Early Pottery from the South Atlantic Region

	Vessel Forms	Temper	Vessel Wall Thick. (mm)*	Rim Profile	Percent Sooted
Early Stallings/ St. Simons	basin	heavy fiber	9.02 ± 1.77	straight	6.7
Classic Stallings – Coastal	bowl, jar	fiber, minor sand	9.42 ± 0.87	straight, incurvate	42.3
– Riverine • Savannah	bowl, jar	fiber, sand	9.48 ± 0.94	straight incurvate carinated	5.0
• Ogeechee	bowl, jar	sand, minor fiber	12.03 ± 2.08	straight incurvate	3.3
Thom's Creek – Coastal	bowl, jar	none, fine sand	7.39 ± 1.05	straight incurvate	no data
– Riverine • Santee- Congaree	bowl, jar	none, fine sand	7.25 ± 0.57	straight incurvate	no data
• Savannah	bowl, jar	fine-medium sand	9.45 ± 0.80	straight incurvate	no data
*Orange*** – Orange 1–2	basin, bowl	heavy fiber	8.00 ± 1.80	straight	3.0
– Orange 3	basin, bowl	heavy fiber	11.30 ± 2.80	straight	67.7
– Orange 4–5	bowl	fiber, sand, spicules	8.50 ± 2.20	straight incurvate	64.4

*   *Measured 3 cm below lip (mean ± one standard deviation)*

** *Based on limited data from five sites in the middle St. Johns Valley; comparable data on assemblages from coastal Florida sites are not yet available (Sassaman 2001)*

Sources:
   Bullen 1972; Espenshade and Brockington 1989; Griffin 1941; Phelps 1968; Sassaman 1993a, 1993c, 2001; Sassaman et al. 1995; Trinkley 1980a

the middle Savannah River valley, beginning at about 5500 B.P., inhabitants began to apply locally available soapstone to their cooking needs. Because it absorbs and dissipates heat very slowly, and is therefore resistant to thermal shock, soapstone makes an excellent thermal medium for indirect-heat cooking. Early forms of soapstone cooking stones consisted of crudely modified nodules. Later, nodules were carefully ground to a flat profile, then perforated so that they could be transferred from fire to container with a stick or antler tine. Clay-lined pits, baskets, and perhaps wooden containers were used with soapstone slabs for indirect-heat moist cooking.

By the time pottery was introduced on the coast and in the lower Coastal Plain at circa 4500 B.P., resident Piedmont populations had a well-established soapstone slab industry. Their Coastal Plain counterparts likewise utilized soapstone slabs, acquiring them either directly, during seasonal rounds to the lower Piedmont, or through exchange with partners near Piedmont sources. The earliest ceramic vessels in these areas were ideally suited to indirect-heat cooking (see Reid 1989; Schiffer and Skibo 1987 for mechanical performance criteria of indirect-heat vessels). Designed to retain internal heat, these shallow basins had thick vessel walls to retard heat loss; insulating, porous pastes provided by fiber temper; and flat, thick bottoms for radiating an internal source of heat. Although the high orifice to volume ratio of this form allowed heat to escape, its wide-mouthed, shallow design was necessary for the manipulation of vessel content, particularly the cooking stones that were cycled through for continuous heating. In essence, these ceramic basins were portable versions of the cooking pits used by countless generations of predecessors. The most likely applications of indirect-heat moist cooking were to render grease from bone and fats from hickory nuts and perhaps to stew small gastropods (Sassaman 1995).

Not long after flat-bottomed basins were introduced, coastal residents began to experiment with forms and manufacturing techniques to develop vessels for direct-heat cooking. It seems likely that this need was stimulated by the high procurement costs of soapstone, accentuated, perhaps, by growing ethnic divisions between riverine and coastal groups, as described earlier. From this point forward, the technological trajectories of early pottery diverged, with innovations enabling direct-heat cooking evolving first on the coast, and indirect-heat cooking techniques persisting for centuries at interior riverine sites.

Technological changes in the coastal Stallings and Thom's Creek series reflect increasing refinement in direct-heat cooking vessels. Vessel forms diversified to include bowl and jar forms with lower orifice to volume ratios than basins, hence lower rates of heat loss. Slightly incurvate rim profiles enhanced thermal efficiency by reducing orifice size without loss of volume. Rounded bases permitted greater air flow to the heat source for better combustion (Hally 1986:280). Thermal conductivity was increased as pastes were made increasingly sandier and less porous. Further improvements in conductivity appeared in the thin vessel walls of Thom's Creek pottery, although initially walls became thicker on average to accommodate taller forms. The innovation of coiling, appearing in the late Stallings and Thom's Creek wares (Trinkley 1980a), alleviated the limitations on thinner walls. Shell-scraped interiors of the Thom's Creek series (Sassaman 1993a:178–79) attest to efforts not only to thin walls for maximum conductivity, but also to achieve uniform thickness for greater thermal shock resistance.

Many of these same innovations for direct-heat cooking had parallel expressions in the riverine contexts of classic Stallings, yet such vessels were not routinely used over fire. Independent evidence for use alteration illustrates the functional distinction. Whereas more than 42 percent of coastal Stallings vessels bear traces of soot on exterior surfaces, only 5 percent of riverine vessels are sooted, a proportion even lower than that seen among flat-bottomed basins of the early Stallings period (Table 18.1). These observations led me to suggest that the tradition of indirect-heat cooking with soapstone persisted among riverine communities of the middle Savannah despite access to technology for direct-heat cooking (Sassaman 1993a). Recent excavations confirm that soapstone cooking stones continued to be made and used during classic Stallings times (Sassaman 1993b).

Elsewhere in riverine contexts, innovations for direct-heat cooking had even less influence. For instance, vessels from Ogeechee River sites are by far the thickest in the region (Table 18.1). Despite forms and temper conducive to direct-heat cooking, these thick wares were undoubtedly poor heat conductors; fewer than 4 percent bear traces of soot. Similarly, Thom's Creek vessels from Savannah River sites have relatively thick vessel walls coupled with sandy or gritty pastes. Quantified data on use alteration are not available for this series, although my own casual inspection has found very few examples with soot.

The only notable exception to the overall trend for traditional cooking practices in riverine contexts is Thom's Creek technology from the Santee-Congaree drainage of central South Carolina. Here, in the Coastal Plain heartland of Thom's Creek wares, we find vessel forms and pastes virtually identical to those from the coast. Most notably, vessel walls are as thin as coastal examples. Although independent data on vessel function are lacking, it is noteworthy that soapstone slabs did not figure prominently in the technological history of Santee-Congaree cooking. Throughout prehistory, this river system formed something of a boundary between regional populations. This was apparently the case during the Thom's Creek era, when Santee-Congaree residents had affiliations with coastal groups to the east, but seemingly little to no affiliation with residents of the middle Savannah River area to the southwest.

Technofunctional data thus far accumulated from sites in the middle St. Johns duplicate the coastal Stallings record in registering: (1) the transition from indirect-heat to direct-heat cooking, and (2) ensuing improvements in the thermal efficiency of vessels. Whereas only 3 percent Orange Plain vessels (n = 231) bear traces of soot, 68 percent of Orange Incised vessels (n = 266) are sooted. A similarly large proportion of fiber-tempered vessels with spiculate paste (n = 73) are sooted. Orifices increased in average size from 21.6 ± 6.7 centimeters for Orange Plain vessels to 29.6 ± 8.8 centimeters for Orange Incised vessels. At 30.6 ± 7.5 centimeters on average, vessels with spiculate paste are comparable to Orange Incised. Presumably vessel height increased as well, although metric data are insufficient to substantiate this. We now have good evidence that coiling was common to Orange Incised vessels (Endonino 2000), an innovation that would have enabled taller vessel profiles. As vessel size increased, wall thickness first increased then decreased. Orange Incised pottery from the middle St. Johns is especially thick, 11.3 ± 2.8 millimeters, compared to Orange Plain at only 8.0 ± 1.8 millimeters. Coupled with the porous paste, thick-walled Orange pottery was not especially efficient in transferring heat. However, by the time spicules were added or selected for in the paste (itself an improvement in thermal conductivity over fiber), average wall thickness dropped to 8.5 ± 2.2 millimeters. Among the techniques used to achieve thinner walls was rigorous scraping of interior vessel walls prior to firing.

Technofunctional data on coastal Orange pottery are yet too few to make definitive statements of comparison with middle St. Johns assemblages. However, Saunders's (2001) vessel data on the 3700–3600 B.P. Rollins Shell Ring, coupled with some preliminary observations from a few other northeast Florida coastal sites, reflect an extremely low incidence of sooted sherds. This stands in sharp contrast to not only the middle St. Johns assemblages of equal age, but also those of coastal Georgia and South Carolina. Saunders (2001) suggests that Orange vessels may have been used routinely over embers, rather than open fires, thus lessening the chances for soot formation on upper portions of vessel walls.

In summary, technofunctional studies of early pottery in Georgia-Carolina and northeast Florida document a history of changing vessel form and paste characteristics that signal a shift from indirect-heat to direct-heat moist cooking. The transition occurred first on the coast of Georgia-Carolina, where access to effective thermal media for indirect-heat cooking was limited. In contrast, occupants of the middle Savannah River area continued to procure and utilize soapstone for cooking stones throughout the early centuries of pottery use, when flat-bottomed, fiber-tempered basins were ideally suited to indirect-heat cooking. Even after innovations for direct-heat cooking with pottery appeared in the middle Savannah, indirect-heat cooking with soapstone slabs persisted. Coastal Florida may likewise be a locus of persistent indirect-heat cooking well after the innovation of direct-heat cooking was embraced in the middle St. Johns area. Additional analyses are required to evaluate this supposition.

Post–3000 B.P. Pottery Typology and Technology

After about 3000 B.P., pottery was made and used widely across the greater Southeast; by 2500 B.P. virtually no populations existed without pottery. The plethora of local and subregional types recognized for this period belies the advanced level of conformity in technology and function after 3000 B.P. With few exceptions, pottery series regionwide consist of tall, globular or conoidal-based vessels that were tempered with either sand or grit and constructed using a coiling technique. Vessel wall thickness generally decreased as vessel height increased, which, together with changes in paste and form, rendered vessels more effective for direct-heat cooking. The actual functions of these new forms are not altogether certain, although such pervasive change in technology would suggest a significant shift in subsistence practices. Irrespective of subsistence change, the shift from circumscribed use of Archaic period pottery to widespread use of Early Woodland pottery was relatively rapid, occurring over a period of about three centuries. Regional traditions of surface treatment, such as cord marking or check stamping, were equally quick and thorough in their diffusion. Social circumstances among populations must have been such that personnel and ideas moved freely from one group to the next. I suggest these circumstances stand in marked contrast to those of the Late Archaic landscape, where at least some cultural configurations (Stallings, Orange, Poverty Point) imposed effective barriers to innovation diffusion.

As Caldwell (1958) observed, the regional landscape of Early Woodland pottery traditions consisted of a complex array of local developments situated within histories of interregional influences. Out of the local traditions of Stallings and Thom's Creek pottery arose the Refuge tradition of coastal and Coastal Plain Georgia–South Carolina (Waring 1968c). Dating from about 3050 B.P., Refuge pottery consists primarily of straight-sided, conoidal or round-bottomed jars averaging 30 centimeters tall and 25 centimeters wide. Temper is generally coarse sand or grit; vessel walls average about 8 millimeters thick. Surface treatments are dominated by simple stamping, with dentate stamping, punctation, and incising comprising minority treatments with chronological significance (Anderson 1987; Anderson [ed.] 1996; Anderson et al. 1982; DePratter 1979, 1991).

In the north Georgia coastal sequence (DePratter 1979), check-stamped pottery of the Deptford series was introduced during the Refuge III phase (2900–2400 B.P.). Located along the Gulf coast of Florida, as well as the south Atlantic coast and Coastal Plain, Deptford culture apparently arose from indigenous Late Archaic populations to become one of the most widespread Woodland traditions, as least in terms of pottery technology. The distinctive check-stamped and simple-stamped surface treatments of Deptford wares occur primarily on conoidal jars, tempered with sand or grit of varying size, and with vessel walls averaging about 7.5 millimeters thick. In the Florida Gulf coastal region, early Deptford pottery sometimes contains fiber, as well as sand or grit, as a tempering agent, a lingering trait that Milanich (1994:129) suggests attests to continuity between local Late Archaic and Woodland populations. Deptford pots from the Gulf Coast sometimes include podal supports on their bases, a trait shared with coeval pottery traditions of the western Gulf Coast and the Piedmont province.

Check stamping and occasional tetrapodal supports also appear later in the St. Johns ceramic sequence of north Florida, which began in Orange 5 times (ca. 3000–2500 B.P.), whereas plain vessels eclipse decorated vessels manyfold in the early assemblages. Distinguishing St. Johns wares from regional counterparts is its fine, chalky paste and prevalence of sponge spicules. Bowl forms continue with appreciable frequency in the St. Johns sequence, although they are routinely thin-walled and often sooted, attesting to use directly over fire.

A second cluster of Early Woodland pottery in the Gulf coastal region and Coastal Plain involves two major series, Bayou La Batre and Alexander. The former is apparently the oldest sand/grit-tempered, coiled pottery in the Gulf region (Wimberly 1953), although absolute chronology for the series is sketchy. Sites with Bayou La Batre pottery, typically shell middens, are centered on Mobile Bay in Alabama. Vessel forms include globular pots and flaring-side jars or beakers, both with annular bases or tetrapodal supports (N. Jenkins and Krause 1986:31; Walthall 1980:95). Random rocker stamping is the most common surface treatment. Poorly documented varieties of fiber-tempered pottery are found in the Mobile Bay area in stratigraphic contexts below Bayou La Batre pottery. These older assemblages suggest a local precedent for pottery reaching back to at least 3200 B.P.

A similar trend from fiber-tempered to sand-tempered pottery exists across much of Alabama and northeast Mississippi in the Alexander pottery series (J. B. Griffin 1939; Haag 1942b). As noted earlier, Wheeler fiber-tempered pottery is widely distributed across Alabama, although it occurs most frequently at sites in the middle Tennessee River valley, where it is thinner and more often decorated than regional counterparts. Local researchers agree that Alexander pottery follows directly from the Wheeler tradition (N. Jenkins and Krause 1986:35; Walthall 1980:100–103; see also O'Hear 1990). Dating as early as 2700 B.P., Alexander pottery consists of sand-tempered globular and straight-sided jars with tetrapodal or annular bases, rim bosses, and surface treatments that include incising, pinching, punctation, rocker stamping, and dentate stamping. A related ware from the Lower Mississippi Valley, Tchefuncte, consists of similar forms with grog or clay temper and diverse surface treatments, some of which, like incising and linear punctate, are possibly the result the influences from the south Atlantic (N. Jenkins et al. 1986:551; cf. J. B. Griffin 1986b:618).

On another front, cord-marked pottery traditions from the north appeared at about 3000 B.P. in the Deep Creek and New River series of coastal and Coastal Plain North Carolina (Phelps 1983) and somewhat later (ca. 2700 B.P.) in the Vincent, Badin, and Yadkin series of Piedmont North Carolina (Coe 1964; Herbert, this volume) and the Swannanoa series of the Appalachian Summit (Keel 1976; Wetmore, this volume). After 2700 B.P., fabric-impressed pottery traditions from the west emerged as distinct Early Woodland wares, such as Dunlap of the Kellogg phase in northwest Georgia (Bowen 1989; Ledbetter 1992). Related traditions appear to have spread rapidly across North Carolina to become part of the Swannanoa, Badin, Vincent, Yadkin, and Deep Creek series. Other subregional expressions of fabric-impressed pottery are seen in the limestone-tempered ceramics of the Long Branch series of western Alabama (DeJarnette et al. 1973) and in the crushed-quartz–tempered Watts Bar series of eastern Tennessee (Lewis and Kneberg 1957).

In sum, Early Woodland pottery series across the Southeast share a variety of technological features that enhanced their functional utility as cooking vessels. Virtually all series consist of tall jars or beakers with conical, rounded, or annular bases. Walls were formed through coiling, a technique that enabled potters to achieve taller profiles. Paddle-and-anvil treatments ensured a compacted ceramic body, and scraping was applied routinely to achieve uniform thickness. Adding sand or crushed quartz to clay afforded resistance to thermal shock in the firing process, as well as in direct-heat applications.

Functions besides cooking no doubt factored into the technical specifications of the Southeast's early potters. Indeed, many Early Woodland ceramics may have embodied a compromise among cooking, dry storage, and liquid storage functions. However, in their choice of temper, vessel profile, and size, Early Woodland potters must have kept the technical specifications of direct-heat cooking foremost in their minds. Continued improvements in cooking vessel design over the Woodland period, such as those described by D. Braun (1983) for the Midwest, likely describes the ensuing history of pottery technology in the Southeast, although data to support this have yet to be compiled.

Conclusion

The advent of the Southeast's oldest pottery traditions—namely Stallings, Orange, and Thom's Creek, as well as lesser-known series of fiber-tempered wares—precedes the regionwide use of pottery by as much as 2000 years. Over these millennia we find evidence for the transition from indirect-heat to direct-heat cooking in the Stallings series of coastal Georgia-Carolina, and perhaps in the Florida Orange series as well. The slow pace of technological change elsewhere is not likely a symptom of social disintegration or economic conservatism, but rather one of regional interaction. As counterintuitive as this may seem, the Stallings culture of the middle Savannah River valley exemplifies how efforts to perpetuate or reinvent traditions of alliance building thwarted significant change in the actual uses of vessels, if not the technology per se.

Other Late Archaic cultural expressions throughout the Southeast may have exerted similar influences that slowed or redirected the pace of change. Poverty Point culture and many of the so-called Shell Mound Archaic cultures involved long-distance alliances and other interregional relations that could have readily accommodated the spread of ceramic technology. Instead, pottery was not adopted among many regional populations until after these cultural entities dissolved. I have suggested elsewhere that the Poverty Point exchange of soapstone vessels thwarted the spread of pottery regionwide (Sassaman 1993a). The precedence of pottery at the Poverty Point site (J. Gibson 1996a) does nothing to undermine this proposal; indeed, it strengthens it, because now we know that Poverty Point residents did not lack knowledge about making and using ceramic pots over the centuries they chose to import and use soapstone for direct-heat cooking. Only after Poverty Point trade ceased, after roughly 2900 B.P., did regional populations embrace ceramic cooking technology in any appreciable fashion.

Refinements in chronology for soapstone vessels in the Southeast show that the technology mostly coincided with the local adoption of direct-heat ceramic vessel technology. In most cases, soapstone vessels were not the technological precursor of pottery. Where soapstone vessels were used before pottery, this was probably not because local populations lacked knowledge of ceramic technology, or access to suitable clays, and not because they lacked a need for durable cooking vessel technology. Why pottery-making populations outside of source areas for soapstone would bother with soapstone vessels would seem to be the more interesting question. Clearly the answer will require more than an understanding of the costs and benefits of alternative cooking technologies in any neofunctionalist sense. As they always do, tradition, history, and culture will take precedence.

Although we are yet to have solid evidence on social organization, I suspect that a contributing factor in the eventual widespread adoption of pottery throughout the Southeast was an erosion of unilineal systems of descent and unilocal postmarital residence patterns (Sassaman and Rudolphi 2001). Inasmuch as pottery was a gender-specific (i.e., women's) technology, changes in descent and postmarital residence would have had potentially marked effects on regional distributions of pottery traits. Notably, changes toward more inclusive social systems, such as bilateral descent and bilocal residence, would have lifted barriers to flows of personnel that perhaps geographically circumscribed cultural traditions such as Stallings, Orange, and Poverty Point. I am optimistic that pottery has the potential to reveal the details of prehistoric social organization, despite the problems recognized in earlier efforts elsewhere (e.g., J. Hill 1970; Longacre 1970). Success in this regard will depend, I think, on continuing efforts to treat technofunctional data not merely as information about technical choice, but as evidence of conscious expressions of cultural identity.

Acknowledgments

Portions of this chapter were published previously in Revista de Arqueología Americana, *volume 14, 1998; used by permission. My thanks to Oscar M. Fonseca Zamora for permission to use this material in modified form. Editors David G. Anderson and Robert C. Mainfort, Jr., and two anonymous reviewers deserve thanks for helping to improve the content and style of this chapter. Technofunctional data on Orange pottery from the middle St. Johns were collected by University of Florida graduate students Mark Donop, Jon Endonino, Jim Mallard, and Christian Russell.*

Chapter 19

Culture-Historical Units and the Woodland Southeast: A Case Study from Southeastern Missouri

Michael J. O'Brien, R. Lee Lyman, and James W. Cogswell

The archaeological record of southeastern Missouri has long been a focus of attention, and there now exists a considerable body of information on that record, especially the part that postdates circa 500 B.C.—the point at which pottery first appeared in the region. Numerous overviews have appeared over the past two decades that address that segment of prehistory in southeastern Missouri (e.g., C. Chapman 1980; Lafferty and Price 1996; R. Lewis 1996; D. Morse and P. Morse 1983; O'Brien and Dunnell [eds.] 1998; O'Brien and Wood 1998), all of which in turn are based on over five decades of survey and excavation in the myriad physiographic zones that comprise the northern end of the Mississippi Embayment (Fisk 1944) (Figure 19.1).

Chronology has long been at the heart of these investigations, and no shortage of schemes exists to keep track of time (and space) in the region—a situation that parallels that for the greater Southeast. In several respects the Southeast has been witness to some of the most innovative archaeology ever undertaken in the United States (see reviews in Dunnell 1985; Lyman et al. 1997; O'Brien 2000; O'Brien and Dunnell 1998; O'Brien and Lyman 1998, 1999). It was in the Mississippi Valley, for example, that a concept central to culture history, the archaeological phase, was widely applied, and it was there that pottery typology reached its zenith (Phillips 1970; Phillips et al. 1951). Somewhere in the process, however, there developed a lack of differentiation between the analytical constructs used by archaeologists to keep track of time, space, and form and the empirical reality they were intended to describe.

Nowhere is this more evident than in southeastern Missouri, where there has arisen an incredible array of archaeological units used to track form over space and through time. Some units perform their intended functions quite well, whereas others do not. Given this assessment, one might think that all that needs to be done to bring better order to the record is to discard

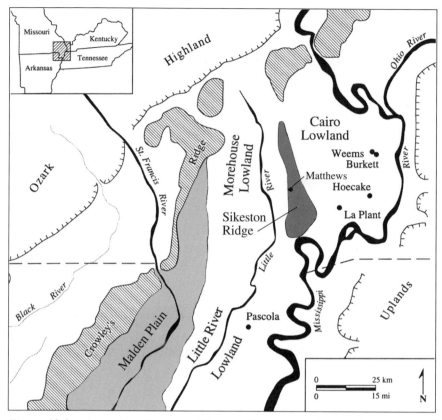

Figure 19.1 — Map of southeastern Missouri showing physiographic features and sites mentioned in the text

the less useful units and either keep the others or modify them. This argument, however, ignores a key epistemological issue: Are the units appropriate for the purposes to which they are being put? This is the critical question we address here by focusing on the three kinds of units—periods, phases, and pottery types—that together comprise archaeological systematics as used in the Southeast. Our comments are directed specifically to units employed by archaeologists working in southeastern Missouri, but they are applicable generally to the greater Southeast. Although we are critical of many of the units, our discussion should not be read as criticism of the researchers who laid the original foundation for time-space systematics. In terms of when they were working and the intellectual climate of the time, what they produced was no different from that produced by many other culture historians. Our point is simply that few efforts have been made in succeeding years to examine the usefulness of the units, most of which exist in unaltered form.

Initial Time-Space Systematics: Phases and Periods

Archaeological interest in southeastern Missouri was sporadic throughout the nineteenth and early twentieth centuries (see O'Brien [1996] for discussion), and it was not until 1941, when Winslow Walker and Robert Adams conducted large-scale excavations at the Matthews site in New Madrid County (W. Walker and Adams 1946) (Figure 19.1), that the region became a focal point of sustained activity. For assistance in analyzing the pottery from Matthews, the investigators turned to James B. Griffin, who at the time was involved with Philip Phillips and James A. Ford in the Lower Mississippi Alluvial Valley Survey (Phillips et al. 1951). Within a few years Griffin, with the help of Albert C. Spaulding, would initiate the Central Mississippi Valley Archaeological Survey as a northward extension of that project (Griffin and Spaulding 1952).

Several projects were carried out in Missouri during the course of the Griffin-Spaulding survey, one of which was a survey-and-excavation program conducted by Stephen Williams (1954). In the course of his analysis, Williams established a series of time-space units—phases—that D. Morse and P. Morse (1983:27) noted "are the basis for those still used in southeast Missouri today." Now, almost two decades later, the Morses' comments still apply, as a more recent summary of the region attests (Lafferty and Price 1996).

Williams's spatial-temporal scheme is shown in Figure 19.2 in modified form. He divided southeastern Missouri into three regions: the Cairo Lowland and the Little River Lowland, both comprising surficial sediments from the Mississippi River, and the Malden Plain, a Pleistocene-age braided-stream surface at the eastern base of Crowley's Ridge (Figure 19.1). The Burkett and Pascola phases marked the initial appearance of pottery in the Cairo Lowland and the Little River Lowland, respectively, and the Barnes Ridge phase marked the appearance in the Cairo River Lowland of pottery carrying stamped and incised designs similar to those on Hopewell vessels from southern Ohio. This phase soon was renamed the La Plant phase (S. Williams 1956) after the site of the same name in New Madrid County (Figure 19.1). Williams added another phase, Black Bayou, in the Cairo Lowland sequence, butting it against the late end of the Barnes Ridge phase (Figure 19.2). He extended the Black Bayou phase spatially into the Little River Lowland, but he inserted the Hoecake phase, named after the Hoecake site in Mississippi County (Figure 19.1), between it and the earlier Pascola phase. Only a single phase—Dunklin—was assigned to the Malden Plain, reflecting in part the lesser amount of work Williams conducted in that area but also the fact that little change in artifact-assemblage composition was evident.

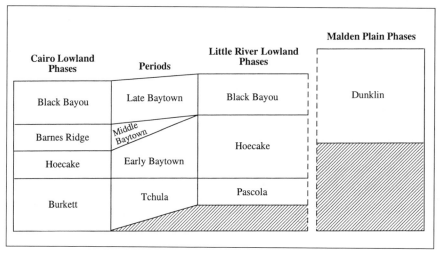

Figure 19.2 — Stephen Williams's correlation of phases and periods for three physiographic regions of southeastern Missouri (after Williams 1954)

Once he had constructed phases, Williams aligned the Cairo Lowland and the Little River Lowland sequences with periods (Figure 19.2)—an earlier Tchula period and a later Baytown period—but assigned no dates to them. He placed the Burkett and Pascola phases in the Tchula period and the Hoecake, Barnes Ridge, and Black Bayou phases in the Baytown period. He then subdivided the Baytown period and equated the Hoecake phase with the Early Baytown period and the Black Bayou phase with the Late Baytown period. He assigned the Barnes Ridge phase, which occurred only in the Cairo Lowland, to the Middle Baytown period. There was no corresponding Middle Baytown phase for the Little River Lowland.

Derivation of the names Tchula and Baytown is of interest here. Concerning Baytown, when Phillips, Ford, and Griffin (1951) undertook their survey of eastern Arkansas and northwestern Mississippi, one of the problems in which they were interested was the chronological placement of the stamped and incised pottery that bore striking resemblances to Hopewell pottery. Similar pottery was even more common in central and southern Louisiana, where it was referred to as Marksville (Setzler 1933a, 1933b, 1934). Sherds of what had become known as Marksville Incised (J. A. Ford and Willey 1940; Haag 1939b) and Marksville Stamped (J. A. Ford and Willey 1940) occurred in Phillips, Ford, and Griffin's survey area, but the farther north a site was, the less frequent the sherds became. Williams found very little of this pottery during the course of his southeastern Missouri survey.

Phillips, Ford, and Griffin used the term *Early Baytown* to refer to the period during which clay- and sand-tempered incised and stamped pottery was manufactured. Because their survey was carried out prior to the advent of radiocarbon dating, they relied on superposition for arranging pottery types chronologically. They found convincing evidence that there was considerable time between the end of the stamped and incised designs of the Early Baytown period and the advent of shell-tempered pottery, which they used as a marker for the beginning of the Late Baytown period. They sandwiched the Middle Baytown period in between, defining it as "the stretch of years that lie between the disappearance of the decorated Marksville types of early Baytown and the first showing of shell-tempered pottery" (Phillips et al. 1951:440). They placed the beginning of the Early Baytown period at A.D. 500, the beginning of the Middle Baytown period at A.D. 700, and the beginning of the Late Baytown period at A.D. 850 (Figure 19.3).

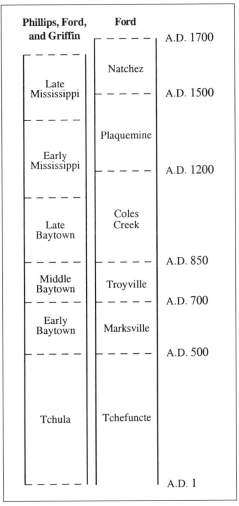

Figure 19.3 — Correlation of chronological arrangement of periods created by Phillips, Ford, and Griffin for the Lower Mississippi Alluvial Valley Survey region (left column) and Ford for the Lower Mississippi Valley (right column) (after Phillips et al. 1951)

More important than the actual spans of time represented by the units was the relation of those units to units in Ford's sequence for the Lower Mississippi Valley—what he eventually referred to as the Red River Mouth chronology (J. A. Ford 1952). Although the last piece of that chronology was not published until 1951, the basic ordering had been in place for a decade (J. A. Ford and Willey 1940, 1941), a product of the WPA excavations in Louisiana directed by Ford (O'Brien and Lyman 1998, 1999). Ford's chronology is shown in the right-hand column in Figure 19.3. When Phillips, Ford, and Griffin aligned their periods with Ford's, they equated Tchula with Tchefuncte, Early Baytown with Marksville, Middle Baytown with Troyville, and Late Baytown with Coles Creek. The earlier periods in the two chronologies were aligned so that their boundaries matched perfectly; the later periods began to diverge at the upper boundary of the Late Baytown and Coles Creek periods (Figure 19.3).

The goal of the Central Mississippi Valley Archaeological Survey was to establish a chronology for eastern Missouri and western Illinois and align it with the other two chronologies. Two sites that figured prominently in the chronological efforts were Weems and Burkett (also known as O'Bryan Ridge), both located in Mississippi County, Missouri (Figure 19.1). Excavations carried out by Williams in 1950 as part of his search for "the solution to nascent Mississippian [culture] mysteries" (S. Williams 1992:195), showed that both sites had levels containing Poverty Point clay objects and other supposedly pre-pottery artifacts that were overlain by pottery-bearing strata. The analysis was never published, but Griffin and Spaulding (1952:2) had this to say about the sites: "Strata pit excavations... suggest that the earliest pottery rather closely follows the clay ball time period.... Some of the sites on this level have a few decorated sherds indicative of a connection with the general Early Woodland horizon in the Lower Mississippi Valley indicating the Tchefuncte culture."[1] This seemingly simple statement merits consideration because it set the tone for the kinds of remarks about the archaeological record of southeastern Missouri that have been made ever since.

Note that Griffin and Spaulding used *Early Woodland* to refer to the horizon of earliest pottery manufacture in southeastern Missouri. By 1952 the term was finding its way into common usage in the archaeology of the Midwest and East, largely at the hand of Griffin. He used it not only in the above-cited publication, but also in several chapters (J. B. Griffin 1952a, 1952d) of his edited volume *Archeology of Eastern United States* (J. B. Griffin [ed.] 1952). He had also used the term as a "stage" several years earlier in a summary article on Eastern prehistory (J. B. Griffin 1946),[2] but by the 1960s

---

[1] *Griffin first reported Stephen Williams's discovery in 1952: "Survey and excavation in southeast Missouri in 1950 by the University of Michigan [Williams] has confirmed the association of a Late Archaic occupation and the clay ball horizon as pre-ceramic" (J. B. Griffin 1952d:228).*

[2] *Although Griffin's article was published in 1946, the paper on which it was based was presented in 1941 (S. Williams 1992:194).*

it had reached the status of a full-fledged period (J. B. Griffin 1967). Griffin's efforts to integrate the entire archaeological record of the Mississippi Valley into a single chronological framework are noteworthy because by the early 1950s there was confusion over which chronology should be used and where. Griffin (1952a) used the Midwestern system of Archaic-Woodland-Mississippi in his article on the Central Mississippi Valley that appeared in *Archeology of Eastern United States,* and Jesse Jennings (1952) did the same in his article on the Lower Mississippi Valley that appeared in the same book.

Subsequent Efforts at Systematics

Beginning in the 1960s, archaeologists became concerned over the increased destruction of sites in the Central Mississippi Valley, especially southeastern Missouri and northeastern Arkansas (McGimsey and Davis [eds.] 1977; Medford 1972), where destruction through agricultural activity was especially severe. Between 1966 and 1968, the University of Missouri examined twenty-two sites during a three-year salvage program, which was directed by J. R. Williams (1967, 1968, 1972; R. Lewis 1972). On the basis of his excavations, J. R. Williams repeatedly modified Stephen Williams's phases; his 1972 summary appears in Figure 19.4. He retained the Burkett and Hoecake phases for the Cairo Lowland and the Pascola and Barnes Ridge phases for the Morehouse Lowland (a northern extension of the Little River Lowland [Figure 19.1]) and discarded the Black Bayou phase. He also inserted the Ten Mile Pond phase in the Cairo Lowland sequence. Slightly later, in a summary of Cairo Lowland phases, J. R. Williams (1974) extended the Barnes Ridge phase into the Cairo Lowland, sliding it in between the Hoecake and Ten Mile Pond phases. He discarded Tchula as a period designation and put all the phases in the Baytown period—a move that extended Baytown from the first appearance of pottery in the region up to the appearance of shell-tempered pottery and the beginning of the Mississippian period. J. R. Williams assigned no dates to his periods, although in his 1974 summary he placed tentative dates on his Cairo Lowland phases: Burkett, 300 B.C.–A.D. 100; Ten Mile Pond, A.D. 1–500; Barnes Ridge, A.D. 300–500; and Hoecake, A.D. 500–1100.

A few pages later, however, J. R. Williams (1974) presented the diagram shown in Figure 19.5. Note that phase boundaries are now shown, with one exception, as slanted lines. He explained that feature as follows:

The lines separating the phases are slanted rather than [horizontal] to emphasize the idea that most of the phases continued longer, temporally, at certain sites in the Cairo Lowland than at other sites. That is, certain cultural traditions constituting a phase may have continued with large numbers of people while other peoples with a similar cultural base may have changed by accepting new cultural traditions. Since there were apparently large numbers of people who never received Hopewellian influence, the Barnes Ridge Phase is illustrated to show that it never completely encompassed the Cairo Lowland. (J. R. Williams 1974:103)

Notice also that J. R. Williams put no boundaries on his periods, noting that there were few cultural traits that marked the end of one period and the beginning of another.

Countless other projects conducted since the late 1960s have contributed to our understanding of the early half of the ceramic period in southeastern Missouri, but for the most part they have relied unquestioningly on earlier work in chronological matters, specifically that of Stephen Williams. For example, when Phillips (1970) published his two-volume synthesis of

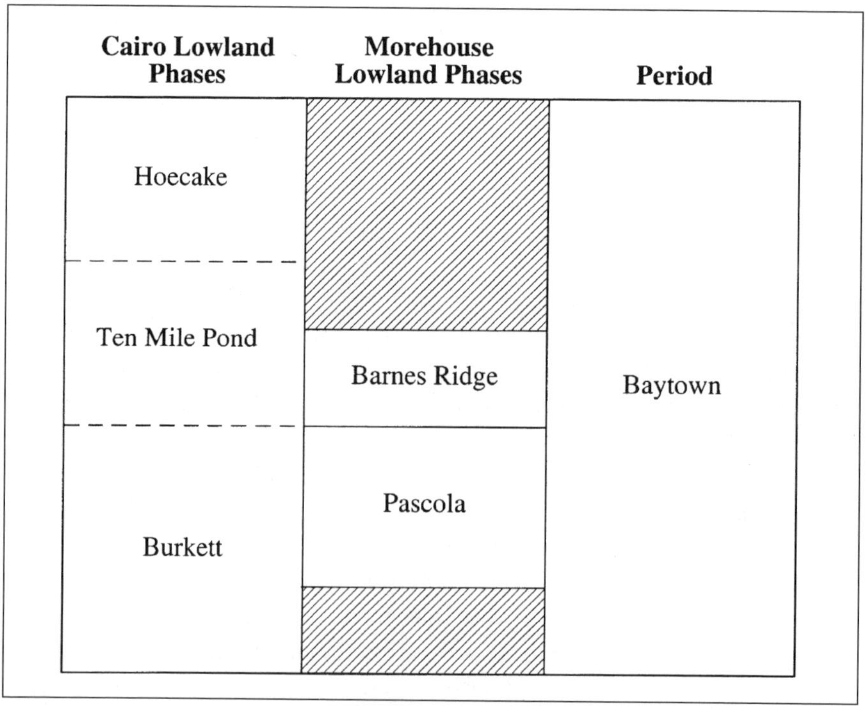

Figure 19.4 — J. R. Williams's correlation of phases and periods for two physiographic regions of southeastern Missouri (after Williams 1972)

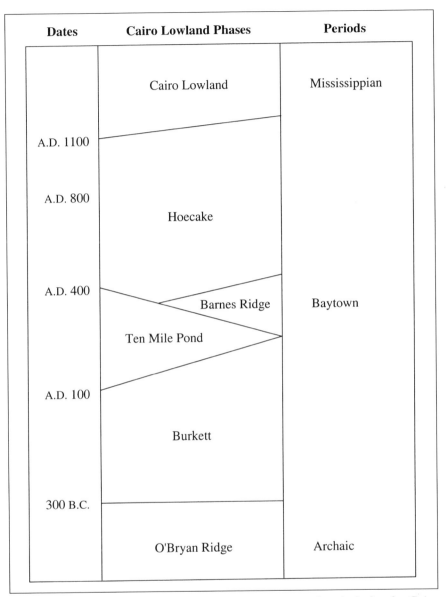

Figure 19.5 — J. R. Williams's correlation of phases and periods for the Cairo Lowland region of southeastern Missouri (after Williams 1974)

the Mississippi Valley, he retained Williams's phases without altering either their spatial extent or order. Phillips organized phases in the Mississippi Valley into the periods shown in the left column in Figure 19.6 and then aligned those periods against other chronological or developmental frame-

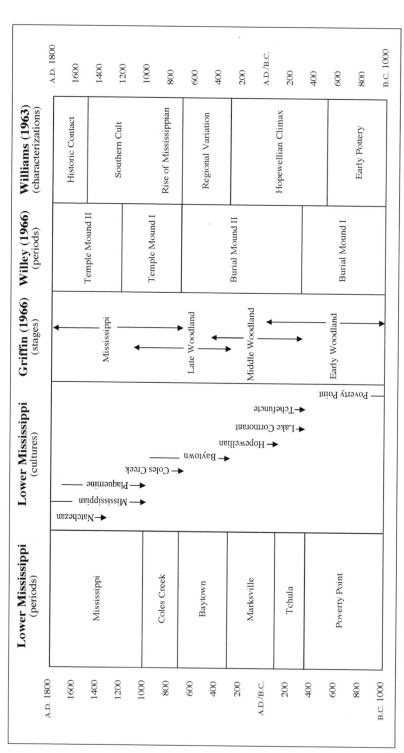

Figure 19.6 — Philip Phillips's correlation of periods in the central and lower Mississippi River valley with various chronological or developmental frameworks consisting of cultures, stages, periods, or characterizations (after Phillips 1970)

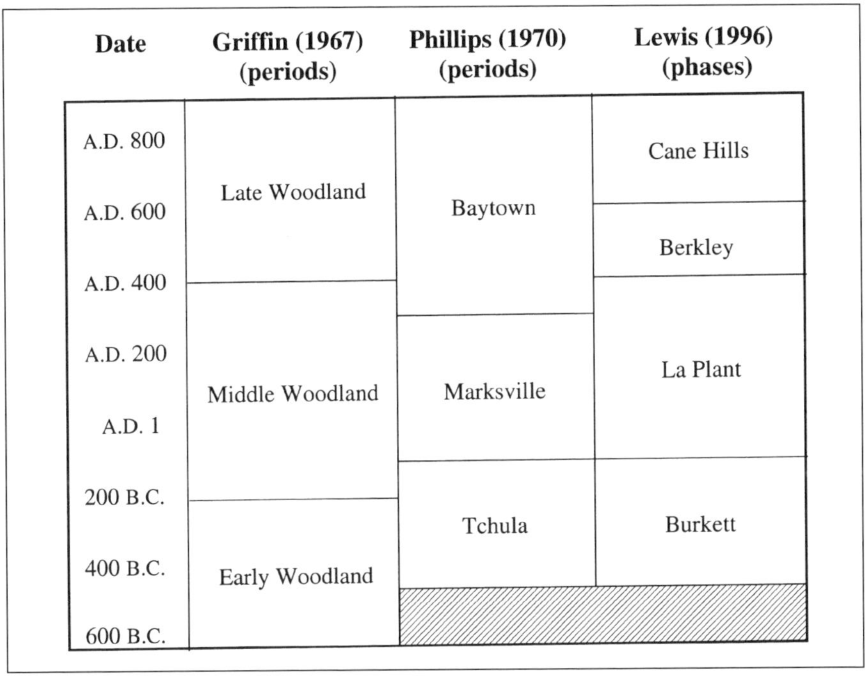

Date	Griffin (1967) (periods)	Phillips (1970) (periods)	Lewis (1996) (phases)
A.D. 800	Late Woodland	Baytown	Cane Hills
A.D. 600			Berkley
A.D. 400	Middle Woodland	Marksville	La Plant
A.D. 200			
A.D. 1			
200 B.C.	Early Woodland	Tchula	Burkett
400 B.C.			
600 B.C.			

Figure 19.7 — Barry Lewis's correlation of phases in the Cairo Lowland region of southeastern Missouri and the western Kentucky border region with chronological sequences proposed by James B. Griffin (1967) and Philip Phillips (1970) (after Lewis 1996)

works consisting of cultures, stages, periods, or characterizations. His period names were derived from both the Phillips, Ford, and Griffin (1951) chronology and the Ford (1951) chronology. Notice that he deleted all mention of Early, Middle, and Late Baytown and inserted Coles Creek after Baytown. Robert Lafferty and James Price (1996) recently imported Phillips's chronology into southeastern Missouri, complete with Williams's phases.

One exception to the status quo is the work by R. Barry Lewis and his colleagues (e.g., R. Lewis 1996; Sussenbach and Lewis 1987) in the Cairo Lowland and western Kentucky. Lewis created two phases to rectify the Baytown period/phase problem discussed above. Lewis's (1996) scheme is shown in Figure 19.7. Notice that Lewis aligned his phases with both J. B. Griffin's (1967) period sequence—the mainstay of Midwestern and Eastern archaeology—and Phillips's (1970) composite sequence—the mainstay of Lower Mississippi Valley archaeology. Lewis changed Phillips's beginning date for the Tchula period (300 B.C.), making it roughly a hundred years earlier in his scheme.

Pottery Types: The Underlying Criteria

Although Phillips (1970) retained Stephen Williams's phases when he published his synthesis of the Mississippi Valley, he apparently had a few reservations about them. For example, with reference to the Pascola and Burkett phases, he expressed "some reservations about the separation of the two phases at this stage of our knowledge of the archaeology" (Phillips 1970:878). Although he did not phrase it as such, implicit in Phillips's skepticism was the question, "What are the necessary and sufficient criteria for defining two separate phases?" To begin to answer that question, we need to have at least a basic knowledge of pottery from southeastern Missouri, in that it is the basis upon which all ceramic-period phases in the region have been created. Two dimensions—paste and decoration—form the core of most pottery types, and we emphasize them in the following discussion.

Phillips, Ford, and Griffin (1951) made no mention of phases in their survey monograph—Phillips, working in conjunction with Gordon Willey, had not yet formally defined the term as a spatio-temporal unit of culture, the way it would be used thereafter (Phillips and Willey 1953; Willey and Phillips 1958)—although spatial and temporal considerations formed the basis of their field and analytical strategies. They did, however, create a series of types to segment the variation in pottery they encountered. Almost all work conducted in southeastern Missouri subsequently has employed their types, although some studies (e.g., Cogswell and O'Brien 1998) have broken with tradition. This does not mean that the type descriptions have remained true to what Phillips and his colleagues envisioned when they created the types. To the contrary, the sometimes rather tight descriptions as originally formulated have been broadened to incorporate considerable variation. There is nothing inherently wrong in so doing, but it makes little sense to use a series of pottery types as the distinguishing characteristics of a phase and then later change the criteria for the types without at least considering what effects such an action might have on phase recognition. Of course, if the phase definitions were never clearly stated in the first place, there is little reason to expect that modifications of type descriptions will have *any* effect.

Concerning the term *Tchula,* one of the first descriptions of pottery from southeastern Missouri was that provided by Griffin and Spaulding (1952) for pottery from Weems and Burkett. Following their lead and with advice from Griffin, Stephen Williams (1954) noted that some of his Tchula period pottery from Weems, Burkett, and sites such as Pascola in Pemiscot County, Missouri (Figure 19.1), was similar to Baumer pottery from southern Illinois, but he emphasized what he saw as stronger connections between the southeastern Missouri sherds and early pottery from farther south in the

Mississippi Valley. He emphasized these southern connections by using the period designation Tchula and placing the sherds in several types created by Phillips, Ford, and Griffin (1951) on the basis of their survey—types such as Cormorant Cord Impressed, Withers Fabric Impressed, and Mulberry Creek Cord Marked. Thus Williams was following Griffin's lead not only in pointing out connections between southeastern Missouri and the Ohio River—the Baumer material—but also in emphasizing connections between southeastern Missouri and locations farther south in the Mississippi Valley. Griffin, remember, had pointed out that a few of the sherds from Weems and Burkett were "indicative of a connection with the general Early Woodland horizon in the Lower Mississippi Valley indicating the Tchefuncte culture" (Griffin and Spaulding 1952:2). Phillips (1970:877) later noted that "I suspect that the key word in this passage is 'general.' I should be surprised if good examples of Tchefuncte types were to be found this far north." He also stated in a footnote that "Griffin's present opinion is that there is no Tchefuncte pottery in Southeast Missouri" (Phillips 1970:877).

Griffin never pursued the Tchefuncte connection. Instead, he commented to Stephen Williams that there were close affinities between some presumably early southeastern Missouri pottery from the Pascola site and Alexander series pottery from northern Alabama—a sandy-paste pottery with an incised and/or punctated (pinched) surface (Griffin and Sears 1950; Haag 1939a). Williams (1954) and Phillips (1970) accepted the designation for southeastern Missouri specimens, with Phillips (1970:878) noting that "no one has yet been able to explain how or why, but these [Alexander series] types have turned up in acceptable purity in many places in the Lower Mississippi Valley as far south as the Lake Pontchartrain region [Louisiana], always in association with local complexes upon which the concept of a Tchula period is based." This is an interesting statement, especially Phillips's mention of "local complexes." What makes it interesting is that Williams was dealing with "local complexes" in his treatment of early pottery from southeastern Missouri. He mentioned that sherds from the Pascola site in Pemiscot County were sand tempered, but he never mentioned the kind of temper in sherds from Weems and Burkett. He used the type designations Cormorant Cord Impressed and Withers Fabric Impressed to refer to some of the sherds from those sites. When Phillips, Ford, and Griffin established those types, one key distinguishing characteristic was the presence of clay, not sand, as temper. With respect to Cormorant Cord Impressed, they noted that "in almost all specimens, particles of clay are clearly present; only a minority would qualify as sand-tempered, in the usual sense of the term" (Phillips et al. 1951:73). Phillips, Ford, and Griffin established a "provisional" type, Twin Lakes Fabric Impressed, as the sand-tempered parallel to

Withers Fabric Impressed. They provided no such parallel to Cormorant Cord Impressed.

Subsequent excavations at Weems by J. R. Williams (1968) and at Burkett by James Hopgood (1967) produced material that is still available for analysis. Inspection of sherds from those excavations demonstrates that several sherds exhibit surface treatments similar to those on sherds Phillips, Ford, and Griffin (1951) placed in the types Cormorant Cord Impressed and Withers Fabric Impressed. It also demonstrates that there is considerable variation in temper, with some sherds tempered exclusively with clay and numerous sherds tempered with either sand or clay and sand. The high frequency of sand-tempered sherds is not surprising, given the location of the two sites on topographically high, Pleistocene-age sediments connected with the ancestral Mississippi-Ohio river system. But do these sherds qualify as Withers Fabric Impressed and/or Cormorant Cord Impressed? On the basis of published criteria, they do not. The designs are similar to those on archetypal examples, but the temper is different. Likewise, some sherds carry surface treatments similar to those found on Baumer and Crab Orchard pottery from southern Illinois (Butler and Jefferies 1986; Muller 1986), but they are tempered with sand, not limestone or other kinds of rock.

Not all clay-tempered pottery in southeastern Missouri falls into the types Cormorant Cord Impressed and Withers Fabric Impressed. Far more common are plain-surface sherds and sherds from vessels that were cord marked over most or all of their exteriors instead of only around the rim, the latter the distinguishing feature of Cormorant Cord Impressed sherds. Phillips, Ford, and Griffin (1951:82) created the type Baytown Plain to house plain-surface, clay-tempered sherds, terming it "the basic, clay-tempered plain ware of the Survey Area." Although clay was the temper highlighted in the type description, the authors recognized that a minor amount of sand often occurred with the clay, possibly the result of "accidental inclusion" (Phillips et al. 1951:76). If the sand appeared to have been added purposely, a sherd or vessel was placed in the type Thomas Plain—a name that never caught on and later was given the status of a variety by Phillips (1970). If a clay-tempered vessel or sherd exhibited cord marking over most if not all of its exterior, it was placed in the type Mulberry Creek Cord Marked, first described by William Haag (1939a) on the basis of sherds from the Pickwick Basin in Alabama. If a clay-tempered sherd was red slipped, it was placed in the type Larto Red Filmed. The dating of these types is imprecise—not only in southeastern Missouri but also in areas to the south—but they certainly span considerable lengths of time, from the pre-Christian era up to perhaps as late as A.D. 600. Mulberry Creek Cord Marked and Larto Red Filmed probably date later in time than Cormorant Cord Impressed and Withers Fabric Impressed, although there undoubtedly was temporal overlap between the two suites of clay-tempered pottery.

We point out that the literature on southeastern Missouri, especially the older literature, is replete with type names for clay-tempered pottery that add nothing to our understanding of the archaeological record and, in fact, confuse matters significantly. For example, three pottery types that are mentioned repeatedly in the literature (e.g., C. Chapman 1980) are Korando Cord Marked, Korando Plain, and Westlake Plain. Korando Cord Marked was a type name coined by Griffin (1941) to refer to pottery from the Korando site in Jackson County, Illinois, and he later used it in reference to pottery from the Matthews site (Walker and Adams 1946). Griffin subsequently dropped the name in favor of Mulberry Creek Cord Marked, but Carl Chapman (1980) and others kept it alive. Korando Plain and Westlake Plain are regional names evidently created by Chapman (e.g., 1980) for Baytown Plain. Phillips (1970) relegated Westlake Plain to a variety of Baytown Plain. In our opinion (see O'Brien and Wood 1998), all of these names should be dropped with the exceptions of Mulberry Creek Cord Marked and Baytown Plain.

What does one do with sand-tempered temporal equivalents of Baytown Plain and Mulberry Creek Cord Marked? If you were Stephen Williams, you would create two new types in which to house such specimens. Thus he created Barnes Plain as the sand-tempered equivalent of Baytown Plain and Barnes Cord Marked as the equivalent of Mulberry Creek Cord Marked. Phillips (1970:43) later changed the type name Barnes Plain to Kennett Plain, but it never stuck. More important, he had this to say about Williams's formulations:

> The types Barnes Plain...and Barnes Cord Marked were set up by Williams...to give classificatory status to a sandy textured ware occurring in Southeast Missouri that seems to be more than merely a sandy variant of the dominant "clay-tempered" ware represented by Baytown and Mulberry Creek. Although this material does occur in minority association with the last-named types in the more easterly portions of the region, it is numerically dominant in the Baytown period sites in the west, particularly those on the Malden Plain, where it carries the main burden for the recognition of a Dunklin phase. (Phillips 1970:43)

In our opinion, Stephen Williams's decision to create separate types for this later sand-tempered pottery was the correct one. It certainly solved the problem of what to do with sand-tempered "varieties" of the earlier types Cormorant Cord Impressed and Withers Fabric Impressed. The problem has been, as Price (1986) pointed out, that far too often investigators unfamiliar with sand-tempered pottery types have tended to refer to any plain-surface, sand-tempered sherd as Barnes Plain and any sand-tempered, cord-marked sherd as Barnes Cord Marked. This has had the effect of masking the variation present in sand-tempered pottery in southeast Missouri, some of which undoubtedly is of chronological significance (Dunnell and Feathers 1991).

What can we make of temper differences in pottery from southeastern Missouri? In discussing the preponderance of sand-tempered Tchula period pottery in the northern and eastern parts of their survey area (northwestern Mississippi), Phillips, Ford, and Griffin (1951:432) stated that "Ford and Phillips interpret this preponderance of sand-tempering as a local specialization without chronological significance, while Griffin sees in it a reflection of the [chronological] priority of sand- over clay-tempering that obtains in northern Alabama." Phillips (1970:887) later made a telling remark regarding the distribution of those two tempers in the northeastern-Arkansas portion of the Little River Lowland:

> *In a brief foray into the Little River Lowland (south) region at the close of the 1940 season, we picked up on several sites a "Baytown" complex that included sizable percentages of the sandy-textured varieties of the familiar clay-tempered types: Baytown Plain, var. Thomas; Mulberry Creek Cord Marked, var. Blue Lake; Withers Fabric Marked, var. Twin Lakes. Samples were small and in all cases mixed with later Mississippian components. We were, and still are, at a loss how to interpret this sandy material—whether a reflection of the priority of sand over "clay" tempering or the effect of local environmental conditions.*

Thus, two decades after Phillips, Ford, and Griffin first pondered the question of why there was a dichotomy in temper in otherwise identical vessels, Phillips was still undecided. He did, however, reiterate his earlier position, assuming that in the "absence of evidence that sandier texture is significant of an earlier date" (Phillips 1970:175), the difference might be environmentally related.

The environmental factors to which Phillips was referring are the two great hydrophysiographic subdivisions evident in the Mississippi Valley: the braided-stream (valley-train) deposits on both sides of Crowley's Ridge that relate to the ancestral Mississippi and Ohio rivers and the more recent meander-belt deposits from the Ohio and Mississippi rivers (Figure 19.1). The Pleistocene braided-stream sediments are in general coarser than those in the meander belt, although local conditions vary significantly. Phillips was suggesting that sites located on the braided-stream surfaces would contain sand-tempered pottery, whereas sites located in the meander-belt zone, with greater access to clays in backwater areas, would contain clay-tempered pottery. This was a reasonable proposition, although perhaps not universally true (D. Morse and P. Morse 1983). We agree that site context did not necessarily dictate what type of temper was used, although one is struck, as Phillips must have been, by the distribution of clay- and sand-tempered pottery relative to the features left by the two fluvial regimes.

Discussion

What are we to make of the various schemes aimed at bringing spatial and temporal control to the archaeological record of southeastern Missouri? In the first place, simply organizing the schemes into some kind of coherent order is difficult because of the way phases appear and disappear in the literature and phase and period boundaries get moved around. Some archaeologists would argue that there is nothing wrong with this, given that the archaeological record of southeastern Missouri is "extremely complex and at best only partially understood [and the schemes] are approximate at very best" (Lafferty and Price 1996:3). Spatial-temporal schemes are *always* going to be approximations, but it is strange that the scheme Lafferty and Price used in their summary of the prehistory of southeastern Missouri—the phases established by Stephen Williams in 1954—was forty-two years old when their summary appeared. It is difficult to escape the conclusion that little progress had been made in the intervening period. More important, we need to ask specifically what it is we are seeking an approximation of. We get caught up in such issues when we treat archaeological constructs—periods, phases, and pottery types—as empirical (real) units rather than as ideational (measurement) units. Only if they are real can we "approximate" them. But such units can never be real; the stuff they are used to measure is real, but the units are not. This critical dichotomy was not lost on Phillips, Ford, and Griffin:

> [T]here is magic in names. Once let a hatful of miserable fragments of fourth-rate pottery be dignified by a "Name," and there will follow inevitably the tendency for the name to become an entity, particularly in the mind of him who gives it. Go a step further and publish a description and the type embarks on an independent existence of its own. At that point the classification ceases to be a "tool," and the archaeologist becomes one. (Phillips et al. 1951:61–62)

Exigencies of language require us to think and talk about pottery types as though they had some sort of independent existence. "This sherd is Baytown Plain." Upon sufficient repetition of this statement, the concept Baytown Plain takes on a massive solidity. The time comes when we are ready to fight for dear old Baytown. What we have to try to remember is that the statement really means something like this: "This sherd sufficiently resembles material which for the time being we have elected to call Baytown Plain." Frequent repetition of this and similar exorcisms we have found to be extremely salutary during the classificatory activities. (Phillips et al. 1951:66)

The equation of measurement units with empirical units is exemplified in reactions to Ford's creation of the Troyville period for his Lower Mississippi Valley sequence. In the latter stages of constructing his chronology, Ford redrew period boundaries, in the process designating a new period, Troyville, between the earlier Marksville period and the later Coles Creek period. Most archaeologists were not happy with Ford's modified scheme, and he answered their criticism:

This readjustment of the named divisions for the time scale in this area seems to have puzzled a few of the archaeologists working in the Mississippi Valley, even some of those who have been best informed as to the field-work which led to this rearrangement. Complaints have been made that pottery types that were formerly classified as Coles Creek in age are now assigned to the Troyville Period. Discussion develops the opinion that if this latest chronological arrangement is correct then the former must have been in error. The adoption of new names for all the periods in the more recent arrangement may have avoided some, but not all, of this confusion. These serious and earnest seekers after truth really believe that we have discovered these periods and that this is a more or less successful attempt to picture the natural divisions in this span of history. This is obviously an incorrect interpretation. This is an arbitrary set of culture chronology units, the limits of each of which are determined by historical accident, and which are named to facilitate reference to them. (J. A. Ford 1951:12–13)

Ford viewed time as a continuum as opposed to a series of natural periods or stages, and it did not matter where one happened to slice that continuum. Years later, Phillips (1970)—clearly unhappy with Ford's procedure of modifying his set of periods—still could not comprehend why Ford had done what he did. Phillips, like most of his contemporaries and successors, believed in the reality of units such as periods and stages and therefore wanted the boundaries of those units to coincide with visible (one might say "objective") junctures in the archaeological record. Given that any number of criteria could be used to designate period boundaries, along with the fact that such criteria did not appear everywhere at the same time, "regional" chronologies sprang up. The next step was to link these chronologies, as Phillips, Ford, and Griffin (1951) attempted to do for the central and lower sections of the Mississippi alluvial valley and Griffin (1952a, 1967) attempted to do for the eastern United States. The results of such exercises often were nightmarish concoctions, as Barry Lewis (1996:49) noted with reference to southeastern Missouri:

> There are few one-to-one correlations between the time slices emphasized in the Griffin and Phillips frameworks, and the archaeological literature of the region contains a certain amount of terminological chaos that reflects the conflicts between them. One finds, for example, confusion about whether the term Baytown in a given context refers to part or all of the Early, Middle, or Late Woodland periods; about whether Tchula is properly considered comparable to the Early Woodland, the Middle Woodland, or parts of both; about whether the Poverty Point period in the northern Lower Valley is appropriately considered Early Woodland, Late Archaic, or part of both; and about how one patches the Lower Valley sequence to accommodate the fact that the Coles Creek period, which has strong trait-based connotations in the Yazoo Basin [of western Mississippi], is meaningless in the Bootheel [of Missouri]. I suspect that everyone who works in this region has felt the frustration of trying to calibrate the two temporal frameworks with sufficient accuracy and precision so that they can get on with their research.

Such problems obtain even at the level of regional chronology. For example, given the way in which Stephen Williams arranged his southeastern Missouri phases, there is no way of illustrating the relation between phases and periods except by showing each set of phases separately (Figure 19.2). This is because the beginning point for the Tchula period and the ending point for the Baytown period were figured differently for each area. Thus, period boundaries did not coincide with phase boundaries for each of the two areas. One could argue that what the formulation is showing is the time-transgressive nature of traits as a result of diffusion, population movements, and the like, and perhaps this is what Phillips, Ford, and Griffin (1951:39) had in mind when they labeled Middle Mississippi as "an archaeological facies." This is difficult to defend when the issue is solely elapsed time, but that was not the only issue at stake. Thus boundaries of time periods were tied directly to events such as the appearance of stamped or incised pottery in a region, and those events could occur at different times in different places. The critical issue is whether those events serving as definitive criteria of phases and periods were in fact the same criteria across all of the included units. Sometimes they were not.

If periods are viewed as real, there is no reason to suspect that phases— those "practical and intelligible unit[s] of study" (Willey and Phillips 1958:22)—are anything other than real. Willey and Phillips set up phases as temporal-spatial units used to keep track of variation in the archaeological record. Components, from which phases were constructed, were vertically bounded excavation units that represented a phase at a particular site. The important point is that phases and components originally were viewed solely as archaeological constructs. Although Phillips and Willey (1953:617) expressed the opinion that "archeo-sociological correlations may eventually be possible," they suggested that "the archaeologist is on firmer footing… with the conception of an archeological culture as an *arbitrarily defined unit* or segment of the total continuum" (emphasis added). But even Willey and Phillips, despite issuing such a caveat, forged ahead and made correlations between archaeological and sociocultural phenomena. Components were more or less equivalent to occupations or communities, and phases were "time-space-culture units" equivalent to societies (Lyman and O'Brien 2001). Thus we have D. Morse and P. Morse (1983:313) equating native provinces in northeastern Arkansas as related in the Hernando de Soto chronicles with archaeological phases.

Artifact types and phases are not the only places where analytical difficulty resides. Precisely the same problems afflict the larger scale, more inclusive units regularly used by culture historians. For example, Gerald Smith (1996:109) stated in a recent paper on the prehistory of western Tennessee that "Late Woodland and Baytown are here regarded as distinct cultural traditions following [the] Middle Woodland [period] and preceding the appearance of local Mississippian culture….The Late Woodland tradition… is regarded as an extension of Midwestern Late Woodland, whereas Baytown is regarded as an extension of the Gulf Coastal tradition." Smith is caught here in a no-man's land in his use of terms such as *Woodland* as both a period and a cultural unit (tradition). When he discusses the Middle Woodland he uses it as a period designation, but when he discusses Late Woodland he uses it as a tradition designation. We empathize with Smith because his study area is complex archaeologically. For the period roughly A.D. 1 to 400, the Middle Woodland period, the archaeological record is relatively homogeneous across the area, but after A.D. 400, the record becomes complicated. Pottery that looks like contemporary materials to the north—Smith's Late Woodland tradition—also looks like contemporary materials to the south—his Baytown tradition. What does one do in such a case? Whatever option one selects, different kinds of units cannot be used interchangeably.

Recall how Griffin attempted to merge his Midwestern chronology with Ford's chronology for the Lower Mississippi Valley by equating the Early Woodland horizon with the Tchefuncte culture. In so doing he went well beyond chronology by using the terms *horizon* and *culture*. What he could have said is that some pottery from southeastern Missouri resembles in certain respects what Ford and Quimby (1945) called Tchefuncte pottery, based on their examination of sherds from southern Louisiana. The term *Early Woodland* started life as a period designation, but it soon became a horizon designation, which apparently was then equated with a cultural designation. This was not unique to Gerald Smith or J. B. Griffin; culture historians working in the Southeast routinely conflate the terms. Perhaps this quote from John W. Griffin (1996:120–21) says it best: "One of the hallmarks of the earliest years of the Southeastern Archaeological Conference…was the definition of and discussion of pottery types in what came to be known, informally at least, as the Southeast Binomial System. We began to take our potsherds seriously. And pottery types and pottery series were soon joined by named cultural units (periods, phases, foci, assemblages, cultures—whatever)." Whatever indeed.

Conclusion

We were amused to read what Lewis (1996:75), using an apologetic tone, said about the archaeology of southeastern Missouri:

> *In my first attempt to sort out the southeast Missouri chronological muddle, I could do little more than describe the disarray of published phase descriptions (Lewis 1972:38–40). I later learned that this affliction—the desire to save the chronological sequence from the legacy of researchers with long experience in the region—is common among new researchers in the Bootheel. In my case I wrote arrogantly, "These phases are in general poorly described and frequently based on little more than surface collections or perhaps one or two lightly tested components. Most, if not all of the phases*

which have been formulated for Southeast Missouri have been erected on a rather shaky archaeological foundation of crossdating [and]...a few radiocarbon dates scattered here and there."

Lewis has nothing to apologize for; his words are as true today as they were in 1972. Southeastern Missouri phases are poorly described, but even worse, they have never been defined. By that we mean that the necessary and sufficient criteria for membership in a phase have never been spelled out. When Stephen Williams created the phases, he used pottery types as tentative phase markers, but he did not define the phases. Almost half a century later, they remain undefined.

Phases can be one of three things (Dunnell 1971; Fox 1998). First, they can be classes, which means that the members of a phase share unique traits—phrased as some abstraction (historical types), such as Phillips, Ford, and Griffin's (1951) pottery types—none of which is shared with members of any other phase. Second, phases can be groups, which means that the actual members of a phase are more similar to one another—again measured in terms of abstractions (historical types)—than any one is to a member of another phase. Third, phases can be historical accidents formed on a loose, ad hoc basis. Fox's (1992, 1998; O'Brien and Fox 1994a, 1994b) examination of late prehistoric phases proposed by researchers working in southeastern Missouri (e.g., Klippel 1969; R. Marshall 1965a; Phillips 1970; G. Smith 1990; J. R. Williams 1967, 1968, 1972; S. Williams 1954, 1956) shows they are neither groups nor classes, but rather inconsistent sets of assemblages. That is, they are historical accidents. If we go back and look at the published criteria for any phase thus far named for southeastern Missouri, it is clear that the necessary and sufficient conditions for membership in those phases are never stated clearly. In other words, phase "definitions" are written so loosely that the criteria are variously ambiguous and overlap.

Once reality is attached to archaeological units, it becomes easy to conflate them (Lyman et al. 1997; O'Brien 1995; O'Brien and Lyman 1998, 2001). Thus, despite the precise definitions that each carries, units such as "period," "stage," "phase," "horizon," and "tradition" often are used interchangeably, sometimes being mixed in with "culture" and "people." This is not what early culture historians intended when the concepts were introduced, but laxity in how units and the terms for them were used was evident almost from the beginning. Beginning with artifact types as the building blocks of larger units, cautions such as those of Phillips, Ford, and Griffin (1951) were overlooked, despite repetition by others such as Alex Krieger (1953:261), who noted that the typological definitions being used by archaeologists were "highly individualistic, determined by inclination or by force of personality in various local situations, without regard to what happens when results must be compared objectively in different areas." And the larger units that rested upon artifact types also were highly individualistic, with some considering a period to comprise only a slice of time (e.g., Rowe 1962), whereas others considered a period as comprising a particular cultural form (e.g., Rouse 1953). Confusing stages with periods and similar problems was a predictable result (e.g., Rowe 1962; Trigger 1968).

Traditional culture-historical units are alive and well in southeastern Missouri, just as they are throughout the Southeast. Despite the fact that they mask variation instead of highlighting it, there are no signs that these units will soon disappear. Archaeologists will continue to use them, often with little regard for the original purpose for which a particular kind of unit—period, phase, type—was created. Nor is there any reason not to suspect that various units will continue to be used interchangeably. As long as we ignore epistemological issues involved in archaeological systematics, we can continue creating audience-friendly stories about the past, but at the same time we should be honest about what we are doing.

Acknowledgments

We thank David Anderson and Robert Mainfort both for inviting us to participate in the Southeastern Archaeological Conference symposium in which this paper was delivered and for their helpful comments. We also thank E. J. O'Brien for extensive editorial assistance, Dan Glover for producing the figures, and Steve Williams for helpful comments on an early draft.

Chapter 20

Shellfish Use during the
Woodland Period in the Middle South

Evan Peacock

O ver the course of 10,000 years, the importance of shellfish in south-eastern aboriginal economies apparently fluctuated a great deal. The first evidence for the intensive exploitation of freshwater mussels occurs during the mid-Holocene Hypsithermal climatic optimum (Dowd 1989; Morrison 1942; B. D. Smith 1986:22–24; Steponaitis 1986:372). This has been attributed to environmental factors, specifically the warmer and drier conditions that led to stabilized aquatic systems with shallower streams and rivers providing optimum habitats for, and easier accessibility to, mussels (B. D. Smith 1986:22–24; see Klippel et al. [1978] and Warren [1995:97, 1996] for discussions of the potential effects of the Hypsithermal on freshwater mussel populations). Freshwater shellfish use is thought by many to have peaked during the subsequent Late Archaic period, when impressively large "shell mounds" appeared alongside many of the major rivers of the Southeast (Cumbaa 1976; J. A. Ford and Willey 1941; T. Lewis and Kneberg 1959; T. Lewis and Lewis 1997:36–37; Marquardt and Watson 1983; Patch 1976; W. Turner n.d.; W. Webb 1939, 1946; W. Webb and DeJarnette 1942, 1948). This apparent focus on freshwater mussels as a dietary staple led archaeologists to adopt the term *Shell Mound Archaic* (a.k.a. "shellheap dwellers," "shellfish eaters") as a general descriptor for post-Hypsithermal, pre-Woodland cultures in the region (J. Chapman 1985a, 1985b; Lyon 1996:197–98; Pope 1956). Freshwater shellfish were considered to represent the major resource tying down one end of a seasonal-round settlement pattern for the hunting-gathering societies that constituted the Shell Mound Archaic (J. Chapman 1985b:150; Pope 1956). This picture has become somewhat modified as the relative dietary importance of mussels has been questioned following research into the nutritive value of unionids and gastropods (Cumbaa 1976; Klippel et al. 1978; Parmalee and Klippel 1974) and as Late Archaic riverine sites in some areas have failed to produce abundant bivalve remains (e.g., J. Chapman 1981:155). Still, the idea of a seasonal pattern that focused on mussels and other riverine resources, as well as "seed gathering and gardening," during the summer months followed by upland nut harvesting and hunting in the fall and winter still holds sway as a general picture of Late Archaic lifeways in the interior riverine areas of the Middle South (e.g., Steponaitis 1986:377). Indeed, the term *Shell Mound Archaic* is still commonly used (e.g., Claassen 1991a, 1992, 1996a, 1996b; Marquardt and Watson 1983, 1997).

The Woodland period typically has been viewed as a time when the subsistence base became diversified (Blitz 1993; Caddell 1981; Futato 1987; C. Jenkins 1993; N. Jenkins 1982; N. Jenkins and Krause 1986; Steponaitis 1986; Walthall 1980; Welch 1990). This suggestion has been bolstered considerably in the past two decades as evidence for the importance of native seed crops in Woodland economies has dramatically increased. While the use of shellfish is known to have continued into and throughout the Woodland period, it generally has not been attributed the same importance that it apparently had during the Archaic. Rather, shellfish have been seen as one resource among many that led to the establishment of floodplain or terrace-edge "base camps" whose inhabitants exploited floodplain resources during the summer and fall before breaking up into "micro-bands" that dispersed into the uplands during the fall and winter—essentially a continuation of, and elaboration on, the previously established Archaic pattern described above (Steponaitis 1986:378–79; Walthall 1980:108).

This pattern of increasing use of second-line resources is thought to have continued throughout the Woodland period (Steponaitis 1986:384), reaching a Late Woodland peak in many parts of the Southeast (e.g., Woodrick 1981:138). For example, N. Jenkins (1982:11) wrote that in the central Tombigbee River valley, "Miller III [Late Woodland] environmental adaptation can best be characterized as a culmination of floodplain forest efficiency" (*sensu* Caldwell 1958). A somewhat circular argument has developed whereby an increased use of second-line resources (and/or the initial appearance of maize in small quantities) led to increased populations, which led to resource stress, which led to still more intensified use of second-line resources, which led to even larger populations, which led to still greater resource stress, and so on until the carrying capacity of the areas under consideration was reached or exceeded (e.g., Scott 1983). "Mississippianization" then took place because Late Woodland groups had locked themselves into an ecological box, the key to which was full-scale, maize-based agriculture (Futato 1987:226–38; M. C. Hill 1987:249; N. Jenkins 1982:143; N. Jenkins and Curren 1975; N. Jenkins and Krause 1986:123; Schroedl and Boyd 1987:144; Scott 1983:322–24; B. D. Smith 1986:50; Walthall 1980:128–29, 136–37, 154–55; Welch 1990; cf. Blitz 1993:36–44).

Many aspects of this idea are speculative, and there are explanations that may serve better to explain the record (e.g., Blitz 1993:38; B. D. Smith

1986:42). For example, many researchers who subscribe to some version of the "resource diversification → population growth → further diversification → further population growth" scenario believe that the Woodland groups in question had a seasonal or "central based wandering" settlement pattern (N. Jenkins 1982:72; Walthall 1980; Welch 1990; see discussion in Futato 1989). An alternative suggestion is that people became sedentary during the Woodland period (J. Rafferty 1986b, 1994, 1996), a change in settlement pattern that is known ethnographically to lead to large increases in population size (J. Rafferty 1985).

While there is doubtless a great deal of regional variability in the timing and nature of Woodland period settlement/subsistence pattern changes (B. D. Smith 1986:41), the case for high population densities and concomitant resource stress has been strongly argued for many areas. For example, in the central Tombigbee River valley, there is a many-fold increase in the number of Late Woodland sites over earlier Woodland sites; Late Woodland components are typically larger as well (N. Jenkins 1982:98; Walthall 1980:154–55; Welch 1990). Besides resource diversification, indirect evidence for resource stress comes from skeletal indicators of poorer health and increased violent conflict (Blitz 1993; Futato 1987; M. C. Hill 1987; N. Jenkins 1982:143–44; K. Turner 1986; Welch 1990). The suggestion that these phenomena result from population increase, rather than a reorganization of the settlement system such as nucleation, is supported by recent surveys in the interior of Mississippi that show Woodland components to be not only abundant but also increasingly abundant through time (Peacock 1995, 1996a, 1996b, 1997a; J. Rafferty 1994, 1996, this volume).

In this chapter, I will attempt to do two things. First, I examine the relative intensity of shellfish harvesting, as represented by shell remains in Archaic, Woodland, and Mississippian deposits, to see whether the resource was being used to a greater or lesser extent through time. Second, I use shell data from Woodland contexts to see whether resource stress was present and territorial constriction is implied. I concentrate primarily on freshwater mussel data from the interior Middle South, simply because I am most familiar with this area both in terms of the archaeological record and the molluscan faunas.

From the "Shell Mound Archaic" to the "Shell Mound Woodland"? Molluscan Use along the Tennessee, Cumberland, and Tombigbee Rivers

There are vast amounts of data available on mussel assemblages from sites of various ages across the Southeast. Unfortunately, most of those data exist as tables or appendices in poorly distributed cultural resource management reports, making it difficult to distinguish regional-scale patterns in shellfish use during Woodland times. At a somewhat anecdotal level, a more-or-less random foray through the literature reveals that freshwater mussel and gastropod remains are found at a wide variety of Woodland site types, from "shell mounds," to large, riverine "base camps" or permanent villages (see below), to smaller villages or hamlets on major rivers and tributary streams (e.g., Bogan 1987; Casey 1987; F. Charles 1973; Curren et al. 1977; Hanley 1983; J. Johnson 1985; T. Lewis and Lewis 1997; D. Morse and P. Morse 1983:146; Parmalee 1990; Parmalee and Bogan 1986; Parmalee et al. 1982; Womochel 1982), to rockshelters and cave sites (e.g., Clench 1974; Parmalee 1994; Parmalee and Klippel 1986; Parmalee et al. 1980; Taylor 1982; Walthall 1980:135; Warren 1995), to mounds and mound/village sites (e.g., Morrison 1951). Brackish-water clam and marine mollusk shells are common constituents of coastal Woodland sites in the region (Curren 1976; Quitmeyer et al. 1985; Steponaitis 1986:380; Trinkley 1985; J. M. Williams 1987).

Recently, I examined temporal changes in the composition of freshwater bivalve assemblages from the Tennessee, Cumberland, and Tombigbee river drainages (Peacock 1998) using shell data that met the following criteria: (1) the shell had to have been recovered using a one-quarter-inch or smaller screen size; (2) there had to be a minimum of 500 identifiable valves in the assemblage; (3) the assemblages had to be from Late Archaic or later contexts in order to avoid confusion that might arise from natural changes in mussel faunas brought on by the Hypsithermal; (4) if data were available from both general strata and features, both types were used; (5) if only data from features were reported, a minimum of five features had to be represented; and (6) data from uncertain cultural contexts (e.g., a pit with mixed Woodland and Mississippian ceramics, a "transitional Woodland/Mississippian" assemblage or level) were not used. These criteria were used to avoid or minimize the various types of bias that might affect archaeological shell assemblages (see Peacock 1998:70–115 for details; cf. Casey 1987; Claassen 1991b; Matteson 1959, 1960; Parmalee et al. 1982:81; Robison 1983; Theler 1991; Warren 1975).

It is assumed that essentially all the shell represented in the analysis, with the exception of a few shell tools, represents food refuse deposits. Claassen (1991a, 1991b, 1992, 1996a) has questioned this common assumption, suggesting that many shell mounds might in fact be intentionally constructed burial facilities. This is based upon the occurrence of large numbers of burials in such mounds and observations made by excavators concerning the frequency of paired (i.e., articulated and unopened) valves at shell mound sites (Claassen 1996a:133–34; cf. Stein 1980). Obviously, unopened valves represent animals that were not consumed, a point that Claassen takes as evidence for the use of shell in lieu of dirt for intentional mound construction. I have disagreed with her assessment (Peacock 1998) for several reasons. First, I believe that the number of articulated valves in shell mounds is much lower than Claassen seems to think. I suspect that excavators mentioned them because they stood out from the mass of (usually unscreened) unarticulated shell, rather than because they were ubiquitous within the deposits. Second, if shell was being used as a construction material, then there would be no reason to expect differential intrasite valve articulation. As Warren (1975) has noted, however, the percentage of paired valves varies considerably from feature to feature at any particular site. Third, at many sites (albeit not always shell "mounds") there is evidence that shells were broken for the extraction of meat (e.g., F. Charles 1973; Peacock 1993). Fourth, if the shell accumulations were intentionally constructed burial mounds, there would be no reason to expect domestic debris or non-mortuary features within the sites. In fact, shell mounds typically contain large numbers and a great variety of artifacts and features. For example, at the Little Bear Creek site on the Tennessee River in northern Alabama, W. Webb and DeJarnette (1948) noted the presence of fire pits, clay hearths, fire basins, pits with animal bone, rock-filled pits, "flint workshops," artifact caches, areas of fire-cracked rock interpreted as "clam bakes," and so on. Artifacts recovered included mortars and pestles, hammerstones, limestone hoes, grooved axes, pitted stones, bifacially flaked axes, celts, discoidals, stone vessel fragments, bannerstones, gorgets, sandstone tablets, abraders, pipes, beads, stone and antler projectile points, vast quantities of debitage, deer ulna awls, bone pins and gouges, fishhooks, and other items. Many of these artifacts were broken, suggesting that they were refuse rather than formal burial accompaniments (W. Webb and DeJarnette 1948:16–49). While shell often was used to cover burial pits (W. Webb and DeJarnette 1948:39), it was probably the shell that was removed from the pits in the first place.

I see no reason to doubt that the shell mounds were built up out of food refuse and domestic waste. The large number of burials recovered from within such mounds can probably be attributed to unusually good bone preservation resulting from the calcareous nature of shell deposits. Milner and Jefferies (1998) examined Claassen's hypothesis using data from an Archaic shell mound in Kentucky and independently reached the same conclusion that I did, for many of the same reasons (see also the discussion in Morey and Crothers 1998).

I realize that there are many shell assemblages from the three river valleys that are still unreported and that I doubtless missed some of the reported data that exist in the gray literature; there also are many assemblages

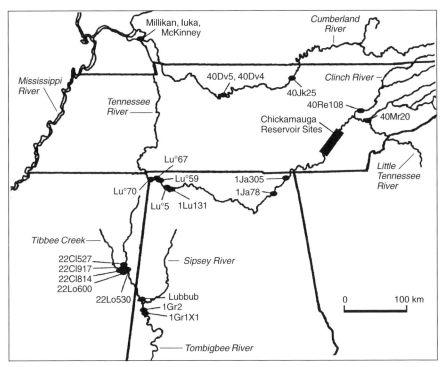

Figure 20.1 — Location map showing rivers and sites in the middle South mentioned in the text

that I purposefully excluded because they did not meet the criteria concerning abundance, recovery methods, number of depositional units represented, or depositional clarity. Still, I examined data from twenty-three sites of various sizes, ranging from deep, multicomponent shell mounds to single-component sites of different periods. I took whatever data I could find that met my criteria, with no effort to favor one cultural period over another, and I believe that a good cross section of the range and types of shell-bearing sites that exist along the three rivers is represented. The data on the number of valves and the attendant references for each assemblage are given in Table 20.1; site locations are shown on Figure 20.1. When all of the data are combined, the total of 203,581 valves can be divided into general Late Archaic, Woodland, and Mississippian categories (Gulf Formational is included with Woodland in this and subsequent analyses when data are thus combined. This decision was based upon continuities in settlement patterns and site occupations, at least in the central Tombigbee River drainage [see J. Rafferty 1980]). Approximately 70 percent of the shell was derived from Woodland contexts, while Late Archaic made up 17 percent and Mississippian 13 per-

Table 20.1 — Assemblages Used in Shell Analysis

Site/Assemblage	Reference	No. Valves
Martin Farm, combined Mississippian assemblages	Bogan and Bogan 1985	707
Clinch River Breeder Reactor Plant site, Mississippian assemblage	Parmalee and Bogan 1986	2,713
Chickamauga Reservoir, combined Mississippian assemblages	Parmalee et al. 1982	2,794
Clinch River Breeder Reactor Plant site, Middle Woodland assemblage	Parmalee and Bogan 1986	20,238
Chickamauga Reservoir, combined Middle and Late Woodland assemblages	Parmalee et al. 1982	12,308
Site Lu°5, combined Late Archaic levels	Morrison 1942	2,968
Site Lu°59, combined Late Archaic levels	Morrison 1942	10,284
Site Lu°67, Late Archaic level	Morrison 1942	1,185
Smith Bottom Cave, Archaic contexts	Parmalee 1994	2,537
Widows Creek site, Archaic contexts	Warren 1975; Peacock 1998	1,938
Site Lu°59, Gulf Formational level	Morrison 1942	7,451
Site Lu°67, Woodland level	Morrison 1942	830
Smith Bottom Cave, Woodland contexts	Parmalee 1994	630
B. B. Corner Bridge site, Late Woodland assemblage	Hanley 1983	3,148
Widows Creek site, combined Woodland contexts	Warren 1975; Peacock 1998	50,913
Penitentiary Branch site, Late Archaic assemblage	Breitburg 1986	16,608
Site 40Dv5, Mississippian assemblage	Peacock 1993	1,642
Site 40Dv4, Mississippian assemblage	Peacock 1993	4,548
McKinney site, Mississippian assemblage	Casey 1987	4,913

Table 20.1 (cont.) — Assemblages Used in Shell Analysis

Site/Assemblage	Reference	No. Valves
Millikan site, Mississippian assemblage	Casey 1987	1,551
Shell Bluff site, Late Woodland assemblage	Peacock 1993	21,679
Tibbee Creek site, Late Woodland assemblage	Peacock 1993	8,620
Kellogg Village site, Late Woodland assemblage	Rummel 1980	2,891
Lubbub Creek Archaeological Locality, Late Woodland contexts	Woodrick 1983	1,686
Site 1Gr1X1, combined Middle and Late Woodland contexts	Woodrick 1981	1,549
Site 1Gr2, combined Middle and Late Woodland contexts	Woodrick 1981	1,282
Sanders site, Gulf Formational assemblage	Hartfield 1990	9,057
Yarborough site, Mississippian assemblage	Hanley 1982	2,791
Lubbub Creek Archaeological Locality, combined Mississippian contexts	Woodrick 1983	4,120
		Total 203,581

cent of the total (Figure 20.2). This suggests that shellfish use was at its peak during the Woodland period along these three rivers.

Where individual sites are concerned, one of the finest molluscan analyses ever conducted in the Southeast remains that reported in J. P. E. Morrison's (1942) chapter in William Webb and David DeJarnette's (1942) classic volume on archaeological excavations of shell mounds along the Tennessee River in the Pickwick Basin. Morrison's sampling and analytic methods (and subsequent interpretations) were considerably ahead of their time in eastern North America. He took large, standardized samples from arbitrary 1-foot levels within the shell mounds; these samples were then screened down to one-quarter-inch mesh. The shells were identified to species and counts were provided in the report. Following the criteria outlined above, I will use Morrison's data only from those levels that produced 500 or more identifiable valves.

Morrison's sampling levels can be directly equated with Webb and DeJarnette's arbitrary excavation levels, and general cultural designations

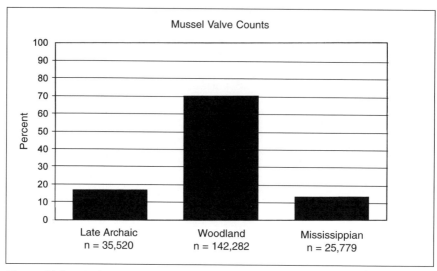

Figure 20.2 — Relative values for reported shell counts by cultural period from the Tennessee, Cumberland, and Tombigbee rivers (data from sources compiled in Peacock 1998)

can be made using the artifact tabulations and illustrations in their report, with the understanding that stratigraphic distinctions were blurred by the use of arbitrary levels. The Bluff Creek site, Lu°59, described as a "typical shell mound," was up to 16 feet (4.88 meters) thick. The top foot* consisted of Gulf Formational to Middle Woodland deposits, while the shell-bearing levels from 6 to 14 feet were Late Archaic (the intervening levels did not have sufficient shell to be included). The Long Branch site, Lu°67, had two levels that can be used in this analysis: Foot Level 2–3, which is considered to be Gulf Formational, and Foot Level 3–4, which is Late Archaic.

When the shell data from the two sites are examined in terms of number of valves, the higher counts might lead one to believe that shellfishing was more important in the Late Archaic than in the subsequent Gulf Formational period (Table 20.2). These data can be adjusted, however, to account for the potential length of time represented by the deposits simply by dividing the valve counts by the number of years that constitute each cultural period, with Late Archaic stretching 2500 years from 3500 to 1000 B.C. and Gulf Formational 750 years from 1000 to 250 B.C. These are, of course, purely arbitrary time lines, and there is no reason to suppose that the entire span of time is represented in the deposits at either site. Still, it may be informative

---

* *This includes Levels 1–1½, 1½–2p, and 1–2p, from Morrison (1942:table 4).*

Table 20.2 — Raw Shell Counts, Shell Counts Adjusted for Time, and Derived Percentages from Tennessee River Sites Lu°59, Lu°67, and 1JA305

		Lu°59	*Lu°67*	*1JA305*
No Valves	Late Archaic	10,284	1,185	1,938
	Gulf Formational/Woodland	7,451	830	50,913
Percent	Late Archaic	58	59	4
	Gulf Formational/Woodland	42	41	96
Shell Quantities	Late Archaic	4.11	0.47	0.78
Corrected by Time	Gulf Formational/Woodland	9.93	1.11	25.46
Corrected Values	Late Archaic	29	30	3
Converted to Percent	Gulf Formational/Woodland	71	70	97

to examine the data in this fashion, and, at the Bluff Creek site at least, the much greater thickness of the Late Archaic deposits argues for a longer depositional time span than that represented in the one level assigned to the Gulf Formational/Middle Woodland. It also should be remembered that Woodland deposits typically make up the surface layers of the Tennessee River shell mounds (Peacock 1998; W. Webb and DeJarnette 1942; Walthall 1980:129) and thus were subject to more postdepositional degradation than the underlying Archaic deposits. If any part of the record is missing from these sites, it is from the Woodland deposits.

When the valve counts are corrected by time, it can be seen that shellfish exploitation was apparently much more intensive during the Gulf Formational/Middle Woodland period (Table 20.2). This is perhaps more effectively illustrated by converting those values into percentage data (Table 20.2 and Figure 20.3). Of the two examples, Bluff Creek is the better one, since multiple Late Archaic levels are being compared to a single Gulf Formational/Middle Woodland level. The similarity between the two sites in terms of percentages is striking, however.

In 1973, the Widows Creek site (1JA305) on the Tennessee River in northeast Alabama was excavated by the University of Tennessee at Chattanooga (Morey 1996; Warren 1975). Arbitrary half-foot levels were used, with 2-foot-square control columns from each level being screened through one-quarter-inch mesh. Twelve stratigraphic zones were recognized and more than 180 features were excavated, the fills of which were screened. The

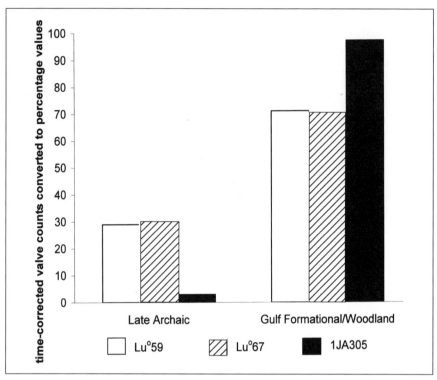

Figure 20.3 — Time-adjusted shell values converted to percentages for Tennessee River sites Lu°59, Lu°67, and 1JA305

shell from the site was analyzed by Bob Warren (1975), and both he and Morey (1996) have made cultural assignments for the depositional zones and features using diagnostic artifacts and a series of ten radiocarbon dates. According to Warren (1975:31), the upper 7 feet of the site represented "a continuum of Woodland occupations" with several feet of Gulf Formational, Late Archaic, and Middle Archaic strata below that.

When the raw valve counts are tabulated and displayed, the combined Gulf Formational, Middle Woodland, and Late Woodland valves far out-number the Late Archaic valves (Table 20.2). This far greater intensity in shellfish use also is seen when the valve counts are corrected for time. In this case, a 2000-year time span was used for the Woodland "continuum" represented by the upper deposits at the site, making the divisor more com-parable to the 2500 years used to divide the Late Archaic shell count. When the time-corrected data are converted to percentages (Table 20.2 and Figure 20.3), it can be seen that Late Archaic shell makes up only 3 percent of the total at this Tennessee River shell-matrix site. The same pattern can be seen at other sites in the area, for example, Russell Cave (Clench 1974). These analyses also suggest that shellfish use reached its peak during the Woodland period in the interior Middle South.

Population Growth and Resource Stress? Evidence from Shell Data

The intensive exploitation of mollusks is often taken as indirect evidence for resource stress and/or territorial constriction (Speth and Scott 1989:77). The "lowly" mussels and snails typically are considered to be a "second-line" resource that was heavily exploited when times were bad (Futato 1987:238; C. Jenkins 1993:47; N. Jenkins 1982; N. Jenkins and Krause 1986:77; Pope 1956:12–13; J. Rudolph 1983:97–98; Warren 1975:210; Woodrick 1983:422). While this characterization may stem in part from our own perceptions of the palatability of mollusks, it is supported by the very limited historical accounts that exist in which mollusk exploitation is mentioned (e.g., Woodrick 1983:422) and by the relatively low nutritive value of freshwater shellfish (Cumbaa 1976; Klippel et al. 1978; Parmalee and Klippel 1974).

Shell data provide an opportunity to test the idea of Woodland period population growth and resource stress by way of the following hypotheses: (1) there would be little or no collection bias by people who were maximizing the use of all available resources—the full range of species available would have been taken, and there would have been no selectivity in terms of the size of mussels obtained and (2) if populations had increased to the extent surmised, then the available space for resource collection would have been constrained; therefore, the mussel species represented at any given site should have come from the immediate environs.

The first hypothesis can be tested by examining the diversity of mussel species typically represented at Woodland period sites. Where it has been possible to compare lists of midden specimens with early Historic period mussel surveys in relatively unmodified waterways, studies have shown that shell-bearing sites tend to produce a good approximation of the range of species that would have been expected prior to extensive modern impacts (e.g., F. Charles 1973:150; J. Rudolph 1983:90; Warren 1975:156; D. White 1977). In other words, prehistoric Native Americans were apparently gathering whatever species were available. This is reflected more generally in the large number of species typically recovered from archaeological sites across the eastern United States (Parmalee 1988; Parmalee and Bogan 1986; Parmalee and Klippel 1984; Parmalee et al. 1980, 1982; Peacock 1993, 1998) and the general similarity of assemblages retrieved from sites located near to one another on any particular waterway (e.g., Hanley 1983:72; Peacock 1993, 1998). These common characteristics of archaeological shell assemblages have led many researchers to state uncategorically that they found no evidence of collection bias, that is, the proportions of taxa represented in the archaeological collections are approximately equivalent to the expected natural proportions (Bogan 1987; Hanley 1984:164; Parmalee 1959:62, 1960:73, 1988:167; Parmalee and Bogan 1986:35; Parmalee and O'Hare 1989:39–42; Parmalee et al. 1972:5; Peacock 1998, 1999; Warren 1975:156, 160).

Some researchers have argued that smaller species or specimens would be relatively hard to retrieve and would yield little meat in return for the labor expended (Murphy 1971:22; Robison 1983:117; Taylor 1989:189), and indeed there are rare instances in which archaeological assemblages seem to have been affected by this type of bias (Taylor 1989:189; Theler 1987:148; Womochel 1982:362). Typically, however, Woodland period assemblages produce an abundance of subadult mussels and small species (e.g., Parmalee and Bogan 1986; W. Turner n.d.). For example, Warren (1975:156) noted at the Widows Creek site "a remarkable quantity of both young and specifically small valves... which indicate specimen selection down to maximum lengths of 25 mm and below," while Parmalee and Bogan (1986:29–30) note that specimens from sites along the Clinch River in Tennessee were as small as about 20 millimeters. Measurements on Late Woodland shell from the Tibbee Creek site, in Lowndes County, Mississippi, showed that mussels as small as 12 to 16 millimeters long were being collected (Peacock 1998). At Woodland period sites in general, size bias seems to have played little role in shaping the shell assemblages, and it seems as though mussels (as well as gastropods) of all sizes were being collected, regardless of the amount of meat that was forthcoming. This can be taken as evidence that Woodland peoples were experiencing resource stress, but it should be noted that this same phenomenon has been noted at pre- and post-Woodland period sites as well (e.g., Peacock 1993, 1999; R. Ray 1994). Determining the extent to which Woodland period sites differ from earlier and later sites in this regard will require a great deal of metric analysis as well as thin-sectioning of valves to see whether the largest specimens being recovered are in fact very old mussels—that the entire size range of mussels present in the environment is represented in the archaeological assemblages.

Mussels often are assumed to have come from the river adjacent to any particular site (Call 1992:249; Peacock 1998; Robison 1983:118), since they were readily available and since their weight (see Parmalee and Klippel 1974:423) makes them difficult to transport overland (Warren 1975). If collection areas were unconstrained, however, there is no reason prehistoric shellfishers could not have harvested mussels from many kilometers upriver or downriver, or up tributary streams, by simply loading the mussels into canoes as they were gathered, then transporting them back to the home site. If collection areas were constrained as a result of population pressure, then only the local mussel beds would have been exploited. Since species proportions change and different species appear or disappear as one moves down a river or up a tributary stream (A. Miller et al. 1994; Parmalee 1990:68; Parmalee and Hughes 1994:22; Parmalee et al. 1980:94; Strayer 1983:256), this question can be explored using mathematical techniques for examining ecological data sets.

Over the past few decades, ecologists have developed statistical means for presenting graphical representations of complex, multivariate data in a simplified two- or three-dimensional fashion (Bray and Curtis 1957; Gauch 1982; Gower 1987; Legendre and Legendre 1983; Ludwig and Reynolds 1988; Pielou 1977; ter Braak and Prentice 1988). This is done using ordination methods such as Principal Components Analysis and Detrended Correspondence Analysis, in which entire assemblages are plotted as individual points, the relative locations of which are based upon similarities to the other assemblages being included in the analysis. Axes are extracted from the data in such a way that the first axis represents as much variation as possible when plotted in n-dimensional hyperspace; the next axis is constructed so as to represent as much of the remaining variation as possible in a position that is perpendicular to the first axis, and so on, up to n axes as determined by the number of variables (e.g., taxa) present in the data matrix (Gower 1987:4; Ludwig and Reynolds 1988:224). The result is "a reduced coordinate system that provides information about the ecological resemblances" (Ludwig and Reynolds 1988:224; see also ter Braak and Prentice 1988) between sample units, in which "the species are axes of multidimensional space and the samples are points located by their abundance for each species" (Gauch 1982:110). Detrending is a complex mathematical procedure that recalculates the position of each lower-order axis relative to the preceding axis so that multiple axes are not needed to account for the natural, clinal variation that typically occurs in ecological data obtained along an environmental gradient such as a river course (see M. O. Hill and Gauch 1980; ter Braak 1985, 1986; ter Braak and Prentice 1988 for a description of the "arch effect").

Detrended Correspondence Analysis was performed with the PC-ORD computer program (McCune and Mefford 1997) using data from Woodland assemblages on the Tennessee and Tombigbee rivers. The resulting ordination diagrams are shown in Figure 20.4. In Figure 20.4, *a,* the Tombigbee River assemblages are strongly separated along Axis 1, the axis that accounts for most of the variation in the data. This separation is obviously

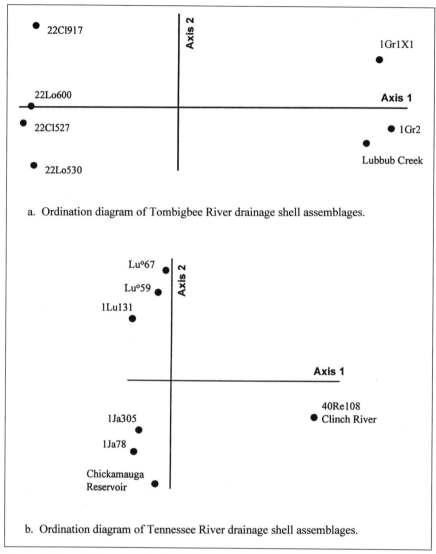

a. Ordination diagram of Tombigbee River drainage shell assemblages.

b. Ordination diagram of Tennessee River drainage shell assemblages.

Figure 20.4 — Ordination diagram showing distribution of Woodland period shell assemblages from (a) the Tombigbee River and (b) the Tennessee River drainage

based on spatial relationships, as the four assemblages that are negative along Axis 1 are from sites located near to one another along the central Tombigbee River and one of its main tributaries, Tibbee Creek, in Mississippi. The other three assemblages, which are strongly positive along Axis 1, come from sites that also are close together, but that lie farther south along the river in Alabama (Figure 20.1). The three assemblages from Alabama also are ordered spatially along Axis 2, following their north-south distribution along the river (Figure 20.1). There is no obvious order to the assemblages from Mississippi, but this may be due to a mix of spatial effects (22Lo600 is on a tributary stream while the other three sites are on the main river) and temporal change (22Cl917 is a single-component Gulf Formational shell midden and is thus earlier than the other three assemblages shown, all of which are Late Woodland). A pattern similar to the Alabama assemblages is seen in the Tennessee River assemblages (Figure 20.4, *b*). In this case, Axis 1 is dominated by differences between sites from the main stem of the river and 40Re108, the Clinch River Breeder Reactor Plant site (the Clinch is a major tributary of the Tennessee). While the main-stem river sites are similar in their placement along Axis 1, spatial differences are readily apparent along Axis 2: moving from negative to positive along that axis, there is an almost perfect ordering of the sites as they occur on the river from east to west (Figure 20.1). Even the three sites located very close together on the river— Lu131, Lu°59, and Lu°67—follow this pattern of spatial separation.

What this analysis implies is that collection areas for mussels were in fact constrained and that only mussels from beds immediately adjacent to the sites are found in the assemblages at these Woodland sites. It could be argued that *low* population levels would lead to the same pattern, since without resource stress it would simply be more convenient to take what was needed from the nearest source. It could also be argued that resource stress would lead people to exploit environments farther away from the site, rather than intensifying use of a local resource. Given the other indicators of population pressure (more and larger sites, skeletal indicators, warfare, etc.), and given the fact that mussels of all species down to 12 millimeters in length were being collected, these arguments can be dismissed in favor of a model of demographic constraint. The indirect evidence from the shell data supports the idea that population pressure played a significant role in determining settlement/subsistence patterns in the Woodland period in the Middle South.

Conclusions

In sum, the data presented herein suggest that prehistoric exploitation of shellfish reached its peak during the Woodland period, at least along the Cumberland, Tennessee, and Tombigbee rivers. On the basis of the number of Woodland period shell assemblages reported in the cultural resource management literature, it is likely that this pattern generally holds true throughout the Southeast. The strong spatial associations revealed in Woodland period shell assemblages using Detrended Correspondence Analysis lend credence to the idea that collection areas were constrained by population pressure during Woodland times, and the consistent presence of very small specimens in shell assemblages suggests that resource stress was indeed present.

The analysis of molluscan remains has come a long way in recent years, with in-depth considerations of the economic and social implications of intensive shellfishing (e.g., Claassen 1996b; Quitmeyer et al. 1985), quantitative methods (e.g., Warren 1991, 1992), contextual concerns (e.g., Morey and Crothers 1998), and other avenues of research (Peacock 1997b). This healthy trend should only continue as traditional settlement/subsistence models are reexamined, as further survey and excavations are carried out away from the main rivers, and as sophisticated computer analysis techniques are brought to bear on the large amounts of data that exist for archaeological shell assemblages in the Southeast.

Acknowledgments

The data presented in this chapter are derived from my doctoral thesis for the Department of Archaeology and Prehistory at the University of Sheffield, England. I am indebted to my supervisors, Paul Halstead and Glynis Jones, for their patience and guidance. I also owe a special thanks to Paul Parmalee for his help over the past few years. He, Walter Klippel, Art Bogan, and Emanuel Breitburg made unpublished data available to me, which I greatly appreciate. Wendell Haag helped me with the identifications of many specimens from the Tombigbee River. Bob Warren very graciously provided me with his original analysis sheets from the Widows Creek site, and Darcy Morey sent an indispensable manuscript relating to that site for which I am most grateful. John Connaway provided me with useful references, as did Kevin Smith, Mike Moore, Eugene Futato, Keith Baca, Sam Brookes, Bob Warren, Danny Olinger, and most especially Rick Walling. As always, I would like to thank Janet Rafferty for her encouragement and support. The Tombigbee River assemblages were made available by the U.S. Army Corps of Engineers, Mobile District. Finally, I would like to thank the editors for asking me to participate in the symposium that led to this volume.

Chapter 21

Woodland Faunal Exploitation in the Midsouth

H. Edwin Jackson and Susan L. Scott

S tudies of Woodland faunal samples from sites in the Southeast have been accumulating during the past 20 years, but there have been few attempts to synthesize the growing body of information (see Wing 1977 for an early exception). In this chapter we begin by identifying factors that likely affected the subsistence strategies of various southeastern Woodland groups and also some issues in zooarchaeological methodology that affect productive intersite comparison and the derivation of broad regional and temporal patterns. We then examine available faunal records in two areas of the Midsouth to illustrate our major points. Recognizing the broad geographic and environmental diversity of the Southeast and the considerable time depth represented by the Woodland era, we have chosen to narrow our focus to zooarchaeological data from the Tombigbee River valley of west-central Alabama and east-central Mississippi and that portion of the Lower Mississippi Valley encompassed by western Mississippi, southeastern Arkansas, and northeastern Louisiana. These two areas provide important contrasts not only in prehistoric animal procurement patterns, but also in the relative potential of zooarchaeological techniques to document important trends.

The broad commonalities among the vast majority of Southeastern faunal assemblages are quite evident. Discounting coastal and certain riverine settings where fishing may have taken on a central role in procurement, deer, rabbit, raccoon, squirrel, and turkey are the most ubiquitous taxa, regardless of site location or temporal affiliation, suggesting their core importance in the meat diet. Deer, as the single and pervasive large mammal in the Southeast for much of Holocene, is unarguably the single most important taxon for its contribution of meat and fat to the diet, in addition to bone and hide as raw materials for clothing, implements, and ornaments.

Beyond these obvious similarities, however, are subtle differences in taxonomic mix that reflect procurement strategies evolving within a complex environmental matrix. By the Woodland era a range of variables affected that mix. Among these are habitat and species distributions (and the

potential effects on them of human population density and cultural practices) and responses to the demands created by specific human demographic
characteristics. A second source of variability derives from potential scheduling conflicts that arose from variably important plant food production and
the labor demands created by increasingly important (or at least
archaeologically more evident) social and ritual activities. As if these variables were not sufficient to make the situation complicated enough, hunting
technology changed near the end of the Woodland period with the introduction of the bow and arrow (Blitz 1988). Not only did the bow enhance effectiveness in procurement of (primarily) terrestrial taxa, but it also made warfare more deadly, just as the potential for intersocietal conflict became more
likely as a result of greater population densities and sociopolitical competition. In sum, beyond a rather simplistic observation that similar taxa were
being utilized, we would not expect to find a single Woodland period faunal
exploitation pattern.

Increasing reliance on cultivated foods must have had a major structuring effect on Woodland hunting strategies. Present evidence suggests considerable variability from region to region in precisely when the threshold
of agricultural dependence was crossed (see Gremillion, this volume). In
some parts of eastern North America, mainly in the Midcontinent region,
much of the Woodland period was characterized by a commitment to at least
horticultural production of indigenous plant taxa. Elsewhere, such as in the
Deep South, the shift occurs at the very end of the Woodland era (C. Scarry
1986). Regardless of timing, when the production and storage of a predictable calorie source became a central feature of the subsistence system, it
resulted in increased sedentism and produced changes in seasonal patterns
of labor demands, thus restructuring opportunities for hunting (e.g., Kent
1989). As agricultural activities such as land clearing, spring planting, and
summer and fall harvesting required greater labor inputs, time available for
hunting during those periods was curtailed (Speth and Scott 1989). Since
the nutrition provided by increased plant food production, particularly in
late prehistoric maize-based systems, contributed primarily calories, it would
have been insufficient to eliminate the need for meat as a source of protein
in the diet. Thus, within the scheduling and labor constraints imposed by the
agricultural calendar, hunting persisted, but probably in somewhat altered
forms.

The impact of agriculture on animal resource distributions has been
hypothesized to have encouraged what is commonly referred to as garden
hunting, based on ethnographic studies of tropical swidden horticulturalists
(e.g., Linares 1976; Neussius 1996). According to the garden hunting hypothesis, the production of edge environments as well as the attractiveness

of crops would have increased the densities of certain taxa in the vicinity of fields, making them more susceptible to hunting.

In the eastern United States, land clearance associated with the intensification of crop production may have initially increased hunting yield, but because settlements probably were not abandoned every few years as is the case in the tropics, degradation of the immediate environment, insofar as hunting is concerned, would have prevailed eventually. Speth and Scott (1989) note that locally available prey are likely to diminish over time as a result of persistent hunting pressure. Eventually, lowered densities of prey in the vicinity of settlements lead to hunting forays at increased distances from the settlement. Speth and Scott argue that these hunting trips focus on large game to compensate for the greater effort expended. At the same time, the risk of failure inherent in large-game hunting is balanced by the security of the food base provided by agriculture. In the southwestern United States, this pattern shows up clearly in the archaeological record of the late prehistoric period as an increase in the proportion of large mammals in faunal samples and suggests the increasing use of logistically organized communal hunting focused on the procurement of large mammal taxa away from the agricultural settlement (Speth and Scott 1989; Szeuter and Bayham 1989).

South of the Tennessee River valley, the intensification of food production appears to have occurred no earlier than the Late Woodland, in contrast to areas farther north for which agricultural dependence appears much earlier (Fritz 1993; Johannessen 1993a, 1993b). According to Caddell (1981, 1983), although maize occurs as early as the Late Woodland Miller III period in the Tombigbee Valley, wild plant resources provided the bulk of plant foods until the very end of the period. C. Margaret Scarry (1986) points to a significant shift in the archaeobotanical record at the very end of the Late Woodland, at roughly A.D. 1050, in the Black Warrior Valley. In the Lower Mississippi Valley, the timing and role of agricultural production is variable. In the Plum Bayou culture area in east-central Arkansas, maize occurs in a number of contexts after A.D. 700, although its presence in different contexts is highly variable (Rolingson 1998c:106, this volume), suggesting that it was not a truly important resource until somewhat later. Unlike elsewhere in the Lower Mississippi Valley, indigenous small seed crops appear to have been important in the Plum Bayou culture (Fritz and Kidder 1993:8). Farther south, indigenous crops do not seem to have been cultivated, and maize, though occurring in contexts after about A.D. 800, does not seem to have been important much before A.D. 1250 (Fritz and Kidder 1993:9).

In addition to agriculture, though closely related to its intensification, increasing human populations also likely played a role in differentiating patterns of faunal exploitation. With increasing population density, size of hunting territory becomes an important factor. Larger populations predictably create a need for larger hunting territories, while simultaneously increasing the potential for intersocietal competition for territory. Reduction in the territory needed for large-game hunting predictably leads to one of two general strategies to solve meat procurement needs (e.g., Earle 1980). Diversification in the species utilized for food provides one solution. In the Southeast, we would expect that where hunting territories were curtailed, increasing numbers of smaller, locally available, taxa would have been pursued. Zooarchaeologically, this shows up as increased diversity, adding unusual species to the list of taxa procured traditionally. In many southeastern locations, this pattern may have included increased use of small mammals and reptiles as well as greater reliance on fishing. A second solution is intensification of procurement of traditionally exploited terrestrial taxa. Intensification requires both increased time for pursuit and also, potentially, greater labor input in the production of nontraditional technologies for capture (such as communal hunting far removed from villages). Despite being more labor intensive, intensification may become necessary, since at some point a strategy relying on increasing diversification may fail to meet the needs of a growing human population. Intensification would show up zooarchaeologically in more complete processing and use of large taxa and potentially in a shift in the age curve, reflecting the inclusion of younger individuals. Intensification of fishing may involve specialized techniques, such as those necessary to procure very large fish, or else nonselective or bulk procurement of smaller sized individuals as a means of increasing total yield. More energy is likely to be expended on this previously underexploited and relatively stationary aquatic resource. Perhaps most important, fishing, where possible, offers an opportunity to safely increase meat procurement through increased labor without the potential complications inherent in other strategies that require increased territory use under conditions of increasing intersocietal conflicts.

To this point we have focused on factors that likely differentiated subsistence systems from one another because of geographic setting. During the Woodland era we might expect early evidence for variation within systems as well, beyond that accountable by seasonal variation in procurement activities. In at least some Woodland societies, increasing social distinctions may have led to variability in patterns of consumption. During the Woodland era, public and ritual contexts—mortuary sites and mound centers, for instance—are either more common or at least easier to recognize archaeologically. These provide opportunities for the collection of faunal samples representing public or ritual meals, which are likely to have differed from everyday fare. The important ritual function of feasting is documented ethnohistorically for later Mississippian societies. Ritual feasting at least by Middle Woodland times is documented by Styles and Purdue (1991) and suspected by others (e.g., Seeman 1979b). Given the long history of corporate earth moving in the Midsouth, it is expectable that fauna from public contexts will reflect prey selection and processing decisions aimed at feeding large groups or providing for ritual consumption, regardless of the time period studied. Bulk meat procurement and processing is likely to distinguish feasting contexts. Similarly, as societies became increasingly differentiated into distinct, ranked social stations, we expect to see evidence for differential access to particular faunal resources, as well as to the quantity of meat in the diet. Patterns of differential access have been established for the subsequent Mississippian period (e.g., H. Jackson and Scott 1995), but the root of socially defined access to different faunal resources is presently incompletely documented.

A final factor to consider is the impact of these changes on the cultural practices and natural processes that created bone accumulations at Woodland sites. Greater sedentism certainly affected the ways in which people disposed of animal refuse, which in turn affected the survival potential of various parts of a faunal assemblage. Field butchering and selective transport of large game, and seasonally distinct methods of handling potentially offensive animal carcasses or rancid fish and mussel shells, may lead to a variety of aboriginally based biases in the representation of fauna that ultimately are examined by the zooarchaeologist.

Methodological Considerations

The validity of quantification techniques continues to be debated among zooarchaeologists, with no certain resolution on the horizon. We feel compelled to enter the fray, since variability in quantitative techniques compromises intersite comparisons. As it presently stands, there is far too much variation in how the contributions of various taxa are characterized. Consistent use of any particular suite of techniques in the analysis of single sites may not lead to great interpretive gaffs. At the level of intersite comparison, however, the variability in quantitative methods and their interaction with the particular qualities of individual assemblages renders comparisons of patterns elicited by different analysts an almost impossible task. A number of problems can be identified that shake confidence in intersite comparisons. Among them are fundamental differences in identification, related to variation in skill, to access to appropriate collections for a particular study region, and to a variety of criteria that guide effort in identifying fragmentary remains unidentifiable to family, genus, or species.

Presentation of quantitative data varies widely among analysts. Most commonly presented are the Number of Identified Specimens (NISP) and Minimum Number of Individuals (MNI). At first glance, NISP would seem to be a reasonable measure for regional comparisons, since it represents primary data. However, it is particularly sensitive to fragmentation, which affects the identification of different taxa differentially. Turtles and certain fish, such as gar, bowfin, and catfish, all have distinctive bone structures that enable identification of even very fragmentary remains.

A more serious problem one encounters with NISP data is the variable way in which analysts deal with fragments that can be identified only above the level of taxonomic family. A great proportion of a sample may be identifiable only to class; when this is the case, some analysts simply categorize this material as unidentifiable. Thus is lost not only a potentially large portion of an assemblage, but also the opportunity to compare assemblages at the level of class, which is necessary when attempting to map broad patterns.

Minimum Number of Individuals seeks to overcome the shortcomings of NISP, but introduces a host of other problems. MNI values are transformations of raw data, and analysts vary greatly in the manner in which they calculate MNI. Two basic categories of variability can be identified easily. The first relates to how bone fragments are considered in the calculation of MNI. More problematic, however, are the variable ways in which assemblages are partitioned to calculate MNI. With increasing partitioning, whether by analytical unit, feature, or some other "logical" cultural unit, more common species increase in their relative contributions to total MNI at the expense of rarer taxa. In village middens, "palimpsests," in the words of Gifford (1981), such techniques are ineffectual at best and potentially quite misleading, being very far removed from the realities of bone accumulation.

Since broad comparisons are most likely to be useful at fairly general taxonomic levels, we believe, and we hope will demonstrate with the data from the Tombigbee region, that bone weight offers the least biased means of comparing the quantities of bone material contributed to an assemblage by different animals or groupings of animals. Although not routinely reported, weight data permit merging of more, less specifically identified material into more general categories, maximizing the information that can be gained from that often significant portion of the sample that cannot be identified at or below the level of family. Furthermore, it is a robust measure not grossly affected by fragmentation (other than as it affects identifiability at more specific levels). It is also a robust measure when interanalyst variability is considered because it provides the opportunity to compare assemblages at the level of general taxonomic categories with greater confidence, thus compensating for differences in analytical skill, the comparative collection available to the analyst, and bone fragmentation, each of which has a significant impact on the characterization of an assemblage. Given that specific circumstances, for example, site catchment, may have considerable effect on the specific taxa procured, intersite comparison at more general taxonomic levels may be more productive for identifying shared patterns.

Present Methods

Having made the pitch for the value of bone weight data, we have to note that it is, unfortunately, not commonly reported by southeastern zooarchaeologists. Thus, in the present study, the summary data gleaned from faunal reports diverge in our two study areas. In the Tombigbee Valley, weight was recorded by the analysts working on the key sites of interest, providing consistent intersite patterns that we believe to be reliable. The value of weight as an analytical tool is emphatically demonstrated by the Tombigbee data set.

For the Lower Mississippi Valley, samples are compared using NISP, since that is the only universally reported primary statistic. A few sites do have weight data; these are presented to facilitate a general impression of differences between the two areas. In tabulating NISP for intersite comparison, identified bone fragment counts were tallied by class. Presumed commensal taxa (for instance, small rodents) were omitted from calculations. Unidentified mammals were tabulated according to size-based subdivisions (e.g., small and medium versus large mammal) if the information was provided in the original report (most often "unidentified mammal" was reported as a single category). In tallying fish, scales were omitted when reported. Gar in particular are subject to overrepresentation when their easily recognized bony scales are included in NISP, since a single individual can contribute hundreds to the count. For Lower Mississippi Valley sites, fish were also tabulated by family, or in the case of perciform fish, superfamily, in order to look at possible fish procurement preferences.

Tombigbee River Valley

Seven sites analyzed by three different zooarchaeologists provide the data set for examining Woodland faunal trends through time in the Tombigbee region (Figure 21.1, Table 21.1). Woodrick (1981) analyzed Woodland components excavated at four sites (1PI33, a portion of the Lubbub Creek Archaeological Locality; 1GR1X1; 1GR2; 1PI61) in the Gainesville Reservoir area in Greene and Pickens counties, Alabama. Scott analyzed fauna from the Late Gulf Formational (ca. 700–100 B.C.) Sanders site, a shell midden in Clay County, Mississippi (Scott 1990), and from Woodland features excavated by the University of Michigan at the Lubbub Creek Archaeological Locality in Pickens County, Alabama (Scott 1983). Finally, C. Jenkins (1993) analyzed fauna from several late Woodland features excavated at the Tibbee Creek site in Lowndes County, Mississippi. Woodland trends are compared with assemblages from two Mississippian settlements, one at the Lubbub Creek Archaeological Locality (Scott 1983), a single-mound center and associated village, and the other the Yarborough site, a single-family farmstead in Clay County, Mississippi (Scott 1982).

The Late Woodland in the central Tombigbee region is subdivided by Ned Jenkins (1982) into four phases: Vienna (A.D. 600–900), Catfish Bend (A.D. 900–1000), Gainesville, and Cofferdam (both dating between A.D. 1000 and 1100). The Gainesville and Cofferdam phases are interpreted as representing culturally distinct units by Ned Jenkins (1982), but as seasonally

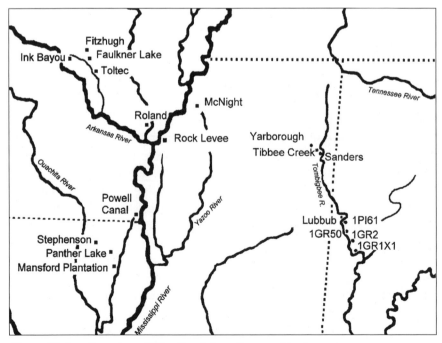

Figure 21.1 — Location of Woodland sites discussed in the text

Table 21.1 — Tombigbee Valley Woodland Faunal Samples

Chronological Unit	Sites	Reference
Late Gulf Formational	Sanders	Scott 1990
Early Miller I	1GR2	Woodrick 1981
Miller II	1GR1X1, 1GR2, 1PI61	Woodrick 1981
Early Miller III	1GR1X1, 1PI61	Woodrick 1981
Middle Miller III	1GR1X1, 1GR2	Woodrick 1981
	Lubbub Creek Archaeological Locality	Scott 1990
Late Miller III	1PI33, 1PI61	Woodrick 1981
	Tibbee Creek	C. Jenkins 1993

differentiated facies of the same settlement system by Welch (1990). All but Catfish Bend, which had not yet been defined at the time of the zooarchaeological analyses, are represented in Woodrick's report. Cliff Jenkins's (1993) analysis of Tibbee Creek identifies features only as being Late Woodland Miller III in age.

Woodrick, Scott, and Cliff Jenkins followed a similar quantitative methodology that included collection of bone weight data, with the result that comparison of the Tombigbee sites is fairly straightforward. Some data massaging was needed to overcome the absence of large and small/medium unidentified mammal categories at Tibbee Creek (C. Jenkins 1993:59). While Scott and Cliff Jenkins both focused on single-site collections, Woodrick's multisite analysis grouped together proveniences from all four sites according to time period, which in effect provides an "averaged" use of fauna by time period. Despite three different analysts of variable experience working independently of one another, the composite database clearly illustrates trends in faunal composition that can be explained in terms of economic and social change in the region. The coherence of the data reflects the robust nature of weight as a method for characterizing quantities of bone material.

Figure 21.2 depicts the chronologically ordered assemblages from the Tombigbee sites included in this discussion. The Late Gulf Formational sample from Sanders and the composite early Miller I sample from the Gainesville sites are virtually identical and are dominated by large mammals, which contribute all but 5 to 7 percent of the total by weight. At no other time does large mammal make such a significant contribution to total bone weight. The remaining portion of the assemblage is comprised of, in order of contribution, turtle, small mammal, fish, and bird.

Beginning in the Middle Woodland Miller II period and continuing through the Terminal Woodland Middle Miller III subperiod, there is a pro-

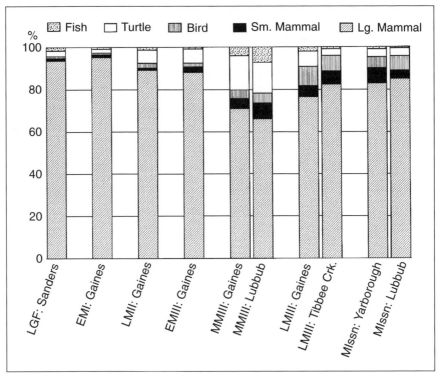

Figure 21.2 — Composition of Tombigbee Valley Woodland samples based on weight; trends in faunal utilization

gressive decline in the contribution made by large mammals and a complementary increase in the percentages of all other categories, but especially turtles and fish. Large mammal bone weight in the collective sample from the Miller II Turkey Paw phase and early Late Woodland Miller III (Vienna phase) sites is 89 percent and 88 percent, respectively. Large mammal drops to less than 80 percent by terminal Miller III. At Lubbub, large mammals make up only 66 percent of the sample. In part, this may reflect a seasonal bias, since fauna recovered from late Miller III features accumulated from spring through fall, based on detailed analysis of stratified feature fill. The composite terminal Miller III data from other Gainesville sites shows essentially an identical drop. At sites included in the Gainesville phase that Welch (1990) interprets as representing cold-weather occupations, large mammal is 76 percent of total bone weight. In the samples from the collective features classified as Gainesville phase, interpreted by Welch to represent warmweather occupations, only 70 percent of the total bone weight was contributed by large mammals. Substantially greater contributions to samples from this subperiod are made by small and medium mammals and birds collectively, but, again, especially turtle and fish. The procurement of very small fish suggests more inclusive or intensive procurement. This pattern has been interpreted to be a reflection of increased subsistence stress as a function of increased regional population (Scott 1983; Welch 1990; Woodrick 1981). The subsistence response was the incorporation of an increasing variety of less-productive, more labor-intensive (but locally available) animal taxa, prior to the transition to food production in the area. A higher regional population is thought to have reduced available territory. Although not included in the present overview, shellfish exploitation shows a corresponding increase (Woodrick 1981:table 37); this was another aquatic resource to boost yields. Interestingly, recent analysis of the species composition of mollusk samples from Woodland features in Tombigbee sites indicates very localized exploitation of shellfish, as would be expected with a reduction in territory (Peacock, this volume). Human skeletal data appear to corroborate an increase in health stress by this time during the Woodland era (Welch 1990:204–5).

It is during the terminal Miller III subperiod that maize begins to appear with some regularity in archaeological contexts (Caddell 1981; Welch 1990:204) as an apparently supplemental resource. Its use increases substantially in the following early Mississippian Summerville I phase. Coincident with this indication of a greater commitment to food production is a reversal in the downward plunge of the large mammals category, which rebounds to between 77 and 80 percent in the two Late Miller III samples. Of even greater interest is a shift in the relative contributions of other taxonomic categories, with proportional increases in small mammals and birds and diminished contributions from turtles and fish. The pattern persists in Mississippian samples from Yarborough and Lubbub. Human osteological data show a corresponding decrease in health stress with one exception: there is a sharp increase in caries rates, an indication of greater amounts of starch in the diet resulting from increased maize consumption (Welch 1990).

The replacement of aquatic taxa by small and medium mammals, most often including rabbits, squirrels, and birds, turkey being the most ubiquitous, may in part be a consequence of habitat changes resulting from agricultural land clearing. Of rabbits and squirrels, conspecifics associated with open habitats dominate: cottontails outnumber swamp rabbits, while fox squirrels outnumber gray squirrels. At Lubbub Creek, commensal mice and rats show a similar shift from those associated with wooded habitats to taxa adapted to more open settings (Scott 1983).

Seasonal variation in Late Woodland procurement emphases is documented by several large stratified Middle Miller III pits at the Lubbub Creek

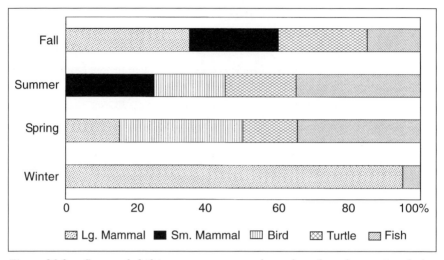

Figure 21.3 — Seasonal shift in procurement emphases based on changes in relative proportions of taxa in middle Miller III stratified Pit 32 contents, Lubbub Creek Archaeological Locality

Archaeological Locality, corroborating in part Welch's interpretation of the Cofferdam and Gainesville phases as seasonally distinct procurement and settlement patterns. Pit 32 from Lubbub illustrates the variable contribution of different taxonomic groups to refuse in pit strata interpreted to have accumulated at different times of the year (Scott 1983)). Excavators identified four distinct strata (Figure 21.3). In the lowest stratum deer refuse comprises more than 70 percent of the fauna by weight and is interpreted as having accumulated in late fall or winter. In the overlying strata, deer declines as fish, reptiles, and birds increase. In the uppermost stratum, deer reappears and the amount of fish declines.

Lower Mississippi Valley

The Lower Mississippi Valley offers environmental and cultural contrasts to the Tombigbee Woodland period. The vast floodplain expanses offered extensive riparian environments with considerable faunal diversity for exploitation (e.g., H. Jackson 1991; B. D. Smith 1975). In particular there is the significantly greater potential of fish as resources. In addition to the environmental differences are localized expressions of an earlier pre-Mississippian shift to greater cultural complexity than that which eventually occurred along the Tombigbee. In particular, the Plum Bayou culture (A.D.

700–1000) in the Arkansas River valley (not technically part of the Lower Mississippi Valley but included here nonetheless), centered on the multi-mound Toltec site, near Little Rock, appears to represent a pre-Mississippian development of greater political complexity. Present evidence suggests a hierarchically organized system ruled by leadership drawn from a high-ranking lineage (Rolingson 1998c:112, this volume), though there is some difference of opinion as to the degree of centralized political control (Nassaney 1992b:125). Four Plum Bayou assemblages are included in the present sample, affording the opportunity to consider the implications for faunal use of greater social and political centralization. Beyond the specific case of Plum Bayou culture, however, the Lower Mississippi Valley exhibits a long history of mound building, beginning well before the Woodland era. This implies a long and rich ceremonial tradition involving corporate labor investment, which we presume took on increasing political connotations over time. Regardless of the degree of political control during any period, group size and its greater food demands during ceremonial aggregations, the seasonality of communal activities, and ritual proscriptions all may have contributed to a divergence between the composition of faunal refuse accumulated at mound sites and that from other communities.

A total of eleven sites, analyzed by seven different zooarchaeologists, were included in the examination of Lower Valley faunal patterns spanning the Middle Woodland Marksville to the Late Coles Creek periods (Table 21.2, Figure 21.1). Marksville period (ca. 100 B.C.–A.D. 500) assemblages are from Mansford Plantation and the Stephenson site, both located in north-

Table 21.2 — Lower Mississippi Valley Woodland Faunal Samples

Chronological Unit	Sites	Reference
Marksville Period	Stephenson	Mariaca 1988
	Mansford Plantation	Mariaca 1988
Early Baytown Period	Panther Lake	Mariaca 1988
	Rock Levee	Scott 1995
Baytown Period	Powell Canal	Carr 1982
	Roland	Butsch 1991
Coles Creek-Plum Bayou	Toltec	Hoffman 1998
	Fitzhugh	Nassaney & Hoffman 1992
	Ink Bayou	Colburn 1987
	Faulkner Lake	Scott 1996
Coles Creek Period	Rock Levee	Scott 1995
	McNight	Breitburg 1998

eastern Louisiana and analyzed by Mariaca (1988). Mansford Plantation is in the Tensas Basin, while the Stephenson site is along Bayou Boeuf. Another Late Marksville Prairie/Porter Bayou phase site sample is from the McNight site, located in Coahoma County, at the northern end of the Yazoo Basin (Breitburg 1998). A Late Marksville–Early Baytown (ca. A.D. 400–600) sample, collected from the Panther Lake site in the Tensas Basin of northeast Louisiana, also analyzed by Mariaca (1988), and a similarly aged sample from the Rock Levee site in the Yazoo Basin, in Bolivar County, Mississippi, analyzed by Scott (1995), are included in the present study. The Panther Lake site sample may represent other than domestic refuse, having been recovered from a mound flank midden. Somewhat later Baytown period (A.D. 500–700) samples include Powell Canal in southeast Arkansas, analyzed by H. Carr (1982), and the Roland site in the Arkansas River valley, analyzed by Butsch (1991).

The Coles Creek period Plum Bayou culture (ca. A.D. 700–1000) is represented by faunal data from four sites: Toltec, Fitzhugh, Ink Bayou, and Faulkner Lake. The Toltec assemblage, analyzed by Robert Hoffman (1998), was excavated from Mound D. Ink Bayou, analyzed by Colburn (1987), the Faulkner Lake site, analyzed by Scott (1996), and the Fitzhugh site, from which a small sample was analyzed by Hoffman (Nassaney and Hoffman 1992), are smaller, presumably residential, sites of the Plum Bayou settlement system.

Two other Yazoo Basin Coles Creek period assemblages are included in our study, one representing a late occupation at Rock Levee and a second being from the McNight site, both dating to the Peabody phase or around A.D. 800 to 1100 (Rock Levee is late in this time range).

There are other Lower Mississippi Valley sites for which faunal samples have been analyzed and reported. We chose not to extend too far south, where significantly different procurement strategies were pursued (e.g., Misner and Reitz 1992). The analysis by Colburn and Styles (1990) of fauna from the Bangs Slough site, located in the Ouachita River valley in south-central Arkansas, was excluded on the basis of their conclusion that the sample represented a specialized primary butchering refuse accumulation and thus may not be representative of domestic consumption patterns. Another Ouachita River valley sample that was excluded from consideration is from the Paw Paw site (Kelley 1992), where nonstandardized excavation recovery procedures produced a faunal collection that was too difficult to reconcile with other samples used here. Finally, the analysis of the Plum Bayou culture Alexander site (Styles et al. 1985) was excluded since it varied significantly from other Plum Bayou samples as a consequence of its upland setting.

Woodland patterns can be contrasted with later Mississippian data drawn from a number of sites analyzed by B. D. Smith (1975). We include here for comparison data from Banks (Arkansas), Chucalissa (Tennessee), and Snodgrass and Lilbourn (Missouri). At the earlier end of the time scale is a single large faunal assemblage from the Poverty Point period J. W. Copes site, in the Tensas Basin of northeast Louisiana (H. Jackson 1986, 1989).

Unlike the case with the Tombigbee sites, quantitative approaches vary widely among the Lower Mississippi Valley samples. Weight data are available for only five sites: Mansford Plantation, Stephenson, Panther Lake, Rock Levee, and Faulkner Lake. Even these are not entirely comparable, since for Mansford, Stephenson, and Panther Lake, large and small mammal were combined in the analysis, while for the two Rock Levee samples, unidentified small and medium mammals and birds (often difficult to confidently distinguish) were lumped together. NISP was the only universally provided quantitative measure, so it is employed in the intersite comparisons presented here. In contrast to the Tombigbee case presented earlier, in which we feel confident that the data are sufficiently comparable to interpret differences in proportional contributions of taxonomic groups as reflecting shifts in subsistence over time, the vagaries of NISP noted earlier preclude the same fine-scale interpretation of the Lower Mississippi Valley samples. We assume that gross differences are sufficiently robust to overcome the confounding effects of fragmentation and identifiability, particularly since we focus on general taxonomic categories.

Before we examine the entire data set, those few sites for which weight data were presented permit us to compare the general character of faunal assemblages in the Lower Mississippi Valley with the character of those from the Tombigbee. Two things are most striking. First is the considerably greater role of fish. For the Tombigbee samples, fish never contribute more than 5 percent to total bone weight, while for Lower Mississippi Valley samples, fish range from 2 to 54 percent. The importance of fish is not surprising given the vast aquatic resources of the Mississippi floodplain, and their use represents a broadly distributed Lower Mississippi Valley adaptation (Springer 1980) with considerable time depth (H. Jackson 1989). A second contrast is the considerably greater variability in contributions made by mammals, which range from 30 to 96 percent.

A similar pattern of variability is exhibited by the entire sample of sites using NISP for comparison. Looking first at the relative contributions of large mammal and fish as percentages of the total NISP of each of the sites, no clear chronological trends are exhibited (Figure 21.4). What does seem to be the case is a dichotomous or inverse relationship in representation: either one or the other makes a more significant contribution to the total

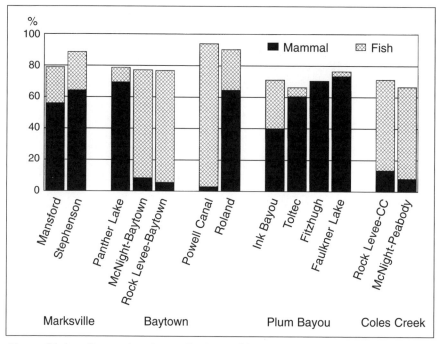

Figure 21.4 — Proportional contributions of large mammals and fish to NISP for Lower Mississippi Valley Woodland samples, ordered chronologically

NISP, but they are never equal. Looking at the combined contribution of fish and large mammals, there appears to be a slight decline over time. Of the Marksville and Baytown period samples, all exceed 76 percent for the combined fish and deer contribution, while only one of the Plum Bayou or other Coles Creek period samples has a fish-deer contribution above 76 percent. The four Plum Bayou sites in central Arkansas are distinguished in sharing among the lowest fish percentages, as well as the greatest contributions of taxa other than deer and fish.

The considerable differences in contributions of fish and deer appear to reflect seasonal emphases in procurement, with fishing primarily a warm-season emphasis and deer hunting occurring mainly during the fall and winter. Fish sizes from Baytown features at Rock Levee indicate spring through summer procurement (Scott 1995). Coles Creek features included basal strata that were interpreted as representing winter disposal episodes, thus contributing to the shift in species contributions. It is relevant to note that the seemingly extreme seasonality distinctions in site assemblages do not necessarily indicate seasonal movements among sites. Although fauna from both components at Rock Levee pointed to warm-season procurement, floral remains

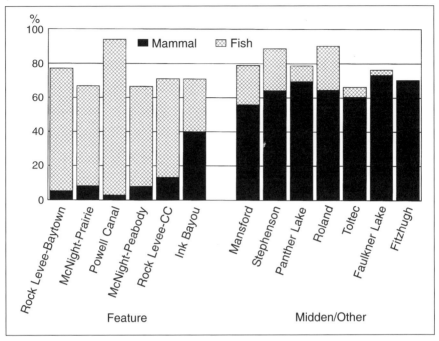

Figure 21.5 — Proportional contributions of large mammals and fish to NISP for Lower Mississippi Valley Woodland samples, grouped by context

analyzed by C. Scarry (1995) demonstrated year-round plant procurement by residents of the site. The disjuncture between faunal and floral remains from Rock Levee seems best accounted for by the fact that the remains were recovered from features, specifically emptied storage pits that subsequently had been filled with refuse. At Rock Levee, sheet middens had been damaged by years of plowing, and excavation emphasized feature excavation, preceded by large-scale mechanical stripping. It is hypothesized that seasonal differences in disposal patterns related to seasonal variation in temperature resulted in seasonally distinct refuse contexts. If we regroup our Woodland samples according to the contexts producing the majority of bone, there are four sites represented by feature fill. Five components, that from Powell Canal, both components at Rock Levee, and both components at McNight, exhibit the high fish–low large mammal pattern expectable during warmer months (Figure 21.5). Samples from sheet middens (general excavation contexts) tend to have smaller percentages of fish. Scott's analysis of the Faulkner Lake sample concluded that this sheet midden–derived fauna was cool-weather refuse. Just to prevent blanket generalizations, the fourth site with a sample from pit contexts, Ink Bayou, is interpreted by

Colburn (1987) on the basis of fish sizes to be a cool-weather assemblage. However, the increments used to categorize length are too large to interpret season of capture confidently, and the site may not be significantly out of line with the seasonality of other high fish samples. Nonetheless, the distinctive difference in faunal composition of samples from pit versus sheet midden contexts (and the seasonality implications of these different accumulations) points out what a critical role excavation strategy plays in producing faunal assemblages. Adequate sampling of these different contexts should be incorporated into the design of excavation whenever possible.

There is some commonality in the contributions made by different fish taxa in samples from the four highest fish-yielding sites, Powell Canal, Rock Levee, Ink Bayou, and McNight-Peabody. Bowfin; catfish including mainly river species (blue, channel, flathead), but also those from small streams (bullheads); and perciform fish (primarily drum, bass, and sunfish) consistently make the greatest contributions. Suckers, gar, and lesser numbers of cyprinids and other small taxa comprise the remainder of the fish fauna. The relative contributions of the major taxa vary from site to site. At Powell Canal, a large number of freshwater drum result in perciform fish ranking first (30 percent of NISP), followed by catfish and bowfin. At Ink Bayou, bowfin contributes more than 30 percent, followed by catfish and perciforms. At Rock Levee and McNight, catfish were caught in greatest numbers, followed by perciforms and bowfin.

Contributions made by taxa other than fish and deer—small and medium mammals, birds, and turtles—were also examined (Figure 21.6). The total contribution of these presumably alternative resources increases over time. There is some hint, though too subtle to be confident using NISP, that the contribution of turtles diminishes near the end of the sequence, as mammals and birds increase in representation. Overall, there appears to be an increase in bird procurement in the late Woodland. At McNight, which is notable for particularly high percentages of mainly ducks in both the earlier and later samples, bird NISP nearly doubles in the Coles Creek samples compared with that from the Middle Woodland component. A similar, though not so dramatic, increase in bird is also seen at Rock Levee. The greatest proportional contribution of bird taxa is at Toltec, a ceremonial center, where birds (including turkey and passenger pigeon) comprise 12 percent of NISP.

Despite this late increase, bird contributes in only a small way to Woodland samples overall, particularly when compared with later Mississippian sites. The number of taxa utilized is also relatively meager and the types relatively uniform, being mainly ducks, geese, and turkey. The avian samples from both the pre-Woodland Copes site (H. Jackson 1989) and the later Mississippian collections reported by B. D. Smith (1975), as well as others

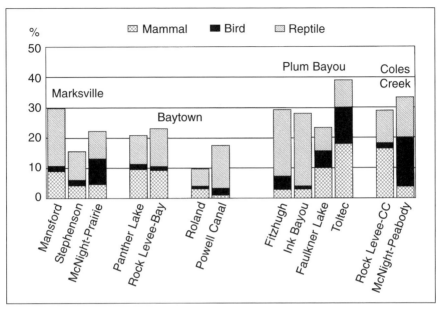

Figure 21.6 — Proportional contributions of small and medium mammals, birds, and reptiles by taxa (other than deer and fish) to Lower Mississippi Valley Woodland samples

(e.g., Guilday and Parmalee 1975; Parmalee 1975), are more diverse and include a variety of wading birds and other migratory waterfowl, plus lesser numbers of raptors and passerines. For example, thirty avian taxa were identified by Guilday and Parmalee (1975) in a sample (NISP = 6082) from the Zebree site in northeastern Arkansas. The most diverse Woodland samples are from Toltec and McNight with fourteen and nine different taxa identified, respectively.

The difficulty of identifying birds without adequate comparative material and the necessarily good bone condition that is required for confident identifications make us hesitant to look systematically at intersite differences in species contributions, or to compare the Woodland samples with earlier and later collections. This is not so for small and medium mammals, which, for the range present in the Lower Mississippi Valley, should be well represented in each analyst's reference materials, thus affording an opportunity to evaluate the breadth of species utilization. As indicated for birds, the Woodland samples included here have a similarly narrow range of small and medium mammals compared with earlier or later collections (Figure 21.7). Dropping the two smallest samples (Faulkner Lake and Fitzhugh), the average number of mammalian taxa other than deer is just above eight, com-

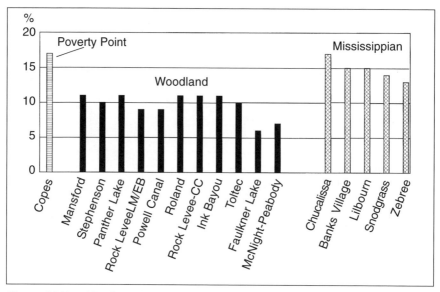

Figure 21.7 — Number of mammalian taxa, including deer, represented in Lower Mississippi Valley samples

pared with twelve at Copes and an average of thirteen mammal taxa at later Mississippian sites. Squirrel, rabbit (cottontail and, when recognized, swamp rabbit), and raccoon are ubiquitous, while beaver, opossum, and muskrat are present in more than half of the samples. Others, including bobcat, fox, bear, mink, and otter occur only sporadically or rarely (weasel, skunk, coyote). Considering both bird and small/medium mammals, the overall impression is that "second line" taxa played a smaller role in the diet during the Woodland era than they did later. The decrease in contributions to NISP made by large mammals and fish in Coles Creek period sites suggests that a shift to greater incorporation of these resources began late in the Woodland time range. Several factors may be involved, the evaluation of which is beyond the scope of this chapter. First, the introduction of the bow and arrow likely increased hunting effectiveness, facilitating procurement of smaller taxa. In those areas where cultivation was becoming more important, resulting in greater forest clearance, open-habitat taxa may have flourished in the vicinity of residential sites. Finally, increasing intersocietal tensions may have resulted in an intensification in localized resource procurement. Were the latter the case, we would expect even greater contributions to the diet by fish.

Two samples offer the opportunity to examine nondomestic meat consumption. The Panther Lake and Toltec samples were collected from mound contexts and are presumed to be feasting refuse. The Panther Lake sample is distinguished from the other Marksville to early Baytown components in having the greatest number of large mammal fragments, the fewest fish specimens, and the greatest contribution to total NISP of small and medium mammals. The later Toltec Mound D sample, in particular, appears to be feasting refuse based on both composition and deer element representation, as well as other artifactual indicators (Rolingson 1998c:108). Deer makes the lowest contribution to NISP for any Plum Bayou culture site, but this is misleading because fragmentation is significantly lower than is true for any other assemblage, underscoring the problems of interpreting NISP data. In addition, element distribution is heavily biased toward those representing high meat value (R. Hoffman 1998:90). If we rely on NISP, the assemblage has a greater amount of both birds and other mammals than any other site. The birds include large amounts of turkey and a greater than "average" variety of waterfowl. Passenger pigeon ranks second among birds in contribution to NISP (first when ranked according to MNI) (R. Hoffman 1998:86), which in Mississippian contexts appears more often in high-status or ritual contexts (H. Jackson and Scott 1995). Passenger pigeon is rare in other Woodland samples.

Conclusions

To summarize, the Lower Mississippi Valley data display greater intersite variability and lack the clear temporal trends identifiable for the Tombigbee sites. Variability is at least in part due to the variable methods used in quantification, but also appears to be a consequence of much greater seasonal differences in resource targets, which ultimately create very different faunal samples in seasonally differentiated depositional contexts. These seasonal emphases in resource targets develop by Late Marksville (and perhaps earlier) and persist into the Coles Creek period. The data point to a shift in the overall mix of resources over time as a consequence of changing demography, technology, or commitment to crop production. Late Woodland samples suggest that diversification, particularly with respect to small mammals and birds, seems to have begun during the Coles Creek period, sometime shortly after A.D. 700, a shift that is more dramatic in the following Mississippian period, perhaps as populations nucleated into larger settlements or as the shift to agriculture created increased forest-edge habitats. This same pattern is noted for the Tombigbee and can be correlated with other indicators of subsistence stress, in particular, those in skeletal remains. There, diversification appears to have been accomplished through increased fishing and reptile (turtle) capture. The Tombigbee trajectory differs from that of the Lower Mississippi Valley in that the role of large mammal rebounded as agricultural production intensified. In the Lower Mississippi Valley, the greater diversity in resource use continued during the Mississippian and, at least in terms of the suite of mammalian and avian resources utilized, broadened. In both areas, birds and other mammals contributed more to that part of the diet that was not provided by deer or fish, as the role of reptiles diminished. What remains to be evaluated is the extent to which nutritional stress may be responsible for the shift noted in Late Woodland samples, as opposed to alternative explanations. Harmon and Rose (1989:331, 337–38), in an overview of available bioarchaeological data from the Lower Mississippi Valley, point to an apparently significant increase in disease load after the Baytown period. They also document evidence for possibly increased incidences of trauma. Further research will be needed to evaluate the impacts of political versus nutritional stressors on the Lower Mississippi Valley subsistence system.

Chapter 22

The Development and Dispersal of Agricultural Systems in the Woodland Period Southeast

Kristen J. Gremillion

As the archaeobotanical record of plant use in eastern North America grows, it becomes increasingly apparent that the economic role of food production during the Woodland period varies considerably across the region (Fritz 1990a; B. D. Smith 1987). The pattern that has attracted the most attention to date is the relative scarcity of evidence for native seed crops in the Southeast, especially prior to the development of maize-based agricultural systems. Current evidence from the lower Southeast (including the Lower Mississippi Valley, the Piedmont to the east of the Appalachians, and the Atlantic and Gulf Coastal Plain) suggests a relatively rapid transition to dependence on maize agriculture during the last centuries of the first millennium A.D. from a forest foraging subsistence base perhaps supplemented by some plant cultivation. In contrast, in the Midwest and Midsouth (north of the Lower Mississippi Valley and west of the Appalachians), the Woodland period is characterized by increasing reliance on cultivated plants and the development of "agricultural economies" (B. D. Smith 1989). Archaeobotanical data show that it is within this so-called "core area" that pre-maize food production developed earliest and had the greatest economic impact in eastern North America. The growing importance of farming in the midcontinent during the Woodland period is further reflected in the paleoenvironmental record of changes in forest composition and patterns of ecological disturbance (Delcourt et al. 1998).

Hypothetical explanations for the contrast between the lower Southeast and the Midsouth have yet to be systematically examined. This chapter aims to review empirical support for some of these explanations in order to identify the factors (cultural, historical, and environmental) most likely to have played a major role in the establishment of regional differences in the development of food production. This task can be approached more efficiently by first ruling out the possibility that the archaeological pattern is primarily a product of the history of research rather than an accurate representation of prehistoric behavioral variability. Assuming that this alternative is unlikely to account fully for the observed patterns (even if it cannot be dismissed as a complicating factor), explanations that link regional differences in the development of prehistoric food production to environmental variability will be examined. These explanations, although sharing an emphasis on environmental influences on behavior, can be separated into those that are based on the goodness of fit between human subsistence behavior and the natural environment and those that focus on historical contingencies that constrain the set of possible responses to environmental variability. All three explanatory elements (research history, adaptation, cultural and environmental history) will be ingredients of any reasonably complete explanation for regional variability in the role of food production.

Variation in Woodland Period Agriculture: A Closer Look

The marked intraregional variability in the archaeobotanical record of Woodland period food production in the Southeast has been characterized in general, relative terms such as late versus early and lesser versus greater dependence. Agricultural systems based on native seed crops appear to be limited geographically to the area north of the Lower Mississippi Valley and central Alabama and west of eastern Tennessee (Fritz 1993; Fritz and Kidder 1993). Fritz (1993:41) cites the low numbers of seeds of crop plants from west-central Alabama and east-central Mississippi relative to those recovered from sites in the Midwest and concludes that "there is reason to doubt that pre-Mississippian gardeners of the deep South produced comparable amounts of food." Johannessen (1993a:66) makes similar observations about the Late Woodland in the Southeast, which has produced only "sparse seed remains" and "little evidence for extensive plant cultivation" prior to the appearance of maize around A.D. 900. The same data led C. Margaret Scarry (1993a:86) to conclude that pre-maize subsistence in the lower Southeast is best characterized as a mix of "foraging and small-scale crop production."

In order to arrive at a more precise characterization of the patterns underlying the current understanding of regional variability in Woodland period food production, it is necessary to compare archaeobotanical data sets. Comparisons across regions that incorporate the work of different analysts and samples of different sizes present many problems for synthesis. Although intersite comparisons should ideally be carried out after norming seed counts, for example by dividing them by liters of soil processed, it is seldom the case that comparable data are available for all of the collections of interest.

Despite these limitations, it can be assumed that relative quantities of seeds of native crops will bear a relationship to their economic importance in different regions that is strong enough to illustrate significant patterns. To this end, raw counts of seeds of the cultivated native taxa of the "starchy" (high carbohydrate) and "oily" (high lipid) varieties were compiled for sites across the Southeast. Included in this analysis are the starchy seed taxa *Chenopodium* (chenopod or goosefoot), *Hordeum pusillum* (little barley), *Phalaris caroliniana* (maygrass), and *Polygonum* sp. (knotweed) and the oily-seeded taxa *Cucurbita pepo* (gourd/squash), *Helianthus annuus* (sunflower), and *Iva annua* (sumpweed). Some of the recorded identifications of these plants may reflect wild or weed forms rather than domesticates or crops, but for simplicity no attempt was made to differentiate remains on the basis of morphological details. Instead, the counts represent records of the taxa that are widely recognized by regional paleoethnobotanists (e.g., Fritz 1990a, 1993) as having been cultivated in the East before the establishment of maize-based agriculture. Table 22.1 and the maps generated from it (Figures 22.1 through 22.4) include only carbonized collections in order to reduce the influence of differential preservation as a result of local environmental factors such as desiccation or water saturation. Archaeological components have been separated into two broad temporal categories, Early and Middle Woodland (ca. 1000 B.C.–A.D. 300) and Late Woodland (ca. 300–800 A.D.). In a few cases this period designation is at variance with local culture-historical sequences, but it serves the purpose of providing a regionwide framework for comparison. Zeros in the table and on the figures indicate areas where the absence of crop seeds has been documented archaeobotanically.

Figure 22.1 plots Early and Middle Woodland counts of native starchy and oily seeds for the Southeast, including data from Illinois and Ohio for comparison. The lowest counts are from southeastern Tennessee, west-central Alabama, the South Carolina Piedmont and Coastal Plain, and the Piedmont of North Carolina. The highest counts outside of the Illinois Valley are from west-central Kentucky and eastern Tennessee. There are no collections of more than 100 seeds that come from the lower Southeast as it is defined here. To the north and west, there is considerable variability but, generally speaking, higher counts of crop seeds are reported. For the Late Woodland, the pattern of intraregional variability is similar, although seed counts for the lower Southeast show an increase over the Early and Middle Woodland (Figure 22.2). There is little evidence, however, for much commitment to food production in the lower Southeast prior to the development of maize-based agriculture in the Late Woodland.

This is a crude assessment of the data that makes no claim to be comprehensive, but it does clarify the empirical basis for the "core area" identified

Table 22.1 — Counts of Crop Seeds by Locality and Time Period

Site(s)	Locality	Source	Period[1]	Starchy[2]	Oily[3]	Total
3 sites	SC coastal plain and piedmont	Wagner 1995	EW	0	0	0
22CL814	east central MS (Tombigbee R. ?)	Yarnell and Black 1985	EW	2	0	2
Salts Cv.	west central KY (Green R.)	Smith 1992b	EW	19,599	730	20,329
44RU14	southwestern VA (Clinch R.)	Gardner 1992	EW	48	0	48
40MI11	eastern TN (Tennessee R.)	Gremillion and Yarnell 1986	EW	1	0	1
3 sites	eastern TN (Little Tennessee R.)	Yarnell and Black 1985	EW	1,350	70	1,420
3 sites	central TN (Duck R./Elk R.)	Yarnell and Black 1985	EW	2	13	15
2 sites	eastern TN (Holston R.)	Yarnell and Black 1985	EW	149	0	149
9CK7	northwest GA (Etowah R.)	Yarnell and Black 1985	EW	8	0	8
15MT8	eastern KY (Tug Fk.)	Fritz 1986b	EW/MW	34	0	34
38BK984	SC coastal plain	Wagner 1997	EW/MW	0	0	0
1GR2	west central AL (Tombigbee R.)	Yarnell and Black 1985	MW	0	0	0
31MC139	western Piedmont, NC (Catawba R.)	Gremillion 1990	MW	15	0	15
3 sites	west central AL (upper Tombigbee R.)	Yarnell and Black 1985	MW	5	3	8
12 sites	central TN (Duck R./Elk R.)	Yarnell and Black 1985	MW	6,988	35	7,023
2 sites	central OH (Scioto R.?)	Wymer 1993	MW	1,055	170	1,225
40MR23	eastern TN (Little Tennessee R.)	Yarnell and Black 1985	MW	180	14	194
7 sites	SC coastal plain and piedmont	Wagner 1995	MW	0	0	0
Walling	northwestern AL (Tennessee R.?)	Fritz 1993	MW	289	?	289?
Smiling Dan	west central IL (lower Illinois R.)	Smith 1992a	MW	12,745	74	12,819
3 sites	American Bottom (Mississippi R.)	Smith 1992a	MW	427	1	428
44RU14	southwestern VA (Clinch R.)	Gardner 1992	MW	42	1	43

Table 22.1 (cont.) — Counts of Crop Seeds by Locality and Time Period

Site(s)	Locality	Source	Period[1]	Starchy[2]	Oily[3]	Total
31CE41	western NC	Gremillion 1989	MW	101	0	101
3 sites	nw AL (Cedar Ck.)	Yarnell and Black 1985	MW	8	0	8
7 sites	SC coastal plain and piedmont	Wagner 1995	LW	0	0	0
31BN335	western NC (French Broad R.?)	Wagner 1991	LW	0	0	0
7 sites	central TN (Duck R./Elk R.)	Yarnell and Black 1985	LW	22	9	31
40MI11	eastern TN (Tennessee R.)	Gremillion and Yarnell 1986	LW	821	0	821
6 sites	west central AL (Tombigbee R.)	Yarnell and Black 1985	LW	380	0	380
7 sites	west central AL (Black Warrior R.)	Scarry 1993a	LW	393	3	396
1CK236	west central AL (Alabama R.?)	Mickelson 1999	LW	12	0	12
2 sites	central OH (Scioto R.?)	Wymer 1993	LW	1,441	5	1,446
11 sites	American Bottom (Mississippi R.)	Johannessen 1993a	LW	21,344	143	21,487
15CR73	eastern KY (Little Sandy R.)	Shea 1991	LW	2	0	2
38GR226	western Piedmont, SC (Saluda R.)	Crites 1998	LW	1,471	0	1,471

[1] EW = Early Woodland (1000–300 B.C.); MW = Middle Woodland (300 B.C.–A.D. 300); LW = Late Woodland (A.D. 300–800) For consistency across the Southeast, these categories are used here as strictly temporal units.

[2] Starchy seed genera: Chenopodium, Phalaris, Polygonum, Hordeum

[3] Oily seed genera: Cucurbita, Iva, Helianthus

Note: Carbonized seeds from flotation and screening of midden and feature fill (excludes exceptional preservation situations, e.g., rockshelter caches and midden)

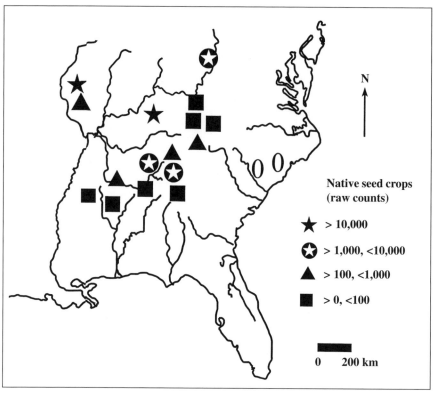

Figure 22.1 — Early and Middle Woodland records of native cultivated plants in the Southeast. Several Midwestern collections are included for comparison. Seed counts and references are found in Table 22.1.

by Fritz (1993) and the regional variation discussed by Johannessen (1993a). This spatial variability is the basis for the three zones depicted in Figure 22.3. These zonal boundaries reflect the data presented in Table 22.1, with some adjustments to incorporate other relevant information. The line that separates the zone of developed food production from the zone of limited food production has been extended to the west in recognition of the archaeobotanical record of the Ozark bluff shelters (Fritz 1986a). In doing so, it is assumed that although seed counts from these sites are not directly comparable to those from carbonized collections, they nonetheless suggest a significant economic role for food production during the Woodland period. Another such adjustment is the eastward displacement of the boundary of the zone of no pre-maize agriculture in recognition of the record of native seed crops dating to the Late Prehistoric and Historic periods in the Piedmont of North Carolina (Gremillion 1995). It should also be recognized that

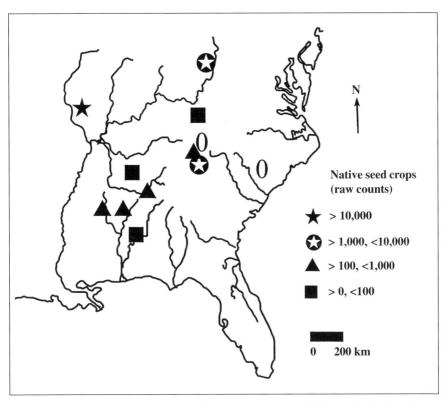

Figure 22.2 — Late Woodland records of native cultivated plants in the Southeast. Several Midwestern collections are included for comparison. Seed counts and references are found in Table 22.1.

assessments of economic importance of native crops in the Midsouth are based on a broad range of archaeological data, not just seed counts (see for example discussions in Fritz 1990a and Watson 1985).

The History of Archaeological Research as an Explanatory Factor

We owe much of our understanding of the origins and early development of food production in eastern North America to a limited set of sites or site clusters. Data from west-central Illinois, particularly the lower Illinois Valley (Asch and Asch 1985a, 1985b) and the American Bottom region (Johannessen 1984), and central and eastern Tennessee (J. Chapman and Shea 1981; Crites 1991) have been especially rich sources of information. Rockshelters of eastern Kentucky and the Arkansas and Missouri Ozarks

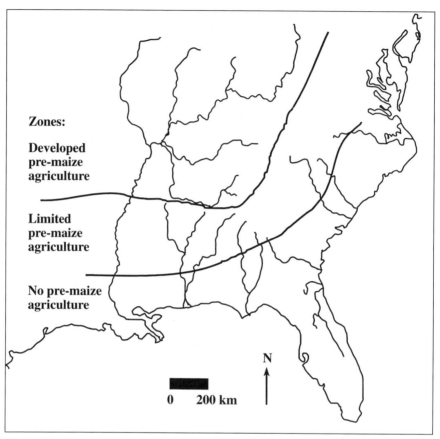

Figure 22.3 — Variation in the intensity of pre-maize food production in the Southeast represented as a series of zones. Zones are delineated on the basis of data presented in Figures 22.1 and 22.2 with adjustments as described in the text.

have yielded large collections of seeds of cultivated plants that have formed the basis of several studies of the domestication process (e.g., Cowan 1985; Gremillion 1993b, 1993c; Yarnell 1978). Most of these data sets emerged from large-scale contract projects that included archaeobotanical recovery as part of their research designs. In comparison, flotation-based reports for the Woodland period from the lower Southeast are relatively few and geographically scattered, with most of the information drawn from sites in west-central Alabama and South Carolina. In light of these historical facts, it is important to determine whether the zones that have been defined with respect to Woodland period food production are largely an artifact of sampling bias and therefore "reflect the areas where work has been done more than anything else" (Johannessen 1993a:58).

It can be shown, however, that the variation in seed quantities is not simply a function of sample size. Table 22.2 compares counts of crop seeds with the total number of samples or features represented in several collections from across the Southeast. The normed values for sites in South Carolina and west-central Alabama are consistently low compared with those from sites to the north and west. For the Middle Woodland, the collections listed form a near transect from Illinois to the South Carolina coast in which seed quantities normed to number of samples decline from west to east. This comparison suggests that it would be premature to dismiss this pattern as a product of sampling error. Instead, it makes sense to proceed on the assumption that populations in this region trod their own distinctive version of the "multiple pathways" to agriculture, one that does not "reflect the intensity of food production practiced farther north" (Fritz 1990a:419).

Table 22.2 — Quantities of Crop Seeds Normed to Number of Samples

	Number of			Crop Seeds per Sample	Reference
	Samples	Sites	Crop Seeds		
Early Woodland					
Eastern TN	75[1]	3	1,032	13.8	Chapman & Shea 1981
SC Coast/Piedmont	10[3]	3	0	—	Wagner 1995
Middle Woodland					
West-Central IL	746	1	12,819	17.2	Asch & Asch 1985b
Central TN	922[2]	7	1,056	11.5	Crites 1978b
Western NC	9	1	101	11.2	Gremillion 1989
NC Piedmont	18	1	15	.8	Gremillion 1990
SC Coast/Piedmont	44[3]	7	0	—	Wagner 1995
West-Central AL	6[3]	1	0	—	Caddell 1982
Late Woodland					
American Bottom	220[3]	12	21,847[4]	97.7	Johannessen 1993a
West-Central AL	76[3]	3	337	4.4	Caddell 1982
SC Coast/Piedmont	77[3]	7	0	—	Wagner 1995

[1] *Each sample represents 10 liters of soil*
[2] *Each sample represents total fill of a feature*
[3] *Number of features and/or units sampled*
[4] *Includes ~ 12,000 seeds from a single feature*

Adaptation in Ecological Context

Next to be considered are explanations that emphasize the adaptive features of food production in different environmental settings. Although these explanations are a mixed bag, each of which identifies its own distinctive set of important variables and mechanisms, they share the (at least implicit) assumption that subsistence change is best understood as an evolutionary process in which selective sorting occurs. Whether and in what manner food production becomes established as part of a population's subsistence pattern depends in large part on its benefits and costs in a particular environmental context. In this view, the slow rate of development of pre-maize agriculture in the lower Southeast is likely to represent an adaptive response to specific local environmental conditions that were significantly different from those found farther to the north and west.

The Floodplain Weed Theory

The floodplain weed theory developed by Bruce Smith (1987, 1992b) to explain the origins of food production in the midcontinent specifies how plant domestication and cultivation grew out of behavioral responses to particular features of the environment. Although the processes of initial domestication and incipient cultivation that form the focal point of Smith's model belong to the mid-Holocene, they set the stage for the later success of agricultural economies in the Midwest. The extent to which similar ecological processes were at work in the lower Southeast may consequently be relevant to explaining the limited impact of Woodland period agriculture there.

Smith's coevolutionary model relies on the interaction of several key types of factors during the Middle Holocene: geomorphological (aggradation of floodplains), biotic (enrichment of aquatic and riverine flora and fauna), demographic (human population growth and settlement aggregation), and ecological (anthropogenic improvement of plant habitats). The chain of events leading to domestication and cultivation originates with the intensification of the ecological relationship between human and plant populations that shared floodplain habitats. Soil disturbance and enrichment in these habitats, which improved growth conditions for several species of weedy annuals, were in turn a direct outcome of a change in human settlement favoring repeated occupation of sites within easy reach of high-yielding concentrations of aquatic and wetland resources. The model developed by Smith for the midwestern case thus hinges on river valleys containing a sufficiently rich resource base to encourage seasonal reuse by a substantial population, although different drainages are expected to reveal "distinct coevolutionary histories" (B. D. Smith 1987:37).

Extrapolation of Smith's model to the Southeast has been questioned on the grounds that primary domestication need not have been restricted to large floodplains; instead, it could have developed simultaneously but independently in localities with "little alluvial soil and few aquatic resources" (Fritz 1997:60; see also Watson 1985). Although Smith's model was developed with a specific ecological situation in mind, the generalizations regarding anthropogenic habitat disturbance at the core of the floodplain weed theory apply in a broad range of environmental contexts (i.e., enrichment of soil nitrogen through the accumulation of organic refuse and the competitive advantage afforded to weedy annuals in disturbed soils exposed to ample sunlight) (B. D. Smith 1992b). In other words, the fact that native crop farming originated when and where it did is a historical fact, not an evolutionary necessity. Cultivation of these crops was adaptable to local conditions outside of their original geographic range and in habitats other than broad, seasonally inundated floodplains in part because anthropogenic disturbance mimicked natural cycles of environmental disruption.

These ecological considerations suggest that it would not be possible to predict the limited economic role of seed crops in the Woodland period lower Southeast on the basis of the river-basin characteristics that were important to the coevolutionary origins of cultivation in the Midwest. If the floodplain weed species of the Midsouth were not available, other suitable protodomesticates may well have been. As Fritz (1990a) points out, there is no reason repeated occupation of river terraces would not have had similar ecological effects south of northern Alabama. The same ecological processes outlined by Smith could have been initiated by a different set of historical events—perhaps the introduction of seedstock and associated knowledge through contact with human groups to the west, or the creation of an anthropogenic disturbance regime by a different pathway involving upland resources, as suggested by Paul Gardner (1997) with respect to forest disturbance related to the management of hickory trees. These possibilities reinforce the point that the characteristics of river basins in the lower Southeast did not somehow preclude the development of farming based on native weedy annuals.

Whether food production arose in the upland areas through a coevolutionary process is still an open question, but it is clear that the production of indigenous seed crops was a successful strategy in very different topographic and hydrological settings. Middle Woodland farming communities developed in river valleys of widely varying scale, within floodplains as large as 16 kilometers across and as narrow as 1 kilometer (perhaps smaller) (B. D. Smith 1992c:215). This pattern, as well as the success of later maize-based farming in the lower Southeast, argues against any limitation on agricultural production stemming from some inherent feature of the environment, such as soil quality. There does not seem to be any individual, easily isolated aspect of river systems that differentiates areas with intensive Woodland farming from those without. It might be more profitable to try to identify more general features of resource distribution, such as patchiness and density (or the "environmental gradient" between valley and upland noted by B. D. Smith [1987:27]), that might underlie and help explain the parallel evolution of food production systems in river basins of different scale.

The Caldwell Effect

An alternative adaptive explanation for the limited importance of Woodland farming in the lower Southeast invokes variations on a causal phenomenon that might be referred to as the "Caldwell effect." Joseph Caldwell (1958) proposed a gradual process of regional adaptation to the Holocene environment of the Southeast, which resulted in a condition he labeled "Primary Forest Efficiency." According to Caldwell, the persistence of this foraging adaptation into the Woodland period despite the presumed availability of crop plants occurred because plant cultivation was not a cost-effective option for human foragers who had access to abundant, seasonally predictable forest resources. Food production was unable to compete successfully "with hunting, with new economic balances based on the acorn, and with older coastal adjustments still relying heavily on shellfish" (Caldwell 1958:19). These adaptive strategies were so effective that dependence on plant cultivation "might have seemed risky or irrelevant" (Caldwell 1958:72).

Although the validity of Caldwell's characterization of Woodland populations as "pure" foragers is challenged by current knowledge, his contention that an effective foraging adaptation will resist significant appropriation of time and energy for farming remains intuitively appealing and can be shown to be consistent with evolutionary theory. Innovation entails some risk, which can be considerable if existing strategies are already providing satisfactory returns. A loss of efficiency is likely to result from adding a new resource to a subsistence base of abundant, high-quality foods, particularly if the new item is costly to produce. Once adopted, a novel food item can remain at a low level of use because of constraints on the economic benefit it can provide (rapidly diminishing returns) or high opportunity costs (the loss incurred by abandoning other, more profitable, activities) (Gremillion 1996b).

An economic interpretation along these lines can be applied to C. Margaret Scarry's (1993a) suggestion that the relatively slow development and limited economic importance of native seed crop agriculture in the lower Southeast might be due to the availability of acorns as a source of carbohydrates. The implication of this statement is that starchy seeds played only a minor dietary role because acorns met the same nutritional needs, presumably at lower cost. In order to evaluate this formulation of the "Caldwell effect" as an explanation for geographical variability in the role of starchy seed crops, it will be necessary first to establish its plausibility. Is acorn harvesting likely to have provided better returns than starchy seed crop cultivation in west-central Alabama during the Woodland period? And if so, did similar conditions of resource abundance characterize areas such as the midwestern river valleys where Woodland farming established a strong early foothold?

There is no doubt that acorns and starchy seeds such as chenopod, maygrass, and knotweed are similar in macronutrient composition. All have high carbohydrate content and thus make suitable staple foods (Gremillion 1998). Acorns, however, usually require extensive processing to remove tannins, a procedure that can cut efficiency considerably ("efficiency" here used to mean energy acquired per unit time spent in procurement and processing), although in raw form the caloric returns are good (Petruso and Wickens 1984). Returns are much higher for species such as live oak (*Quercus virginiana* L.) that do not require extensive processing. Starchy seeds, in contrast, can be eaten raw or with minimal preparation (Gremillion and Sobolik 1996), although cooking undoubtedly increases the availability of nutrients (A. Stahl 1989). Planting, harvesting, and garden maintenance add to the costs of obtaining carbohydrate calories from starchy seed crops. Even taking such costs into account, however, most starchy seed crops seem to provide superior caloric returns to those obtainable from acorns (Gremillion 1998).

This analysis does not offer much support to the hypothesis that acorns would have been preferred to at least some of the native crop plants as a source of calories in carbohydrate form. What Scarry (1993a) seems to be suggesting, however, is that the abundance of acorns in west-central Alabama had a strong influence on the economic utility of exploiting this resource to the virtual exclusion of cultivated alternatives. This proposal is a reasonable one, since resource density affects the costs and benefits of subsistence options (although absolute abundance does not translate inevitably into dietary importance). If availability of acorns made starchy seed crops superfluous, we might actually expect the midcontinent (which lies within the oak-hickory forest zone) to reflect less intensive food production than west-central Alabama, where mixed pine-oak-hickory forests predominate.

There are many other factors not considered here, for example, the possibility that acorn yields may have been higher in the lower Southeast than in the midcontinent, despite the fact that oak trees represented a smaller percentage of stems. There is also a good bit of evidence for a complementary relationship between acorns and agriculture; when starchy crops (most notably corn) become dietary staples, it is common to see a decline in acorn shell in the archaeobotanical record. This has been noted for the Late Prehistoric and Historic in parts of the Southeast (C. Scarry 1986; Yarnell and Black 1985) and hypothesized for eastern Kentucky (Gremillion 1998). It may turn out to be the case that starchy seeds were actually an improvement over acorns in some parts of the Southeast, but decidedly less cost effective in others.

To investigate further the assertion that an effective foraging economy (perhaps including small-scale cultivation) limited the spread or development of pre-maize farming in the lower Southeast, it is necessary to isolate and characterize specific elements of subsistence systems in environmental context. One example of this kind of analysis is the comparison of the relative economic benefits of naturally occurring and cultivated plant resources that meet the same nutritional needs (as in the case of acorns and starchy seeds presented above). A similar approach might be used to investigate the relationship between availability of marine and estuarine resources and the late adoption of agriculture in coastal areas. Analyses of this kind have the advantage of translating general propositions about the utility of subsistence options into specific testable hypotheses.

Seasonality and Storage

The importance of native seed crops as stored foods for winter use has been well established on the basis of the seasonality of consumption of pollen and seeds (Cowan 1978; Gremillion and Sobolik 1996; Yarnell 1974a, 1974b) in conjunction with archaeological evidence in the form of storage features (Cowan 1985; Gremillion 1993a, 1993d; Johannessen 1984). It has been argued that the role of seed crops as a buffer against seasonal food shortage played a key role in the early success of farming in some areas, such as the uplands of eastern Kentucky (Cowan 1985). Seasonal variation has been suggested as an important influence on the geographical distribution of Woodland period farming economies (Fritz 1990a).

If adjustment to seasonal variation was a key causal factor in the development of food production, we would expect a relationship between the timing, spread, and importance of cultivated plants and environmental variables such as length of the growing season. To test this hypothesis, isotherms were plotted representing the average number of days per year in which temperatures drop below 32° Fahrenheit (that is, average number of

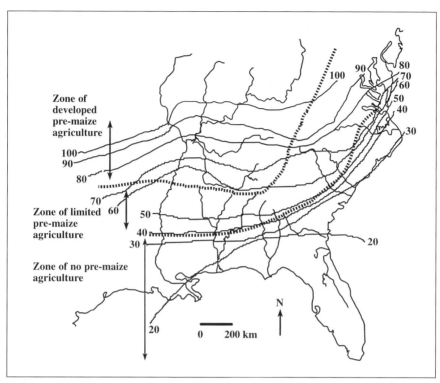

Figure 22.4 — Food production zones superimposed on isotherms of the average number of days annually in which temperatures drop below 32° Fahrenheit. Data are from National Climatic Data Center (1999).

days in which frost occurs). I used data from the National Weather Service for twenty-three southeastern data collection stations (National Climatic Data Center 1999). When this isotherm map is placed over the map of Woodland period plant-use regions presented earlier (Figure 22.3), it is apparent that the bulk of existing evidence for developed farming comes from sites that fall between the 100- and 60-day isotherms (Figure 22.4). This area includes the Ozark bluff shelters, the caves and shelters of Kentucky, and central and eastern Tennessee, all of which have provided evidence of economically important Woodland farming including storage of seeds and in some cases their consumption out of season. The area between 50 and 60 days includes the sites in west-central and northwest Alabama that have produced evidence of only limited cultivation until the Late Woodland. South of the 50-day line is a zone virtually lacking in evidence for Woodland pre-maize farming (Fritz 1990a). If the data collection stations are divided into those that fall within the zone of developed food production and those that lie beyond it, there is a significant difference between the two groups in average length of growing season ($t = 5.42$, $df = 21$, n = 23, $p < .01$).

The 60-day isotherm has less predictive power east of the Appalachians than it does along its southern margin. South of it the expected pattern of little or no Woodland agriculture holds, but to the north and west it breaks down; there is little indication that native seed crop farming was important in the Piedmont or along the eastern slopes of the Appalachians (with the exception of the Pumpkin site in the western South Carolina Piedmont [Crites 1998]). On the other hand, this is an area from which there is little relevant archaeobotanical information, although by the Late Prehistoric native crops such as sunflower, sumpweed, and chenopod were cultivated, albeit on a small scale (Gremillion 1995). The Piedmont of North and South Carolina is a region to watch in the coming years because it offers an opportunity to assess further the relationship between farming and seasonal variability in length of the growing season.

Incipient agriculture developed where and how it did in part because of the conjunction of particular environmental features and human responses to them. The evolutionary and ecological processes involved (such as the effects of anthropogenic disturbance and increasing yields under domestication) are not, however, restricted to the river valleys of the Midwest. Ecological correlates of river basin geomorphology do not adequately explain the late development of pre-maize food production in the lower Southeast. Patterns of plant-resource availability need to be evaluated more precisely to determine whether the abundance of mast or other alternative plant foods limited the dietary role of seed crops. Intra-annual variation in plant resource availability as measured by the length of the growing season appears to have been a key influence on the importance of seed crops, which were stored for use during times of scarcity. The relatively mild temperatures of the lower Southeast limit the length and severity of the winter season and therefore the degree of reliance on stored foods.

History and the Rise of Food Production

Although adaptive explanations are likely to be important, particularly where such a basic survival mechanism as food acquisition is concerned, it would be shortsighted to ignore the influence of history. Evolutionary biologists have taken their colleagues to task for assuming that adaptation can account for any and all traits, when in fact some traits persist not because of functional superiority over alternatives, but as a result of the constriction of the range of possibilities by antecedent events and processes (Gould and

Lewontin 1978). An evolving entity's history constrains the set of possible options for the future. That history includes unpredictable environmental events, patterns of the flow of information (whether cultural or genetic), and the limitations imposed by selection as it weeds out unsuccessful variants and shapes successful ones into functional systems. The adaptive explanations discussed above incorporate historical aspects of the natural environment (river development, forest growth, anthropogenesis), but do not consider how these factors might affect the transmission of materials and information between human populations. Such transmission acts to constrain possibilities, much as barriers to gene flow influence the genotypic composition of natural populations.

For example, the plants brought under domestication in the Southeast may not have occurred naturally in every locality where food production became established, despite the operation of similar ecological and evolutionary processes across the region. Therefore, it seems reasonable to ask whether the absence of natural populations of the species that were domesticated elsewhere could account for the limited success of Woodland period farming in the lower Southeast. *Chenopodium* and *Iva annua* form large stands in broad, seasonally inundated floodplains in the Midwest (Asch and Asch 1985a; B. D. Smith 1987), but both also have a large geographical range that includes most of the Southeast. Sunflower was domesticated in the midcontinent from a weed form native to the Plains (Heiser 1978). In contrast, maygrass is native to the Southeast and appears to have been dispersed farther north and west as a consequence of its cultivation (Cowan 1978). Modern distribution data suggest that natural populations of most of the species that formed the basis for pre-maize farming across much of the Eastern Woodlands were probably present in the lower Southeast. Presence alone, however, is a poor predictor of economic importance; density, yield, and distribution of available plants play a critical role.

Dispersal of plants by humans presents another interesting historical wrinkle in the story of food production in the lower Southeast. Such dispersal routes may have influenced the distribution of developed Woodland farming with respect to river drainages (Figure 22.3). All but one of the sites that have produced evidence of developed farming lie within drainages that connect to the Mississippi and its tributaries (i.e., the Tennessee, the Ohio, and the Illinois). They are situated in a variety of topographic settings. The one exception is the Pumpkin site, which lies in the extreme western Piedmont of South Carolina; it provides the only instance of economically significant pre-maize Woodland farming that lies within river valleys that drain into the Atlantic and Gulf coast regions (the Cape Fear, Savannah, Pensacola) east of the Mississippi. It is too soon to tell whether this pattern will hold up under further investigation, but at present there is a significant contrast in the role (if not the presence) of food production across the Appalachian divide, although the distinction is less clear to the west where the mountains are not a factor. Although this pattern does not suggest that communication along connected drainages was determinative of the development of food production, it does seem to call for closer attention to the dynamics of exchange of goods and information along natural travel routes. It is likely that the history of interaction influenced the form taken by food production systems in different subregions and affected the spread of plants and of cultural knowledge about them.

Another historical concern is that of systemic constraints. An individual cultural trait exists as part of a larger system, elements of which might be considered part of the environment on which its evolutionary fate depends. Traits cannot always be simply added to and subtracted from a complex system, whether an organism or a subsistence regime, without having ramifying effects. Cultural systems are extremely flexible, but not infinitely so. Thus it makes sense to ask whether subsistence systems throughout the lower Southeast were so tightly integrated that significant food production was incompatible with survival. I doubt that this is the case, mainly because cultural systems are so much more fluid than, say, anatomical and physiological ones. A basic structural feature such as bilateral symmetry with a very deep history is essentially built into a lineage. In contrast, radical shifts in human diet and subsistence can take place, and have taken place, in the space of a single generation. For this reason it is unlikely that the limited development of pre-maize agriculture in the lower Southeast was the result of a systemic constraint.

Conclusions and Recommendations

Within the Southeast, considerable variation existed in the character and rate of development of plant cultivation during the Woodland period. This variability can be used to define zones reflecting different degrees of commitment to food production within the Southeast. Quantities of carbonized seeds from across the region are highest in the Midsouth, especially within the drainages of major streams such as the Tennessee, Mississippi, and Illinois rivers. To the south and west, evidence for food production prior to the transition to maize agriculture at the end of the Woodland period is much weaker. The differences between these two areas cannot be fully attributed either to the emphasis on major river valleys in archaeological research or to sampling bias.

Explanations for spatial variability in the role of food production within the Southeast have been suggested but not systematically examined. The suggestion that the cultivation of crops was not as cost effective as the use of alternative food sources available in the lower Southeast deserves further consideration. Such work might take the form of analyzing environments in which human populations developed contrasting degrees of reliance on food production and using economic/ecological models to understand better the costs and benefits involved. Such adaptation-centered theories cannot afford to ignore historical factors that influence the rate of transmission of innovations and the natural distribution of plant populations.

My recommendations for future research into the development of food production in the Woodland period Southeast include the following:

1. Continue to encourage the employment of effective techniques for the recovery of macrobotanical remains on archaeological sites. Federal and state agencies have an important role to play in this endeavor by demanding and enforcing standards of data recovery and analysis. Programs for archaeobotanical data recovery should be fully integrated into research programs, not carried out as an afterthought. The Piedmont of the Carolinas is a potentially rich source of information on Woodland period plant use that deserves more intensive investigation.

2. Continue to formulate and test hypotheses to explain regional variation in the role of food production. Hypothesis development will be more likely to contribute to knowledge if it is informed by an explicit theoretical framework that can be used to relate test implications to general explanatory models. Testing will require precise measurement of environmental as well as behavioral (archaeological) variables.

3. Carry out studies of environmental influences on the preservation of archaeobotanical remains and how they may be affecting archaeological reconstructions of subsistence (especially food production).

Chapter 23

Woodland Cave Archaeology in Eastern North America

George M. Crothers, Charles H. Faulkner, Jan F. Simek, Patty Jo Watson, and P. Willey

There are hundreds of thousands of caves throughout the vast limestone-bedrock region of the United States that extends from Missouri through southern Illinois and Indiana to the Virginias, Kentucky, Tennessee, Alabama, Georgia, Arkansas, Texas, and Florida. Beginning at least as early as 4500 years ago, the people who lived in this karstic area traveled into and through dozens of these caves, using them as quarries, mines, cemeteries, and places to communicate with the spirit world. In this chapter, we describe and discuss highlights of Woodland archaeology in caves, focusing on the kinds of materials left there, current interpretations of those materials, and regional patterning in cave use during the Woodland period. We are concerned specifically with subterranean archaeology in deep pits not accessible without special equipment and skills, and with the dark zones of cave interiors, not with rockshelters, cave entrances, or the twilight zones provided by small and/or shallow caves.

The Nature of Cave Archaeology in Eastern North America

In basic method and theory, cave archaeology is just like any other kind of archaeology (Watson 2001), but issues of preservation, of access, and of documentation techniques differ from those of above-ground archaeology. Limestone caves in eastern North America are much older (by a million years or more) than the earliest period of human presence in the New World. Preservation conditions for fragile, ordinarily highly perishable materials in the older, inactive, hence dry, passages (i.e., those with no flowing or dripping water, even though humidity may be quite high) are often extremely favorable. This is because of the absence of decay organisms, as well as the stable environment with consequent lack of weathering (Crothers and Watson 1993). Ferns, grass, fabrics and cordage, wooden artifacts, fuel for torches and fires, human hair, human fecal matter, and human bodies are desiccated but otherwise kept in a state of complete integrity for thousands of years. This is a tremendous archaeological advantage, but also may pose significant curational problems when these items are removed from the cave.

Another corollary of the optimal preservation in dry cave passages is that recent and very ancient materials (e.g., wood, leaves, bark) look exactly alike. Torch or campfire debris from a few cave trips by a few people over many generations cannot be distinguished visually from such debris resulting from one or two trips by a larger group. Moreover, because of the geological and hydrogeological processes involved in cave formation, most cave passages of any size are primarily rock-floored rather than being filled wholly or partially with sediment. Even when sediment deposits are present, sedimentation is often very slow, with rates commonly on the order of a few centimeters per millennium. Hence, deep cave archaeology usually addresses large and complex "surface" sites where nearly all the debris is scattered on the substrate, not piled up in stratified sequences. Of course, later cave trips alter or destroy much evidence of earlier ones because most cave passages are constrained spaces without a great many possibilities for optimal movement in and through them.

Accessibility to archaeological remains in karstic pits and in the dark zones of cave interiors is frequently physically difficult, but it is the total and perpetual lack of light that distinguishes field work in caves from aboveground work. All illumination must be brought in and carefully maintained during all work periods. This necessity manifests itself primarily as a supply problem (of lights, batteries, lanterns, fuel), but also as a survival issue that requires unremitting attention from every crew member throughout the course of every field trip.

The complete absence of all but imported, artificial light also always affects documentation techniques (especially photography). A more serious logistical problem, however, is posed by the small spaces and lengthy routes field crews must traverse to reach the work locale. It is often impossible to transport or use theodolites, alidades, plane tables, and surveying rods, so mapping small, remote cave passages and the archaeological remains in them is often done with compasses and tapes.

There is a fourth issue that should be noted briefly because it must be addressed for every subterranean archaeological project: what is the relation of cultural remains found in cave interiors to those left by the same human groups above ground? There are many facets of this problem, but one of the most fundamental is distinguishing the archaeological material essential to ancient people entering and working in caves (i.e., caving gear) from remains that are clues to specific activities undertaken by them in cave environments rather than on the surface. Sometimes the above-ground and below-ground activities are similar (e.g., burying the dead, quarrying chert); sometimes they are significantly different (e.g., procuring substances, especially those of symbolic significance because of their subterranean origin, or those available only in caves). Cave-specific materials often help explain why ancient people went into deep caves.

The advantages and disadvantages of cave archaeology are further illustrated in the next section, which contains summary accounts of archaeological work in a wide variety of cave interiors.

The Sites

Late Archaic Cave Exploration in the Midsouth

The earliest dates so far known from the dark zone of a big cave in the Eastern Woodlands are those from Jaguar Cave in north-central Tennessee (Figure 23.1, Table 23.1; Robbins et al. 1981; Watson et al. n.d.). Jaguar has about 13 kilometers of passages and was entered a few times (perhaps no more than twice) by one or two small groups who found their way out of the entrance, stream-passage mazeway up a massive breakdown pile through a kilometer and a half of cave, with some very tricky intersections, to a passage now called Aborigine Avenue. They walked the circa 400-meter length of this passage, which is decorated with stalactites, stalagmites, soda straws, and calcite floor crusts, looked around at the end of it, then went back to the entrance and left the cave. A scattering of soot smudges on passage walls, and a thin scatter of cane charcoal (some of which yielded three radiocarbon determinations: 4695 ± 85 B.P., 4590 ± 75 B.P., and 4530 ± 85 B.P., as well as some 275 foot impressions in the soft mud of Aborigine Avenue, make up the evidential record for the earliest cave exploration in eastern North America.

Similar isolated exploratory episodes probably took place in many other midwestern and southeastern caves, but at present we have records for only eight other well-dated examples prior to 3000 B.P. (Figure 23.1, Table 23.1). All but two of these are in Kentucky and four of the eight are within the borders of Mammoth Cave National Park: Marshall Avenue in Lee Cave (Freeman et al. 1973); Jessup Avenue in Mammoth Cave (Watson 1983, 1996; Watson [ed.] 1974); the Upper Crouchway in Unknown Cave; and Lower Salts Cave (Watson [ed.] 1974). The other Kentucky caves outside Mammoth Cave National Park are Fisher Ridge Cave (Watson 1983) and Adair Glyph Cave (DiBlasi 1996). Outside Kentucky are 3rd Unnamed Cave in Tennessee (Simek et al. 1998) and Wyandotte Cave in southern Indiana

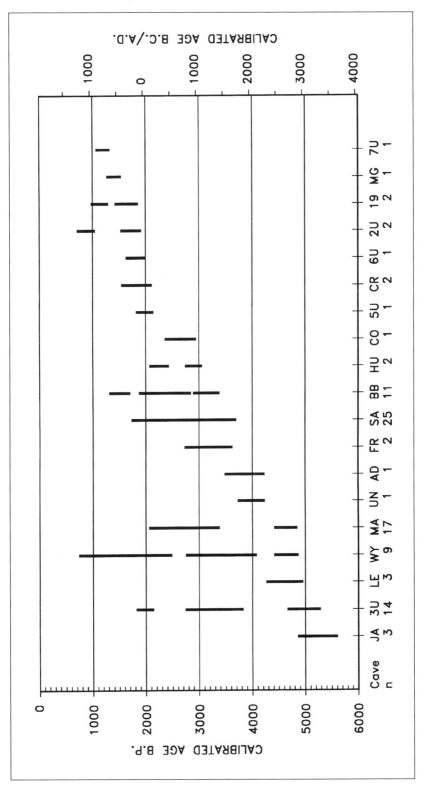

Figure 23.1 — Calibrated age ranges of radiocarbon determinations (n = number) listed in Table 23.1

Table 23.1 — Archaic and Woodland Period Radiocarbon Dates from Cave Sites in the Eastern Woodlands

Laboratory Number	Material	Determination			Reference
		Assay	σ	ƒ	
Jaguar Cave, Tennessee					
1 SI-3006	charcoal	4695	85	60	Robbins et al. 1981
2 SI-3003	charcoal	4590	75	60	Robbins et al. 1981
3 SI-3005	charcoal	4530	85	60	Robbins et al. 1981
3rd Unnamed Cave, Tennessee					
1 SI-5067	charcoal	4350	60	60	Watson unpublished
2 Beta-126041	charcoal	3360	60	60	Simek unpublished
3 Beta-126038	charcoal	3330	70	60	Simek unpublished
4 SI-5064	charcoal	3115	65	60	Watson unpublished
5 Beta-96624	charcoal	3060	50	60	Simek et al. 1998
6 ISGS-4234	charcoal	3060	70	60	Simek unpublished
7 ISGS-4232	charcoal	3050	70	60	Simek unpublished
8 Beta-114172	charcoal	2970	40	60	Simek et al. 1998
9 Beta-114173	charcoal	2970	40	60	Simek et al. 1998
10 SI-5066	charcoal	2950	65	60	Watson unpublished
11 Beta-96623	charcoal	2950	110	60	Simek et al. 1998
12 SI-5063	charcoal	2805	75	60	Watson unpublished
13 SI-5065	charcoal	2745	75	60	Watson unpublished
14 Beta-126040	cane	2010	60	50	Simek unpublished
Lee Cave, Kentucky					
1 UCLA-1729A	cane	4200	65	60	Watson, ed. 1974
2 Beta-81338	cane	4100	60	60	Crothers unpublished
3 Beta-81337	cane	4050	70	60	Crothers unpublished
Wyandotte Cave, Indiana					
1 Beta-17350	hickory bark	4150	90	60	Munson & Munson 1990
2 SFU-200	hickory bark	3160	260	60	Munson & Munson 1990
3 UCLA-1731B	hickory bark	2890	60	60	Watson, ed. 1974
4 Beta-17351	hickory bark	2190	120	50	Munson & Munson 1990
5 UCLA-1731A	hickory bark	1710	80	50	Watson, ed. 1974
6 SFU-222	hickory bark	1560	150	50	Munson & Munson 1990
7 SFU-199	oak charcoal	1400	270	50	Munson & Munson 1990
8 Beta-17349	oak & hickory bark	1260	50	50	Munson & Munson 1990
9 Beta-17352	oak wood	1150	50	50	Munson & Munson 1990
Mammoth Cave, Kentucky					
1 UCLA-1730A	twigs	4120	70	60	Watson, ed. 1974
2 UCLA-1730B	wood	3000	70	60	Watson, ed. 1974
3 SI-6890A	cane charcoal	2920	60	60	Munson et al. 1989
4 AA-10085	paleofece	2700	80	60	Gremillion & Sobolik 1996
5 AA-16566	paleofece	2675	50	50	Watson unpublished
6 Beta-47292	split-cane basket	2630	55	50	Watson unpublished
7 AA-10084	paleofece	2605	70	50	Gremillion & Sobolik 1996
8 AA-10081	paleofece	2575	65	50	Gremillion & Sobolik 1996
9 Beta-47470	bark lashing	2500	55	50	Kennedy 1992
10 SI-6890B	cane charcoal	2495	80	50	Munson et al. 1989

Table 23.1 (cont.) — Archaic and Woodland Period Radiocarbon Dates from Cave Sites in the Eastern Woodlands

Laboratory Number		Material	Determination			Reference
			Assay	σ	ƒ	
Mammoth Cave, Kentucky (cont.)						
11	AA-10080	paleofece	2485	70	50	Gremillion & Sobolik 1996
12	AA-10083	paleofece	2485	70	50	Gremillion & Sobolik 1996
13	SI-3007A	matting	2395	75	50	Watson unpublished
14	X-9	cane	2370	60	50	Watson, ed. 1974
15	AA-10082	paleofece	2365	70	50	Gremillion & Sobolik 1996
16	AA-10079	paleofece	2335	75	50	Gremillion & Sobolik 1996
17	X-8	twined slipper	2230	40	50	Watson, ed. 1974
Unknown Cave, Kentucky						
1	Beta-96145	cane	3670	50	60	Watson unpublished
Adair Cave, Kentucky						
1	Beta-16932	cane charcoal	3560	110	60	DiBlasi 1996
Fisher Ridge Cave, Kentucky						
1	Smithsonian	cane charcoal	3175	80	60	Kennedy et al. 1984
2	Smithsonian	oak	2750	85	60	Kennedy et al. 1984
Salts Cave, Kentucky						
1	M-1589	wood & bark	3140	150	60	Watson, ed. 1974
2	I-256	wall soot	3075	140	60	Watson, ed. 1974
3	M-1586	cane	2840	150	60	Watson, ed. 1974
4	Beta-32685	cane torch bundle	2790	70	60	Tankersley et al. 1994
5	Beta-87915	climbing pole	2760	40	60	Kennedy & Watson 1997
6	M-1588	wood	2720	140	60	Watson, ed. 1974
7	AA-11738	paleofece	2705	60	60	Gremillion & Sobolik 1996
8	M-1770	paleofece	2660	140	50	Watson, ed. 1974
9	AA-10088	paleofece	2605	80	50	Gremillion & Sobolik 1996
10	AA-10089	paleofece	2590	70	50	Gremillion & Sobolik 1996
11	AA-10090	paleofece	2580	70	50	Gremillion & Sobolik 1996
12	M-1574	paleofece	2570	140	50	Watson, ed. 1974
13	AA-10086	paleofece	2570	70	50	Gremillion & Sobolik 1996
14	M-1587	wood	2520	140	50	Watson, ed. 1974
15	M-1584	cane	2510	140	50	Watson, ed. 1974
16	AA-10091	paleofece	2500	80	50	Gremillion & Sobolik 1996
17	Beta-47472	cedar climbing pole	2495	60	50	Tankersley et al. 1994
18	Beta-47471	tip of digging stick	2490	60	50	Tankersley et al. 1994
19	M-1585	cane	2430	130	50	Watson, ed. 1974
20	Beta-60067	paleofece	2410	90	50	Ruppert 1994
21	AA-10087	paleofece	2410	70	50	Gremillion & Sobolik 1996
22	Beta-32684	cane charcoal	2410	60	50	Tankersley et al. 1994
23	M-1577	paleofece	2350	140	50	Watson, ed. 1974
24	M-1777	paleofece	2270	140	50	Watson, ed. 1974
25	M-1573	paleofece	2240	200	50	Watson, ed. 1974

Table 23.1 (cont.) — Archaic and Woodland Period Radiocarbon Dates from Cave Sites in the Eastern Woodlands

Laboratory Number	*Material*	*Determination*			*Reference*
		Assay	*σ*	*f*	
Big Bone Cave, Tennessee					
1 Beta-13968	cane	3000	70	60	Crothers 1987
2 Beta-32546	paleofece	2550	80	50	C. T. Faulkner 1991
3 Beta-13967	twigs	2380	70	50	Crothers 1987
4 Beta-13969	twigs	2340	60	50	Crothers 1987
5 Beta-13971	wood, cf. *Carya*	2230	70	50	Crothers 1987
6 Beta-106302	twined bag	2190	60	50	Crites unpublished
7 Beta-13970	cane	2170	60	50	Crothers 1987
8 Beta-13972	twigs	2120	60	50	Crothers 1987
9 Beta-124966	gourd container	2060	50	50	Crites unpublished
10 SI-6012	grape vine	1615	60	50	Crothers 1987
11 SI-6013	*Prunus* twigs	1595	55	50	Crothers 1987
Hubbards Cave, Tennessee					
1 Beta-116409	cane	2730	60	60	Simek unpublished
2 Beta-126034	cane	2260	60	50	Simek unpublished
Crystal Onyx Cave, Kentucky					
1 Teledyne	bone	2630	95	50	Haskins 1987
5th Unnamed Cave, Tennessee					
1 Beta-106695	bone	2030	50	50	Simek unpublished
Crumps Cave, Kentucky					
1 unknown	cane	1980	60	50	Davis and Haskins 1993
2 Beta-116408	torch charcoal	1840	80	50	Simek unpublished
6th Unnamed Cave, Tennessee					
1 Beta-109675	bone	1890	50	50	Simek unpublished
2 Beta-106697	burnt bone	630	50	50	Simek unpublished
2nd Unnamed Cave, Tennessee					
1 Beta-126036	burnt bone	1800	60	50	Simek unpublished
2 AA-15811	cane	970	60	50	Simek unpublished
19th Unnamed Cave, Alabama					
1 Beta-126044	cane	1740	60	50	Cressler et al. 1999
2 Beta-126043	wood charcoal	1240	60	50	Cressler et al. 1999
Mud Glyph Cave, Tennessee					
1 SI-5468	cane charcoal	1485	60	50	C. H. Faulkner, ed. 1986
7th Unnamed Cave, Tennessee					
1 Beta-106698	bone	1320	40	50	Simek unpublished

(Munson and Munson 1990). In Fisher Ridge Cave and in each of the Mammoth Cave National Park caves, only a few people were involved (just two in Unknown Cave, where they left a short trail of foot impressions), and in each case the objective seems to have been simply exploring or reconnoitering. At Wyandotte Cave, a radiocarbon determination of 4150 ± 90 B.P. and another of 3160 ± 260 B.P. are thought to be associated with the outcrops of Wyandotte chert in the Dining Room and Coon's Council Chamber, respectively (Munson and Munson 1990:48–49). The most striking facts about all of these earliest eastern North American cave trips, however, are that the groups involved went so far into the dark zone (one or more kilometers) and—in at least one case (Aborigine Avenue in Jaguar)—they successfully navigated their way in and out of some quite variegated, wet and muddy, confusing, and demanding cave passages (also probably true of the Fisher Ridge group), but they apparently did not spend much time at the end points of their journeys, nor did they make repeated trips to those locales. Just a little later, however (ca. 3600 B.P., in Adair Glyph Cave, Kentucky (DiBlasi 1996), several visits of a very different kind were made to a mud-floored passage more than 1 kilometer from the entrance where no foot impressions have been noted, but where the entire substrate was covered with geometric markings (see summary below under Woodland Period Ceremonial Caves).

At about 3000 B.P., a few people (perhaps only two) also left torch debris, some geometric markings, and about eighteen foot impressions in parts of Fisher and Raccoon avenues and Aborigine Way in Fisher Ridge Cave, an approximately 135-kilometer-long system just outside the eastern boundary of Mammoth Cave National Park. This cave was discovered by Euroamericans in 1981. It has been explored and mapped, over the past seventeen years, by members of the Detroit Urban Grotto of the National Speleological Society. It is unlikely that the prehistoric explorers entered via the natural openings that are now known, but just where they gained access is unclear.

A number of impressions left by unshod human feet were discovered in 1979 at the top of a narrow climb near a waterfall deep inside 3rd Unnamed Cave (referred to in earlier accounts as "Saltpeter Cave") in northern Tennessee (Simek et al. 1998; Watson 1986). In passages below the level of that with the foot impressions, river cane torch fragments and numerous torch smudges or stoke marks on cave walls testify to the long and tortuous, sometimes dangerous, path the lightly shod or barefoot explorers took to get to the place where a wet mud substrate preserved a few imprints of their feet. Radiocarbon dates on some of the torch fragments indicate that much, if not all, prehistoric visitation to 3rd Unnamed Cave occurred during the Terminal Archaic, around 3000 B.P. In addition to their footprints, prehistoric visitors to this cave left evidence for a range of other complicated activities, suggesting that at least some caves were perceived as more than curiosities during the Archaic period of Southeastern prehistory.

In a remote passage of 3rd Unnamed Cave, more than 1 kilometer from the entrance, prehistoric toolmakers found great quantities of high-quality chert in the limestone walls and in secondary position in floor sediments. Over a relatively short time period (Simek et al. 1998), they turned over several hundred cubic meters of chert-bearing deposits in this mining chamber in search of raw material. They unearthed thousands of nodules that either were abandoned immediately as too small or too poor in quality, or that were simply tested using a hard hammer-and-anvil technique. Collecting in discrete knapping areas and refitting the nodule fragments has enabled identification of the raw material sought by the prehistoric miners. To illuminate their work, the ancient knappers lit small fires of dry pine sticks at each work area: these have yielded a series of tightly clustered radiocarbon age determinations (Figure 23.1, Table 23.1), all of which indicate Terminal Archaic activity.

On the ceiling above the chert quarry and on several large breakdown blocks scattered through the chamber, abstract and representational images were engraved into the bare limestone. Rayed circles and semicircles, concentric ovals, and checkerboard and chevron patterns (Figure 23.2), along with numerous enigmatic groups of lines and figures, compose an extensive petroglyph assemblage that is one of the earliest examples of dark-zone cave art in the Southeast. Several of the images recall some from Adair Glyph Cave (see below).

That the underground landscape of the Appalachian Plateau saw its first economic exploitation during the latter part of the Archaic period is not too surprising given cultural and ecological changes characteristic of this time (see Delcourt et al. 1998). The remains in 3rd Unnamed Cave, however, reflect a complex range of dark-zone activities, possibly including ceremony as well as exploration and mining, by Terminal Archaic foragers.

Between 4500 and 3000 B.P., there were at least four categories of activity in the big caves and deep pits of the Midsouth, three of which have been briefly discussed above: simple exploration, exploration plus ritual or ceremony, chert quarrying (sometimes accompanied by creation of graffiti, petroglyphs, or mud glyphs), and use of subterranean locales for mortuary purposes. The latter activity is widely distributed—Kentucky, Virginia, Tennessee, Texas (D. Boyd and Boyd 1997; Haskins 1987; Hubbard and Barber 1997; Turpin 1985; Willey et al. 1988)—with quite a few bodies represented in total and at some individual sites (see the section Woodland Period Mortuary Pits and Caves below).

Figure 23.2 — Chevron petroglyph from 3rd Unnamed Cave, Tennessee (photo by Alan Cressler)

Early Woodland Miners in the Mammoth Cave System

With the exception of chert quarrying in 3rd Unnamed Cave, and probably also in Wyandotte Cave, the earliest and most extensive prehistoric extractive activity in the caves of eastern North America is the mining of various sulfate minerals from the walls, ceilings, and sediments of Salts Cave and Mammoth Cave in the Mammoth Cave System (Kennedy and Watson 1997; Munson et al. 1989; Watson [ed.] 1969, 1974). This subterranean industry began about 3000 years ago and continued for several centuries throughout the last millennium B.C. (Table 23.1, Figure 23.1). Although we do not have empirical evidence for all the details of the processing, distribution, and uses of the products after they were removed from the cave, we do know a considerable amount about the subterranean activities involved in obtaining them. Owing to the geological and geochemical characteristics of the Mammoth Cave System, a complex suite of cave minerals is naturally available in the dry, upper-level passages. Most abundant among them is gypsum (hydrated calcium sulfate, $CaSO_4 \cdot 2H_2O$), but hydrated sodium sulfate or mirabilite ($Na_2SO_4 \cdot 10\ H_2O$) is present as well. Gypsum was sought in the form of a powder battered off the walls and ceilings, or crystals broken from the walls and pried out of crevices, or dug from the sediment (in the form of selenite). Mirabilite could have been and probably was scooped up off the cave floor and out of breakdown hollows, or brushed off ceilings and walls where it forms abundantly. Epsomite ($MgSO_4 \cdot 7H_2O$) is also probably present here and there in Upper Salts as it is in Lower Salts and in Mammoth Cave (Palmer 1981:123; Watson [ed.] 1974:69; W. White 1969).

Gypsum is—in human terms—a nonrenewable resource (that is, it forms very slowly), whereas mirabilite forms more or less continuously in several parts of Upper Mammoth and Upper Salts caves.

Sulfate-mining technology was simple, requiring only portable lighting (probably the same techniques and materials used after dark above ground), digging sticks, and containers for the mined minerals. The various cave minerals were obtained using a variety of techniques: digging into floor sediments for selenite crystals, breaking off natural speleothem features such as gypsum crust and gypsum flowers, brushing or scraping mirabilite and epsomite from walls and breakdown blocks, and battering satin spar (a fibrous form of gypsum) from crevices in walls and ceilings.

Perhaps the most demanding aspects of cave mining in Salts and Mammoth were the navigational abilities required to get to and from various work locales within the labyrinthine passages and the logistical capability to maintain sufficient light, food, and water for extended periods underground. These problems were solved in a highly successful manner, however. It is abundantly clear that Early Woodland cave miners were thoroughly familiar with many kilometers of cave passages and were perfectly capable of going to, working in, and returning from any destination they chose. We know of only two fatal accidents during several hundred years of prehistoric cave use: one of a young boy, probably a result of inexperience (Robbins 1971; Tankersley et al. 1994), and one of a mature man, apparently a result of judgmental error (Munson et al. 1989; Neumann 1938; Pond 1937).

Our inferences about why the various cave minerals were so persistently sought can be briefly summarized as follows. Gypsum powder may have been used to make white paint (by mixing it with water or grease). Gypsum crystals (satin spar and selenite), like other crystalline substances, might have been desired for ritual or ceremonial purposes. Mirabilite and epsomite are both laxatives and have the other medicinal properties of Glauber's salt and Epsom salts, which are their anhydrous forms. In addition, mirabilite tastes salty and could be used as seasoning and perhaps even as a preservative for meat.

Beyond a description of mineral mining techniques, and the medicinal or other properties of specific cave minerals that may have made them attractive to prehistoric peoples, there is the deeper question of how and why cave mining was developed into an intensive and coordinated activity. Crothers (2001) has hypothesized that intensive cave use was related to larger cultural developments during the Early Woodland, which coincides with the beginning of agricultural delayed-return economies. Why was the mining population seemingly dominated by males? What are the potential social implications this has for understanding Early Woodland society? We are only able to begin asking such questions now, however, after a long and continuing effort to document evidence of Early Woodland cave mining and its recurring features. With new insights from this prolonged program of data gathering, we can begin to seek broader understanding of the Early Woodland societies within which cave mining was embedded.

Woodland Period Mining and Quarrying of Caves Elsewhere in the Midwest and Midsouth

Cave mineral mining in the Mammoth Cave System was the first example noted and is the most thoroughly documented, but there are several other caves now known to have served as mines or quarries. We briefly describe three of them here: Wyandotte Cave in Indiana and Big Bone Cave and Hubbards Cave in Tennessee.

• *Wyandotte Cave, Indiana*
Wyandotte Cave was entered, explored, and variously mined for chert, aragonite, and probably epsomite between 4150 and 1150 B.P. (Munson and Munson 1990). Outcrops of Wyandotte chert in several cave rooms or passages are thought to have been the main focus of attention during the earlier part of the span (4150 to 2190 B.P., but the masses of epsomite could have been important medicinal sources at any time, as they were historically. Quarrying of aragonite fragments from a large stalagmite (some 10 meters high and 7 meters in diameter), known historically as the Pillar of the Constitution, apparently took place primarily in the Middle Woodland period. Forty artifacts made of Wyandotte Cave aragonite have been identified at sites in Indiana, Illinois, Ohio, and Iowa (Munson and Munson 1990:67–71), suggesting that this cave resource was widely valued. The prehistoric people who explored and worked in Wyandotte Cave used hickory bark torches for light and were skilled, agile cavers familiar with somewhat more than 8 kilometers of passageways.

• *Big Bone Cave, Tennessee*
Big Bone Cave is a large cave system (approximately 15.5 kilometers of passages) in middle Tennessee that has extensive dry passages where gypsum and other sulfate minerals can be found. Like other dry caves in eastern

North America with easily accessible entrances, it was mined historically for saltpeter (calcium nitrate), a process that destroyed much of the prehistoric archaeological context. A systematic archaeological survey of the cave (Crothers 1987), however, found three passages totaling some 1000 meters in length that contained numerous and relatively intact prehistoric remains. This material is consistent with that found in Mammoth and Salts caves: torch debris of various kinds (cane, sticks, weed stalks), gourd containers, a woven bag, a pair of woven slippers, digging sticks, and numerous paleofecal specimens (C. T. Faulkner 1991). Unlike Mammoth and Salts (and Hubbards Cave, described below), Big Bone shows no appreciable evidence for the mining of gypsum crust from the walls or ceiling. Much of the best gypsum crust appears to be beyond the currently known limits of prehistoric activity. Selenite needles, however, are abundant in intact sediments within the passages entered prehistorically. This was the primary mineral form of interest to the prehistoric explorers of Big Bone Cave (Crothers 1987). Eight of eleven radiocarbon determinations (Figure 23.1, Table 23.1) firmly date Big Bone mining activity to the Early Woodland period (calibrated age range 2850–1900 B.P., overlapping with the mining activity in Mammoth and Salts caves. One date is slightly older (age range 3390–2890 B.P.) but is still consistent with other mining and cave exploration dates. Two of the eleven dates are slightly younger (calibrated age range 1710–1310 B.P.) but are problematic because this split coincides with determinations from different dating laboratories and hence may be due to a systematic laboratory offset. Only additional dating will determine whether the later determinations are indeed correct in showing Middle Woodland as well as Early Woodland activity in Big Bone Cave.

- *Hubbards Cave, Tennessee*

In 1997, a group of conservationists working with Joe Douglas, a historian interested in early Tennessee saltpeter mines, found burnt river cane fragments and saw gypsum battering on the walls of Hubbards Cave in Warren County, Tennessee (Douglas [ed.] 1997). They alerted archaeologists from the University of Tennessee, who visited the cave and confirmed evidence for extensive prehistoric gypsum mining in Hubbards. Over a distance of more than a kilometer, gypsum coatings on the passage walls have been removed by battering as high as a human being can reach without assistance. Natural river cobble hammerstones used to remove the minerals are scattered over the floor below the mined walls; no formal tools have been found, as is also the case in Salts and Mammoth caves, where conveniently sized pieces of breakdown were used as hammerstones. Gypsum was exploited even in narrow crevices, and the length and width of the human arm seem to have been the only limiting factors in obtaining mineral crystals. In some areas where more recent saltpeter mining removed sedimentary deposits in the search for niter, gypsum battering is 4 to 5 meters above the present floor level. These surfaces presumably were mined when the floor was in its prehistoric configuration prior to the saltpeter excavations, as no battering is present below the original sediment level. A prehistoric ladder is known from Mammoth Cave, and climbing poles were found in both Salts and Mammoth caves (the ladder and two of the Salts Cave climbing poles date to the Early Woodland period; see Table 23.1, Figure 23.1), but such tools were not used here, or were removed after use (either prehistorically or by the saltpeter workers). No broken gypsum coatings or accumulations of gypsum powder were observed on the cave floor beneath the battered surfaces, suggesting that containers may have been positioned below the areas where coatings were battered to catch the falling fragmented and powdered gypsum. The scale of prehistoric exploitation at Hubbards Cave is impressive. Cave walls were mined for hundreds of meters, and very large quantities of gypsum were removed from the cave.

The Woodland age of mining in Hubbards Cave is affirmed by two carbon 14 determinations made on large cane torch fragments from the north passage. The torches were recovered from below a mined wall in a narrow and dusty passage that has not seen postdepositional alteration since prehistoric times. One Early Woodland age of 2730 ± 60 B.P. yields a calibrated age range of 3060 to 2740 B.P. A second determination of 2260 ± 60 gives a calibrated range of 2430 to 2070 B.P. These dates accord very well with the bulk of those from Salts and Mammoth caves (see Kennedy and Watson 1997) (see Table 23.1, Figure 23.1). The Hubbards Cave dates are also in line with five determinations from Big Bone Cave in Van Buren County, Tennessee, associated with aboriginal mining there (see Big Bone discussion above, and Figure 23.1, Table 23.1).

Although historic niter mining has reworked many of the sedimentary deposits in Hubbards Cave, one agent has acted to preserve the prehistoric record in a rather remarkable fashion. Eastern wood rats (*Neotoma floridana*) constructed numerous nests in the cave, on ledges running high above both ancient and modern cave floors. These nests are composed of debris recovered from the cave by the rats. Literally thousands of cane torch fragments, some 30 to 40 centimeters long, are incorporated into them. Other prehistoric artifacts like cordage and gourd container fragments similar to those recovered from Big Bone Cave also are conserved in these features, and, therefore, the prospects for better chronological information from Hubbards Cave are quite good. In any case, Hubbards Cave significantly expands our knowledge of Woodland cave mineral mining in the Eastern Woodlands.

Woodland Period Mortuary Pits and Caves

The use of pit caves or vertical shafts as repositories for human remains appears to be a widespread phenomenon in eastern North America, possibly with distinct regional expressions. Only a few systematic studies have been carried out to document these sites, however. Human remains have been identified from caves in Tennessee, Kentucky, Virginia, Georgia, Alabama, and Texas (D. Boyd and Boyd 1997; Haskins 1987; Hubbard and Barber 1997; Turpin 1985; Willey et al. 1988) and from at least one Indiana cave (D. Cook 1986). The caves vary from small features that can be entered horizontally or through short vertical drops (<10 meters) to deep vertical shafts (>30 meters in some cases) that require ropes and climbing gear. Human beings who entered these deep pits prehistorically must have been dead before deposition, or they would have died soon after entry. Vertical shafts with openings to the surface have extremely complex depositional environments, in which bodies (and burial artifacts) are incorporated into dynamic talus cones at the bases of the shafts, which then may be reworked by water flowing horizontally through the cave. These deposits also are sometimes obscured by dead cows, horses, dogs, and quantities of trash thrown into the pits by modern inhabitants of the region. The last and most problematic aspect of these sites is that they are also the targets of looters, especially in those cases in which exotic artifacts are found with the bodies. The Copena burial caves (see below) are a well-known example, but artifacts (e.g., pipes, gorgets, beads, bifaces, pottery) also were apparently deposited with bodies placed in pit caves (e.g., Hubbard and Barber 1997; Whyte and Kimball 1997).

Use of inner cave areas for burial may also have considerable antiquity. An inner chamber of a small cave in middle Tennessee (Meadows Hill Saltpetre Cave) was dug by a collector in the 1950s, who found at least four flexed burials associated with diagnostic Archaic period bannerstones, projectile points, ground gastropod (*Anculosa*) and mussel shell beads, and other worked shell and bone artifacts (Owen 1958). The 2nd, 5th, and 6th Unnamed caves in Tennessee are three small caves with vertical and/or horizontal entrances that are known to contain human remains, a Woodland ceramic sherd, and either petroglyphs (5th and 6th Unnamed Caves; Simek 1998; Willey et al. 1988) or mud glyphs (2nd Unnamed Cave). Three of the five radiocarbon determinations (Figure 23.1, Table 23.1) from these sites date approximately 2000 years B.P.; a fourth date (from 6th Unnamed Cave) is 630 ± 50 radiocarbon years B.P., and a fifth date (from 2nd Unnamed Cave) is 970 ± 60 B.P. The relationships among the artifacts, radiocarbon dates, burials, and cave art in these sites are unclear partly because of the nature of the evidence (relating parietal art to cave deposits), but mainly because of the extensive looting of these sites. The 2nd, 5th, and 6th Un-named caves are described further below.

One of the few burial caves excavated by archaeologists is Ausmus Cave in Tennessee (Tucker 1989; W. Webb 1938), a small cave with relatively easy access. A minimum number of twenty individuals were identified, apparently dating to the Mississippian according to a few associated artifacts.

The talus deposit of a deep pit cave in Alabama was excavated by Oakley (1971) as his master's thesis project. More than ninety individuals were identified among these remains. Diagnostic artifacts (primarily Hamilton projectile points) also seemed to indicate a Late Woodland or possibly late prehistoric age for these remains.

Haskins (1987) undertook a master's thesis project on a series of burial pit caves in Prewitts Knob, central Kentucky. Her research did not involve extensive excavation, but she was able to identify numerous individuals (of various ages and both sexes) among material found on or near the floor surfaces of two of the larger pit caves (Pit of the Skulls and Crystal Onyx). A radiocarbon determination of 2630 ± 95 B.P. on human bone, previously obtained from Crystal Onyx Cave by University of Kentucky archaeologists, indicates use contemporary with activities in nearby Mammoth and Salts caves.

A number of other pit caves in east Tennessee have been investigated by Willey and Crothers, but for the most part we have only descriptions of material found *in situ* on the passage floors of these caves. There is little or no evidence for age of use, but we suspect most are Late Woodland or later. An even larger number of burial pit caves are known for southwest Virginia (Hubbard and Barber 1997), and systematic efforts have recently begun to examine these sites in greater detail (e.g., D. Boyd and Boyd 1997; Whyte and Kimball 1997). In general, the current evidence supports a conclusion that primary use of mortuary pit caves falls between 500 and 1000 years ago.

• *Copena Mortuary Caves*
Perhaps the best-known example of Woodland use of caves for human burial is from the Copena culture of north Alabama and northwest Georgia (Beck 1995; Turner 1980; Walthall 1973; Walthall and DeJarnette 1974). Confined to the middle reaches of the Tennessee River valley, Copena cave use was recognized in the 1970s as part of a wider burial complex, including above-ground mounds in addition to several caves, all dating to the Middle Woodland period (Walthall and DeJarnette 1974). At the time of their discovery, Copena burial caves were, with a few exceptions, the only burial caves known in the Southeast, and they were viewed as a regional "tradi-

tion" that distinguished the Copena culture from neighboring Woodland groups (Beck 1995). Use of caves for burial outside the core Copena area was seen as evidence for direct Copena influence (Walthall and DeJarnette 1974:55).

Copena burials, whether in caves or in mounds, share certain defining characteristics. Interments were fleshed, and the burial site often was prepared with imported puddled clay and woven fabrics or mats (Beck 1995:172). In caves, a few burials were placed on the natural floor surface and covered with puddled clay brought in from elsewhere. A rather specific artifact assemblage, consisting of imported raw materials, such as copper and galena, and artifacts produced from mica, marine shells, greenstone, and steatite (including one platform and several elbow pipes), is associated with Copena mortuary contexts (Walthall 1973). On the basis of these characteristics, Copena was seen as a "Southern Hopewell," joined with the northern version by extensive trade networks that developed throughout the Eastern Woodlands during the Middle Woodland period (Beck 1995).

Woodland Period Ceremonial Caves

Over the past few years, it has become increasingly apparent that the kind of prehistoric dark-zone ceremonialism first identified at Mud Glyph Cave (C. H. Faulkner 1986), involving the production and perhaps use of parietal art, is more widespread in space and time than previously thought (C. H. Faulkner 1997; Simek 2001). There are more than thirty glyph caves now known in the Midsouth and Southeast (Simek et al. 2001), and there is reason to believe that cave art may have its roots in the Late Archaic period. Several cave art sites probably date to the Woodland period, and several others may have Woodland art in association with later Mississippian work. What is clear now is that Woodland people made and used cave art and that their iconography was complex, beautiful, and sometimes suggestive of later Mississippian imagery.

The earliest pre-Woodland, clearly ceremonial use of a deep cave interior known at present is that manifested in Adair Glyph Cave in Kentucky (DiBlasi 1996; C. H. Faulkner 1997). A large room (150 meters long by 4 meters wide) about 1 kilometer from the cave entrance was discovered in 1986 by recreational cavers who noticed that the mud floor was covered with incised geometric figures. A single radiocarbon determination on cane charcoal from the passage yielded a date of 3560 ± 110 (Figure 23.1, Table 23.1). DiBlasi (1996:42–43) provides a short summary description of the glyphs, which are abundant and intricate. Zigzags are very common, as is cross-hatching. Cross-hatching and other linear markings have also been noted at several places in the upper-level trunk passages of Salts Cave, and there is at least one occurrence of cross-hatching in Fisher Ridge Cave (DiBlasi 1996:43–46). Possibly prehistoric rectilinear and curvilinear pictographs have been recorded for Mammoth Cave as well (DiBlasi 1996:46). In at least one place in Salts Cave there are three zoomorphic figures drawn with charcoal on a rock face that may be prehistoric (DiBlasi 1996:43–45), and we have already cited the petroglyphs from 3rd Unnamed Cave. Thus, it seems that at least some kinds of ceremonial activities were taking place in deep cave interiors as early as the Late Archaic and Early Woodland periods.

At present, nineteen cave art sites have yielded associated artifacts amenable to radiocarbon determination. Nine sites have Woodland radiocarbon ages (Figure 23.1, Table 23.1), but only three have *only* Woodland period determinations. The most recently discovered cave art site, 19th Unnamed Cave in Alabama, has two radiocarbon age determinations, both Woodland (Table 23.1), and the ceramic assemblage found in the dark-zone chamber where the cave art occurs contains exclusively Woodland types. Thus, there *is* Woodland cave art, and it occurs, on the present evidence, more commonly than caves decorated in the Archaic period. Mississippian period cave art remains by far the most common, but continuity in cave art production from the Archaic to the Mississippian is now indicated for the Southeast.

The earliest Woodland art comes from 5th Unnamed Cave in middle Tennessee. This small cave was a burial pit with a second, horizontal entrance, but it was severely looted in 1997. Several bodies, including males and females, adults and children, had been placed in the cave from above. A radiocarbon determination of 2030 ± 50 B.P. (2150 to 1820 B.P. calibrated range) from these deposits indicates early Middle Woodland mortuary use. No artifacts were found in the looters' tailings, but the complete lack of galena, mica, and similar items leads us to suspect that this was not a classic Copena burial cave, as defined farther to the south in Alabama (Walthall 1973). On the wall of the chamber originally containing the burials are two petroglyphs (Figure 23.3): a "toothy mouth" and a box-like human effigy (Simek 1998). Simple in style, these images have no real correlates among later Mississippian iconography. After recovery and reburial of the human remains, this cave was permanently sealed to protect it from further looting.

A complex assemblage of glyphs incised into alluvial mud banks in Crumps Cave in Kentucky also has Woodland age determinations. A piece of cane torch recovered from inside a mud glyph line, probably used to draw the glyph itself, yielded an age of 1980 ± 60 B.P. (D. B. Davis and Haskins 1993). A second assay of 1840 ± 80 B.P., recently obtained from a torch smudge above the glyphs, agrees well with the first and confirms a probable Woodland age for the mud glyphs from Crumps. The Crumps Cave glyphs

Figure 23.3 — "Toothy Mouth" from 5th Unnamed Cave, Tennessee (photo by Alan Cressler)

are elaborate, and they comprise box-like human effigies, representations of animals, including serpents and a terrapin, and more abstract patterns and lines. Nothing in the iconography precludes a Woodland style, although one possible serpent image has horns or antlers, a characteristic of some Mississippian icons both in caves (Simek et al. 1997) and on mobiliary objects found in other ceremonial contexts (e.g., Phillips and Brown 1978). Thus, both petroglyphs and mud glyphs are associated with Woodland age determinations in 5th Unnamed Cave and Crumps Cave.

Nineteenth Unnamed Cave was discovered in July 1998 on the north side of the Tennessee River valley in Alabama (Cressler et al. 1999). In a large room about 100 meters from the cave entrance, numerous mud glyphs were incised into a thin mud veneer coating the ceiling, using a technique we call "digital tracing" (C. H. Faulkner and Simek 2001) because the artists' fingers were used to produce the images. The mud glyph assemblage from 19th Unnamed Cave consists of hundreds of images, including meandering lines, representations of animals, and human effigies. In subject matter, if not execution, these glyphs resemble those from Crumps Cave in Kentucky.

All the 19th Unnamed Cave glyphs are very large, some covering tens of square meters. Animal images include coiled rattlesnakes (Figure 23.4),

Figure 23.4 — Rattlesnake effigy from 19th Unnamed Cave, Alabama (photo by Alan Cressler)

flying creatures, and a very large bear. Human effigies range from 10 centimeters to 3.0 meters in size, and several have rayed semicircles attached to or exiting from their midsections (Figure 23.5). One large panel of meandering lines and circles resembles nothing more than Woodland complicated stamped ceramic decorations found in the same region (Broyles 1968; T. Lewis and Lewis 1997). The imagery of this assemblage bears some similarity to Mississippian icons seen in the dark zones of caves (e.g., C. H. Faulkner 1986, 1997; Simek et al. 1997), but its simple execution and the particular subject matter of some of the glyphs differ from those in most Mississippian cave art contexts. In any case, this is the southernmost manifestation of the mud glyph cave art tradition now known from eleven caves in the Southeast (C. H. Faulkner 1986; C. H. Faulkner and Simek 2001).

Two radiocarbon determinations have been obtained for wood charcoal fragments found in the cave: 1740 ± 60 and 1240 ± 60 B.P. Both fall into the Woodland period. The cave mouth has been washed clean of sedimentary deposits, so no archaeological material remains there, but a few sherds have been recovered from the cave floor below the glyphs. It is important to note that these artifacts are found in the cave's dark zone, and they cannot have been washed into the cave from outside. Moreover, there are no lithic items in proximity to the glyphs, as would be expected in a habitation site, even if it were only briefly occupied. The ceramics from 19th Unnamed Cave, therefore, have a good chance of being associated with glyph production and/or use. All sherds are limestone tempered; two temporally diagnostic sherds indicate Early and Middle Woodland manufacture (Cressler et al. 1999). Thus, the chronological indications presently available, and the subject matter of the art, all suggest an exclusively Woodland period use of 19th Unnamed Cave for ceremonial purposes.

Five other cave art sites, all in Tennessee, have both Woodland and Mississippian age determinations. One of these, 6th Unnamed Cave, is another burial cave located near 5th Unnamed Cave. One carbon 14 determina-

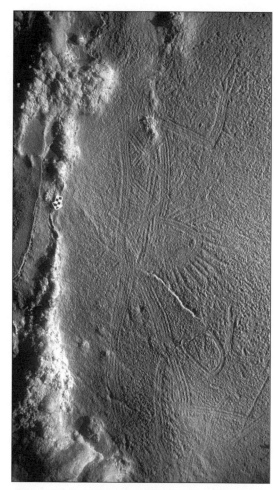

Figure 23.5 — Human effigy with a rayed semi-circle in the abdomen from 19th Unnamed Cave, Alabama (photo by Alan Cressler)

tion on cultural material from the cave places prehistoric use at 1890 ± 50 B.P. (calibrated range 1990 to 1630 B.P.), but another yielded an age of 630 ± 50 B.P. (calibrated range 690 to 520 B.P.), fully within the classic Mississippian in this area. A series of petroglyphs on the cave wall show human head effigies, some with iconographic elements, like the "weeping eye," usually attributed to the later time period. Thus, 6th Unnamed Cave may have served as a mortuary pit during the Woodland, but its parietal art assemblage probably relates to Mississippian use. What is interesting, nevertheless, is that Mississippian peoples probably also used this cave for burial, making it the only confirmed example of cave burial from Mississippian times in the Appalachian Plateau. This suggests more continuity in cave use from early periods into the later Mississippian cultures.

Another cave in the same area, 2nd Unnamed Cave, has human burials associated with artifacts; farther into the cave, cane torch smudges on the ceiling within an array of mud glyphs have a Mississippian age. Here, differing uses of the cave over time are indicated. Seventh Unnamed Cave, near the multi-use sites just noted, has a Late Woodland date (1320 ± 40 B.P.), along with Early Mississippian style artifacts in cave fill, and petroglyphs on the cave walls. This date overlaps the Emergent Mississippian in the area, so a Woodland attribution is problematic.

Elsewhere, a single Woodland period date was obtained from Mud Glyph Cave itself (1485 ± 60 B.P.). It is possible that Woodland mud glyphs are present in the cave under the sometimes bewildering array of Mississippian art, but seven other age determinations indicate Mississippian dominance of activity in Mud Glyph Cave (C. H. Faulkner 1986).

Finally, 3rd Unnamed Cave has yielded a single Woodland age determination, but the cane sample used for this date came from the passage floor at a place more than 1 kilometer from the cave art chamber. It is unlikely that Woodland people created the 3rd Unnamed Cave art. Thus, ceremonial use of caves in the Midsouth and Southeast during Woodland times has been confirmed at several sites. Caves were variously used for mortuary ritual and for purposes resulting in art production. In several cases, both activities are indicated for a single cave. Continuity from the preceding Archaic and with the succeeding Mississippian period in cave art production, and even in subject matter, indicate long adherence to this tradition and probably a local origin for it within this region.

Summary and Conclusions: Woodland Period Activities in Caves

Woodland period activities in caves were abundant and diverse, ranging from extractive (minerals, flowstone, chert; in at least one Florida cave there was some evidence for prehistoric removal of clay thought to be raw material for pottery manufacture [Bullen 1949]), to mortuary, to creation of graphic representations by incising mud or stone surfaces and by drawing on walls or breakdown blocks. All of these activities are documented by 3000 B.P. and continue throughout most of the Woodland period. In several caves there is evidence for both graphics creation and extractive work, the combination of mortuary use and production of graphics being less common.

There is evidence for continuity in some patterns (chert procurement; graphics production, presumably in association with ritual practices) into the Late Woodland and even the Mississippian period. In the realm of cave art or graphic representation there seem to be long-term trends and even shared symbol systems that span several millennia, some of them perhaps implying developmental relationships. Cave mineral mining, however, seems to be restricted to the Early and Middle Woodland periods. The tendency has been to think of this mining as supplying trade networks, some of which were established during the Late Archaic period. That suggestion may be plausible for Wyandotte Cave and the Middle Woodland Hopewell Interaction Sphere, but the Salts/Mammoth, Big Bone, and Hubbards cave gypsum-mining evidence is more difficult to fit into what is known of Early Woodland developments in west-central Kentucky (Railey 1991) and central Tennessee. Neither region is known to be involved in whatever exchange networks provided copper, mica, and marine shell for elaborate Adena burials (if some of these are indeed Early rather than Middle Woodland). Hence, it behooves us to formulate some alternative possibilities (e.g., Crothers 2001).

In any case, it is clear that for more than 4500 years caves were recognized by southeastern peoples as integral parts of the landscape: places that could be explored, exploited, and included in ceremonial observances as were various above-ground locales. Cave archaeology is an essential aspect of research on the Woodland Southeast.

Acknowledgments

Over the years our work has been supported by a number of institutions, but we would particularly like to acknowledge the National Park Service and the staff of Mammoth Cave National Park, the Cave Research Foundation, and the National Speleological Society for their continuing efforts to protect cave sites and promote scientific investigations. We owe a large debt of gratitude to the many cavers who have assisted us directly in our work and are responsible for alerting the archaeological community to many of the sites discussed here. Gary Crites kindly gave us permission to use his two unpublished radiocarbon dates from Big Bone Cave. Some of the work reported here was funded by grants to Jan Simek from the National Science Foundation (SBR-9903076), the National Geographic Society, and the Tennessee Historical Commission.

Chapter 24

Domesticating Self and Society
in the Woodland Southeast

Charles R. Cobb and Michael S. Nassaney

U nraveling the nature of social organization in the Woodland Southeast has traditionally been approached from a number of different directions, notably mortuary practices, exchange networks, and settlement patterns. Earthworks have also constituted an important venue for addressing social complexity. Mound-building traditions such as Poverty Point, Marksville, Coles Creek, and Mississippian have been used by archaeologists to draw inferences about the mobilization of labor, ceremonial behavior, and other correlates of complexity. In this chapter, we suggest that long-term changes in earthwork construction during the Woodland era may have been linked to changes in world view among indigenous groups in the Southeast—changes that involved societies enacting increasingly stronger notions of discipline and domestication of the self. In addition, we consider how these changes may have permeated the everyday world of domestic architecture and subsistence.

Researchers elsewhere have observed that the process of plant domestication involved dramatic shifts in human perceptions of self in addition to alterations in plant genomes and food practices (Hodder 1990; P. Wilson 1988). In other words, societies domesticated themselves while they were domesticating plants. This suggests to us that addressing social organization in the Woodland Southeast requires a consideration of both the ceremonial dimensions of earthworks and the more mundane daily practices that reproduce everyday existence. Only by considering the complementarity of ritual and quotidian life—the sacred and the profane—is it possible to comprehend the reproduction of the social body.

In making this argument, we adopt a perspective akin to that espoused by Julian Thomas (1993a) in his studies of Neolithic landscapes: that it is possible to develop a historical phenomenology that encompasses transformations in world view and power from the view of the long term. With regard to the Woodland era, we suggest that, similar to the Neolithic, groups may have been experiencing a revolution in subjectivity that set the stage for dramatic changes in perceptions of the social body, which corresponded in turn to important shifts in social organization. These social transformations were manifested, in part, in the physical landscape of earthworks and the built environment.

These perspectives perhaps come closer to *interpreting* the archaeological record than to *explaining* it, as is the more common objective among southeastern archaeologists. We do not, however, believe that proposed shifts in Woodland world view constituted purely a revolution of the mind; they were, in fact, strongly articulated with material dimensions of society. As a consequence, we believe that it is possible to argue that recurrent patterning in the landscape (visible and measurable to archaeologists) is the result of habits that transmitted ideas and practices from one generation to another. In particular, we will argue that the increasing instillation of social discipline is evident in changing land-use practices in the Woodland period built environment. Further, this built environment extended beyond architecture to the landscape of subsistence practices.

In this chapter we take on two orders of business. First, we consider transformations in human attitudes toward, and perceptions of, the natural and social world that occurred in tandem with plant domestication in the Southeast. Second, we scrutinize how those changes corresponded with increasing conditions of cultural and social domestication, which, in turn, we believe can be viewed as a form of cultural discipline. In particular, we argue that, while there is a long-term trend toward intensification of agriculture, changes in monumentality and houses indicate that the imposition of discipline oscillated between the ritual and domestic worlds. To understand this process, it is first important to consider changing notions of land use between hunters and gatherers on one hand and agricultural groups on the other.

Land and Labor

In the study of political economy the distinction has been made between land as an object of labor and land as an instrument of labor (Meillassoux 1978:160; Wolf 1982:91–92). As an object of labor, land serves as a reservoir of resources exploited by human groups. This conceptualization is characteristically associated with hunters and gatherers, who are more prone to live off the land, so to speak, rather than attempt to harness the productivity of land by actively modifying the landscape and its flora and fauna. Simply put, hunters and gatherers practice territoriality rather than the tenure associated with cultivators (Ingold 1986:134–36ff.). This does not mean that mobile societies make no impact on the landscape. Intentional fires, the construction of fish weirs, and similar energy investments by hunters and gatherers demonstrate that human beings have a long history of altering their surroundings (Lourandos 1983; Nicholas 1999; W. Patterson and Sassaman 1988; P. Stahl 1996).

When land is an instrument of labor, human beings manipulate the landscape on a sustained basis with the express purpose of intensifying food production. Further, "nature itself becomes a means of production, an instrument on which labor is expended" (Wolf 1982:92). The development of irrigation canals, agricultural tools, ridged fields, and similar technologies speaks not only to attempts to raise the threshold of food production, but also, just as important, to a notion of a delayed return on investment. Landscape is modified with the expectation that the ultimate yield may not be immediately forthcoming, but it will occur on a somewhat routine and predictable basis.

This simple dichotomy—land as object of labor and land as instrument of labor—tends to obscure two important points. First, there is not a clean historical break between the use of land as object and as instrument. Most agricultural societies underwent a period when foraging and collecting were carried out in concert with cultivation; indeed, most agricultural societies never totally forsake hunting and gathering. In the Woodland Southeast (and Midwest) there are numerous examples of communities that were adopting cultigens at differing rates and in different ways. In many locales the horticultural complex did not appear closely tied to the growth of cultural complexity, whereas in other regions permanently nucleated settlements occurred in tandem with the use of tropical and indigenous cultigens (Fritz 1990a; Gremillion, this volume; Nassaney 2000; Nassaney and Cobb 1991; Simon 2000; Watson 1985). Yet, in both sets of cases, wild plant species remained a substantial portion of the diet. This evidence suggests that Woodland communities do not fit neatly into either the object of labor or instrument of labor category.

The "multiple pathways" perspective (Fritz 1990a) shows that it is misleading to view human groups as moving along a unilinear continuum between hunting and gathering at one end and agriculture at the other, whereby societies "in transition" represent some average of these two subsistence strategies. Horticultural Woodland groups were something quite distinct from either hunters and gatherers or large-scale agriculturists; we might say they were using land as a "subject of labor." By this we mean that human groups, by virtue of some reliance on cultigens, imposed a stronger sense of structure over the means of production. They had begun the process of landscape modification (however minor) and scheduling practices that attend plant cultivation. At the same time, they had set into motion a new set of subsis-

tence interdependencies. These involve potential scheduling and organizational conflicts between the different demands of wild resources found scattered in the environment versus domesticated resources that are more fixed
(e.g., K. Flannery 1968). Such conflicts might also extend to the organization of labor, in which new sets of duties have to be negotiated between men
and women, elders and youth, and other interest groups. In short, there is a
dynamic tension between foraging and cultivating that must be mediated by
both logistical and cultural practices. Consequently, when land is a subject
of labor there is a qualitatively different arena of social relations than that
typified by either hunters and gatherers (where land is an object of labor) or
groups who use cultigens as a staple (where land is an instrument of labor).
It is that arena that typified Woodland communities in the Southeast.

A second difficulty with the object of labor/instrument of labor dichotomy
is that it focuses too narrowly on production, meanwhile overlooking the
transformations in ideology, ritual, and ceremony that accompany shifts in
labor. In the remainder of this chapter we explore more specifically the ideological alterations manifested in the emergence of land as a subject of labor
in the Southeast and how these were played out in the domestication of
society. We contend that the process of domestication incorporated a notion
of discipline, whereby human groups, for various reasons, began to impose
a stronger sense of order on their natural and cultural worlds. This sense of
order, both sacred and secular, was often manifested in the use of space and
the built environment. In the case of the Woodland Southeast, earthworks
and domestic structures became media for discipline, domestication, and
social reproduction.

Historical Contexts of Social Discipline

The process of social discipline or domestication appeared in many times
and places around the world. It also appeared in many guises and can be
attributed to a variety of causes and effects. Thus, while social discipline
appears to be tied to plant domestication, that does not represent the only
link. Perhaps the most well-known association is the work and time discipline that is seen as so important to the growth of industrial capitalism (e.g.,
Leone 1995; Nassaney and Abel 2000; Shackel 1993; Thompson 1967).

We see variations of time and space discipline played out elsewhere in
both the Old and New Worlds. In medieval Italy, for example, the creation
of hilltop nucleated and fortified villages circa A.D. 1000–1100 is referred to
as *incastellamento,* a process that involved an increase in monastic patri-
mony and closer regulation over local production to stimulate surplus pro-

duction (Moreland 1992). Such communities facilitated the capabilities of surveillance and centralized regulation, combining the elements of space and power along the lines argued by Foucault (1979). In feudal England the regimentation of space was played out in a somewhat different way, but with similar results (M. Johnson 1996). There, landscape was used to impose order on society and nature through enclosure, in turn stimulating the growth of individual farming and a growing body of landless laborers who were instrumental to the development of English capitalism.

Clearly, these cases are not all perfectly analogous, for they occurred in very different social and natural contexts. What they do suggest, though, is that the interaction of societies with their surroundings creates a "technology of self" (J. Thomas 1993a). In other words, the practices involved in the transformation of landscape and home are social as well as physical, and they serve to reproduce the social body and perceptions about the social body. The social landscape is not just a passive reflection of human production; it was created to be seen, experienced, and "consumed" (Nassaney et al. 2000). Moreover, notions of time and space are not mere backdrops to processes of earthwork and home construction; they in fact constitute society. When and where activities and events occurred are not only markers for the construction of archaeological time-space systematics, they are manifestations of habitus, comprised of the relations, daily practices, construction of the built environment, and ritual that serve to transmit meaning from one generation to another (Bourdieu 1977).

So too Native Americans of the Woodland era mapped their social relations on the ground, using landscape and mounds as ways to identify with a particular locale. One of the unintended consequences of this process was that these groups created a world of reduced mobility and internal discipline that was further accelerated by the gradual adoption of cultivated plants. We may debate the motivations and conditions that lead to the adoption of horticulture (e.g., population increase, pressures on surplus production), but without question the consequences of altered subsistence practices are new tensions, opportunities, and constraints that potentially alter the conditions of reproduction (Friedman 1975:165).

Disciplining the Natural World: Mounds and the Ritual Landscape

Before the widespread use of flotation techniques, the mound-building societies associated with Poverty Point, Ohio Hopewell, and Coles Creek were thought to have been largely agricultural (J. A. Ford 1969; Jennings 1952; C. Webb 1968). As Jon Gibson (1994:163) points out, it was commonly believed that "mound building, pottery, agriculture, sedentism, and large populations were integral aspects of a Formative way of life and they were an integrated complex." As the logic went, the surplus made possible by food production had several important impacts. First, it stimulated the growth of population and thereby labor for erecting earthworks. Second, it released a segment of society from primary production so that they could oversee monumental construction. Third, it created the leisure time that allowed for cultural and artistic development. As we now know, dependence upon cultivated plants appears to have been minor for many mound-building groups, even if they were "complex-looking" (Fritz and Kidder 1993).

The revised perspective on the spurious relationship between cultigens and earthworks has been supported by the realization that the labor requirements to build mounds and embankments may have been overestimated. It is now fairly well established that prior to the Middle Woodland period most earthworks did not require that much energy investment. It is even debatable how much labor was required at any one time for many of the large earthworks associated with later sites such as Toltec Mounds or large Mississippian mound centers (Muller 1997:272–74; Nassaney 1996b). For most mound sites, their importance lies not so much in the amount of vested effort, but in the fact that people participated in a communal construction activity that likely had strong ceremonial and ritual implications. As Knight's ethnohistoric research shows, "Mounds possess symbolic associations with autochthony, the underworld, birth, fertility, death, burial, the placation of spirits, emergence, purification, and supernatural protection" (Knight 1989:283). Moreover, the practice of erecting a mound, or adding a mantle, also involved a physical dimension that may have habituated or routinized a population to certain tasks, even if the means of persuasion were ritual in nature. In this way, certain groups may willingly surrender surplus labor that may benefit others, creating a "subjectivity of discipline" (Paynter and McGuire 1991).

Even in the absence of mounds or megaliths, hunters and gatherers are known to attribute the natural environment with transcendent or ritual qualities (Tilley 1994); for such groups, we might say that landscape is an *object* of ritual belief rather than an *instrument*. In other words, the landscape is not usually actively manipulated to any great extent with the purpose of fixing the ritual process, although it is endowed with supernatural qualities. Alternatively, the creation of monumentality symbolized an attachment to and control over the landscape (Hodder 1990)—much in the way Middle Archaic burials may have created a territorial claim, but in a more ostentatious manner (e.g., D. Charles and Buikstra 1983).

This link with a specific place on the landscape stands in contrast to the occupation of a *zone,* such as a first terrace or upland ridge system, which

refers more to a group's use and occupation of a locality because of its resource potential (Whittle 1996:52). With earthworks, an imprint on the landscape is established by human agency, rather than the natural agency of
tectonic uplift or riverine hydrology. Furthermore, the construction of
earthworks regiments the location and timing of the ritual process, which in
turns promotes the discipline of the social and natural worlds (e.g., Bender
1993; Cooney 1999; Edmonds 1999; Mainfort and Sullivan 1998; J. Thomas 1993b).

The ties of earthworks to ritual processes likely had repercussions in
other aspects of daily life as well. It has been pointed out that there is little
evidence for the genesis of classes and alienation of workers from land or
production during the Woodland—or even Mississippian—period (e.g.,
Muller 1997). However, access to ritual knowledge and power can lead to
control over the economy (Keesing 1987; McGuire and Saitta 1996; Nassaney
1992a:269; Pauketat 1994; J. Thomas 1993a), albeit in a less direct fashion
than control over the means of production. Here we move into the realm of
what Bourdieu (1977) has termed "symbolic" capital. In effect, small-scale
societies are more likely to practice an ideological or ritual alienation rather
than economic alienation as a means of manipulation and discipline; we see
this in the Southeast with the growth of earthworks and attendant ceremonial activities, in addition to the rise of ritualized exchange, which reached
its peak during the Middle Woodland period.

Landscape as a form of discipline, particularly in the guise of earthworks,
continued unabated in the history of the Southeast, from the likes of Poverty
Point to Swift Creek to Marksville to Plum Bayou. Importantly, the notion
that terrain could be modified for the reproduction of ritual occurred well
before the idea that the earth could also be modified by agriculture for the
reproduction of biology. Our best evidence in this regard is a series of Middle
Archaic mound sites in northeast Louisiana, as well as Archaic mounds at
other locations in the Southeast (H. Jackson and Jeter 1994; Piatek 1994; J.
Saunders et al. 1994; R. Saunders 1994).

After the Archaic period, earthworks seem to have assumed an even
more active role in the landscape and literally began to impose structure on
the world of those living or moving within the shadow of mounds. In the
Middle Woodland period, for example, there are embankments and formal
configurations of earthworks that were more likely to structure ritual practices and beliefs than Archaic mound arrangements (Mainfort and Sullivan
1998:11–12). Clay (1987) argues that Hopewell mound building was coordinated with other modifications to community space and landscape, pointing to a wide-ranging relationship between disciplining the built environment and the cultures associated with earthworks. Similar arguments have

been forwarded for more southerly Middle Woodland sites, such as Pinson Mounds (Thunen 1998) and Marksville (D. Jones and Kuttruff 1998) (Figures 24.1 and 24.2). Middle Woodland earthworks also may have acted to segregate the untamed world—the space outside of the mounds—from the orderly world of ritual inside the earthworks.

Interestingly, builders often attempted to enhance this sense of separation through the use of natural features of the landscape: at Pinson Mounds the circular earthwork is built on a peninsula of land (Thunen 1998) (see Figure 2.2 herein), whereas at Marksville both a bluff and a ravine demarcate large sections of the site (D. Jones and Kuttruff 1998) (Figure 24.2). While mounds at certain times may have helped to serve as a point of gravitation and interaction for dispersed populations (Clay 1986:594; Mainfort and Sullivan 1998:15; Nassaney 1996b), Middle Woodland enclosures seem to have served a dialectical role of attracting populations at one level (at least for their construction) yet maintaining a sense of segregation between ritual specialists or elites on the one hand and the hoi polloi on the other. The active and complex structuring of space also may have elevated the ambiguity of signification (see J. Thomas 1993a), underscoring the likeli-

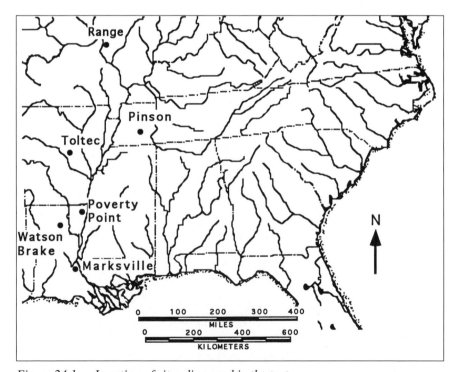

Figure 24.1 — Location of sites discussed in the text

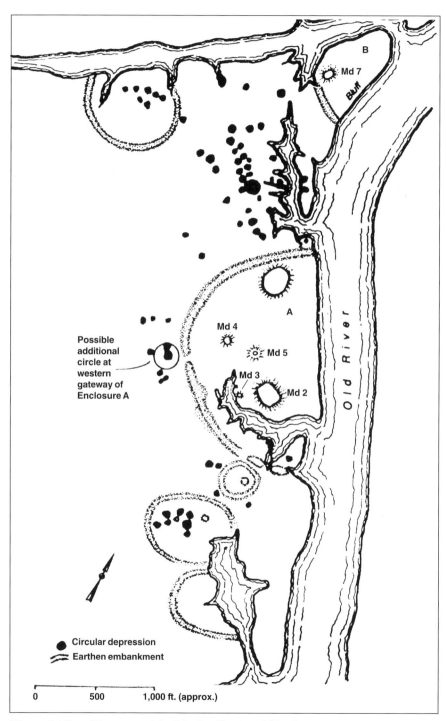

Figure 24.2 — Plan map of the Marksville site (16Av-1)

hood that not all persons or interest groups attached the same meaning to earthworks. Differential perceptions of space, mounds, and ritual likely occurred through the history of the Southeast and may have been a major source of social tensions.

The formalization of enclosures and mound sites declined in many areas with the waning of the Hopewell Interaction Sphere. However, sites such as Toltec Mounds in Arkansas and Coles Creek period sites in the Lower Mississippi Valley continued this practice. At the other end of the time line, Poverty Point is perhaps the earliest well-known example in the Southeast of the capacity of earthworks to actively reshape the surroundings of daily life (J. Gibson 1998). Poverty Point also is somewhat of an anomaly because it reflects a high degree of planning at such an early date, that is, in the Late Archaic. However, the loose arrangement of mounds in a ring at Watson Brake may reflect even earlier attempts at the formalization of ritual space (J. Saunders et al. 1994:143).

Earthworks clearly were not static entities in the Southeast; their form and configuration varied greatly—and presumably their meaning did so as well. The construction cycles of individual mounds or mound sites may have altered through time. Also, the use of earthworks waxed and waned throughout the history of the entire Southeast. There do seem to be some very broad trends, however, that have long been recognized and codified in Willey's (1966) Burial and Temple Mound periodizations. Early in the Woodland period, mounds were often used for interments, perhaps reflecting attempts to control death and come to terms with the afterlife through the ritual landscape (e.g., Parker Pearson 1984). Furthermore, the reuse of mounds by adding new mantles, as seen at sites like Greenhouse (J. A. Ford 1951), often had connotations of death and rebirth. Although it is unclear how often this pattern occurred in the Woodland Southeast, it likely reflects an indigenous perspective on the cyclicity of time, further situating a mound within the reproduction of the ritual system. In other words, mounds and earthworks served to evoke the *past* through buried ancestors, reproduce the *present* through ritual, and point to the *future* as a landmark that would attract others at a later date.

From the view of the long term, earthworks appear to go through at least three phases in the Southeast. First, they were closely wedded to the natural landscape, where there was still a notion that they constituted an object of ideology. Second, mounds began to structure the world on a routine basis, but they still were not integrated into daily life. They were more a subject of ideology. In this regard, we find sites like Marksville and Pinson Mounds in the Middle Woodland, and Toltec Mounds somewhat later, with elaborate configurations of space and order, but relatively small amounts of domestic debris. These communities appear to have been points of regular visitation and cyclical ritual rather than long-term occupations, giving rise to the popular term "vacant centers." Finally, in a stage that only reached its full expression during the Mississippian period, mounds became instruments of ceremony that played a pivotal role in the daily life of communities. These long-term trends also may be intimately involved with the nature and display of Woodland period social inequality, in that the prevalence of corporate burial mounds early in the Southeast (e.g., Blitz 1986; Brookes 1976; J. A. Ford and Willey 1940; N. Jenkins and Krause 1986:58–60) may have disguised achievement and authority, whereas platform mounds later in time appear to have been more closely linked with individuals or interest groups (Nassaney 1992a:269). It should be pointed out, nonetheless, that these two patterns overlap and are not sequential in a clearly staged way.

The progression of artificial landscapes that we present is not a universal one in the Southeast. Mound building was not experienced by all regions, nor was mound building continuous in all parts of the Southeast. Yet we do believe it is important that mounds occur when cultivated plants were a very minor component—or even absent—in the diet of many regions. The idea that the natural world could be disciplined or structured was an important transformation in world view that would have made possible other daily practices involving regimentation. In particular, with the groundwork laid for the domestication of society, horticulture would have been a more viable cultural option in the face of population pressure, demands for surplus, or other stimuli for food production.

Agriculture gradually did become more important through time in the Southeast, while the use of mounds and earthworks oscillated greatly. The small scale of Late Woodland earth moving throughout much of the Southeast is particularly noteworthy in this regard. Nevertheless, while disciplining the natural world through earthworks and ritual may have played a major role in the development of agricultural societies, cultures could, and did, discipline their domestic world too.

Disciplining the Domestic World: Community and Houses

"The most readily available means whereby great quantities of labor may be used to convert to prestige, a means that is the great invention of domesticated society, is architecture in general and the house specifically" (P. Wilson 1988:87). This quotation from Peter Wilson summarizes a perspective that sees the built environment, particularly in the form of domestic structures, as an end product of labor and the processes of social differentiation that accompany the mobilization of surplus. Thus, certain characteristics of the house, such as size or decor, at times may be emblematic of status, a principle well established by architectural historians and historical archaeologists (e.g., Clark 1988; M. Johnson 1993; Rotman and Nassaney 1997), but documented for some small-scale societies, too (John Chapman 1990; T. Gibson 1995; Loftfield and Jones 1995; Waterson 1995). Domestic structures may also ensure continuity and the transmission of wealth and may serve to facilitate endeavors that promote social power (Waterson 1995). For these reasons, the house may serve as an important unit of study that is much more available to the archaeologist than is the household, which is a social construct.

Yet the house is more than an outward manifestation of power relations. It also is both a nexus of the social group and a cultural concept. Furthermore, like mounds, houses constitute a social rendering of space. In contrast to earthworks, houses create an immediate sense of inside and outside, of belonging and not belonging, that is more closely tied to the domestic world. The interior of houses may be integral to a notion of shared identity, and the everyday activities that occur within the house form the basis of the habitus—those taken-for-granted practices that structure and are structured by daily life (Bourdieu 1977; T. Gibson 1995; Hodder 1990; Robben 1989). This perspective refocuses issues of power to a smaller scale, one that emphasizes the give and take of everyday domestic life.

Studies of the Eurasian Neolithic have been most prominent in linking the house and notions of the domestic; a relationship that—if not preceding agriculture—coincides so closely with it that it forms part of the larger bundle of practices that paved the way for a sedentary life-style and corresponding transformations in social organization (Hodder 1990; Whittle 1996). Various interpretations have been attached to the growth of the *domus*—habitus played out within the household—within the built environment and the process of domestication. Hodder (1990) suggests that the house resolves conflicts between the inner and the outer worlds. The inner world of the domicile becomes a metaphor for the domus as well as the process of domestication; the outer world represents the untamed and dangerous world outside of the home and the community. Others have argued that the house serves as a similar point of conflict and mediation, but involving different opposing forces, such as descent versus alliance (Levi-Strauss 1987) or gender relations (Janowski 1995).

Houses in the Woodland Southeast are often difficult to detect. Nevertheless, there are widely reported cases of post-mold structures of various sizes dating to Early Woodland components and even earlier (e.g., Ledbetter 1991; Sassaman 1993b; Sassaman and Ledbetter 1996; Schambach 1982).

In many instances, these presumed residences are associated with hearths, large pits, and processing technology such as metates, evidence that points to the increasing sedentism and settling in that are hallmarks of the domestication of human beings. However, there are few signs of planned communities early in the Woodland period; most structures seem to be scattered in small numbers. Further, the evidence for long-term occupation of these settlements is still ambiguous (Sassaman 1993c:244–46). The lack of strongly aggregated communities in the Southeast contrasts strongly with the investment in domestic architecture and nucleation evident at Neolithic sites also involved in plant domestication, such as Çatal Hüyük, Jericho, and Varna. Most of the labor-intensive early architecture in eastern North America appears to be related to ritual, rather than domestic, activities, especially the presumed mortuary complexes associated with Adena "sacred circles" in the lower Midwest and Midsouth (Clay 1986, 1987).

Although there do seem to be some Archaic sites with significant houses in the Southeast (Sassaman and Ledbetter 1996), the wholesale commitment to substantial vernacular architecture appears to be loosely tied to a corresponding commitment to cultigens. For example, during the Terminal Woodland Patrick phase of the American Bottom, the Range site was characterized by keyhole and rectilinear structures, large numbers of pits, and an apparent "community square" (J. Kelly 1990b) (see Figure 7.5 herein). Domesticates of the Eastern Agricultural Complex were also common at this site. A similar pattern is seen at Miller III phase (also Terminal Woodland) sites in Alabama, where square, semi-subterranean structures replaced the oval houses of earlier times (N. Jenkins and Krause 1986:77–80). It is noteworthy that maize does not appear to become a staple in either region until a few centuries later; apparently spatial discipline in the domestic sphere preceded the regimentation associated with a heavy investment in plant cultivation.

Although houses were likely part and parcel of the reproduction of everyday life, it is problematic whether we can speak of a segregated world of secular domiciles versus ceremonial mounds. It is likely that the two were closely entwined and we are dealing more with a matter of emphasis rather than true separation (J. Gibson 1998). In this vein, the courtyard, and later the plaza, may have served to bridge the sacred and the profane. Open spaces in the middle of structure complexes may appear as early as the Archaic period (Sassaman 1993c:266), occur occasionally in the Woodland period, and are a regular feature of Mississippian communities. Although the most secure evidence for courtyards dates to Late Woodland occupations such as the Range site noted above, there are possible Middle Woodland sites with this feature (e.g., Maher 1991). The formalization of open space circumscribed by residences may be a very important trend in the evolution of the domestic, in that such areas may represent the institutionalization of a wider social field involved in a corporate sense of discipline.

Discussion and Conclusion

We have elsewhere devoted some effort to pondering the Late Woodland period (C. Cobb and Nassaney 1995; Nassaney 2000; Nassaney and Cobb 1991) and why it appears to represent a transition from the Middle Woodland period beyond the usual typological criteria. From the long-term perspective afforded by this overview we believe that we have gained a better insight into the historical dynamics of the Woodland Southeast. What is noteworthy is that the domestication of society through the built environment appears to have occurred much earlier in the ritual world, as manifested in earthworks, than in the household where it penetrated later in time. The archaeological record suggests to us that, during the Early Woodland and Middle Woodland periods, there was very little formalization of domestic space through the use of either substantial houses or planned living communities. Thus, despite the veneer of formality suggested by earthworks, particularly those of the Middle Woodland period, the discipline of the domestic world as seen in the Eurasian Neolithic did not seem to take hold during the Woodland era in the Southeast until extremely late. In contrast, there seems to have been continuing attempts to rein in the world of the supernatural, through the construction of earthworks, the formalization of burial ceremonies, and the use of shamanistic practices such as smoking.

Nevertheless, the discipline associated with the ritual order appears to have occurred only intermittently over much of the Woodland period. Highly formal mound sites such as those associated with the Middle Woodland period are not common. Importantly, mounds and mound sites in general seem to have been used on a recurring, but not continuous, basis, and often do not display evidence for significant associated habitations. Consequently, the taming of the supernatural did not involve the daily practices that would necessarily have involved the development of the domus that we associate with houses. In contrast, many Neolithic structures have evidence of figurines and possible ceremonial behavior that may reflect the penetration of ritual into everyday life. That kind of transformation may have been a necessary prelude to the organic domestication of society that accompanied qualitative changes in social organization.

To close our discussion, we believe that it is instructive to extend our time line beyond the Woodland era to follow out the various trends and patterns we have enumerated. It appears that the key architectural transformation associated with the Mississippian period was not necessarily the widespread occurrence of earthworks, which after all have a lengthy history in the Southeast. Perhaps even more important was the institutionalization of domestic space that we see in the development of wall-trench structures, the internal segmentation of domestic space within houses, and the arrangement of structures into formal barrios at some sites. We think it noteworthy that the well-documented decline in Mississippian mound-building following the thirteenth century A.D. appears to have had few repercussions in the domestic sphere. Hamlets, villages, and towns appear to have thrived, in many cases as very formal spatial entities, up until the time of European contact and even afterwards. Apparently, the seeds of human domestication and discipline sown during the Woodland era had flourished to the point where the spatial discipline of the ritual world became secondary in the process of cultural domestication.

Chapter 25

Epilogue: Future Directions for Woodland Archaeology in the Southeast

David G. Anderson and Robert C. Mainfort, Jr.

The contributors to this volume examine the Woodland period occupation of the Southeast from a variety of perspectives, ranging from geographical and topical overviews of cultural developments and archaeological research, to considerations of how this record of research and interpretation has been shaped by our approaches to systematics and taxonomy, to how the world view and cosmology of the Southeast's prehistoric Woodland inhabitants underlay and structured their societies and helped shape transformations that were occurring within them.

As editors, our goal has been not only to present a summary of current knowledge, but also to show the array of approaches by which this knowledge has been obtained and interpreted. At our direction, many of the authors herein suggest avenues for future research in their regional areas or topics of concern. Here we offer our own suggestions and concluding thoughts on the current state of Woodland period archaeology in the Southeast.

First and foremost, we believe that far more problem-oriented and theoretically well-informed primary research on the Woodland period is needed all across the region, covering both existing collections (many of which remain unanalyzed) and fieldwork. The latter is a particularly urgent need given the rate of archaeological site destruction throughout the region. Field research is at the core of our discipline and it should remain so. If we are to successfully evaluate our ideas about the past and develop new ones, evidence must continue to be collected and older data reexamined. But we must be flexible in our thinking about what we are recovering and be open to new ideas and approaches in field research, analysis, and interpretation. In our theoretical and analytical diversity there is indeed strength, and southeastern archaeology's tolerance of differing approaches to archaeological inquiry should by all means continue (I. Brown 1994), albeit closely linked to our region's equally strong insistence that interpretations of the past be well grounded—securely linked to data compiled and evaluated in the field and in the laboratory (e.g., Peebles 1990; Watson 1990).

Perhaps the most influential monograph on southeastern archaeology produced in the twentieth century, *Archaeological Survey in the Lower Mississippi Alluvial Valley, 1940–1947* (Phillips et al. 1951), exemplified these ideals and yielded appreciable insight about Woodland as well as later occupations in the region. The work is a monument to careful field data collection, analysis, and interpretation, and the differing theoretical approaches and interpretations of the three authors are clearly evident and candidly presented, producing a standard of scientific reporting that should be read and emulated by every southeastern archaeologist (see especially Phillips et al. 1951:425–29). As archaeology is increasingly a multidisciplinary team endeavor, presenting the views of teams rather than individuals will become a hallmark of our work. Open and honest debate between project participants, and among scholars in the regional professional community in general, is an important part of this process.

Also in the realm of primary data compilation, we must develop a better handle on site and artifact distributions at local to regional scales if we are to successfully construct models of settlement, subsistence, and political geography. This can be facilitated by careful attention to collections and record management, including efforts to ensure data comparability from state to state and between researchers. Such data will allow us to examine empirically such questions as where people were on the landscape during various Woodland subperiods; whether there were buffer zones between societies, as unquestionably occurred during the subsequent Mississippian period; and what geographic and organizational scales of the societies were present in the region.

The full potential of the suggestions offered above cannot be fully realized if analysis of archaeological materials remains mired in the quagmire of culture history that has dominated southeastern archaeology for over half a century (Dunnell 1990). The call for reevaluating and perhaps discarding current systematics (O'Brien et al., this volume) clearly is a challenge that must be met if we are to increase our understanding of the Woodland Southeast. The same approaches to artifact typology and the formulation of culture-historical units (phases) that have been used successfully to identify long-term changes over broad areas are not well suited for measuring variation on the finer scales necessary for addressing many of the research topics mentioned by the contributors to this volume. For example, it is time to revisit pottery type definitions through attribute/mode analysis, as well as technological and compositional studies. Such research will necessarily lead to examining the basis for and validity of existing phase constructs. Multivariate statistical methods, which have not seen wide application in the Southeast, hold considerable promise for identifying analytically defensible groups of sites on the basis of artifact frequency data (e.g., Mainfort 1999b). It seems unlikely that culture histories grounded in traditional phases can significantly advance our understanding of most research questions posed by the contributors to this volume.

Another area to which future research might be profitably directed is examination of the impacts Woodland societies had on the physical landscape. While the construction of monumental architecture and the maintenance of trail networks are obvious and dramatic examples, whether and how biotic communities were manipulated or actively managed warrants further investigation. That is, were certain plant and animal species encouraged through controlled burning, planting, or culling? Linked to this would be evaluation of the role of agricultural food production in the diet and in the generation of surplus that may have fueled tributary economies. Flotation and fine screening, and the collection of appropriate samples for detailed paleoethnobotanical and zooarchaeological analyses, should be commonplace during all excavations. The domestication of plants and the transformation of the physical landscape over time are topics that can and should receive increasing attention, particularly from researchers working in a world where climate and the physical landscape are changing so dramatically. The role of global climate change on Woodland cultures across the region itself needs further examination (Anderson 2001; Gunn [ed.] 2000).

Finally, publication of research conducted at Woodland sites and with Woodland assemblages needs to be encouraged, including the many fine reports produced by cultural resource management firms and agencies that typically have very limited distribution. Full publication includes thorough descriptions of what was done, what was found (by provenience), and what measurements were taken or results were obtained during associated analyses. It also includes the reporting of all samples collected and processed in specialized analyses, including absolute dating, as well as provision of sufficient photographs, floor plans, and profiles so researchers can understand the assemblage's context. When interpretive claims are made, these should be backed by analyses that can be replicated using the collected data. Authors of good site reports are to be cherished as exemplars of responsible archaeological behavior, for they are producing records that will last far beyond their lifetimes and be used for generations to come. When we excavate, write, and curate our collections and records properly, we are upholding the highest ethical standards of our profession, meeting the responsibility we have to the archaeological record, and hence to the people of the past whose lives our work has touched and brought to light. We must never forget that our research is, after all, ultimately about people, and directed to understanding the lives of those who inhabited the region before us.

References Cited

Abbott, Lawrence E., Jr., Erica E. Sanborn, Leslie E. Raymer, Lisa D. O'Steen, W. J. Cleary, and G. C. Turner
    1999   *Data Recovery at 31CB114, Columbus County, North Carolina: Prehistoric Settlement and Subsistence Practices within the Lower Cape Fear River Valley.* Draft Report, New South Associates Technical Report No. 618. Submitted to International Paper Company, Inc., by New South Associates, Inc., Mebane, N.C.

Abrams, Elliot M.
    1992a   Woodland Settlement Patterns in the Southern Hocking River Valley, Southeastern Ohio. In *Cultural Variability in Context: Woodland Settlements of the Mid-Ohio Valley,* edited by Mark F. Seeman, pp. 19–23. Midcontinental Journal of Archaeology Special Paper 7, Kent State University Press, Kent, Ohio.
    1992b   Archaeological Investigation of the Armitage Mound (33AT434). *Midcontinental Journal of Archaeology* 17(1):80–111.

Adams, Natalie, and Michael Trinkley
    1993   *Archaeological Survey of the Seaside Farms Tract, Charleston County, South Carolina.* Research Series 35, Chicora Foundation, Inc., Columbia, S.C.

Adams, Robert McCormack, and Frank Magre
    1939   Archaeological Surface Survey of Jefferson County. *The Missouri Archaeologist* 5(2):11–23.

Adams, Robert McCormack, and W. Walker
    1942   Archeological Surface Survey of New Madrid County, Missouri. *The Missouri Archaeologist* 8(2).

Adams, William H. (editor)
    1985   *Aboriginal Subsistence and Settlement Archaeology of the Kings Bay Locality.* Vol. 1, *The Kings Bay and Devils Walkingstick Sites.* Report of Investigations 1, Department of Anthropology, University of Florida, Gainesville.

Ahler, Steven R.
    1988   *Excavations at the Hansen Site.* Archaeological Report 173, University of Kentucky Program for Cultural Resource Assessment, Lexington.

Ahler, Steven R., and Paul E. Albertson
    1996   *Development, Testing, and Refinement of a Predictive Locational Model for Prehistoric Sites at Fort Leonard Wood, Missouri.* Illinois State Museum Quaternary Studies Program Technical Report No. 96-1019-1. Submitted to the U.S. Army Corps of Engineers Waterways Experiment Station Geotechnical Laboratory (GL-6), Vicksburg, Miss. (Contract No. DACA39–95-K-0099).

Ahler, Steven R., Paul P. Kreisa, Jacqueline M. McDowell, and Kevin P. McGowan
    1995a   *Phase II Evaluation and Paleoenvironmental Investigations at Fifteen Selected Sites at Fort Leonard Wood, Pulaski County, Missouri.* Research Report No. 10, Public Service Archaeology Program, University of Illinois at Urbana-Champaign. Submitted to the U.S. Army Construction Engineering Research Laboratory, Champaign, Ill.

Ahler, Steven R., Paul P. Kreisa, James L. Theler, Gregory R. Walz, Robert E. Warren, Eve A. Hargrave, Brian Adams, and Cynthia L. Balek
    1995b   *Excavation and Resource Evaluation of Sites 23PU2, 23PU255 and 23PU235 (Miller Cave Complex), Fort Leonard Wood, Pulaski County, Missouri.* Research Report No. 19, Public Service Archaeology Program, University of Illinois at

Urbana-Champaign. Submitted to the U.S. Army Construction Engineering Research Laboratory, Champaign, Ill.

Ahler, Steven R., Marjorie B. Schroeder, Bonnie W. Styles, Robert E. Warren, and Karli White
  1996 *Phase II Evaluation of Three Sites in the Ramsey Peninsula Complex, Fort Leonard Wood, Pulaski County, Missouri.* Quaternary Studies Program Technical Report 96-1048-37, Illinois State Museum, Springfield. Submitted to the U.S. Army Corps of Engineers Waterways Experiment Station, Vicksburg, Miss.

Ahler, Steven R., Dawn E. Harn, Margot Neverett, Marjorie B. Schroeder, Bonnie W. Styles, Robert E. Warren, Karli White, James L. Theler, and Robert A. Dunn
  1997 *Interdisciplinary Data Recovery and Analyses at Four Sites in the Ramsey Complex, Fort Leonard Wood, Pulaski County, Missouri.* Quaternary Studies Program Technical Report 97-1066-18, Illinois State Museum, Springfield. Submitted to the U.S. Army Corps of Engineers Waterways Experiment Station, Vicksburg, Miss.

Ahler, Steven R., Dawn E. Harn, Margot Neverett, Marjorie B. Schroeder, Bonnie W. Styles, Robert E. Warren, Karli White, and Paul E. Albertson
  1998 *Archaeological Assessment and Geotechnical Stabilization of Three Cave Sites at Fort Leonard Wood, Missouri.* Quaternary Studies Program Technical Report 98-1173-20, Illinois State Museum, Springfield. Submitted to the U.S. Army Corps of Engineers Waterways Experiment Station, Vicksburg, Miss.

Ahler, Steven R., David L. Asch, Dawn E. Harn, Bonnie W. Styles, Karli White, Carol Diaz-Granados, and David Ryckman
  1999 *National Register Eligibility Assessments of Seven Prehistoric Archaeological Sites at Fort Leonard Wood, Missouri.* Quaternary Studies Program Technical Report 98-1202-28, Illinois State Museum, Springfield. Submitted to the U.S. Army Construction Engineering Research Laboratories, Champaign, Ill.

Albert, L. E., and D. G. Wyckoff
  1984 Oklahoma Environments Past and Present. In *Prehistory of Oklahoma,* edited by R. E. Bell, pp. 1–44. Orlando: Academic Press.

Allen, R.
  1948 The Big Circle Mounds. *Florida Anthropologist* 1:17–21.

Allen, Ralph, and Sarah E. Pennell
  1978 Rare Earth Element Distribution Patterns to Characterize Soapstone Artifacts. In *Archaeological Chemistry II,* edited by G. F. Giles, pp. 230–57. Advances in Chemistry Series No. 171, American Chemical Society, Washington, D.C.

Allen, W. L., and James B. Richardson
  1971 The Reconstruction of Kinship from Archaeological Data: The Concepts, the Methods, and the Feasibility. *American Antiquity* 36:41–53.

Allman, John
  1957 A New Late Woodland Culture for Ohio, the Lichliter Village near Dayton. *Ohio Archaeologist* 7(2):59–68.

Altschul, Jeffrey H.
  1983 *Bug Hill: Excavation of a Multicomponent Midden Mound in the Jackfork Valley, Southeast Oklahoma.* Report of Investigations No. 81-1, New World Research, Inc., Pollock, La.

Ambrose, Steven
  1998 *Lewis and Clark: The Voyage of Discovery.* Washington, D.C.: National Geographic Society.

Anderson, David G.
  1975a Inferences from Distributional Studies of Prehistoric Artifacts in the Coastal Plain of South Carolina. *Southeastern Archaeological Conference Bulletin* 18:180–94.

1975b *The Distribution of Prehistoric Ceramics in the Coastal Plain of South Carolina.* Manuscript, appendices, and data sheets on file at the Institute of Archaeology and Anthropology, University of South Carolina, Columbia, and The Charleston Museum, Charleston, S.C.

1977a *Zebree Archeological Project Data Appendices.* Ms. on file, Arkansas Archeological Survey, Fayetteville.

1977b *Archeological Investigations at the Knapp (Toltec) Mound Group: 1966 Test Excavations at Mound C.* Ms. on file, Arkansas Archeological Survey, Toltec Mounds Research Station, Scott.

1978 *The Robert Chowning and Frank E. Chowning Collection: Lithic Artifacts from the Surface of the Toltec Site.* Ms. on file, Arkansas Archeological Survey, Toltec Mounds Research Station, Scott.

1979 *Excavations at Four Fall Line Sites: The Southeastern Beltway Project.* Submitted to South Carolina Department of Highways and Public Transportation, Columbia, by Commonwealth Associates, Inc., Jackson, Mich.

1980 Post Depositional Modification of the Zebree Behavioral Record. In *Zebree Archeological Project Excavation, Data Interpretation, and Report on the Zebree Homestead Site, Mississippi County, Arkansas,* edited by Dan F. Morse and Phyllis A. Morse, pp. 8-1 to 8-28. Report submitted to the U.S. Army Corps of Engineers, Memphis District, by Arkansas Archeological Survey, Fayetteville.

1983 The Ceramic Sequence from the Mattassee Lake Sites: Towards a Cultural Sequence for the Lower Santee River, South Carolina. *South Carolina Antiquities* 15:31–41.

1985 Middle Woodland Societies on the Lower South Atlantic Slope: A View from Georgia and South Carolina. *Early Georgia* 13(1, 2):29–66.

1987 Prehistoric Ceramics from Four Sites along the Middle Savannah River, 38BR259, 38BR495, 38BR527, and 38BR528. In *Late Archaic–Late Woodland Adaptive Stability and Change in the Steel Creek Watershed, South Carolina,* edited by Mark J. Brooks and Glen T. Hanson, appendix III, pp. 1–15. Savannah River Archaeological Research Program, South Carolina Institute of Archaeology and Anthropology, University of South Carolina, Columbia. Submitted to Savannah River Operations Office, U.S. Department of Energy.

1990 *Political Change in Chiefdom Societies: Cycling in the Late Prehistoric Southeastern United States.* Ph.D. dissertation, Department of Anthropology, University of Michigan, Ann Arbor.

1994 *The Savannah River Chiefdoms: Political Change in the Late Prehistoric Southeast.* Tuscaloosa: University of Alabama Press.

1998 Swift Creek in a Regional Perspective. In *A World Engraved: Archaeology of the Swift Creek Culture,* edited by J. Mark Williams and Daniel T. Elliott, pp. 274–300. Tuscaloosa: University of Alabama Press.

2001 Climate and Culture Change in Prehistoric and Early Historic Eastern North America. *Archaeology of Eastern North America* 29:143–86.

2002 The Evolution of Tribal Social Organization in the Southeastern United States. In *The Archaeology of Tribal Societies,* edited by William A. Parkinson. International Monographs in Prehistory, Ann Arbor, Mich., in press.

Anderson, David G. (editor)

1996 *Indian Pottery of the Carolinas: Observations from the March 1995 Ceramic Workshop at Hobcaw Barony.* Council of South Carolina Professional Archaeologists, Columbia.

Anderson, David G., and Virginia Horak (editors)

1995 *Archaeological Site File Management: A Southeastern Perspective.* Interagency

Archeological Services Division, National Park Service, Southeast Regional Office, Atlanta, Ga.

Anderson, David G., and J. W. Joseph
  1988   *Prehistory and History along the Upper Savannah River: Technical Synthesis of Cultural Resource Investigations, Richard B. Russell Multiple Resource Area.* Russell Papers, Interagency Archeological Services Division, National Park Service, Atlanta.

Anderson, David G., Charles E. Cantley, and A. Lee Novick
  1982   *The Mattassee Lake Sites: Archaeological Investigations along the Lower Santee River in the Coastal Plain of South Carolina.* Special Publication 1, Archaeological Services Branch, National Park Service, Atlanta.

Anslinger, C. M.
  1993   *Bratfish: A Stratified Prehistoric Site in the Central Ohio Valley, Dearborn County, Indiana.* Technical Report No. 15, Anthropology Laboratory, Indiana State University, Terre Haute.

Asch, David, and Nancy Asch
  1978   The Economic Potential of *Iva annua* and Its Prehistoric Importance in the Lower Illinois Valley. In *The Nature and Status of Ethnobotany,* edited by Richard I. Ford, pp. 300–341. Anthropological Papers No. 67, Museum of Anthropology, University of Michigan, Ann Arbor.
  1985a   Prehistoric Plant Cultivation in West-Central Illinois. In *Prehistoric Food Production in North America,* edited by Richard I. Ford, pp. 149–203. Anthropological Papers No. 75, Museum of Anthropology, University of Michigan, Ann Arbor.
  1985b   Archeobotany. In *Excavation at the Smiling Dan Site: Delineation of Site Structure and Function during the Middle Woodland Period,* edited by Barbara D. Stafford and Mark B. Sant, pp. 635–725. Reports of Investigations No. 137, Center for American Archaeology, Kampsville, Ill.

Asch, David L., and Nancy Asch Sidell
  1992   Archeobotany. In *Early Woodland Occupations at the Ambrose Flick Site in the Sny Bottom of West-Central Illinois,* edited by C. R. Stafford, pp. 177–293. Research Series, Vol. 10, Center for American Archeology, Kampsville Archeological Center, CAA Press, Kampsville, Ill.

Ashley, Keith H.
  1992   Swift Creek Manifestations along the Lower St. Johns River. *Florida Anthropologist* 45:127–38.
  1995   The Dent Mound: A Coastal Woodland Period Burial Mound near the Mouth of the St. Johns River, Florida. *Florida Anthropologist* 48:13–34.
  1998   Swift Creek Traits in Northeast Florida: Ceramics, Mounds, and Middens. In *A World Engraved: Archaeology of the Swift Creek Culture,* edited by J. Mark Williams and Daniel T. Elliott, pp. 197–221. Tuscaloosa: University of Alabama Press.

Aswell, James R., and William H. Bunce (editors)
  1939   *Tennessee: A Guide to the State.* Federal Writers Project of WPA for the State of Tennessee, Knoxville.

Athens, William P., Charlotte Donald, Susan B. Smith, Paul Heinrich, Tom Fenn, Jennifer Cohen, Stephen Hinks, Julie McClay, and Thomas Neuman
  1993   *Phase I Cultural Resources Investigation of the Mississippi Portion of the Florida Gas Transmission Company Phase II Expansion Project.* Report submitted to the Florida Gas Transmission Company, Houston, by R. Christopher Goodwin and Associates, Inc., New Orleans.

Atkinson, James R., and Crawford H. Blakeman
  1975 *Archaeological Site Survey in the Tallahalla Reservoir Area, Jasper County, Mississippi: 1975.* Report submitted to the U.S. Army Corps of Engineers, Mobile District, by the Department of Anthropology, Mississippi State University, Starkville.
Atkinson, James R., and Jack D. Elliott, Jr.
  1978 *A Cultural Resources Survey of Selected Construction Areas in the Tennessee-Tombigbee Waterway: Alabama and Mississippi.* Report submitted to the U.S. Army Corps of Engineers, Mobile District, by the Department of Anthropology, Mississippi State University, Starkville.
  1979 *A Cultural Resources Survey and Evaluation in the Tallahalla Creek Lake, Jasper County Mississippi.* Report submitted to the U.S. Army Corps of Engineers, Mobile District, by Department of Anthropology, Mississippi State University, Starkville.
Atkinson, James R., John C. Phillips, and Richard Walling
  1980 *The Kellogg Village Site Investigations, Clay County, Mississippi.* Report submitted to the U.S. Army Corps of Engineers, Mobile District, by the Department of Anthropology, Mississippi State University, Starkville.
Atwater, Caleb
  1820 Description of the Antiquities Discovered in the State of Ohio and Other Western States. *Transactions and Collections of the American Antiquarian Society* 1:105–267.
Atwood, W. W.
  1940 *The Physiographic Provinces of North America.* Boston: Ginn.
Autin, Whitney J., Scott F. Burns, Bobby J. Miller, Roger T. Saucier, and John I. Snead
  1991 Quaternary Geology of the Lower Mississippi Valley. In *The Geology of North America.* Vol. K-2, *Quaternary Nonglacial Geology; Coterminous United States,* edited by R. B. Morrison, pp. 547–82. Boulder: Geological Society of America.
Baby, Raymond S., and Suzanne M. Langlois
  1979 Seip Mound State Memorial: Nonmortuary Aspects of Hopewell. In *Hopewell Archaeology: The Chillicothe Conference,* edited by D. Brose and N. Greber, pp. 16–18. Kent, Ohio: Kent State University Press.
Baca, Keith A.
  1993 Test Excavations at a Pre-Mississippian Platform Mound in the North-Central Hills of Mississippi. Presented at the 14th annual meeting of the Mid-South Archaeological Conference, Memphis, Tenn.
Baca, Keith A., and Evan Peacock
  1996 The Brogan Mound, a Middle Woodland Site in Clay County, Mississippi. In *Mounds, Embankments, and Ceremonialism in the Midsouth,* edited by Robert C. Mainfort and R. Walling, pp. 12–21. Arkansas Archeological Survey Research Series No. 46, Fayetteville.
Bacon, Willard S.
  1975 Additional Data on Site 40-FR-47, Franklin County, Tennessee. *Tennessee Archaeologist* 31(2):98–103.
  1982 Structural Data Recovered from the Banks III Site (40-CF-108) and the Parks Site (40-CF-5), Normandy Reservoir, Coffee County, Tennessee. *Tennessee Anthropologist* 7(2):176–97.
Bacon, Willard S., and H. L. Merryman
  1973 *Salvage Archaeology at 40-FR-47.* Miscellaneous Paper 11, Tennessee Archaeological Society, Knoxville.

Bailey, Garrick A. (editor)
  1995   *The Osage and the Invisible World: From the Works of Francis La Flesche.* Norman
          and London: University of Oklahoma Press.
Baker, Charles M.
  1974   Preliminary Investigations at the Mill Creek Site, 3ST12, Stone County, Arkansas.
          Arkansas Archeologist 15:1–17.
Bareis, Charles J., and James W. Porter (editors)
  1984   *American Bottom Archaeology: A Summary of the FAI-270 Project Contribution
          to the Culture History of the Mississippi River Valley.* Urbana: University of Illi-
          nois Press.
Barker, Alex W.
  1992   Powhatan's Pursestrings: On the Meaning of Surplus in a Seventeenth Century
          Algonkian Chiefdom. In *Lords of the Southeast: Social Inequality and the Native
          Elites of Southeastern North America,* edited by Alex W. Barker and Timothy R.
          Pauketat, pp. 61–80. Archaeological Papers of the American Anthropological As-
          sociation No. 3, Washington, D.C.
  1999   *Chiefdoms and the Economics of Perversity.* Ph.D. dissertation, Department of
          Anthropology, University of Michigan, Ann Arbor.
Barker, Alex W., and Timothy R. Pauketat (editors)
  1992   *Lords of the Southeast: Social Inequality and the Native Elites of Southeastern
          North America.* Archeological Papers of the American Anthropological Associa-
          tion No. 3, Washington, D.C.
Barry, Roger G.
  1992   *Mountain Weather and Climate.* 2d ed. New York: Rutledge.
Bass, Quentin R. II
  1977   *Prehistoric Settlement and Subsistence Patterns in the Great Smoky Mountains.*
          University of Tennessee. Report submitted to the National Park Service (Contract
          No. CX500050211).
Baugh, S. T.
  1982   Radiocarbon Dates for the McCutchan-McLaughlin Site, 34LT-11. *Bulletin of the
          Oklahoma Anthropological Society* 30(2):4–8.
Beck, Lane A.
  1995   Regional Cults and Ethnic Boundaries in "Southern Hopewell." In *Regional Ap-
          proaches to Mortuary Analysis,* edited by Lane Beck, pp. 167–87. New York and
          London: Plenum Press.
Beers, Bridget A.
  1997   *Middle Woodland Subsistence: Floral Remains from 8Le120A, A Swift Creek Site
          in Leon County, Florida.* Master's thesis, Department of Anthropology, Florida
          State University, Tallahassee.
Bell, James
  1883   Mounds in Alachua County, Florida. *Annual Report of the Smithsonian Institu-
          tion, 1880–1881,* pp. 636–37. Washington, D.C.
Bell, Robert E.
  1980   Fourche Maline: An Archaeological Manifestation in Eastern Oklahoma. *Louisi-
          ana Archaeology* 6:83–125.
  1984   Arkansas Valley Caddoan: The Harlan Phase. In *Prehistory of Oklahoma,* edited
          by R. E. Bell, pp. 221–40. Orlando: Academic Press.
Bell, Robert E., and David A. Baerreis
  1951   A Survey of Oklahoma Archaeology. *Bulletin of the Texas Archaeological and
          Paleontological Society* 22:7–100.

Bell, Robert E., and C. Dale
1953   The Morris Site, CK-39, Cherokee County, Oklahoma. *Bulletin of the Texas Ar-cheological and Paleontological Society* 24:69–140.
Belmont, John S.
1961   *The Peabody Excavations, Coahoma County, Mississippi, 1901–1902.* Bachelor's thesis, Department of Anthropology, Harvard University, Cambridge.
1967   The Culture Sequence at the Greenhouse Site, Louisiana. *Southeastern Archaeo-logical Conference Bulletin* 6:27–34.
1980   *Gold Mine (16RI13): Preliminary Report on the 1980 Season.* Ms. on file, Center for Archaeology, Department of Anthropology, Tulane University, New Orleans.
1983   Appendix D: Faunal Remains. D.1 Analysis of the Bone and Shell. In *Excavations at the Lake George Site, Yazoo County, Mississippi, 1958–1960,* edited by Stephen Williams and Jeffery P. Brain, pp. 453–69. Papers of the Peabody Museum of Archaeology and Ethnology, Vol. 74, Harvard University, Cambridge.
1984   The Troyville Concept and the Gold Mine Site. *Louisiana Archaeology* 9:65–98.
1985   A Reconnaissance of the Boeuf Basin, Louisiana.*Louisiana Archaeology*10:271–84.
Belmont, John S., and Stephen Williams
1981   Painted Pottery Horizons in the Southern Lower Mississippi Valley. In *Traces of Prehistory: Papers in Honor of William G. Haag,* edited by F. H. West and Robert W. Neuman, pp. 19–42. Geoscience and Man 22, Geoscience Publications, De-partment of Geography and Anthropology, Louisiana State University, Baton Rouge.
Belovich, Stephanie J.
1998   Defensive or Sacred? An Early Late Woodland Enclosure in Northeastern Ohio. In *Ancient Earthen Enclosures of the Eastern Woodlands,* edited by Robert C. Main-fort, Jr., and Lynne P. Sullivan, pp. 154–80. Gainesville: University Press of Florida.
Bender, Barbara
1993   *Landscape Politics and Perspectives.* Oxford: Berg.
Bense, Judith A.
1969   *Excavations at the Bird Hammock Site (8Wa30), Wakulla County, Florida.* Master's thesis, Department of Anthropology, Florida State University, Tallahassee.
1985   *Hawkshaw: Prehistory and History in an Urban Neighborhood in Pensacola, Florida.* Reports of Investigations 7, University of West Florida, Office of Cul-tural and Archaeological Research, Pensacola.
1994   *Archaeology of the Southeastern United States: Paleoindian to World War I.* San Diego: Academic Press.
1998   Santa Rosa–Swift Creek in Northwest Florida. In *A World Engraved: Archaeol-ogy of the Swift Creek Culture,* edited by J. Mark Williams and Daniel T. Elliott, pp. 247–73. Tuscaloosa: University of Alabama Press.
Bense, Judith A., and Thomas C. Watson
1977   *A Swift Creek–Weeden Island Village Complex in the St. Andrew Bay System of the Northwest Florida Gulf Coast: Analysis and Implications.* Ms. on file, Depart-ment of Sociology, Anthropology, and Social Sciences, University of West Florida, Pensacola.
1979   A Swift Creek and Weeden Island "Ring Midden" in the St. Andrews Bay Drain-age System on the Northwest Florida Gulf Coast. *Journal of Alabama Archaeol-ogy* 25:85–137.
Bentz, Charles, Jr.
1986   *Middle and Late Woodland Settlements in Selected Areas of the Mid-South: A View from the Middle Duck River Drainage of Tennessee.* Master's thesis, Depart-ment of Anthropology, University of Tennessee, Knoxville.

Bentz, Charles, Jr. (editor)

1995 *The Aenon Creek Site (40MU493): Late Archaic, Middle Woodland, and Historic Settlement and Subsistence in Middle Duck River Drainage of Tennessee.* Miscellaneous Publication 1, Tennessee Division of Archaeology, and Tennessee Department of Transportation, Publications in Archaeology 1, Nashville.

Bergman, Christopher A., Donald A. Miller, John F. Doershuk, Ken Duerksen, and Teresa W. Tune

1998 Early Woodland Occupation of the Northern Bluegrass: The West Runway Site (15Be391), Boone County, Kentucky. *North American Archaeologist* 19(1):13–33.

Binford, Lewis R.

1964 *Archaeological and Ethnohistorical Investigation of Cultural Diversity and Progressive Development among Aboriginal Cultures of Coastal Virginia and North Carolina.* Ph.D. dissertation, Department of Anthropology, University of Michigan, Ann Arbor.

1980 Willow Smoke and Dogs' Tails: Hunter-Gatherer Settlement Systems and Archaeological Site Formation. *American Antiquity* 45:4–20.

Bitgood, Mark J.

1989 *The Baytown Period in the Upper Tensas Basin.* Bulletin 12, Lower Mississippi Survey, Peabody Museum, Harvard University, Cambridge.

Blake, Leonard W.

1942 Survey of a Hopewell-like Site near St. Louis. *The Missouri Archaeologist* 8(1):2–7.

Blakeman, Crawford H., Jr.

1975a *Archaeological Investigations in the Upper-Central Tombigbee Valley: 1974 Season.* Submitted to the National Park Service by the Department of Anthropology, Mississippi State University.

1975b Activities of the Mississippi State University Field School in Archaeology: 1975 Season. Presented at the 32nd annual meeting of the Southeastern Archaeological Conference, Gainesville, Fla.

1976 *A Cultural Resources Survey of the Aberdeen Lock and Dam and Canal Section Areas of the Tennessee-Tombigbee Waterway: 1975.* Submitted to the National Park Service by the Department of Anthropology, Mississippi State University.

Blakeman, Crawford H., Jr., James R. Atkinson, and G. Gerald Berry

1976 *Archaeological Excavations at the Cofferdam Site, 22Lo599, Lowndes County, Mississippi.* Submitted to U.S. Army Corps of Engineers, Mobile District, by the Department of Anthropology, Mississippi State University.

Blanton, Dennis B., Christopher T. Espenshade, and Paul E. Brockington, Jr.

1986 *An Archaeological Study of 38Su83: A Yadkin Phase Site in the Upper Coastal Plain of South Carolina.* Submitted to the South Carolina Department of Transportation by Garrow and Associates, Inc., Atlanta, Ga.

Blanton, Richard

1995 Patterns of Exchange and the Social Production of Pigs in Highland New Guinea: Their Relevance to Questions about the Origins and Evolution of Agriculture. *Journal of Archaeological Research* 3:113–45.

Blitz, John H.

1984 *A Cultural Resources Survey in the Tombigbee National Forest, Mississippi.* USDA Forest Service, National Forests in Mississippi, Jackson.

1986 The McRae Mound: A Middle Woodland Site in Southeastern Mississippi. *Mississippi Archaeology* 21(2):11–40.

1988   Adoption of the Bow in Prehistoric North America. *North American Archaeologist* 9(2):123–45.

1993   *Ancient Chiefdoms of the Tombigbee.* Tuscaloosa: University of Alabama Press.

Blitz, John, and C. Baxter Mann

2000   *Fisherfolk, Farmers, and Frenchmen: Archaeological Explorations on the Mississippi Gulf Coast.* Archaeological Report 30, Mississippi Department of Archives and History, Jackson.

Bogan, Arthur E.

1982   Archeological Evidence of Subsistence Patterns in the Little Tennessee River Valley. *Tennessee Anthropologist* 7(1):38–50.

1987   Molluscan Remains from the Milner Site (22YZ515) and the O'Neil Site (22YZ624), Yazoo County, Mississippi. Appendix D in *Data Recovery at the Milner (22YZ515) and O'Neil Creek (22YZ624) Sites, Yazoo County, Mississippi,* edited by Lorraine Heartfield, G. R. Dennis Price, and Glen S. Greene, pp. D-1 to D-11. Submitted to the U.S. Army Corps of Engineers, Vicksburg District, by Heartfield, Price and Greene, Inc., Monroe, La.

Bogan, Arthur E., and Cynthia M. Bogan

1985   Faunal Remains. In *Archaeological Contexts and Assemblages at Martin Farm,* edited by Gerald F. Schroedl, R. P. Stephen Davis, Jr., and C. Clifford Boyd, Jr., pp. 369–410. Report of Investigations 39, University of Tennessee, Department of Anthropology, Knoxville.

Bohannon, Charles P.

1972   *Excavations at the Pharr Mounds, Prentiss and Itawamba Counties, Mississippi, and Excavations at the Bear Creek Site, Tishomingo County, Mississippi.* National Park Service, Washington, D.C.

Bond, C. L.

1977   Spinach Patch Site and the River Bank Site. In *Ozark Reservoir Papers: Archeology in West-Central Arkansas, 1965–1970,* edited by M. P. Hoffman, pp. 81–137. Arkansas Archeological Survey Research Series No. 10, Fayetteville.

Booth, Donald L., and Brad Koldehoff

1999   *The EWF Project: Archaeological Investigations for the 1998 Metro East Ditch Cleanout Project in Madison and St. Clair Counties, Illinois.* Research Reports No. 62, Illinois Transportation Archaeological Research Program, University of Illinois, Urbana.

Borremans, Nina T.

1991   North Peninsular Gulf Coast, 500 B.C.–A.D. 1600. In *Florida's Comprehensive Historic Preservation Plan* (draft version of March 18, 1991), pp. 81–88. Division of Historical Resources, Florida Department of State, Tallahassee.

Bourdieu, Pierre

1977   *Outline of a Theory of Practice.* Cambridge: Cambridge University Press.

Bowen, William Rowe

1982   *Archaeological Investigations at 9Ck(DOT)7 Cherokee County, Georgia.* Occasional Papers in Cultural Resource Management 1, Georgia Department of Transportation, Atlanta.

1989   *An Examination of Subsistence, Settlement, and Chronology during the Early Woodland Kellogg Phase in the Piedmont Physiographic Province of the Southeastern United States.* Ph.D. dissertation, Department of Anthropology, University of Tennessee, Knoxville.

Boyd, Clifford C., Jr.

1986   *Archaeological Investigations in the Watauga Reservoir, Carter and Johnson Coun-*

ties, Tennessee. Report of Investigations 44, Department of Anthropology, University of Tennessee, Knoxville.

Boyd, C. Clifford, Jr., and Donna C. Boyd
  1997   Osteological Comparison of Prehistoric Native Americans from Southwest Virginia and East Tennessee Mortuary Caves. *Journal of Cave and Karst Studies (National Speleological Society Bulletin)* 59:160–65.

Boyd, Donna, and Clifford Boyd
  1992   Late Woodland Mortuary Variability in Virginia. In *Middle and Late Woodland Research in Virginia,* edited by Theodore Reinhart and M. E. Hodges, pp. 249–76. Special Publication No. 29, Archaeological Society of Virginia, Richmond.

Brain, Jeffrey P.
  1978   Late Prehistoric Settlement Patterning in the Yazoo Basin and Natchez Bluffs Regions of the Lower Mississippi Valley. In *Mississippian Settlement Patterns,* edited by Bruce D. Smith, pp. 331–68. New York: Academic Press.
  1989   *Winterville: Late Prehistoric Culture Contact in the Lower Mississippi Valley.* Archaeological Report 23, Mississippi Department of Archives and History, Jackson.

Brandewie, Ernest
  1991   The Place of the Big Man in Traditional Hagen Society in the Central Highlands of New Guinea. In *Anthropological Approaches to Political Behavior,* edited by F. McGlynn and A. Tuden, pp. 62–82. Pittsburgh: University of Pittsburgh Press.

Braun, David P.
  1977   *Middle Woodland–(Early) Late Woodland Social Change in the Prehistoric Central Midwestern United States.* University Microfilms, Ann Arbor, Mich.
  1983   Pots as Tools. In *Archaeological Hammers and Theories,* edited by J. A. Moore and A. S. Keene, pp. 107–34. New York: Academic Press.
  1985a   Ceramic Decorative Diversity and Illinois Woodland Regional Integration. In *Decoding Prehistoric Ceramics,* edited by Ben A. Nelson, pp. 128–53. Carbondale and Edwardsville: Southern Illinois University Press.
  1985b   Absolute Seriation: A Time-Series Approach. In *For Concordance in Archaeological Analysis: Bridging Data Structure, Quantitative, Technique, and Theory,* edited by Christopher Carr, pp. 509–39. Kansas City: Westview Press.

Braun, David P., and Stephen Plog
  1982   Evolution of "Tribal" Social Networks: Theory and Prehistoric North American Evidence. *American Antiquity* 47(3):504–25.

Braun, E. Lucy
  1950   *Deciduous Forests of Eastern North America.* Philadelphia: Blakiston.

Bray, J. R., and J. T. Curtis
  1957   An Ordination of the Upland Forest Communities of Southern Wisconsin. *Ecological Monographs* 27:325–49.

Breitburg, Emanuel
  1986   Paleoenvironmental Exploitation Strategies: The Faunal Data. In *Penitentiary Branch: A Late Archaic Cumberland River Shell Midden in Middle Tennessee,* by Patricia A. Cridlebaugh, pp. 87–125. Report of Investigations 4, Division of Archaeology, Tennessee Department of Conservation, Nashville.
  1998   Faunal Remains. In *Archaeological Data Recovery at the McNight Site (22Co560), Coahoma County, Mississippi,* by S. Chapman and R. Walling, pp. 209–16. Report prepared for the Mississippi Department of Transportation by Panamerican Consultants, Inc., Memphis.

Bronk Ramsey, C.
  1994   Analysis of Chronological Information and Radiocarbon Calibration: The Pro-
          gram OxCal. *Archaeological Computing Newsletter* 41:11–16.
  1995   Radiocarbon Calibration and Analysis of Stratigraphy: The OxCal Program. *Ra-
          diocarbon* 37(2):425–30.
Brookes, Samuel O.
  1976   *The Grand Gulf Mound: Salvage Excavation of an Early Marksville Burial Mound
          in Claiborne County, Mississippi.* Archaeological Report 1, Mississippi Depart-
          ment of Archives and History, Jackson.
  1980   *The Peabody Phase in the Upper Sunflower Region.* Master's thesis, Department
          of Anthropology, University of Mississippi, Oxford.
  1988   Foreword. In *Early Marksville Phases in the Lower Mississippi Valley: A Study of
          Culture Contact Dynamics,* by E. A. Toth, pp. ix–xiv. Archaeological Report 21,
          Mississippi Department of Archives and History, Jackson.
Brookes, Samuel O., and John Connaway
  1977   *Mississippi Archaeological Survey, Lowndes County, Mississippi.* Ms. on file,
          Mississippi Department of Archives and History, Jackson.
Brookes, Samuel O., and C. Taylor
  1986   Tchula Period Ceramics in the Upper Sunflower Region. In *The Tchula Period in
          the Mid-South and Lower Mississippi Valley,* edited by David H. Dye and R. C.
          Brister, pp. 23–27. Archaeological Report 17, Mississippi Department of Archives
          and History, Jackson.
Brooks, Mark J., and Veletta Canouts (assemblers)
  1984   *Modeling Subsistence Change in the Late Prehistoric Period in the Interior Lower
          Coastal Plain of South Carolina.* Anthropological Studies 6, Occasional Papers of
          the South Carolina Institute of Archaeology and Anthropology, University of South
          Carolina, Columbia.
Brooms, R. McDonald
  1980   Investigations at 1JE37, a West Jefferson Phase Site in Jefferson County, Ala-
          bama. *Journal of Alabama Archaeology* 26:87–98.
Brose, David S.
  1979a   A Speculative Model of the Role of Exchange in the Prehistory of the Eastern
          Woodlands. In *Hopewell Archaeology: The Chillicothe Conference,* edited by D.
          Brose and N. Greber, pp. 3–8. Kent, Ohio: Kent State University Press.
  1979b   An Interpretation of the Hopewellian Traits in Florida. In *Hopewell Archaeology:
          The Chillicothe Conference,* edited by D. Brose and N. Greber, pp. 141–49. Kent,
          Ohio: Kent State University Press.
  1985   The Woodland Period. In *Ancient Art of the American Woodland Indians,* by David
          S. Brose, James A. Brown, and David W. Penny, pp. 42–91. New York: Harry N.
          Abrams.
  1988   Seeing the Mid South from the Southeast: Second Century Stasis and Status. In
          *Middle Woodland Settlement and Ceremonialism in the Mid South and Lower
          Mississippi Valley,* edited by Robert C. Mainfort, Jr., pp. 147–57. Archaeological
          Report 22, Mississippi Department of Archives and History, Jackson.
Brose, David S., and N'omi Greber (editors)
  1979   *Hopewell Archaeology: The Chillicothe Conference.* Kent, Ohio: Kent State Uni-
          versity Press.
Brose, David S., and George W. Percy
  1974   Weeden Island Settlement—Subsistence and Ceremonialism: A Reappraisal in

Systemic Terms. Presented at the 37th annual meeting of the Society for American Archaeology, Washington, D.C.

Broster, John B., and Lee Schneider
1977   Settlement and Subsistence: An Analysis of Middle Woodland Sites on the South Fork of the Forked Deer River, West Tennessee. *Journal of Alabama Archaeology* 23:58–69.

Brown, C. T., C. A. Darby, J. A. Green, C. Davies, M. Williams, G. Gordon, F. Vento, and W. P. Athens
1996   *Phase III Data Recovery at Site 22PR533 for the Proposed Florida Gas Transmission Company Phase III Expansion Project, Pearl River County, Mississippi.* R. Christopher Goodwin and Associates, Inc., New Orleans.

Brown, Ian W.
1981   The Morgan Site: An Important Coles Creek Mound Complex on the Chenier Plain of Southwest Louisiana. *North American Archaeologist* 2:207–37.
1982   *The Southeastern Check Stamped Pottery Tradition: A View from Louisiana.* Midcontinental Journal of Archaeology Special Paper 4, Kent State University Press, Kent, Ohio.
1984   Late Prehistory in Coastal Louisiana: The Coles Creek Period. In *Perspectives on Gulf Coast Prehistory,* edited by Dave D. Davis, pp. 94–124. Gainesville: University Presses of Florida.
1985   Plaquemine Architectural Patterns in the Natchez Bluffs and Surrounding Regions of the Lower Mississippi Valley. *Midcontinental Journal of Archaeology* 10:251–305.
1994   Recent Trends in the Archaeology of the Southeastern United States. *Journal of Archaeological Research* 2:45–111.

Brown, James A.
1979   Charnel Houses and Mortuary Crypts: Disposal of the Dead in the Middle Woodland Period. In *Hopewell Archaeology: The Chillicothe Conference,* edited by D. Brose and N. Greber, pp. 211–19. Kent, Ohio: Kent State University Press.
1981   The Search for Rank in Prehistoric Burials. In *The Archaeology of Death,* edited by R. Chapman, I. Kinnes, and K. Randsborg, pp. 25–37. Cambridge: Cambridge University Press.
1984   *Prehistoric Southern Ozark Marginality: A Myth Exposed.* Special Publications No. 6, Missouri Archaeological Society, Columbia, Mo.
1992   Closing Commentary. In *Cultural Variability in Context: Woodland Settlements of the Mid-Ohio Valley,* edited by Mark F. Seeman, pp. 80–82. Midcontinental Journal of Archaeology Special Paper 7, Kent State University Press, Kent, Ohio.
1996   *The Spiro Ceremonial Center, the Archaeology of Arkansas Valley Caddoan Culture in Eastern Oklahoma.* Memoirs No. 29, Museum of Anthropology, University of Michigan, Ann Arbor.
1997   The Archaeology of Ancient Religion in the Eastern Woodlands. *Annual Review of Anthropology* 26:465–85.

Brown, James A., R. A. Kerber, and Howard D. Winters
1990   Trade and the Evolution of Exchange Relations at the Beginning of the Mississippian Period. In *The Mississippian Emergence,* edited by B. D. Smith, pp. 251–63. Washington, D.C.: Smithsonian Institution Press.

Brown, Malaina L.
1996   *Plant Remains from the Taylor Mounds (3DR2) Site, Southeastern Arkansas.* Master's thesis, Department of Anthropology, Washington University, St. Louis.

Brown, Margaret K. (editor)
1981   *Predictive Models in Illinois Archaeology.* Illinois Department of Conservation, Springfield.

Brown, Paul, James P. Kennett, and B. Lynn Ingram
1999   Marine Evidence for Episodic Holocene Megafloods in North America and the Northern Gulf of Mexico. *Paleoceanography* 14:498–510.

Brown, Tracy C.
1982a   Archaeological Components at the Parks Site. In *Seventh Report of the Normandy Archaeological Project,* edited by Charles H. Faulkner and Major C. R. McCollough, pp. 353–537. Report of Investigations 32, Department of Anthropology, University of Tennessee, and TVA Publications in Anthropology 29, Knoxville.
1982b   *Prehistoric Mortuary Patterning and Change in the Normandy Reservoir, Coffee County, Tennessee.* Master's thesis, Department of Anthropology, University of Tennessee, Knoxville.

Broyles, Bettye
1967   Bibliography of Pottery Type Descriptions from the Eastern United States. *Southeastern Archaeological Conference Bulletin* (Morgantown, West Virginia) 4.
1968   Reconstructed Designs from Swift Creek Complicated Stamped Sherds. *Southeastern Archaeological Conference Bulletin* (Morgantown, West Virginia) 8:49–75.

Bruseth, James E.
1998   The Development of Caddoan Polities along the Middle Red River Valley of Eastern Texas and Oklahoma. In *The Native Culture History of the Caddo: Their Place in Southeastern Archeology and Ethnography,* edited by Timothy K. Perttula and James E. Bruseth, pp. 47–68. Studies in Archeology, vol. 30, Texas Archeological Research Laboratory, University of Texas at Austin.

Buikstra, Jane E., Lyle W. Konigsberg, and Jill Burlington
1986   Fertility and the Development of Agriculture in the Prehistoric Midwest. *American Antiquity* 51(3):528–46.

Bullen, Ripley P.
1949   Indian Sites at Florida Caverns State Park. *Florida Anthropologist* 2:1–9.
1955   Stratigraphic Tests at Bluffton, Volusia County, Florida. *Florida Anthropologist* 8:1–16.
1958   *Six Sites near the Chattahoochee River in the Jim Woodruff Reservoir Area, Florida.* River Basin Survey Papers No. 14, Bulletin 169, Bureau of American Ethnology, Smithsonian Institution, Washington, D.C.
1959   The Transitional Period of Florida. *Southeastern Archaeological Conference Newsletter* 6(1):43–53.
1966   Stelae at the Crystal River Site, Florida. *American Antiquity* 31:861–65.
1972   The Orange Period of Peninsular Florida. *Florida Anthropologist* 25(2):9–33.

Burnett, B. A.
1990   The Bioarcheological Synthesis. In *Human Adaptation in the Ozark and Ouachita Mountains,* by George Sabo III, Ann M. Early, Jerome C. Rose, B. A. Burnett, L. Vogele, Jr., and J. P. Harcourt, pp. 193–220. Arkansas Archeological Survey Research Series No. 31, Fayetteville.

Bush, Deborah E.
1975   A Ceramic Analysis of the Late Adena Buckmeyer Site, Perry County, Ohio. *Michigan Archaeologist* 21:9–23.

Butler, Brian M.
1968   The Brickyard Site (40Fr–13). In *Archaeological Investigations in the Tims Ford*

Reservoir, Tennessee, edited by Charles H. Faulkner, pp. 142–213. Report of Investigations 6, Department of Anthropology, University of Tennessee, Knoxville.

1979   Hopewell Contacts in Southern Middle Tennessee. In *Hopewell Archaeology: The Chillicothe Conference,* edited by D. Brose and N. Greber, pp. 150–56. Kent, Ohio: Kent State University Press.

Butler, Brian M., and Richard W. Jefferies

1986   Crab Orchard and Early Woodland Cultures in the Middle South. In *Early Woodland Archeology,* edited by Kenneth B. Farnsworth and Thomas E. Emerson, pp. 524–34. Kampsville Seminars in Archeology No. 2, Center for American Archeology, Kampsville, Ill.

Butsch, E. A.

1991   Vertebrate Faunal Remains from the Roland Site, 3AR30, Arkansas County, Arkansas. *Arkansas Archeologist* 30:51–56.

Byrd, Kathleen M.

1974   *Tchefuncte Subsistence Patterns: Morton Shell Mound, Iberia Parish, Louisiana.* Master's thesis, Department of Geography and Anthropology, Louisiana State University, Baton Rouge.

1976a   Tchefuncte Subsistence: Information Obtained from the Excavation of the Morton Shell Mound, Iberia Parish, Louisiana. *Southeastern Archaeological Conference Bulletin* 19:70–75.

1976b   The Brackish Water Clam (*Rangea cuneata*): A Prehistoric "Staff of Life" or a Minor Food Resource. *Louisiana Archaeology* 3:23–31.

1979   Marksville Faunal Use: Material from Mansford Plantation. Presented at the 4th annual meeting of the Louisiana Archaeological Society, Baton Rouge.

1994   Tchefuncte Subsistence Practices at the Morton Shell Mound, Iberia Parish, Louisiana. *Louisiana Archaeology* 16:1–128.

Byrd, John E.

1997   The Analysis of Diversity in Archaeological Faunal Assemblages: Complexity and Subsistence Strategies in the Southeast during the Middle Woodland Period. *Journal of Anthropological Archaeology* 16:49–72.

1999   Ceramic Types and Typology in Northeastern North Carolina: The View from the Davenport Site (31BR39). *North Carolina Archaeology* 48:95–106.

Byrd, John E., and Charles L. Heath

1997   *The Rediscovery of the Tuscarora Homeland: A Final Report of the Archaeological Survey of the Contentnea Creek Drainage.* Submitted to the Office of State Archaeology, Raleigh, by David S. Phelps Archaeology Laboratory, East Carolina University, Greenville.

Cable, John S., and Charles E. Cantley

1998   *Shaw Air Force Base: Archeological Data Recovery at Sites 38SU45, 38SU133, and 38SU145, with Results of Test Excavations Conducted at Sites 38SU136, 38SU137, and 38SU141, Poinsett Electronic Combat Range, Sumter County, South Carolina.* Submitted to the U.S. Army Corps of Engineers, Fort Worth District, by Geo-Marine, Plano, Texas.

Cable, John S., and Leslie E. Raymer

1991   *Archeological Test Excavations at the Lake Acworth (9Co45) and Butler Creek (9Co46) Sites: Two Prehistoric Settlements in the Piedmont Uplands, Allatoona Lake, Cobb County, Georgia.* NSA Technical Report 54, New South Associates, Stone Mountain, Ga.

Cable, John S., Kenneth F. Styer, and Charles E. Cantley

1998   *Data Recovery Excavations at the Maple Swamp (38HR309) and Big Jones*

(38HR315) Sites on the Conway Bypass, Horry County, South Carolina. Submitted to the South Carolina Department of Transportation, Columbia, by New South Associates, Inc., Stone Mountain, Ga.

Caddell, Gloria M.

1981 Plant Resources, Archaeological Plain Remains, and Prehistoric Plant Use Patterns in the Central Tombigbee Valley. In *Biocultural Studies in the Gainesville Lake Area,* by Gloria Caddell, Anne Woodrick, and Mary C. Hill, pp. 1–90. Report of Investigations 14, University of Alabama Office of Archaeological Research, Tuscaloosa.

1982 *Plant Resources, Archaeological Plant Remains, and Prehistoric Plant-Use Patterns in the Central Tombigbee River Valley.* Alabama Museum of Natural History Bulletin 7, Tuscaloosa.

1983 Floral Remains from the Lubbub Creek Archaeological Locality. In *Prehistoric Agricultural Communities in West Central Alabama,* vol. 2, edited by C. S. Peebles, pp. 194–271. U.S. Army Corps of Engineers, Mobile District.

Calabrese, F. A.

1976 *Excavations at 40RH6, Watts Bar Area, Rhea County, Tennessee.* Department of Sociology and Anthropology, University of Tennessee at Chattanooga (TVA Contract TV-37351A). Published by the Tennessee Valley Authority, Knoxville.

Caldwell, Joseph R.

1952 The Archaeology of Eastern Georgia to South Carolina. In *Archeology of Eastern United States,* edited by James B. Griffin, pp. 312–21. Chicago: University of Chicago Press.

1958 *Trend and Tradition in the Prehistory of the Eastern United States,* American Anthropological Association Memoir 88, Menasha, Wis.

1964 Interaction Spheres in Prehistory. In *Hopewellian Studies,* edited by Joseph R. Caldwell and Robert L. Hall, pp. 133–43. Scientific Papers 12, Illinois State Museum, Springfield.

1970 Chronology of the Georgia Coast. *Southeastern Archaeological Conference Bulletin* 13:88–92.

1971 *Historical and Archaeological Investigation in the Wallace Reservoir of the Georgia Power Company. Contract proposal submitted to the Georgia Power Company.* Ms. on file, Department of Anthropology, University of Georgia, Athens.

1978 *Report of the Excavations at Fairchild's Landing and Hare's Landing, Seminole County, Georgia,* edited by B. A. Smith. Kennesaw College. Submitted to Southeast Archeological Center, National Park Service, Tallahassee, Fla. (Contract No. 589070204).

Caldwell, Joseph R., and Antonio J. Waring, Jr.

1939 Some Chatham County Pottery Types and Their Sequence. *Southeastern Archaeological Conference Newsletter* 1(5–6). Reprinted in 1968 in *The Waring Papers: The Collected Works of Antonio J. Waring, Jr.,* edited by Stephen Williams, pp. 110–33. Papers of the Peabody Museum of Archaeology and Ethnology, Vol. 58, Harvard University, Cambridge.

Caldwell, Joseph R., Catherine McCann, and H. T. Cain

n.d. *The Deptford Site, Chatham County, Georgia.* Ms. on file, Laboratory of Archaeology Research Manuscript No. 272, University of Georgia, Athens.

Call, S. M.

1992 Molluscan Faunal Remains. In *Fort Ancient Cultural Dynamics in the Middle Ohio Valley,* edited by A. G. Henderson, pp. 243–50. Monographs in World Archaeology 8. Madison, Wis.: Prehistory Press.

Cambron, James W., and David C. Hulse
  1975   *Handbook of Alabama Archaeology: Part 1, Point Types.* Tuscaloosa: Alabama
          Archaeological Society.
Cameron, Catherine M.
  1993   Abandonment and Archaeological Interpretation. In *Abandonment of Settlements
          and Regions,* edited by C. M. Cameron and S. A. Tomka, pp. 3–7. Cambridge:
          Cambridge University Press.
Campbell, L. Janice, Christopher Hays, Paul V. Heinrich, James H. Mathews, Gregory Mikell,
A. Frank Servello, Prentice M. Thomas, Jr., and Eugene Wilson
  1988   *Cultural Resources Testing on the Mobile Bay Pipeline Project, Choctaw, Wash-
          ington and Mobile Counties, Alabama,* vol. 1. Report of Investigations No. 167,
          New World Research, Inc. Prepared for EMANCO, Inc., Fort Walton Beach, Fla.
Cantley, Charles E., Leslie E. Raymer, Johannes H. N. Loubser, and Mary Beth Reed
  1997   *Phase III Data Recovery at Four Prehistoric Sites in the Horton Creek Reservoir
          Project Area, Fayette County, Georgia,* 2 vols. NSA Technical Report 316, New
          South Associates, Stone Mountain, Ga.
Cantwell, Anna-Marie
  1980   *Dickson Camp and Pond: Two Early Havana Tradition Sites in the Central Illi-
          nois Valley.* Illinois State Museum Reports of Investigations No. 36, Springfield.
Carleton, Kenneth H.
  1999   Nanih Waiya Mounds (22Wi500): An Archaeological and Historical Overview.
          Mississippi Archaeology 34:125–55.
Carneiro, R. L.
  1967   On the Relationship between Size of Population and Complexity of Social Orga-
          nization. *Southwestern Journal of Anthropology* 23:234–43.
Carpenter, Edmund S.
  1950   Five Sites of the Intermediate Period. *American Antiquity* 15:298–314.
Carr, Christopher, and Herbert Haas
  1996   Beta-Count and AMS Radiocarbon Dates of Woodland and Fort Ancient Period
          Occupations in Ohio, 1350 B.C.– A.D. 1650. *West Virginia Archaeologist* 48(1,
          2):19–53.
Carr, Holly Ann
  1982   Preliminary Analysis of the Faunal Remains. In *Powell Canal,* edited by John H.
          House. Arkansas Archeological Survey Research Series 19, Fayetteville.
Carr, R. S.
  1975   *An Archaeological and Historical Survey of Lake Okeechobee.* Miscellaneous
          Project Report Series Number 22, Division of Archives, History and Records
          Management, Bureau of Historic Sites and Properties, Tallahassee, Fla.
  1985   Prehistoric Circular Earthworks in South Florida. *Florida Anthropologist* 38:288–
          301.
Carr, R. S., and J. G. Beriault
  1984   Prehistoric Man in South Florida. In *Environments of South Florida Present and
          Past II,* edited by Patrick J. Gleason, pp. 1–19. Coral Gables, Fla.: Miami Geo-
          logical Society.
Carskadden, Jeff, and Tim Gregg
  1974   Excavation of an Adena Open Site, Duncan Falls, Ohio. *Ohio Archaeologist* 24:4–
          7.
Casey, Joanna L.
  1987   Aboriginal and Modern Mussel Assemblages of the Lower Cumberland River.
          Southeastern Archaeology 6(2):115–24.

Chapman, Carl H.
1948a A Preliminary Survey of Missouri Archaeology: Part 3, Woodland Cultures and the Ozark Bluff Dwellers. *The Missouri Archaeologist* 10(3).
1948b A Preliminary Survey of Missouri Archaeology: Part 4, Ancient Cultures and Sequences. *The Missouri Archaeologist* 10(4).
1980 *The Archaeology of Missouri, II.* Columbia: University of Missouri Press.
Chapman, Jefferson
1973 *The Icehouse Bottom Site, 40MR23.* Report of Investigations 13, Department of Anthropology, University of Tennessee, Knoxville.
1975 *The Rose Island Site and the Bifurcate Tradition.* Report of Investigations 14, Department of Anthropology, University of Tennessee, Knoxville.
1979 *Archaeological Investigations at the Howard (40MR66) and Calloway Island (40MR41) Sites.* Report of Investigations 27, Department of Anthropology, University of Tennessee, and TVA Publications 23, Knoxville.
1981 *The Bacon Bend and Iddins Sites: The Late Archaic Period in the Lower Little Tennessee River Valley.* Report of Investigations 31, Department of Anthropology, University of Tennessee, and TVA Publications in Anthropology 25, Knoxville.
1985a *Tellico Archaeology: 12,000 Years of Native American History.* Report of Investigations 43, Department of Anthropology, University of Tennessee, Knoxville. Published by the Tennessee Valley Authority.
1985b Archaeology and the Archaic Period in the Southern Ridge-and-Valley Province. In *Structure and Process in Southeastern Archaeology,* edited by Roy S. Dickens, Jr., and H. Trawick Ward, pp. 137–53. Tuscaloosa: University of Alabama Press.
1987 The Kittrell Mound and an Assessment of Burial Mound Construction in the Southern Ridge and Valley Province. *Tennessee Anthropologist* 12:51–73.
Chapman, Jefferson, and Gary D. Crites
1987 Evidence for Early Maize (*Zea mays*) from the Icehouse Bottom Site, Tennessee. *American Antiquity* 52:352–54.
Chapman, Jefferson, and Bennie C. Keel
1979 Candy Creek–Connestee Components in Eastern Tennessee and Western North Carolina and Their Relationship with Adena-Hopewell. In *Hopewell Archaeology: The Chillicothe Conference,* edited by D. Brose and N. Greber, pp. 157–61. Kent, Ohio: Kent State University Press.
Chapman, Jefferson, and Andrea Brewer Shea
1981 The Archaeobotanical Record: Early Archaic Period to Contact in the Lower Little Tennessee River Valley. *Tennessee Anthropologist* 6:61–84.
Chapman, Jefferson, Paul A. Delcourt, Patricia A. Cridlebaugh, Andrea Shea, and Hazel R. Delcourt
1982 Man-Land Interaction: 10,000 Years of American Indian Impact on Native Ecosystems in the Lower Little Tennessee River Valley, Eastern Tennessee. *Southeastern Archaeology* 1:115–21.
Chapman, John
1990 Social Inequality on Bulgarian Tells and the Varna Problem. In *The Social Archaeology of Houses,* edited by R. Samson, pp. 49–92. Edinburgh: Edinburgh University Press.
Charles, Douglas K., and Jane E. Buikstra
1983 Archaic Mortuary Sites in the Central Mississippi Drainage: Distribution, Structure, and Behavioral Implications. In *Archaic Hunters and Gatherers in the American Midwest,* edited by J. L. Phillips and J. A. Brown, pp. 117–45. New York: Academic Press.

Charles, Frank N., III
    1973   Analysis of Molluscan Remains from the Higgs and Doughty Sites. Appendix IV
            in *Excavation of the Higgs and Doughty Sites, I-75 Salvage Archaeology,* by Ma-
            jor C. R. McCollough and Charles H. Faulkner, pp. 149–62. Miscellaneous Paper
            12, Tennessee Archaeological Society, Knoxville.
Chase, David W.
    1957   *The Quartermaster Site, 9CE42.* Ms. on file, Columbus Museum of Arts and Sci-
            ence, Columbus, Ga.
    1963   *Background of the Archeology of the Middle Chattahoochee Valley 1955–1963.*
            Ms. on file, Columbus Museum of Arts and Science, Columbus, Ga.
    1978a   Uchee Creek Site 4: 1Ru58. *Journal of Alabama Archaeology* 24(1): 52–59.
    1978b   Weeden Island–Swift Creek Affinities in the Middle Chattahoochee Valley. *Jour-
            nal of Alabama Archaeology* 24(1):60–64.
    1990   Carbon 14 Dates from Miner's Creek. *Newsletter of the Greater Atlanta Archaeo-
            logical Society* 55:1–2.
    1991   *Miner's Creek Site, 9DA91.* Report submitted to DeKalb County Parks and Recre-
            ation, Decatur, Ga.
    1998   Swift Creek: Lineage and Diffusion. In *A World Engraved: Archaeology of the
            Swift Creek Culture,* edited by J. Mark Williams and Daniel T. Elliott, pp. 48–60.
            Tuscaloosa: University of Alabama Press.
Childress, Mitchell R., and Guy G. Weaver
    1998   *National Register Eligibility Assessment of Four Archaeological Sites on Upper
            Roubidoux Creek (23PU483, 23PU458, 23PU354, 23PU264), Fort Leonard Wood,
            Pulaski County, Missouri.* Brockington and Associates, Inc., Memphis, Tennes-
            see. Submitted to the U.S. Army Construction Engineering Research Laboratory,
            Champaign, Ill.
Claassen, Cheryl
    1991a   New Hypotheses for the Demise of the Shell Mound Archaic. In *The Archaic
            Period in the Mid-South,* edited by Charles M. McNutt, pp. 66–71. Archaeologi-
            cal Report 24, Mississippi Department of Archives and History, Jackson.
    1991b   Normative Thinking and Shell-Bearing Sites. In *Archaeological Method and
            Theory,* vol. 3, edited by Michael B. Schiffer, pp. 249–98. Tucson: University of
            Arizona Press.
    1992   Shell Mounds as Burial Mounds: A Revision of the Shell Mound Archaic. In *Cur-
            rent Archaeological Research in Kentucky: Volume Two,* edited by D. Pollack and
            A. G. Henderson, pp. 1–11. Frankfort: Kentucky Heritage Council.
    1996a   Research Problems with Shells from Green River Shell Matrix Sites. In *Of Caves
            and Shell Mounds,* edited by Kenneth C. Carstens and Patty Jo Watson, pp. 132–
            39. Tuscaloosa: University of Alabama Press.
    1996b   A Consideration of the Social Organization of the Shell Mound Archaic. In *Ar-
            chaeology of the Mid-Holocene Southeast,* edited by Kenneth E. Sassaman and
            David G. Anderson, pp. 235–58. Gainesville: University Press of Florida.
Claflin, William H., Jr.
    1931   *The Stalling's Island Mound, Columbia County, Georgia.* Papers of the Peabody
            Museum of Archaeology and Ethnology, Vol. 14(1), Harvard University, Cambridge.
Claggett, Stephen R., and John S. Cable
    1982   *The Haw River Sites: Archeological Investigation at Two Stratified Sites in the
            North Carolina Piedmont,* vols. 1–3. Submitted to the U.S. Army Corps of Engi-
            neers, Wilmington District, by Commonwealth Associates, Inc. (Contract No.
            DACW54-79-C-0052).

Clark, Clifford E., Jr.

1988   Domestic Architecture as an Index to Social History: The Romantic Revival and the Cult of Domesticity in America, 1840–1870. In *Material Life in America, 1600–1860,* edited by R. B. S. George, pp. 535–49. Boston: Northeastern University Press.

Clay, R. Berle

1980   The Culture Historical Placement of Fayette Thick Ceramics in Central Kentucky. *Tennessee Anthropologist* 5:166–78.

1984   Styles of Stone Graves. In *Late Prehistoric Research in Kentucky,* edited by David Pollack, Charles Hockensmith, and Thomas Sanders, pp. 131–44. Frankfort: Kentucky Heritage Council.

1985   Peter Village 164 Years Later: A Summary of 1983 Excavations. In *Woodland Period Archaeology in Kentucky,* edited by David Pollack, Thomas Sanders, and Charles Hockensmith, pp. 1–41. Frankfort: Kentucky Heritage Council.

1986   Adena Ritual Spaces. In *Early Woodland Archaeology,* edited by Kenneth B. Farnsworth and Thomas E. Emerson, pp. 581–95. Center for American Archaeology, Kampsville, Ill.

1987   Circles and Ovals: Two Types of Adena Space. *Southeastern Archaeology* 6(1):46–55.

1988a   The Ceramic Sequence at Peter Village and Its Significance. In *New Deal Era Archaeology and Current Research in Kentucky,* edited by David Pollack and Mary Powell, pp. 105–13. Frankfort: Kentucky Heritage Council.

1988b   Peter Village: An Adena Enclosure. In *Middle Woodland Settlement and Ceremonialism in the Mid-South and Lower Mississippi Valley,* edited by Robert C. Mainfort, Jr., pp. 19–30. Archaeological Report 22, Mississippi Department of Archives and History, Jackson.

1991   Adena Ritual Development: An Organizational Type in a Temporal Perspective. In *The Human Landscape in Kentucky's Past,* edited by Charles Stout and Christine Hensley, pp. 30–39. Frankfort: Kentucky Heritage Council.

1992   Chiefs, Big Men, or What? Economy, Settlement Patterns, and Their Bearing on Adena Political Models. In *Cultural Variability in Context: Woodland Settlements of the Mid-Ohio Valley,* edited by Mark Seeman, pp. 77–80. Midcontinental Journal of Archaeology Special Paper 7, Kent State University Press, Kent, Ohio.

1998   The Essential Features of Adena Ritual and Their Implications. *Southeastern Archaeology* 17(1):1–21.

Clay, R. Berle, and Charles Niquette

1989   *Phase III Excavations at the Niebert Site (46MS103) in the Gallipolis Locks and Dam Replacement Project, Mason County, West Virginia.* Contract Publication Series 89–06, Cultural Resource Analysts, Inc., Lexington.

1992   Middle Woodland Mortuary Rituals in the Gallipolis Locks and Dam Vicinity, Mason County, West Virginia. *West Virginia Archaeologist* 44(1, 2):1–25.

Clench, William J.

1974   Mollusca from Russell Cave. In *Investigations in Russell Cave,* by John W. Griffin, pp. 86–90. Publications in Archeology 13, U.S. Department of the Interior, National Park Service, Washington, D.C.

Cobb, Charles R., and Michael S. Nassaney

1995   Interaction and Integration in the Late Woodland Southeast. In *Native American Interactions,* edited by Michael S. Nassaney and Kenneth E. Sassaman, pp. 205–26. Knoxville: University of Tennessee Press.

Cobb, James E.

1978   The Middle Woodland Occupations of the Banks V Site, 40CF111. In *Fifth Report of the Normandy Archaeological Project,* edited by Charles H. Faulkner and Major C. R. McCollough, pp. 72–327. Report of Investigations 20, Department of Anthropology, University of Tennessee, Knoxville.

1982   The Late Middle Woodland Occupation of the Eoff I Site 40CF32. In *Eighth Report of the Normandy Archaeological Project,* edited by Charles H. Faulkner and Major C. R. McCollough, pp. 149–301. Report of Investigations 33, Department of Anthropology, University of Tennessee, and TVA Publications in Anthropology 30, Knoxville.

1985   *Late Middle Woodland Settlement and Subsistence Patterns in the Eastern Highland Rim of Tennessee.* Ph.D. dissertation, Department of Anthropology, University of Tennessee, Knoxville.

Cobb, James E., and Charles H. Faulkner

1978   *The Owl Hollow Project: Middle Woodland Settlement and Subsistence Patterns in the Eastern Highland Rim of Tennessee.* Final technical report submitted to the National Science Foundation in accordance with the requirements of Grant BNS76-11266.

Cockrell, Wilburn A.

1970   *Glades I and Pre-Glades Settlement and Subsistence Patterns on Marco Island (Collier County, Florida).* Master's thesis, Department of Anthropology, Florida State University, Tallahassee.

Coe, Joffre L.

1952   The Cultural Sequence of the Carolina Piedmont. In *Archeology of Eastern United States,* edited by James B. Griffin, pp. 301–11. Chicago: University of Chicago Press.

1961   Cherokee Archaeology. In *Symposium on Cherokee and Iroquois Culture,* edited by William M. Fenton and John Gulick, pp. 53–60. Bulletin 180, Bureau of American Ethnology, Smithsonian Institution, Washington, D.C.

1964   The Formative Culture of the Carolina Piedmont. *Transactions of the American Philosophical Society* (Philadelphia) 5(5).

1995   *Town Creek Indian Mound: A Native American Legacy.* Chapel Hill: University of North Carolina Press.

Cogswell, J. W., and Michael J. O'Brien

1998   Analysis of Early Mississippian-Period Pottery from Kersey, Pemiscot County, Missouri. *Southeastern Archaeology* 17:39–52.

Colburn, Mona L.

1987   Faunal Exploitation at the Ink Bayou Site. In *Results of Final Testing for Significance at the Ink Bayou Site (3PU252), Pulaski County, Arkansas,* by D. B. Waddell, J. House, F. King, M. L. Colburn, and M. K. Marks, pp. 250–79. Submitted to the Arkansas Highway and Transportation Department by Arkansas Archeological Survey, Fayetteville.

Colburn, Mona L., and Bonnie W. Styles

1990   Faunal Remains from the Bangs Slough Site. In *Coles Creek and Mississippi Period Foragers in the Felsenthal Region of the Lower Mississippi Valley,* edited by Frank F. Schambach, pp. 95–108. Arkansas Archeological Survey Research Series No. 39, Fayetteville.

Cole, Fay Cooper, Robert Bell, J. Bennett, James R. Caldwell, N. Emerson, Richard S. MacNeish, K. Orr, and R. Willis

1951   *Kincaid: A Prehistoric Metropolis.* Chicago: University of Chicago Press.

Cole, Patricia E.

1975   *A Synthesis and Interpretation of the Hamilton Mortuary Pattern in East Tennessee.* Master's thesis, Department of Anthropology, University of Tennessee, Knoxville.

Collins, Henry B., Jr.
1927 *Archeological Work in Louisiana and Mississippi.* Smithsonian Miscellaneous Collections 78(7), U.S. Government Printing Office, Washington, D.C.
1932 Excavations at a Prehistoric Indian Village Site in Mississippi. *Proceedings of the United States National Museum* 79(32):1–22.
1941 Relationships of an Early Indian Cranial Series from Louisiana. *Washington Academy of Science Journal* 31(4):145–55.

Collins, Susan M.
1977 *A Prehistoric Community at the Macon County Industrial Park.* North Carolina Archaeological Council Publications in Archaeology 2, Division of Archives and History, North Carolina Department of Cultural Resources, Raleigh.

Connaway, John M.
1980 The Baldwin-O'Neal Dilemma. *Mississippi Archaeology* 15(1):22–29.
1981 *Archaeological Investigations in Mississippi, 1969–1977.* Archaeological Report 6, Mississippi Department of Archives and History, Jackson.

Connaway, John M., and S. O. McGahey
1971 *Archaeological Excavation at the Boyd Site, Tunica County, Mississippi.* Technical Report No. 1, Mississippi Department of Archives and History, Jackson.

Conner, Michael D.
1995 Ceramic Assemblage. In *Occupations at the Hayti Bypass Site, Pemiscot County, Missouri,* edited by Michael D. Conner, pp. 122–70. Special Publication No. 1, Center for Archaeological Research, Southwest Missouri State University, Springfield.

Conner, Michael D. (editor)
1995 *Occupations at the Hayti Bypass Site, Pemiscot County, Missouri.* Special Publication No. 1, Center for Archaeological Research, Southwest Missouri State University, Springfield.

Conner, Michael D., and Jack H. Ray
1995 Site Formation and Structure. In *Occupations at the Hayti Bypass Site, Pemiscot County, Missouri,* edited by Michael D. Conner, pp. 61–121. Special Publication No. 1, Center for Archaeological Research, Southwest Missouri State University, Springfield.

Connolly, Robert P.
1997 The Evidence for Habitation at the Fort Ancient Earthworks. In *Ohio Hopewell Community Organization,* edited by William S. Dancey and Paul J. Pacheco, pp. 251–83. Kent, Ohio: Kent State University Press.

Converse, Robert N.
1993 The Troyer Site: A Hopewell Habitation Site, and a Secular View of Hopewell Villages. *Ohio Archaeologist* 43(3):4–12.

Cook, Della C.
1986 Prehistoric Mortuary Use of a Pit Cave in Southeastern Indiana. Presented at the 51st annual meeting of the Society for American Archaeology, New Orleans.

Cook, Fred C.
1995 *An Archaeological Survey of Sidon Plantation.* Submitted to Magnolia, Outlet Mall, Brunswick, Ga.

Cooney, Gabriel
1999 Social Landscapes in Irish Prehistory. In *The Archaeology and Anthropology of Landscape,* edited by P. J. Ucko and R. Layton, pp. 46–64. New York: Routledge.

Cordell, A. S.
1992 Technological Investigation of Pottery Variability in Southwest Florida. In *Cul-*

ture and Environment in the Domain of the Calusa, edited by William H. Marquardt, pp. 105–89. Monograph No. 1, Institute of Archaeology and Paleoenvironmental Studies, University of Florida, Gainesville.

1993   Chronological Variability in Ceramic Paste: A Comparison of Deptford and Savannah Period Pottery in the St. Marys River Region of Northeast Florida and Southeast Georgia. *Southeastern Archaeology* 12:33–58.

Cotter, John L., and John M. Corbett

1951   *Archeology of the Bynum Mounds, Mississippi.* Archeological Research Series 1, National Park Service, Washington, D.C.

Cowan, C. Wesley

1975   *An Archaeological Survey and Assessment of the Proposed Red River Reservoir in Wolfe, Powell, and Menifee Counties, Kentucky.* Museum of Anthropology, University of Kentucky, Lexington.

1978   Seasonal Nutritional Stress in a Late Woodland Population: Suggestions from Some Eastern Kentucky Coprolites. *Tennessee Anthropologist* 3:117–28.

1979   Excavations at the Haystack Rockshelters. *Midcontinental Journal of Archaeology* 4:3–33.

1985   Understanding the Evolution of Plant Husbandry in Eastern North America: Lessons from Botany, Ethnography, and Archaeology. In *Prehistoric Food Production in North America,* edited by Richard I. Ford, pp. 205–43. Anthropological Papers No. 75, Museum of Anthropology, University of Michigan, Ann Arbor.

Cowan, C. Wesley, and Patty Jo Watson

1992   *Agricultural Origins in World Perspective.* Washington, D.C.: Smithsonian Institution Press.

Cox, P. E.

1929   Preliminary Report of Exploration at Old Stone Fort, Manchester, Tennessee. *Journal of the Tennessee Academy of Science* 4(1):1–8.

Cramer, Ann C.

1989   *The Dominion Land Company Site: An Early Adena Mortuary Manifestation in Franklin County, Ohio.* Master's thesis, Department of Anthropology, Kent State University, Kent, Ohio.

Crane, H. R.

1956   University of Michigan Radiocarbon Dates I. *Science* 124:665–72.

Crane, H. R., and J. B. Griffin

1963   University of Michigan Radiocarbon Dates VIII. *Radiocarbon* 5:228–53.

1966   University of Michigan Radiocarbon Dates XI. *Radiocarbon* 8:256–85.

Crawford, Robert G. H.

1966   *An Archaeological Survey of Lenoir County, North Carolina.* Master's thesis, Department of Anthropology, University of Florida, Gainesville.

Cressler, Alan M., Jan F. Simek, Todd M. Ahlman, Joanne L. Bennett, and Jay D. Franklin

1999   Prehistoric Mud Glyph Cave Art from Alabama. *Southeastern Archaeology* 18(1):35–44.

Cridlebaugh, Patricia A.

1981   *The Icehouse Bottom Site (40MR23): 1977 Excavations.* Report of Investigations 35, Department of Anthropology, University of Tennessee, Knoxville.

1984   *American Indian and Euro-American Impact upon Holocene Vegetation in the Lower Little Tennessee River Valley, East Tennessee.* Ph.D. dissertation, Department of Anthropology, University of Tennessee, Knoxville.

Crites, Gary D.

1978a   *Paleoethnobotany of the Normandy Reservoir in the Upper Duck River Valley,*

Tennessee. Master's thesis, Department of Anthropology, University of Tennessee, Knoxville.

1978b Plant Food Utilization Patterns during the Middle Woodland Owl Hollow Phase in Tennessee: A Preliminary Report. *Tennessee Anthropologist* 3:80–92.

1985 *Middle Woodland Paleoethnobotany of the Eastern Highland Rim of Tennessee: An Evolutionary Perspective on Change in Human-Plant Interaction.* Ph.D. dissertation, Department of Anthropology, University of Tennessee, Knoxville.

1991 Investigations into Early Plant Domesticates and Food Production in Middle Tennessee: A Status Report. *Tennessee Anthropologist* 16:69–87.

1997 Plant Remains from Site 31JK291. In *Archeological Data Recovery at Site 31JK291, Jackson County, North Carolina,* by Brett H. Riggs, M. Scott Shumate, and Patti Evans-Shumate, pp. 93–98. Ms. on file, Office of State Archaeology, Raleigh, N.C.

1998 Plant Remains from the Pumpkin Site (38GR226): Middle Woodland Ethnobotany on the South Carolina Piedmont. Presented at the 55th annual meeting of the Southeastern Archaeological Conference, Greenville, S.C.

Crook, Morgan R., Jr.
1990 *The Rae's Creek Site: A Multicomponent Archaeological Site at the Fall Line along the Savannah River.* Submitted to the Environmental Analysis Bureau, Georgia Department of Transportation by Department of Anthropology, Georgia State University, Atlanta.

Crothers, George M.
1987 *An Archaeological Survey of Big Bone Cave, Tennessee, and Diachronic Patterns of Cave Utilization in the Eastern Woodlands.* Master's thesis, Department of Anthropology, University of Tennessee, Knoxville.

2001 Mineral Mining and Perishable Remains in Mammoth Cave, Kentucky: Examining Social Process during the Early Woodland Period. In *Fleeting Identities: Perishable Material Culture in Archaeological Research,* edited by Penelope B. Drooker, pp. 314–34. Occasional Paper 28, Center for Archaeological Investigations, Southern Illinois University-Carbondale.

Crothers, George M., and Patty Jo Watson
1993 Archaeological Contexts in Deep Cave Sites: Examples from the Eastern Woodlands of North America. In *Formation Processes in Archaeological Context,* edited by Paul Goldberg, D. T. Nash, and D. Petraglia, pp. 53–60. Madison, Wis.: Prehistory Press.

Culpepper, Stacy, Charles L. Heath, Jeffrey D. Irwin, and Joseph M. Herbert
2000 *From Drowning Creek to Sicily: Archaeological Investigations at Fort Bragg, North Carolina.* Research Report No. 2, Cultural Resources Management Series, Fort Bragg Cultural Resources Program, Fort Bragg, N.C.

Cumbaa, Stephen L.
1972 *An Intensive Harvest Economy in North-Central Florida.* Master's thesis, Department of Anthropology, University of Florida, Gainesville.

1976 A Reconsideration of Freshwater Shellfish Exploitation in the Florida Archaic. *Florida Archaeologist* 29(2, pt. 1):49–59.

Curren, Cailup B., Jr.
1976 Prehistoric and Early Historic Occupation of the Mobile Bay and Mobile Delta Area of Alabama with an Emphasis on Subsistence. *Journal of Alabama Archaeology* 22(1):61–84.

Curren, Cailup B., Jr., Betsy Reitz, and James Walden
1977 Faunal Remains, Bone and Shell Artifacts. In *The Bellefonte Site, 1JA300,* by

Eugene M. Futato, pp. 173–91. Research Series No. 2, Office of Archaeological Research, University of Alabama, Tuscaloosa.

Curry, Dennis
  1999   *Feast of the Dead: Aboriginal Ossuaries in Maryland.* Crownsville, Md.: Maryland Historical Trust Press.
Curry, Dennis, and Maureen Kavanagh
  1991   The Middle to Late Woodland Transition in Maryland. *North American Archaeologist* 12:3–28.
Cushing, Frank H.
  1896   Explorations of Ancient Key Dwellers' Remains on the Gulf Coast of Florida. *Proceedings of the American Philosophical Society* 35:329–432.
Cusik, James G., Todd McMakin, Shannon Dawdy, and Jill-Karen Yakubik
  1994   *Environmental Assessment and Cultural Resources Documentation, Black River Bridge at Jonesville Jct. LA 3037 to LA 565, Catahoula and Concordia Parishes Route LA-US 84.* Earth Search, Inc., New Orleans.
Custer, Jay F.
  1984   *Prehistoric Delaware Archaeology: An Ecological Approach.* Newark: University of Delaware Press.
  1987a   Problems and Prospects in Northeastern Prehistoric Ceramics. *North American Archaeologist* 8(2):97–123.
  1987b   New Perspectives on the Delmarva Adena Complex. *Midcontinental Journal of Archaeology* 12:33–53.
  1989   *Prehistoric Cultures of the Delmarva Peninsula: An Archaeological Study.* Newark: University of Delaware Press.
  1994   Current Archaeological Research in the Middle Atlantic Region of the Eastern United States. *Journal of Archaeological Research* (2):329–60.
  1996   *Prehistoric Cultures of Eastern Pennsylvania.* Anthropological Series No. 7, Pennsylvania Historical and Museum Commission, Harrisburg.
Custer, Jay F., S. C. Watson, and C. A. DeSantis
  1987   An Early Woodland Household Cluster from the Clyde Farm Site (7NC-E-6), Delaware. *Journal of Field Archaeology* 4:229–35.
Custer, Jay F., Karen Rosenberg, G. Mellin, and A. Washburn
  1992   A Re-examination of the Island Field Site (7K-F-17), Delaware. *Archaeology of Eastern North America* 18:145–212.
Cutler, H. C.
  1975   Two Kinds of Gourds from Marco Island. Appendix D in *The Material Culture of Key Marco,* by M. S. Gilliland, pp. 255–56. Gainesville: University Presses of Florida.
Damon, P. E., C. W. Ferguson, A. Long, and E. T. Wallick
  1972   Dendrochronologic Calibration of the Carbon-14 Time Scale. In *Proceedings of the Eighth International Radiocarbon Dating Conference,* vol. 1, edited by T. A. Rafter and T. Grant-Taylor, pp. 44–59. Lower Hutt, New Zealand.
Dancey, William S.
  1988   The Community Plan of an Early Late Woodland Village in the Middle Scioto River Valley. *Midcontinental Journal of Archaeology* 13(2):223–58.
  1991   A Middle Woodland Settlement in Central Ohio: A Preliminary Report on the Murphy Site (33Li212). *Pennsylvania Archeologist* 61:37–72.
  1992   Village Origins in Central Ohio: The Results and Implications of Recent Middle and Late Woodland Research. In *Cultural Variability in Context: Woodland Settlements of the Mid-Ohio Valley,* edited by Mark F. Seeman, pp. 24–29. Midcontinental Journal of Archaeology Special Paper 7, Kent State University Press, Kent, Ohio.

1996   Putting an End to Ohio Hopewell. In *A View from the Core: A Synthesis of Ohio Hopewell Archaeology,* edited by Paul J. Pacheco, pp. 396–405. Columbus: Ohio Archaeological Council.

Dancey, William S., and Paul J. Pacheco
1997   A Community Model of Ohio Hopewell Settlement. In *Ohio Hopewell Community Organization,* edited by William S. Dancey and Paul J. Pacheco, pp. 3–40. Kent, Ohio: Kent State University Press.

Dancey, William S., and Paul J. Pacheco (editors)
1997   *Ohio Hopewell Community Organization.* Kent, Ohio: Kent State University Press.

Dancey, William S., Mary Lou Fricke, and Flora Church
1987   *The Water Plant Site and Other Sites in Southeastern Hamilton Township, Franklin County, Ohio.* Columbus, Ohio: The Ohio State University Research Foundation.

Davis, Dave D., Marco J. Giardino, Vickie Carpenter, and Ken Jones
1982   *Archaeological Survey of Grand Bayou, St. Charles Parish, Louisiana.* Ms. on file, Office of the State Archaeologist, Louisiana Division of Archaeology, Baton Rouge.

Davis, Donald B., and Valerie A. Haskins
1993   A Preliminary Investigation of Mississippian Mud Glyphs in a Warren County Cave. Presented at the Eastern States Rock Art Conference, Natural Bridge State Park, Kentucky.

Davis, Hester A.
1966   Nine Days at the Toltec Site, the Society's Third Successful Dig. *Field Notes* (Arkansas Archeological Society, Fayetteville) 20:2–5.
1967   The Puzzle of Point Remove. *Field Notes* (Arkansas Archeological Society, Fayetteville) 33:2–7.
1996   Life in the Foothills: Archeology of the Little Red River in North-Central Arkansas. Presented at the 61st annual meeting of the Society for American Archaeology, New Orleans.

Davis, Hester A., Don G. Wyckoff, and M. A. Holmes (editors)
1971   *Proceedings of the Eighth Caddo Conference.* Occasional Publication No. 2, Oklahoma Archeological Society, University of Oklahoma, Norman.

Davis, R. P. Stephen, Jr.
1978   1975 Excavations at the Wiser-Stephens I Site (40CF81). In *Sixth Report of the Normandy Archaeological Project,* edited by Major C. R. McCollough and Charles H. Faulkner, pp. 291–547. Report of Investigations 21, University of Tennessee, Department of Anthropology/Notes in Anthropology 4, Laboratory of Anthropology, Wright State University/TVA Publications in Anthropology 19, Knoxville.
1990   *Aboriginal Settlement Patterns in the Lower Little Tennessee River Valley.* Report of Investigations 50, Department of Anthropology, University of Tennessee, and TVA Publications in Anthropology 54, Knoxville.

DeJarnette, David L., Edward B. Kurjack, and Bennie C. Keel
1973   Weiss Reservoir. *Journal of Alabama Archaeology* 19(2).

Delcourt, Hazel R.
1976   Presettlement Vegetation of the North of Red River Land District, Louisiana. *Castanea* 41:122–39.

Delcourt, Hazel R., and Paul A. Delcourt
1985   Quaternary Palynology and Vegetational History of the Southeastern United States. In *Pollen Records of Late-Quaternary North American Sediments,* edited by V. M. Bryant, Jr., and R. G. Holloway, pp. 1–37. American Association of Stratigraphic Palynologists Foundation, Dallas, Texas.

1996   Quaternary Paleoecology of the Lower Mississippi Valley. *Engineering Geology* 45:219–42.

Delcourt, Paul A., Hazel R. Delcourt, Cecil R. Ison, William E. Sharp, and Kristen J. Gremillion
1998   Prehistoric Human Use of Fire, the Eastern Agricultural Complex, and Appalachian Oak-Chestnut Forests: Paleoecology of Cliff Palace Pond, Kentucky. *American Antiquity* 63:263–78.

DeLeon, Mark F.
1981   *A Study of the Environment and Prehistoric Occupation in the Black Creek Basin of the Piney Woods of South Mississippi.* Master's thesis, Department of Anthropology and Sociology, University of Southern Mississippi, Hattiesburg.

Denny, Sidney
1976   *A Report of Archaeological Inventory Reconnaissance for the Proposed Richland Creek Abatement Project in the Vicinity of Belleville, Illinois.* Department of Anthropology, Southern Illinois University, Edwardsville. Submitted to the Illinois Department of Transportation, Springfield.

Denny, Sidney G., and James Anderson
1972   An Archaeological Survey of the Upland Areas Adjacent to the American Bottoms Region. In *Preliminary Report of 1972 Historic Sites Survey Archaeological Reconnaissance of Selected Areas in the State of Illinois: Part I, Summary Section B,* pp. 126–28. Illinois Department of Conservation, Springfield.
1974   An Archaeological Survey of the Upland Areas Adjacent to the American Bottoms Region. In *Preliminary Report of 1973 Historic Sites Survey Archaeological Reconnaissance of Selected Areas in the State of Illinois; Part I, Summary Section B,* pp. 126–28. Illinois Department of Conservation, Springfield.

Dent, Richard J.
1995   *Chesapeake Prehistory: Old Traditions, New Directions.* New York: Plenum Press.

DePratter, Chester B.
1979   Ceramics. In *The Anthropology of St. Catherines Island: The Refuge-Deptford Mortuary Complex,* edited by David H. Thomas and Clark S. Larsen, pp. 109–32. Anthropological Papers of the American Museum of Natural History 56(1), New York.
1991   *W.P.A. Archaeological Excavations in Chatham County, Georgia: 1937–1942.* Laboratory of Archaeology Series 29, Department of Anthropology, University of Georgia, Athens.

Derley, J.
1979   The Honey Creek Point: A Prairie County Original? *Field Notes* (Arkansas Archeological Society, Fayetteville) 170:5.

Dewar, Robert E.
1991   Incorporating Variation in Occupation Span into Settlement Pattern Analysis. *American Antiquity* 56:604–20.

Dewar, Robert E., and Kevin A. McBride
1992   Remnant Settlement Patterns. In *Space, Time, and Archaeological Landscapes,* edited by J. Rossignol and L. Wandsnider, pp. 227–55. New York: Plenum Press.

Diaz-Granados, Carol
1993   *The Petroglyphs and Pictographs of Missouri: A Distributional, Stylistic, Contextual, Functional, and Temporal Analysis of the State's Rock Graphics.* Ph.D. dissertation, Department of Anthropology, Washington University, St. Louis.
1999   Interpretation of the Rock Art Images. In *National Register Eligibility Assessments of Seven Prehistoric Archaeological Sites at Fort Leonard Wood, Missouri,* by Steven R. Ahler, David L. Asch, Dawn E. Harn, Bonnie W. Styles, Karli White, Carol Diaz-Granados, and David Ryckman, pp. 215–18. Quaternary Studies Pro-

gram Technical Report 98-1202-28, Illinois State Museum, Springfield.

DiBlasi, Philip J.

1996 Prehistoric Expressions from the Central Kentucky Karst. In *Of Caves and Shell Mounds,* edited by Kenneth C. Carstens and Patty Jo Watson, pp. 40–47. Tuscaloosa: University of Alabama Press.

Dickens, Roy S., Jr.

1971 Archaeology in the Jones Bluff Reservoir of Central Alabama. *Journal of Alabama Archaeology* 17:1–107.

1975 A Processual Approach to Mississippian Origins on the Georgia Piedmont. *Southeastern Archaeological Conference Bulletin* 18:31–42.

1976 *Cherokee Prehistory: The Pisgah Phase in the Appalachian Summit Region.* Knoxville: University of Tennessee Press.

Dickens, Roy S., Jr., H. Trawick Ward, and R. P. Stephen Davis, Jr. (editors)

1987 *The Siouan Project: Seasons I and II.* Monograph Series No. 1, Research Laboratories of Anthropology, University of North Carolina, Chapel Hill.

Dickinson, S. D., and H. J. Lemley

1939 Evidences of the Marksville and Coles Creek Complexes at the Kirkham Place, Clark County, Arkansas. *Texas Archeological and Paleontological Society Bulletin* 11:139–89.

Doran, Glen H., and Bruce J. Piateck

1985 *Archaeological Investigations at Naval Live Oaks, Studies in Spatial Patterning and Chronology in the Gulf Coast of Florida.* Ms. on file, Southeast Archeological Center, National Park Service, Tallahassee, Fla.

Douglas, Joe (editor)

1997 *Hubbard's Cave: Preliminary Historic Preservation Report.* Report to the Nature Conservancy, Arlington, Va.

Dowd, John T.

1989 *The Anderson Site: Middle Archaic Adaptation in Tennessee's Central Basin.* Miscellaneous Paper No. 13, Tennessee Anthropological Association, Knoxville.

Dragoo, Don W.

1963 *Mounds for the Dead.* Annals of the Carnegie Museum 37, Pittsburgh.

1964 The Development of Adena and Its Role in the Formation of Ohio Hopewell. In *Hopewellian Studies,* edited by Joseph R. Caldwell and Robert L. Hall, pp. 2–34. Scientific Papers 12, Illinois State Museum, Springfield.

1976 Some Aspects of Eastern North American Prehistory: A Review 1975. *American Antiquity* 41(1):3–27.

Drucker, Lesley M., and Susan Jackson

1984 *Shell in Motion: An Archaeological Study of Minim Island National Register Site, Georgetown County, South Carolina.* Resource Studies Series 73, Carolina Archaeological Services, Columbia.

Duerksen, Ken, John F. Doershuk, Christopher A. Bergman, Teresa W. Tune, and Donald A. Miller

1995 Fayette Thick Ceramic Chronology at the West Runway Site (15Be391), Boone County, Kentucky. In *Current Archaeological Research in Kentucky: Volume 3,* edited by John F. Doershuk, Christopher A. Bergman, and David Pollack, pp. 70–88. Frankfort: Kentucky Heritage Council.

Duggan, Betty J.

1982 *A Synthesis of the Late Woodland Mason Phase in the Normandy and Tims Ford Reservoirs in Middle Tennessee.* Master's thesis, Department of Anthropology, University of Tennessee, Knoxville.

Dunavan, S. L.
   1992   Archeobotanical Remains from the 1990 Excavations at 3MR80-D Buffalo Na-
           tional River, Arkansas. In *Archeological Investigations at 3MR80-Area D in the
           Rush Development Area, Buffalo National River, Arkansas,* vol. 2., by R. L.
           Guendling, George Sabo III, M. J. Guccione, S. L. Dunavan, and Susan L. Scott,
           pp. 87–98. Southwest Cultural Resources Center Professional Papers No. 50, Santa
           Fe.
Dunbar, Gary S.
   1966   Thermal Belts in North Carolina. *Geographical Review* 56:516–26.
Dunham, Gary
   1994   *Common Ground, Contested Visions: The Emergence of Burial Mound Ritual in
           Late Prehistoric Central Virginia.* Ph.D. dissertation, Department of Anthropol-
           ogy, University of Virginia, Charlottesville. University Microfilms, Ann Arbor, Mich.
Dunn, Michael C.
   1999   *An Analysis of Lithic Artifacts from the Swamp Child Site (22FO666): An Investi-
           gation into Site Function and Adaptive Strategies.* Master's thesis, University of
           Southern Mississippi, Hattiesburg.
Dunnell, Robert C.
   1970   Seriation Method and Its Evaluation. *American Antiquity* 35:305–19.
   1971   *Systematics in Prehistory.* New York: Free Press.
   1985   Archaeological Survey in the Lower Mississippi Alluvial Valley, 1940–1947: A
           Landmark Study in American Archaeology. *American Antiquity* 50:297–300.
   1990   The Role of the Southeast in American Archaeology. *Southeastern Archaeology*
           9(1):11–22.
   1992   The Notion Site. In *Space, Time, and Archaeological Landscapes,* edited by J.
           Rossignol and L. Wandsnider, pp. 21–41. New York: Plenum Press.
Dunnell, Robert C., and William S. Dancey
   1983   The Siteless Survey: A Regional Scale Data Collection Strategy. In *Advances in
           Archaeological Method and Theory,* vol. 6, pp. 267–87. New York: Academic Press.
Dunnell, Robert C., and James K. Feathers
   1991   Late Woodland Manifestations of the Malden Plain, Southeast Missouri. In *Stabil-
           ity, Transformation, and Variation: The Late Woodland Southeast,* edited by
           Michael S. Nassaney and Charles R. Cobb, pp. 21–45. New York: Plenum Press.
Durham, J. H., and M. K. Davis
   1975   Report on Burials Found at Crenshaw Mound "C," Miller County, Arkansas. *Bul-
           letin of the Oklahoma Anthropological Society* 23:1–90.
DuVall, Glyn D.
   1977   *The Ewell III Site (40CF118): An Early Middle Woodland McFarland Phase Site
           in the Normandy Reservoir, Coffee County, Tennessee.* Master's thesis, Depart-
           ment of Anthropology, University of Tennessee, Knoxville.
   1982   The Ewell III Site (40CF118). In *Seventh Report of the Normandy Archaeological
           Project,* edited by Charles H. Faulkner and Major C. R. McCollough, pp. 8–151.
           Report of Investigations 32, Department of Anthropology, University of Tennes-
           see, and TVA Publications in Anthropology 29, Knoxville.
Earle, Timothy
   1980   A Model of Subsistence Change. In *Modeling Change in Prehistoric Subsistence
           Economies,* edited by Timothy Earle and A. Christenson, pp. 1–29. New York:
           Academic Press.
   1991   The Evolution of Chiefdoms. In *Chiefdoms: Power, Economy, and Ideology,* ed-
           ited by Timothy Earle, pp. 1–15. Cambridge: Cambridge University Press.

Early, Ann M.
1982 SW Study Unit 27: Dutchman's Garden Phase, Fourche Maline Culture. In *A State Plan for the Conservation of Archeological Resources in Arkansas,* edited by Hester A. Davis, pp. 85–87. Arkansas Archeological Survey Research Series No. 21, Fayetteville.
2000 The Caddos of the Trans-Mississippi South. In *Indians of the Greater Southeast,* edited by Bonnie G. McEwan, pp. 121–42. Gainesville: University Press of Florida.
Early, Ann M. (editor)
1993 *Caddoan Saltmakers in the Ouachita Valley: The Hardman Site.* Arkansas Archeological Survey Research Series No. 43, Fayetteville.
Eastman, Jane M.
1994a The North Carolina Radiocarbon Date Study (Part 1). *Southern Indian Studies* 42:1–63.
1994b The North Carolina Radiocarbon Date Study (Part 2). *Southern Indian Studies* 43:1–117.
Eastman, Jane, Loretta Lautzenheiser, and Mary Ann Holm
1997 A Re-evaluation of Ceramics from the Tower Hill Site (31LR1), Lenoir County, North Carolina. *North Carolina Archaeology* 46:109–20.
Edging, Richard
2000 Epilogue. In *A Cultural Affiliation Overview for Fort Leonard Wood, Pulaski County, Missouri.* Report prepared for the U.S. Army Construction Engineering Research Laboratory, Champaign, Ill.
Edmonds, Mark
1999 *Ancestral Geographies of the Neolithic.* New York: Routledge.
Egloff, Keith T.
1985 Spheres of Cultural Interaction across the Coastal Plain of Virginia in the Woodland Period. In *Structure and Process in Southeastern Archaeology,* edited by Roy S. Dickens and H. Trawick Ward, pp. 229–42. Tuscaloosa: University of Alabama Press.
1991 Development and Impact of Ceramics in Virginia. In *Late Archaic and Early Woodland Research in Virginia: A Synthesis,* edited by T. R. Reinhart and M. E. N. Hodges, pp. 243–52. Archaeological Society of Virginia Special Publication No. 23, Richmond.
Egloff, Keith T., and Steven R. Potter
1982 Indian Ceramics from Coastal Plain Virginia. *Archaeology of Eastern North America* 10:95–117.
Egloff, Keith T., and Deborah Woodward
1992 *First People: The Early Indians of Virginia.* Charlottesville: University Press of Virginia.
Egloff, Keith T., Mary Ellen N. Hodges, Jay F. Custer, Keith R. Doms, and Leslie D. McFaden
1988 *Archaeological Investigations at Croaker Landing 44JC70 and 44JC71.* Research Report Series 4, Department of Conservation and Historic Resources, Division of Historic Landmarks, Commonwealth of Virginia, Richmond.
Ehrenhard, John E., and R. C. Taylor
1980 *The Big Cypress National Preserve: Archaeological Survey Season 3.* Southeastern Archaeological Center, National Park Service, U.S. Department of the Interior, Tallahassee.
Ehrenhard, John E., R. S. Carr, and R. C. Taylor
1978 *The Archaeological Survey of the Big Cypress National Preserve: Phase I.* Southeastern Archaeological Center, National Park Service, U.S. Department of the Interior, Tallahassee.

1979   *The Big Cypress National Preserve: Archaeological Survey Season 2.* Southeast-
        ern Archaeological Center, National Park Service, U.S. Department of the Inte-
        rior, Tallahassee.

Ehrenhard, John E., R. C. Taylor, and G. Komara
1980   *Big Cypress National Preserve Cultural Resource Inventory Season 4.* Southeast-
        ern Archaeological Center, National Park Service, U.S. Department of the Inte-
        rior, Tallahassee.
1981   *Big Cypress National Preserve Cultural Resource Inventory Season 5.* Southeast-
        ern Archaeological Center, National Park Service, U.S. Department of the Inte-
        rior, Tallahassee.

Elliott, Daniel T.
1998   The Northern and Eastern Expression of Swift Creek Culture: Settlement in the
        Tennessee and Savannah River Valleys. In *A World Engraved: Archaeology of the
        Swift Creek Culture,* edited by J. Mark Williams and Daniel T. Elliott, pp. 19–35.
        Tuscaloosa: University of Alabama Press.

Elliott, Daniel T., and Kenneth E. Sassaman
1995   *Archaic Period Archaeology of the Georgia Coastal Plain and Coastal Zone.* Geor-
        gia Archaeological Research Design Paper No. 11, University of Georgia, Athens.

Elliott, Daniel T., R. Jerald Ledbetter, and Elizabeth A. Gordon
1994   *Data Recovery at Lovers Lane, Phinizy Swamp and the Old Dike Sites Bobby
        Jones Expressway Extension Corridor Augusta, Georgia.* Occasional Papers in
        Cultural Resource Management 7, Georgia Department of Transportation, Atlanta.

Elliott, Daniel T., Jeffrey T. Holland, Phil Thomason, Michael Emrick, and Richard W. Stoops,
Jr.
1995   *Historic Preservation Plan for the Cultural Resources on U.S. Army Installations
        at Fort Benning Military Reservation, Chattahoochee and Muscogee Counties,
        Georgia, and Russell County, Alabama.* Vol. 2, *Technical Synthesis.* Submitted to
        the National Park Service, Southeast Regional Office, Atlanta, by Garrow and
        Associates, Atlanta (Contract No. 1443CX500093048).

Emerson, Thomas E.
1983   The Florence Street Site: An Early Woodland Florence Phase Occupation in the
        American Bottom. In *The Florence Street Site,* by Thomas E. Emerson, G. R. Milner,
        and D. K. Jackson, pp. 19–178. American Bottom Archaeology FAI-270 Site Re-
        ports, Vol. 2, University of Illinois Press, Urbana.
1986   A Retrospective Look at the Earliest Woodland Cultures in the American Heart-
        land. In *Early Woodland Archaeology,* edited by Kenneth B. Farnsworth and Tho-
        mas E. Emerson, pp. 621–31. Center for American Archaeology, Kampsville, Ill.

Emerson, Thomas E., and Andrew C. Fortier
1986   Early Woodland Cultural Variation, Subsistence, and Settlement in the American
        Bottom. In *Early Woodland Archaeology,* edited by Kenneth Farnsworth and Tho-
        mas Emerson, pp. 475–522. Kampsville Seminars in Archaeology Vol. 2,
        Kampsville, Ill.

Emerson, Thomas, George Milner, and Douglas K. Jackson (editors)
1983   *The Florence Street Site.* American Bottom Archaeology FAI-270 Site Reports,
        Vol. 2, University of Illinois Press, Urbana.

Endonino, Jon C.
2000   Manufacturing Techniques and Vessel Forms of Late Archaic Fiber-Tempered Pot-
        tery: An Analysis of Orange Period Pottery from Two Sites in the Vicinity of Silver
        Glen Springs, Marion and Lake Counties, Florida. Ms. on file, Laboratory of South-
        eastern Archaeology, University of Florida, Gainesville.

Ensor, H. Blaine
  1981   *Gainesville Lake Area Lithics: Chronology, Technology, and Use.* Report of Inves-
         tigations 14, Office of Archaeological Research, University of Alabama, Univer-
         sity.
Esarey, Duane
  1986   Red Ochre Mound Building and Marion Phase Associations: A Fulton County
         Perspective. In *Early Woodland Archeology,* edited by Kenneth B. Farnsworth
         and Thomas E. Emerson, pp. 231–43. Kampsville Seminars in Archeology No. 2,
         Center for American Archeology, CAA Press, Kampsville, Ill.
Espenshade, Christopher T.
  1993   *A Few Visits in Prehistory: Data Recovery Excavation at 9Rh18, Randolph County,
         Georgia.* Submitted to the Georgia Department of Transportation, Atlanta. Occa-
         sional Papers in Cultural Resource Management No. 5, Brockington and Associ-
         ates, Atlanta and Charleston.
  n.d.   Data Recovery at Bethea Tract, Hilton Head Island, Beaufort County, South Caro-
         lina. Brockington and Associates, Atlanta.
Espenshade, Christopher T., and Paul E. Brockington
  1989   *An Archaeological Study of the Minim Island Site: Early Woodland Dynamics in
         Coastal South Carolina.* Submitted to U.S. Army Corps of Engineers by
         Brockington and Associates, Atlanta.
Espenshade, Christopher T., Linda Kennedy, and Bobby G. Southerlin
  1994   *What Is a Shell Midden? Data Recovery Excavations of Thom's Creek and Deptford
         Shell Middens, 38BU2, Spring Island, South Carolina.* Submitted to Spring Island
         Plantation by Brockington and Associates, Atlanta.
Evans, Bryant
  1994   The Late Archaic to Early Woodland Transition in the American Bottom. Pre-
         sented at the Joint Southeast–Midwest Archaeological Conference, Lexington, Ky.
  1995   Cultural Discontinuity in the American Bottom during the Late Archaic-Early
         Woodland Transition. Presented at the 60th annual meeting of the Society for
         American Archaeology, Minneapolis.
Evans, Bryant J., Madeleine G. Evans, Mary Simon, and Thomas E. Berres
  1997   *Ringering: A Multi-Component Site in the American Bottom.* Ms. on file, Illinois
         Department of Transportation Archaeological Research Program, University of
         Illinois, Champaign.
Evans, Clifford
  1955   *A Ceramic Study of Virginia Archeology.* Bulletin 160, Bureau of American Eth-
         nology, Washington, D.C.
Fagan, Brian M.
  1991   *Ancient North America: The Archaeology of a Continent.* New York: Thomas and
         Hudson.
Farnsworth, Kenneth B.
  1986   Black Sand Culture Origins and Distribution. In *Early Woodland Archeology,* ed-
         ited by Kenneth B. Farnsworth and Thomas E. Emerson, pp. 634–41. Kampsville
         Seminars in Archeology No. 2, Center for American Archeology, CAA Press,
         Kampsville, Ill.
Farnsworth, Kenneth B., and David L. Asch
  1986   Early Woodland Chronology, Artifact Styles, and Settlement Distribution in the
         Lower Illinois Valley Region. In *Early Woodland Archeology,* edited by Kenneth
         B. Farnsworth and Thomas E. Emerson, pp. 326–457. Kampsville Seminars in
         Archeology No. 2, Center for American Archeology, CAA Press, Kampsville, Ill.

Farnsworth, Kenneth B., and Thomas E. Emerson (editors)
   1986   *Early Woodland Archeology.* Kampsville Seminars in Archaeology No. 2, Center for American Archeology, CAA Press, Kampsville, Ill.
Faulkner, Charles H.
   1968   The Mason Site (40Fr-8). In *Archaeological Investigations in the Tims Ford Reservoir, Tennessee, 1966,* edited by Charles H. Faulkner, pp. 12–140. Report of Investigations 6, Department of Anthropology, University of Tennessee, Knoxville.
   1977a Eoff I Site (40CF32). In *Fourth Report of the Normandy Archaeological Project,* edited by Charles H. Faulkner and Major C. R. McCollough, pp. 64–278. Report of Investigations 19, Department of Anthropology, University of Tennessee, Knoxville.
   1977b The Winter House: An Early Southeast Tradition. *Midcontinental Journal of Archaeology* 2(2):141–59.
   1982   The McFarland Occupation at 40CF32: Interpretations from the 1975 Field Season. In *Eighth Report of the Normandy Archaeological Project,* edited by Charles H. Faulkner and Major C. R. McCollough, pp. 302–88. Report of Investigations 33, Department of Anthropology, University of Tennessee, and TVA Publications in Anthropology 30, Knoxville.
   1988   Middle Woodland Community and Settlement Patterns on the Eastern Highland Rim, Tennessee. In *Middle Woodland Settlement and Ceremonialism in the Mid-South and Lower Mississippi Valley,* edited by Robert C. Mainfort, Jr., pp. 76–98. Archaeological Report 22, Mississippi Department of Archives and History, Jackson.
   1996   The Old Stone Fort Revisited: New Clues to an Old Mystery. In *Mounds, Embankments, and Ceremonialism in the Midsouth,* edited by Robert C. Mainfort and Richard Walling, pp. 7–11. Arkansas Archeological Survey Research Series 46, Fayetteville.
   1997   Four Thousand Years of Native American Cave Art in the Southern Appalachians. *Journal of Cave and Karst Studies (National Speleological Society Bulletin)* 59:148–53.
Faulkner, Charles H. (editor)
   1986   *The Prehistoric Native American Art of Mud Glyph Cave.* Knoxville: University of Tennessee Press.
Faulkner, Charles H., and J. B. Graham
   1966   *Westmoreland-Barber Site (40MI11), Nickajack Reservoir: Season II.* Report of Investigations 11, Department of Anthropology, University of Tennessee, Knoxville.
Faulkner, Charles H., and Major C. R. McCollough
   1973   *Introductory Report of the Normandy Reservoir Salvage Project: Environmental Setting, Typology, and Survey.* Report of Investigations 11, Department of Anthropology, University of Tennessee, Knoxville.
   1974   *Excavations and Testing, Normandy Reservoir Salvage Project: 1972 Season.* Report of Investigations 12, Department of Anthropology, University of Tennessee, Knoxville.
   1982   Excavation of the Jernigan II Site (40CF37). In *Seventh Report of the Normandy Archaeological Project,* edited by Charles H. Faulkner and Major C. R. McCollough, pp. 153–311. Report of Investigations 32, Department of Anthropology, University of Tennessee, and TVA Publications in Anthropology 29, Knoxville.
Faulkner, Charles H., and Major C. R. McCollough (editors)
   1978   *Fifth Report of the Normandy Archaeological Project.* Report of Investigations 20, Department of Anthropology, University of Tennessee, Knoxville.

1982a   *Seventh Report of the Normandy Archaeological Project.* Report of Investigations 32, Department of Anthropology, University of Tennessee, and TVA Publications in Anthropology 29, Knoxville.

1982b   *Eighth Report of the Normandy Archaeological Project.* Report of Investigations 33, Department of Anthropology, University of Tennessee, and TVA Publications in Anthropology 30, Knoxville.

Faulkner, Charles H., and Jan Simek

2001   Variability in the Production and Preservation of Prehistoric Mud Glyphs from Southeastern Caves. In *Fleeting Identities: Perishable Material Culture in Archaeological Research,* edited by Penelope B. Drooker, pp. 335–56. Occasional Paper 28, Center for Archaeological Investigations, Southern Illinois University-Carbondale.

Faulkner, Charles T.

1991   Prehistoric Diet and Parasitic Infection in Tennessee: Evidence from the Analysis of Desiccated Human Paleofeces. *American Antiquity* 56:687–700.

Fenenga, Franklin

1938   Pottery Types from Pulaski County. *The Missouri Archaeologist* 4:5–7.

Fenneman, Nevin M.

1938   *Physiography of the Eastern United States.* New York: McGraw-Hill.

Fewkes, Jesse W.

1924   Preliminary Archeological Investigations at Weeden Island, Florida. *Smithsonian Miscellaneous Collections* (Washington, D.C.) 76(13):1–26.

Figley, C. A

1968   The Soc Site, 3WH34. *Arkansas Archeologist* 9:41–58.

Finn, Michael R.

1996   *Data Recovery at the Blackburn Fork Site: A Prehistoric Occupation in the Murphrees Valley of Northeast Alabama.* Report of Investigations (draft), Office of Archaeological Research, University of Alabama, Moundville.

Finn, Michael R., and Nurit Goldman-Finn

1997   Steatite Exchange, Ceramics, and Mobility at the Archaic/Woodland Transition in the Midsouth. Presented at the 62nd annual meeting of the Society for American Archaeology, Nashville.

Finney, Fred A.

1983   Middle Woodland Cement Hollow Phase. In *The Mund Site (11-S-435),* by Andrew C. Fortier, Fred A. Finney, and R. B. Lacampagne, pp. 40–107. American Bottom Archaeology FAI-270 Site Reports, Vol. 5, University of Illinois Press, Urbana.

Fish, Suzanne K., and Richard W. Jefferies

1983   The Site Plan at Cold Springs, 9Ge10. *Early Georgia* 11:61–73.

Fisk, Harold N.

1944   *Geological Investigation of the Alluvial Valley of the Lower Mississippi River.* U.S. Army Corps of Engineers, Mississippi River Commission, Vicksburg, Miss.

Flannery, Kent

1968   Archaeological Systems Theory and Early Mesoamerica. In *Anthropological Archaeology in the Americas,* edited by B. J. Meggers, pp. 67–87. Anthropological Society of Washington, Washington, D.C.

Flannery, Regina

1943   Some Notes on a Few Sites in Beaufort, S.C. *Bureau of American Ethnology Bulletin* 133:147–53.

Fontaneda, D°. d'E.

1944   *Memoir of D° d'Escalante Fontaneda Respection Florida,* translated by B. Smith.

Originally published 1854; reprinted with revisions. Coral Gables, Fla.: University of Miami Press.

Ford, James A.

1951   *Greenhouse: A Troyville–Coles Creek Period Site in Avoyelles Parish, Louisiana.* Anthropological Papers of the American Museum of Natural History 44, pp. 5–132, New York, N.Y.

1952   *Measurements of Some Prehistoric Design Developments in the Southeastern States.* Anthropological Papers of the American Museum of Natural History 44(3), New York, N.Y.

1963   *Hopewell Culture Burial Mounds Near Helena, Arkansas.* Anthropological Papers of the American Museum of Natural History 50(1), New York.

1969   *A Comparison of Formative Cultures in the Americas: Diffusion or the Psychic Unity of Man?* Smithsonian Contributions to Anthropology 11, Smithsonian Institution, Washington, D.C.

Ford, James A., and G. I. Quimby, Jr.

1945   *The Tchefuncte Culture, an Early Occupation of the Lower Mississippi Valley.* Memoirs No. 2, Society for American Archaeology, Menasha, Wis.

Ford, James A., and Gordon R. Willey

1940   *Crooks Site, a Marksville Period Burial Mound in La Salle Parish, Louisiana.* Anthropological Study No. 3, Louisiana Department of Conservation.

1941   An Interpretation of the Prehistory of the Eastern United States. *American Anthropologist* 43:325–63.

Ford, James A., Philip Phillips, and William G. Haag

1955   *The Jaketown Site in West-Central Mississippi.* Anthropological Papers Vol. 45, Pt. 1, American Museum of Natural History, New York.

Ford, Janet L.

1989   Time and Temper in the North-Central Hills of Mississippi. *Journal of Alabama Archaeology* 27:57–69.

1990   The Tchula Connection: Early Woodland Culture and Burial Mounds in North Mississippi. *Southeastern Archaeology* 9:103–15.

Ford, Richard I.

1997   Preliminary Report on the Plant Remains from the George C. Davis Site, Cherokee County, Texas: 1968–1970 Excavations. *Bulletin of the Texas Archeological Society* 68:104–7.

Fortier, Andrew C.

1981   Kaskaskia River Unit (VII). In *Predictive Models in Illinois Archaeology,* edited by M. K. Brown, pp. 81–105. Illinois Department of Conservation, Springfield.

1983   Early Woodland Marion Phase. In *The Mund Site (11-S-435),* by A. C. Fortier, F. A. Finney, and R. B. Lacampagne, pp. 36–39. American Bottom Archaeology FAI 270 Site Reports, Vol. 5, University of Illinois Press, Urbana.

1985a   Early Woodland Occupations at the Carbon Monoxide Site. In *Selected Sites in the Hill Lake Locality,* by Andrew C. Fortier, pp. 25–116. American Bottom Archaeology FAI-270 Site Reports, Vol. 13, University of Illinois Press, Urbana.

1985b   Early Woodland Occupations at the Fiege Site. In *Selected Sites in the Hill Lake Locality,* by Andrew C. Fortier, pp. 117–38. American Bottom Archaeology FAI-270 Site Reports, Vol. 13, University of Illinois Press, Urbana.

1985c   Middle Woodland Occupations at the Truck #7 and Go-Kart South Sites. In *Selected Sites in the Hill Lake Locality,* by Andrew C. Fortier, pp. 163–280. American Bottom Archaeology FAI-270 Site Reports, Vol. 13, University of Illinois Press, Urbana.

1991 The Late Woodland/Emergent Mississippian Transition in the American Bottom. In *The Sponemann Site: The Formative Emergent Mississippian Sponemann Occupations*. American Bottom Archaeology FAI-270 Site Reports, Vol. 23, University of Illinois Press, Urbana.

1998 Pre-Mississippian Economies in the American Bottom of Southwestern Illinois, 3000 B.C.–A.D. 1050. In *Research in Economic Anthropology*, vol. 19, edited by Barry L. Isaac, pp. 341–92. Stamford, Conn.: JAI Press.

Fortier, Andrew C., and Douglas K. Jackson

2000 The Formation of a Late Woodland Heartland in the American Bottom. In *Late Woodland Societies: Tradition and Transformation across the Midcontinent*, edited by Thomas E. Emerson, Dale L. McElrath, and Andrew C. Fortier, pp. 123–48. Lincoln: University of Nebraska Press.

Fortier, Andrew C., Thomas E. Emerson, and Fred A. Finney

1984 Early and Middle Woodland Periods. In *American Bottom Archaeology: A Summary of the FAI-270 Project Contribution to the Culture History of the Mississippi River Valley*, edited by C. J. Bareis and J. W. Porter, pp. 59–103. Urbana: University of Illinois Press.

Fortier, Andrew C., Thomas O. Maher, Joyce A. Williams, and Michael C. Meinkoth

1989a Site Interpretation. In *The Holding Site*, by Andrew C. Fortier, Thomas O. Maher, Joyce A. Williams, Michael C. Meinkoth, Kathryn E. Parker, and Lucretia S. Kelly, pp. 555–79. Urbana: University of Illinois Press.

Fortier, Andrew C., Thomas O. Maher, Joyce A. Williams, Michael C. Meinkoth, Kathryn E. Parker, and Lucretia S. Kelly

1989b *The Holding Site (11-Ms-118): A Hopewell Community in the American Bottom*. American Bottom Archaeology FAI-270 Site Reports, Vol. 19, University of Illinois Press, Urbana.

Fortier, Andrew, Thomas E. Emerson, and Katie Parker

1998 The Meyer Site: A Terminal Late Archaic Residential Camp in the American Bottom. *Illinois Archaeology* 10:195–228.

Foucault, Michel

1979 *Discipline and Punish: The Birth of the Prison*. New York: Vintage.

Fowke, Gerard

1894 *Archaeologic Investigations in the James and Potomac Valleys*. Bulletin No. 23, Bureau of American Ethnology, Washington, D.C.

1902 *Archaeological History of Ohio*. Columbus: Ohio State Archaeological and Historical Society.

1922 *Archaeological Investigations*. Bulletin No. 56, Bureau of American Ethnology, Smithsonian Institution, Washington, D.C.

1928 *Archaeological Investigations II*. Forty-fourth Annual Report of the Bureau of American Ethnology: 1926–1927, pp. 399–540. Smithsonian Institution, Washington, D.C.

Fowler, Melvin. L.

1959 *Summary Report of Modoc Rock Shelter: 1952, 1953, 1955, 1956*. Illinois State Museum Reports of Investigations No. 8, Springfield.

1991 Mound 72 and Early Mississippian at Cahokia. In *Monographs in World Archaeology No. 2*, edited by James B. Stoltman, pp. 1–28. Prehistory Press Monographs in Archaeology No. 2, Madison, Wis.

1997 *The Cahokia Atlas: A Historical Atlas of Cahokia Archaeology*. Studies in Archaeology Number 2, University of Illinois at Urbana-Champaign. Illinois Transportation Archaeological Research Program, Urbana.

Fowler, Melvin L., Jerome Rose, Barbara Vander Leest, and Steven R. Ahler
   1999   *The Mound 72 Area: Dedicated and Sacred Space in Early Cahokia.* Illinois State
         Museum Reports of Investigations No. 54, Springfield.

Fox, G. L.
   1992   *A Critical Evaluation of the Interpretive Framework of the Mississippi Period in*
         Southeast Missouri. Ph.D. dissertation, Department of Anthropology, University
         of Missouri-Columbia.
   1998   An Examination of Mississippian-Period Phases in Southeastern Missouri. In
         Changing Perspectives on the Archaeology of the Central Mississippi Valley, ed-
         ited by M. J. O'Brien and R. C. Dunnell, pp. 31–58. Tuscaloosa: University of
         Alabama Press.

Freeman, John P., Gordon L. Smith, Thomas L. Poulson, Patty Jo Watson, and William B. White
   1973   Lee Cave, Mammoth Cave National Park, Kentucky. *National Speleological Soci-*
         ety Bulletin 35:109–25.

Friedman, Jonathan
   1975   Tribes, States, and Transformations. In *Marxist Analyses and Social Anthropol-*
         ogy, edited by M. Bloch, pp. 161–202. New York: Tavistock.

Fritz, Gayle J.
   1986a *Prehistoric Ozark Agriculture, The University of Arkansas Rockshelter Collec-*
         tions. Ph.D. dissertation, University of North Carolina, Chapel Hill.
   1986b Carbonized Plant Remains. In *The Calloway Site (15MT8): A Transitional Early to*
         Middle Woodland Camp in Martin County, Kentucky, by Charles M. Niquette and
         Randall D. Boedy, pp. 90–102. Publication Series 86–12, Cultural Resource Ana-
         lysts, Inc., Lexington, Ky. Report prepared for Brighton Engineering Co., Inc.,
         Frankfort, Ky. Lead Agency: U.S. Army Corps of Engineers, Huntington District.
   1988   Adding the Plant Remains to Assessments of Late Woodland/Early Mississippi
         Period Plant Husbandry. Presented to the 53rd annual meeting of the Society for
         American Archaeology, Phoenix.
   1989   Evidence of Plant Use from Copple Mound at the Spiro Site. In *Contributions to*
         Spiro Archaeology: Mound Excavations and Regional Perspectives, edited by J.
         Daniel Rogers, Donald G. Wyckoff, and D. A. Peterson, pp. 65–87. Studies in
         Oklahoma's Past No. 16, Oklahoma Archeological Survey, Norman.
   1990a Multiple Pathways to Farming in Precontact Eastern North America. *Journal of*
         World Prehistory 4(4):387–435.
   1990b Archeobotanical Remains from the Dirst Site, Buffalo National River, Arkansas.
         In *Archeological Investigations at 3MR80-Area D in the Rush Development Area,*
         Buffalo National River, Arkansas, by George Sabo III, R. L. Guendling, W. Fred
         Limp, M. J. Guccione, Susan L. Scott, Gayle J. Fritz, and P. A. Smith. Southwest
         Cultural Resources Center Professional Papers No. 38, Santa Fe.
   1993   Early and Middle Woodland Paleoethnobotany. In *Foraging and Farming in the*
         Eastern Woodlands, edited by C. Margaret Scarry, pp. 39–56. Gainesville: Uni-
         versity Press of Florida.
   1997   A Three-Thousand-Year-Old Cache of Crop Seeds from Marble Bluff, Arkansas.
         In *People, Plants, and Landscapes: Studies in Paleoethnobotany,* edited by Kristen
         J. Gremillion, pp. 42–62. Tuscaloosa: University of Alabama Press.

Fritz, Gayle J., and Tristram R. Kidder
   1993   Recent Investigations into Prehistoric Agriculture in the Lower Mississippi Val-
         ley. *Southeastern Archaeology* 12:1–14.

Fritz, Gayle J., and G. Powell
   1998   Seeds, Plants, and Cultigens. In *Toltec Mounds and Plum Bayou Culture: Mound*

    D Excavations, by Martha A. Rolingson, pp. 135–36. Arkansas Archeological Survey Research Series No. 54, Fayetteville.

Fritz, Gayle J., and Bruce D. Smith

1988   Old Collections and New Technology: Documenting the Domestication of *Chenopodium* in Eastern North America. *Midcontinental Journal of Archaeology* 12(1):3–27.

Fuller, Richard S.

1998   Indian Pottery and Cultural Chronology of the Mobile-Tensaw Basin and Alabama Coast. *Journal of Alabama Archaeology* 44:1–51.

Fuller, Richard S., Jr., and Diane S. Fuller

1987   *Excavations at Morgan: A Coles Creek Period Mound Complex in Coastal Louisiana.* Bulletin 11, Lower Mississippi Survey, Peabody Museum, Harvard University, Cambridge.

Fulton, R. L., and C. H. Webb

1953   The Bellevue Mound: A Pre-Caddoan Site in Bossier Parish, Louisiana. *Bulletin of the Texas Archeological and Paleontological Society* 24:18–42.

Funkhouser, William D., and William S. Webb

1935   *The Ricketts Site in Montgomery County, Kentucky.* University of Kentucky Reports in Anthropology and Archaeology 3(6), Lexington.

1937   *The Chilton Site.* University of Kentucky Reports in Archaeology and Anthropology 3(5), Lexington.

Furst, Peter T.

1968   The Olmec Were-Jaguar Motif in Light of Ethnographic Reality. In *Dumbarton Oaks Conference on the Olmec,* edited by Elizabeth P. Benson, pp. 143–74. Dumbarton Oaks Research Library and Collections, Washington, D.C.

Futato, Eugene M.

1982   An Outside View of Middle Woodland Chronology in the Normandy Reservoir. *Tennessee Anthropologist* 7(2):105–13.

1987   *Archaeological Investigations at Shell Bluff and White Springs, Two Late Woodland Sites in the Tombigbee River Multi-Resource District.* Report of Investigations 50, Office of Archaeological Research, Alabama State Museum of Natural History, University of Alabama, University.

1988   Continuity and Change in the Middle Woodland Occupation of the Northwest Alabama Uplands. In *Middle Woodland Settlement and Ceremonialism in the Mid-South and Lower Mississippi Valley,* edited by Robert C. Mainfort, Jr., pp. 31–48. Archaeological Report 22, Mississippi Dept. of Archives and History, Jackson.

1989   *An Archaeological Overview of the Tombigbee River Basin, Alabama and Mississippi.* University of Alabama, State Museum of Natural History, Division of Archaeology, Report of Investigations 59.

Gallivan, Martin D.

1999   *The Late Prehistoric James River Village: Household, Community, and Regional Dynamics.* Ph.D. dissertation, Department of Anthropology, University of Virginia. University Microfilms, Ann Arbor, Mich.

Gallivan, Martin, and Jeffrey L. Hantman

1998   *The Spessard Site: A Stratified Floodplain Site Dating to the Woodland Period.* Ms. on file, Department of Anthropology, University of Virginia, Charlottesville.

Galm, J. R.

1984   Arkansas Valley Caddoan Formative: The Wister and Fourche Maline Phases. In *Prehistory of Oklahoma,* edited by R. E. Bell, pp. 199–220. Orlando: Academic Press.

Gardner, Paul S.
 1987 New Evidence Concerning the Chronology and Paleoethnobotany of Salts Cave, Kentucky. *American Antiquity* 52(2):358–67.
 1992 *Diet Optimization Models and Prehistoric Subsistence Change in the Eastern Woodlands.* Ph.D. dissertation, University of North Carolina, Chapel Hill.
 1997 The Ecological Structure and Behavioral Implications of Mast Exploitation Strategies. In *People, Plants, and Landscapes: Studies in Paleoethnobotany,* edited by Kristen J. Gremillion, pp. 161–78. Tuscaloosa: University of Alabama Press.
Gardner, William M.
 1986 *Lost Arrowheads and Broken Pottery.* Thunderbird Museum Publication, Manassas, Va.
 1993 Early/Middle Woodland Mounds in the Upper Shenandoah Valley and Contiguous Regions in West Virginia: Observations on Distribution and Variations in Internal Structure. Presented at the 1993 Middle Atlantic Archaeological Conference, Ocean City, Md.
Gauch, H. G., Jr.
 1982 *Multivariate Analysis in Community Ecology.* Cambridge: Cambridge University Press.
Geier, Clarence R.
 1975 *The Kimberlin Site: The Ecology of a Late Woodland Population.* Research Series No. 12, Missouri Archaeological Society, Columbia.
Geller, J. Elaine Hardy, and David B. Crampton
 1987 *The Boschert Site (23SC609). A Late Woodland Extraction Site in the Uplands of St. Charles County, Missouri.* Submitted to the Missouri Highway and Transportation Department.
Gentry, R. C.
 1984 Hurricanes in South Florida. In *Environments of South Florida: Present and Past II,* 2d ed., edited by P. J. Gleason, pp. 510–19. Coral Gables, Fla.: Miami Geological Society.
Gertjejansen, Doyle J., and J. Richard Shenkel
 1983 Laboratory Simulation of Tchefuncte Period Ceramic Vessels from the Pontchartrain Basin. *Southeastern Archaeology* 2:37–63.
Giardino, Marco J.
 1984 Temporal Frameworks: Archaeological Components and Burial Styles: The Human Osteology of the Mt. Nebo Site in North Louisiana. *Louisiana Archaeology* 9:99–126.
Gibson, Jon L.
 1970 The Hopewellian Phenomenon in the Lower Mississippi Valley. *Louisiana Studies* 9:176–92.
 1976 *Archaeological Survey of Bayou Teche, Vermilion River, and Freshwater Bayou, South Central Louisiana.* Report 2, Center for Archaeological Studies, University of Southwestern Louisiana, Lafayette.
 1984 Old Creek, a Troyville Period Ossuary in LaSalle Parish, Louisiana: Reflections after a Quarter Century. *Louisiana Archaeology* 9:127–204.
 1985a Mounds on the Ouachita. *Louisiana Archaeology* 10:171–270.
 1985b Ouachita Prehistory. *Louisiana Archaeology* 10:319–35.
 1994 Before Their Time? Early Mounds in the Lower Mississippi Valley. *Southeastern Archaeology* 13:162–86.
 1996a Poverty Point and Greater Southeastern Prehistory: The Culture That Did Not Fit. In *Archaeology of the Mid-Holocene Southeast,* edited by Kenneth E. Sassaman and David G. Anderson, pp. 288–305. Gainesville: University Press of Florida.

1996b   *Ancient Earthworks of the Ouachita Valley in Louisiana.* Technical Reports 5, Southeast Archeological Center, National Park Service, Tallahassee, Fla.

1998   Broken Circles, Owl Monsters, and Black Earth Midden: Separating Sacred and Secular at Poverty Point. In *Ancient Earthen Enclosures of the Eastern Woodlands,* edited by Robert C. Mainfort and L. P. Sullivan, pp. 17–30. Gainesville: University Press of Florida.

Gibson, Jon L., and J. Richard Shenkel

1988   Louisiana Earthworks: Middle Woodland and Predecessors. In *Middle Woodland Settlement and Ceremonialism in the Mid-South and Lower Mississippi Valley,* edited by Robert C. Mainfort, pp. 7–18. Archaeological Report 22, Mississippi Department of Archives and History, Jackson.

Gibson, Thomas

1995   Having Your House and Eating It: Houses and Siblings in Ara, South Sulawesi. In *About the House,* edited by J. Carsten and S. Hugh-Jones, pp. 129–48. Cambridge: Cambridge University Press.

Gifford, Diane

1981   Taphonomy and Paleoecology: A Critical Review of Archaeology's Sister Disciplines. *Advances in Archaeological Method and Theory* 4:365–438.

Giles, Eric G.

2001   *A Design Contact Analysis of Swift Creek Complicated Stamped Pottery from the Borklund Mound Site (8TA35) in Northwest Florida.* Master's thesis, Department of Anthropology, East Carolina University, Greenville, N.C.

Gilliland, M. S.

1975   *The Material Culture of Key Marco.* Gainesville: University Presses of Florida.

Gleeson, Paul F. (editor)

1970   *Archaeological Investigations in the Tellico Reservoir, Interim Report, 1969.* Report of Investigations 8, Department of Anthropology, University of Tennessee, Knoxville.

1971   *Archaeological Investigations in the Tellico Reservoir, Interim Report, 1970.* Report of Investigations 9, Department of Anthropology, University of Tennessee, Knoxville.

Goad, Sharon I.

1979   Middle Woodland Exchange in the Prehistoric Southeastern United States. In *Hopewell Archaeology: The Chillicothe Conference,* edited by D. Brose and N. Greber, pp. 239–46. Kent, Ohio: Kent State University Press.

Goatley, Daniel B., Kenneth B. Farnsworth, Karen A. Atwell, Marjorie B. Schroeder, and Karli White

1996   *Phase III Archaeological Excavation of Area G of the O'Donnell Site (11-JY-290) within the Proposed Grafton Relocation Project, Jersey County, Illinois.* Contract Archaeology Program Report of Investigations No. 226, Center for American Archaeology, Kampsville, Ill.

Goggin, John M.

1948   A Revised Temporal Chart of Florida Archeology. *Florida Anthropologist* 1:57–60.

1949   Cultural Traditions in Florida Prehistory. In *The Florida Indian and His Neighbors,* edited by John W. Griffin, pp. 13–44. Rollins College Inter-American Center, Winter Park, Fla.

1950   Florida Archeology—1950. *Florida Anthropologist* 3:9–20.

1952   *Space and Time Perspectives in Northern St. Johns Archaeology, Florida.* Yale University Publications in Anthropology 47, New Haven, Conn.

Goggin, J. W., and W. T. Sturtevant
    1964   The Calusa: A Stratified Nonagricultural Society (With Notes on Sibling Marriage).
            In *Explorations in Cultural Anthropology: Essays in Honor of George Peter
            Murdock,* edited by W. H. Goodenough, pp. 179–219. New York: McGraw-Hill.
Gold, Debra L.
    1999   *Subsistence, Health and Emergent Inequality in Late Prehistoric Interior, Virginia.*
            Ph.D. dissertation, Department of Anthropology, University of Michigan. Univer-
            sity Microfilms, Ann Arbor, Mich.
Goodwin, Gary C.
    1977   *Cherokees in Transition: A Study of Changing Culture and Environment prior to
            1775.* University of Chicago Department of Geography Research Paper No. 181.
Gould, Stephen Jay, and Richard C. Lewontin
    1978   The Spandrels of San Marco and the Panglossian Paradigm: A Critique of the Adap-
            tationist Programme. *Proceedings of the Royal Society in London* 205:581–98.
Gower, J. C.
    1987   Introduction to Ordination Techniques. In *Developments in Numerical Ecology,*
            edited by P. Legendre and L. Legendre, pp. 3–64. Berlin: Springer-Verlag.
Gray, Bruce J.
    1993   *Cultural Resources Survey of the Proposed Relocation of U.S. Highway 82, Mis-
            sissippi Highway 25 and Mississippi Highway 12 at Starkville, Oktibbeha County,
            Mississippi.* Mississippi Department of Transportation, Jackson.
Greber, N'omi
    1983   *Recent Excavations at the Edwin Harness Mound.* Midcontinental Journal of Ar-
            chaeology Special Paper 5, Kent State University Press, Kent, Ohio.
    1994   A Study of Continuity and Contact between Central Scioto Adena and Hopewell
            Sites. *West Virginia Archaeologist* 43(1, 2):1–26.
    1997   Two Geometric Enclosures in the Paint Creek Valley: An Estimate of Possible
            Changes in Community Patterns through Time. In *Ohio Hopewell Community
            Organization,* edited by William S. Dancey and Paul J. Pacheco, pp. 207–30. Kent,
            Ohio: Kent State University Press.
Green, William
    1993   A Prehistoric Frontier in the Prairie Peninsula: Late Woodland Upland Settlement
            and Subsistence Patterns. *Illinois Archaeology* 5:201–14.
Greengo, Robert E.
    1964   *Issaquena: An Archaeological Phase in the Yazoo Basin of the Lower Mississippi
            Valley.* Memoirs No. 18, Society for American Archaeology, Salt Lake City.
Greenman, Emerson
    1932   Excavation of the Coon Mound and an Analysis of the Adena Culture. *Ohio Ar-
            chaeological and Historical Quarterly* 51(3).
Gremillion, Kristen J.
    1989   Plant Remains from 31Ce41, Cherokee County, North Carolina. Appendix 1 in
            *Archaeological Excavations within the Alternate Pipeline Corridor Passing through
            the Harshaw Bottom Site (31Ce41), Cherokee County, North Carolina,* by Ken-
            neth W. Robinson. Report on file at Office of State Archaeology, Raleigh, N.C.
            (CH-87-C-0000-0882).
    1990   *Paleoethnobotanical Remains from 31MC139, McDowell County, North Caro-
            lina.* Ms. on file, Paleoethnobotany Laboratory, Department of Anthropology, Ohio
            State University, Columbus.
    1993a   Paleoethnobotany. In *The Development of Southeastern Archaeology,* edited by
            Jay K. Johnson, pp. 132–59. Tuscaloosa: University of Alabama Press.

1993b   The Evolution of Seed Morphology in Domesticated *Chenopodium:* An Archaeo-
        logical Case Study. *Journal of Ethnobiology* 13:149–69.
1993c   Crop and Weed in Prehistoric Eastern North America: The *Chenopodium* Example.
        American Antiquity 58:496–509.
1993d   Plant Husbandry at the Archaic/Woodland Transition: Evidence from the Cold
        Oak Shelter, Kentucky. *Midcontinental Journal of Archaeology* 18:161–89.
1995   Comparative Paleoethnobotany of Three Native Southeastern Communities of the
        Historic Period. *Southeastern Archaeology* 14:1–16.
1996a   The Paleoethnobotanical Record for the Southeastern United States. In *Archaeol-
        ogy of the Mid-Holocene Southeast,* edited by Kenneth E. Sassaman and David G.
        Anderson, pp. 99–115. Gainesville: University Press of Florida.
1996b   Diffusion and Adoption of Crops in Evolutionary Perspective. *Journal of Anthro-
        pological Archaeology* 15:183–204.
1998   Changing Roles of Wild and Cultivated Plant Resources among Early Farmers of
        Eastern Kentucky. *Southeastern Archaeology* 17:140–57.
Gremillion, Kristen J., and Kristin D. Sobolik
1996   Dietary Variability among Prehistoric Forager-Farmers of Eastern North America.
        Current Anthropology 37:529–39.
Gremillion, Kristen J., and Richard A. Yarnell
1986   Plant Remains from the Westmoreland-Barber and Pittman-Alder Sites, Marion
        County, Tennessee. *Tennessee Anthropologist* 11:1–20.
Gresham, Thomas H., W. Dean Wood, Chad O. Braley, and Kay G. Wood
1985   *The Carmouche Site: Archeology in Georgia's Western Fall Line Hills.* Submitted
        to the U.S. Army Corps of Engineers, Savannah District, Savannah, Ga., by South-
        eastern Archeological Services, Inc., Athens, Ga.
Griffin, James B.
1939   Report of the Ceramics of the Wheeler Basin. In *An Archaeological Survey of
        Wheeler Basin on the Tennessee River in Northern Alabama,* by W. S. Webb, pp.
        127–65. Bulletin 122, Bureau of American Ethnology, Smithsonian Institution,
        Washington, D.C.
1941   Report on Pottery from the St. Louis Area. *The Missouri Archaeologist* 7(2):1–17.
1943a   *Adena Village Pottery from Fayette County, Kentucky.* University of Kentucky
        Reports in Anthropology and Archaeology 5(7):667–72, Lexington.
1943b   An Analysis and Interpretation of Ceramic Remains from Two Sites near Beaufort,
        South Carolina. *Bureau of American Ethnology Bulletin* 133:159–68.
1945a   *The Ceramic Affiliation of the Ohio Valley Adena Culture.* University of Kentucky
        Reports in Anthropology and Archaeology 6:220–46, Lexington.
1945b   *Ceramic Collections from Two South Carolina Sites.* Papers of the Michigan Acad-
        emy of Science, Arts, and Letters 30:465–78.
1946   Change and Continuity in Eastern United States Archaeology. In *Man in North-
        eastern North America,* edited by Frederick Johnson, pp. 37–95. Papers of the
        Robert S. Peabody Foundation for Archaeology 3, Andover.
1952a   Culture Periods in Eastern United States Archeology. In *Archeology of Eastern
        United States,* edited by James B. Griffin, pp. 352–64. Chicago: University of
        Chicago Press.
1952b   Some Early and Middle Woodland Pottery Types in Illinois. In *Hopewellian Com-
        munities in Illinois,* edited by Thorne Deuel, pp. 93–129. Scientific Papers 5, Illi-
        nois State Museum, Springfield.
1952c   The Late Prehistoric Cultures of the Ohio Valley. *Ohio State Archaeological and
        Historical Quarterly* 61(2):166–95.

1952d   Prehistoric Cultures of the Central Mississippi Valley. In *Archeology of Eastern United States,* edited by James B. Griffin, pp. 226–38. Chicago: University of Chicago Press.

1958   *The Chronological Position of the Hopewellian Culture in the Eastern United States.* Anthropological Papers No. 12, Museum of Anthropology, University of Michigan, Ann Arbor.

1960   Climatic Change: A Contributory Cause of the Growth and Decline of Northern Hopewellian Culture. *Wisconsin Archeologist* 41(1):21–33.

1966   Mesoamerica and the Eastern United States in Prehistoric Times. In *Handbook of Middle American Indians.* Vol. 4, *Archaeological Frontiers and External Connections,* edited by R. Wauchope, pp. 111–31. Austin: University of Texas Press.

1967   Eastern North American Archeology: A Summary. *Science* 15(3772):175–91.

1979   An Overview of the Chillicothe Hopewell Conference. In *Hopewell Archaeology: The Chillicothe Conference,* edited by D. Brose and N. Greber, pp. 266–79. Kent, Ohio: Kent State University Press.

1986a   The Tchula Period in the Mississippi Valley. In *The Tchula Period in the Midsouth and Lower Mississippi Valley,* edited by David H. Dye and Ronald C. Brister, pp. 40–42. Proceedings of the 1982 Mid-south Archaeological Conference, Mississippi Department of Archives and History, Jackson.

1986b   Comments on the Kampsville Early Woodland Conference. In *Early Woodland Archaeology,* edited by Kenneth B. Farnsworth and Thomas E. Emerson, pp. 609–20. Center for American Archaeology Press, Kampsville, Ill.

1997   Interpretations of Ohio Hopewell 1845–1984 and the Recent Emphasis on the Study of Dispersed Hamlets. In *Ohio Hopewell Community Organization,* edited by William S. Dancey and Paul J. Pacheco, pp. 405–26. Kent, Ohio: Kent State University Press.

Griffin, James B. (editor)
1952   *Archaeology of Eastern United States.* Chicago: University of Chicago Press.

Griffin, James B., and W. H. Sears
1950   Certain Sand-Tempered Pottery Types of the Southeast. In *Prehistoric Pottery of the Eastern United States,* edited by James B. Griffin. Museum of Anthropology, University of Michigan, Ann Arbor.

Griffin, James B., and Albert C. Spaulding
1952   The Central Mississippi River Valley Archaeological Survey, Season 1950: A Preliminary Report. In *Prehistoric Pottery of Eastern United States,* edited by James B. Griffin, pp. 1–7. Museum of Anthropology, University of Michigan, Ann Arbor.

Griffin, James B., Richard E. Flanders, and Paul F. Titterington
1970   *The Burial Complexes of the Knight and Norton Mounds in Illinois and Michigan.* Memoirs No. 2, Museum of Anthropology, University of Michigan, Ann Arbor.

Griffin, John W.
1972   Fiber-Tempered Pottery in the Tennessee Valley. *Florida Anthropologist* 25(2):34–36.

1985   Conclusions. In *Excavations at the Granada Site: Archaeology and History of the Granada Site,* vol. 1, edited by John W. Griffin, S. B. Richardson, Mary Pohl, C. D. McMurray, C. Margaret Scarry, Susan K. Fish, E. S. Wing, L. Jill Loucks, and M. K. Welch, pp. 365–94. Florida Division of Archives, History and Records Management, Tallahassee.

1988   *The Archaeology of Everglades National Park.* National Park Service, Southeastern Archaeological Center, Tallahassee.

1996   Some Highlights in the History of Florida Archaeology. In *Fifty Years of South-eastern Archaeology: Selected Works of John W. Griffin,* edited by P. C. Griffin, pp. 115–23. Gainesville: University Press of Florida.

Guendling, Randy L.
1996   *Test Excavations at the Faulkner Lake Sites: 3PU115, 3PU163, and 3PU410, Pulaski County, Arkansas.* Arkansas Archeological Survey (Project No. 939), Fayetteville. Submitted to the Arkansas Highway and Transportation Department.

Guendling, Randy L., George Sabo III, M. J. Guccione, S. L. Dunavan, and Susan L. Scott
1992   *Archeological Investigations at 3MR80-Area D in the Rush Development Area, Buffalo National River, Arkansas, Volume II.* Professional Papers 50, Southwest Cultural Resources Center, Santa Fe.

Guilday, John E., and Paul W. Parmalee
1975   Faunal Remains from the Zebree Site. Appendix I in *Report of Excavations at the Zebree Site 1969,* by D. F. Morse, pp. 228–34. Arkansas Archeological Survey Research Report No. 4, Fayetteville.

Gunn, Joel D. (editor)
2000   *The Years Without Summer: Tracing A.D. 536 and Its Aftermath.* British Archaeological Reports International Series 872, Archaeopress, London.

Gunn, Joel D., Thomas G. Lilly, Cheryl Claassen, John Byrd, and Andrea Brewer Shea
1995   *Archaeological Data Recovery Investigations at Sites 38BU905 and 38BU921 along the Hilton Head Cross Island Expressway, Beaufort County, South Carolina.* Submitted to the South Carolina Department of Transportation, Columbia, by Garrow and Associates, Inc., Raleigh.

Haag, William G.
1939a   Pickwick Basin Pottery Type Descriptions. *Southeastern Archaeological Conference Newsletter* 1(1):1–17.
1939b   Description of Pottery Types. *Southeastern Archaeological Conference Newsletter* 1(3).
1942a   *The Pottery from the C and O Mounds at Paintsville.* Reports in Anthropology and Archaeology 5(4):341–49, Department of Anthropology and Archaeology, University of Kentucky, Lexington.
1942b   Pickwick Basin Pottery. In *An Archaeological Survey of the Pickwick Basin in the Adjacent Portions of the Sates of Alabama, Mississippi, and Tennessee,* by William S. Webb and David L. DeJarnette, pp. 509–26. Bulletin 129, Bureau of American Ethnology, Smithsonian Institution, Washington, D.C.
1958   *The Archaeology of Coastal North Carolina.* Louisiana State University Studies, Coastal Studies Series Number Two, Louisiana State University Press, Baton Rouge.

Hall, G. D.
1981   *Allen's Creek: A Study in the Prehistory of the Lower Brazos River Valley, Texas.* Research Report 61, Texas Archeological Survey, University of Texas at Austin.

Hall, Linda, and C. Michael Baker
1993   *Data Recovery at 31BN175, The Biltmore Estate, Buncombe County, North Carolina.* Ms. on file at Office of State Archaeology, Raleigh (ER 93-7128).

Hall, Robert L.
1979   In Search of the Ideology of the Adena-Hopewell Climax. In *Hopewell Archaeology: The Chillicothe Conference,* edited by D. Brose and N. Greber, pp. 258–65. Kent, Ohio: Kent State University Press.
1980   An Interpretation of the Two Climax Model of Illinois Prehistory. In *Early Native Americans: Prehistoric Demography, Economy, and Technology,* edited by David Browman, pp. 401–62. The Hague: Mouton.

1997   *An Archaeology of the Soul: North American Indian Belief and Ritual.* Urbana and Chicago: University of Illinois Press.

Hally, David J.

1972   *The Plaquemine and Mississippian Occupations of the Upper Tensas Basin, Louisiana.* Ph.D. dissertation, Department of Anthropology, Harvard University, Cambridge.

1975   Complicated Stamped Pottery and Platform Mounds: The Origins of South Appalachian Mississippian. Discussion. *Southeastern Archaeological Conference Bulletin* 18:43–47.

1986   The Identification of Vessel Function: A Case Study from Northwest Georgia. *American Antiquity* 51:267–95.

Hanley, Robert W.

1982   An Analysis of the Mollusk Remains from Site 22Cl814. In *Archaeological Investigations at the Yarborough Site (22Cl814), Clay County, Mississippi,* by C. Solis and R. Walling, pp. 153–55. Report of Investigations 30, Office of Archaeological Research, University of Alabama, University.

1983   Mollusk Remains. In *Archaeological Investigations at the B. B. Comer Bridge Site, 1Ja78, Jackson County, Alabama,* by Eugene M. Futato and Carlos Solis, pp. 67–72. Report of Investigations 31, Office of Archaeological Research, University of Alabama, University.

1984   Invertebrate Animal Remains [1Tu4]. In *The Protohistoric Period in Central Alabama,* by Cailup B. Curren, Jr., pp. 162–65. Alabama Tombigbee Regional Commission, Camden.

Hann, John H.

1991   *Missions to the Calusa.* Gainesville: University Presses of Florida.

Hanson, Glen T.

1988   The George S. Lewis Site (38AK228) West Area: The Deptford Component. Presented at the 11th annual meeting of the Archeological Society of South Carolina, Columbia.

Hanson, Lee H.

1960   *The Analysis, Distribution and Seriation of Pottery from the Green River Drainage as a Basis for an Archaeological Sequence of That Area.* Department of Anthropology, University of Kentucky, Lexington.

Hantman, Jeffrey L.

1985   *The Archaeology of Albemarle County.* University of Virginia Archaeological Survey Monograph No. 2, Department of Anthropology, University of Virginia, Charlottesville.

1990   Between Powhatan and Quirank: Reconstructing Monacan Culture and History in the Context of Jamestown. *American Anthropologist* 92:676–90.

1993   Powhatan's Relations with the Piedmont Monacans. In *Powhatan Foreign Relations,* edited by Helen Rountree, pp. 94–111. Charlottesville: University Press of Virginia.

Hantman, Jeffrey L., and Michael Klein

1992   Middle and Late Woodland Archaeology in Piedmont Virginia. In *Middle and Late Woodland Archaeology in Virginia: A Synthesis,* edited by T. Reinhart and M. E. N. Hodges, pp. 137–64. Archaeological Society of Virginia Special Publication No. 24, Richmond.

Harden, P., and D. Robinson

1975   A Descriptive Report of the Vanderpool Site, CK-32, Cherokee County, Oklahoma. *Bulletin of the Oklahoma Anthropological Society* 23:91–168.

Hargrave, Michael L., Charles R. Cobb, and Paul A. Webb
1991 Late Prehistoric Style Zones in Southern Illinois. In *Stability, Transformation, and Variation: The Late Woodland Southeast,* edited by Michael S. Nassaney and Charles R. Cobb, pp. 149–76. New York: Plenum Press.

Hargrove, Thomas H.
1993 *Archaeological Excavations at 31NH142, Hamp's Landing, River Road Park, New Hanover County, North Carolina.* Submitted to New Hanover County, Department of Parks and Recreation, Wilmington, S.C.

Hargrove, Thomas H., and Jane M. Eastman
1997 Limestone- or Marl-Tempered Ceramics from the Lower Cape Fear River Region, New Hanover County, North Carolina. *North Carolina Archaeology* 46:91–108.
1998 Limestone- or Marl-Tempered Ceramics from the Lower Cape Fear River Region, New Hanover County, North Carolina. Presented at the 55th annual meeting of the Southeastern Archaeological Conference, Greenville, S.C.

Harl, Joseph L.
1995 *Master Plan for the Management of Archaeological Cultural Resources within St. Louis City and County, Missouri.* Research Report No. 203, Archaeological Services, University of Missouri-St. Louis.

Harmon, Anna M., and Jerome C. Rose
1989 Bioarchaeology of the Louisiana and Arkansas Study Area. In *Archaeology and Bioarchaeology of the Lower Mississippi Valley and Trans-Mississippi South in Arkansas and Louisiana,* by Marvin D. Jeter, Jerome C. Rose, G. Ismael Williams, and A. M. Harmon, pp. 323–54. Arkansas Archeological Survey Research Series No. 37, Fayetteville.

Harn, Alan
1971 *An Archaeological Survey of the American Bottoms and Wood River Terrace.* Illinois State Museum Reports of Investigation No. 21, Pt. 1, Springfield.

Hart, John P.
1999 Maize Agriculture Evolution in the Eastern Woodlands of North America: A Darwinian Perspective. *Journal of Archaeological Method and Theory* 6:137–80.

Hartfield, Paul
1990 Mussels. In *Archaeological Investigations at the Sanders Site (22CL917), an Alexander Midden on the Tombigbee River, Clay County, Mississippi,* by John W. O'Hear, pp. 76–79. Report of Investigations 6, Cobb Institute of Archaeology, Mississippi State University.

Haskins, Valerie A.
1987 *The Prehistory of Prewitts Knob, Kentucky.* Master's thesis, Department of Anthropology, Washington University, St. Louis.

Hawkins, Rebecca Anne
1996 Revising the Ohio Middle Woodland Ceramic Typology: New Information from the Twin Mounds West Site. In *A View from the Core: A Synthesis of Ohio Hopewell Archaeology,* edited by Paul J. Pacheco, pp. 70–91. Columbus: Ohio Archaeological Council.

Hayden, Brian
1995 Pathways to Power: Principles for Creating Socioeconomic Inequalities. In *Foundations of Social Inequality,* edited by T. Douglas Price and Gary Feinman, pp. 15–86. New York: Plenum Press.

Hays, Chris
1995 *1995 Annual Report for Management Units IV and V.* Louisiana Division of Archaeology, Baton Rouge.

Heiser, Charles
  1978   Taxonomy of Helianthus and Origin of Domesticated Sunflower. In *Sunflower Science and Technology,* edited by Jack F. Carter, pp. 31–53. American Society of Agronomy, Madison, Wis.
Hemmings, E. Thomas
  1975   An Archaeological Survey of the South Prong of the Alafia River, Florida. *Florida Anthropologist* 28:41–51.
  1978   Cades Pond Subsistence, Settlement, and Ceremonialism. *Florida Anthropologist* 31:141–50.
  1982   *Human Adaptation in the Grand Marais Lowland: Intensive Archeological Survey and Testing in the Felsenthal Navigation Pool, Ouachita and Saline Rivers, Southern Arkansas.* Arkansas Archeological Survey Research Series No. 17, Fayetteville.
Hemmings, E. Thomas, and John H. House (editors)
  1985   *The Alexander Site, Conway County, Arkansas.* Arkansas Archeological Survey Research Series No. 24, Fayetteville.
Henderson, A. Gwynn, and David Pollack
  1985   The Late Woodland Occupation at the Bentley Site. In *Woodland Period Research in Kentucky,* edited by David Pollack, Thomas Sanders, and Charles Hockensmith, pp. 140–64. Frankfort: Kentucky Heritage Council.
Herbert, Joseph M.
  1997   *Refining Prehistoric Culture Chronology in Southern North Coastal Carolina: Pottery from the Papanow and Pond Trail Sites.* Submitted to the State of North Carolina, Department of Cultural Resources, Division of Archives and History, Office of State Archaeology, Raleigh.
  1999   Prehistoric Pottery Taxonomy and Sequence on the Southern Coast of North Carolina. *North Carolina Archaeology* 48:37–58.
  2000   Sequencing Ceramics from the Carolina Sandhills. Presented at the 65th annual meeting of the Society for American Archaeology, Philadelphia.
Herbert, Joseph M., and Mark A. Mathis
  1996   An Appraisal and Re-evaluation of the Prehistoric Pottery Sequence of Southern Coastal North Carolina. In *Indian Pottery of the Carolinas: Observations from the March 1995 Ceramic Workshop at Hobcaw Barony,* edited by David G. Anderson, pp. 136–89. Council of South Carolina Professional Archaeologists, Columbia.
Hill, James K.
  1970   *Broken K Pueblo: Prehistoric Social Organization in the American Southwest.* Anthropological Papers 18, Museum of Anthropology, University of Arizona, Tucson.
Hill, Mary Cassandra
  1981   Analysis, Synthesis, and Interpretation of the Skeletal Material Excavated for the Gainesville Section of the Tennessee-Tombigbee Waterway. In *Biocultural Studies in the Gainesville Lake Area,* by G. M. Caddell, A. Woodrick, and M. C. Hill, pp. 211–334. Report of Investigations 14, University of Alabama Office of Archaeological Research, University.
  1987   Emergent Mississippian Cultures. In *The Emergent Mississippian: Proceedings of the Sixth Mid-South Archaeological Conference,* edited by Richard A. Marshall, pp. 239–52. Occasional Papers 87-01, Cobb Institute of Archaeology, Mississippi State University.
Hill, M. O., and H. G. Gauch
  1980   Detrended Correspondence Analysis: An Improved Ordination Technique. *Vegetatio* 42:47–58.

Hodder, Ian
1990 *The Domestication of Europe: Structure and Contingency in Neolithic Societies.* Oxford: Basil Blackwell.

Hodder, Ian, and Clive Orton
1976 *Spatial Analysis in Archaeology.* Cambridge: Cambridge University Press.

Hoffman, Curtiss
1998 Pottery and Steatite in the Northeast: A Reconsideration of Origins. *Northeast Anthropology* 56:43–68.

Hoffman, Michael P.
1977 An Archeological Survey of the Ozark Reservoir in West-Central Arkansas. In *Ozark Reservoir Papers: Archeology in West-Central Arkansas, 1965–1970,* edited by Michael P. Hoffman, pp. 1–44. Arkansas Archeological Survey Research Series No. 10, Fayetteville.

Hoffman, Robert W.
1998 The Faunal Material. In *Toltec Mounds and Plum Bayou Culture: Mound D Excavations,* by Martha A. Rolingson, pp. 84–94. Arkansas Archeological Survey Research Series No. 54, Fayetteville.

Hoffman, T. L.
1998 The Lithic Assemblage: A Technological Approach. In *Toltec Mounds and Plum Bayou Culture: Mound D Excavations,* by Martha A. Rolingson, pp. 54–79. Arkansas Archeological Survey Research Series No. 54, Fayetteville.

Hofman, Jack L.
1980 Twenhafel Archaeology: The Southeastern Connection. *Tennessee Anthropologist* 5(2):185–201.

Hogue, S. Homes, and William Erwin
1993 A Preliminary Analysis of Diet Change Using Small Burial Samples from Three Sites in Mississippi. *Mississippi Archaeology* 28(1):1–19.

Holden, Patricia Padgett
1966 *An Archaeological Survey of Transylvania County, North Carolina.* Master's thesis, University of North Carolina at Chapel Hill.

Holland, C. G., S. Pennell, and R. Allen
1981 Geographical List of Soapstone Artifacts from Twenty-One Aboriginal Quarries in the Eastern United States. *Quarterly Bulletin of the Archaeological Society of Virginia* 35:200–208.

Holland-Lilly, Mimi
1996 Batesville Mounds: Recent Investigations at a Middle Woodland Site. *Mississippi Archaeology* 31(1):40–55.

Holley, George R.
2000 Late Woodland on the Edge of Looking Glass Prairie: A Joint-Use Archaeological Project Perspective. In *Late Woodland Societies: Tradition and Transformation across the Midcontinent,* edited by Thomas E. Emerson, Dale L. McElrath, and Andrew C. Fortier, pp. 149–62. Lincoln: University of Nebraska Press.

Holm, Mary Ann
n.d. Identification of Faunal Remains, 31BN174. Manuscript prepared for Western Office of North Carolina Department of Archives and History, Asheville.

Holmes, William H.
1903 Aboriginal Pottery of the Eastern United States. *Bureau of American Ethnology, Annual Report* 20:1–201.

Hopgood, J. F.
1967 The Burkett Site (23MI-20). In *Land Leveling Salvage Archaeological Work in*

Southeast Missouri: 1966, by J. R. Williams, pp. 293–304. Submitted to the National Park Service, Midwest Archeological Center, Lincoln, Neb.

1969 *Continuity and Change in the Baytown Pottery Tradition of the Cairo Lowland, Southeast Missouri.* Master's thesis, Department of Anthropology, University of Missouri, Columbia.

House, John H.

1975 Summary of Archeological Knowledge Updated with Newly Gathered Data. In *The Cache River Archeological Project: An Experiment in Contract Archeology,* edited by Michael B. Schiffer and John H. House, pp. 153–62. Arkansas Archeological Survey Research Series No. 8, Fayetteville.

1982a *Powell Canal: Baytown Period Occupation on Bayou Macon in Southeast Arkansas.* Arkansas Archeological Survey Research Series No. 19, Fayetteville.

1982b Evolution of Complex Societies in East-Central Arkansas: An Overview of Environments and Regional Data Bases. In *Arkansas Archeology in Review,* edited by N. L. Trubowitz and Marvin D. Jeter, pp. 37–47. Arkansas Archeological Survey Research Series No. 15, Fayetteville.

1990 Powell Canal: Baytown Period Adaptation on Bayou Macon, Southeast Arkansas. In *The Mississippian Emergence,* edited by Bruce D. Smith, pp. 9–26. Washington, D.C.: Smithsonian Institution Press.

1996 East-Central Arkansas. In *Prehistory of the Central Mississippi Valley,* edited by Charles H. McNutt, pp. 137–54. Tuscaloosa: University of Alabama Press.

House, John H., and Marvin D. Jeter

1994 Excavations at Boydell Mound A (3AS58), Southeast Arkansas. *Arkansas Archeologist* 33:1–82.

House, John H., and Michael B. Schiffer

1975 Significance of the Archeological Resources of the Cache River Basin. In *The Cache River Archeological Project: An Experiment in Contract Archeology,* edited by Michael B. Schiffer and John H. House, pp. 163–86. Arkansas Archeological Survey Research Series No. 8, Fayetteville.

Hubbard, David A., Jr., and Michael B. Barber

1997 Virginia Burial Caves: An Inventory of a Desecrated Resource. *Journal of Cave and Karst Studies (National Speleological Society Bulletin)* 59:154–59.

Hudson, Charles

1970 *The Catawba Nation.* Athens: University of Georgia Press.

1997 *Knights of Spain, Warriors of the Sun: Hernando de Soto and the South's Ancient Chiefdoms.* Athens: University of Georgia Press.

Hunter, Donald G., and William S. Baker, Jr.

1979 Excavations in the Atkins Midden at the Troyville Site, Catahoula Parish, Louisiana. *Louisiana Archaeology* 4:21–52.

Hunter, Donald G., Gayle J. Fritz, Whitney J. Autin, and Kam-biu Liu

1995 *Manifest East: Cultural Resources Investigations along Portions of Highway 8, Catahoula Parish, Louisiana.* Baton Rouge: Coastal Environments.

Ingold, Tim

1986 *The Appropriation of Nature.* Manchester, U.K.: Manchester University Press.

Irwin, Jeffrey C., Wayne C. J. Boyko, Joseph M. Herbert, and Chad Braley

1999 Woodland Burial Mounds in the North Carolina Sandhills and Southern Coastal Plain. *North Carolina Archaeology* 48:59–86.

Jackson, Douglas K.

1996 *The Vaughn Branch Site (11-Ms-1437): Late Woodland and Mississippian Occupations in the American Bottom.* Research Reports No. 42, Illinois Transportation

Archaeological Research Program, University of Illinois, Urbana.

Jackson, H. Edwin

1986 *Sedentism and Hunter-Gatherer Adaptations in the Lower Mississippi Valley: Subsistence Strategies during the Poverty Point Period.* Ph.D. dissertation, University of Michigan, Ann Arbor. University Microfilms, Ann Arbor.

1989 Adaptive Systems in the Lower Mississippi Valley during the Poverty Point Period: Subsistence Remains from the J. W. Copes Site. *North American Archaeologist* 10(3):174–204.

1991 Bottomland Resources and Exploitation Strategies during the Poverty Point Period: Implications of the Archaeological Record from the J. W. Copes Site. In *The Poverty Point Culture: Local Manifestations, Subsistence Practices and Trade Networks,* edited by K. M. Byrd, pp. 131–57. Geoscience and Man 29, Geoscience Publications, Department of Geography and Anthropology, Louisiana State University, Baton Rouge.

1995 *Archaeological Investigations at the Burkett's Creek Site (22-FO-748), Hattiesburg, Mississippi.* Scott and Associates, Hattiesburg, Miss.

1998 Little Spanish Fort: An Early Middle Woodland Enclosure in the Lower Yazoo Basin, Mississippi. *Midcontinental Journal of Archaeology* 23:199–220.

Jackson, H. Edwin, and Rita D. Fields

2000 *Phase II Testing of 22GN668, Greene County, Mississippi.* Report prepared for Mississippi Department of Transportation, Jackson.

Jackson, H. Edwin, and Marvin D. Jeter

1994 Preceramic Earthworks in Arkansas: A Report on the Poverty Point Period Lake Enterprise Mound (3AS379). *Southeastern Archaeology* 13:153–62.

Jackson, H. Edwin, and Susan L. Scott

1995 The Faunal Record of the Southeastern Elite: The Implications of Economy, Social Relations, and Ideology. *Southeastern Archaeology* 14(2):103–19.

Jackson, H. Edwin, and Kate E. McLaurin-Wright

2000 *Phase II Testing of 22FO1023, The Chief Cato Site, Forrest County, Mississippi.* Report prepared for Environmental Division, Mississippi Department of Transportation, Jackson.

Jackson, H. Edwin, Melissa Reams, and Robert Reams

1995 Cultural and Chronological Trends of the Mississippi Gulf Coastal Plain: A Synthesis of Recent Research. Presented at the 52nd annual meeting of the Southeastern Archaeological Conference, Knoxville, Tenn.

Jackson, H. Edwin, Melissa Reams, and Kate Wright

1999 Prehistoric Upland Occupation and Notions of Significance: Investigations at 22-Jo-699, an Insignificant Site in the Pine Hills of Mississippi. Presented at the 56th annual meeting of the Southeastern Archaeological Conference, Pensacola, Fla.

Jackson, Paul D.

1996 *An Examination of Late Woodland Features in the Tombigbee, Black Warrior, and Tennessee River Valleys.* Master's thesis, Department of Anthropology, University of Alabama, Tuscaloosa.

Janowski, Monica

1995 The Hearth-Group, the Conjugal Couple and the Symbolism of the Rice Meal among the Kelabit of Sarawak. In *About the House,* edited by J. Carsten and S. Hugh-Jones, pp. 84–104. Cambridge: Cambridge University Press.

Janus Research

1995 *Archaeological Investigations at the Summer Haven Site (8SJ46), An Orange Period and St. Johns Period Midden Site in Southeastern St. Johns County, Florida.*

Report prepared for Florida Department of Transportation, District Two, Lake City, Fla., by Janus Research, St. Petersburg, Fla.

Jefferies, Richard W.

1976 *The Tunacunnhee Site: Evidence of Hopewell Interaction in Northwest Georgia.* Anthropological Papers of the University of Georgia No. 1, Athens.

1979 The Tunacunnhee Site: Hopewell in Northwest Georgia. In *Hopewell Archaeology: The Chillicothe Conference,* edited by D. Brose and N. Greber, pp. 162–70. Kent, Ohio: Kent State University Press.

1994 The Swift Creek Site and Woodland Platform Mounds in the Southeastern United States. In *Ocmulgee Archaeology, 1936–1986,* edited by D. J. Hally, pp. 71–83. Athens: University of Georgia Press.

1996 The Emergence of Long-Distance Exchange Networks in the Southeastern United States. In *Archaeology of the Mid-Holocene Southeast,* edited by Kenneth E. Sassaman and David G. Anderson, pp. 222–34. Gainesville: University Press of Florida.

Jenkins, Cliff

1993 The Use of Vertebrate Fauna in the Subsistence System during the Transition from Late Woodland to Mature Mississippian: The Tibbee Creek Site (22-Lo-600), Lowndes County, Mississippi. *Mississippi Archaeology* 28(2):45– 73.

Jenkins, Cliff, Kevin L. Bruce, Philip J. Carr, and Bruce J. Gray

1997 *Cultural Resources Survey of Proposed Relocation of Mississippi Highway 6 between Pontotoc and Tupelo, Pontotoc and Lee Counties, Mississippi.* Mississippi Department of Transportation, Jackson.

Jenkins, Ned J.

1974 Subsistence and Settlement Patterns in the Western Middle Tennessee Valley during the Transitional Archaic-Woodland Period. *Journal of Alabama Archaeology* 20:183–93.

1981 *Gainesville Lake Area Ceramic Description and Chronology. Archaeological Investigations of the Gainesville Lake Area of the Tennessee-Tombigbee Waterway,* vol. 2. Report of Investigations 12, Office of Archaeological Research, University of Alabama, Tuscaloosa.

1982 *Archaeology of the Gainesville Lake Area: Synthesis.* Report of Investigations 23, Office of Archaeological Research, University of Alabama, Tuscaloosa.

Jenkins, Ned J., and Cailup B. Curren, Jr.

1975 Archaeological Investigations on the Central Tombigbee River, Alabama: Chronology, Subsistence, and Settlement Patterns: A Preliminary Report. Presented at 32nd annual meeting of the Southeastern Archaeological Conference, Gainesville, Fla.

Jenkins, Ned J., and H. Blaine Ensor

1981 *The Gainesville Lake Area Excavations.* Report of Investigations 11, Office of Archaeological Research, University of Alabama, Tuscaloosa.

Jenkins, Ned J., and Richard A. Krause

1986 *The Tombigbee Watershed in Southeastern Prehistory.* Tuscaloosa: University of Alabama Press.

Jenkins, Ned J., Cailup B. Curren, and Mark R. DeLeon

1975 *Archaeological Site Survey of the Demopolis and Gainesville Lake Navigation Channels and Additional Construction Areas.* Submitted to the National Park Service by the University of Alabama Department of Anthropology.

Jenkins, Ned J., David H. Dye, and John A. Walthall

1986 Early Ceramic Development in the Gulf Coastal Plain. In *Early Woodland Archeology,* edited by Kenneth B. Farnsworth and Thomas E. Emerson, pp. 546–63.

Kampsville Seminars in Archeology 2, Center for American Archeology, Kampsville, Ill.

Jennings, Jesse D.
1941   Chickasaw and Earlier Indian Cultures of Northeast Mississippi. *Journal of Mississippi History* 3:155–226.
1952   Prehistory of the Lower Mississippi Valley. In *Archeology of Eastern United States,* edited by James B. Griffin, pp. 256–71. Chicago: University of Chicago Press.

Jennings, Jesse D., and Charles H. Fairbanks
1939   Pottery Type Description for Swift Creek Complicated Stamped. *Southeastern Archaeological Conference Newsletter* 1(2).

Jeter, Marvin D.
1977   Late Woodland Chronology and Change in Central Alabama. *Journal of Alabama Archaeology* 23:112–36.
1982   The Archeology of Southeast Arkansas: An Overview for the 1980s. In *Arkansas Archeology in Review,* edited by N. Trubowitz and M. Jeter, pp. 76–131. Arkansas Archeological Survey Research Series No. 15, Fayetteville.

Jeter, Marvin D. (editor)
1990   *Edward Palmer's Arkansaw Mounds.* Fayetteville: University of Arkansas Press.

Jeter, Marvin D., and G. Ishmael Williams, Jr.
1989   Ceramic-Using Cultures, 600 B.C.–A.D. 700. In *Archeology and Bioarcheology of the Lower Mississippi Valley and Trans-Mississippi South in Arkansas and Louisiana,* edited by Marvin D. Jeter, Jerome C. Rose, G. Ishmael Williams, Jr., and A. M. Harmon, pp. 111–70. Arkansas Archeological Survey Research Series No. 37, Fayetteville.

Jeter, Marvin D., Jerome C. Rose, G. Ishmael Williams, Jr., and A. M. Harmon
1989   *Archeology and Bioarcheology of the Lower Mississippi Valley and Trans-Mississippi South in Arkansas and Louisiana.* Arkansas Archeological Survey Research Series No. 37, Fayetteville.

Johannessen, Sissel
1984   Paleoethnobotany. In *American Bottom Archaeology,* edited by Charles J. Bareis and James W. Porter, pp. 197–214. Urbana: University of Illinois Press.
1993a   Farmers of the Late Woodland. In *Foraging and Farming in the Eastern Woodlands,* edited by C. Margaret Scarry, pp. 57–77. Gainesville: University Press of Florida.
1993b   Food, Dishes, and Society in the Mississippi Valley. In *Foraging and Farming in the Eastern Woodlands,* edited by C. Margaret Scarry, pp. 182–205. Gainesville: University Press of Florida.

Johnson, Allen W., and Timothy Earle
1987   *The Evolution of Human Society: From Forager Group to Agrarian State.* Palo Alto: Stanford University Press.

Johnson, G. Michael
1985   *Lithic Technology and Social Complexity at a North Florida Weeden Island Period Site.* Master's thesis, Department of Anthropology, Washington State University, Pullman.

Johnson, G. Michael, and Timothy A. Kohler
1987   Toward a Better Understanding of North Peninsular Gulf Coast Florida Prehistory: Archaeological Reconnaissance in Dixie County. *Florida Anthropologist* 40:275–86.

Johnson, Hunter, and Edmond A. Boudreaux
1998   The Florence Mound: A Middle Woodland Platform Mound in the Middle Tennes-

see Valley. Presented at the 55th annual meeting of the Southeastern Archaeological Conference, Greenville, S.C.

Johnson, Jay K.
  1985 Upland Subsistence Data from Colbert Ferry Park, Northwest Alabama. *Journal of Alabama Archaeology* 31(1):48–63.
  1988 Woodland Settlement in Northeast Mississippi: The Miller Tradition. In *Middle Woodland Settlement and Ceremonialism in the Mid-South and Lower Mississippi Valley: Proceedings of the 1984 Mid-South Archaeological Conference,* edited by Robert C. Mainfort, pp. 49–60. Archaeological Report 22, Mississippi Department of Archives and History, Jackson.
  1996 Excavations at the Batesville Mound Group, Panola County, Mississippi. Presented at the 53rd annual meeting of the Southeastern Archaeological Conference, Birmingham, Ala.

Johnson, Jay K., and James R. Atkinson
  1987 New Data on the Thelma Mound Group in Northeast Mississippi. In *The Emergent Mississippian,* edited by R. A. Marshall, pp. 63–70. Occasional Papers 87-01, Cobb Institute of Archaeology, Mississippi State University.

Johnson, Jay K., and Robert M. Thorne
  1987 *Cultural Resource Studies of Six Watersheds, Demonstration Erosion Control Project, Yazoo Basin, Mississippi, Phase I.* Submitted to the U.S. Army Corps of Engineers, Vicksburg, by the Center for Archaeological Research, University of Mississippi.

Johnson, Jay K., H. K. Curry, James R. Atkinson, and John T. Sparks
  1984 *Cultural Resources Survey in the Line Creek Watershed, Chickasaw, Clay and Webster Counties, Mississippi.* Submitted to the Soil Conservation Service by the Center for Archaeological Research, University of Mississippi.

Johnson, Jay K., Geoffrey R. Lehmann, James R. Atkinson, Susan L. Scott, and Andrea Shea
  1991 *Protohistoric Chickasaw Settlement Patterns and the De Soto Route in Northeast Mississippi.* Submitted to the National Endowment for the Humanities by the Center for Archaeological Research, University of Mississippi.

Johnson, Jay K., Gena M. Aleo, Rodney T. Stuart, and John Sullivan
  2001 *The 1996 Excavations at the Batesville Mounds: A Woodland Period Platform Mound Complex in Northwest Mississippi.* Archaeological Report 32, Mississippi Department of Archives and History, Jackson.

Johnson, Kenneth W.
  1986 *Archaeological Survey of Contact and Mission Period Sites in Northern Peninsular Florida.* Miscellaneous Project Report 37, Department of Anthropology, Florida Museum of Natural History, Gainesville.
  1987 *The Search for Aguacaleyquen and Cali.* Miscellaneous Project Report 33, Department of Anthropology, Florida Museum of Natural History, Gainesville.
  1991 *The Utina and the Potano Peoples of Northern Florida: Changing Settlement Systems in the Spanish Colonial Period.* Ph.D. dissertation, Department of Anthropology, University of Florida, Gainesville.

Johnson, Kenneth W., and Bruce C. Nelson
  1990 The Utina: Seriations and Chronology. *Florida Anthropologist* 43:48–62.
  1992 *High Plain Swamps and Flatwoods: Archaeological Survey of Portions of Baker, Columbia, and Union Counties in North Florida.* Miscellaneous Project Report 49, Department of Anthropology, Florida Museum of Natural History, Gainesville.

Johnson, Kenneth W., Bruce C. Nelson, and Keith A. Terry
  1988 *The Search for Early Spanish-Indian Sites in North Florida: Archaeological Sur-*

vey of Portions of Columbia, Suwannee, Union, and Adjacent Counties, Season II. Miscellaneous Project Report 38, Department of Anthropology, Florida Museum of Natural History, Gainesville.

Johnson, Matthew
1993 *Housing Culture: Traditional Architecture in an English Landscape.* Smithsonian Institution Press, Washington, D.C.
1996 *An Archaeology of Capitalism.* Oxford: Blackwell.

Jolly, Fletcher, III
1971 A Single Component, Alexander Assemblage from the Mingo Mound Site in the Bear Creek Watershed of N. E. Mississippi. *Tennessee Archaeologist* 27:1–38.

Jones, B. Calvin, and Louis D. Tesar
1996 *Emergency Archaeological Salvage Excavation within the Swift Creek Subarea of the Block-Sterns Site (8LE148), Leon County, Florida: A Public Archaeology Project.* Bureau of Archaeological Research, Division of Historical Resources, Florida Department of State, Tallahassee.

Jones, B. Calvin, Daniel T. Penton, and Louis D. Tesar
1998 1973 and 1994 Excavations at the Block-Sterns Site, Leon County, Florida. In *A World Engraved: Archaeology of the Swift Creek Culture,* edited by M. Williams and D. T. Elliott, pp. 222–46. Tuscaloosa: University of Alabama Press.

Jones, David C., Christopher T. Espenshade, and Linda Kennedy
1997 *Archaeological Investigation at 31ON190, Cape Island, Onslow County, North Carolina.* Submitted to The Island Development Group, Inc., Ringgold, Va., by Garrow and Associates, Atlanta. Copies available from the Office of State Archaeology, Raleigh.

Jones, Dennis, and Carl Kuttruff
1998 Prehistoric Enclosures in Louisiana and the Marksville Site. In *Ancient Earthen Enclosures of the Eastern Woodlands,* edited by Robert C. Mainfort, Jr., and Lynne P. Sullivan, pp. 31–56. Gainesville: University Press of Florida.

Jones, George T., and Charlotte Beck
1992 Chronological Resolution in Distributional Archaeology. In *Space, Time, and Archaeological Landscapes,* edited by J. Rossignol and L. Wandsnider, pp. 167–92. New York: Plenum Press.

Jones, Kenneth R., Herschel A. Franks, and Tristram R. Kidder
1994 *Cultural Resources Survey and Testing for Davis Pond Freshwater Diversion, St. Charles Parish, Louisiana,* 2 vols. Cultural Resources Series Report No. COELMN/PD-93/01, Earth Search, Inc., New Orleans.

Jones, Paul L., and Nina T. Borremans
1991 *An Archaeological Survey of the Gulf Hammock, Florida.* Report of Investigations submitted to the Division of Historical Resources, Dept. of State, Tallahassee, Fla.

Jones, Reca B.
1979 Human Effigy Vessels from Gold Mine Plantation. *Louisiana Archaeology* 4:117–21.

Jones, Volney H.
1949 Appendix in Maize from the Davis Site: Its Nature and Interpretation. *American Antiquity* 19(4):241–49.

Justice, Noel D.
1987 *Stone Age Spear and Arrow Points of the Midcontinental and Eastern United States: A Modern Survey and Reference.* Bloomington: Indiana University Press.

Kay, Marvin
1980 *The Central Missouri Hopewell Subsistence-Settlement System.* Research Series No. 15, Missouri Archaeological Society, Columbia.

Keel, Bennie C.
  1970   Excavations at the Red Springs Mound RB°4, Robeson County 1971. *Southern Indian Studies* 22:16–22.
  1976   *Cherokee Archaeology: A Study of the Appalachian Summit.* Knoxville: University of Tennessee Press.
  1978   1974 Excavations at the Nowlin II Site (40CF35). In *Sixth Report of the Normandy Archaeological Project,* edited by Major C. R. McCollough and Charles H. Faulkner, pp. ix–290. Report of Investigations 21, University of Tennessee, Department of Anthropology/Notes in Anthropology 4, Laboratory of Anthropology, Wright State University/TVA Publications in Anthropology 19, Knoxville.
Keel, Bennie C., and Brian J. Egloff
  1984   The Cane Creek Site, Mitchell County, North Carolina. *Southern Indian Studies* 33:1–44.
Keeler, Robert W.
  1971   An Archaeological Survey of the Upper Catawba River Valley. Bachelor of Arts Honors thesis, Dept. of Anthropology, University of North Carolina, Chapel Hill.
Keesing, Roger M.
  1987   Anthropology as Interpretive Quest. *Current Anthropology* 28:161–76.
Keith, Grace F.
  1997   *A Technological Analysis of Ceramics from the Leaf River Drainage, Southeast Mississippi.* Master's thesis, Department of Anthropology and Sociology, University of Southern Mississippi, Hattiesburg.
Keith, Scot
  1998   *Settlement and Lithic Organization from the Paleoindian through Late Woodland at the Sandhill Site (22-Wa-676), Southeast Mississippi.* Master's thesis, Department of Anthropology and Sociology, University of Southern Mississippi, Hattiesburg.
Kellar, James H.
  1979   The Mann Site and "Hopewell" in the Lower Wabash-Ohio Valley. In *Hopewell Archaeology: The Chillicothe Conference,* edited by D. Brose and N. Greber, pp. 100–107. Kent, Ohio: Kent State University Press.
Kellar, James H., A. R. Kelly, and Edward V. McMichael
  1961   *Final Report to the National Park Service, Mandeville Site, Georgia.* Ms. on file, Department of Anthropology, University of Georgia, Athens.
  1962a   The Mandeville Site in Southwest Georgia. *American Antiquity* 28:338–55.
  1962b   *Final Report on Archaeological Explorations at the Mandeville Site, 9Cla1 Clay County, Georgia, Seasons 1959, 1960, 1961.* Laboratory of Archaeology Series, Report No. 8, University of Georgia, Athens.
Keller, John E.
  1982   Lithic Scatters and Longleaf Pine: Limited Activity Areas in Pyrogenic Environments. *Southeastern Archaeology* 1:40–51.
Kelley, David B.
  1992   Coles Creek Period Faunal Exploitation in the Ouachita River Valley of Southern Arkansas. *Midcontinental Journal of Archaeology* 17:227–64.
Kelly, Arthur R.
  1938   *Preliminary Report on Archeological Explorations at Macon, Georgia.* Bulletin 119, Bureau of American Ethnology, Smithsonian Institution, Washington, D.C.
  1953   *A Weeden Island Burial Mound in Decatur County, Georgia, and Related Sites on the Lower Flint River.* Laboratory of Archaeology Series, Report 1, University of Georgia, Athens.

Kelly, Arthur R., and Betty A. Smith
    1975   The Swift Creek Site, 9-Bi-3, Macon, Georgia. Ms. 333 on file, Laboratory of Archaeology, University of Georgia, Athens. Submitted to the Southeast Archeological Center, National Park Service, Tallahassee, Fla.

Kelly, John E.
    1980   *Formative Developments at Cahokia and the Adjacent American Bottom: A Merrell Tract Perspective.* Ph.D. dissertation, Department of Anthropology, University of Wisconsin, Madison.

    1987   Emergent Mississippian and the Transition from Late Woodland to Mississippian: The American Bottom Case for a New Concept. In *The Emergent Mississippian: Proceedings of the Sixth Mid-South Archaeological Conference, June 6–9, 1985,* edited by R. A. Marshall, pp. 212–26. Occasional Papers 87-01. Mississippi State: Cobb Institute of Archaeology, Mississippi State University.

    1990a The Emergence of Mississippian Culture in the American Bottom Region. In *The Mississippian Emergence,* edited by Bruce D. Smith, pp. 113–52. Smithsonian Institution Press, Washington, D.C.

    1990b Range Site Community Patterns and the Mississippian Emergence. In *The Mississippian Emergence,* edited by Bruce D. Smith, pp. 67–112. Smithsonian Institution Press, Washington, D.C.

    1992   The Impact of Maize on the Development of Nucleated Settlements: An American Bottom Example. In *Late Prehistoric Agriculture: Observations from the Midwest,* edited by William I. Woods, pp. 167–97. Studies in Illinois Archaeology No. 8, Illinois Historic Preservation Agency, Springfield.

    1999   Notes of Moorehead's 1922–23 Investigations outside Cahokia. Ms. in possession of author.

    2000   The Grassy Lake Site: An Historical and Archaeological Overview. In *Mounds, Modoc, and Mesoamerica: Papers in Honor of Melvin L. Fowler,* edited by Steve R. Ahler, pp. 141–78. Scientific Papers 28, Illinois State Museum, Springfield.

    2001   *A Report on the Archaeological Mitigation of the Mozel Site (11MO858), Monroe County, Illinois.* Central Mississippi Valley Archaeological Research Institute. Submitted to the Illinois Historic Preservation Agency, Springfield.

Kelly, John E., Steven J. Ozuk, Douglas K. Jackson, Dale L. McElrath, Fred A. Finney, and Duane Esarey
    1984   Emergent Mississippian Period. In *American Bottom Archaeology: A Summary of the FAI-270 Project Contribution to the Culture History of the Mississippi River Valley,* edited by Charles J. Bareis and James W. Porter, pp. 128–57. Urbana: University of Illinois Press.

Kelly, John E., Andrew C. Fortier, Steven J. Ozuk, and Joyce A. Williams
    1987   *The Range Site: Archaic through Late Woodland Occupations.* American Bottom Archaeology FAI-270 Site Reports, Vol. 16, University of Illinois Press, Urbana.

Kelly, John E., Steven O. Ozuk, and Joyce A. Williams
    1990   *The Range Site 2: The Emergent Mississippian Dohack and Range Phase Occupations.* American Bottom Archaeology FAI-270 Site Reports, Vol. 20, University of Illinois Press, Urbana.

Kenion, Rita B.
    1989   *A Functional Analysis of the Middle to Late Woodland Ceramic Assemblage of the G. S. Lewis-West Site.* Master's thesis, Department of Anthropology, University of South Carolina, Columbia.

Kennedy, Mary C.
  1992   Aboriginal Dates from Mammoth Cave. *CRF Newsletter* (Cave Research Founda-
          tion, Yellow Springs, Ohio) 20(4):2–3.
Kennedy, Mary C., and Patty Jo Watson
  1997   The Chronology of Early Agriculture and Intensive Mineral Mining in the Salts
          Cave and Mammoth Cave Region, Mammoth Cave National Park, Kentucky. *Jour-
          nal of Cave and Karst Studies (National Speleological Society Bulletin)* 59:5–9.
Kennedy, Mary C., Christine Hensley-Martin, and Patty Jo Watson
  1984   CRF Archeological Project: 1983. In *Cave Research Foundation Annual Report
          for 1983,* pp. 22–23, Barbourville, Ky.
Kent, Susan (editor)
  1989   *Farmers as Hunters: The Implications of Sedentism.* Cambridge: Cambridge Uni-
          versity Press.
Kidder, T. R.
  1990   *Final Report on the 1989 Archaeological Investigations at the Osceola (16TE2)
          and Reno Brake (16TE93) Sites, Tensas Parish, Louisiana.* Archaeological Report
          1, Tulane University Center for Archaeology, New Orleans.
  1992a   Coles Creek Period Social Organization and Evolution in Northeast Louisiana. In
          *Lords of the Southeast: Social Inequality and the Native Elites of Southeastern
          North America,* edited by A. W. Barker and T. R. Pauketat, pp. 145–62. Archeologi-
          cal Papers of the American Anthropological Association No. 3, Washington, D.C.
  1992b   Timing and Consequences of the Introduction of Maize Agriculture in the Lower
          Mississippi Valley. *North American Archaeologist* 13:15–41.
  1994   Matheny: A Multicomponent Site on Bayou Bartholomew, Northeast Louisiana.
          Midcontinental Journal of Archaeology 19:137–69.
  1996   Perspectives on the Geoarchaeology of the Lower Mississippi Valley. *Engineering
          Geology* 45:305–23.
  1998a   Mississippi Period Mound Groups and Communities in the Lower Mississippi
          Valley. In *Mississippian Towns and Sacred Spaces,* edited by R. Barry Lewis and
          Charles Stout, pp. 123–50. Tuscaloosa: University of Alabama Press.
  1998b   Rethinking Caddoan–Lower Mississippi Valley Interaction. In *The Native History
          of the Caddo: Their Place in Southeastern Archeology and Ethnohistory,* edited
          by Timothy K. Perttula and James E. Bruseth, pp. 129–43. Studies in Archeology
          30, Texas Archeological Research Laboratory, University of Texas at Austin.
Kidder, Tristram R., and Gayle J. Fritz
  1993   Subsistence and Social Change in the Lower Mississippi Valley: The Reno Brake
          and Osceola Sites, Louisiana. *Journal of Field Archeology* 20:281–97.
Kidder, Tristram R., and Diane M. Ring
  1986   The Stevenson Site (16RI14 [22-J-2]). In *Final Report on Archaeological Test
          Excavations in the Central Boeuf Basin, Louisiana, 1985,* edited by T. R. Kidder,
          pp. 85–165. Bulletin 10, Lower Mississippi Survey, Peabody Museum, Harvard
          University, Cambridge.
Kimball, Larry R. (editor)
  1985   *The 1977 Archaeological Survey: An Overall Assessment of the Archaeological Re-
          sources of Tellico Reservoir.* Report of Investigations 40, Department of Anthropol-
          ogy, University of Tennessee, and TVA Publications in Anthropology 39, Knoxville.
King, Frances B.
  1985   Presettlement Vegetation and Plant Remains. In *The Alexander Site, Conway
          County, Arkansas,* edited by E. Thomas Hemmings and John H. House, pp. 49–
          57. Arkansas Archeological Survey Research Series No. 24, Fayetteville.

1987   Presettlement Vegetation and Plant Remains from the Ink Bayou Site. In *Results of Final Testing for Significance at the Ink Bayou Site (3PU252), Pulaski County, Arkansas,* by David B. Waddell, John H. House, Frances B. King, M. L. Colburn, and M. K. Marks, pp. 235–49. Arkansas Archeological Survey (Project No. 577), Fayetteville. Submitted to the Arkansas Highway and Transportation Department.

Kirchen, Roger
1997   Woodland Beginnings in the Western Piedmont of North Carolina. Presented at the 54th annual meeting of the Southeastern Archaeological Conference, Baton Rouge.

Kirkland, S. Dwight, and Robert E. Johnson
2001   *Archeological Data Recovery at the Greenfield Site No. 5 (8DU5541), Wonderwood Road Project (Arlington to Mayport Connector), Duval County, Florida.* Florida Archeological Services, Jacksonville. Submitted to Aerostar Environmental Services, Jacksonville.

Kitchline, Herbert E.
1941   Supplemental Climatic Notes for North Carolina. In *Yearbook of Agriculture: Climate and Man,* pp. 1043–44. U.S. Department of Agriculture, Washington, D.C.

Klein, Michael
1997   The Transition from Soapstone Bowls to Marcey Creek Ceramics in the Middle Atlantic Region: A Consideration of Vessel Technology, Ethnographic Data, and Regional Exchange. *Archaeology of Eastern North America* 25:143–58.

Klein, Terry H., Joseph M. Herbert, and Suzanne S. Pickens
1994   *Phase I Archaeological Survey: Wilmington Bypass, New Hanover and Brunswick Counties.* Submitted to Planning and Environmental Branch, North Carolina Department of Transportation (State Project No. 8u25091, TIP No. R-2633), Raleigh.

Kline, Gerald W., Gary D. Crites, and Charles H. Faulkner
1982   *The McFarland Project: Early Middle Woodland Settlement and Subsistence in the Upper Duck River Valley in Tennessee.* Miscellaneous Paper 8, Tennessee Anthropological Association, Knoxville.

Klippel, Walter E.
1969   The Hearnes Site: A Multicomponent Occupation Site and Cemetery in the Cairo Lowland Region of Southeast Missouri. *The Missouri Archaeologist* 31:1–120.

Klippel, Walter E., Gail Celmer, and James R. Purdue
1978   The Holocene Naiad Record at Rodgers Shelter in the Western Ozark Highland of Missouri. *Plains Anthropologist* 23(82, pt. 1):257–71.

Knapp, Mrs. Gilbert
1878   *Earth-works on the Arkansas River, Sixteen Miles below Little Rock.* Annual Report of the Board of Regents of the Smithsonian Institution 1877, p. 251, Washington, D.C.

Kneberg, Madeline
1952   The Tennessee Area. In *Archeology of Eastern United States,* edited by James B. Griffin, pp. 190–98. Chicago: University of Chicago Press.

Knight, Vernon James, Jr.
1984   Late Prehistoric Adaptation in the Mobile Bay Region. In *Perspectives on Gulf Coast Prehistory,* edited by Dave D. Davis, pp. 198–215. Gainesville: University Presses of Florida.

1989   Symbolism of Mississippian Mounds. In *Powhatan's Mantle: Indians in the Colonial Southeast,* edited by P. H. Wood, G. A. Waselkov, and M. T. Hatley, pp. 279–91. Lincoln and London: University of Nebraska Press.

1990a   *Excavation of the Truncated Mound at the Walling Site: Middle Woodland Culture and Copena in the Tennessee Valley.* Report of Investigations 56, University of Alabama Division of Archaeology, Tuscaloosa.

1990b   Social Organization and the Evolution of Hierarchy in Southeastern Chiefdoms. *Journal of Anthropological Research* 46:1–23.

Knight, Vernon James, Jr., and Tim S. Mistovich

1984   *Walter F. George Lake: Archaeological Survey of Fee Owned Lands, Alabama and Georgia.* Report of Investigations 42, Office of Archaeological Research, University of Alabama, Tuscaloosa. Submitted to the U.S. Army Corps of Engineers, Mobile District, Mobile (Contract No. DACWO1-83-C-0173).

Knox, James C.

1983   Responses of River Systems to Holocene Climates. In *Late-Quaternary Environments of the United States,* vol. 2, edited by H. E. Wright, pp. 26–41. Minneapolis: University of Minnesota Press.

1985   Responses of Floods to Holocene Climatic Change in the Upper Mississippi Valley. *Quaternary Research* 23:287–300.

Köppen, W.

1931   *Grundriss der Klimakunde.* Leipzig: Grundriss.

Kohler, Tim A.

1978   *The Social and Chronological Dimensions of Village Occupation at a North Florida Weeden Island Period Site.* Ph.D. dissertation, Department of Anthropology, University of Florida, Gainesville.

1980   The Social Dimensions of Village Occupation of the McKeithen Site, North Florida. *Southeastern Archaeological Conference Bulletin* 22:5–10.

Kozarek, Sue Ellen

1987   *A Hopewellian Homestead in the Ohio River Valley.* Master's thesis, University of Cincinnati.

1997   Determining Sedentism in the Archaeological Record. In *Ohio Hopewell Community Organization,* edited by William S. Dancey and Paul J. Pacheco, pp. 131–52. Kent, Ohio: Kent State University Press.

Kreinbrink, Jeannine

1992a   The Rogers Site Complex in Boone County, Kentucky. In *Current Archaeological Research in Kentucky: Volume Two,* edited by David Pollack and Gwen Henderson, pp. 79–102. Frankfort: Kentucky Heritage Council.

1992b   *The Rogers Site Complex and Its Relationship to the Late Woodland Period in the Ohio Valley.* Master's thesis, Department of Anthropology, University of Cincinnati.

Kreisa, Paul P.

2000   *The Lohraff Peninsula Site Complex: An NRHP Evaluation of Three Prehistoric Sites at Fort Leonard Wood, Pulaski County, Missouri.* Research Report No. 47. Public Service Archaeology Program, University of Illinois at Urbana-Champaign.

Kreisa, Paul P. (editor)

1995   *Phase II Excavations and Evaluation of Seven Sites at Fort Leonard Wood, Pulaski County, Missouri.* Research Report No. 21, Public Service Archaeology Program, University of Illinois at Urbana-Champaign. Submitted to the U.S. Army Construction Engineering Research Laboratory, Champaign, Ill.

Kreisa, Paul P., and Brian Adams

1999   *Phase I Archaeological Survey of 3,511 Acres at Fort Leonard Wood, Pulaski County, Missouri.* Research Report No. 39, Public Service Archaeology Program, University of Illinois at Urbana-Champaign. Submitted to the U.S. Army Construction Engineering Research Laboratory, Champaign, Ill.

Kreisa, Paul P., Gregory R. Walz, Brian Adams, Kevin P. McGowan, and Jacqueline M. McDowell
  1996   *Phase II Excavation and Evaluation of Eight Sites at Fort Leonard Wood, Pulaski County, Missouri.* Research Report No. 24, Public Service Archaeology Program, University of Illinois at Urbana-Champaign. Submitted to the U.S. Army Construction Engineering Research Laboratory, Champaign, Ill.

Krieger, A. D.
  1946   *Culture Complexes and Chronology in Northern Texas with Extensions of Puebloan Dating to the Mississippi Valley.* Publication 4640, University of Texas, Austin.
  1953   New World Culture History: Anglo-America. In *Anthropology Today,* edited by A. L. Kroeber, pp. 238–64. Chicago: University of Chicago Press.

Kroeber, A. L.
  1939   *Cultural and Natural Areas of Native North America.* University of California Publications in American Archaeology and Ethnology 38, pp. 1–242, University of California Press, Berkeley.

Kwas, Mary L., and Robert C. Mainfort, Jr.
  1986   The Johnston Site: Precursor to Pinson Mounds? *Tennessee Anthropologist* 11(1):29–41.

Lafferty, Robert H., III
  1981   *The Phipps Bend Archaeological Project.* Research Series 4, Office of Archaeological Research, University of Alabama, and TVA Publications in Anthropology 26, Knoxville.

Lafferty, Robert H., III, and K. M. Hess (editors)
  1996   *Archeological Investigations in the New Madrid Floodway, Volume I, Report of Findings.* Mid-Continental Research Associates, Inc., Report 95-7. Submitted to the U.S. Army Corps of Engineers, Memphis District (Contract No. DACW-66-89-D-0053).

Lafferty, Robert H., III, and J. E. Price
  1996   Southeast Missouri. In *Prehistory of the Central Mississippi Valley,* edited by Charles H. McNutt, pp. 1–45. Tuscaloosa: University of Alabama Press.

Larson, Lewis H.
  1959   Middle Woodland Manifestations in North Georgia. *Southeastern Archaeological Conference Newsletter* 6:54–62.
  1980   *Aboriginal Subsistence Technology of the Southeastern Coastal Plain during the Late Prehistoric Period.* Gainesville: University Presses of Florida.

Lazarus, William C.
  1965a   Effects of Land Subsidence and Sea Level Changes on Elevation of Archaeological Sites on the Florida Gulf Coast. *Florida Anthropologist* 18:49–58.
  1965b   Alligator Lake, a Ceramic Horizon Site on the Northwest Florida Coast. *Florida Anthropologist* 23:83–124.

Ledbetter, R. Jerald
  1991   Late Archaic/Early Woodland Structures from the Mill Branch Sites, Warren County, Georgia. *Early Georgia* 19:34–46.
  1992   *Archaeological Investigations at the Pumpkin Pile Site (9PO27), Polk County, Georgia.* Reported submitted to Soil Conservation Service by Southeastern Archaeological Services, Athens.
  1995   *Archaeological Investigations at Mill Branch Sites 9WR4 and 9WR11, Warren County, Georgia.* Technical Report No. 3, Interagency Archeological Services Division, National Park Service, Atlanta.

Lee, Aubra L., Rhonda L. Smith, Jill-Karen Yakubik, Tristram R. Kidder, Ruben Saenz II, Benjamin Maygarden, Gayle J. Fritz, and Roger T. Saucier
  1997   *Archaeological Data Recovery at the Birds Creek Site (16CT416), Catahoula Parish, Louisiana.* Earth Search, Inc., New Orleans.

Lee, William D.
  1955   *The Soils of North Carolina: Their Formation, Identification and Use.* North Carolina Agricultural Experiment Station Technical Bulletin No. 115, Raleigh.

Legendre, L., and P. Legendre
  1983   *Numerical Ecology.* New York: Elsevier Scientific.

Leone, Mark P.
  1995   A Historical Archaeology of Capitalism. *American Anthropologist* 97:251–68.

Lepper, Bradley T.
  1996   The Newark Earthworks and the Geometric Enclosures of the Scioto Valley: Connections and Conjectures. In *A View from the Core: A Synthesis of Ohio Hopewell Archaeology,* edited by Paul J. Pacheco, pp. 224–41. Columbus: Ohio Archaeological Council.

Lepper, Bradley T., and Richard W. Yerkes
  1997   Hopewellian Occupations at the Northern Periphery of the Newark Earthworks: The Newark Expressway Sites Revisited. In *Ohio Hopewell Community Organization,* edited by William S. Dancey and Paul J. Pacheco, pp. 175–206. Kent, Ohio: Kent State University Press.

Levi-Strauss, Claude
  1987   *Anthropology and Myth: Lectures 1951–1982.* Oxford: Blackwell.

Lewis, Barbara A.
  1991   *Analysis of Pathologies Present in the 16ST1 Tchefuncte Indian Skeletal Collection.* Master's thesis, Department of Geography and Anthropology, Louisiana State University, Baton Rouge.

Lewis, R. Barry
  1972   *Land Leveling Salvage Archaeology in Portions of Stoddard and Scott Counties, Missouri: 1969.* Submitted to the National Park Service, Midwest Archeological Center, Lincoln, Neb.
  1991   The Early Mississippi Period in the Confluence Region and Its Northern Relationships. In *Cahokia and the Hinterlands,* edited by Thomas E. Emerson and R. Barry Lewis, pp. 274–96. Urbana: University of Illinois Press.
  1996   The Western Kentucky Border and the Cairo Lowland. In *Prehistory of the Central Mississippi Valley,* edited by Charles H. McNutt, pp. 47–76. Tuscaloosa: University of Alabama Press.

Lewis, Thomas M. N., and Madeline Kneberg
  1941   *The Prehistory of the Chickamauga Basin in Tennessee.* Tennessee Anthropology Papers No. 1, Knoxville.
  1946   *Hiwassee Island.* Knoxville: University of Tennessee Press.
  1957   The Camp Creek Site. *Tennessee Archaeologist* 13(1):1–48.
  1959   The Archaic Culture of the Middle South. *American Antiquity* 25:161–83.

Lewis, Thomas M. N., and Madeline D. Kneberg Lewis
  1997   *The Prehistory of the Chickamauga Basin in Tennessee,* 2 vols. Compiled and edited by Lynne P. Sullivan. Knoxville: University of Tennessee Press.

Lightfoot, Kent G., and Gary Feinman
  1981   Sociopolitical Development of Early Mogollon Pithouse Villages. In *Mogollon Archaeology,* edited by P. H. Beckett, pp. 27–36. Boulder: Acoma Books.

1982   Social Differentiation and Leadership Development in Early Pithouse Villages in the Mogollon Region of the American Southwest. *American Antiquity* 47:64–86.

Lilly, Thomas G., and Joel D. Gunn

1996   An Analysis of Woodland and Mississippian Period Ceramics from Osprey Marsh, Hilton Head Island, South Carolina. In *Indian Pottery of the Carolinas: Observations from the March 1995 Ceramic Workshop at Hobcaw Barony,* edited by David G. Anderson, pp. 63–115. Council of the South Carolina Professional Archaeologists, Columbia.

Linares, Olga F.

1976   "Garden Hunting" in the American Tropics. *Human Ecology* 4(4):331–49.

Linder, Jean Rita

1974   The Jean Rita Site: An Early Woodland Site in Monroe County, Illinois. *Wisconsin Archeologist* 55(2):99–162.

Linder, Jean R., Teresa J. Cartmell, and John E. Kelly

1978   *Preliminary Archaeological Reconnaissance of the Segments Under Study for FAP-413 in Madison County, Illinois.* Illinois Department of Transportation, District 8, Fairview Heights.

Little, Barbara

1995   *National Capital Area Archaeological Overview and Survey Plan.* Occasional Report No. 13, U.S. Department of the Interior, National Park Service, National Capital Area, Washington, D.C.

Loftfield, Thomas C.

1976   *"A Briefe and True Report . . ." An Archaeological Interpretation of the Southern North Carolina Coast.* Ph.D. dissertation, Department of Anthropology, University of North Carolina, Chapel Hill.

1987   *Excavations at 31ON305, the Flynt Site at Sneads Ferry, North Carolina.* Ms. on file, Department of Sociology and Anthropology, University of North Carolina, Wilmington. Copies available from the Office of State Archaeology, Raleigh.

1990   Ossuary Interments and Algonkian Expansion on the North Carolina Coast. *Southeastern Archaeology* 9(2):116–23.

Loftfield, Thomas C., and David C. Jones

1995   Late Woodland Architecture on the Coast of North Carolina: Structural Meaning and Environmental Adaptation. *Southeastern Archaeology* 14:120–35.

Longacre, William A.

1970   *Archaeology as Anthropology: A Case Study.* Anthropological Papers 17, Museum of Anthropology, University of Arizona, Tucson.

Lopinot, Neal H.

1990   *Archaeology of the Little Hills Expressway Site (23SC572), St. Charles County, Missouri.* Contract Archaeology Program Research Report No. 6, Southern Illinois University, Edwardsville.

1995   Archaeobotanical Remains. In *Occupations at the Hayti Bypass Site, Pemiscot County, Missouri,* edited by Michael D. Conner, pp. 221–62. Special Publication No. 1, Center for Archaeological Research, Southwest Missouri State University, Springfield.

1999   Floral Analysis. In *Data Recovery (Mitigation) of Sites 23MI578, 23MI605, 23MI651, 23MI652 and 23MI797 in the New Madrid Floodway, Mississippi County, Missouri,* by Shawn Chapman, Emanuel Breitberg, and Neal Lopinot, pp. 121–32. Submitted to the U.S. Army Corps of Engineers, Memphis District, by Panamerican Consultants, Inc., Memphis.

Lopinot, Neal H., Michael D. Conner, and Jack H. Ray
    1995   Conclusions. In *Occupations at the Hayti Bypass Site, Pemiscot County, Missouri,* edited by Michael D. Conner, pp. 290–98. Special Publication No. 1, Center for Archaeological Research, Southwest Missouri State University, Springfield.
Lopinot, Neal H., Michael D. Conner, Jack H. Ray, and Jeffrey K. Yelton
    1998   *Prehistoric and Historic Properties on Mitigation Lands, Horseshoe Lake Peninsula, Madison County, Illinois.* St. Louis District Historic Properties Management Report No. 55, U.S. Army Corps of Engineers, St. Louis District.
Loubser, J. H. N., John S. Cable, Leslie E. Raymer, David S. Leith, Lisa D. O'Steen, Laurie C. Steponaitis, and M. R. Marquez
    2000   *Phase III Mitigation of Area B at Site 38Bu927, Marine Corps Air Station, Beaufort, South Carolina.* New South Associates, Stone Mountain, Georgia. Submitted to Gulf South Research Corporation, Baton Rouge, La.
Lourandos, Harry
    1983   Intensification and Australian Prehistory. In *Prehistoric Hunter-Gatherers,* edited by T. D. Price and J. A. Brown, pp. 385–423. Orlando: Academic Press.
Ludwig, J. A., and J. F. Reynolds
    1988   *Statistical Ecology.* New York: John Wiley and Sons.
Luer, George M.
    1989   Calusa Canals in Southwest Florida: Routes of Tribute and Exchange. *Florida Anthropologist* 42:89–130.
Luer, George M., and Marion M. Almy
    1981   Temple Mounds of the Tampa Bay Area. *Florida Anthropologist* 34:127–55.
    1982   A Definition of the Manasota Culture. *Florida Anthropologist* 35:34–58.
Luer, George M., and R. J. Wheeler
    1997   How the Pine Island Canal Worked: Topography, Hydraulics, and Engineering. *Florida Anthropologist* 50:115–32.
Lyman, R. Lee, and Michael J. O'Brien
    2001   Introduction. In *Method and Theory in American Archaeology,* by Gordon R. Willey and P. Phillips. Tuscaloosa: University of Alabama Press.
Lyman, R. Lee, Michael J. O'Brien, and Robert C. Dunnell
    1997   *The Rise and Fall of Culture History.* New York: Plenum Press.
Lynott, Mark J.
    1989   *An Archeological Evaluation of the Gooseneck and Owls Bend Sites.* Occasional Studies in Anthropology No. 23, U.S. National Park Service, Midwest Archeological Center, Lincoln, Neb.
Lynott, Mark J., Thomas W. Boutton, James E. Price, and Dwight E. Nelson
    1986   Stable Carbon Evidence for Maize Agriculture in Southeast Missouri and Northeast Arkansas. *American Antiquity* 51(1):51–65.
Lyon, Edwin A.
    1996   *A New Deal for Southeastern Archaeology.* Tuscaloosa: University of Alabama Press.
McClurkan, B. B., E. B. Jelks, and H. P. Jensen
    1980   Jonas Short and Coral Snake Mounds: A Comparison. *Louisiana Archaeology* 6:173–97.
McCollough, Major C. R., and Glyn D. DuVall
    1976   Results of 1973 Testing. In *Third Report of the Normandy Reservoir Salvage Project,* edited by Major C. R. McCollough and Charles H. Faulkner, pp. 27–139. Report of Investigations 16, Department of Anthropology, University of Tennessee, Knoxville.

McCollough, Major C. R., and Charles H. Faulkner
1973 *Excavation of the Higgs and Doughty Sites: I-75 Salvage Archaeology.* Miscellaneous Paper 12, Tennessee Archaeological Society, Knoxville.
McCollough, Major C. R., and Charles H. Faulkner (editors)
1976 *Third Report of the Normandy Reservoir Salvage Project.* Report of Investigations 16, University of Tennessee, Department of Anthropology, Knoxville.
1978 *Sixth Report of the Normandy Archaeological Project.* Report of Investigations 21, Department of Anthropology, University of Tennessee/Notes in Anthropology 4, Laboratory of Anthropology, Wright State University/TVA Publications in Anthropology 19, Knoxville.
McCollough, Major C. R., Glyn D. DuVall, Charles H. Faulkner, and Tracy C. Brown
1979 A Late Woodland Shaft and Chamber Grave in the Normandy Reservoir, Tennessee. *Tennessee Anthropologist* 4(2):175–88.
McConaughty, Mark
1990 Early Woodland Mortuary Practices in Western Pennsylvania. *West Virginia Archaeologist* 42(2):1–10.
MacCord, Howard A., Sr.
1966 The McLean Mound, Cumberland County, North Carolina. *Southern Indian Studies* 18:3–45.
1985 *The Lewis Creek Mound Culture.* Privately printed, Richmond, Va.
McCormick, Olin F.
1969 *Archaeological Resources of the New Hope Reservoir Area, North Carolina.* Master's thesis, Department of Anthropology, University of North Carolina, Chapel Hill.
McCune, B., and M. J. Mefford
1997 PC-ORD. Multivariate Analysis of Ecological Data, Version 3.0. MjM Software Design, Gleneden Beach, Ore.
McElrath, Dale L., and Andrew C. Fortier
2000 The Early Late Woodland Occupation of the American Bottom. In *Late Woodland Societies: Tradition and Transformation across the Midcontinent,* edited by Thomas E. Emerson, Dale L. McElrath, and Andrew C. Fortier, pp. 97–121. Lincoln: University of Nebraska Press.
McGahey, Samuel O.
1971 *Archaeological Survey in the Tombigbee River Drainage Area, May–June 1970.* Preliminary Report 2, Mississippi Archaeological Survey, Jackson.
1999 Use and Avoidance of Kosciusko Quartzite in Prehistoric Mississippi Flaked Stone Assemblages. In *Raw Materials and Exchange in the Mid-South,* edited by Evan Peacock and Samuel O. Brookes, pp. 1–11. Archaeological Report 29, Mississippi Department of Archives and History, Jackson.
2000 *Mississippi Projectile Point Guide.* Archaeological Report 31, Mississippi Department of Archives and History, Jackson.
McGimsey, Charles R.
1999 *Excavating the Past: Archaeology and the Marksville Site (16AV1).* 1998/1999 Annual Report of the Regional Archaeology Program, Management Unit III, Louisiana Division of Archaeology, Baton Rouge.
McGimsey, C. R., III, and H. A. Davis (editors)
1977 *The Management of Archaeological Resources: The Airlie House Report.* Society for American Archaeology, Washington, D.C.
McGrath, Kerry C.
1977 *Cultural Resource Survey Report: Route 63, Maries County.* Submitted to the

Missouri Highway and Transportation Department, Jefferson City.

McGuire, Randall H., and Dean J. Saitta
1996   Although They Have Petty Captains, They Obey Them Badly: The Dialectics of Prehispanic Western Pueblo Social Organization. *American Antiquity* 61:197–216.

McIlvenna, Noeleen
1994   *Late Archaic–Middle Woodland Cultural Change in South Central Tennessee.* Final report to the Tennessee Department of Transportation, Transportation Center, University of Tennessee, Knoxville.

McKern, W. C.
1939   The Midwestern Taxonomic Method as an Aid to Archaeological Culture Study. *American Antiquity* 4:301–13.

McLearen, Douglas
1991   Late Archaic and Early Woodland Material Culture in Virginia. In *Late Archaic and Early Woodland Research in Virginia: A Synthesis,* edited by T. Reinhart and M. E. Hodges. Special Publication No. 23, Archaeological Society of Virginia, Richmond.

McMahan, Joe D.
1983   *Paleoethnobotany of the Late Woodland Mason Phase in the Elk and Duck River Valleys, Tennessee.* Master's thesis, Department of Anthropology, University of Tennessee, Knoxville.

McMakin, Todd A.
1995   *Residential Mobility and Its Impact on Lithic Use Strategies: A Comparison of a Late Archaic Assemblage and a Gulf Formational Assemblage from South Mississippi.* Master's thesis, Department of Sociology and Anthropology, University of Southern Mississippi, Hattiesburg.
1996   Changes in Mobility Patterns in South Mississippi from the Late Archaic to the Late Gulf Formational Stage: An Example from Forrest County, Mississippi. *Mississippi Archaeology* 31(2):51–63.

McMichael, Edward V.
1960   *The Anatomy of a Tradition: A Study of Southeastern Stamped Pottery.* Dissertation, Department of Anthropology, Indiana University, Bloomington.
1971   Adena-East, an Appraisal of the More Easterly Extensions of the Spread of the Adena Phenomenon. In *Adena: The Seeking of an Identity,* edited by B. K. Swartz, Jr., pp. 83–95. Muncie, Ind.: Ball State University.

McMillan, R. Bruce
1963   *A Survey and Evaluation of the Archaeology of the Central Gasconade River Valley in Missouri.* Master's thesis, Department of Sociology and Anthropology, University of Missouri, Columbia.
1965   Gasconade Prehistory: A Survey and Evaluation of the Archaeological Resources. *The Missouri Archaeologist* 23(3–4):1–114.

McNutt, Charles H.
1996a   The Upper Yazoo Basin in Northwest Mississippi. In *Prehistory of the Central Mississippi Valley,* edited by Charles H. McNutt, pp. 155–86. Tuscaloosa: University of Alabama Press.
1996b   The Central Mississippi Valley: A Summary. In *Prehistory of the Central Mississippi Valley,* edited by Charles H. McNutt, pp. 187–258. Tuscaloosa: University of Alabama Press.

McNutt, Charles H. (editor)
1996   *Prehistory of the Central Mississippi Valley.* Tuscaloosa: University of Alabama Press.

McNutt, Charles H., and Guy G. Weaver
  1983   *The Duncan Tract Site (40TR27), Trousdale County, Tennessee.* TVA Publications in Anthropology 33, Knoxville.
Maher, Thomas O.
  1991   Time and Community Patterns at Holding, A Middle Woodland Site in the American Bottom. *Southeastern Archaeology* 10:114–33.
  1996   *Time, Space, and Social Dynamics during the Hopewell Occupation of the American Bottom.* Ph.D. dissertation, Department of Anthropology, University of North Carolina at Chapel Hill.
Mainfort, Robert C., Jr.
  1986   *Pinson Mounds: A Middle Woodland Ceremonial Site.* Research Series No. 7, Tennessee Department of Conservation, Division of Archaeology, Nashville.
  1988a Middle Woodland Ceremonialism at Pinson Mounds. *American Antiquity* 53(1):158–73.
  1988b Middle Woodland Mortuary Patterning at Helena Crossing, Arkansas. *Tennessee Anthropologist* 13(1):35–50.
  1988c Pinson Mounds: Internal Chronology and External Relationships. In *Middle Woodland Settlement and Ceremonialism in the Mid-South and Lower Mississippi Valley,* edited by Robert C. Mainfort, Jr., pp. 132–46. Archaeological Report 22, Mississippi Department of Archives and History, Jackson.
  1989   Adena Chiefdoms: Evidence from the Wright Mound. *Midcontinental Journal of Archaeology* 14:164–78.
  1994   *Archaeological Investigations in the Obion River Drainage: The West Tennessee Tributaries Project.* Research Series No. 10, Tennessee Division of Archaeology, Nashville.
  1996a Pinson Mounds and the Middle Woodland Period in the Midsouth and Lower Mississippi Valley. In *A View from the Core: A Synthesis of Ohio Hopewell Archaeology,* edited by Paul J. Pacheco, pp. 370–91. Columbus: Ohio Archaeological Council.
  1996b The Reelfoot Lake Basin, Kentucky and Tennessee. In *Prehistory of the Central Mississippi Valley,* edited by Charles H. McNutt, pp. 77–96. Tuscaloosa: University of Alabama Press.
  1997a Putative Poverty Point Phases in Western Tennessee: A Reappraisal. *Tennessee Anthropologist* 22(1):72–91.
  1997b An Historical Overview of Marksville Research. Presented at the Mid-South Archaeological Conference, Jonesboro, Ark.
  1999a Swift Creek Ceramics at Pinson Mounds. *Southeastern Archaeological Conference Newsletter* 41(2):3–4.
  1999b Late Period Phases in the Central Mississippi Valley: A Multivariate Approach. In *Arkansas Archaeology: Essays in Honor of Dan and Phyllis Morse,* edited by R. C. Mainfort, Jr., and M. D. Jeter, pp. 143–67. Fayetteville: University of Arkansas Press.
Mainfort, Robert C., Jr. (editor)
  1980   *Archaeological Investigations at Pinson Mounds State Archaeological Area: 1974, 1975, and 1978 Field Seasons.* Research Series No. 1, Tennessee Department of Conservation, Division of Archaeology, Nashville.
  1988   *Middle Woodland Settlement and Ceremonialism in the Mid-South and Lower Mississippi Valley.* Archaeological Report 22, Mississippi Department of Archives and History, Jackson.
Mainfort, Robert C., Jr., and Kenneth C. Carstens
  1987   A Middle Woodland Embankment and Mound Complex in Western Kentucky. *Southeastern Archaeology* 6(1):57–61.

Mainfort, Robert C., Jr., and J. Shawn Chapman
  1994   West Tennessee Ceramic Typology, Part I: Tchula and Middle Woodland Periods. *Tennessee Anthropologist* 19:148–79.
Mainfort, Robert C., Jr., and Lynne P. Sullivan
  1998   Explaining Earthen Enclosures of the Eastern Woodlands. In *Ancient Earthen Enclosures of the Eastern Woodlands,* edited by Robert C. Mainfort, Jr., and Lynne P. Sullivan, pp. 1–16. Gainesville: University Press of Florida.
Mainfort, Robert C., Jr., and Lynne P. Sullivan (editors)
  1998   *Ancient Earthen Enclosures of the Eastern Woodlands.* Gainesville: University Press of Florida.
Mainfort, Robert C., Jr., and Richard Walling
  1992   1989 Excavations at Pinson Mounds: Ozier Mound. *Midcontinental Journal of Archaeology* 17(1):112–36.
Mainfort, Robert C., Jr., and Richard Walling (editors)
  1996   *Mounds, Embankments, and Ceremonialism in the Midsouth.* Arkansas Archeological Survey Research Series No. 46, Fayetteville.
Mainfort, Robert C., Jr., George W. Shannon, Jr., and Jack E. Tyler
  1985   1983 Excavations at Pinson Mounds: The Twin Mounds. *Midcontinental Journal of Archaeology* 10(1):49–75.
Mainfort, Robert C., Jr., James W. Cogswell, Michael J. O'Brien, Hector Neff, and Michael D. Glascock
  1997   Neutron Activation Analysis of Pottery from Pinson Mounds and Nearby Sites in Western Tennessee: Local Production vs. Long Distance Importation. *Midcontinental Journal of Archaeology* 22:43–68.
Mann, Cyril Baxter
  1988   *An Archaeological Classification of Ceramics from the Pearl Mounds (22LW510), Lawrence County, Mississippi.* Master's thesis, University of Southern Mississippi, Hattiesburg.
Manson, Carl
  1948   Marcey Creek Site: An Early Manifestation in the Potomac Valley. *American Antiquity* 13(3):223–27.
Mariaca, Maria Teresa
  1988   *Late Marksville/Early Baytown Period Subsistence Economy: Analysis of Three Faunal Assemblages from Northeastern Louisiana.* Master's thesis, Department of Archaeology, Boston University.
Markman, Charles W.
  1993   *Miller Cave (23PU2), Fort Leonard Wood, Pulaski County, Missouri: Report of Archaeological Testing and Assessment of Damage.* Research Report No. 9, Markman and Associates, Inc., St. Louis. Submitted to the U.S. Army Corps of Engineers, Kansas City District (Contract Number DACA41-91-0016, Delivery Order 2).
Marquardt, William H. (editor)
  1992   *Culture and Environment in the Domain of the Calusa.* Institute of Archaeology and Paleoenvironmental Studies Monograph 1, Florida Museum of Natural History, Gainesville.
Marquardt, William H., and Patty Jo Watson
  1983   The Shell Mound Archaic of Western Kentucky. In *Archaic Hunters and Gatherers in the American Midwest,* edited by James A. Phillips and James A. Brown, pp. 323–39. New York: Academic Press.
  1997   The Green River Shell Mound Archaic: Interpretive Trajectories. Presented at the

54th annual meeting of the Southeastern Archaeological Conference, Baton Rouge, La.

Marrinan, Rochelle
1975 *Ceramics, Mollusks, and Sedentism: The Late Archaic Period on the Georgia Coast.* Ph.D. dissertation, Department of Anthropology, University of Florida, Gainesville. University Microfilms, Ann Arbor, Mich.

Marshall, Adam
1999 Interior Rim Impressions as an Indicator of Typological Relationships. *North Carolina Archaeology* 48:87–94.

Marshall, James A.
1996 Towards the Definition of the Ohio Hopewell Core and Periphery Utilizing the Geometric Earthworks. In *A View from the Core,* edited by Paul J. Pacheco, pp. 210–23. Columbus: Ohio Archaeological Council.

Marshall, Richard A.
1963 *A Preliminary Report on the Meramec Spring Focus in the Central Missouri Highlands.* Ms. on file, American Archaeology Division, University of Missouri, Columbia.

1965a *An Archaeological Investigation of Interstate Route 55 through New Madrid and Pemiscot Counties, Missouri, 1964.* Highway Archaeology Report No. 1, University of Missouri, Columbia.

1965b *Archaeological Investigations in Meramec Spring, St. James, Missouri Locality.* American Archaeology Division, University of Missouri-Columbia. Submitted to the James Foundation. Copies available from the American Archaeology Division, University of Missouri, Columbia.

1966 *Prehistoric Indians at Meramec Spring Park.* University of Missouri-Columbia and the Lucy Wortham James Foundation.

1982a *Survey and Excavation along Archusa Creek.* Archaeological Report 11, Mississippi Department of Archives and History, Jackson.

1982b *A Report on Archaeological Test Excavations at Goode Lake, Jackson County, Mississippi.* Archaeological Report 10, Mississippi Department of Archives and History, Jackson.

1987 A Brief Comparison of Two Emergent Mississippi Substage Settlement Patterns in Southeast Missouri and Northwest Mississippi. In *The Emergent Mississippian,* edited by Richard A. Marshall, pp. 160–66. Occasional Papers 87-01, Cobb Institute of Archaeology, Mississippi State University.

1988 The Burial Pattern in Story Mound 1: Hoecake Site, Southeast Missouri. In *Middle Woodland Settlement and Ceremonialism in the Mid-South and Lower Mississippi Valley,* edited by Robert C. Mainfort, Jr., pp. 117–31. Archaeological Report 22, Mississippi Department of Archives and History, Jackson.

Maslowski, Robert
1984 The Significance of Cordage Attributes in the Analysis of Woodland Pottery. *Pennsylvania Archaeologist* 54(1–2):51–60.

Mathews, James H.
1998 Changes in Swift Creek Rim Forms. Presented at the 55th annual meeting of the Southeastern Archaeological Conference, Greenville, S.C.

Mathis, Mark A.
1999 Oak Island: A Retiring Type. *North Carolina Archaeology* 48:18–36.

Matteson, Max R.
1959 An Analysis of the Shells of Fresh-water Mussels Gathered by Indians in Southwestern Illinois. *Transactions of the Illinois State Academy of Science* 52:52–58.

1960   Reconstruction of Prehistoric Environments through the Analysis of Molluscan Collections from Shell Middens. *American Antiquity* 26(1):117–20.

Maxwell, Moreau S.
1951   *The Woodland Cultures in Southern Illinois: Archaeological Excavations in the Carbondale Area.* Bulletin 7, Logan Museum Publications in Anthropology, Beloit College, Beloit, Wis.

Medford, Larry D.
1972   *Site Destruction due to Agricultural Practices in Northeast Arkansas.* Arkansas Archeological Survey Research Series No. 3, Fayetteville.

Meillassoux, Claude
1978   The Social Organization of the Peasantry: The Economic Basis of Kinship. In *Relations of Production: Marxist Approaches to Economic Anthropology,* edited by D. Seddon, pp. 159–69. London: Frank Cass.

Merrell, James
1989   *The Indians' New World.* Chapel Hill: University of North Carolina Press.

Metcalf, Ashley
1992   Materials Analysis of Sand-Tempered Pottery from Northeast Mississippi. *Mississippi Archaeology* 27(1):19–43.

Mickelson, Katherine R.
1999   Plant Remains from 1CK236, Clarke County, Alabama. Submitted to Archaeological Research Program, University of South Alabama, Mobile.

Mikell, Gregory A.
1992   *Cultural Resources Impact Assessment of the Santa Rosa Island Pipeline Project, Eglin Air Force Base, Florida.* Report of Investigations No. 211, New World Research, Inc., Fort Walton Beach, Fla.
1993   The Little's Bayou West Site: Evidence of the Late Weeden Island–Fort Walton Transition in Northwest Florida. *Florida Anthropologist* 46:12–19.
1997   A Case of Direct Association between Fiber-Tempered Pottery, Late Archaic Stemmed Points, and Sante Fe Points at the Reddick Bluff Site, Walton County. *Florida Anthropologist* 50(2):83–93.

Milanich, Jerald T.
1971a   *The Deptford Phase: An Archeological Reconstruction.* Ph.D. dissertation, University of Florida. University Microfilms, Ann Arbor, Mich.
1971b   Conclusions from the Excavation of Two Transitional-Deptford Sites on Cumberland Island, Georgia. *Southeastern Archaeological Conference Bulletin* 12:55–63.
1973a   The Southeastern Deptford Culture: A Preliminary Definition. *Bureau of Historic Sites and Properties, Division of Archives, History and Records Management, Bulletin 2,* pp. 35–61. Florida Department of State, Tallahassee.
1973b   A Deptford Phase House Structure, Cumberland Island, Georgia. *Florida Anthropologist* 26:105–13.
1974   Life in a Ninth Century Indian Household, a Weeden Island Fall-Winter Site on the Upper Apalachicola River, Florida. *Bureau of Historic Sites and Properties, Division of Archives, History and Records Management, Bulletin 4,* pp. 1–44. Florida Department of State, Tallahassee.
1978   Two Cades Pond Sites in North-Central Florida: The Occupational Nexus as a Model of Settlement. *Florida Anthropologist* 31:151–73.
1980   Weeden Island Studies—Past, Present, and Future. *Southeastern Archaeological Conference Bulletin* 22:11–18.
1994   *Archaeology of Precolumbian Florida.* Gainesville: University Press of Florida.

1996   *The Timucua.* Oxford, U.K.: Blackwell Publishers.

1998   Native Chiefdoms and the Exercise of Complexity in Sixteenth-Century Florida. In *Chieftains and Chieftaincy in the Americas,* edited by Elsa M. Redmond, pp. 245–64. Gainesville: University Press of Florida.

1999   Introduction. In *Famous Florida Sites: Mt. Royal and Crystal River,* edited by Jerald T. Milanich, pp. i–xx. Gainesville: University Press of Florida.

Milanich, Jerald T., and Charles H. Fairbanks

1980   *Florida Archaeology.* Orlando: Academic Press.

Milanich, Jerald T., Carlos A. Martinez, Karl T. Steinen, and Ronald L. Wallace

1976   Georgia Origins of the Alachua Tradition. *Bureau of Historic Sites and Properties, Division of Archives, History and Records Management, Bulletin 5,* pp. 47–56. Florida Department of State, Tallahassee.

Milanich, Jerald T., Ann S. Cordell, Vernon J. Knight, Jr., Timothy A. Kohler, and Brenda J. Sigler-Lavelle

1984   *McKeithen Weeden Island: The Culture of Northern Florida, A.D. 200–900.* Orlando: Academic Press.

1997   *Archaeology of Northern Florida, A.D. 200–900: The McKeithen Weeden Island.* Gainesville: University Press of Florida.

Miller, Andrew C., Barry S. Payne, and Larry T. Neill

1994   A Recent Re-evaluation of the Bivalve Fauna of the Lower Green River, Kentucky. *Transactions of the Kentucky Academy of Science* 55(1–2):46–54.

Miller, Carl F.

1949   The Lake Springs Site, Columbia County, Georgia. *American Antiquity* 15:254–58.

Miller, J. E., III

1982   Construction of Site Features: Tests of Mounds C, D, E, B, and the Embankment. In *Emerging Patterns of Plum Bayou Culture: Preliminary Investigations of the Toltec Mounds Research Project,* edited by Martha A. Rolingson, pp. 30–43. Arkansas Archeological Survey Research Series No. 18, Fayetteville.

Miller, James J.

1998   *An Environmental History of Northeast Florida.* Gainesville: University Press of Florida.

Mills, William C.

1902   Excavations of the Adena Mound. *Ohio Archaeological and Historical Publications* 10:452–79.

1917   Exploration of the Westenhaver Mound. *Ohio Archaeological and Historical Publications* 26:226–66.

Milner, George R.

1998   *The Cahokia Chiefdom.* Washington, D.C.: Smithsonian Institution Press.

1999   Warfare in Prehistoric and Early Historic North America. *Journal of Archaeological Research* 7:105–51.

Milner, George R., and Richard W. Jefferies

1987   A Reevaluation of the WPA Excavation of the Robbins Mound in Boone County, Kentucky. In *Current Archaeological Research in Kentucky, Volume One,* edited by David Pollack, pp. 33–42. Frankfort: Kentucky Heritage Council.

1998   The Read Archaic Shell Midden in Kentucky. *Southeastern Archaeology* 17(2):119–32.

Misner, Elizabeth J., and Elizabeth J. Reitz

1992   Vertebrate Fauna from Pump Canal (16SC27), Louisiana. Ms. in possession of authors.

Mistovich, Tim S.

1987   *Archaeological Survey of the Town Creek Watershed, Mississippi.* Report of Investigations 55, University of Alabama Office of Archaeological Research, Moundville.

1988   Early Mississippian in the Black Warrior Valley: The Pace of Transition. *Southeastern Archaeology* 7:21–38.

Mitchem, Jeffrey M.

1989   *Redefining Safety Harbor: Late Prehistoric/Protohistoric Archaeology in West Peninsular Florida.* Ph.D. dissertation, Department of Anthropology, University of Florida, Gainesville.

Mocas, Stephen T.

1988   Pinched and Punctated Pottery of the Falls of the Ohio River Region: A Reappraisal of the Zorn Punctate Ceramic Type. In *New Deal Era Archaeology and Current Research in Kentucky,* edited by David Pollack and Mary Lucas Powell, pp. 115–42. Frankfort: Kentucky Heritage Council.

Mooney, James

1894   *The Siouan Tribes of the East.* Bulletin No. 22, Bureau of American Ethnology, Washington, D.C.

Moore, Clarence B.

1900   Certain Antiquities of the Florida West Coast. *Journal of the Academy of Natural Sciences of Philadelphia* 11:349–94.

1901a   Certain Aboriginal Remains of the Tombigbee River. *Journal of the Academy of Natural Sciences of Philadelphia* 9(4):498–514.

1901b   Certain Aboriginal Remains of the Northwest Florida Coast, Part I. *Journal of the Academy of Natural Sciences of Philadelphia* 11:419–97.

1902   Certain Aboriginal Remains of the Northwest Florida Coast, Part II. *Journal of the Academy of Natural Sciences of Philadelphia* 12:127–358.

1903a   Certain Aboriginal Mounds of the Apalachicola River. *Journal of the Academy of Natural Sciences of Philadelphia* 12:439–92.

1903b   Certain Aboriginal Mounds of the Central Florida West Coast. *Journal of the Academy of Natural Sciences of Philadelphia* 12:361–438.

1905a   Certain Aboriginal Remains of the Lower Tombigbee River. *Journal of the Academy of Natural Sciences of Philadelphia* 13(2):245–78.

1905b   Miscellaneous Investigations in Florida. *Journal of the Academy of Natural Sciences of Philadelphia* 13:298–325.

1907   Crystal River Revisited. *Journal of the Academy of Natural Sciences of Philadelphia* 13:406–25.

1908   Certain Mounds of Arkansas and of Mississippi, Part I. Mounds and Cemeteries of the Lower Arkansas River. *Journal of the Academy of Natural Sciences of Philadelphia* 13:481–563.

1910   Antiquities of the St. Francis, White, and Black Rivers, Arkansas. *Journal of the Academy of Natural Sciences of Philadelphia* 14:255–364.

1913   Some Aboriginal Sites in Louisiana and Arkansas. *Journal of the Academy of Natural Sciences of Philadelphia* 16:7–99.

1918   The Northwestern Florida Coast Revisited. *Journal of the Academy of Natural Sciences of Philadelphia* 16:513–81.

Moore, David G.

1984   Biltmore Estate Archaeological Survey: Final Report. Report on file, Western Office of North Carolina Department of Archives and History, Asheville.

1986   The Pisgah Phase: Cultural Continuity in the Appalachian Summit. In *The Confer-*

ence on Cherokee Prehistory, edited by David G. Moore, pp. 73–80. Swannanoa, N.C.: Warren Wilson College.

Moorehead, Warren K.
  1892   *Primitive Man in Ohio,* New York: G. P. Putnam and Sons.
  1909   A Study of Primitive Culture in Ohio. In *Putnam Anniversary Volume,* pp. 137–50. New York: G. E. Stechert.
  1929   The Cahokia Mounds: Part I, Explorations of 1922, 1923, 1924, and 1927 in the Cahokia Mounds. *University of Illinois Bulletin* (Urbana) 26(4):7–106.

Moreland, John F.
  1992   Restoring the Dialectic: Settlement Patterns and Documents in Medieval Central Italy. In *Archaeology, Annales, and Ethnohistory,* edited by A. B. Knapp, pp. 112–29. Cambridge: Cambridge University Press.

Morey, Darcy F.
  1996   *Vertebrate Resource Utilization at the Widows Creek Site (1JA305), Jackson County, Alabama.* Submitted to the Tennessee Valley Authority by the Department of Anthropology, University of Tennessee, Knoxville.

Morey, Darcy F., and George M. Crothers
  1998   Clearing Up Clouded Waters: Paleoenvironmental Analysis of Freshwater Mussel Assemblages from the Green River Shell Middens, Western Kentucky. *Journal of Archaeological Science* 25(9):907–26.

Morgan, David T.
  1992   Ceramics. In *Early Woodland Occupations at the Ambrose Flick Site in the Sny Bottom of West-Central Illinois,* edited by C. Russell Stafford, pp. 127–49. Research Series, Vol. 10, Center for American Archeology, Kampsville Archeological Center, CAA Press, Kampsville, Ill.

Morgan, Richard G.
  1952   Outline of Cultures in the Ohio Region. In *Archaeology of Eastern United States,* edited by James B. Griffin, pp. 83–98. Chicago: University of Chicago.

Morrell, L. Ross
  1960   Oakland Mound (Je53), Florida: A Preliminary Report. *Florida Anthropologist* 13:101–8.

Morrison, J. P. E.
  1942   Preliminary Report on Mollusks Found in the Shell Mounds of the Pickwick Landing Basin in the Tennessee River Valley. In *An Archaeological Survey of Pickwick Basin in the Adjacent Portions of the States of Alabama, Mississippi, and Tennessee,* by William S. Webb and David L. DeJarnette, pp. 341–92. Bulletin 129, Bureau of American Ethnology, Smithsonian Institution, Washington, D.C.
  1951   Shell Material. In *Archeology of the Bynum Mounds, Mississippi,* by John L. Cotter and John M. Corbett, p. 50. Archeological Research Series Number 1, U.S. Department of the Interior, National Park Service, Washington, D.C.

Morse, Dan F.
  1980   Other Aspects of the Barnes Occupation. In *Zebree Archeological Project Excavation, Data Interpretation, and Report on the Zebree Homestead Site, Mississippi County, Arkansas,* edited by Dan F. Morse and Phyllis A. Morse, pp. 17-1 to 17-33. Submitted to the U.S. Army Corps of Engineers, Memphis District, by the Arkansas Archeological Survey, Fayetteville.
  1986   McCarty (3-Po-467): A Tchula Period Site near Marked Tree, Arkansas. In *The Tchula Period in the Mid-South and Lower Mississippi Valley,* edited by David H. Dye and R. C. Brister, pp. 70–92. Archaeological Report 17, Mississippi Department of Archives and History, Jackson.

1988   The Keller Site: Its Implications for Interpreting the Late Marksville Period Occu-
         pation of Northeast Arkansas. In *Middle Woodland Settlement and Ceremonialism
         in the Mid-South and Lower Mississippi Valley,* edited by Robert C. Mainfort, Jr.,
         pp. 68–75. Archaeological Report 22, Mississippi Department of Archives and
         History, Jackson.

Morse, Dan F., and Phyllis A. Morse
1983   *Archaeology of the Central Mississippi Valley.* New York: Academic Press.
1990   Emergent Mississippian in the Central Mississippi Valley. In *The Mississippian
         Emergence,* edited by Bruce D. Smith, pp. 153–73. Washington, D.C.: Smithsonian
         Institution Press.
1996   Northeast Arkansas. In *Prehistory of the Central Mississippi Valley,* edited by
         Charles H. McNutt, pp. 119–36. Tuscaloosa: University of Alabama Press.

Morse, Dan F., and Phyllis A. Morse (editors)
1980   *Zebree Archeological Project Excavation, Data Interpretation, and Report on the
         Zebree Homestead Site, Mississippi County, Arkansas.* Submitted to the U.S. Army
         Corps of Engineers, Memphis District, by the Arkansas Archeological Survey,
         Fayetteville.

Morse, Phyllis A., and Dan F. Morse
1990   The Zebree Site, An Emerged Early Mississippian Expression in Northeast Arkan-
         sas. In *The Mississippian Emergence,* edited by Bruce D. Smith, pp. 51–66. Wash-
         ington, D.C.: Smithsonian Institution Press.

Mouer, L. Daniel
1991   The Formative Transition in Virginia. In *Late Archaic and Early Woodland Re-
         search in Virginia: A Synthesis,* edited by T. Reinhard and M. E. Hodges, pp. 1–
         88. Special Publication No. 23, Archaeological Society of Virginia, Richmond.

Muller, Jon
1986   *Archaeology of the Lower Ohio River Valley.* Orlando: Academic Press.
1997   *Mississippian Political Economy.* New York: Plenum Press.

Munson, Patrick J.
1966   The Sheets Site: A Late Archaic–Early Woodland Occupation in West-Central Illi-
         nois. *Michigan Archaeologist* 12:111–20.
1971   An Archaeological Survey of the Wood River Terrace and Adjacent Bottoms and
         Bluffs in Madison County. In *An Archaeological Survey of the American Bottoms
         and Wood River Terrace.* Illinois State Museum Reports of Investigations No. 21,
         Pt. 2, Springfield.
1986   Black Sand and Havana Tradition Ceramic Assemblages and Culture History in
         the Central Illinois River Valley. In *Early Woodland Archeology,* edited by Ken-
         neth B. Farnsworth and Thomas E. Emerson, pp. 280–300. Kampsville Seminars
         in Archeology No. 2, Center for American Archaeology, CAA Press, Kampsville,
         Ill.

Munson, Patrick J., and Cheryl Ann Munson
1990   *The Prehistoric and Early Historic Archaeology of Wyandotte Cave and Other
         Caves in Southern Indiana.* Prehistory Research Series 7, No. 1, Indiana Histori-
         cal Society, Indianapolis.

Munson, Patrick J., Kenneth B. Tankersley, Cheryl A. Munson, and Patty Jo Watson
1989   Prehistoric Selenite and Satin Spar Mining in the Mammoth Cave System, Ken-
         tucky. *Midcontinental Journal of Archaeology* 14:119–45.

Murphy, J. L.
1971   Molluscan Remains from Four Archaeological Sites in Northeastern Ohio. *Sterkiana*
         43:21–25.

Nance, C. Roger
1976   *The Archaeological Sequence at Durant Bend, Dallas County, Alabama.* Special Publications of the Alabama Archaeological Society 2, University.
Naroll, R.
1962   Floor Area and Settlement Population. *American Antiquity* 27:587–89.
Nassaney, Michael S.
1991   Spatial-Temporal Dimensions of Social Integration during the Coles Creek Period in Central Arkansas. In *Stability, Transformation, and Variation: The Late Woodland Southeast,* edited by Michael S. Nassaney and Charles R. Cobb, pp. 177–220. New York: Plenum Press.
1992a   *Experiments in Social Ranking in Prehistoric Central Arkansas.* Ph.D. dissertation, Department of Anthropology, University of Massachusetts. University Microfilms, Ann Arbor, Mich.
1992b   Communal Societies and the Emergence of Elites in the Prehistoric American Southeast. In *Lords of the Southeast: Social Inequality and the Native Elites of Southeastern North America,* edited by A. W. Barker and T. R. Pauketat, pp. 111–43. Archeological Papers of the American Anthropological Association No. 3, Washington, D.C.
1994   The Historical and Archaeological Context of Plum Bayou Culture in Central Arkansas. *Southeastern Archaeology* 13:36–55.
1996a   The Contributions of the Plum Bayou Survey Project, 1988–1994, to the Native Settlement History of Central Arkansas. *Arkansas Archeologist* 35:1–50.
1996b   Aboriginal Earthworks in Central Arkansas. In *Mounds, Embankments, and Ceremonialism in the Midsouth,* edited by Robert C. Mainfort and R. Walling, pp. 22–35. Arkansas Archeological Survey Research Series No. 46, Fayetteville.
2000   The Late Woodland Southeast. In *Late Woodland Societies: Tradition and Transformation across the Midcontinent,* edited by Thomas E. Emerson, Dale L. McElrath, and Andrew C. Fortier, pp. 713–30. Lincoln: University of Nebraska Press.
Nassaney, Michael S., and Charles R. Cobb
1991   Patterns and Processes of Late Woodland Development in the Greater Southeastern United States. In *Stability, Transformation, and Variation: The Late Woodland Southeast,* edited by Michael S. Nassaney and Charles R. Cobb, pp. 285–322. New York: Plenum Press.
Nassaney, Michael S., and Robert Hoffman
1992   Archaeological Investigations at the Fitzhugh Site (3LN212): A Plum Bayou Culture Household in Central Arkansas. *Midcontinental Journal of Archaeology* 17:139–65.
Nassaney, Michael S., and Kendra Pyle
1999   The Adoption of the Bow and Arrow in Eastern North America: A View from Central Arkansas. *American Antiquity* 64(2):243–63.
Nassaney, Michael S., Deborah L. Rotman, Daniel O. Sayers, Carol A. Nickolai
2000   *The Southwest Michigan Historical Landscape Project: Exploring Class, Gender, and Ethnicity from the Ground Up.* Ms. on file, Department of Anthropology, Western Michigan University, Kalamazoo.
National Climatic Data Center
1999   Mean Number of Days with Minimum Temperature 32 Degrees F or Less. National Oceanographic and Atmospheric Administration, Climatic Data Online. www.ncdc.noaa.gov.ol.climate/online/ccd/ min32temp.html.

Nelson, P. W.
   1987   *The Terrestrial Natural Communities of Missouri.* Missouri Natural Areas Com-
           mittee, Jefferson City.
Neuman, Robert W.
   1981   Complicated Stamped Pottery in Louisiana: Its Spatial Distribution and Chronol-
           ogy. In *Traces of Prehistory: Papers in Honor of William G. Haag,* edited by F. H.
           West and R. W. Neuman, pp. 71–76. Geoscience and Man 22, Geoscience Publi-
           cations, Department of Geography and Anthropology, Louisiana State University,
           Baton Rouge.
   1984   *An Introduction to Louisiana Archaeology.* Baton Rouge: Louisiana State Univer-
           sity Press.
Neumann, Georg K.
   1938   The Human Remains from Mammoth Cave, Kentucky. *American Antiquity* 3:339–
           53.
Neumann, Georg K., and Melvin L. Fowler
   1952   Hopewellian Sites in the Lower Wabash Valley. In *Hopewellian Communities in
           Illinois,* edited by Thorne Deuel, pp. 175–248. Scientific Papers 5, Illinois State
           Museum, Springfield.
Neussius, Sarah
   1996   Garden Hunting: Is the Model Relevant in the Southeast? Presented at the 53rd
           annual meeting of the Southeastern Archaeological Conference, Birmingham, Ala.
Newell, H. P., and A. D. Krieger
   1949   *The George C. Davis Site, Cherokee County, Texas.* Memoirs No. 5, Society for
           American Archaeology, Menasha, Wis.
Newkumet, P. J.
   1940   Preliminary Report of Excavations of the Williams Mound, LeFlore County, Okla-
           homa. *Oklahoma Prehistorian* 3(2):2–10.
Nicholas, George P.
   1999   A Light but Lasting Footprint: Human Influences on the Northeastern Landscape.
           In *The Archaeological Northeast,* edited by Mary A. Levine, Kenneth E. Sassaman,
           and Michael S. Nassaney, pp. 25–38. Westport, Conn.: Bergin and Garvey Press.
Niquette, Charles M.
   1984   *Archaeological Survey and Testing: The 1983 Field Season at Fort Leonard Wood,
           Pulaski County, Missouri.* Submitted to the U.S. Army Corps of Engineers, Kan-
           sas City District, by Cultural Resource Analysts, Inc., Lexington. Copies available
           from Cultural Resource Analysts, Inc.
Niquette, Charles M., and Jonathan P. Kerr
   1993   Late Woodland Archaeology at the Parkline Site, Putnam County, West Virginia.
           West Virginia Archaeologist 45(1-2):43–59.
Norton, Mark R.
   1997   Pinson Mounds: New Pieces of the Puzzle. Presented at the 54th annual meeting
           of the Southeastern Archaeological Conference, Baton Rouge, La.
O'Brien, Michael J.
   1985   Archaeology of the Central Salt River Valley: An Overview of the Prehistoric
           Occupation. *The Missouri Archaeologist* 46.
   1995   Archaeological Research in the Central Mississippi Valley: Culture History Gone
           Awry. *Review of Archaeology* 16:23–36.
   1996   *Paradigms of the Past: The Story of Missouri Archaeology.* Columbia: University
           of Missouri Press.
   2000   The Legacy of Culture History in the Southeastern United States. *Reviews in*

Anthropology 29:111–39.

O'Brien, Michael J., and Robert C. Dunnell

1998   A Brief Introduction to the Archaeology of the Central Mississippi River Valley. In *Changing Perspectives on the Archaeology of the Central Mississippi Valley,* edited by Michael J. O'Brien and Robert C. Dunnell, pp. 1–30. Tuscaloosa: University of Alabama Press.

O'Brien, Michael J., and Robert C. Dunnell (editors)

1998   *Changing Perspectives on the Archaeology of the Central Mississippi Valley.* Tuscaloosa: University of Alabama Press.

O'Brien, Michael J., and G. L. Fox

1994a   Sorting Artifacts in Space and Time. In *Cat Monsters and Head Pots: The Archaeology of Missouri's Pemiscot Bayou,* by Michael J. O'Brien, pp. 25–60. Columbia: University of Missouri Press.

1994b   Assemblage Similarities and Dissimilarities. In *Cat Monsters and Head Pots: The Archaeology of Missouri's Pemiscot Bayou,* by Michael J. O'Brien, pp. 61–93. Columbia: University of Missouri Press.

O'Brien, Michael J., and R. Lee Lyman

1998   *James A. Ford and the Growth of Americanist Archaeology.* Columbia: University of Missouri Press.

1999   *Measuring the Flow of Time: The Works of James A. Ford, 1935–1941.* Tuscaloosa: University of Alabama Press.

2001   The Epistemological Nature of Archaeological Units. *Anthropological Theory,* in press.

O'Brien, Michael J., and W. Raymond Wood

1998   *The Prehistory of Missouri.* Columbia: University of Missouri Press.

O'Hear, John W.

1990   *Archaeological Investigations at the Sanders Site (22Cl917).* Report of Investigations 6, Cobb Institute of Archaeology, Mississippi State University.

1996   Reanalysis of Major Wheeler and Alexander Assemblages in Pickwick Basin. Presented at the 53rd annual meeting of the Southeastern Archaeological Conference, Birmingham.

O'Hear, John W., and Thomas L. Conn

1978   *Archaeological Salvage Excavations at the L. A. Strickland I Site (22Ts765), Tishomingo County, Mississippi.* Submitted to the U.S. Army Corps of Engineers, Nashville District, by the Department of Anthropology, Mississippi State University.

O'Hear, John W., Clark Larsen, Margaret M. Scarry, John Phillips, and Erica Simons

1981   *Archaeological Salvage Excavations at the Tibbee Creek Site (22Lo600), Lowndes County, Mississippi.* Submitted to the U.S. Army Corps of Engineers, Mobile District, by the Department of Anthropology, Mississippi State University.

O'Neill, Brian

1981   *Kansas Rock Art.* Topeka: Kansas State Historical Society.

Oakley, Carey B., Jr.

1971   *An Archaeological Investigation of Pinson Cave (1Je20).* Master's thesis, Department of Anthropology, University of Alabama, Tuscaloosa.

Oehler, Charles

1973   *Turpin Indians.* Popular Publication Series No. 1, Cincinnati Museum of Natural History.

Oliver, Billy

1985   Tradition and Typology: Basic Elements of the Carolina Projectile Point Sequence.

In *Structure and Process in Southeastern Archaeology,* edited by Roy S. Dickens, Jr., and H. Trawick Ward, pp. 195–211. Tuscaloosa: University of Alabama Press.

1988   Ethnobotanical Analysis, 31Bn174. Manuscript prepared for David G. Moore, Western Office of the North Carolina Department of Archives and History.

Orr, K. G.
1952   Survey of Caddoan Area Archeology. In *Archeology of Eastern United States,* edited by James B. Griffin, pp. 239–55. Chicago: University of Chicago Press.

Owen, V. S.
1958   A Bedford County Cavern Investigation. *Tennessee Archaeologist* 14:16–22.

Owsley, Douglas W., and Jerome C. Rose (editors)
1997   *Bioarchaeology of the North Central United States: A Volume in the Central and Northern Plains Overview.* Arkansas Archeological Survey Research Series No. 49, Fayetteville.

Pace, Robert E.
1973   *Archaeological Salvage, Daughtery-Monroe Site: Island Levee Local Protection Project, Sullivan County, Indiana.* Submitted to the Northeast Regional Office, U.S. National Park Service.

Pacheco, Paul J.
1996   Ohio Hopewell Regional Settlement Patterns. In *A View from the Core: A Synthesis of Ohio Hopewell Archaeology,* edited by Paul J. Pacheco, pp. 16–35. Columbus: Ohio Archaeological Council.

1997   Ohio Middle Woodland Intracommunity Settlement Variability: A Case Study from the Licking Valley. In *Ohio Hopewell Community Organization,* edited by William S. Dancey and Paul J. Pacheco, pp. 41–84. Kent, Ohio: Kent State University Press.

Pacheco, Paul J. (editor)
1996   *A View from the Core: A Synthesis of Ohio Hopewell Archaeology.* Columbus: Ohio Archaeological Council.

Padgett, Thomas J.
1976   Hinderland Exploitation in the Central Gulf Coast–Manatee Region during the Safety Harbor Period. *Florida Anthropologist* 29:39–48.

Padgett, Thomas J., and David M. Heisler
1979   *A Predictive Model of Archaeological Site Location in the Central Leaf River Basin, Mississippi.* Submitted to the Mississippi Department of Archives and History by the Department of Sociology and Anthropology, University of Southern Mississippi, Hattiesburg.

Palmer, Arthur N.
1981   *A Geological Guide to Mammoth Cave National Park.* Teaneck, N.J.: Zephyrus Press.

Palmer, Edward
1917   Arkansas Mounds. *Arkansas Historical Association Publications* (Little Rock) 4:390–448.

Parker, Garald G.
1984   Hydrology of the Pre-drainage System of the Everglades in Southern Florida. In *Environments of South Florida: Present and Past II,* edited by Patrick J. Gleason, pp. 28–37. Coral Gables, Fla.: Miami Geological Society.

Parker, Kathryn E.
1989   Archaeobotanical Assemblage. In *The Holding Site (11 Ms 118): A Hopewell Community in the American Bottom,* by A. C. Fortier, T. O. Maher, J. A. Williams, M. C. Meinkoth, K. E. Parker, and L. S. Kelly, pp. 429–64. American Bottom Archaeology FAI-270 Site Reports, Vol. 19, University of Illinois Press, Urbana.

Parker Pearson, Michael
   1984   Economic and Cyclical Change: Cyclical Growth in the Pre-State Societies of
           Jutland. In *Ideology, Power, and Prehistory,* edited by D. Miller and C. Tilley, pp.
           69–92. Cambridge: Cambridge University Press.
Parks, A. M.
   1985   *Where the River Found the Bay: Archaeology and History of the Granada Site,
           Volume 2.* Florida Division of Archives, History and Records Management, Talla-
           hassee.
Parmalee, Paul W.
   1959   Animal Remains from the Modoc Rock Shelter Site, Randolph County, Illinois. In
           Summary Report of Modoc Rock Shelter, 1952, 1953, 1955, 1956, by Melvin L.
           Fowler, pp. 61–65. Illinois State Museum Reports of Investigations No. 8, Spring-
           field.
   1960   Mussels from the Angel Site, Indiana. *The Nautilus* 74(2):70–75.
   1975   A General Summary of the Vertebrate Fauna from Cahokia. In *Perspectives in
           Cahokia Archaeology,* edited by Melvin L. Fowler, pp. 137–55. Bulletin 10, Illi-
           nois Archaeological Survey, Urbana.
   1988   A Comparative Study of Late Prehistoric and Modern Molluscan Faunas of the
           Little Pigeon River System, Tennessee. *American Malacological Bulletin*
           62(2):165–78.
   1990   Animal Remains from the 40LD207 Site, Loudon County, Tennessee. In *The Kim-
           berly-Clark Site (40LD208) and Site 40LD207,* by Jefferson Chapman, Appendix
           3, pp. 65–73. Report of Investigations 51, Department of Anthropology, Univer-
           sity of Tennessee, Knoxville.
   1994   Freshwater Mussels from Dust and Smith Bottom Caves, Alabama. In *Preliminary
           Archaeological Papers on Dust Cave, Northwest Alabama,* edited by Nurit S.
           Goldman-Finn and Boyce N. Driskell. *Journal of Alabama Archaeology* 40(1 and
           2):135–62.
Parmalee, Paul W., and Arthur E. Bogan
   1986   Molluscan Remains from Aboriginal Middens at the Clinch River Breeder Reac-
           tor Plant Site, Roane County, Tennessee. *American Malacological Bulletin* 4(1):25–
           37.
Parmalee, Paul W., and Mark Hughes
   1994   Freshwater Mussels (Bivalvia: Unionidae) of the Hiwassee River in East Tennes-
           see. *American Malacological Bulletin* 11(1):21–27.
Parmalee, Paul W., and Walter E. Klippel
   1974   Freshwater Mussels as a Prehistoric Food Resource. *American Antiquity* 39(3):421–
           34.
   1984   The Naiad Fauna of the Tellico River, Monroe County, Tennessee. *American Mala-
           cological Bulletin* 3(1):41–44.
   1986   A Prehistoric Aboriginal Freshwater Mussel Assemblage from the Duck River in
           Middle Tennessee. *The Nautilus* 100(4):134–40.
Parmalee, Paul W., Walter E. Klippel, and Arthur E. Bogan
   1980   Notes on the Prehistoric and Present Status of the Naiad Fauna of the Middle
           Cumberland River, Smith County, Tennessee. *The Nautilus* 94(3):93–105.
   1982   Aboriginal and Modern Freshwater Mussel Assemblages (Pelecypoda: Unionidae)
           from the Chickamauga Reservoir, Tennessee. *Brimleyana* 8:75–90.
Parmalee, Paul W., and Constance O'Hare
   1989   Snails and Freshwater Mussels from the Anderson Site. In *The Anderson Site:
           Middle Archaic Adaptation in Tennessee's Central Basin,* by John T. Dowd, pp.

37–42. Tennessee Anthropological Association Miscellaneous Paper 13, Knox-ville.

Parmalee, Paul W., A. A. Paloumpis, and N. Wilson
1972   *Animals Utilized by Woodland Peoples Occupying the Apple Creek Site, Illinois.* Illinois State Museum Reports of Investigations No. 23, Springfield.

Patch, Diana Craig
1976   *An Analysis of the Archaeological Shell of Fresh Water Mollusks from the Carlston Annis Shellmound, West Central Kentucky.* Honors thesis, Washington University, St. Louis.

Patterson, Paul L.
1990   *An Archaeological Reconnaissance of Selected Areas of the Black Prairie Region of West Central Alabama.* Submitted to the Alabama DeSoto Commission by the Division of Archaeology, University of Alabama, Tuscaloosa.

Patterson, William A., III, and Kenneth E. Sassaman
1988   Indian Fires in the Prehistory of New England. In *Holocene Human Ecology in Northeastern North America,* edited by G. P. Nicholas, pp. 107–35. New York: Plenum Press.

Pauketat, Timothy R.
1993   *Temples for Cahokia Lords: Preston Holder's 1955–1956 Excavations of Kunnemann Mound.* Memoir No. 26, Museum of Anthropology, University of Michigan, Ann Arbor.
1994   *The Ascent of Chiefs: Cahokia and Mississippian Politics in Native North America.* Tuscaloosa: University of Alabama Press.

Pauketat, Timothy R., Mark A. Rees, and Stephanie L. Pauketat
1998   *An Archaeological Survey of the Horseshoe Lake State Park, Madison County, Illinois.* Illinois State Museum Reports of Investigation No. 55, Springfield.

Paynter, Robert W., and Randall H. McGuire
1991   The Archaeology of Inequality: Material Culture, Domination and Resistance. In *The Archaeology of Inequality,* edited by R. H. McGuire and R. W. Paynter, pp. 1–11. Oxford: Basil Blackwell.

Peabody, Charles
1904   *Exploration of Mounds, Coahoma County, Mississippi.* Papers of the Peabody Museum of Archaeology and Ethnology 3(2), Harvard University, Cambridge.

Peacock, Evan
1986   A Comparison of Late Woodland, Mississippian, and Protohistoric Triangular Points from the Central Tombigbee River Drainage. *Journal of Alabama Archaeology* 32:108–29.
1993   Molluscan Analysis. In *Archaeological Data Recovery, Jefferson Street (FAU-3258) Bridge: The East Nashville Mounds (40DV4) and French Lick/Sulphur Dell (40DV5) Sites, Nashville, Davidson County, Tennessee, Vol. II,* by Richard Wall-ing, Lawrence Alexander, and Evan Peacock, pp. 12-1 to 12-18. Draft report sub-mitted to the Tennessee Department of Transportation by Panamerican Consult-ants, Inc., Tuscaloosa, Ala.
1995   *Shovel-Test Screening and Survey Methodology: A Field Study from the Tombigbee National Forest, North Mississippi.* USDA Forest Service, Jackson.
1996a Tchula Period Sites on the Holly Springs National Forest, North-Central Missis-sippi. In *Proceedings of the 14th Annual Mid-South Archaeological Conference,* edited by R. Walling, C. Wharey, and C. Stanley, pp. 13–23. Special Publications 1, Panamerican Consultants, Tuscaloosa, Ala.
1996b Archaeological Site Survey in Wooded Environments: A Field Study from the

Tombigbee National Forest, North-Central Mississippi. *North American Archaeologist* 17:61–79.

1997a Woodland Ceramic Affiliations and Settlement Pattern Change in the North Central Hills of Mississippi. *Midcontinental Journal of Archaeology* 22:237–61.

1997b Current and Future Directions in the Analysis of Freshwater Bivalve Remains in Archaeology. In *Results of Recent Archaeological Investigations in the Greater Mid-South,* edited by Charles M. McNutt, pp. 71–93. Occasional Paper 18, Anthropological Research Center, University of Memphis.

1998 *Fresh-Water Mussels as Indicators of Prehistoric Human Environmental Impact in the Southeastern United States.* Doctoral thesis, Department of Archaeology and Prehistory, University of Sheffield, England.

1999 Molluscan Analysis. In *Cultural Resources Survey, Rehabilitation, and Repairs, Sterlington to Monroe, and Testing of 16Ou97, Ouachita River Levees, Louisiana,* by Shawn Chapman, Richard Walling, Les Seago, and Paul D. Jackson. Submitted to the U.S. Army Corps of Engineers, Vicksburg District, by Panamerican Consultants, Inc., Memphis, Tenn.

Peacock, Evan, and David W. Fant

1998 Artifact Translocation in Upland Sandy Soils: An Example for the Holly Spring National Forest, North-Central Mississippi. Presented at the 63rd annual meeting of the Society for American Archaeology, Seattle.

Pearsall, James E., and Clyde D. Malone

1991 A Middle Woodland Solstice Alignment at Old Stone Fort? *Tennessee Anthropologist* 16(1):20–28.

Peebles, Christopher S.

1990 From History to Hermeneutics: The Place of Theory in the Later Prehistory of the Southeast. *Southeastern Archaeology* 9(1):23–34.

Peebles, Christopher S., and Susan M. Kus

1977 Some Archaeological Correlates of Ranked Societies. *American Antiquity* 42:421–48.

Penman, John T.

1980 *Archaeological Survey in Mississippi, 1974–1975.* Archaeological Report 2, Mississippi Department of Archives and History, Jackson.

Penny, David W.

1985 Continuities of Imagery and Symbolism in the Art of the Woodlands. In *Ancient Art of the American Woodland Indians,* by David S. Brose, James A. Brown, and David W. Penny, pp. 147–98. New York: Harry N. Abrams.

Penton, Daniel T.

1970 *Excavations in the Early Swift Creek Component at Bird Hammock (8-Wa-30).* Master's thesis, Dept. of Anthropology, Florida State University, Tallahassee.

Percy, George W.

1971 *Preliminary Report to the Division of Recreation and Parks, Department of Natural Resources, State of Florida, on Archaeological Work in the Torreya State Park during the Year of 1971 by the Department of Anthropology at Florida State University.* Ms. on file, Florida Department of Natural Resources, Tallahassee.

Percy, George W., and David S. Brose

1974 Weeden Island Ecology, Subsistence, and Village Life in Northwest Florida. Presented at the 39th annual meeting of the Society for American Archaeology, Washington, D.C.

Percy, George W., and M. Katherine Jones

1976 An Archaeological Survey of Upland Locales in Gadsden and Liberty Counties, Florida. *Florida Anthropologist* 29:105–25.

Perino, Gregory L.
    1966   A Preliminary Report on the Peisker Site: Part 1—The Early Woodland Occupa-
               tion. *Central States Archaeological Journal* 13:47–51.
Perino, Gregory L., and W. J. Bennett, Jr.
    1978   *Archaeological Investigations at the Mahaffey Site, Ch-1, Hugo Reservoir, Choctaw
               County, Oklahoma.* Museum of the Red River, Idabel, Okla.
Perttula, Timothy K.
    1992   *"The Caddo Nation," Archaeological and Ethnohistoric Perspectives.* Texas Ar-
               chaeology and Ethnohistory Series. Austin: University of Texas Press.
    1999   Environment and Cultural Setting. In Vol. 1 of *The Hurricane Hill Site (41HP106):
               The Archaeology of a Late Archaic/Early Ceramic and Early-Middle Caddoan
               Settlement in Northeast Texas,* 2 vols., edited by Timothy K. Perttula, pp. 10–33.
               Pittsburg, Texas: Friends of Northeast Texas Archaeology.
Perttula, Timothy K. (editor)
    1999   *The Hurricane Hill Site (41HP106): The Archaeology of a Late Archaic/Early
               Ceramic and Early-Middle Caddoan Settlement in Northeast Texas,* volume 1 (of
               2). Pittsburg, Texas: Friends of Northeast Texas Archaeology.
Peterson, Drexel A., Jr.
    1979a *An Archaeological Survey and Assessment of the Loosahatchie Watershed.* Sub-
               mitted to the Soil Conservation Service, Nashville, Tenn., by Memphis State Uni-
               versity.
    1979b *An Archaeological Survey and Assessment of the Wolf River Watershed.* Submit-
               ted to the Soil Conservation Service, Nashville, Tenn., by Memphis State University.
Petruso, Karl M., and Jere M. Wickens
    1984   The Acorn in Aboriginal Subsistence in Eastern North America: A Report on Mis-
               cellaneous Experiments. In *Experiments and Observations on Aboriginal Wild
               Plant Food Utilization in Eastern North America,* edited by Patrick J. Munson,
               pp. 360–78. Prehistory Research Series 6, No. 2, Indiana Historical Society, India-
               napolis.
Phelps, David S.
    1965   The Norwood Series of Fiber-Tempered Ceramics. *Southeastern Archaeological
               Conference Bulletin* 2:65–69.
    1966   Early and Late Components of the Tucker Site. *Florida Anthropologist* 19:11–38.
    1968   Thom's Creek Ceramics in the Central Savannah River Locality. *Florida Anthro-
               pologist* 21(1):17–30.
    1969   Swift Creek and Santa Rosa in Northwest Florida. *Notebook* 1(6–9):14–24. South
               Carolina Institute of Archeology and Anthropology, University of South Carolina,
               Columbia.
    1980   *Archaeological Salvage of the Thorpe Site and Other Investigations along the US
               64 Bypass, Rocky Mount, North Carolina.* East Carolina University Archaeologi-
               cal Research Report No. 3, Archaeology Laboratory, Department of Sociology
               and Anthropology, East Carolina University, Greenville.
    1981   *Archaeological Survey of Four Watersheds in the North Carolina Coastal Plain.*
               North Carolina Archaeological Council Publication 16, Raleigh.
    1983   Archaeology of the North Carolina Coast and Coastal Plain: Problems and Hy-
               potheses. In *The Prehistory of North Carolina: An Archaeological Symposium,*
               edited by Mark A. Mathis and J. J. Crow, pp. 1–51. Division of Archives and
               History, North Carolina Department of Cultural Resources, Raleigh.
Phelps, David S., and Charles L. Heath
    1998   Cashie Series Ceramics from the Interior Coastal Plain of North Carolina. Pre-

sented at the 55th annual meeting of the Southeastern Archaeological Conference, Greenville, S.C.

Phillips, Philip
1970 *Archaeological Survey in the Lower Yazoo Basin, Mississippi, 1949–1955.* Papers of the Peabody Museum of Archaeology and Ethnology, Vol. 60, Pt. I, Harvard University, Cambridge.

Phillips, Philip, and James A. Brown
1978 *Pre-Columbian Shell Engravings from the Craig Mound at Spiro, Oklahoma.* Peabody Museum Press, Peabody Museum of Archaeology and Ethnology, Harvard University, Cambridge.

Phillips, Philip, and Gordon R. Willey
1953 Method and Theory in American Archaeology: An Operational Basis for Culture-Historical Integration. *American Anthropologist* 55:615–33.

Phillips, Philip, James A. Ford, and James B. Griffin
1951 *Archaeological Survey in the Lower Mississippi Alluvial Valley, 1940–1947.* Papers of the Peabody Museum of Archaeology and Ethnology, Vol. 25, Harvard University, Cambridge.

Piatek, Bruce John
1994 The Tomoka Mound Complex in Northeast Florida. *Southeastern Archaeology* 13:109–18.

Pielou, E. C.
1977 *Mathematical Ecology.* New York: John Wiley and Sons.

Pluckhahn, Thomas J.
1996 Joseph Caldwell's Summerour Mound (9FO16) and Woodland Platform Mounds in the Southeastern United States. *Southeastern Archaeology* 15:191–211.
1998 *Highway 61 Revisited: Archeological Evaluation of Eight Sites in Bartow County, Georgia.* Submitted to the Georgia Department of Transportation, Office of Environment/Location, Atlanta, by Southeastern Archeological Services, Athens, Ga.
2000 Fifty Years since Sears: Deconstructing the Domestic Sphere at Kolomoki. *Southeastern Archaeology* 19:145–55.

Pollack, David, and Gwyn Henderson
1984 A Mid-Eighteenth Century Historic Indian Occupation in Greenup County, Kentucky. In *Late Prehistoric Research in Kentucky,* edited by David Pollack, Charles Hockensmith, and Thomas Sanders, pp.1–24. Frankfort: Kentucky Heritage Council.

Pollack, David, Thomas Sanders, and Charles Hockensmith (editors)
1985 *Woodland Period Research in Kentucky.* Frankfort: Kentucky Heritage Council.

Pond, Alonzo
1937 Lost John of Mummy Ledge. *Natural History* 39:174–76.

Pope, G. D., Jr.
1956 *Ocmulgee.* National Park Service Historical Handbook Series No. 24, Washington, D.C.

Poplin, Eric C., Christopher T. Espenshade, and D. C. Jones
1993 *Archaeological Investigations at the Buck Hall Site (38CH644), Francis Marion National Forest, South Carolina.* Brockington and Associates, Atlanta and Charleston. Francis Marion and Sumter National Forests Cultural Resources Management Report 92–08.

Porter, James W.
1963 Southern Illinois University Museum Projects. In *Second Annual Report: American Bottom Archaeology,* edited by Melvin L. Fowler, pp. 31–39. Urbana: Illinois Archaeological Survey.

1972   An Archaeological Survey of the Mississippi Valley in St. Clair, Monroe, and
        Randolph Counties. In *Preliminary Report of 1972 Historic Sites Archaeological
        Reconnaissance of Selected Areas in the State of Illinois: Part I, Summary Section
        A,* pp. 25–33. Illinois Department of Conservation, Springfield.
1974   Thin Section Analysis of the Jean Rita Marion Thick Pottery. *Wisconsin Archaeolo-
        gist* 55(2):163–72.
Potter, Stephen
    1989   Early English Effects on Virginia Exchange and Tribute Systems in the Seven-
            teenth Century: An Example from the Tidewater Potomac. In *Powhatan's Mantle:
            Indians in the Colonial Southeast,* edited by P. Wood, G. Waselkov, and T. Hatley,
            pp. 151–72. Lincoln: University of Nebraska Press.
    1993   *Commoners, Tribute and Chiefs: The Development of Algonquian Culture in the
            Potomac Valley.* Charlottesville: University Press of Virginia.
Potts, Thomas D., and Samuel O. Brookes
    1981   The Bobo Site (22-Co-535). *Mississippi Archaeology* 16(1):2–24.
Powell, Mary L.
    1989   The People of Nodena. In *Nodena: An Account of 90 Years of Archeological In-
            vestigation in Southeast Mississippi County, Arkansas,* edited by D. F. Morse, pp.
            65–95. Arkansas Archeological Survey Research Series No. 30, Fayetteville.
Prentice, Guy
    1986   Origins of Plant Domestication in the Eastern United States: Promoting the Indi-
            vidual in Archaeological Theory. *Southeastern Archaeology* 5:103–19.
Prezzano, Susan C.
    1997   Warfare, Women, and Households: The Development of Iroquois Culture. In *Women
            in Prehistory,* edited by Cheryl Claassen, pp. 88–99. Philadelphia: University of
            Pennsylvania Press.
Price, James E.
    1986   Tchula Period Occupation along the Ozark Border in Southeast Missouri. In *Early
            Woodland Archaeology,* edited by Kenneth B. Farnsworth and Thomas E. Emerson,
            pp. 535–45. Center for American Archaeology Press, Kampsville, Ill.
Price, James E., and Cynthia R. Price
    1984   *Phase II Testing of the Shell Lake Site, 23WE627, near Wappapello Dam, Wayne
            County, Missouri.* Cultural Resource Management Report No. 11, U.S. Army Corps
            of Engineers, St. Louis District.
Proctor, C.
    1957   The Sam Site, Lf-28, of LeFlore County, Oklahoma. *Bulletin of the Oklahoma
            Anthropological Society* 5:45–91.
Prufer, Olaf H.
    1964   The Hopewell Complex of Ohio. In *Hopewellian Studies,* edited by James R.
            Caldwell and Robert L. Hall, pp. 35–84. Scientific Papers 12, Illinois State Mu-
            seum, Springfield.
    1967a   The Scioto Valley Archaeological Survey. In *Studies in Ohio Archaeology,* edited
            by Olaf H. Prufer and Douglas H. McKenzie, pp. 267–328. Kent, Ohio: Kent State
            University Press.
    1967b   Chesser Cave: A Late Woodland Phase in Southeastern Ohio. In *Studies in Ohio
            Archaeology,* edited by Olaf Prufer and Douglas McKenzie, pp. 1–62. Kent, Ohio:
            Kent State University Press.
    1968   *Ohio Hopewell Ceramics: An Analysis of the Extant Collections.* Anthropological
            Papers No. 33, Museum of Anthropology, University of Michigan, Ann Arbor.
    1997   How to Construct a Model: A Personal Memoir. In *Ohio Hopewell Community*

Organization, edited by William S. Dancey and Paul J. Pacheco, pp. 105–30. Kent, Ohio: Kent State University Press.

Prufer, Olaf, and Douglas H. McKenzie
1965   *The McGraw Site: A Study in Hopewellian Dynamics.* Cleveland Museum of Natural History Scientific Publications 3:1.

Pullins, Stevan C., James B. Stoltman, Veronica L. Deitrick, Dennis B. Blanton, and Anna L. Gray
1996   *Ceramic Technology, Early Woodland Settlement and Enfield Plantation Phase III Archaeological Data Recovery for Mitigation of Effects to Site 44KW81 Associated with the Route 629 Bridge Replacement, King William County, Virginia.* Technical Report Series No. 21, William and Mary Center for Archaeological Research, Department of Anthropology, The College of William and Mary, Williamsburg, Va.

Purrington, Burton L.
1976   Soils and Site Distribution in the Upper Watauga Valley, North Carolina: A Preliminary Report. Presented at the 6th Middle Atlantic Archaeology Conference, Front Royal, Va.
1983   Ancient Mountaineers: An Overview of the Prehistoric Archaeology of North Carolina's Western Mountain Region. In *The Prehistory of North Carolina: An Archaeological Symposium,* edited by Mark A. Mathis and Jeffrey J. Crow, pp. 83–160. North Carolina Department of Archives and History, Raleigh.

Quimby, George I.
1951   *The Medora Site, West Baton Rouge Parish, Louisiana.* Anthropological Series 24, Field Museum of Natural History, Chicago.

Quitmeyer, Irvy R., H. Stephen Hale, and Douglas S. Jones
1985   Paleoseasonality Determination Based on Incremental Shell Growth in the Hard Clam, *Mercenaria mercenaria,* and Its Implications for the Analysis of Three Southeast Georgia Coastal Shell Middens. *Southeastern Archaeology* 4(1):27–40.

Radin, Paul
1923   *The Winnebago Tribe* (reprinted in 1990). Lincoln: University of Nebraska Press.

Radiocarbon Dates Association, Inc.
1958   Key-Sort Cards of Radiocarbon Dates. Quincy Mail Advertising Company, Braintree, Mass.

Rafferty, Janet
1980   Surface Collections and Settlement Patterns in the Central Tombigbee Valley. *Southeastern Archaeological Conference Bulletin* 22:90–94.
1985   The Archaeological Record on Sedentariness: Recognition, Development, and Implications. In *Advances in Archaeological Method and Theory,* vol. 8, edited by Michael B. Schiffer, pp. 113–56. New York: Academic Press.
1986a   A Critique of the Type-Variety System as Used in Ceramic Analysis. *Mississippi Archaeology* 21(2):40–49.
1986b   Summary and Conclusions. In *Test Excavations at Two Woodland Sites, Lowndes County, Mississippi,* by Janet Rafferty and Mary Evelyn Starr, pp. 135–39. Report of Investigations 3, Cobb Institute of Archaeology, Mississippi State University.
1987   The Ingomar Mounds Site: Internal Structure and Chronology. *Midcontinental Journal of Archaeology* 12:147–73.
1990   Test Excavations at Ingomar Mounds, Mississippi. *Southeastern Archaeology* 9:93–102.
1994   Gradual or Step-Wise Change: The Development of Sedentary Settlement Patterns in Northeast Mississippi. *American Antiquity* 59:405–25.

1995a   A Seriation of Historic Period Aboriginal Pottery from Northeast Mississippi. *Journal of Alabama Archaeology* 41:180–207.

1995b   *Owl Creek Mounds: Test Excavations at a Vacant Mississippian Mound Center.* Report of Investigations 7, Cobb Institute of Archaeology, Mississippi State University.

1996   Continuity in Woodland and Mississippian Settlement Patterning in Northeast Mississippi. *Southeastern Archaeology* 15:230–43.

1998   Tracking Change in Pottery Temper through Late Prehistory in the Tombigbee Valley. Presented at the 63rd annual meeting of the Society for American Archaeology, Seattle.

Rafferty, Janet, and Mary Evelyn Starr

1986   *Test Excavations at Two Woodland Sites, Lowndes County, Mississippi.* Report of Investigations 3, Cobb Institute of Archaeology, Mississippi State University.

Rafferty, Milton D.

1980   *The Ozarks, Land and Life.* Norman: University of Oklahoma Press.

Rafinesque, Constantine S.

1824   *Ancient History, or Annals of Kentucky; With a Survey of the Ancient Monuments of North America, and a Tabular View of the Principal Languages and Primitive Nations of the Whole Earth.* Printed for the author, Frankfort, Ky.

Railey, Jimmy

1991   Woodland Settlement Trends and Symbolic Architecture in the Kentucky Bluegrass. In *The Human Landscape in Kentucky's Past,* edited by Charles Stout and Christine K. Hensley, pp. 56–77. Frankfort: Kentucky Heritage Council.

1996   Woodland Cultivators. In *Kentucky Archaeology,* edited by R. Barry Lewis, pp. 79–125. Lexington: University of Kentucky Press.

Railey, Jimmy (editor)

1984   *The Pyles Site (15MS28), a Newtown Village in Mason County, Kentucky.* Occasional Paper 1, William S. Webb Archaeological Society, Lexington, Ky.

Ray, Jack H.

1995   Lithic Analysis. In *Occupations at the Hayti Bypass Site, Pemiscot County, Missouri,* edited by Michael D. Conner, pp. 171–220. Special Publication No. 1, Center for Archaeological Research, Southwest Missouri State University, Springfield.

Ray, Robert

1994   Freshwater Bivalve Shell Remains. In *Excavations at Boydell Mound A (3AS58), Southeast Arkansas,* by John H. House and Marvin D. Jeter, pp. 66–71. *Arkansas Archeologist* 33(for 1992):1–82.

Reams, Melissa

1996   Tanya's Knoll. Presented at the annual meeting of the Mississippi Archaeological Association, Greenwood.

Reams, Robert E.

1995   *A Red Flag Predictive Model for the Black Creek and Biloxi Ranger Districts, De Soto National Forest.* Master's thesis, Department of Anthropology, Wake Forest University, Winston-Salem, N.C.

Reeder, Robert L.

1982   *The Feeler Site, 23MS12: A Multi-Component Site in the Central Gasconade Drainage.* Submitted to the Missouri State Highway Commission, Jefferson City.

1988   *Prehistory of the Gasconade River Basin.* Ph.D. dissertation, University of Missouri, Columbia. University Microfilms, Ann Arbor.

1999   The Meramec Spring Phase. Ms. in possession of author.

Reid, Kenneth C.
1989   A Materials Science Perspective on Hunter-Gatherer Pottery. In *Pottery Technology: Ideas and Approaches,* edited by G. Bronitsky, pp. 167–80. Boulder: Westview Press.

Reid, William H., and Kay Simpson
1996   *Phase II Investigation of Nine Prehistoric Sites and Phase I Survey of the P-028 Range Area, Greater Sandy Run Acquisition Area, Marine Corps Base, Camp Lejeune, Onslow County, North Carolina.* Submitted to the Marine Corps Base, Camp Lejeune, North Carolina. Copies available from The Cultural Resources Group, Louis Berger and Associates, Inc., Richmond, Va.

Reidhead, Van A.
1981   *A Linear Programming Model of Prehistoric Subsistence Optimization: A Southeastern Indiana Example.* Prehistory Research Series 5, No. 1, Indiana Historical Society, Indianapolis.

Reidhead, Van A., and William F. Limp
1974   *The Haag Site (12D19): A Preliminary Report.* Indiana Archaeological Bulletin 1, No. 1 (August), Indiana Historical Society, Indianapolis.

Rein, Judith S.
1974   *The Complicated Stamped Pottery of the Mann Site, Posey County, Indiana.* Master's thesis, Department of Anthropology, Indiana University, Bloomington.

Riggs, Brett H.
1985   Dated Contexts from Watauga Reservoir: Cultural Chronology Building for Northeast Tennessee. In *Exploring Tennessee Prehistory: A Dedication to Alfred K. Guthe,* edited by T. R. Whyte, C. C. Boyd, Jr., and Brett H. Riggs, pp. 169–84. Report of Investigations 42, Department of Anthropology, University of Tennessee, Knoxville.

Riggs, Brett H., M. Scott Shumate, and Patti Evans-Shumate
1997   *Archaeological Data Recovery at Site 31JK291, Jackson County, North Carolina.* Technical Report prepared for Tribal Casino Gaming Enterprise, Cherokee, N.C.

Riggs, Rodney E.
1986   New Stratigraphic Sequences from the Lower Little Miami River. *West Virginia Archaeologist* 38(2):1–21.
1998   *Ceramics, Chronology and Cultural Change in the Lower Little Miami River Valley, Southwestern Ohio, circa 100 B.C. to circa A.D. 1650.* Ph.D. dissertation, University of Wisconsin-Madison.

Riley, Thomas J., Gregory R. Walz, Charles J. Bareis, Andrew C. Fortier, and Kathryn E. Parker
1994   Accelerator Mass Spectrometry (AMS) Dates Confirm Early *Zea mays* in the Mississippi River Valley. *American Antiquity* 59(3):490–98.

Rindos, David, and Sissel Johannessen
1991   Human-Plant Interaction and Cultural Change in the American Bottom. In *Cahokia and the Hinterlands,* edited by Thomas Emerson and R. Barry Lewis, pp. 35–45. Urbana and Chicago: University of Illinois Press.

Ring, Diane M.
1986   *Evaluation of the Hegwood Bayou Phase as a Late Marksville Period Phase in the Northern Boeuf Basin, Louisiana.* Bachelor's thesis, Department of Anthropology, Harvard University, Cambridge.

Riordan, Robert
1995   A Construction Sequence for a Middle Woodland Hilltop Enclosure. *Midcontinental Journal of Archaeology* 20(1):40–61.

1996   The Enclosed Hilltops of Southern Ohio. In *A View from the Core: A Synthesis of Ohio Hopewell Archaeology,* edited by Paul J. Pacheco, pp. 242–57. Columbus: Ohio Archaeological Council.

1998   Boundaries, Resistance, and Control: Enclosing the Hilltops in Middle Woodland Ohio. In *Ancient Earthen Enclosures of the Eastern Woodlands,* edited by Robert C. Mainfort, Jr., and Lynne P. Sullivan, pp. 68–84. Gainesville: University Press of Florida.

Robben, A.

1989   Habits of the Home: Spatial Hegemony and the Structuration of House and Society in Brazil. *American Anthropologist* 91:570–88.

Robbins, Louise M.

1971   A Woodland "Mummy" from Salts Cave, Kentucky. *American Antiquity* 36:200–205.

Robbins, Louise M., Ronald C. Wilson, and Patty Jo Watson

1981   Paleontology and Archaeology of Jaguar Cave, Tennessee. In *Proceedings: Eighth International Congress of Speleology, Bowling Green, Kentucky,* edited by Barry Beck, pp. 377–80. Atlanta, Georgia: Georgia State University and the National Speleological Society.

Roberts, Katherine M.

2000   Plant Remains. In *Data Recovery Excavations at the Hedgeland Site (16CT19), Catahoula Parish, Louisiana,* edited by J. Ryan, pp. 10.1–10.33. Submitted to the U.S. Army Corps of Engineers, Vicksburg District, by Coastal Environments, Inc., Baton Rouge, La. (Contract No. DACW 38-91-D-0014, Delivery Order Nos. 0018 and 0025).

Roberts, Marian D., and Paul E. Brockington, Jr.

1996   *Archaeological Data Recovery at Selected Prehistoric Sites on Dataw Island, Beaufort, South Carolina.* Submitted to ALCOA, South Carolina, by Brockington and Associates, Atlanta.

Roberts, Marian D., and Connie Huddleston

1998   *Data Recovery at the 38BU1302 Shell Midden, Belfair Plantation Tract, Beaufort County, South Carolina.* Submitted to Belfair Plantation L.L.C., by Brockington and Associates, Atlanta.

Roberts, Ralph G.

1965   Tick Creek Cave, an Archaic Site in the Gasconade River Valley of Missouri. *The Missouri Archaeologist* 27(2):1–52.

Robinson, Kenneth W.

1989   *Archaeological Excavations within the Alternate Pipeline Corridor Passing through the Harshaw Bottom Site (31Ce41), Cherokee County, North Carolina.* Clearing House Project No. CH-87-C-0000-0882, prepared for the Cherokee County Commissioners, Murphy, N.C.

Robison, Neil D.

1983   Archeological Records of Naiad Mussels along the Tennessee-Tombigbee Waterway. In *Report of Freshwater Mussels Workshop 26–27 October 1982,* compiled by Andrew C. Miller, pp. 115–29. U.S. Army Corps of Engineers Waterways Experiment Station, Vicksburg, Miss.

Rogers, J. Daniel

1989   Settlement Contexts for Shifting Authority in the Arkansas Basin. In *Contributions to Spiro Archeology: Mound Excavations and Regional Perspectives,* edited by J. Daniel Rogers, Don G. Wyckoff, and D. A. Peterson, pp. 160–76. Studies in Oklahoma's Past No. 16, Oklahoma Archeological Survey, Norman.

1991 Patterns of Change on the Western Margin of the Southeast, A.D. 600–900. In *Stability, Transformation, and Variation: The Late Woodland Southeast,* edited by Michael S. Nassaney and Charles R. Cobb, pp. 221–48. New York: Plenum Press.

Rogers, Robert
1988 *A Cultural Resources Reconnaissance of the Black Creek Wilderness Area, De Soto National Forest, Perry County, MS.* Heartfield, Price and Greene, Inc., Monroe, La.

Rogers, Ronnie H., Karen G. Wood, and W. Dean Wood
1991 *A Cultural Resource Survey of the Plant Scherer Alternate Railroad Route, Monroe and Butts Counties, Georgia.* Submitted to the Georgia Power Company, Atlanta, by Southeastern Archeological Services, Athens, Ga.

Rolingson, Martha A.
1980 Toltec Mounds Research Project. *Arkansas Archeologist* 21:35–56.
1982a Public Archeology: Research and Development of the Toltec Mounds Site. In *Arkansas Archeology in Review,* edited by Neal L. Trubowitz and Marvin D. Jeter, pp. 48–75. Arkansas Archeological Survey Research Series No. 15, Fayetteville.
1982b The Toltec Mounds Site and Research Program. In *Emerging Patterns of Plum Bayou Culture: Preliminary Investigations of the Toltec Mounds Research Project,* edited by Martha A. Rolingson, pp. 1–10. Arkansas Archeological Survey Research Series No. 18, Fayetteville.
1982c Emerging Cultural Patterns at the Toltec Mounds Site. In *Emerging Patterns of Plum Bayou Culture: Preliminary Investigations of the Toltec Mounds Research Project,* edited by M. A. Rolingson, pp. 60–63. Arkansas Archeological Survey Research Series 18, Fayetteville.
1990 The Toltec Mounds Site, a Ceremonial Center in the Arkansas River Lowland. In *The Mississippian Emergence,* edited by Bruce D. Smith, pp. 27–49. Washington, D.C.: Smithsonian Institution Press.
1993 Archeology along Bayou Bartholomew, Southeast Arkansas. *Arkansas Archeologist* 32:1–138.
1998a *Toltec Mounds and Plum Bayou Culture: Mound D Excavations.* Arkansas Archeological Survey Research Series No. 54, Fayetteville.
1998b Excavation, Stratigraphy, and Chronometry. In *Toltec Mounds and Plum Bayou Culture: Mound D Excavations,* by Martha A. Rolingson, pp. 10–25. Arkansas Archeological Survey Research Series No. 54, Fayetteville.
1998c Plum Bayou Culture at Toltec Mounds and Vicinity Sites. In *Toltec Mounds and Plum Bayou Culture: Mound D Excavations,* by Martha A. Rolingson, pp. 95–112. Arkansas Archeological Survey Research Series No. 54, Fayetteville.
1998d Plum Bayou Borders and Neighbors. In *Toltec Mounds and Plum Bayou Culture: Mound D Excavations,* by Martha A. Rolingson, pp. 113–32. Arkansas Archeological Survey Research Series No. 54, Fayetteville.
1998e Antler, Bone, and Shell Artifacts. In *Toltec Mounds and Plum Bayou Culture: Mound D Excavations,* by Martha A. Rolingson, pp. 80–83. Arkansas Archeological Survey Research Series No. 54, Fayetteville.
1998f The Ceramic Assemblage. In *Toltec Mounds and Plum Bayou Culture: Mound D Excavations,* by Martha A. Rolingson, pp. 26–53. Arkansas Archeological Survey Research Series No. 54, Fayetteville.

Rolingson, Martha A., and Douglas W. Schwartz
1966 *Late Paleo-Indian and Early Archaic Manifestations in Western Kentucky.* Studies in Anthropology No. 3, University of Kentucky, Lexington.

Romain, William F.
  1996   Hopewellian Geometry: Forms at the Interface of Time and Eternity. In *A View from the Core: A Synthesis of Ohio Hopewell Archaeology,* edited by Paul J. Pacheco, pp. 194–209. Columbus: Ohio Archaeological Council.
Rose, Jerome C.
  1984   Bioarcheology of the Cedar Grove Site. In *Cedar Grove: An Interdisciplinary Investigation of a Late Caddo Farmstead in the Red River Valley,* edited by N. M. Trubowitz, pp. 227–56. Arkansas Archeological Survey Research Series No. 23, Fayetteville.
Rose, Jerome C. (editor)
  1999   *Bioarcheology of the South Central United States.* Arkansas Archeological Survey Research Series 55, Fayetteville.
Rose, Jerome C., M. K. Marks, and E. B. Kiddick
  1983   Bioarchaeology of the Bug Hill Site. In *Bug Hill: Excavation of a Multicomponent Midden Mound in the Jackfork Valley, Southeast Oklahoma,* edited by J. H. Altschul, pp. 241–78. Report of Investigations No. 81-1, New World Research, Inc., Pollock, La.
Rose, Jerome C., B. A. Burnett, M. W. Blaeuer, and Michael S. Nassaney
  1984   Paleopathology and the Origins of Maize Agriculture in the Lower Mississippi Valley and Caddoan Areas. In *Paleopathology at the Origins of Agriculture,* edited by Mark N. Cohen and George J. Armelagos, pp. 393–424. Orlando: Academic Press.
Rose, Jerome C., M. P. Hoffman, B. A. Burnett, A. M. Harmon, and J. E. Barnes
  1998   Skeletal Biology of the Prehistoric Caddo. In *The Native History of the Caddo: Their Place in Southeastern Archeology and Ethnohistory,* edited by Timothy K. Perttula and James E. Bruseth, pp. 113–26. Studies in Archeology 30, Texas Archeological Research Laboratory, University of Texas at Austin.
Rose, Jerome C., B. A. Burnett, and J. P. Harcourt
  1999a   Ouachita Mountains, Arkansas River Valley and Ozark Mountains. In *Bioarcheology of the South Central United States,* edited by Jerome C. Rose, pp. 1–34. Arkansas Archeological Survey Research Series No. 55, Fayetteville.
Rose, Jerome C., D. G. Steele, B. A. Burnett, K. J. Reinhard, and B. W. Olive
  1999b   Gulf Coastal Plain. In *Bioarcheology of the South Central United States,* edited by Jerome C. Rose, pp. 83–132. Arkansas Archeological Survey Research Series No. 55, Fayetteville.
Rossen, Jack, and Richard Edging
  1987   East Meets West: Patterns in Kentucky Late Prehistoric Subsistence. In *Current Archaeological Research in Kentucky: Volume One,* edited by D. Pollack, pp. 225–34. Frankfort: Kentucky Heritage Council.
Rotman, Deborah L., and Michael S. Nassaney
  1997   Class, Gender, and the Built Environment: Deriving Social Relations from Cultural Landscapes in Southwest Michigan. *Historical Archaeology* 31:42–62.
Rountree, Helen
  1992   Indian Virginians on the Move. In *Indians of the Southeastern United States in the Late Twentieth Century,* edited by J. Anthony Paredes, pp. 9–28. Tuscaloosa: University of Alabama Press.
Rountree, Helen, and E. Randolph Turner
  1994   On the Fringe of the Southeast: The Powhatan Paramount Chiefdom in Virginia. In *The Forgotten Centuries: Indians and Europeans in the American South, 1521–*

1704, edited by C. Hudson and C. Tesser, pp. 355–72. Athens: University of Georgia Press.

1998 The Evolution of the Powhatan Paramount Chiefdom in Virginia. In *Chiefdoms and Chieftaincy in the Americas,* edited by E. Redmond, pp. 265–96. Gainesville: University Press of Florida.

Rouse, I. B.

1953 The Strategy of Culture History. In *Anthropology Today,* edited by A. L. Kroeber, pp. 57–76. Chicago: University of Chicago Press.

Rowe, J. H.

1962 Stages and Periods in Archaeological Interpretations. *Southwestern Journal of Anthropology* 18:40–54.

Ruby, Bret J.

1997 *The Mann Phase: Hopewellian Subsistence and Settlement Adaptations in the Wabash Lowlands of Southwestern Indiana.* Ph.D. dissertation, Department of Anthropology, Indiana University, Bloomington.

Ruby, Bret J., and Christine M. Shriner

2000 Hopewellian Ceramic Production and Exchange at the Mann Site, Southwestern Indiana: A Petrological Approach to Identifying Local and Non-Local Production. Presented at the 65th annual meeting of the Society for American Archaeology, Philadelphia.

Rucker, Marc D.

1974 *Archaeological Survey and Test Excavations in the Upper-Central Tombigbee River Valley: Aliceville-Columbus Lock and Dam and Impoundment Areas, Alabama and Mississippi.* Submitted to the National Park Service by the Department of Anthropology, Mississippi State University.

Rudolph, James L.

1983 Lamar Period Exploitation of Aquatic Resources in the Middle Oconee River Valley. *Early Georgia* 11(1 and 2):86–103.

1984 Earthlodges and Platform Mounds: Changing Public Architecture in the Southeastern United States. *Southeastern Archaeology* 3:33–45.

Rudolph, Teresa P.

1985 Late Swift Creek and Napier Settlement in Northern Georgia. Presented at the 42nd annual meeting of the Southeastern Archaeological Conference, Birmingham.

1986 Regional and Temporal Variability in Swift Creek and Napier Ceramics from North Georgia. Presented at the Ocmulgee National Monument 50th Anniversary Conference, Macon, Ga.

1991 The Late Woodland "Problem" in Northern Georgia. In *Stability, Transformation, and Variation: The Late Woodland Southeast,* edited by Michael S. Nassaney and Charles R. Cobb, pp. 259–83. New York: Plenum Press.

Ruhl, Donna L.

2000 Archaeobotany of Bernath Place (8SR986) and Other Santa Rosa/Swift Creek–Related Sites in Coastal and Non-Coastal Southeastern U.S. Locations. *Florida Anthropologist* 53:190–202.

Ruhl, Katharine C., and Mark F. Seeman

1998 The Temporal and Social Implications of Ohio Hopewell Ear Spool Design. *American Antiquity* 63(4):651–62.

Rummel, R.

1980 Mussel Shells from Kellogg Site Features. Appendix D in *The Kellogg Village Site*

Investigations, Clay County, Mississippi, by James R. Atkinson, John C. Phillips, and Richard Walling. Submitted to the U.S. Army Corps of Engineers, Mobile District, by the Department of Anthropology, Mississippi State University.

Ruppert, Lisa
1994   *Evidence for the Endoparasite* Giardia lambilia *in Human Paleofeces from Salts Cave, Mammoth Cave National Park, Kentucky.* Master's thesis, Department of Anthropology, Western Michigan University, Kalamazoo.

Russo, Michael
1991   *Archaic Sedentism on the Florida Coast: A Case Study from Horr's Island.* Ph.D. dissertation, Department of Anthropology, University of Florida, Gainesville.
1992   Chronologies and Cultures of the St. Marys Region of Northeast Florida and Southeast Georgia. *Florida Anthropologist* 45:107–26.
1994   Why We Don't Believe in Archaic Ceremonial Mounds and Why We Should: The Case from Florida. *Southeastern Archaeology* 13:93–109.
1996a   Southeastern Archaic Mounds. In *Archaeology of the Mid-Holocene Southeast,* edited by Kenneth E. Sassaman and David G. Anderson, pp. 259–87. Gainesville: University Press of Florida.
1996b   Southeastern Mid-Holocene Coastal Settlements. In *Archaeology of the Mid-Holocene Southeast,* edited by Kenneth E. Sassaman and David G. Anderson, pp. 177–99. Gainesville: University Press of Florida.

Ryan, Thomas M.
1972   *Archaeological Survey of the Columbia Zoological Park, Richland and Lexington Counties, South Carolina.* Research Manuscript Series 37, South Carolina Institute of Archaeology and Anthropology, University of South Carolina, Columbia.

Sabo, George, III, and Ann M. Early
1990   Prehistoric Culture History. In *Human Adaptation in the Ozark and Ouachita Mountains,* edited by George Sabo III, Ann M. Early, Jerome C. Rose, B. A. Burnett, L. Vogele, Jr., and J. P. Harcourt, pp. 34–120. Arkansas Archeological Survey Research Series No. 31, Fayetteville.

Sabo, George, III, Ann M. Early, Jerome C. Rose, B. A. Burnett, L. Vogele, Jr., and J. P. Harcourt
1990b   *Human Adaptation in the Ozark and Ouachita Mountains.* Arkansas Archeological Survey Research Series No. 31, Fayetteville.

Sabo, George, III, Randy L. Guendling, W. Fred Limp, M. J. Guccione, Susan L. Scott, Gail J. Fritz, and P. A. Smith
1990a   *Archeological Investigations at 3MR80-Area D in the Rush Development Area, Buffalo National River, Arkansas.* Professional Papers 38, pp. 231–68, National Park Service Southwest Cultural Resources Center, Santa Fe.

Sahlins, Marshall
1963   Poor Man, Rich Man, Big Man, Chief: Political Types in Melanesia and Polynesia. *Comparative Studies in Society and History* 5:285–303.
1972   *Stone Age Economics.* Chicago: Aldine Publishing.

Salo, Lawr. V. (editor)
1969   *Archaeological Investigations in the Tellico Reservoir, Tennessee, 1967–1968: An Interim Report.* Report of Investigations 7, Department of Anthropology, University of Tennessee, Knoxville.

Sanborn, Erica E., and Lawrence E. Abbott
1999   Early Archaic Ceramic Traditions on the Southern Coastal Plain of North Carolina: Radiocarbon Data from 31CB114. *North Carolina Archaeology* 48:3–17.

Sanders, W. T., and R. S. Santley
  1985 A Tale of Three Cities: Energetics and Urbanization in Prehispanic Central Mexico. In *Prehistoric Settlement Pattern Studies: Retrospect and Prospect,* edited by E. Z. Vogt. Albuquerque: University of New Mexico Press.

Sassaman, Kenneth E.
  1989 Prehistoric Settlement in the Aiken Plateau: Summary of Archaeological Investigations at 38AK158 and 38AK159, Aiken County, South Carolina. *South Carolina Antiquities* 21:31–64.
  1993a *Early Pottery in the Southeast: Tradition and Innovation in Cooking Technology.* Tuscaloosa: University of Alabama Press.
  1993b *Mims Point 1992: Archaeological Investigations at a Prehistoric Habitation Site in the Sumter National Forest, South Carolina.* Savannah River Archaeological Research Papers 4, South Carolina Institute of Archaeology and Anthropology, University of South Carolina, Columbia.
  1993c *Early Woodland Settlement in the Aiken Plateau: Archaeological Investigations at 38AK157, Savannah River Site, Aiken County, South Carolina.* Savannah River Archaeological Research Papers 3, South Carolina Institute of Archaeology and Anthropology, University of South Carolina.
  1995 The Social Contradictions of Traditional and Innovative Cooking Technologies in the Prehistoric American Southeast. In *The Emergence of Pottery: Technology and Innovation in Ancient Societies,* edited by W. K. Barnett and J. W. Hoopes, pp. 223–40. Washington, D.C.: Smithsonian Institution Press.
  1997 Refining Soapstone Vessel Chronology in the Southeast. *Early Georgia* 25(1):1–20.
  2001 Common Origins and Divergent Histories in the Early Pottery Traditions of the American Southeast. Presented at the 66th annual meeting of the Society for American Archaeology, New Orleans.

Sassaman, Kenneth E., and David G. Anderson
  1995 *Middle and Late Archaic Archaeological Records of South Carolina: A Synthesis for Research and Resource Management.* Savannah River Archaeological Research Papers 6, South Carolina Institute of Archaeology and Anthropology, University of South Carolina.

Sassaman, Kenneth E., and David G. Anderson (editors)
  1996 *The Archaeology of the Mid-Holocene Southeast.* Gainesville: University Presses of Florida.

Sassaman, Kenneth E., and R. Jerald Ledbetter
  1996 Middle and Late Archaic Architecture. In *Archaeology of the Mid-Holocene Southeast,* edited by Kenneth E. Sassaman and David G. Anderson, pp. 75–98. Gainesville: University Press of Florida.

Sassaman, Kenneth E., and Wictoria Rudolphi
  2001 Communities of Practice in the Early Pottery Traditions of the American Southeast. *Journal of Anthropological Research* 57(4).

Sassaman, Kenneth E., Mark J. Brooks, Glen T. Hanson, and David G. Anderson
  1990 *Native American Prehistory of the Middle Savannah River Valley: A Synthesis of Archaeological Investigations on the Savannah River Site, Aiken and Barnwell Counties, South Carolina.* Savannah River Archaeological Research Papers 1, Occasional Papers of the Savannah River Archaeological Program, South Carolina Institute of Archaeology and Anthropology, University of South Carolina.

Sassaman, Kenneth E., Kristin Wilson, and Frankie Snow
  1995 Putting the Ogeechee in Its Place. *Early Georgia* 23:20–40.

Saucier, Roger T.
  1974   *Quaternary Geology of the Lower Mississippi Valley.* Arkansas Archeological
          Survey Research Series No. 6, Fayetteville.
  1994   *Geomorphology and Quaternary Geologic History of the Lower Mississippi Val-
          ley.* U.S. Army Corps of Engineers Waterways Experiment Station, Vicksburg, Miss.
Saucier, Roger T., Lawson M. Smith, and Whitney J. Autin (editors)
  1996   *Geology in the Lower Mississippi Valley: Implications for Engineering, the Half
          Century since Fisk, 1944.* Engineering Geology 45. Amsterdam: Elsevier.
Sauer, Carl O.
  1920   *The Geography of the Ozark Highlands.* Bulletin No. 7, The Geographic Society
          of Chicago, University of Chicago Press.
Saunders, Joe W., and Thurman Allen
  1994   Hedgepeth Mounds, an Archaic Mound Complex in North-Central Louisiana.
          American Antiquity 59:471–89.
Saunders, Joe W., Thurman Allen, and Roger T. Saucier
  1994   Four Archaic? Mound Complexes in Northeast Louisiana. *Southeastern Archae-
          ology* 13:134–53.
Saunders, Joe, Rolfe D. Mandel, Roger T. Saucier, E. Thurman Allen, C. T. Hallmark, Jay K.
Johnson, Edwin H. Jackson, Charles M. Allen, Gary L. Stringer, Douglas S. Frink, James K.
Feathers, Stephen Williams, Kristen J. Gremillion, Malcolm F. Vidrine, and Reca Jones
  1997   A Mound Complex in Louisiana at 5400–5000 Years Before the Present. *Science*
          19:1796–99.
Saunders, Rebecca
  1986   *Attribute Variability in Late Swift Creek Phase Ceramics from Kings Bay, Geor-
          gia.* Master's thesis, Department of Anthropology, University of Florida,
          Gainesville.
  1994   The Case for Archaic Period Mounds in Southeastern Louisiana. *Southeastern
          Archaeology* 13:118–34.
  1997   Stylistic Influences on the Gulf Coastal Plain: New Evidence from Paddle Stamped
          Pottery in Louisiana. *Louisiana Archaeology* 22:93–123.
  1998   Swift Creek Phase Design Assemblages from Two Sites on the Georgia Coast. In *A
          World Engraved: Archaeology of the Swift Creek Culture,* edited by J. Mark Wil-
          liams and Daniel T. Elliott, pp. 154–80. Tuscaloosa: University of Alabama Press.
  2001   Spatial Variation in Orange Culture Pottery: Prestige and Interaction. Presented at
          the 66th annual meeting of the Society for American Archaeology, New Orleans.
Saunders, Rebecca, Thomas DesJean, and Karen Jo Walker
  1985   Descriptive Archeology of the Kings Bay Site (9CAM171). In *The Kings Bay and
          Devils Walkingstick Sites,* vol. 1 of *Aboriginal Subsistence and Settlement Arche-
          ology of the Kings Bay Locality,* edited by W. H. Adams, pp. 169–293. Reports of
          Investigations No. 1. Department of Anthropology, University of Florida,
          Gainesville.
Scarry, C. Margaret
  1985   Paleoethnobotany of the Granada Site. In *Excavations at the Granada Site: Ar-
          chaeology and History of the Granada Site,* vol. 1, edited by John W. Griffin, S. B.
          Richardson, Mary Pohl, C. D. McMurray, C. Margaret Scarry, Susan K. Fish, E. S.
          Wing, L. Jill Loucks, and M. K. Welch, pp. 181–248. Florida Division of Ar-
          chives, History and Records Management, Tallahassee.
  1986   *Change in Plant Procurement and Production during the Emergence of the
          Moundville Chiefdom.* Ph.D. dissertation, University of Michigan. University
          Microfilms, Ann Arbor.

1990   Plant Remains. In *Archaeological Investigations at the Sanders Site (22Cl917), an Alexander Midden on the Tombigbee River, Clay County, Mississippi,* by J. W. O'Hear, pp. 80–96. Report of Investigations 6, Cobb Institute of Archaeology, Mississippi State University.

1993a   Variability in Mississippian Crop Production Strategies. In *Foraging and Farming in the Eastern Woodlands,* edited by C. Margaret Scarry, pp. 78–90. Gainesville: University Press of Florida.

1993b   Agricultural Risk and the Development of the Moundville Chiefdom. In *Foraging and Farming in the Eastern Woodlands,* edited by C. Margaret Scarry, pp. 157–81. Gainesville: University Press of Florida.

1995   Plant Remains. In *The Rock Levee Site: Late Marksville through Late Mississippi Period Settlement, Bolivar County, Mississippi,* by Richard A. Weinstein, R. S. Fuller, Susan L. Scott, C. Margaret Scarry, and S. T. Duay, pp. 263–86. Report prepared for the U.S. Army Corps of Engineers, Vicksburg District, by Coastal Environments, Inc., Baton Rouge, La.

Scarry, C. Margaret (editor)
1993   *Foraging and Farming in the Eastern Woodlands.* Gainesville: University Press of Florida.

Scarry, C. Margaret, and L. A. Newsom
1992   Archaeobotanical Research in the Calusa Heartland. In *Culture and Environment in the Domain of the Calusa,* edited by William H. Marquardt, pp. 375–402. Monograph No. 1, Institute of Archaeology and Paleoenvironmental Studies, University of Florida, Gainesville.

Scarry, John F.
1990a   Mississippian Emergence in the Fort Walton Area: The Evolution of the Cayson and Lake Jackson Phases. In *Mississippian Emergence: The Evolution of Ranked Agricultural Societies in Eastern North America,* edited by Bruce D. Smith, pp. 227–50. Washington, D.C.: Smithsonian Institution Press.

1990b   The Rise, Transformation, and Fall of Apalachee: A Case Study of Political Change in a Chiefly Society. In *Lamar Archaeology: Mississippian Chiefdoms in the Deep South,* edited by J. Mark Williams and Gary Shapiro, pp. 175–86. Tuscaloosa: University of Alabama Press.

1996   The Nature of Mississippian Societies. In *Political Structure and Change in the Prehistoric Southeastern United States,* edited by John F. Scarry, pp. 12–24. Gainesville: University Press of Florida.

Scarry, John F. (editor)
1996   *Political Structure and Change in the Prehistoric Southeastern United States.* Gainesville: University Press of Florida.

Schambach, Frank F.
1970   *Pre-Caddoan Cultures in the Trans-Mississippi South: A Beginning Sequence.* Ph.D. dissertation, Harvard University, Cambridge, Mass.

1972   Preliminary Report on the 1972 Excavations at the Ferguson Site (3HE63). *Arkansas Archeologist* 13(1 and 2):1–15.

1982   An Outline of Fourche Maline Culture in Southwest Arkansas. In *Arkansas Archeology in Review,* edited by Neal L. Trubowitz and Marvin D. Jeter, pp. 132–97. Arkansas Archeological Survey Research Series No. 15, Fayetteville.

1991   Coles Creek Culture in the Trans-Mississippi South. *Caddoan Archeology Newsletter* 2(3):2–8.

1993a   Some New Interpretations of Spiroan Culture History. In *Archaeology of Eastern North America: Papers in Honor of Stephen Williams,* edited by James B. Stoltman, pp. 187–230. Archaeological Report 25, Mississippi Department of Archives and History, Jackson.

1993b   A Summary of the History of the Caddo People. *Notes on Northeast Texas Archaeology* 2:1–7.

1995   A Probable Spiroan Entrepot in the Red River Valley in Northeast Texas. *Caddoan Archeology Newsletter* 6(1):9–25.

1996a   The Development of the Burial Mound Tradition in the Caddo Area. *Journal of Northeast Texas Archaeology* 9:53–72.

1996b   Mounds, Embankments and Ceremonialism in the Trans-Mississippi South. In *Mounds, Embankments and Ceremonialism in the Midsouth,* edited by Robert C. Mainfort, Jr., and R. C. Walling, pp. 36–43. Arkansas Archeological Survey Research Series No. 46, Fayetteville.

1997   The Development of the Burial Mound Tradition in the Caddo Area. *Journal of Northwest Texas Archaeology* 9:53–72.

1998a   Introduction. In *Pre-Caddoan Cultures in the Trans-Mississippi South: A Beginning Sequence,* pp. xi–xxi. Arkansas Archeological Survey Research Series No. 53, Fayetteville.

1998b   *Pre-Caddoan Cultures in the Trans-Mississippi South: A Beginning Sequence.* Arkansas Archeological Survey Research Series No. 53, Fayetteville.

1999a   Spiro and the Tunica: A New Interpretation of the Role of the Tunica in the Culture History of the Southeast and the Southern Plains, A.D. 1100–1750. In *Arkansas Archeology: Essays in Honor of Dan and Phyllis Morse,* edited by Robert C. Mainfort, Jr., and Marvin D. Jeter, pp. 169–224. Fayetteville: University of Arkansas Press.

1999b   Deconstructing the "Sanders Focus" and the "Sanders Phase": A Reply to Perttula Regarding the Taxonomy and Significance of the So-Called Sanders Focus or Sanders Phase Pottery of Northeast Texas and Southeast Oklahoma. *Caddoan Archeology* 9(3/4):3–55.

2000a   The Significance of the Sanders Site in the Culture History of the Mississippi Period Southeast and the Southern Plains. In *The 1931 Excavations at the Sanders Site, Lamar County Texas: Notes on the Field Work, Human Osteology, and Ceramics by A. T. Jackson, Marcus S. Goldstein, and Alex Krieger.* Archival Series 2, Texas Archeological Research Laboratory, University of Texas at Austin.

2000b   Spiroan Traders, the Sanders Site, and the Plains Interaction Sphere: A Reply to Bruseth, Wilson, and Perttula. *Plains Anthropologist* 45(171):7–33.

2001   Fourche Maline and Its Neighbors: Observations on an Important Woodland Period Culture of the Trans-Mississippi South. *Arkansas Archeologist* 40:21–50.

Schambach, Frank F. (editor)

1990   *Coles Creek and Mississippi Period Foragers in the Felsenthal Region of the Lower Mississippi Valley.* Arkansas Archeological Survey Research Series No. 39, Fayetteville.

Schiffer, Michael B., and James M. Skibo

1987   Theory and Experiment in the Study of Technological Change. *Current Anthropology* 28:595–622.

Schmitt, Karl

1952   Archaeological Chronology of the Middle Atlantic States. In *Archeology of Eastern United States,* edited by James B. Griffin, pp. 59–70. Chicago: University of Chicago Press.

Scholtz, James A.

1986   Preliminary Testing at the Powell Site, 3CL9: A Temple Mound Site in Clark County, Arkansas. *Arkansas Archeologist* 23–24:11–42.

1991 Investigations at the Roland Site. *Arkansas Archeologist* 30:7–56.

Schoolcraft, Henry R.
1853 *Historical and Statistical Information Respecting the History, Conditions, and Prospects of the Indian Tribes of the United States,* vol. 2. Philadelphia: Lippincott, Grambo.

Schroeder, Sissel
1997 *Place, Productivity, and Politics: The Evolution of Cultural Complexity in the Cahokia Area.* Ph.D. dissertation, Pennsylvania State University, University Park.

Schroedl, Gerald F.
1973 Radiocarbon Dates from Three Burial Mounds at the McDonald Site in East Tennessee. *Tennessee Archaeologist* 29:3–11.
1978a *The Patrick Site (40MR40), Tellico Reservoir, Tennessee.* Report of Investigations 25, Department of Anthropology, University of Tennessee, and TVA Publications in Anthropology 22, Knoxville.
1978b *Excavations of the Leuty and McDonald Site Mounds.* Report of Investigations 22, Department of Anthropology, University of Tennessee, Knoxville.
1990 *Archaeological Research at 40RE107, 40RE109 and 40RE124 in the Clinch River Breeder Plant Area, Tennessee.* Report of Investigations 49, Department of Anthropology, University of Tennessee, and TVA Publications in Anthropology 53, Knoxville.

Schroedl, Gerald F., and C. Clifford Boyd, Jr.
1987 Mississippi Origins in East Tennessee. In *The Emergent Mississippian: Proceedings of the Sixth Mid-South Archaeological Conference,* edited by Richard A. Marshall, pp. 137–48. Occasional Papers 87–01, Cobb Institute of Archaeology, Mississippi State University.
1991 Late Woodland Period Culture in East Tennessee. In *Stability, Transformation and Variation: The Late Woodland Southeast,* edited by Michael S. Nassaney and Kenneth E. Sassaman, pp. 69–90. Knoxville: University of Tennessee Press.

Schroedl, Gerald F., C. Clifford Boyd, Jr., and R. P. Stephen Davis, Jr.
1990 Explaining Mississippian Origins in East Tennessee. In *The Mississippian Emergence,* edited by Bruce D. Smith, pp. 175–96. New York: Plenum Press.

Schroedl, Gerald F., R. P. Stephen Davis, Jr., and C. Clifford Boyd
1985 *Archaeological Contexts and Assemblages at Martin Farm.* Report of Investigations 39, Department of Anthropology, University of Tennessee, Knoxville.

Scott, Susan L.
1982 Yarborough Site Faunal Remains. In *Archaeological Investigations at the Yarborough Site (22CL814), Clay County, Mississippi,* edited by Carlos Solis and Richard Walling, pp. 140–52. Report of Investigations 30, Office of Archaeological Research, University of Alabama, Tuscaloosa.
1983 Analysis, Synthesis, and Interpretation of Faunal Remains from the Lubbub Creek Archaeological Locality. In *Prehistoric Agricultural Communities in West Central Alabama,* edited by Christopher S. Peebles, pp. 272–379. U.S. Army Corps of Engineers, Mobile District.
1990 Vertebrate Fauna. In *Archaeological Investigations at the Sanders Site (22Cl917), An Alexander Midden on the Tombigbee River, Clay County, Mississippi,* edited by J. W. O'Hear, pp. 60–71. Report of Investigations 6, Cobb Institute of Archaeology, Mississippi State University.
1992 Zooarcheological Remains, Lower Midden Area. In *Archeological Investigations at 3MR80-Area D in the Rush Development Area, Buffalo National River, Arkansas Vol II,* by Randy L. Guendling, George Sabo III, M. J. Guccione, S. L. Dunavan,

and Susan L. Scott, pp. 99–118. Southwest Cultural Resources Center Professional Papers No. 50, Santa Fe.

1995   Vertebrate Faunal Remains. In *The Rock Levee Site: Late Marksville through Late Mississippi Period Settlement, Bolivar County, Mississippi,* by Richard A. Weinstein, Richard S. Fuller, Susan L. Scott, C. Margaret Scarry, and S. T. Duay, pp. 243–62. Report prepared for the U.S. Army Corps of Engineers, Vicksburg District, by Coastal Environments, Inc., Baton Rouge, La.

1996   Faunal Remains. In *Test Excavations at the Faulkner Lake Sites: 3PU115, 3PU163, and 3PU410, Pulaski County, Arkansas,* edited by Randy D. Guendling. Submitted to the Arkansas Highway and Transportation Department by the Arkansas Archeological Survey, Fayetteville.

Sears, Elsie
1982   Pollen Analysis. In *Fort Center: An Archaeological Site in the Lake Okeechobee Basin,* edited by William H. Sears, pp. 118–29. Gainesville: University Press of Florida.

Sears, William H.
1948   What Is the Archaic? *American Antiquity* 14(2):122–24.

1952   An Archaeological Manifestation of a Natchez-type Burial Ceremony. *Florida Anthropologist* 5:1–7.

1954   The Sociopolitical Organization of Pre-Columbian Cultures of the Gulf Coastal Plain. *American Anthropologist* 56:339–46.

1956a   *Excavations at Kolomoki, Final Report.* University of Georgia Series in Anthropology 5, Athens.

1956b   Melton Mound Number 3. *Florida Anthropologist* 9:87–100.

1958   Burial Mounds on the Gulf Coastal Plain. *American Antiquity* 23:274–84.

1961   The Study of Social and Religious Systems in North American Archaeology. *Current Anthropology* 2:223–46.

1962a   Hopewellian Affiliations of Certain Sites on the Gulf Coast of Florida. *American Antiquity* 28:5–18.

1962b   The State in Certain Areas and Periods of the Prehistoric Southeastern United States. *Ethnohistory* 9:109–25.

1966   Deptford in Florida. *Southeastern Archaeological Conference Newsletter* 10(1):3–8.

1968   The State and Settlement Patterns in the New World. In *Settlement Archaeology,* edited by K. C. Chang, pp. 134–53. Palo Alto, Calif.: National Press Books.

1973   The Sacred and the Secular in Prehistoric Ceramics. In *Variation in Anthropology: Essays in Honor of John McGregor,* edited by D. Lathrop and J. Douglas, pp. 31–42. Urbana: Illinois Archaeological Survey.

1982   *Fort Center: An Archaeological Site in the Lake Okeechobee Basin.* Gainesville: University Press of Florida.

1992   Mea Culpa. *Southeastern Archaeology* 11(1):66–71.

n.d.   *An Investigation of Prehistoric Processes on the Gulf Coastal Plain.* Undated report to the National Science Foundation (NSF-G-5019). On file, James A. Ford Library, Florida Museum of Natural History, Gainesville.

Sears, William H., and James B. Griffin
1950   Type Descriptions: Fiber Tempered Pottery. In *Prehistoric Pottery of the Eastern United States,* edited by James B. Griffin. Museum of Anthropology, University of Michigan, Ann Arbor.

Seeman, Mark F.
1979a   *The Hopewell Interaction Sphere: The Evidence for Interregional Trade and Struc-*

tural Complexity. Prehistory Research Series 5, Indiana State Historical Society, Indianapolis.

1979b   Feasting with the Dead: Ohio Hopewell Charnel House Ritual as a Context for Redistribution. In *Hopewell Archaeology: The Chillicothe Conference,* edited by D. Brose and N. Greber, pp. 39–46. Kent, Ohio: Kent State University Press.

1981a   *Phase I (Literature Search) and Phase II (Locational Survey) Investigations of the Chillicothe Correctional Institute, Chillicothe, Ohio.* Report prepared for the Bureau of Prisons, United States Department of Justice, Contract No. J100c-068.

1981b   A Late Woodland Steatite Pipe from the Catlin Site, Vermillion County, Indiana: The Implications for East-West Trade. *Archaeology of Eastern North America* 9:103–9.

1986   Adena "Houses" and Their Implications for Early Woodland Settlement Models in the Ohio Valley. In *Early Woodland Archaeology,* edited by Kenneth B. Farnsworth and Thomas E. Emerson, pp. 564–80. Center for American Archaeology, Kampsville, Ill.

1992a   Woodland Traditions in the Midcontinent: A Comparison of Three Regional Sequences. *Research in Economic Anthropology, Supplement* 6:3–46.

1992b   The Bow and Arrow, The Intrusive Mound Complex and a Late Woodland Jack's Reef Horizon in the Mid-Ohio Valley. In *Cultural Variability in Context: Woodland Settlements of the Mid-Ohio Valley,* edited by Mark F. Seeman, pp. 41–51. Midcontinental Journal of Archaeology Special Paper 7, Kent State University Press, Kent, Ohio.

1996   The Ohio Hopewell Core and Its Many Margins: Deconstructing Upland and Hinterland Relations. In *A View from the Core: A Synthesis of Ohio Hopewell Archaeology,* edited by Paul J. Pacheco, pp. 304–15. Columbus: Ohio Archaeological Council.

Seeman, Mark, and Olaf Prufer
1988   A Late Woodland Jar from Stanhope Cave, Jackson County, Ohio. *Pennsylvania Archaeologist* 58:61–68.

Service, Elman R.
1962   *Primitive Social Organization.* New York: Random House.

Setzler, F. M.
1933a   Hopewell Type Pottery from Louisiana. *Washington Academy of Sciences, Journal* 23:149–53.

1933b   Pottery of the Hopewell Type from Louisiana. *Proceedings of the United States National Museum,* vol. 81, art. 22, pp. 1–21, pls. 1–7. Washington, D.C.: Smithsonian Institution.

1934   A Phase of Hopewell Mound Builders in Louisiana. *Explorations and Fieldwork of the Smithsonian Institution in 1933,* pp. 38–40. Washington, D.C.: Smithsonian Institution.

Setzler, Frank M., and Jesse D. Jennings
1941   *Peachtree Mound and Village Site, Cherokee County, North Carolina.* Bulletin 131, Bulletin of American Ethnology, Smithsonian Institution, Washington, D.C.

Shackel, Paul A.
1993   *Personal Discipline and Material Culture: An Archaeology of Annapolis, Maryland, 1695–1870.* Knoxville: University of Tennessee Press.

Shane, Orrin C., III
1971   The Scioto Hopewell. In *Adena: The Seeking of an Identity,* edited by B. K. Swartz, pp. 142–57. Muncie, Ind.: Ball State University.

Shannon, George, Jr.
  1986   The Southeastern Fiber-Tempered Ceramic Tradition Reconsidered. In *Papers in
          Ceramic Analysis,* edited by P. M. Rice, pp. 47–80. Ceramic Notes No. 3, Florida
          State Museum, Gainesville.
Sharrock, F. W.
  1960   The Wann Site, Lf-27 of the Fourche Maline Focus. *Bulletin of the Oklahoma
          Anthropological Society* 8:17–47.
Shea, Andrea
  1991   Archaeobotanical Remains. In *The Grayson Site: Phase III Investigations of
          15CR73, Carter County, Kentucky,* edited by R. Jerald Ledbetter and Lisa D.
          O'Steen, pp. 131–48. Report prepared by Southeastern Archaeological Services,
          Inc., Athens, Ga. (Project No. 174) for City of Grayson, Kentucky. Lead Federal
          Agency, Economic Development Administration.
Shenkel, J. Richard
  1974   Big Oak and Little Oak Islands: Excavations and Interpretations. *Louisiana Ar-
          chaeology* 1:37–65.
  1981   *Oak Island Archaeology: Prehistoric Estuarine Adaptations in the Mississippi
          River Delta.* National Park Service, Jean Lafitte National Historical Park, New
          Orleans.
  1984a   Early Woodland in Coastal Louisiana. In *Perspectives on Gulf Coast Prehistory,*
          edited by Dave D. Davis, pp. 41–71. Gainesville: University Presses of Florida.
  1984b   An Early Marksville Burial Component in Southeastern Louisiana. *Midcontinental
          Journal of Archaeology* 9:105–34.
Shenkel, J. Richard, and Jon L. Gibson
  1974   Big Oak Island: An Historical Perspective of Changing Site Function. *Louisiana
          Studies* 8:173–86.
Sherrod, P. Clay, and Martha A. Rolingson
  1987   *Surveyors of the Ancient Mississippi Valley: Modules and Alignments in Prehis-
          toric Mound Sites.* Arkansas Archeological Survey Research Series No. 28,
          Fayetteville.
Shetrone, Henry C.
  1920   The Culture Problem in Ohio Archaeology. *American Anthropologist* 22(1):144–72.
  1930   *The Mound-Builders.* New York: D. Appleton.
Shott, Michael J.
  1990   *Childers and Woods: Two Late Woodland Sites in the Upper Ohio Valley, Mason
          County, West Virginia.* Archaeological Reports 20, University of Kentucky Pro-
          gram for Cultural Resource Assessment, Lexington.
  1993   Spears, Darts, and Arrows: Late Woodland Hunting Techniques in the Upper Ohio
          Valley. *American Antiquity* 58(3):425–43.
Shott, Michael J., and Richard W. Jefferies
  1992   Late Woodland Economy and Settlement in the Mid-Ohio Valley: Recent Results
          from the Childers/Woods Project. In *Cultural Variability in Context: Woodland
          Settlements of the Mid-Ohio Valley,* edited by Mark F. Seeman, pp. 52–64.
          Midcontinental Journal of Archaeology Special Paper 7, Kent State University
          Press, Kent, Ohio.
Shumate, Scott M., and Patti Evans-Shumate
  2000   *Archaeological Investigations at Long Point (31JN2) and Haywood Landing
          (31JN3) on the Croatan National Forest, Jones County, North Carolina.* Appala-
          chian State University Laboratories of Archaeological Science and Blue Ridge

Cultural Resources. USDA Forest Service, Asheville, N.C.

Sierzchula, Michael C., Robert H. Lafferty III, and Neal H. Lopinot
1994 *Cultural Resources Mitigation by Data Recovery of Site 23RI192, Fourche Creek Watershed Dam Site 8, Ripley County, Missouri.* Mid-Continental Research Associates Report No. 94-2, Lowell, Ark.

Sigler-Lavelle, Brenda J.
1980a On the Non-Random Distribution of Weeden Island Period Sites in North Florida. *Southeastern Archaeological Conference Bulletin* 22:22–29.
1980b *The Political and Economic Implications of the Distribution of Weeden Island Period Sites in North Florida.* Ph.D. dissertation, New School for Social Research, New York, N.Y.

Simek, Jan F.
1998 Images from the Darkness: Prehistoric Cave Art from Southeastern North America. Presented at the 62nd annual meeting of the Society for American Archaeology, Seattle.

Simek, Jan F., and Alan Cressler
2001 Issues in the Study of Southeastern Prehistoric Cave Art. In *Cave Archaeology: Theory, Method, and Techniques,* edited by Sarah Sherwood and Jan Simek. *Midcontinental Journal of Archaeology* 26(2), in press.

Simek, Jan F., Charles H. Faulkner, Susan R. Frankenberg, Walter E. Klippel, Todd M. Ahlman, Nicholas P. Herrmann, Sarah C. Sherwood, Renee B. Walker, W. Miles Wright, and Richard Yarnell
1997 A Preliminary Report on the Archaeology of a New Mississippian Cave Art Site in Eastern Tennessee. *Southeastern Archaeology* 16:51–73.

Simek, Jan F., Jay D. Franklin, and Sarah C. Sherwood
1998 The Context of Early Southeastern Prehistoric Cave Art: A Report on the Archaeology of 3rd Unnamed Cave. *American Antiquity* 63:663–77.

Simek, Jan F., Susan R. Frankenberg, and Charles H. Faulkner
2001 Towards an Understanding of Southeastern Cave Art. In *Archaeology of the Appalachian Highlands,* edited by Lynne P. Sullivan and Susan C. Prezzano. Knoxville: University of Tennessee Press.

Simon, Mary L.
2000 Regional Variations in Plant Use Strategies in the Midwest During the Late Woodland. In *Late Woodland Societies: Tradition and Transformation across the Midcontinent,* edited by Thomas E. Emerson, Dale L. McElrath, and Andrew C. Fortier, pp. 37–75. Lincoln: University of Nebraska Press.

Skibo, James M., David J. Hally, and Michael B. Schiffer
1988 The Manufacture and Use of Fiber-Tempered Pottery from the Southeastern United States. Presented at the 53rd annual meeting of the Society for American Archaeology, New Orleans.

Smith, Betty A.
1972 *An Analysis of Regional Variants of Deptford Pottery.* Master's thesis, Department of Anthropology, University of Georgia, Athens.
1975a The Relationship between Deptford and Swift Creek Ceramics as Evidenced at the Mandeville Site, 9Cla1. *Southeastern Archeological Conference Bulletin* 18:195–200.
1975b *A Reanalysis of the Mandeville Site, 9Cla1: Focusing on Its Internal History and External Relations.* Ph.D. dissertation, Department of Anthropology, University of Georgia, Athens.

1977 Southwest Georgia Prehistory: An Overview. *Early Georgia* 5(1 and 2):61–87.

1979 The Hopewell Connection in Southwest Georgia. In *Hopewell Archaeology: The Chillicothe Conference,* edited by D. Brose and N. Greber, pp. 181–87. Kent, Ohio: Kent State University Press.

1998 Neutron Activation Analysis of Ceramics from Mandeville and Swift Creek. In *A World Engraved: Archaeology of the Swift Creek Culture,* edited by J. Mark Williams and Daniel T. Elliott, pp. 112–29. Tuscaloosa: University of Alabama Press.

Smith, Bruce D.

1975 *Middle Mississippi Exploitation of Animal Populations.* Anthropological Papers No. 57, Museum of Anthropology, University of Michigan, Ann Arbor.

1985a *Chenopodium berlandieri* ssp. *jonesianum:* Evidence for a Hopewellian Domesticate from Ash Cave, Ohio. *Southeastern Archaeology* 4:107–33.

1985b The Role of *Chenopodium* as a Domesticate in Pre-Maize Garden Systems of the Eastern United States. *Southeastern Archaeology* 4:51–72.

1986 The Archaeology of the Southeastern United States: From Dalton to de Soto, 10,500–500 B.P. In *Advances in World Prehistory,* vol. 5, edited by F. Wendorf and A. Close, pp. 1–92. Orlando: Academic Press.

1987 Independent Domestication of Indigenous Seed-Bearing Plants in Eastern North America. In *Emergent Horticultural Economies of the Eastern Woodlands,* edited by William F. Keegan, pp. 3–47. Occasional Paper No. 7, Center for Archaeological Investigations, Southern Illinois University, Carbondale.

1989 Origins of Agriculture in Eastern North America. *Science* 246:1566–71.

1992a Agricultural Origins in Eastern North America. In *Agricultural Origins in World Perspective,* edited by C. Wesley Cowan and Patty Jo Watson, pp. 101–20. Washington, D.C.: Smithsonian Institution Press.

1992b The Floodplain Weed Theory of Plant Domestication in Eastern North America. In *Rivers of Change: Essays on Early Agriculture in Eastern North America,* edited by Bruce D. Smith, pp. 19–34. Washington, D.C.: Smithsonian Institution Press.

1992c Hopewellian Farmers of Eastern North America. In *Rivers of Change,* by Bruce D. Smith, pp. 201–48. Washington, D.C.: Smithsonian Institution Press.

1993 Reconciling the Gender-Credit Critique and the Floodplain Weed Theory of Plant Domestication. In *Archaeology of Eastern North America: Papers in Honor of Stephen Williams,* edited by James B. Stoltman, pp. 111–26. Archaeological Report 25, Mississippi Department of Archives and History, Jackson.

Smith, Bruce D. (editor)

1990 *The Mississippian Emergence.* Washington D.C.: Smithsonian Institution Press.

Smith, Christopher J.

1993 *The Analysis of Plant Remains from Mound S at the Toltec Site.* Master's thesis, Department of Anthropology, Washington University, St. Louis.

1996 Analysis of Plant Remains from Mound S at the Toltec Mounds Site. *Arkansas Archeologist* 35:51–76.

Smith, D. C., and F. M. Hodges

1968 The Rankin Site, Cocke County, Tennessee. *Tennessee Anthropologist* 24(2):37–91.

Smith, Gerald P.

1971 *Protohistoric Sociopolitical Organization of the Nottoway in the Chesapeake Bay–Carolina Sounds Region.* Ph.D. dissertation, University of Missouri, Columbia. University Microfilms, Ann Arbor, Mich.

1979 *Archaeological Surveys in the Obion–Forked Deer and Reelfoot–Indian Creek*

Drainages: 1966 through Early 1975. Occasional Papers 9, Memphis State University Anthropological Research Center, Memphis, Tenn.

1990　The Walls Phase and Its Neighbors. In *Towns and Temples along the Mississippi,* edited by David H. Dye and C. A. Cox, pp. 135–69. Tuscaloosa: University of Alabama Press.

1996　The Mississippi River Drainage of Western Tennessee. In *Prehistory of the Central Mississippi Valley,* edited by Charles H. McNutt, pp. 97–118. Tuscaloosa: University of Alabama Press.

Smith, Karen

1999　*From Pots to Potters: Ceramic Manufacture at Fairchild's Landing, Seminole County, Georgia.* Master's thesis, Department of Anthropology, University of Alabama, Tuscaloosa.

Smith, Marvin T.

1978　*Excavations at Several Woodland and Archaic Camp and Workshop Sites in Laurens County, Georgia.* Report No. 16, Laboratory of Archaeology Series, University of Georgia, Athens.

Smith, Rhonda L.

1996　*Vertebrate Subsistence in Southeastern Louisiana between A.D. 700 and 1500.* Master's thesis, Department of Anthropology, University of Georgia, Athens.

Smith, Samuel D.

1971　*A Reinterpretation of the Cades Pond Archeological Period.* Master's thesis, Department of Anthropology, University of Florida, Gainesville.

Snow, Dean

1980　*The Archaeology of New England.* New York: Academic Press.

Snow, Frankie

1975　Swift Creek Designs and Distributions: A South Georgia Study. *Early Georgia* 3:38–59.

1977a　*An Archaeological Survey of the Ocmulgee Big Bend Region.* Occasional Papers from South Georgia 3, South Georgia College, Douglas.

1977b　A Survey of the Ocmulgee Big Bend Region. *Early Georgia* 5:37–60.

1992a　Swift Creek Subphase Dated A.D. 580. In *The Profile Papers,* edited by Patrick H. Garrow and George S. Lewis, pp. 40–42. Society for Georgia Archaeology Special Publication 1, Atlanta (originally published in *The Profile* 27).

1992b　Kolomoki and Milamo: Some Synchronic Evidence. In *The Profile Papers,* edited by Patrick H. Garrow and George S. Lewis, pp. 49–52. Society for Georgia Archaeology Special Publication 1, Atlanta (originally published in *The Profile* 36).

1994　Swift Creek Art: An Anthropological Tool for Investigating Middle Woodland Society in Southern Georgia. Presented at the 51st annual meeting of the Southeastern Archaeological Conference, Lexington.

1998　Swift Creek Design Investigations: The Hartford Case. In *A World Engraved: Archaeology of the Swift Creek Culture,* edited by J. Mark Williams and Daniel T. Elliott, pp. 61–98. Tuscaloosa: University of Alabama Press.

Snow, Frankie, and Keith Stephenson

1990　Hartford: A 4th-Century Swift Creek Mound Site on the Interior Coastal Plain of Georgia. Presented at the 47th annual meeting of the Southeastern Archaeological Conference, Mobile.

1998　Swift Creek Designs: A Tool for Monitoring Interaction. In *A World Engraved: Archaeology of the Swift Creek Culture,* edited by J. Mark Williams and Daniel T. Elliott, pp. 99–111. Tuscaloosa: University of Alabama Press.

Snow, Frankie, and Chris T. Trowell
   1992   Ocmulgee Big Bend Swift Creek Site Dated A.D. 215 ± 70. In *The Profile Papers,* edited by Patrick H. Garrow and George S. Lewis, p. 31. Society for Georgia Archaeology Special Publication 1, Atlanta (originally published in *The Profile* 20:7).

Snow, Frankie, Eli Willcox, and Chris T. Trowell
   1992   Some Preliminary Observations on Milamo. In *The Profile Papers,* edited by Patrick H. Garrow and George S. Lewis, pp. 35–38. Society for Georgia Archaeology Special Publication 1, Atlanta (originally published in *The Profile* 26).

South, Stanley
   1959   *A Study of the Prehistory of the Roanoke Rapids Basin.* Master's thesis, Department of Sociology and Anthropology, University of North Carolina, Chapel Hill.
   1960   *An Archaeological Survey of Southeastern Coastal North Carolina.* Ms. on file, North Carolina Office of State Archaeology, Raleigh.
   1966   Exploratory Excavation of the McFayden Mound, Brunswick County, N.C. *Southern Indian Studies* 18:59–61.
   1976   An Archaeological Survey of Southeastern Coastal North Carolina. *Notebook* 8. South Carolina Institute of Archeology and Anthropology, University of South Carolina, Columbia.

Sparks, John T.
   1987   *Prehistoric Settlement Patterns in Clay County, Mississippi.* Archaeological Report 20, Mississippi Department of Archives and History, Jackson.

Spears, Carol S.
   1978   *The DeRossitt Site (3SF49): Application of Behavioral Archeology to a Museum Collection.* Master's thesis, University of Arkansas, Fayetteville.

Speth, John D., and Susan L. Scott
   1989   Horticulture and Large Mammal Hunting: The Role of Resource Depletion and the Constraints of Time and Labor. In *Farmers as Hunters: The Implications of Sedentism,* edited by S. Kent, pp. 71–79. Cambridge: Cambridge University Press.

Springer, James W.
   1980   An Analysis of Prehistoric Food Remains from the Bruly-St. Martin Site, Louisiana, with a Comparative Discussion of Mississippi Valley Faunal Studies. *Midcontinental Journal of Archaeology* 5(2):193–223.

Squier, Ephraim G., and E. H. Davis
   1848   *Ancient Monuments of the Mississippi Valley.* Smithsonian Contributions to Knowledge 1, New York.

Stafford, C. Russell (editor)
   1992   *Early Woodland Occupations at the Ambrose Flick Site in the Sny Bottom of West-Central Illinois.* Research Series Vol. 10, Center for American Archeology, Kampsville Archeological Center, CAA Press, Kampsville, Ill.

Stahl, Ann B.
   1989   Plant Food Processing: Implications for Dietary Quality. In *Foraging and Farming: The Evolution of Plant Exploitation,* edited by D. R. Harris and G. C. Hillman, pp. 171–96. London: Unwin-Hyman.

Stahl, Peter
   1996   Holocene Biodiversity. *Annual Review of Anthropology* 25:105–26.

Stahle, David W., M. K. Cleaveland, and J. G. Hehr
   1985   A 450-Year Drought Reconstruction for Arkansas, United States. *Nature* 316:530–32.

Stanyard, William F., and Richard W. Stoops, Jr.
1995   *The Archaeology of the Chase Site (9RO53), Rockdale County, Georgia.* 2 vols. Submitted to the City of Conyers, Ga., by Garrow and Associates, Atlanta.

Stein, J. K.
1980   *Geoarchaeology of the Green River Shell Mounds, Kentucky.* Ph.D. thesis, Center for Ancient Studies, University of Minnesota, Minneapolis. University Microfilms, Ann Arbor, Mich.

Steinen, Karl T.
1976   *The Weeden Island Ceramic Complex: An Analysis of Distribution.* Ph.D. dissertation, Department of Anthropology, University of Florida, Gainesville.
1977   Weeden Island in Southwest Georgia. *Early Georgia* 5:73–99.
1989   The Balfour Mound and Weeden Island Culture in South Georgia. *Early Georgia* 17:1–23.
1998   Kolomoki and the Development of Sociopolitical Organization on the Gulf Coastal Plain. In *A World Engraved: Archaeology of the Swift Creek Culture,* edited by J. Mark Williams and Daniel T. Elliott, pp. 181–96. Tuscaloosa: University of Alabama Press.

Stephenson, Keith, and Frankie Snow
1993   Hartford Revisited: Surface Reconnaissance at a Swift Creek Village. Presented at the Meeting of the Society for Georgia Archaeology, Red Top Mountain State Park.
1994   The Hartford Site: Feasting and Trade in the Georgia Coastal Plain. Presented at 51st annual meeting of the Southeastern Archaeological Conference, Lexington.

Steponaitis, Vincas
1983   *Ceramics, Chronology, and Community Patterns: An Archaeological Study at Moundville.* New York: Academic Press.
1986   Prehistoric Archaeology in the Southeastern United States, 1970–1985. *Annual Review of Anthropology* 15:363–404.
1991   Contrasting Patterns of Mississippian Development. In *Chiefdoms: Power, Economy, and Ideology,* edited by Timothy K. Earle, pp. 193–228. Cambridge: Cambridge University Press.

Stewart, R. Michael
1981   Prehistoric Burial Mounds in the Great Valley of Maryland. *Maryland Archaeology* 17:1–16.
1989   Trade and Exchange in Middle Atlantic Region Prehistory. *Archaeology of Eastern North America* 17:47–78.
1990   Clemson's Island Studies in Pennsylvania: A Perspective. *Pennsylvania Archaeologist* 60:79–107.
1992   Observations on the Middle Woodland Period of Virginia: A Middle Atlantic Region Perspective. In *Middle and Late Woodland Research in Virginia,* edited by T. Reinhart and M. E. Hodges, pp. 1–38. Special Publication No. 29, Archaeological Society of Virginia, Richmond.
1995   The Status of Woodland Prehistory in the Middle Atlantic Region. *Archaeology of Eastern North America* 23:177–206.
1998a   Thoughts on the Origins of Ceramic Use and Variation. *Journal of Middle Atlantic Archaeology* 14:1–12.
1998b   Unraveling the Mystery of Zoned Decorated Pottery: Implications for Middle Woodland Society in the Middle Atlantic Region. *Journal of Middle Atlantic Archaeology* 14:161–84.

Steyermark, Julian A.
   1963   *Flora of Missouri.* Ames: Iowa State University Press.
Stoltman, James B.
   1972   The Late Archaic in the Savannah River Region. In *Fiber-Tempered Pottery in Southeastern United States and Northern Columbia: Its Origins, Context and Significance,* edited by Ripley P. Bullen and James B. Stoltman, pp. 37–62. Florida Anthropological Society Publications 6, Tallahassee.
   1974   *Groton Plantation: An Archaeological Study of a South Carolina Locality.* Monograph of the Peabody Museum No. 1, Cambridge.
   1978   Temporal Models in Prehistory: An Example from Eastern North America. *Current Anthropology* 19:703–46.
   1998   Hopewell Interaction in the Southeast as Reflected in Ceramics. Presented at 55th annual meeting of the Southeastern Archaeological Conference, Greenville, S.C.
Stoltman, James B., and Robert C. Mainfort, Jr.
   1999   Elements and Minerals: Reconciling the Differential Findings of Neutron Activation and Petrography in the Compositional Analysis of Ceramics from Pinson Mounds. Presented to the 64th annual meeting of the Society for American Archaeology, Chicago.
Stoltman, James B., and Frankie Snow
   1998   Cultural Interaction within Swift Creek Society: People, Pots, Paddles. In *A World Engraved: Archaeology of the Swift Creek Culture,* edited by J. Mark Williams and Daniel T. Elliott, pp. 130–53. Tuscaloosa: University of Alabama Press.
Story, D. A.
   1990   Culture History of the Native Americans. In *The Archeology and Bioarcheology of the Gulf Coastal Plain,* vol. 1, edited by D. A. Story, pp. 162–365. Arkansas Archeological Survey Research Series No. 38, Fayetteville.
Story, D. A., J. A. Guy, B. A. Burnett, M. D. Freeman, Jerome C. Rose, D. G. Steele, B. W. Olive, and K. J. Reinhard
   1990   *The Archeology and Bioarcheology of the Gulf Coastal Plain: Volume 1.* Arkansas Archeological Survey Research Series No. 38, Fayetteville.
Strayer, D.
   1983   The Effects of Surface Geology and Stream Size on Freshwater Mussel (Bivalvia, Unionidae) Distribution in Southeastern Michigan, U.S.A. *Freshwater Biology* 13:253–64.
Streuver, Stuart
   1964   The Hopewell Interaction Sphere in Riverine–Western Great Lakes Culture History. In *Hopewellian Studies,* edited by Joseph R. Caldwell and Robert L. Hall, pp. 85–106. Scientific Papers 12, Illinois State Museum, Springfield.
Streuver, Stuart, and Gail L. Houart
   1972   An Analysis of the Hopewell Interaction Sphere. In *Social Exchange and Interaction,* edited by Edwin N. Wilmsen, pp. 47–49. Anthropological Papers No. 46, Museum of Anthropology, University of Michigan, Ann Arbor.
Stubbs, John D., Jr.
   1983   *A Report Presenting the Results of Archaeological Survey in Lee County, Mississippi, June 1981 to June 1983.* Submitted to the Chickasaw Indian Cultural Center Foundation, Tupelo, by the Mississippi Dept. of Archives and History, Jackson.
Stuckey, J. L.
   1965   *North Carolina: Its Geology and Mineral Resources.* North Carolina Division of Mineral Resources, Raleigh.

Stuiver, Minze, and Paula J. Reimer
  1993   Extended 14C Database and Revised CALIB Radiocarbon Calibration Program. *Radiocarbon* 35:215–30.
Stuiver, Minze, Paula J. Reimer, Edouard Bard, J. Warren Beck, G. S. Burr, Konrad A. Hughen, Bernd Kromer, Gerry McCormac, Johannes van der Plicht, and Marco Spurk
  1998   INTCAL98 Radiocarbon Age Calibration, 24,000–0 cal B.P. *Radiocarbon* 40(3):1041–83.
Styles, Bonnie W., and James R. Purdue
  1991   Ritual and Secular Use of Fauna by Middle Woodland Peoples in Western Illinois. In *Beamers, Bobwhites, and Blue-Points: Tributes to the Career of Paul W. Parmalee,* edited by J. R. Purdue, W. E. Klippel, and B. W. Styles, pp. 421–34. Scientific Papers 23, Illinois State Museum, Springfield.
Styles, Bonnie W., James R. Purdue, and Mona L. Colburn
  1985   Analysis of Faunal Remains. In *The Alexander Site, Conway County, Arkansas,* edited by E. Thomas Hemmings and John H. House, pp. 58–75. Arkansas Archeological Survey Research Series No. 24, Fayetteville.
Suhm, D. A., and E. B. Jelks
  1962   *Handbook of Texas Archeology: Type Descriptions.* Texas Memorial Museum Bulletin Number 4.
Sullivan, Lynne P.
  1989   Cultural Change and Continuity in the Late Woodland and Mississippian Occupations of the Mouse Creeks Site. *Tennessee Anthropologist* 14(1):33–63.
Sussenbach, T., and R. Barry Lewis
  1987   *Archaeological Investigations in Carlisle, Hickman, and Fulton Counties, Kentucky.* Western Kentucky Project Report No. 4, Department of Anthropology, University of Illinois, Urbana.
Swanton, John R.
  1946   *The Indians of the Southeastern United States.* Bulletin 137, Bureau of American Ethnology, Washington, D.C.
Swartz, B. K., Jr. (editor)
  1971   *Adena: The Seeking of an Identity.* Muncie, Ind.: Ball State University.
Szuter, Christine R., and Frank E. Bayham
  1989   Sedentism and Prehistoric Animal Procurement among Desert Horticulturalists of the North American Southwest. In *Farmers as Hunters: The Implications of Sedentism,* edited by S. Kent, pp. 80–95. Cambridge: Cambridge University Press.
Tainter, Joseph A.
  1977   Woodland Social Change in West Central Illinois. *Midcontinental Journal of Archaeology* 2:67–98.
Tankersley, Kenneth B., Samuel S. Frushour, Frank Nagy, Stephen L. Tankersley, and Kevin Tankersley
  1994   The Archaeology of Mummy Valley, Salts Cave, Mammoth Cave National Park, Kentucky. *North American Archaeologist* 15:129–46.
Taylor, Ralph W.
  1982   Mollusk Shells Associated with Evidence of Habitation by Prehistoric Native Americans in a Hardin County, Kentucky, Cave. *Transactions of the Kentucky Academy of Science* 43(3–4):155–57.
  1989   Changes in Freshwater Mussel Populations of the Ohio River: 1,000 B.P. to Recent Times. *Ohio Journal of Science* 89(5):188–91.

Tedesco, L. P., H. R. Wanless, L. A. Scusa, J. A. Risi, and S. Gelsanliter
  1995   Impact of Hurricane Andrew on South Florida's Sandy Coastlines. *Journal of Coastal Research* (Special Issue) 21:59–82.
ter Braak, C. J. F.
  1985   Correspondence Analysis of Incidence and Abundance Data: Properties in Terms of a Unimodal Response Model. *Biometrics* 41:859–73.
  1986   Canonical Correspondence Analysis: A New Eigenvector Technique for Multivariate Direct Gradient Analysis. *Ecology* 67(5):1167–79.
ter Braak, C. J. F., and I. C. Prentice
  1988   A Theory of Gradient Analysis. *Advances in Ecological Research* 18:272–317.
Tesar, Louis D.
  1974   *Archaeological Assessment Survey of the Tallahalla Reservoir Area, Jasper County, Mississippi.* Submitted to the National Park Service by the Department of Anthropology, Mississippi State University.
  1980   *The Leon County Bicentennial Survey Report: An Archaeological Survey of Selected Portions of Leon County, Florida.* Miscellaneous Project Report Series 49, Bureau of Historic Sites and Properties, Florida Division of Archives, History and Records Management, Florida Department of State, Tallahassee.
Theler, James L.
  1987   Prehistoric Freshwater Mussel Assemblages of the Mississippi River in Southwestern Wisconsin. *The Nautilus* 101(3):143–50.
  1991   Aboriginal Utilization of Freshwater Mussels at the Aztalan Site, Wisconsin. In *Beamers, Bobwhites, and Blue-Points: Tributes to the Career of Paul W. Parmalee,* edited by James R. Purdue, Walter E. Klippel, and Bonnie W. Styles, pp. 315–32. Scientific Papers 23, Illinois State Museum, Springfield.
Thomas, Cyrus
  1894   Report on the Mound Explorations of the Bureau of Ethnology. *Bureau of Ethnology, Annual Report* 12:3–742 (reprinted in 1994 by Smithsonian Institution Press, Washington, D.C.).
Thomas, David H., and C. S. Larsen (editors)
  1979   *The Anthropology of St. Catherines Island 2: The Refuge-Deptford Mortuary Complex.* Anthropological Papers of the American Museum of Natural History 56, New York, N.Y.
Thomas, Julian
  1993a The Hermeneutics of Megalithic Space. In *Interpretative Archaeology,* edited by C. Tilley, pp. 73–97. New York: Berg.
  1993b The Politics of Vision and the Archaeology of Landscape. In *Landscape: Politics and Perspective,* edited by B. Bender, pp. 19–48. New York: Berg.
Thomas, Prentice M., Jr., and L. Janice Campbell
  1985   The Deptford to Santa Rosa/Swift Creek Transition in the Florida Panhandle. *Florida Anthropologist* 38:110–19.
  1987   *Site Distribution and Cultural Chronology in a Portion of Southwestern Alabama: Results of Cultural Resources Survey on the Mobile Bay Pipeline Project, Choctaw, Washington and Mobile Counties.* Report of Investigations 158, New World Research, Inc., Fort Walton Beach, Fla.
  1990   Santa Rosa/Swift Creek Culture on the Northwest Florida Gulf Coast: The Horseshoe Bayou Phase. Presented at the 47th annual meeting of the Southeastern Archaeological Conference, Mobile.
  1991   The Elliott's Point Complex: New Data Regarding the Localized Poverty Point Expression on the Northwest Florida Gulf Coast, 2000 B.C.–500 B.C. In *The Pov-*

erty Point Culture: Local Manifestations, Subsistence Practices, and Trade Networks, edited by K. M. Byrd, pp. 102–20. Geoscience and Man 29, Geoscience Publications, Department of Geography and Anthropology, Louisiana State University, Baton Rouge.

Thomas, Prentice M., Jr., and L. Janice Campbell (editors)
1993   Technical Synthesis of Cultural Resources Investigations at Eglin Santa Rosa, Okaloosa and Walton Counties. Report of Investigations 192, New World Research, Inc., Fort Walton Beach, Fla.

Thomas, Prentice M., Jr., Maria L. Schleidt Peñalva, L. Janice Campbell, and Mathilda Cox (editors)
1996   Completing the Compliance Process at Eglin Air Force Base, Okaloosa, Santa Rosa and Walton Counties: Controlled Excavation at 8WL58, The Old Homestead Site. Submitted to Eglin Air Force Base by Prentice Thomas and Associates, Fort Walton.

Thomas, Ronald
1971   Adena Influence in the Middle Atlantic Coast. In Adena: The Seeking of an Identity, edited by B. K. Swartz, pp. 56–87. Muncie, Ind.: Ball State University.
1987   Prehistoric Mortuary Complexes of the Delmarva Peninsula. Journal of Middle Atlantic Archaeology 3:35–47.

Thomas, T. M.
1974   A Detailed Analysis of Climatological and Hydrological Records of South Florida with Reference to Man's Influences upon Ecosystem Evolution. In Environments of South Florida: Present and Past, edited by P. J. Gleason, pp. 82–122. Memoir 2, Miami Geological Society.

Thompson, E. P.
1967   Time, Work-Discipline, and Industrial Capitalism. Past and Present 38:56–97.

Thorne, Robert M.
1976   A Cultural Resources Survey of the Divide-Cut Section, Tennessee-Tombigbee Waterway, Tishomingo County, Mississippi: 1975. Submitted to the National Park Service by the Department of Sociology and Anthropology, University of Mississippi.

Thunen, Robert L.
1988   Geometric Enclosures in the Mid-South: An Architectural Analysis of Enclosure Form. In Middle Woodland Settlement and Ceremonialism in the Mid-South and Lower Mississippi Valley, edited by Robert C. Mainfort, Jr., pp. 99–116. Archaeological Report 22, Mississippi Department of Archives and History, Jackson.
1990   Planning Principles and Earthwork Architecture: The Pinson Mounds Enclosure. Ph.D. dissertation, Northwestern University, Evanston, Ill.
1998   Defining Space: An Overview of the Pinson Mounds Enclosure. In Ancient Earthen Enclosures of the Eastern Woodlands, edited by Robert C. Mainfort, Jr., and L. P. Sullivan, pp. 57–67. Gainesville: University Press of Florida.

Tilley, Christopher
1994   A Phenomenology of Landscape. Oxford: Berg.

Toth, Edwin Alan
1974   Archaeology and Ceramics at the Marksville Site. Anthropological Papers No. 56, Museum of Anthropology, University of Michigan, Ann Arbor.
1979a   The Lake St. Agnes Site: A Multi-Component Occupation of Avoyelles Parish, Louisiana. Melanges No. 13, Museum of Geoscience, Louisiana State University, Baton Rouge.
1979b   The Marksville Connection. In Hopewell Archaeology: The Chillicothe Confer-

ence, edited by D. Brose and N. Greber, pp. 188–99. Kent, Ohio: Kent State University Press.

1988   *Early Marksville Phases in the Lower Mississippi Valley: A Study of Culture Contact Dynamics.* Archaeological Report 21, Mississippi Department of Archives and History, Jackson.

Trachtenberg, Samuel

1999   *Macrobotanical Remains from the Raffman Site (16MA20).* Master's thesis, Department of Anthropology, Tulane University, New Orleans.

Trickey, E. B.

1958   A Chronological Framework for the Mobile Bay Region. *American Antiquity* 23:388–96.

Trickey, E. B., and N. J. Holmes

1971   A Chronological Framework for the Mobile Bay Region. *American Antiquity* 23:388–96.

Trigger, B. G.

1968   *Beyond History: The Methods of Prehistory.* New York: Holt, Rinehart and Winston.

Trinkley, Michael B.

1980a   A Typology of Thom's Creek Pottery for the South Carolina Coast. *South Carolina Antiquities* 12:1–35.

1980b   *Investigation of the Woodland Period along the South Carolina Coast.* Ph.D. dissertation, University of North Carolina at Chapel Hill. University Microfilms, Ann Arbor, Mich.

1980c   *Additional Investigations at Site 38LX5.* Submitted to South Carolina Department of Highways and Public Transportation by the Chicora Foundation, Columbia, S.C.

1981   *Studies of Three Woodland Period Sites in Beaufort County, South Carolina.* Submitted to South Carolina Department of Highways and Public Transportation by the Chicora Foundation, Columbia, S.C.

1983   Ceramics of the Central South Carolina Coast. *South Carolina Antiquities* 15:43–53.

1985   The Form and Function of South Carolina's Early Woodland Shell Rings. In *Structure and Process in Southeastern Archaeology,* edited by Roy S. Dickens, Jr., and H. Trawick Ward, pp. 102–18. Tuscaloosa: University of Alabama Press.

1989   An Archaeological Overview of the Woodland Period: It's the Same Old Riddle. In *Studies in South Carolina Archaeology: Essays in Honor of Robert L. Stephenson,* edited by A. C. Goodyear III and G. T. Hanson, pp. 53–72. Anthropological Studies 9, South Carolina Institute of Archaeology and Anthropology, University of South Carolina, Columbia.

1990   *An Archaeological Context for the South Carolina Woodland Period.* Chicora Foundation Research Series 22. Prepared for South Carolina Department of Archives and History, Columbia.

1991   *Further Investigations of Prehistoric and Historic Lifeways on Callawassie and Spring Islands, Beaufort County, South Carolina,* Chicora Foundation Research Series 23, Columbia, S.C.

Trinkley, Michael (editor)

1990   *The Second Phase of Archaeological Survey on Spring Island, Beaufort County, South Carolina, Investigation of Prehistoric and Historic Settlement Patterns on an Isolated Sea Island.* Chicora Foundation Research Series 20, Columbia, S.C.

Trinkley, Michael, and Natalie Adams

1994 *Middle and Late Woodland Life at Old House Creek, Hilton Head Island, South Carolina.* Chicora Foundation Research Series 42, Columbia, S.C.

Trowell, Chris T.

1979 *A Reconnaissance of Aboriginal Okefenokee: An Outline of the Prehistoric Geography of the Okefenokee Swamp and an Inventory of Prehistoric Archaeological Sites in the Okefenokee National Wildlife Refuge, Part I.* Okefenokee Area Survey Working Paper 1, South Georgia College, Douglas.

1992 The Seasholtz Site: 9WE11. In *The Profile Papers,* edited by Patrick H. Garrow and George S. Lewis, pp. 23–24. Society for Georgia Archaeology Special Publication 1, Atlanta.

1998 A Kolomoki Chronicle: History of a Plantation, a State Park and the Archaeological Search for Kolomoki's Prehistory. *Early Georgia* 26(1):12–81.

Tucker, Carol

1989 *A Reanalysis of the Osteological and Cultural Remains from Ausmus Burial Cave, Claiborne County, Tennessee (3CE20).* Master's thesis, Department of Anthropology, University of Tennessee, Knoxville.

Turner, E. Randolph

1976 *An Archaeological and Ethnohistorical Study of the Evolution of Rank Societies in the Virginia Coastal Plain.* Ph.D. dissertation, Department of Anthropology, Pennsylvania State University. University Microfilms, Ann Arbor, Mich.

Turner, Kenneth R.

1980 Affinities of the Copena Skeletal Series from Site 1SE42. In *The Skeletal Biology of Aboriginal Populations in the Southeastern United States,* edited by P. S. Willey and F. H. Smith, pp. 15–27. Miscellaneous Paper 5, Tennessee Anthropological Association, Knoxville.

1986 Human Skeletal Remains, 22Lo860. In *Test Excavations at Two Woodland Sites, Lowndes County, Mississippi,* by Janet E. Rafferty and Mary Evelyn Starr, pp. 131–34. Report of Investigations 3, Cobb Institute of Archaeology, Mississippi State University.

Turner, William B.

n.d. *A Preliminary Analysis of Prehistoric Fresh-Water Bivalve Species Composition Changes from ca. 7500 to 2500 B.P.: A View from the Central Duck River Drainage.* Ms. on file, Department of Anthropology, University of Tennessee, Knoxville.

Turpin, Solveig A.

1985 *Seminole Sink (41VV620): Excavation of a Vertical Shaft Tomb, Val Verde County, Texas.* University of Texas Research Report 93, Texas Archaeological Survey, Austin.

Upchurch, S. B., P. Jewell IV, and E. DeHaven

1992 Stratigraphy of India "Mounds" in the Charlotte Harbor Area, Florida: Sea-level Rise and Paleoenvironments. In *Culture and Environment in the Domain of the Calusa,* edited by William H. Marquardt, pp. 59–103. Monograph No. 1, Institute of Archaeology and Paleoenvironmental Studies, University of Florida, Gainesville.

Van Beck, J. C., and L. M. Van Beck

1965 The Marco Midden, Marco Island, Florida. *Florida Anthropologist* 18:37–54.

Vescelius, Gary S.

1957 Mound 2 at Marksville. *American Antiquity* 22:416–20.

Waddell, David B., John H. House, F. B. King, M. L. Colburn, and M. K. Marks

1987 *Results of Final Testing for Significance at the Ink Bayou Site (3PU252), Pulaski*

County, Arkansas. Submitted to the Arkansas Highway and Transportation Department by the Sponsored Research Program, Arkansas Archeological Survey, Fayetteville (Project No. 577).

Waddell, Eugene
  1965   A C-14 Date for Awendaw Punctate. *Southeastern Archaeological Conference Bulletin* 3:82–85.

Wagner, Gail E.
  1991   *Late Woodland Plant Remains from 31BN335, Buncombe County, North Carolina.* Submitted to Dr. Michael Baker, Archaeological Consultants, Weaverville, N.C.
  1995   The Prehistoric Sequence of Plant Utilization in South Carolina. Presented at the 52nd annual meeting of the Southeastern Archaeological Conference, Knoxville.
  1997   *Early-Middle Woodland Plant Remains from 38BK984, Berkeley County, South Carolina.* Submitted to Brockington and Associates, Atlanta.

Wagner, Mark J.
  1980   *The Aaron Shelton Site (40CF69): A Multicomponent Site in the Lower Normandy Reservoir.* Master's thesis, Department of Anthropology, University of Tennessee, Knoxville.

Wagner, Mark J., Mary R. McCorvie, and Charles A. Swenlund
  1999   The Korando Site (11J334): A Mississippian Ritual Cave and Rock Art Site in Southwestern Illinois. *Illinois Archaeology* 11:149–86.

Walker, Karen J.
  1992   The Zooarchaeology of Charlotte Harbor's Prehistoric Maritime Adaptation: Spatial and Temporal Perspectives. In *Culture and Environment in the Domain of the Calusa,* edited by William H. Marquardt, pp. 265–367. Monograph No. 1, Institute of Archaeology and Paleoenvironmental Studies, University of Florida, Gainesville.

Walker, Karen J., F. W. Stapor, Jr., and William H. Marquardt
  1994a   Archaeological Evidence for a 1750–1450 Higher-than-Present Sea Level along Florida's Gulf Coast. In *Holocene Cycles: Climate, Sea Levels, and Sedimentation,* pp. 205–18. *Journal of Coastal Research* (Special Issue No. 17).
  1994b   Episodic Sea Levels and Human Occupation at Southwest Florida Wightman Site. *Florida Anthropologist* 47:161–79.

Walker, Winslow M.
  1936   *The Troyville Mounds, Catahoula Parish, Louisiana.* Bulletin 113, Bureau of American Ethnology, Washington, D.C.

Walker, Winslow M., and R. M. Adams
  1946   Excavations in the Matthews Site, New Madrid County, Missouri. *Academy of Science of St. Louis, Transactions* 31(4):75–120.

Walling, R., Robert C. Mainfort, Jr., and James Atkinson
  1991   Radiocarbon Dates for the Bynum, Pharr, and Miller Sites, Northeast Mississippi. *Southeastern Archaeology* 10(1):54–62.

Walthall, John A.
  1973   *Copena: A Tennessee Valley Middle Woodland Culture.* Ph.D. dissertation, Department of Anthropology, University of North Carolina, Chapel Hill.
  1979   Hopewell and the Southern Heartland. In *Hopewell Archaeology: The Chillicothe Conference,* edited by D. Brose and N. Greber, pp. 200–208. Kent, Ohio: Kent State University Press.
  1980   *Prehistoric Indians of the Southeast: Archaeology of Alabama and the Middle South.* Tuscaloosa: University of Alabama Press.

1981   *Galena and Aboriginal Trade in Eastern North America.* Scientific Papers 17, Illinois State Museum, Springfield.

1985   Early Hopewellian Ceremonial Encampments in the South Appalachian Highlands. In *Structure and Process in Southeastern Archaeology,* edited by R. S. Dickens, Jr., and H. T. Ward, pp. 243–62. Tuscaloosa: University of Alabama Press.

Walthall, John A., and David DeJarnette
1974   Copena Burial Caves. *Journal of Alabama Archaeology* 20:1–59.

Walthall, John A., and Ned J. Jenkins
1976   The Gulf Formational Stage in Southeastern Prehistory. *Southeastern Archaeological Conference Bulletin* 19:43–49.

Wanless, H. R.
1982   Sea Level Is Rising—So What? *Journal of Sedimentary Petrology* 52:1051–54.

Wanless, H. R., R. W. Parkinson, and L. P. Tedesco
1994   Sea Level Control on the Stability of Everglades Wetlands. In *Everglades, the Ecosystem and Its Restoration,* edited by S. M. Davis and J. C. Ogden, pp. 199–222. Delray, Fla.: St. Lucie Press.

Wanless, H. R., L. P. Tedesco, J. A. Risi, B. G. Bischof, S. Gelsanliter
1995   The Role of Storm Processes on the Growth and Evolution of Coastal and Shallow Marine Sedimentary Environments in South Florida. The 1st SEPM Congress on Sedimentary Geology, Pre-Congress Field Trip Guide, August 11–13, 1995.

Ward, H. Trawick
1983   A Review of Archaeology in the North Carolina Piedmont: A Study of Change. In *The Prehistory of North Carolina: An Archaeological Symposium,* edited by Mark A. Mathis and Jeffery J. Crow, pp. 53–81. North Carolina Division of Archives and History, Raleigh.

Ward, H. Trawick, and R. P. Stephen Davis, Jr.
1993   *Indian Communities on the North Carolina Piedmont, A.D. 1000–1700.* Monograph No. 2, Research Laboratories of Anthropology, University of North Carolina, Chapel Hill.

1999   *A Time before History: The Archaeology of North Carolina.* Chapel Hill: University of North Carolina Press.

Ward, H. Trawick, and Jack H. Wilson, Jr.
1980   Archaeological Investigations at the Cold Morning Site. *Southern Indian Studies* 32:5–40.

Waring, Antonio J., Jr.
1968a   The Bilbo Site, Chatham County, Georgia (originally 1940). In *The Waring Papers: The Collected Works of Antonio J. Waring, Jr.,* edited by Stephen Williams, pp. 152–97. Papers of the Peabody Museum of Archaeology and Ethnology, Vol. 58, Harvard University, Cambridge.

1968b   Fiber-Tempered Pottery and Its Cultural Affiliations on the Georgia-Carolina Coast (originally 1952). In *The Waring Papers: The Collected Works of Antonio J. Waring, Jr.,* edited by Stephen Williams, pp. 253–55. Papers of the Peabody Museum of Archaeology and Ethnology, Vol. 58, Harvard University, Cambridge.

1968c   The Refuge Site, Jasper County, South Carolina (originally 1940). In *The Waring Papers: The Collected Works of Antonio J. Waring, Jr.,* edited by Stephen Williams, pp. 198–208. Papers of the Peabody Museum of Archaeology and Ethnology, Vol. 58, Harvard University, Cambridge.

Waring, Antonio J., Jr., and Preston Holder
1968   The Deptford Ceramic Complex. In *The Waring Papers: The Collected Works of Antonio J. Waring, Jr.,* edited by Stephen Williams, pp. 135–51. Papers of the

Peabody Museum of Archaeology and Ethnology, Vol. 58, Harvard University, Cambridge.

Waring, Antonio J., Jr., and Lewis H. Larson, Jr.

1968   The Shell Ring on Sapelo Island (originally 1955–1960). In *The Waring Papers: The Collected Works of Antonio J. Waring, Jr.,* edited by Stephen Williams, pp. 263–78. Papers of the Peabody Museum of Archaeology and Ethnology, Vol. 58, Harvard University, Cambridge.

Warren, Robert E.

1975   *Prehistoric Unionacean (Freshwater Mussel) Utilization at the Widows Creek Site (1JA305), Northeast Alabama.* Master's thesis, Department of Anthropology, University of Nebraska, Lincoln.

1991   Freshwater Mussels as Paleoenvironmental Indicators: A Quantitative Approach to Assemblage Analysis. In *Beamers, Bobwhites, and Blue-Points: Tributes to the Career of Paul W. Parmalee,* edited by James R. Purdue, Walter E. Klippel, and Bonnie W. Styles, pp. 23–66. Scientific Papers 23, Illinois State Museum, Springfield.

1992   *UNIO: A Spreadsheet Program for Reconstructing Aquatic Environments Based on the Species Composition of Freshwater Mussel (Unionoidea) Assemblages.* Quaternary Studies Program Technical Report 92-000-3, Illinois State Museum, Springfield.

1995   Prehistoric Mussel Faunas from the Northern Ozark Highland of Missouri: Cultural and Geological Implications. *The Missouri Archaeologist* 53:80–100.

1996   Paleoenvironmental Implications of Freshwater Mussel Faunas from Two Caves in the Northern Ozark Highland of Missouri. Presented at the 41st Midwest Archaeological Conference, Beloit, Wis.

Waselkov, Gregory A.

1982   *Shellfish Gathering and Shell Midden Archaeology.* Ph.D. dissertation, Department of Anthropology, University of North Carolina, Chapel Hill. University Microfilms, Ann Arbor, Mich.

Waterson, Roxana

1995   Houses and Hierarchies in Island Southeast Asia. In *About the House,* edited by J. Carsten and S. Hugh-Jones, pp. 47–68. Cambridge: Cambridge University Press.

Watson, Patty Jo

1977   Design Analysis of Painted Pottery. *American Antiquity* 42:381–93.

1983   CRF Archeological Project and Shellmound Archeological Project: 1982. *Cave Research Foundation Annual Report for 1982,* pp. 13–15, Barbourville, Ky.

1985   The Impact of Early Horticulture in the Upland Drainages of the Midwest and Midsouth. In *Prehistoric Food Production in North America,* edited by Richard I. Ford, pp. 99–147. Anthropological Papers No. 75, Museum of Anthropology, University of Michigan, Ann Arbor.

1986   Prehistoric Cavers of the Eastern Woodlands. In *The Prehistoric Native American Art of Mud Glyph Cave,* edited by C. H. Faulkner, pp. 109–16. Knoxville: University of Tennessee Press.

1990   Trend and Tradition in Southeastern Archaeology. *Southeastern Archaeology* 9(1):43–54.

1996   Of Caves and Shell Mounds in West-Central Kentucky. In *Of Caves and Shell Mounds,* edited by Kenneth C. Carstens and P. J. Watson, pp. 159–64. Tuscaloosa: University of Alabama Press.

2001   Theory in Cave Archaeology. In *Cave Archaeology: Theory, Method, and Tech-*

niques, edited by Sarah Sherwood and Jan Simek. *Midcontinental Journal of Archaeology* 26(2), in press.

Watson, Patty Jo (editor)
1969 *The Prehistory of Salts Cave, Kentucky.* Illinois State Museum Reports of Investigations No. 16, Springfield.
1974 *Archeology of the Mammoth Cave Area.* New York: Academic Press (reprinted in 1997, with a new foreword and updated reference list, by Cave Books, St. Louis).

Watson, Patty Jo, and Mary C. Kennedy
1991 The Development of Horticulture in the Eastern Woodlands of North America: Women's Role. In *Engendering Archaeology: Women and Prehistory,* edited by Joan M. Gero and Margaret W. Conkey, pp. 255–75. Chicago: Blackwell.

Watson, Patty Jo, Mary C. Kennedy, P. Willey, Louise Robbins, and Ronald Wilson
n.d. Prehistoric Footprints in Jaguar Cave, Tennessee. Ms. in possession of author.

Wauchope, Robert
1966 *Archaeological Survey of Northern Georgia.* Memoirs No. 21, Society for American Archaeology, Menasha, Wis.

Wayne, Lucy B.
1987 Swift Creek Occupation in the Altamaha Delta. *Early Georgia* 15(1 and 2):46–65.

Weaver, E. C.
1963 Technological Analysis of Prehistoric Lower Mississippi Valley Ceramic Material: A Preliminary Report. *American Antiquity* 29(1):49–56.

Weaver, Guy G., Mitchell R. Childress, C. Andrew Buchner, and Mary E. Starr
1996 *Archaeological Investigations at Three Sites near Arlington, State Route 385 (Paul Barrett Parkway), Shelby County, Tennessee.* Submitted to Parsons De Leuw, Inc., and Tennessee Department of Transportation by Garrow and Associates, Inc., Memphis.

Webb, Clarence H.
1968 The Extent and Content of Poverty Point Culture. *American Antiquity* 33:297–321.
1982 The Bellevue Focus: A Marksville-Troyville Manifestation in Northwestern Louisiana. *Louisiana Archaeology* 9:251–74.

Webb, Clarence H., and Monroe Dodd, Jr.
1939 Further Excavations of the Gahagan Mound: Connections with a Florida Culture. *Bulletin of the Texas Archeological Society* 11:92–126.

Webb, Clarence H., and R. R. McKinney
1975 Mounds Plantation (16CD12), Caddo Parish, Louisiana. *Louisiana Archaeology* 2:39–127.

Webb, Clarence H., F. E. Murphey, W. G. Ellis, and H. R. Green
1969 The Resch Site, 41HS16, Harrison County, Texas. *Bulletin of the Texas Archeological Society* 40:3–106.

Webb, Robert S., J. T. Doolin, Mary E. Gantt, and B. D. Gumbert
1994 *Upper Towaliga Reservoir, Data Recovery at Three Prehistoric Sites within the Henry County Water Supply Reservoir System, Henry and Spalding Counties, Georgia.* Law Engineering and Environmental Services, Inc., Kennesaw, Ga.

Webb, William S.
1938 *An Archaeological Survey of the Norris Basin in Eastern Tennessee.* Bulletin 118, Bureau of American Ethnology, Smithsonian Institution, Washington, D.C.
1939 *An Archaeological Survey of Wheeler Basin on the Tennessee River in Northern Alabama.* Bulletin 122, Bureau of American Ethnology, Smithsonian Institution, Washington, D.C.

1940   *The Wright Mounds, Sites 6 and 7, Montgomery County, Kentucky.* University of
        Kentucky Reports in Anthropology and Archaeology 5(1), Lexington.

1941a   *The Morgan Stone Mound, Site 15, Bath County, Kentucky.* University of Ken-
        tucky Reports in Anthropology and Archaeology 5(2), Lexington.

1941b   *Mt. Horeb Earthworks, Site 1, and the Drake Mound, Site 11, Fayette County,
        Kentucky.* University of Kentucky Reports in Anthropology and Archaeology 5(2),
        Lexington.

1943a   *A Note on the Mt. Horeb Earthworks, Site Fa 1, and Two New Adjacent Sites, Fa
        14 and Fa 15, Fayette County, Kentucky.* University of Kentucky Reports in An-
        thropology and Archaeology 5(7), pp. 666–70, Lexington.

1943b   *The Crigler Mounds and the Hartman Mound.* University of Kentucky Reports in
        Anthropology and Archaeology 5(6), Lexington.

1943c   *The Riley Mound Site Be 15, and the Landing Mound, Site Be 17, Boone County,
        Kentucky.* University of Kentucky Reports in Anthropology and Archaeology 5(7),
        Lexington.

1946   *Indian Knoll, Site Oh2, Ohio County, Kentucky.* University of Kentucky Reports
        in Anthropology and Archaeology 4(3, Part 1), Lexington.

Webb, William S., and Raymond S. Baby

1957   *The Adena People #2.* The Ohio Historical Society, Columbus.

Webb, William S., and David L. DeJarnette

1942   *An Archaeological Survey of Pickwick Basin in the Adjacent Portions of the States
        of Alabama, Mississippi, and Tennessee.* Bulletin 129, Bureau of American Eth-
        nology, Smithsonian Institution, Washington, D.C.

1948   *Little Bear Creek Site Cto8, Colbert County, Alabama.* Alabama Museum of Natu-
        ral History Museum Paper 26, University.

Webb, William S., and John Elliot

1942   *The Robbins Mounds, Sites Be 3 and Be 14, Boone County, Kentucky.* University
        of Kentucky Reports in Anthropology and Archaeology 5(5), Lexington.

Webb, William S., and William D. Funkhouser

1940   *Ricketts Site Revisited.* University of Kentucky Reports in Anthropology and Ar-
        chaeology 3(6), Lexington.

Webb, William S., and William G. Haag

1947   *The Fischer Site, Fayette County, Kentucky.* University of Kentucky Reports in
        Anthropology and Archaeology 7(2), Lexington.

Webb, William S., and Charles Snow

1945   *The Adena People.* University of Kentucky Reports in Anthropology and Archae-
        ology 6, Lexington.

Weinstein, Richard A.

1986   Tchefuncte Occupation of the Lower Mississippi Delta and Adjacent Coastal Zone.
        In *The Tchula Period in the Mid-South and Lower Mississippi Valley,* edited by
        David H. Dye and R. C. Brister, pp. 102–27. Archaeological Report 17, Missis-
        sippi Department of Archives and History, Jackson.

1995   The Tchula Period in the Lower Mississippi Valley and Adjacent Coastal Zone: A
        Brief Summary. *Louisiana Archaeology* 18:153–87.

Weinstein, Richard A., and Thurston G. H. Hahn III

1992   *Cultural Resources Survey of the Lake Beulah Landside Berm, Item L-583, Bolivar
        County, Mississippi.* The Beulah Levee Project: Archaeology and History, Vol. 1.
        Coastal Environments, Inc., Baton Rouge.

Weinstein, Richard A., and David B. Kelley

1984   *Archaeology and Paleogeography of the Upper Felsenthal Region: Cultural Re-*

sources Investigations in the Calion Navigation Pool, South-Central Arkansas. Coastal Environments, Inc., Baton Rouge.

1992   *Cultural Resources Investigations in the Terrebonne Marsh, South-Central Louisiana.* Cultural Resources Series Report No. COELMN/PD-89/06, Coastal Environments, Inc., Baton Rouge.

Weinstein, Richard A., and Philip G. Rivet

1978   *Beau Mire: A Late Tchula Period Site of the Tchefuncte Culture, Ascension Parish, Louisiana.* Anthropological Report 1, Louisiana Archaeological Survey and Antiquities Commission, Baton Rouge.

Weinstein, Richard A., Eileen K. Burden, Katherine L. Brooks, and Sherwood M. Gagliano

1978   *Cultural Resource Survey of the Proposed Relocation Route of U.S. 90 (LA 3052), Ascension, St. Mary, and Terrebonne Parishes, Louisiana.* Coastal Environments, Inc., Baton Rouge.

Weinstein, Richard A., Richard S. Fuller, Jr., Susan L. Scott, C. Margaret Scarry, and Sylvia T. Duay

1995   *The Rock Levee Site: Late Marksville through Late Mississippi Period Settlement, Bolivar County, Mississippi.* The Beulah Levee Project: Archaeology and History, Vol. 3. Coastal Environments, Inc., Baton Rouge.

Weisman, Brent R.

1995   *Crystal River: A Ceremonial Mound Center on the Florida Gulf Coast.* Division of Historical Resources, Florida Bureau of Archaeological Research, Tallahassee.

Welch, Paul D.

1990   Mississippian Emergence in West Central Alabama. In *The Mississippian Emergence,* edited by Bruce D. Smith, pp. 197–225. Washington, D.C.: Smithsonian Institution Press.

1998   Middle Woodland and Mississippian Occupations of the Savannah Site in Tennessee. *Southeastern Archaeology* 17:79–92.

Wells, Douglas C.

1997   Political Competition and Site Placement: Late Prehistoric Settlement in the Tensas Basin of Northeast Louisiana. *Louisiana Archaeology* 22:71–91.

1998   *The Early Coles Creek Period and the Evolution of Social Inequality in the Lower Mississippi Valley.* Ph.D. dissertation, Department of Anthropology, Tulane University, New Orleans.

Wendland, Wayne M., and Reid A. Bryson

1974   *Cultural Sensitivity to Environmental Change IV: Dating Climatic Episodes of the Holocene.* Report 21, Institute for Environmental Studies, University of Wisconsin, Madison.

Wetmore, Ruth Y.

1979   Report on Excavations at the Buie Mound, Robeson County, North Carolina. *Notebook* 10:30–71. Institute of Archeology and Anthropology, University of South Carolina, Columbia.

1990   *The Ela Site (31Sw5): Archaeological Data Recovery of Connestee and Qualla Phase Occupations at the East Elementary School Site, Swain County, North Carolina.* Draft report on file, Office of State Archaeology, Raleigh.

1993   *An Archaeological Survey of Transylvania County, North Carolina.* Report prepared for the Transylvania County Historical Properties Commission. Report on file, Office of State Archaeology, Raleigh.

1996   The Connestee Component from the Ela Site (31Sw5). In *Upland Archeology in the East, Symposium Five,* edited by Eugene B. Barfield and Michael B. Barber. Special Publication No. 38, Part 5, Archeological Society of Virginia, Richmond.

Wetmore, Ruth Y., Kenneth W. Robinson, and David G. Moore
   1996   Woodland Adaptations in the Appalachian Summit of Western North Carolina:
          Exploring the Influence of Climatic Change. Presented at the Southeastern Ar-
          chaeological Conference, Birmingham, Ala.
   2000   Woodland Adaptations in the Appalachian Summit of Western North Carolina:
          Exploring the Influence of Climatic Change. In *The Years Without Summer: Trac-
          ing A.D. 536 and Its Aftermath,* edited by Joel D. Gunn, pp. 139–49. BAR Interna-
          tional Series 872. Oxford, England: Archaeopress.
Wheeler, R. J.
   1998   Aboriginal Canals of Cape Sable. *Florida Anthropologist* 51:15–24.
White, D. S.
   1977   Changes in the Freshwater Mussel Populations of the Poteau River System, Le
          Flore County, Oklahoma. *Proceedings of the Oklahoma Academy of Science*
          57:103–5.
White, Nancy M.
   1981   *Archaeological Survey at Lake Seminole, Jackson and Gadsden Counties, Florida,
          Seminole and Decatur Counties, Georgia.* Cleveland Museum of Natural History
          Archaeological Research Report. Final report submitted to the U.S. Army Corps
          of Engineers, Mobile District (Contract No. DACW01-78-C-0163).
   1992   The Overgrown Road Site (8Gu38): A Swift Creek Camp Site in the Lower
          Apalachicola Valley. *Florida Anthropologist* 45(1):18–38.
White, William B.
   1969   Mineralogy of the Salts Cave Archaeological Site. In *The Prehistory of Salts Cave,
          Kentucky,* edited by Patty Jo Watson, appendix, pp. 79–82. Illinois State Museum
          Reports of Investigations No. 16, Springfield.
Whittle, Alasdair
   1996   *Europe in the Neolithic: The Creation of New Worlds.* Cambridge: Cambridge
          University Press.
Whittlesey, Charles C.
   1850   *Descriptions of Ancient Works in Ohio.* Smithsonian Contributions to Knowledge
          3(7), Washington, D.C.
Whyte, Thomas R., and Larry R. Kimball
   1997   Science Versus Grave Desecration: The Saga of Lake Hole Cave. *Journal of Cave
          and Karst Studies (National Speleological Society Bulletin)* 59:143–47.
Wiant, Michael D., and Dawn Harn
   1994   *Human Skeletal Remains Protection Act Investigations: 11Ms37 at Horseshoe Lake
          State Park, Madison County, Illinois.* Illinois State Museum, Springfield.
Widmer, R. J.
   1986a *Prehistoric Estuarine Adaptation at the Solana Site, Charlotte County, Florida.*
          Florida Division of Archives, History, and Records Management, Bureau of Ar-
          chaeological Research, Tallahassee.
   1986b Sociopolitical Implications of Off-shore Fishing in Aboriginal Southeast Florida.
          Florida Anthropologist 39:244–52.
   1988   *The Evolution of the Calusa: A Nonagricultural Chiefdom on the Southwest Florida
          Coast.* Tuscaloosa: University of Alabama Press.
   1996   Recent Excavation at the Key Marco Site, 8CR48, Collier County, Florida. *Florida
          Anthropologist* 49:10–26.
Wilde-Ramsing, Mark
   1978   *A Report on the New Hanover County Archaeological Survey: A C.E.T.A. Project.*
          Submitted to the North Carolina Office of State Archaeology, Raleigh.

Willey, Gordon R.
  1945   The Weeden Island Culture: A Preliminary Definition. *American Antiquity* 10:225–54.
  1949a   *Excavations in Southeast Florida.* Yale University Publications in Anthropology 42, New Haven, Conn.
  1949b   *Archeology of the Florida Gulf Coast.* Smithsonian Miscellaneous Collections 113, Washington, D.C.
  1966   *An Introduction to American Archaeology.* Vol. 1, *North and Middle America.* Englewood Cliffs, N.J.: Prentice-Hall.
Willey, Gordon R., and Philip Phillips
  1958   *Method and Theory in American Archaeology.* Chicago: University of Chicago Press.
Willey, Gordon R., and Richard B. Woodbury
  1942   A Chronological Outline for the Northwest Florida Coast. *American Antiquity* 7:232–54.
Willey, P., George M. Crothers, and Charles H. Faulkner
  1988   Aboriginal Skeletons and Petroglyphs in Officer Cave, Tennessee. *Tennessee Anthropologist* 13:51–75.
Williams, J. Mark
  1987   *Archaeological Excavations at the Jackson Landing/Mulatto Bayou Earthwork.* Archaeological Report 19, Mississippi Dept. of Archives and History, Jackson.
  1996   *Archaeological Investigations at the Sawyer Site (9LS1).* LAMAR Institute Publication 32, LAMAR Institute, Watkinsville, Ga.
Williams, J. Mark, and Daniel T. Elliott
  1998   Swift Creek Research: History and Observations. In *A World Engraved: Archaeology of the Swift Creek Culture,* edited by J. Mark Williams and Daniel T. Elliott, pp. 1–11. Tuscaloosa: University of Alabama Press.
Williams, J. Mark, and Daniel T. Elliott (editors)
  1998   *A World Engraved: Archaeology of the Swift Creek Culture.* Tuscaloosa: University of Alabama Press.
Williams, J. Mark, and Gary Shapiro
  1990   *Archaeological Excavations at Little River (9MG46): 1984 and 1987.* LAMAR Institute, Watkinsville, Ga.
Williams, J. Raymond
  1967   *Land Leveling Salvage Archaeological Work in Southeast Missouri: 1966.* Submitted to the National Park Service, Midwest Archeological Center, Lincoln, Neb.
  1968   *Southeast Missouri Land Leveling Salvage Archaeology: 1967.* Submitted to the National Park Service, Lincoln, Neb.
  1972   *Land Leveling Salvage Archaeology in Missouri: 1968.* Submitted to the National Park Service, Midwest Archeological Center, Lincoln, Neb.
  1974   The Baytown Phases in the Cairo Lowland of Southeast Missouri. *The Missouri Archaeologist* 36.
Williams, Joyce A.
  1993   Meridian Hills: An Upland Holding Phase Middle Woodland Habitation Site. *Illinois Archaeology* 5(1 and 2):193–200.
Williams, Joyce A., and Richard Lacampagne
  1982   *Final Investigations on the Adler Site (11-S-64).* FAI-270 Archaeological Mitigation Report 43, Department of Anthropology, University of Illinois-Urbana.
Williams, Stephen
  1954   *An Archeological Study of the Mississippian Culture in Southeast Missouri.* Ph.D. dissertation, Yale University. University Microfilms, Ann Arbor, Mich.

1956   Settlement Patterns in the Lower Mississippi Valley. In *Prehistoric Settlement Patterns in the New World,* edited by Gordon R. Willey, pp. 52–62. Viking Fund Publications in Anthropology No. 23, New York, N.Y.

1963   The Eastern United States. In *Early Indian Farmers and Villages and Communities,* edited by W. G. Haag, pp. 267–325. U.S. Department of the Interior, National Park Service, Washington, D.C.

1992   Obion Retrospective and Prospective. In *The Obion Site: An Early Mississippian Center in Western Tennessee,* by E. B. Garland, pp. 193–201. Report of Investigations 7, Cobb Institute of Archaeology, Mississippi State University.

Williams, Stephen, and Jeffrey P. Brain

1983   *Excavations at the Lake George Site, Yazoo County, Mississippi, 1958–1960.* Papers of the Peabody Museum of Archaeology and Ethnology, Vol. 74, Harvard University, Cambridge.

Williamson, Robert M.

1941   Climatic Data with Special Reference to Agriculture in the United States: Supplemental Climatic Notes for Tennessee. Part 5 of *Climate and Man: Yearbook of Agriculture, 1941,* edited by Robert M. Williamson, pp. 663–1128. Washington, D.C.: U.S. Government Printing Office.

Willis, Roger K.

1941   The Baumer Focus. *Society for American Archaeology, Notebook* 2(2):28.

Wilson, Jack L.

1976   *Final Report: 1974 Excavations within the New Hope Reservoir.* Ms. on file, Research Laboratories of Archaeology, University of North Carolina, Chapel Hill.

Wilson, Peter J.

1988   *The Domestication of the Human Species.* New Haven and London: Yale University Press.

Wimberly, Steve B.

1953   Bayou La Batre Tchefuncte Series. In *Prehistoric Pottery of the Eastern United States,* edited by James B. Griffin, pp. 2-1 to 2-2. Museum of Anthropology, University of Michigan, Ann Arbor.

1960   *Indian Pottery from Clarke County and Mobile County, Southern Alabama.* Museum Paper 36, Alabama Museum of Natural History, University.

Wimberly, Steve, and Harry A. Tourtelot

1941   *The McQuorquodale Mound: A Manifestation of the Hopewellian Phase in South Alabama.* Museum Paper 19, Geological Survey of Alabama, Tuscaloosa.

Wing, Elizabeth S.

1977   Subsistence Systems in the Southeast. *Florida Anthropologist* 30:81–87.

Winters, Howard D.

1963   *An Archaeological Survey of the Wabash Valley in Illinois.* Illinois State Museum Report of Investigations 10, Springfield.

Witthoft, John

1953   Broad Spearpoints and Transitional Period Cultures. *Pennsylvania Archaeologist* 23:4–31.

Witty, Charles O.

1993   *Fingerhut (11-S-34/7): A Lohmann/Stirling Phase Cemetery, Mississippian Occupation with an Early Woodland Component.* Submitted in partial fulfillment of the degree of Master of Science, Department of Environmental Studies, Southern Illinois University at Edwardsville.

Wobst, H. Martin

1977   Stylistic Behavior and Information Exchange. In *For the Director: Research Es-*

says in Honor of James B. Griffin, edited by Charles E. Cleland, pp. 317–42. Anthropological Papers No. 61, Museum of Anthropology, University of Michigan, Ann Arbor.

Wolf, Eric R.
1982 *Europe and the People without History.* Berkeley: University of California Press.

Wolforth, Thomas R., Mary L. Simon, and Richard L. Alvey
1990 The Widman Site (11-Ms-866): A Small Middle Woodland Settlement in the Wood River Valley, Illinois. *Illinois Archaeology* 2(1 and 2):45–69.

Womochel, Daniel R.
1982 Mollusks from 1Au139 and the Ivy Creek Locality, Autauga County, Alabama. In *The Archaeology of Ivy Creek,* by John W. Cottier, pp. 354–65. Auburn University Archaeological Monograph 3.

Wood, W. Dean, and William R. Bowen
1995 *Woodland Period Archaeology of Northern Georgia.* Laboratory of Archaeology Series Report No. 33, Dept. of Anthropology, University of Georgia, Athens.

Wood, W. Dean, Dan T. Elliott, Teresa P. Rudolph, and Dennis B. Blanton
1986 *Prehistory in the Richard B. Russell Reservoir: The Archaic and Woodland Periods of the Upper Savannah River.* Russell Papers, Archaeological Services Branch, National Park Service, Atlanta.

Wood, W. Raymond
1963a A Preliminary Report on the 1962 Excavations at the Crenshaw Site: 3MI6. In *Arkansas Archeology, 1962,* edited by Charles R. McGimsey III, pp. 1–14. Arkansas Archeological Society, Fayetteville.
1963b *The Poole Site: Components of the Fourche Maline and Mid-Ouachita Foci in Garland County, Arkansas.* Ms. on file, University of Arkansas Museum, Fayetteville.
1963c *The Crenshaw Site: A Coles Creek and Caddoan Mound Group in Miller County, Arkansas.* Ms. on file at the University of Arkansas Museum, Fayetteville.

Wood, W. Raymond, and Ann M. Early
1981 The Poole Site, 3GA3, with a new Foreword and Summary by Ann M. Early. *Arkansas Archeologist* 22:7–62.

Woodall, J. Ned
1984 *The Donnaha Site: 1973, 1975 Excavations.* Publication 22, North Carolina Archaeological Council, Raleigh.

Woodiel, Deborah K.
1980 *St. Gabriel: Prehistoric Life on the Mississippi.* Master's thesis, Department of Geography and Anthropology, Louisiana State University, Baton Rouge.

Woodland Conference
1943 The First Archaeological Conference on the Woodland Pattern. *American Antiquity* 8:392–400.

Woodrick, Anne
1981 An Analysis of the Faunal Remains from the Gainesville Lake Area. In *Biocultural Studies in the Gainesville Lake Area,* by Gloria Caddell, Anne Woodrick, and Mary C. Hill, pp. 91–168. Report of Investigations 14, University of Alabama Office of Archaeological Research, Tuscaloosa.
1983 Molluscan Remains and Shell Artifacts. In *Studies of Material Remains from the Lubbub Creek Archaeological Locality.* Volume 2 of *Prehistoric Agricultural Communities in West Central Alabama,* edited by Christopher S. Peebles, pp. 391–429. Submitted to the U.S. Army Corps of Engineers, Mobile District, by the University of Michigan, Ann Arbor.

Worth, John E.
  1992   Revised Aboriginal Ceramic Typology for the Timucua Mission Province. In *Excavations of the Franciscan Frontier, Archaeology of the Fig Springs Mission,* by Brent R. Weisman, pp. 188–205. Gainesville: University Press of Florida.
  1998   *Timucuan Chiefdoms of Spanish Florida.* Vol. 1., *Assimilation.* Gainesville: University Press of Florida.

Wyckoff, D. G.
  1974   *The Caddoan Area: An Archaeological Perspective.* New York: Garland Press.
  1980   *Caddoan Adaptive Strategies in the Arkansas Basin, Eastern Oklahoma.* Ph.D. dissertation, Department of Anthropology, Washington State University, Pullman.
  1984   The Cross Timbers: An Ecotone in Historic Perspective. In *Contributions to Cross Timbers Prehistory,* edited by P. L. Kawecki and D. G. Wyckoff, pp. 1–19. Studies in Oklahoma's Past No. 12, Oklahoma Archeological Survey, Norman.

Wyckoff, D. G., and R. L. Brooks
  1983   *Oklahoma Archeology: A 1981 Perspective of the State's Archeological Resources, Their Significance, Their Problems, and Some Proposed Solutions.* Archeological Resources Survey Report No. 16, Oklahoma Archeological Survey, University of Oklahoma, Norman.

Wymer, Dee Ann
  1987   The Middle Woodland–Late Woodland Interface in Central Ohio: Subsistence Continuity Amid Cultural Change. In *Emergent Horticultural Economies of the Eastern Woodlands,* edited by William F. Keegan, pp. 201–42. Occasional Paper No. 7, Center for Archaeological Investigations, Southern Illinois University, Carbondale.
  1992   Trends and Disparities: The Woodland Paleoethnobotanical Record of the Mid-Ohio Valley. In *Cultural Variability in Context: Woodland Settlements of the Mid-Ohio Valley,* edited by Mark F. Seeman, pp. 65–76. Midcontinental Journal of Archaeology Special Paper 7, Kent State University Press, Kent, Ohio.
  1993   Cultural Change and Subsistence: The Middle Woodland and Late Woodland Transition in the Mid-Ohio Valley. In *Foraging and Farming in the Eastern Woodlands,* edited by C. Margaret Scarry, pp. 138–56. Gainesville: University Press of Florida.
  1997   Paleoethnobotany in the Licking River Valley, Ohio: Implications for Understanding Ohio Hopewell. In *Ohio Hopewell Community Organization,* edited by William S. Dancey and Paul J. Pacheco, pp. 153–75. Kent, Ohio: Kent State University Press.

Wynn, Jack T., and James R. Atkinson
  1976   *Archaeology of the Okashua and Self Sites, Mississippi.* Submitted to the National Park Service by the Department of Anthropology, Mississippi State University.

Yarnell, Richard A.
  1974a   Intestinal Contents of the Salts Cave Mummy and Analysis of the Initial Salts Cave Flotation Series. In *Archaeology of the Mammoth Cave Area,* edited by Patty Jo Watson, pp. 109–12. New York: Academic Press.
  1974b   Plant Foods and Cultivation of the Salts Cavers. In *Archaeology of the Mammoth Cave Area,* edited by Patty Jo Watson, pp. 113–22. New York: Academic Press.
  1976   Plant Remains from the Warren Wilson Site. Appendix A in *Cherokee History: The Pisgah Phase in the Appalachian Summit Region,* by Roy S. Dickens, Jr., pp. 217–24. Knoxville: University of Tennessee Press.
  1978   Domestication of Sunflower and Sumpweed in Eastern North America. In *The Nature and Status of Ethnobotany,* edited by Richard I. Ford, pp. 289–300. An-

thropological Papers No. 67, Museum of Anthropology, University of Michigan, Ann Arbor.

1993 The Importance of Native Crops during the Late Archaic and Woodland Periods. In *Foraging and Farming in the Eastern Woodlands,* edited by C. Margaret Scarry, pp. 13–26. Gainesville: University Press of Florida.

Yarnell, Richard A., and M. Jean Black

1985 Temporal Trends Indicated by a Survey of Archaic and Woodland Plant Food Remains from Southeastern North America. *Southeastern Archaeology* 4:93–106.

Yelton, J. K.

1995a Vertebrate Remains. In *Occupations at the Hayti Bypass Site, Pemiscot County, Missouri,* edited by Michael D. Conner, pp. 263–89. Special Publication No. 1, Center for Archaeological Research, Southwest Missouri State University, Springfield.

1995b *The 1993 Passports-in-Time Program at Merrell Cave, 23PH64, Phelps County, Missouri.* Submitted to the Mark Twain National Forest, Rolla, Mo.

Contributors

Steven R. Ahler is Senior Archaeologist at the Illinois State Museum Society in Springfield. He has worked extensively in Illinois and Missouri over the past 20 years, with research interests focusing on Late Woodland settlement systems, potential cultural effects of Archaic period environmental changes, and lithic analyses.

David G. Anderson is an archaeologist with the Southeast Archeological Center of the National Park Service, based in Tallahassee, Florida. His home is in Williston, South Carolina.

Judith A. Bense is a professor of anthropology and Director of the Archaeology Institute at the University of West Florida in Pensacola. She founded the archaeology program there in 1980 and conducts research in the lower southeastern United States in the Woodland, Archaic, and Historic Colonial periods. She has studied the Swift Creek culture since the 1960s and has excavated four shell midden rings of this period on the northern Gulf Coast.

R. Berle Clay is Supervisory Archaeologist with Cultural Resource Analysts, Inc., in Lexington, Kentucky.

Charles R. Cobb is an associate professor of anthropology at State University of New York at Binghamton. His research interests include political economy, the organization of technology, and lithic studies. He is the author of *From Quarry to Cornfield: The Political Economy of Mississippian Hoe Production* (2000, University of Alabama Press). Currently, he is the editor of *Northeast Anthropology*.

James W. Cogswell is a research archaeologist with Northland Research, Inc., in Tempe, Arizona. His research interests include pottery technology and ceramic sourcing through neutron-activation analysis.

George M. Crothers is the 2000–2001 Visiting Scholar at the Center for Archaeological Investigations, Southern Illinois University, Carbondale. His research interests include the prehistory of eastern North America, cave archaeology, and the archaeology of hunter-gatherer groups.

Richard Edging is a University of Missouri, Columbia, archaeologist assigned as cultural resource manager at Fort Leonard Wood, Missouri. He has over 25 years of experience in archaeology and historic preservation with interests that include Native American cultures, pre-Columbian Midwestern archaeology, iconography, NAGPRA, prehistoric and historic contexts, and historic archaeology.

Charles H. Faulkner, professor of anthropology and Distinguished Professor of Humanities at the University of Tennessee, Knoxville, has conducted archaeological research in east and middle Tennessee for the past 36 years. During this time his research has focused on Woodland ceramics and community patterning, prehistoric activity in the dark zone of caves, and historical archaeology.

Debra L. Gold is assistant professor of anthropology at St. Cloud State University, Minnesota. She received her doctorate in anthropology from the University of Michigan. Her research interests include the late prehistory of the Eastern Woodlands, early agricultural communities, the emergence of inequality, bioarchaeology, and mortuary analysis. Recent publications include "Utmost Confusion Reconsidered: Bioarchaeology and Secondary Burial in Late Prehistoric Interior Virginia" in *Bioarchaeological Studies of Life in the Age of Agriculture,* edited by P. M. Lambert and published by the University of Alabama Press.

Kristen J. Gremillion is associate professor of anthropology at Ohio State University.

Jeffrey L. Hantman is associate professor of anthropology at the University of Virginia. He received his doctorate from Arizona State University. His research interests include Eastern Woodlands archaeology, colonialism, cultural identity, and the writing of history. He is currently directing excavations at the site of Monasukapanough in Virginia, part of a larger research program focused on the archaeology and ethnohistory of the Monacan Indian communities. Recent writings include "Monacan History at the Dawn of Colonization" in *Societies in Eclipse* published by the Smithsonian Institution Press.

Joseph M. Herbert is currently employed as an archaeologist with the Cultural Resources Management Program at Fort Bragg and is a Ph.D. candidate at the University of North Carolina at Chapel Hill.

Melissa L. Higgins received her bachelor of arts degree from Wake Forest University in 1990 and her master's degree in anthropology from the University of Mississippi in 1994. She worked as an archaeologist for the U.S. Forest Service in south Mississippi from 1992 until June 2000. She now resides in northern Minnesota along the shore of Lake Superior.

H. Edwin Jackson is professor of anthropology at the University of Southern Mississippi. He received his doctorate in anthropology from the University of Michigan in 1986. He is interested in the ecological, social, political, and ritual patterning in the prehistoric use of animal resources, as well as in broader issues of southeastern prehistory.

John E. Kelly is a lecturer in archaeology at Washington University in St. Louis.

Tristram R. Kidder is an associate professor at Tulane University in New Orleans.

Paul P. Kreisa is Program Coordinator of the Public Service Archaeology Program, University of Illinois at Urbana-Champaign. He has worked extensively in Illinois and Missouri, including 9 years of research at Fort Leonard Wood. His research interests center on developmental trends in the late prehistoric cultures of the Southeast and Midwest.

R. Lee Lyman is professor and chairman of the Department of Anthropology, University of Missouri-Columbia. His research interests include evolutionary theory, Americanist culture history, and zooarchaeology.

Robert C. Mainfort, Jr., is Sponsored Research Administrator, Arkansas Archeological Survey, and professor of anthropology, University of Arkansas.

Jerald T. Milanich is an archaeologist at the Florida Museum of Natural History in Gainesville.

Michael S. Nassaney is an associate professor of anthropology at Western Michigan University. His research interests include social archaeology, political economy, ethnohistory, and material analysis in eastern North America. He recently co-edited *Interpretations of Native*

North American Life: Material Contributions to Ethnohistory (2000, University Press of Florida and the Society for Historical Archaeology).

Michael J. O'Brien is professor of anthropology and associate dean of the College of Arts and Science, University of Missouri-Columbia. His research interests include evolutionary theory, Americanist culture history, and ceramic technology.

Evan Peacock received a bachelor of arts degree in anthropology from Mississippi State University in 1988, a master's in environmental archaeology and paleoeconomy from the University of Sheffield, England, in 1990, and a doctorate in archaeology from Sheffield in 1999. He is currently a Senior Research Associate with the Cobb Institute of Archaeology and an assistant professor at Mississippi State University.

Janet Rafferty received a doctorate in anthropology in 1974 from the University of Washington, Seattle. She has taught since 1977 at Mississippi State University. Her major research interests are evolutionary archaeology and prehistoric settlement pattern change in the southeastern United States.

Robert E. Reams is a district archaeologist for the National Forests in Mississippi in the De Soto Ranger District. He received his master's degree from Wake Forest University in 1995. His research includes local turpentine and logging industries and prehistoric landscape studies, and he has conducted public excavations involving volunteers, foreign archaeologists, and students.

Martha Ann Rolingson is Arkansas Archeological Survey Station Archeologist at Toltec Mounds Archeological State Park and professor of anthropology at the University of Arkansas. She received her Ph.D. from the University of Michigan in 1967. Her research interests are multiple mound sites, settlement patterns, and ceramics of the lower Mississippi River valley.

Kenneth E. Sassaman is assistant professor of anthropology at the University of Florida. After working for a decade in the middle Savannah River valley of Georgia and South Carolina, he recently began long-term research on the Archaic prehistory of the St. Johns Basin of northeast Florida. His interests center on technological change, social interactions, and historical process.

Frank F. Schambach (Ph.D. Harvard University) has been the Arkansas Archeological Survey's station archeologist in southwest Arkansas since 1968. His main research interests are the culture history of the Trans-Mississippi South and adjacent parts of the Lower Mississippi, and the question of trade between the Southeast and the southern Plains during the Mississippi period.

Susan L. Scott is a private consulting zooarchaeologist. Her work includes the analyses of numerous assemblages from the Southeast and Midwest, as well as Texas, New Mexico, and the Plains. She is currently focusing on long-term trends in human adaptation on the south Texas coast and mid-Holocene subsistence in the Midsouth.

Jan F. Simek is professor of anthropology at the University of Tennessee. His life-long research interests include cave archaeology in Europe and North America and the evolution of human behavior.

Frankie Snow, of the Science and Math Division at South Georgia College, is a native of South Georgia who has spent decades studying the region's cultural and natural history. His archaeological investigations have dealt primarily with revealing a wealth of information about Swift Creek culture as seen through the artwork available on its distinctive pottery.

Keith Stephenson is an archaeologist with the Savannah River Archaeological Research Program of the South Carolina Institute of Archaeology and Anthropology. He received his bachelor of arts degree in anthropology from the University of Georgia and is a doctoral student at the University of Kentucky. His research area includes the interior Coastal Plain of Georgia and South Carolina and his archaeological interests focus on the social structure and political organization of Woodland period societies.

Patty Jo Watson is the Edward M. Mallinckrodt Professor of Anthropology at Washington University in St. Louis, where she has been a faculty member for 30 years. She earned her master's degree and doctorate in anthropology at the University of Chicago, where she specialized in Near Eastern prehistory, turning to cave archaeology and eastern North American prehistory later in her career.

Ruth Y. Wetmore is an archaeologist affiliated with Brevard College, with research interests in southeastern prehistory and historic Indian groups. Publications include *First on the Land: The North Carolina Indians,* monographs, and journal articles in several fields. She has authored or co-authored over twenty unpublished archaeological survey and data recovery reports.

Randolph J. Widmer is an associate professor of anthropology at the University of Houston. He received his doctoral degree from Pennsylvania State University. He works in South Florida and Mesoamerica and has conducted excavations at Teotihuacan, Copan, Key Marco, and Brickell Point. His research interests include the evolution of complex society, craft specialization, and coastal adaptations.

P. Willey is a professor of anthropology at Chico State University, California, where he has taught for the past twelve years. He has studied human skeletons for more than thirty-five years, including those from the Little Bighorn and the victims of the prehistoric Crow Creek Massacre.

Index